THE COLUMBIA DICTIONARY OF QUOTATIONS FROM SHAKESPEARE

THE COLUMBIA DICTIONARY OF

⸺ FROM ⸺

QUOTATIONS

SHAKESPEARE

MARY AND REGINALD FOAKES

BARNES
&NOBLE
BOOKS
NEW YORK

Copyright © 1998 by Columbia University Press

This edition published by Barnes & Noble, Inc.,
by arrangement with Columbia University Press

All rights reserved. No part of this book may be used or reproduced in any
manner whatsoever without the written permission of the Publisher.

2000 Barnes & Noble Books

ISBN 0-7607-1903-9 *casebound*
ISBN 0-7607-1904-7 *trade paperback*

Printed and bound in the United States of America

00 01 02 03 04 MC 9 8 7 6 5 4 3 2 1
00 01 02 03 04 MT 9 8 7 6 5 4 3 2 1

FG

Contents

Introduction

In the English-speaking world William Shakespeare and his works have an extraordinary status. He has long been accepted as a figure of enormous cultural authority. This is evidenced both in the education provided by schools and colleges, where his works are widely studied, and in the theaters, summer festivals and libraries dedicated to preserving his achievements. This cultural authority has paradoxically ensured that Shakespeare has been democratized as a representative consciousness, whose works embody in memorable language much of the wisdom of our civilization. Passages from his plays and poems are frequently cited in all sorts of contexts to support legal or political arguments, validate advertisements, justify prejudices, and generally sanction a whole range of beliefs and opinions. In this process, his words have floated free of their moorings in the context of his plays, have become detached from the characters for whom the lines were written, and are treated as if they represent Shakespeare's own convictions.

So in support of their nominees or arguments politicians may quote speeches from *Othello* or *Richard III* without realizing that the words may be appropriate in ways they have not imagined, since they were written to be spoken by Iago and Richard, characters noted for their manipulation of others and their consummate hypocrisy. Such mindless use of quotations is encouraged by dictionaries that do not identify the speaker of particular lines, or indicate what sort of character he or she represents. However much we may feel Shakespeare put a lot of himself into figures like Hamlet, we cannot be sure that any character speaks for him as embodying his beliefs. He was steeped in the Bible and in folk-wisdom as represented, for instance, by proverbs, and he lived in an age when people noted down clever sayings or "sentences" (Latin "*sententiae*") in their commonplace books. His plays certainly contain many such sayings, and some memorable formulations of accepted wisdom that have passed into the language. However, many other quotations need to be understood in context if their full implications are to be appreciated. This new selection identifies characters for each citation, and provides annotations designed to help the reader to understand the dramatic context and meaning of passages that offer any kind of difficulty. For an example, consider the line "Respect and reason wait on wrinkled age," from *The Rape of Lucrece*, which might seem to need no explanation as stating a general truth. It makes a lot of difference, however, if we know that these words are spoken by Tarquin as he premeditates raping Lucrece, and tries to justify his deed by arguing that it is proper for the young to follow their heart's desire and reject reason. The line should give us food for thought; it is not simply expressing received wisdom.

So much of Shakespeare's language is quotable that every collection of quotations from his works differs from earlier ones, and there is no sense in which any collection can be "complete." What makes a quotation? In going through Shakespeare's works for the present collection, our first thought was that in general quotations should be brief, not more than six lines or so, and memorable. In fact we found we could not make this a rule, and we include a few longer passages as well as two sonnets. We had in mind several other criteria in choosing passages. Some were selected for their current aptness, as in this entry from *Antony and Cleopatra* under "Business":

To business that we love we rise betime,
And go to't with delight.

Antony is preparing for battle, but the lines may seem appealing or ironic as they might relate to commuters rushing towards another day in the office; the word "business" has taken on wider meanings since Shakespeare's day. Others were selected for their descriptive beauty, for their pithy expression of an opinion or wise saying, or for their wit and forcefulness of style, or their sheer quality as poetry. Shakespeare was brilliant at rewording proverbial sayings and recycling phrases from the Bible in such a way that his formulations have often passed into common use. The more notable allusions to the Bible are recorded in commentary notes on the passages, and there is a section devoted to proverbs which do not fit easily under another topic heading.

The quotations are arranged under topics, which are in alphabetical order. Topic headings are necessarily arbitrary, and it is often the case that a single passage of a few lines could be linked to several topics. For example, the line cited above, "Respect and reason wait on wrinkled age," could be placed under "Respect" or "Reason," but in fact appears under "Old Age." Some quotations are printed under two different topics, but to do this with every one that could be located under two or more possible headings would swell the collection enormously. So as a further aid to the reader this collection has an exceptionally full index to significant words in quotations, an index that offers a more thorough guide to the collection than the list of topics which is also provided. A further index ties each quotation by topic heading to the work from which it is cited, identifying in the case of Shakespeare's plays the character who speaks the words. It is thus possible, by looking up the play in this index, to trace what passages are cited from it, and also what passages attributed to any particular character are quoted. The list of topics, index of words, and index of plays and characters together provide a full reference guide to what is contained in the quotations.

The text of the quotations has been modernized. Line references, for convenience, are to the *Riverside Shakespeare* (Boston: Houghton Mifflin), and may be slightly different in other editions. Shakespeare's plays and poems were written between about 1588 and 1613, when the English language was being greatly enriched by an influx of new coinages. Shakespeare had a huge vocabulary, and seems to have introduced a great many words that have remained current; but there have been many changes since his day, both in the meanings of some words, and in grammatical usage. The annotations to quotations in this collection provide explanations of changes in meaning or style. Thus the indexes and annotations are intended to give the reader all possible help in finding and in appreciating the passages quoted. Their relevance for our own time is best left to the individual reader.

I am grateful to Curt Whitaker for assistance in checking and proof-reading.

The basic selection of quotations in this volume was made by my dear wife, Mary (F. Mary White), who, sadly, did not live to see its completion; the book is lovingly dedicated to her memory.

Reginald Foakes

List of Topics

THE COLUMBIA
DICTIONARY OF
QUOTATIONS
•FROM•
SHAKESPEARE

Quotations

Absence

1   Shall I abide
In this dull world, which in thy
     absence is
No better than a sty?

Cleopatra in *Antony and Cleopatra*,
4.15.60–2

On the death of Antony.

2   I shall be loved when I am lacked.

Coriolanus in *Coriolanus*, 4.1.15

Referring to his banishment from Rome.

3   There is not one among them but I
     dote on his very absence.

Portia in *The Merchant of Venice*,
1.2.109–10

Dismayed by all her suitors, she wishes they
would go away.

4   How like a winter hath my absence
     been
From thee, the pleasure of the fleet-
     ing year!
What freezings have I felt, what
     dark days seen,

What old December's bareness
     everywhere!

Sonnet 97, 1–4

For the speaker, the absence of his lover has
turned summer into winter.

Achievement

1   All's well that ends well; still the
     fine's the crown.
Whate'er the course, the end is the
     renown.

Helena in *All's Well That Ends Well*,
4.4.35–6

The play's proverbial title is repeated at
5.4.35; "the end crowns all" ("fine" = end,
from the Latin) is also proverbial.

Acting
(see also Plays, Theater)

1   When good will is showed, though
     it come too short,
The actor may plead pardon.

Cleopatra in *Antony and Cleopatra*,
2.5.8–9

2   You have put me now to such a
       part which never
    I shall discharge to the life.

Coriolanus in *Coriolanus*, 3.2.105–6

Speaking of the requirement that he stand in
the gown of humility and ask the public for
votes.

3   Like a dull actor now
    I have forgot my part, and I am out,
    Even to a full disgrace.

Coriolanus in *Coriolanus*, 5.3.40–2

Coriolanus, about to make war on Rome, is
ashamed to be at a loss for words ("out")
when confronted by his family, come to plead
with him.

4   How strange or odd some'er I bear
       myself,
    As I perchance hereafter shall think
       meet
    To put an antic disposition on.

Hamlet in *Hamlet*, 1.5.170–2

Announcing to Horatio and Marcellus his idea
of pretending to be mad whenever it suits him
("shall think meet").

5   He that plays the king shall be wel-
       come.

Hamlet in *Hamlet*, 2.2.319

Welcoming the actors who come to play at
court.

6   The best actors in the world,
    either for tragedy, comedy, history,
    pastoral, pastoral-comical, histori-
    cal-pastoral, tragical-historical,
    tragical-comical-historical-pastoral,
    scene individable, or poem
    unlimited.

Polonius in *Hamlet*, 2.2.396–400

Listing every kind of play, and then some.

7   Will you see the players well
    bestowed? Do you hear, let them
    be well used, for they are the
    abstracts and brief chronicles of the
    time. After your death you were
    better have a bad epitaph than their
    ill report while you live.

Hamlet in *Hamlet*, 2.2.522–6

Speaking to Polonius about the actors who
have just arrived in Elsinore; "bestowed" =
lodged.

8   What's Hecuba to him, or he to
       Hecuba,
    That he should weep for her? What
       would he do
    Had he the motive and the cue for
       passion
    That I have?

Hamlet in *Hamlet*, 2.2.559–62

Meditating on the player who weeps as he
narrates the death of Hecuba, Queen of Troy,
and on his own failure to act.

9   Speak the speech, I pray you, as I
    pronounced it to you, trippingly
    on the tongue; but if you mouth it
    as many of your players do, I had
    as lief the town-crier spoke my
    lines.

Hamlet in *Hamlet*, 3.2.1–4

To the actors, who are to perform a play with
a speech by Hamlet inserted; "as lief" = just as
willingly.

10   Be not too tame neither, but let
    your own discretion be your tutor.
    Suit the action to the word, the
    word to the action, with this special
    observance, that you o'erstep not
    the modesty of nature.

Hamlet in *Hamlet*, 3.2.16–19

Instructing the actors; "modesty" =
moderation.

11 The purpose of playing, whose end,
both at the first and now, was and
is, to hold as 'twere the mirror up
to nature: to show virtue her feature, scorn her own image, and the
very age and body of the time his
form and pressure.

Hamlet in *Hamlet*, 3.2.20–4

Hamlet's advice to the actors has its origins in
classical rhetoric; they are to show plainly the
appearance (feature) of virtue and of vice, and
reflect the present state of affairs; "pressure" =
impression, as if in wax.

12 O Jesu, he doth it as like one of
these harlotry players as ever I see!

Hostess in *Henry IV, Part 1*, 2.4.395–6

On Falstaff's extempore portrayal of King
Henry IV; "harlotry" = rascal.

13   But pardon, gentles all,
The flat unraisèd spirits that hath
dared
On this unworthy scaffold to bring
forth
So great an object.

Chorus in *Henry V*, Prologue, 8–11

Apologizing to the audience ("gentles" = gentlemen and gentlewomen) for the inadequacy
of the actors on their stage ("scaffold").

14   Still be kind,
And eke out our performance with
your mind.

Chorus in *Henry V*, 3.Prologue, 34–5

Appealing to the audience.

15 Good gentlemen, look fresh and
merrily.
Let not our looks put on our purposes,
But bear it as our Roman actors do,

With untired spirits and formal
constancy.

Brutus in *Julius Caesar*, 2.1.224–7

As the conspirators set off towards the Capitol.

16   How many ages hence
Shall this our lofty scene be acted
over
In states unborn and accents yet
unknown!

Cassius in *Julius Caesar*, 3.1.111–13

Referring to the assassination of Caesar.

17 I hold the world but as the world,
Gratiano,
A stage, where every man must play
a part,
And mine a sad one.

**Antonio in *The Merchant of Venice*,
1.1.77–9**

18 *Bottom.* What is Pyramus? A lover
or a tyrant?
Quince. A lover that kills himself,
most gallant, for love.
Bottom. That will ask some tears in
the true performing of it. If I do
it, let the audience look to their
eyes.

***A Midsummer Night's Dream*, 1.2.22–6**

Peter Quince is casting Bottom for the play of
Pyramus and Thisbe.

19 My chief humor is for a tyrant.
I could play Ercles rarely, or a part
to tear a cat in, to make all split.

**Bottom in *A Midsummer Night's
Dream*, 1.2.28–30**

"Humor" = inclination; "Ercles" is Bottom's
corruption of Hercules; to "tear a cat" on the
stage is to rant and bluster.

20 *Snug.* Have you the lion's part
written? Pray you, if it be, give it
me; for I am slow of study.
Quince. You may do it extempore,
for it is nothing but roaring.

A Midsummer Night's Dream, 1.2.66–9

21 I will aggravate my voice so that I
will roar you as gently as any suck-
ing dove. I will roar you and 'twere
any nightingale.

**Bottom in A Midsummer Night's
Dream,** 1.2.81–4

Bottom offers the gentlest of lions' roars so
as not to frighten ladies; he means to say
"moderate."

22 There we may rehearse most
obscenely and courageously.

**Bottom in A Midsummer Night's
Dream,** 1.2.107–8

"Obscenely" is Bottom's mistake for "seemly"
(fitly), or some such word.

23 You speak all your part at once,
cues and all.

**Quince in A Midsummer Night's
Dream,** 3.1.99–100

On Flute, who is rehearsing for the part of
Thisbe in the play they are to stage for the
wedding of Theseus and Hippolyta.

24 We do not come, as minding to
content you,
Our true intent is. All for your
delight
We are not here.

**Quince in A Midsummer Night's
Dream,** 5.1.113–15

He wrecks the sense of his prologue by confusing the punctuation.

25 *Theseus.* The best in this kind are
but shadows; and the worst are no
worse, if imagination amend
them.
Hippolyta. It must be your imagination then, and not theirs.
Theseus. If we imagine no worse of
them than they of themselves,
they may pass for excellent men.

A Midsummer Night's Dream,
5.1.211–16

Watching "Pyramus and Thisbe" as staged by
Bottom, Quince and their crew.

26 I can counterfeit the deep trage-
dian,
Speak, and look back, and pry on
every side,
Tremble and start at wagging of a
straw,
Intending deep suspicion. Ghastly
looks
Are at my service like enforcèd
smiles,
And both are ready in their offices
At any time to grace my stratagems.

Buckingham in Richard III, 3.5.5–11

"Intending" = pretending; Buckingham is
putting his ability to act a part at the service of
Richard.

27 They thought it good you hear a
play,
And frame your mind to mirth and
merriment,
Which bars a thousand harms and
lengthens life.

**Messenger in The Taming of the
Shrew,** Induction, 2.134–6

Inviting the tinker Sly to watch the play.

28 Our revels now are ended. These
our actors,

As I foretold you, were all spirits, and
Are melted into air, into thin air.

Prospero in *The Tempest*, 4.1.148–50

Dismissing the masquers who have entertained Ferdinand and Miranda.

29   *Olivia.* Whence came you, sir?
Viola. I can say little more than I
have studied, and that question's
out of my part.

Twelfth Night, 1.5.177–9

Olivia thinks Viola is a man, Cesario; Viola is indeed playing a part, that of Orsino's messenger of love.

30   I see the play so lies
That I must bear a part.

Perdita in *The Winter's Tale*, 4.4.655

Spoken as she is asked to disguise herself as a man.

31   We may leisurely
Each one demand and answer to his
part
Performed in this wide gap of time
since first
We were dissevered.

Leontes in *The Winter's Tale*, 5.3.152–5

Winding up the play; only the audience knows the whole story.

Action

1   In such business
Action is eloquence, and the eyes of
th' ignorant
More learned than the ears.

Volumnia in *Coriolanus*, 3.2.75–7

Coriolanus's mother advises him to look humble in front of the Roman people in order to win votes.

2   She stripped it from her arm. I see
her yet:
Her pretty action did outsell her
gift,
And yet enriched it too.

Jachimo in *Cymbeline*, 2.4.101–3

A charming description of an imaginary act; Jachimo is lying about how he came by Imogen's bracelet.

3   Duller shouldst thou be than the fat
weed
That roots itself in ease on Lethe
wharf,
Wouldst thou not stir in this.

Ghost in *Hamlet*, 1.5.32–4

Urging Hamlet to revenge his murder; "Lethe" = the underworld river of forgetfulness.

4   I am not yet of Percy's mind, the
Hotspur of the north, he that kills
me some six or seven dozen of
Scots at a breakfast, washes his
hands, and says to his wife,
"Fie upon this quiet life! I want
work."

Prince Hal in *Henry IV, Part 1*,
2.4.101–5

Mocking Hotspur's devotion to fighting.

5   The undeserver may sleep when the
man of action is called on.

Falstaff in *Henry IV, Part 2*, 2.4.376–7

Falstaff, late as usual, is summoned to help fight rebels.

6   A very little little let us do
And all is done.

Constable in *Henry V*, 4.2.33–4

Convinced the French will have an easy victory.

7   Strike now, or else the iron cools.

**Richard of Gloucester in *Henry VI,
Part 3*, 5.1.49**

Proverbial; the idea is that iron is malleable
and can be worked by the smith while it is
hot.

8   He's sudden if a thing comes in his
head.

King Edward in *Henry VI, Part 3*, 5.5.86

On Richard, soon to be Richard III;
"sudden" = quick to act, impetuous.

9   We must not stint
Our necessary actions in the fear
To cope malicious censurers.

Cardinal Wolsey in *Henry VIII*, 1.2.76–8

Defending the imposition of a savage tax;
"to cope" = of encountering.

10   If we shall stand still
In fear our motion will be mocked
or carped at,
We should take root here where we
sit, or sit
State-statues only.

Cardinal Wolsey in *Henry VIII*, 1.2.85–8

On hearing of complaints made about his use
of power; "motion" = proposals, actions.

11   'Tis a kind of good deed to say well,
And yet words are no deeds.

King Henry in *Henry VIII*, 3.2.153–4

On discovering the gap between Wolsey's
words and his actions.

12   If it were done when 'tis done, then
'twere well
It were done quickly. If the assassination
Could trammel up the consequence, and catch
With his surcease success—that but
this blow

Might be the be-all and the end-
all!—here,
But here, upon this bank and shoal
of time,
We'd jump the life to come.

Macbeth in *Macbeth*, 1.7.1–7

"If it were done when 'tis done" = if the deed
were at an end, completely finished, at the
moment it is done; Macbeth thinks that if he
could avoid ("trammel up" = catch in a net)
the consequences of murder with the death
("surcease") of Duncan, he would take a
chance on the life to come (on earth, and in
heaven or hell).

13   O, what men dare do! What men
may do! What men daily do, not
knowing what they do!

**Claudio in *Much Ado About Nothing*,
4.1.19–20**

His words reflect ironically on himself, as he
is about to reject Hero as they are due to be
married.

14   Pleasure and action make the hours
seem short.

Iago in *Othello*, 2.3.379

Iago has just contrived to get Cassio, his superior officer, dismissed by Othello.

15   A stirring dwarf we do allowance
give
Before a sleeping giant.

**Agamemnon in *Troilus and Cressida*,
2.3.137–8**

Achilles is the "sleeping giant," who refuses to
fight; "allowance" = praise, honor.

16   This action I now go on
Is for my better grace.

Hermione, *The Winter's Tale*, 2.1.121–2

She is being sent to prison by her husband,
Leontes, an "action" that will elicit her fortitude and patience.

Adoration

1   She speaks!
O, speak again, bright angel, for
    thou art
As glorious to this night, being o'er
    my head,
As is a wingèd messenger of heaven.

Romeo in *Romeo and Juliet*, 2.2.25–8

On Juliet at her window.

Adultery

1   What was thy cause? Adultery?
Thou shalt not die. Die for adul-
    tery? No,
The wren goes to't, and the small
    gilded fly
Does lecher in my sight.
Let copulation thrive.

King Lear in *King Lear*, 4.6.109–14

Addressing Gloucester, who fathered the bastard Edmund.

2   There have been,
Or I am much deceived, cuckolds
    ere now,
And many a man there is, even at
    this present,
Now, while I speak this, holds his
    wife by th'arm,
That little thinks she has been
    sluiced in's absence,
And his pond fished by his next
    neighbor, by
Sir Smile, his neighbor.

Leontes in *The Winter's Tale*, 1.2.190–6

Beginning to believe the worst of his own wife.

3   Should all despair
That have revolted wives, the tenth
    of mankind

Would hang themselves.

Leontes in *The Winter's Tale*, 1.2.198–200

Suspecting his own wife of adultery.

Adversity

1   O how full of briers is this working-
    day world!

Rosalind in *As You Like It*, 1.3.11–12

Sighing for love, she finds the everyday world thorny.

2   Sweet are the uses of adversity,
Which like the toad, ugly and ven-
    omous,
Wears yet a precious jewel in his
    head.

Duke Senior in *As You Like It*, 2.1.12–14

A common belief about toads; it was proverbial that adversity makes men wise.

3   A wretched soul, bruised with
    adversity,
We bid be quiet when we hear it
    cry;
But were we burdened with like
    weight of pain,
As much, or more, we should our-
    selves complain.

Adriana in *The Comedy of Errors*, 2.1.34–7

4   Adversity's sweet milk, philosophy,
To comfort thee, though thou art
    banished.

Friar Lawrence in *Romeo and Juliet*, 3.3.55–6

Seeking to comfort the banished Romeo.

5   O, give me thy hand,
One writ with me in sour misfortune's book!

Romeo in *Romeo and Juliet*, 5.3.81–2

Addressing Paris, whom he has just fought
and killed.

6   Let's shake our heads and
say,
As 'twere a knell unto our master's
fortunes,
We have seen better days.

Flavius in *Timon of Athens*, 4.2.25–7

To Timon's servants as they depart from his
house.

Advice

1   Love all, trust a few,
Do wrong to none.

**Countess of Rossillion in *All's Well
That Ends Well*, 1.1.64–5**

A mother's advice to her young son Bertram,
as he is summoned by the King to Paris.

2   Be checked for silence,
But never taxed for speech.

**Countess of Rossillion in *All's Well
That Ends Well*, 1.1.67–8**

Advice to her son on how to behave at court:
don't mind being rebuked for saying nothing,
but never be charged with saying too much.

3   For I must tell you friendly in your
ear,
Sell when you can, you are not for
all markets.

Rosalind in *As You Like It*, 3.5.59–60

To Phebe, who rejects Silvius's love.

4   Do not, as some ungracious pastors
do,
Show me the steep and thorny way
to heaven,
Whilst like a puffed and reckless
libertine
Himself the primrose path of dalliance treads,
And recks not his own rede.

Ophelia in *Hamlet*, 1.3.47–51

To her brother, Laertes, who has been urging
her not to listen to Hamlet's advances; "ungracious" = lacking grace; "puffed" = bloated;
"recks" = heeds; "rede" = advice.

5   Give every man thy ear, but few thy
voice,
Take each man's censure, but
reserve thy judgment.

Polonius in *Hamlet*, 1.3.68–9

Advice to his son; "censure" = opinion.

6   Neither a borrower nor a lender be,
For loan oft loses both itself and
friend,
And borrowing dulls the edge of
husbandry.

Polonius in *Hamlet*, 1.3.75–7

Advice to his son, going to live abroad; "husbandry" = thrift.

7   This above all: to thine own self be
true,
And it must follow, as the night the
day,
Thou canst not then be false to any
man.

Polonius in *Hamlet*, 1.3.78–80

The last of a list of precepts addressed to his
son, who is going to live abroad.

8   You shall be as a father to my
youth,

My voice shall sound as you do
prompt mine ear,
And I will stoop and humble my
intents
To your well-practiced wise directions.

Prince Hal in *Henry IV, Part 2,*
5.2.118–121

Accepting the guidance of the Chief Justice.

9   Heat not a furnace for your foe so
hot
That it do singe yourself.

Norfolk in *Henry VIII,* 1.1.140–1

To Buckingham, who has proclaimed his
enmity to Wolsey.

10   Let go thy hold when a great wheel
runs down a hill lest it break thy
neck with following; but the great
one that goes upward, let him draw
thee after.

Fool in *King Lear,* 2.4.71–4

Giving Kent politic advice, to abandon Lear;
he goes on to say "I would have none but
knaves follow it."

11   It is a good divine that follows his
own instructions; I can easier teach
twenty what were good to be done,
than to be one of the twenty to follow mine own teaching.

Portia in *The Merchant of Venice,*
1.2.14–17

Echoing the proverb, "practice what you
preach."

12   Pause awhile,
And let my counsel sway you in this
case.

Friar Francis in *Much Ado About
Nothing,* 4.1.200–1

Trying to help the distraught Leonato.

13   I pray thee, cease thy counsel,
Which falls into mine ears as profit-
less
As water in a sieve.

Leonato in *Much Ado About Nothing,*
5.1.3–5

Refusing his brother's attempt to comfort him.

14   And what's he then that says I play
the villain,
When this advice is free I give, and
honest,
Probal to thinking, and indeed the
course
To win the Moor again?

Iago in *Othello,* 2.3.336–9

Addressing the audience after advising
Cassio to apply to Desdemona; "probal" =
reasonable.

15   Wise men ne'er sit and wail their
woes,
But presently prevent the ways to
wail.

Bishop of Carlisle in *Richard II,*
3.2.178–9

Giving the downcast Richard some good
advice.

16   O Lord, I could have stayed here all
the night
To hear good counsel. O, what
learning is!

Nurse in *Romeo and Juliet,* 3.3.159–60

On hearing Friar Lawrence counseling
Romeo, who has tried to kill himself.

17   Thou dost advise me
Even so as I mine own course have
set down.

Leontes in *The Winter's Tale,* 1.2.339–40

On hearing Camillo's advice to treat
Hermione well.

Affectation

1   *Holofernes.* He is too picked, too spruce, too affected, too odd as it were, too peregrinate as I may call it.
Nathaniel. A most singular and choice epithet.
Love's Labor's Lost, 5.1.12–15

Speaking of Armado; "picked" = fastidious; "peregrinate" = outlandish.

Affliction (see also Grief, Misery, Suffering)

1   You do draw my spirits from me
With new lamenting ancient over-sights.
Northumberland in *Henry IV, Part 2*, 2.3.46–7

Hearing old mistakes lamented saps his courage.

2   *Cassius.* I did not think you could have been so angry.
Brutus. O Cassius, I am sick of many griefs.
Julius Caesar, 4.3.143–4

Cassius does not know that Portia, Brutus's wife, has taken her own life.

3   O madam, my old heart is cracked, it's cracked!
Gloucester in *King Lear*, 2.1.90

Supposing his son Edgar has sought to kill him.

4   You see me here, you gods, a poor old man,
As full of grief as age, wretched in both.
King Lear in *King Lear*, 2.4.272–3

The old king is cast out by his daughters, Goneril and Regan.

5   The worst is not
So long as we can say, "This is the worst."
Edgar in *King Lear*, 4.1.27–8

6   Henceforth I'll bear
Affliction till it do cry out itself
"Enough, enough," and die.
Gloucester in *King Lear*, 4.6.75–7

Believing he has miraculously survived falling off a cliff.

7   O, full of scorpions is my mind, dear wife!
Macbeth in *Macbeth*, 3.2.36

8   My heart is turned to stone; I strike it, and it hurts my hand.
Othello in *Othello*, 4.1.182–3

9   Had it pleased Heaven
To try me with affliction, had they rained
All kind of sores and shames on my bare head,
Steeped me in poverty to the very lips,
Given to captivity me and my utmost hopes,
I should have found in some place of my soul
A drop of patience.
Othello in *Othello*, 4.2.47–53

No affliction could match that of Desdemona's supposed adultery.

10   O ill-starred wench,
Pale as thy smock! When we shall
   meet at compt,
This look of thine will hurl my soul
   from heaven,
And fiends will snatch at it. Cold,
   cold, my girl,
Even like thy chastity.

Othello in _Othello_, 5.2.272–6

Looking at Desdemona's lifeless body;
"compt" = the Day of Judgment.

11 Comfort's in heaven, and we are on
   the earth,
Where nothing lives but crosses,
   cares and grief.

York in _Richard II_, 2.2.78–9

He is left alone to cope with rebellion;
"crosses" = vexations.

12 Affliction is enamored of thy parts,
And thou art wedded to calamity.

Friar Lawrence in _Romeo and Juliet_,
3.3.2–3

Telling the newly-married Romeo that he is
banished.

13 _Camillo._ Prosperity's the very bond
   of love,
Whose fresh complexion and
   whose heart together
Affliction alters.
Perdita.   One of these is true:
I think affliction may subdue the
   cheek,
But not take in the mind.

The Winter's Tale, 4.4.573–7

Camillo is trying to help Perdita escape from
the anger of Polixenes.

14 It easeth some, though none it ever
   cured,

To think their dolor others have
   endured.

The Rape of Lucrece, 1581–2

Afterlife (see also Heaven)

1 But this eternal blazon must not be
To ears of flesh and blood.

Ghost in _Hamlet_, 1.5.21–2

Refusing to describe to Hamlet his afterlife;
"eternal blazon" = revelation of eternal things.

2   Who would fardels bear
To grunt and sweat under a weary
   life
But that the dread of something
   after death,
The undiscovered country, from
   whose bourn
No traveler returns, puzzles the will,
And makes us rather bear those ills
   we have,
Than fly to others that we know not
   of?

Hamlet in _Hamlet_, 3.1.75–81

The "fardels" or burdens of this life are made
tolerable by fear of worse after death.

3 Would I were with him, wheresoe'er he is, either in heaven or in
   hell!

Bardolph in _Henry V_, 2.3.7–8

On hearing that Falstaff is dead.

4 Nay sure, he's not in hell; he's in
   Arthur's bosom, if ever man went
   to Arthur's bosom. 'A made a finer
   end, and went away an it had been
   any christom child.

Mistress Quickly in _Henry V_, 2.3.9–12

On Falstaff: she confuses King Arthur with
Abraham (a beggar is carried by angels to
"Abraham's bosom" in Luke 16:22); by "chris-
tom child" she means new christened baby.

5   So part we sadly in this troublous
    world
    To meet with joy in sweet
    Jerusalem.

Queen Margaret in *Henry VI, Part 3*,
5.5.7–8

Parting from her allies who are about to be
executed; "sweet Jerusalem" is heaven, the
holy city of the new Jerusalem promised in
Revelation 21:2 and 10.

6   Beating and hanging are terrors to
    me. For the life to come, I sleep out
    the thought of it.

Autolycus, *The Winter's Tale*, 4.3.29–30

Age (see also Middle Age, Old Age)

1   Unregarded age in corners thrown.

Adam in *As You Like It*, 2.3.42

On being dismissed at the age of "almost
fourscore" from the household where he has
served all his life.

2   He that doth the ravens feed,
    Yea, providently caters for the spar-
    row,
    Be comfort to my age!

Adam in *As You Like It*, 2.3.43–5

Calling on God's help.

3   Therefore my age is as a lusty win-
    ter,
    Frosty, but kindly.

Adam in *As You Like It*, 2.3.52–3

4   The sixth age shifts
    Into the lean and slippered pan-
    taloon,

With spectacles on nose, and pouch
    on side,
His youthful hose, well saved, a
    world too wide
For his shrunk shank, and his big
    manly voice,
Turning again toward childish tre-
    ble, pipes
And whistles in his sound.

Jaques in *As You Like It*, 2.7.157–63

The sixth of the "seven ages" of man;
"pantaloon" = old fool, from a character type
in Italian comedy.

5   Last scene of all,
    That ends this strange eventful his-
    tory,
    Is second childishness, and mere
    oblivion,
    Sans teeth, sans eyes, sans taste,
    sans everything.

Jaques in *As You Like It*, 2.7.163–6

The seventh of the "seven ages" of man.

6   The satirical rogue says here that
    old men have grey beards, that their
    faces are wrinkled, their eyes purg-
    ing thick amber and plum-tree
    gum, and that they have a plentiful
    lack of wit, together with most
    weak hams.

Hamlet in *Hamlet*, 2.2.196–200

Mocking the aging Polonius by pretending to
quote from a book he is reading.

7   What doth gravity out of his bed at
    midnight?

Falstaff in *Henry IV, Part 1*, 2.4.294

On an old nobleman arriving with a message
for Hal.

8   That he is old, the more the pity,
    his white hairs do witness it.

Falstaff in *Henry IV, Part 1*, 2.4.467–8

Inviting sympathy because of old age.

9 If sack and sugar be a fault, God help the wicked! If to be old and merry be a sin, then many an old host that I know is damned.

Falstaff in *Henry IV, Part 1*, 2.4.470–2

Defending himself against Prince Henry's denunciation.

10 Your lordship, though not clean past your youth, have yet some smack of age in you, some relish of the saltness of time in you.

Falstaff in *Henry IV, Part 2*, 1.2.96–9

Insulting the Chief Justice; "saltness" = sharp or bitter taste.

11 You that are old consider not the capacities of us that are young.

Falstaff in *Henry IV, Part 2*, 1.2.173–4

In fact Falstaff is as old as the Chief Justice he is teasing.

12 Have you not a moist eye, a dry hand, a yellow cheek, a white beard, a decreasing leg, an increasing belly? Is not your voice broken, your wind short, your chin double, your wit single, and every part about you blasted with antiquity? And will you yet call yourself young?

Chief Justice in *Henry IV, Part 2*, 1.2.180–5

Rebuking old Falstaff for calling himself young.

13 A man can no more separate age and covetousness than 'a can part young limbs and lechery.

Falstaff in *Henry IV, Part 2*, 1.2.228–30

14 *Shallow.* Doth she hold her own well?
Falstaff. Old, old, Master Shallow.
Shallow. Nay, she must be old, she cannot choose but be old, certain she's old.

Henry IV, Part 2, 3.2.205–8

Recalling what happened fifty-five years previously.

15 Lord, Lord, how subject we old men are to this vice of lying!

Falstaff in *Henry IV, Part 2*, 3.2.303–4

Falstaff speaking truth for once.

16 The old folk, time's doting chronicles.

Clarence in *Henry IV, Part 2*, 4.4.126

"Doting" implies they are extravagantly fond of recalling the past.

17 I know thee not, old man. Fall to thy prayers.
How ill white hairs becomes a fool and jester!

Prince Hal, now King Henry V, in *Henry IV, Part 2*, 5.5.47–8

His famous rejection of his old companion, Falstaff.

18 A good soft pillow for that good white head
Were better than a churlish turf of France.

King Henry in *Henry V*, 4.1.14–15

Addressing the old soldier Erpingham.

19 My comfort is that old age, that ill layer-up of beauty, can do no more spoil upon my face.

King Henry in *Henry V*, 5.2.229–31

Apologizing for his plainness.

20 You see how full of changes his age is.

Goneril in *King Lear* , 1.1.288

Speaking of her father, King Lear.

21   Idle old man,
That still would manage those authorities
That he hath given away!

Goneril in *King Lear*, 1.3.16–18

She is speaking about her father, King Lear.

22 Old fools are babes again, and must be used
With checks as flatteries.

Goneril in *King Lear*, 1.3.19–20

Speaking about her father, King Lear, and varying the proverb "an old man is twice a child"; "checks" or rebukes are the flattery they require.

23 As you are old and reverend, should be wise.

Goneril in *King Lear*, 1.4.240

To her father, implying he is anything but wise.

24 Thou shouldst not have been old till thou hadst been wise.

Fool in *King Lear*, 1.5.44–5

Addressing King Lear.

25   O sir, you are old;
Nature in you stands on the very verge
Of his confine.

Regan in *King Lear*, 2.4.146–8

"Confine" = limit, bounds.

26 Do you but mark how this becomes the house!
"Dear daughter, I confess that I am old;
Age is unnecessary. On my knees I beg
That you'll vouchsafe me raiment, bed, and food."

King Lear in *King Lear*, 2.4.153–6

Scorning the idea of begging his daughter's forgiveness; "becomes the house" = befits the decorum of the royal house.

27 I am a very foolish fond old man,
Fourscore and upward, not an hour more nor less;
And to deal plainly,
I fear I am not in my perfect mind.

King Lear in *King Lear*, 4.7.59–62

"Fond" = silly, in my dotage.

Air

1 Hover through the fog and filthy air.

The Witches (Weird Sisters) in *Macbeth*, 1.1.12

2 *Adrian.* The air breathes upon us here most sweetly.
Sebastian. As if it had lungs, and rotten ones.
Antonio. Or as 'twere perfumed by a fen.

The Tempest, 2.1.47–9

Shipwrecked courtiers, whose characters are reflected in their attitudes to the island on which they find themselves.

Ambition

1
                    Ambition
(The soldier's virtue) rather makes
    choice of loss
Than gain which darkens him.

Ventidius in *Antony and Cleopatra*,
3.1.22–4

Having won a victory, he decides not to do
more, so as not to outshine the emperor,
Antony.

2   Ill-weaved ambition, how much art
        thou shrunk!
When that this body did contain a
    spirit,
A kingdom for it was too small a
    bound,
But now two paces of the vilest
    earth
Is room enough.

Prince Hal in *Henry IV, Part 1*,
5.4.88–92

On the death of Hotspur.

3   These days are dangerous;
Virtue is choked with foul ambi-
    tion,
And charity chased hence by ran-
    cor's hand.

Gloucester in *Henry VI, Part 2*,
3.1.142–4

On plots against the king.

4   No man's pie is freed
From his ambitious finger.

Buckingham in *Henry VIII*, 1.1.52–3

On Cardinal Wolsey.

5   Cromwell, I charge thee, fling away
        ambition,
By that sin fell the angels; how can
    man then,
The image of his maker, hope to
    win by it?

Cardinal Wolsey in *Henry VIII*,
3.2.440–2

Lucifer's sin is usually called pride, but he was
ambitious too: "I will exalt my throne above
the stars of God" (Isaiah 14:13).

6   Love and meekness,
        lord,
Become a churchman better than
    ambition.

Archbishop Cranmer in *Henry VIII*,
5.2.97–8

Rebuking the Bishop of Winchester.

7   'Tis a common proof
That lowliness is young ambition's
    ladder.

Brutus in *Julius Caesar*, 2.1.21–2

8   Ambition's debt is paid.

Brutus in *Julius Caesar*, 3.1.83

Meaning the ambition of the assassinated
Caesar.

9   But Brutus says he was ambitious,
And Brutus is an honorable man.

Mark Antony in *Julius Caesar*, 3.2.86–7

Speaking to the people after the death of
Caesar.

10   When that the poor have cried,
        Caesar hath wept;
Ambition should be made of
    sterner stuff.

Mark Antony in *Julius Caesar*, 3.2.91–2

11   Thou wouldst be great;
Art not without ambition, but
   without
The illness should attend it. What
   thou wouldst highly
That wouldst thou holily; wouldst
   not play false,
And yet wouldst wrongly win.

Lady Macbeth in *Macbeth,* 1.5.18–22

"Illness" = wickedness; describing the moral
confusion in Macbeth as they think about
murdering Duncan.

12   I have no spur
To prick the sides of my intent, but
   only
Vaulting ambition, which o'erleaps
   itself,
And falls on th' other.

Macbeth in *Macbeth,* 1.7.25–8

The image is of a rider vaulting into the saddle
and falling on the other side of the horse;
Macbeth is contemplating the murder of
Duncan.

13   Thriftless ambition, that will raven
   up
Thine own life's means!

Ross in *Macbeth,* 2.4.28–9

Supposing Duncan's sons have killed their
father, and hence their means of subsistence;
"raven up" = devour greedily.

14   The aim of all is but to nurse the
   life
With honor, wealth and ease in
   waning age.

The Rape of Lucrece, 141–2

Anarchy (see also Chaos, Disorder)

1   If that the heavens do not their visible spirits

Send quickly down to tame these
   vile offenses,
It will come:
Humanity must perforce prey on
   itself,
Like monsters of the deep.

Albany in *King Lear,* 4.2.46–9

Albany is horrified by what King Lear's daughters, Goneril and Regan, have done to their
father, thrust out into a wild storm; but his
words carry a more general meaning, impli-
cating everyone.

2   Force should be right, or, rather,
   right and wrong—
Between whose endless jar justice
   resides—
Should lose their names, and so
   should justice too.
Then everything includes itself in
   power,
Power into will, will into appetite;
And appetite, an universal wolf,
So doubly seconded with will and
   power,
Must make perforce an universal
   prey,
And last eat up himself.

Ulysses in *Troilus and Cressida,*
1.3.116–24

Ulysses' vision of anarchy if social ranks and
hierarchy are abolished.

Androgyny

1   They shall yet belie thy happy years
That say thou art a man. Diana's
   lip
Is not more smooth and rubious;
   thy small pipe
Is as the maiden's organ, shrill and
   sound,
And all is semblative a woman's
   part.

Orsino in *Twelfth Night*, 1.4.30–4

Almost penetrating Viola's disguise as his page Cesario; "rubious" = red; "pipe" = voice; "is semblative" = resembles. (Viola was originally played by a boy).

2   A woman's face with Nature's own
    hand painted
    Hast thou, the master-mistress of
    my passion;
    A woman's gentle heart, but not
    acquainted
    With shifting change as is false
    women's fashion.

Sonnet 20, 1–4

Addressing his male "friend."

Angels

1   Angels are bright still, though the
    brightest fell.
    Though all things foul would wear
    the brows of grace,
    Yet grace must still look so.

Malcolm in *Macbeth*, 4.3.22–4

Referring to Lucifer; see Isaiah 14:12.

2   For every man that Bolingbroke
    hath pressed
    To lift shrewd steel against our
    golden crown,
    God for his Richard hath in heav-
    enly pay
    A glorious angel. Then if angels
    fight,
    Weak men must fall; for heaven still
    guards the right.

King Richard in *Richard II*, 3.2.58–62

Trying to comfort himself.

Anger

1   Anger's my meat; I sup upon
    myself,
    And so shall starve with feeding.

Volumnia in *Coriolanus*, 4.2.50–1

Refusing an invitation to supper after Coriolanus's banishment.

2   Must I give way and room to your
    rash choler?
    Shall I be frighted when a madman
    stares?

Brutus in *Julius Caesar*, 4.3.39–40

Responding to the angry Cassius.

3   Sir, sir, impatience hath his privi-
    lege.

Pembroke of *King John*, 4.3.32

Meaning that strong emotion permits a freedom from the restraints of good manners.

4   Come not between the dragon and
    his wrath.

King Lear in *King Lear*, 1.1.122

King Lear himself is the "dragon," the absolute monarch, speaking to Kent.

5   O, when she is angry she is keen
    and shrewd;
    She was a vixen when she went to
    school,
    And though she be but little, she is
    fierce.

**Helena in *A Midsummer Night's
Dream*, 3.2.323–5**

On Hermia; "keen and shrewd" = caustic and malicious.

6 Now you strike like the blind man;
'twas the boy that stole your meat,
and you'll beat the post.
Benedick in *Much Ado About Nothing*,
2.1.198–200

Claudio lashes out wildly on thinking he has
been betrayed.

7 O God, that I were a man! I would
eat his heart in the market-place.
Beatrice in *Much Ado About Nothing*,
4.1.306–7

Angry with Claudio for abandoning Hero.

8 Like an unseasonable stormy day,
Which makes the silver rivers
drown their shores,
As if the world were all dissolved to
tears,
So high above his limits swells the
rage
Of Bolingbroke.
Sir Stephen Scroop in *Richard II*,
3.2.106–10

Bringing news that the whole country has
gone over to Henry Bolingbroke.

9 To be in anger is impiety;
But who is man that is not angry?
Alcibiades in *Timon of Athens*, 3.5.56–7

Seeking mercy for a friend who has killed, he
claims, in self-defense.

Animals (see also Creatures, Dogs, Horses)

1 A lioness, with udders all drawn
dry,
Lay couching, head on ground,
with cat-like watch

When that the sleeping man should
stir; for 'tis
The royal disposition of that beast
To prey on nothing that doth seem
as dead.
Oliver in *As You Like It*, 4.3.114–18

Describing the danger from which Orlando
rescued him.

2 Pray you no more of this, 'tis like
the howling of Irish wolves against
the moon.
Rosalind in *As You Like It*, 5.2.109–10

Dogs or wolves barking at the moon offered a
proverbial image of ineffectual outcry. She is
calling on the lovers to stop complaining.

3 The cat will mew, and dog will have
his day.
Hamlet in *Hamlet*, 5.1.292

Meaning that one cannot stop a creature from
acting according to its nature. Hamlet may
refer to Laertes (as the cat), and himself (as the
dog whose turn will come). The saying about
the dog was proverbial.

4 Wanton as youthful goats, wild as
young bulls.
Vernon in *Henry IV, Part 1*, 4.1.103

Prince Hal and his companions, ready for
war against the rebels; "wanton" = merry,
frolicsome.

5 The fox barks not when he would
steal the lamb.
Suffolk in *Henry VI, Part 2*, 3.1.55

6 But when the fox hath once got in
his nose,
He'll soon find means to make the
body follow.
**Richard of Gloucester in *Henry VI,
Part 3*,** 4.7.25–6

7   And when the lion fawns upon the
       lamb,
    The lamb will never cease to follow
       him.

King Henry in *Henry VI, Part 3*,
4.8.49–50

Henry wrongly imagines that the people will
support him because of his mild rule.

8   A harmless necessary cat.

Shylock in *The Merchant of Venice*,
4.1.55

Commenting on what some people for no reason dislike.

9   *King Richard.* Lions make leopards
       tame.
    Mowbray. Yea, but not change his
       spots.

***Richard II*, 1.1.174–5**

Richard sees himself as a lion, king of beasts.

10   The lion dying thrusteth forth his
       paw
    And wounds the earth, if nothing
       else, with rage
    To be o'erpowered.

Queen in *Richard II*, 5.1.29–31

Urging the woebegone Richard to behave like
the lion, the king of beasts.

11   Villain, thou know'st nor law of
       God nor man;
    No beast so fierce but knows some
       touch of pity.

Lady Anne in *Richard III*, 1.2.70–1

To Richard, displaying the corpse of Henry VI,
slain by him; "nor law" = neither law.

12   *Exit pursued by a bear.*

Stage direction in *The Winter's Tale*,
3.3.58

A famous stage direction, thought to be
Shakespeare's own, for the exit of Antigonus;
probably an actor dressed in a bear-skin was
used.

Answers

1   Your answer, sir, is enigmatical.

Benedick in *Much Ado about Nothing*,
5.4.27

He is puzzled by Leonato's reference to the
trick played on him to make him fall in love
with Beatrice.

Anticipation

1   All things that are
    Are with more spirit chasèd than
       enjoyed.

Gratiano in *The Merchant of Venice*,
2.6.12–13

Referring to Lorenzo's plan to elope with Jessica.

2   A day in April never came so sweet,
    To show how costly summer was at
       hand,
    As this fore-spurrer comes before
       his lord.

Messenger in *The Merchant of Venice*,
2.9.93–5

On the messenger who announces the coming
of Bassanio; "costly" = rich, splendid.

3   Gallop apace, you fiery-footed
       steeds,
    Towards Phoebus' lodging.

Juliet in *Romeo and Juliet*, 3.2.1–2

Trying to hurry on the horses of the sun (Phoebus) towards nightfall, when she expects
Romeo to come.

4   I am giddy; expectation whirls me
     round.
     Th'imaginary relish is so sweet
     That it enchants my sense.

Troilus in *Troilus and Cressida*,
3.2.18–20

Anticipating his first chance to make love to
Cressida.

Anti-Semitism

1   You call me misbeliever, cut-throat
     dog,
     And spit upon my Jewish gaber-
     dine,
     And all for use of that which is
     mine own.

Shylock in *The Merchant of Venice*,
1.3.111–13

"Gaberdine" = loose cape or cloak.

2   He hath disgraced me, and hin-
     dered me half a million, laughed at
     my losses, mocked at my gains,
     scorned my nation, thwarted my
     bargains, cooled my friends, heated
     mine enemies; and what's his rea-
     son? I am a Jew.

Shylock in *The Merchant of Venice*,
3.1.54–8

On the Christian merchant, Antonio.

Anxiety

1   Undone, and forfeited to cares for
     ever!

Bertram in *All's Well That Ends Well*,
2.3.266

On being forced to marry Helena.

2   So shaken as we are, so wan with
     care,
     Find we a time for frighted peace to
     pant.

King Henry in *Henry IV, Part 1*, 1.1.1–2

Hoping for a breathing-space and the end of
civil war.

3   Care is no cure, but rather corro-
     sive.
     For things that are not to be reme-
     died.

Joan la Pucelle in *Henry VI, Part 1*,
3.3.3–4

Speaking to the French leaders, after the English have taken Rouen.

4   Between the acting of a dreadful
     thing
     And the first motion, all the interim
     is
     Like a phantasma or a hideous
     dream.
     The genius and the mortal instru-
     ments
     Are then in council, and the state of
     man,
     Like to a little kingdom, suffers
     then
     The nature of an insurrection.

Brutus in *Julius Caesar*, 2.1.63–9

A marvelous expression of a tormented mind
living as it were a hallucination ("phantasma"), while the soul ("genius") on the one
hand, and the mental and physical functions
of the body on the other, are at odds.

5   You have some sick offense within
     your mind,
     Which by the right and virtue of
     my place
     I ought to know of.

Portia in *Julius Caesar*, 2.1.268–70

Demanding, as Brutus's wife, to know what troubles him.

6   Better be with the dead,
Whom we, to gain our peace, have
      sent to peace,
Than on the torture of the mind to
      lie
In restless ecstasy.

Macbeth in *Macbeth*, 3.2.19–22

To Lady Macbeth; those they have murdered have gone to "peace" or heaven, but their deeds have not brought peace of mind to Macbeth, only "ecstasy," or a frenzied anxiety.

7   Then comes my fit again. I had else
      been perfect,
Whole as the marble, founded as
      the rock,
As broad and general as the casing
      air.
But now I am cabined, cribbed,
      confined, bound in
To saucy doubts and fears.

Macbeth in *Macbeth*, 3.4.20–4

On learning that his murderers failed to kill Fleance; "broad and general" = free and unconfined; "casing" = surrounding.

8   You have too much respect upon
      the world.
They lose it that do buy it with
      much care.

**Gratiano in *The Merchant of Venice*,
1.1.74–5**

Telling Antonio he has too anxious a regard ("respect") for his business affairs ("upon the world").

9   Although I joy in thee,
I have no joy of this contract
      tonight.

It is too rash, too unadvised, too
      sudden,
Too like the lightning which doth
      cease to be
Ere one can say it lightens.

Juliet in *Romeo and Juliet*, 2.2.116–20

To Romeo; she already has a premonition that their love may not last.

10 O, the thorns we stand upon!

Florizel in *The Winter's Tale*, 4.4.585

To Perdita; a proverbial expression for anxiety about the problems they face.

11 Not mine own fears, nor the
      prophetic soul
Of the wide world, dreaming on
      things to come,
Can yet the lease of my true love
      control,
Supposed as forfeit to a confined
      doom.

***Sonnet* 107, 1–4**

Anxiety about the future in these lines may have been sparked by the uncertainties of the last years of the reign of Queen Elizabeth I; the "lease" or allotted term may be of the speaker's life and love, or of the loved one's life and love, or both; "forfeit to a confined doom" is usually taken to mean "subject to a fixed term."

Aphorisms and Epigrams

1   He that wants money, means, and
    content is without three good
    friends.

Corin in *As You Like It*, 3.2.24–6

"Means" = opportunity.

2   He's mad that trusts in the tame-
    ness of a wolf, a horse's health, a
    boy's love, or a whore's oath.

Fool in *King Lear*, 3.6.18–19

3 Wisdom and goodness to the vile
  seem vile.

Albany in *King Lear*, 4.2.38

Pretending he has a toothache in order to avoid confessing he is in love; "grief" = pain or anguish.

4 Things without all remedy
  Should be without regard: what's
  done is done.

Lady Macbeth in *Macbeth*, 3.2.11–12

"Be without regard" = not be brooded on. She speaks as though it is easy to forget the past, but see 7 below.

5 Things bad begun make strong
  themselves by ill.

Macbeth in *Macbeth*, 3.2.55

6 Receive what cheer you may;
  The night is long that never finds
  the day.

Malcolm in *Macbeth*, 4.3.239–40

7 What's done cannot be undone.

Lady Macbeth in *Macbeth*, 5.1.68

Her involvement in murders returns to haunt her; compare 4 above.

8 Shall quips and sentences and
  these paper bullets of the brain awe
  a man from the career of his
  humor? No, the world must be
  peopled.

Benedick in *Much Ado About Nothing*, 2.3.240–2

Refusing to be intimidated by mocking words ("sentences" = maxims) from pursuing his inclination, and loving Beatrice.

9 Everyone can master a grief but he
  that has it.

Benedick in *Much Ado About Nothing*, 3.2.28–9

10 She never yet was foolish that was
  fair,
  For even her folly helped her to an
  heir.

Iago in *Othello*, 2.1.136–7

No matter how silly, a beautiful woman may win a rich husband and have a child; "heir" may carry both senses.

11 Poor and content is rich, and rich
  enough,
  But riches fineless is as poor as winter
  To him that ever fears he shall be
  poor.

Iago in *Othello*, 3.3.172–4

"Fineless" = unlimited.

Apologies (see also Excuses)

1   I would I could
  Quit all offenses with as clear
  excuse
  As well as I am doubtless I can
  purge
  Myself of many I am charged
  withal.

Prince Hal in *Henry IV, Part 1*, 3.2.18–21

Apologizing to his father, King Henry; "quit" = be clear of.

2 I should not urge thy duty past thy
  might.
  I know young bloods look for a
  time of rest.

Brutus in *Julius Caesar*, 4.3.261–2

To his servant Lucius.

3 Pardon this fault, and by my soul I
   swear
   I never more will break an oath
   with thee.

Bassanio in *The Merchant of Venice,*
5.1.247–8

The "fault" lay in giving Portia's ring away.

4 I have been long a sleeper; but I
   trust
   My absence doth neglect no great
   design
   Which by my presence might have
   been concluded.

King Richard in *Richard III,* 3.4.23–5

Apologizing for his late arrival at a council
meeting; "great design" = important proposal
or business.

5 My business was great, and in such
   a case as mine a man may strain
   courtesy.

Romeo in *Romeo and Juliet,* 2.4.49–51

Apologizing for dodging away from Mercutio;
his "business" was to make love to Juliet.

Apparitions (see also Ghosts)

1 What, has this thing appeared again
   tonight?

Horatio in *Hamlet,* 1.1.21

Addressed to the sentinels at the king's castle,
regarding the ghost of the dead King Hamlet
of Denmark.

2 What art thou that usurp'st this
   time of night,
   Together with that fair and warlike
   form
   In which the majesty of buried
   Denmark
   Did sometimes march? By heaven I
   charge thee speak!

Horatio in *Hamlet,* 1.1.46–9

Addressing the ghost of Hamlet's father, the
dead King of Denmark; Horatio questions the
ghost's right to assume that likeness, and its
right to invade the night, by the use of the
term "usurp'st."

3 In the most high and palmy state of
   Rome,
   A little ere the mightiest Julius fell,
   The graves stood tenantless and the
   sheeted dead
   Did squeak and gibber in the
   Roman streets.

Horatio in *Hamlet,* 1.1.113–16

The apparition of the dead King Hamlet suggests some impending calamity, like portents
before the assassination of Julius Caesar.

4 How ill this taper burns! Ha! Who
   comes here?
   I think it is the weakness of mine
   eyes
   That shapes this monstrous apparition.

Brutus in *Julius Caesar,* 4.3.275–7

On the entry of the ghost of Caesar.

5 Art thou some god, some angel, or
   some devil,
   That mak'st my blood cold, and my
   hair to stare?

Brutus in *Julius Caesar,* 4.3.279–80

Seeing the ghost of Caesar.

6 Is this a dagger which I see before
   me,
   The handle toward my hand?
   Come, let me clutch thee:
   I have thee not, and yet I see thee
   still.

Macbeth in *Macbeth,* 2.1.33–5

The imaginary dagger that symbolizes his anxiety about killing Duncan.

7   Art thou not, fatal vision, sensible
     To feeling as to sight? Or art thou
        but
     A dagger of the mind, a false cre-
        ation
     Proceeding from the heat-
        oppressèd brain?

Macbeth in *Macbeth*, 2.1.36–9

The vision is "fatal" as prompting him to murder; "heat-oppressed" = fevered.

8   Can such things be
     And overcome us like a summer's
        cloud,
     Without our special wonder?

Macbeth in *Macbeth*, 3.4.109–11

On seeing the ghost of the murdered Banquo.

Appearance

1   *Gertrude.* Why seems it so particu-
        lar with thee?
     Hamlet. Seems, madam? Nay, it is,
        I know not "seems."

***Hamlet*, 1.2.75–6**

Gertrude has attempted to console Hamlet for
his father's death by urging that death is common, i.e., universal, not "particular."

2   There's no art
     To find the mind's construction in
        the face:
     He was a gentleman on whom I
        built
     An absolute trust.

Duncan in *Macbeth*, 1.4.11–14

Referring to the traitor Cawdor.

3   Mislike me not for my complexion,
     The shadowed livery of the bur-
        nished sun,
     To whom I am a neighbor and near
        bred.

**Prince of Morocco in *The Merchant of
Venice*, 2.1.1–3**

Asking Portia to be color-blind as he is black.

4   Lord worshipped might he be, what
        a beard hast thou got!

**Old Gobbo in *The Merchant of Venice*,
2.2.93–4**

The blind old man mistakes his son's long hair
for a beard.

5   O wise and upright judge!
     How much more elder art thou
        than thy looks!

**Shylock in *The Merchant of Venice*,
4.1.150–1**

On Portia, who has led him to think he can
have his pound of flesh.

6   *Claudio.* The old ornament of his
        cheek hath already stuffed tennis-
        balls.
     Leonato. Indeed, he looks younger
        than he did, by the loss of a beard.

***Much Ado About Nothing*, 3.2.46–9**

Benedick appears clean-shaven for the sake of
Beatrice, who said she could not stand a
bearded man.

7   Give not this rotten orange to your
        friend;
     She's but the sign and semblance of
        her honor.

**Claudio in *Much Ado About Nothing*,
4.1.32–3**

Rejecting Hero as unchaste at the wedding
ceremony; "sign and semblance" = outward
appearance.

8   Men should be what they seem,
     Or those that be not, would they
        might seem none.

Iago in *Othello*, 3.3.126

Ironic in relation to his own hypocrisy.

9   Opinion's but a fool that makes us
    scan
    The outward habit for the inward
    man.
    Simonides in *Pericles*, 2.2.56–7

    Or judge people by appearances.

10 I think there's never a man in
    Christendom
    Can lesser hide his love or hate than
    he,
    For by his face straight shall you
    know his heart.
    Hastings in *Richard III*, 3.4.51–3

    Showing his mistaken trust in Richard.

11 I will believe thou hast a mind that
    suits
    With this thy fair and outward
    character.
    Viola in *Twelfth Night*, 1.2.50–1

    To the captain of the ship that brought her to
    Illyria.

12 He's as tall a man as any's in Illyria.
    **Sir Toby Belch in *Twelfth Night*,
    1.3.20**

    Defending his friendship with Sir Andrew
    Aguecheek.

13 *Mamillius.* What color are your
    eyebrows?
    First Lady. Blue, my lord.
    Mamillius. Nay, that's a mock. I
    have seen a lady's nose
    That has been blue, but not her eye-
    brows.
    The Winter's Tale, 2.1.13–15

    Hermione's little son talks with court ladies.

Appetite

1   The sweetest honey
     Is loathsome in his own delicious-
     ness,
     And in the taste confounds the
     appetite.
     **Friar Lawrence in *Romeo and Juliet*,
     2.6.11–13**

     Varying the proverb, "too much honey cloys
     the stomach," and hinting at the idea of love
     turning into hate.

Argument (see also Reason)

1   You shall have time to wrangle in
     when you have nothing else to do.
     **Enobarbus in *Antony and Cleopatra*,
     2.2.105–6**

     Intervening to stop Antony and Octavius
     arguing about who is to blame for their
     differences.

2   He is too disputable for my com-
     pany. I think of as many matters as
     he, but I give heaven thanks, and
     make no boast of them.
     Jaques in *As You Like It*, 2.5.35–7

     "Disputable" = fond of argument.

3   Your reasons at dinner have been
     sharp and sententious, pleasant
     without scurrility, witty without
     affection, audacious without
     impudency, learned without
     opinion, and strange without
     heresy.
     Nathaniel in *Love's Labor's Lost*, 5.1.2–6

     The curate praises the conversation of the
     pedant; "affection" = affectation; "without
     opinion" = without being opinionated.

4　He draweth out the thread of his verbosity finer than the staple of his argument.

Holofernes in *Love's Labor's Lost*, 5.1.16–17

Describing Armado's extravagant language; "staple" = fiber.

5　You have both said well,
And on the cause and question now in hand
Have glozed, but superficially—not much
Unlike young men whom Aristotle thought
Unfit to hear moral philosophy.

Hector in *Troilus and Cressida*, 2.2.163–7

Referring to Paris and Troilus in the debate about whether to keep Helen; "glozed" = commented. Aristotle lived long after the Trojan War took place.

6　The reasons you allege do more conduce
To the hot passion of distempered blood
Than to make up a free determination
'Twixt right and wrong; for pleasure and revenge
Have ears more deaf than adders to the voice
Of any true decision.

Hector in *Troilus and Cressida*, 2.2.168–73

Criticizing Troilus and Paris for being besotted on Helen; "free" = unbiased.

Arithmetic

1　*Moth.* How many is one, thrice told?

Armado. I am ill at reckoning; it fitteth the spirit of a tapster.

***Love's Labor's Lost*, 1.2.39–41**

"Tapster" = barman.

Arrogance

1　But most it is presumption in us when
The help of heaven we count the act of men.

Helena in *All's Well That Ends Well*, 2.1.151–2

She is urging the King of France, who has refused her offer to treat his illness, to think of her as heaven's agent.

2　Possessed he is with greatness,
And speaks not to himself but with a pride
That quarrels at self-breath.

Ulysses in *Troilus and Cressida*, 2.3.170–2

Commenting on Achilles; "quarrels at self-breath" = finds fault with what he says about himself (as not measuring up to his greatness).

Asceticism

1　A man whose blood
Is very snow-broth; one who never feels
The wanton stings and motions of the sense,
But doth rebate and blunt his natural edge
With profits of the mind, study, and fast.

Lucio in *Measure for Measure*, 1.4.57–61

Describing Angelo as an ascetic who never feels sexual passion ("wanton stings and motions of the sense").

Aspiration

1 Why, then, I do but dream on sovereignty
Like one that stands upon a promontory
And spies a far-off shore where he would tread,
Wishing his foot were equal with his eye.

Richard of Gloucester in *Henry VI, Part 3*, 3.2.134–7

Already dreaming of becoming King Richard III.

Assassination

1 Let's kill him boldly, but not wrathfully;
Let's carve him as a dish fit for the gods,
Not hew him as a carcass fit for hounds.

Brutus in *Julius Caesar*, 2.1.172–4

On the idea of killing Caesar.

2 Let our hearts, as subtle masters do,
Stir up their servants to an act of rage
And after seem to chide 'em. This shall make
Our purpose necessary, and not envious;
Which so appearing to the common eyes,
We shall be called purgers, not murderers.

Brutus in *Julius Caesar*, 2.1.175–80

"Servants" = bodily agents; "envious" = malicious; he is trying to make the murder of Caesar look like a sacrifice.

Assault

1 These hands do lack nobility that they strike
A meaner than myself.

Cleopatra in *Antony and Cleopatra*, 2.5.82–3

On losing dignity in striking the messenger who brings bad news.

Astrology

1 We make guilty of our disasters the sun, the moon, and stars, as if we were villains on necessity, fools by heavenly compulsion.

Edmund in *King Lear*, 1.2.120–2

Edmund's contempt for astrology passes into a rejection of religion and morality; "on" = by.

2 My father compounded with my mother under the Dragon's tail, and my nativity was under Ursa Major, so that it follows, I am rough and lecherous. Fut, I should have been that I am, had the maidenliest star in the firmament twinkled on my bastardizing.

Edmund in *King Lear*, 1.2.128–33

The constellations Draco ("Dragon's tail") and Ursa Major, or Great Bear, were supposed to have a malignant influence. Edmund's belief contrasts with that of Kent in the same play; see the next entry

3 It is the stars,
The stars above us, govern our conditions.

Kent in *King Lear*, 4.3.32–3

He cannot explain the difference between King Lear's two wicked elder daughters and his youngest, the gentle Cordelia; "conditions" = natures, dispositions.

4   I find my zenith doth depend upon
A most auspicious star, whose
    influence
If now I court not, but omit, my
    fortunes
Will ever after droop.

Prospero in *The Tempest*, 1.2.181–4

"Zenith" = height of fortune.

Authority

1   I must be patient; there is no fettering of authority.

Parolles in *All's Well That Ends Well*,
2.3.236–7

Referring to Lord Lafew, who has seen
through his affectations, and treats him with
contempt.

2   Hear you this Triton of the minnows? Mark you
His absolute "shall"?

Coriolanus in *Coriolanus*, 3.1.89–90

Showing his contempt for Sicinius, a tribune
of the people; Triton was a minor sea-god in
ancient Greece.

3   He'll shake
Your Rome about your ears.

Cominius in *Coriolanus*, 4.6.98–9

Said of Coriolanus, when news comes that he
has joined with the Volscians against Rome.

4   I think he'll be to Rome
As is the osprey to the fish, who
    takes it
By sovereignty of nature.

Aufidius in *Coriolanus*, 4.7.33–5

Speaking of Coriolanus; fish were said to sur-
render themselves to the osprey.

5   O, sir, your presence is too bold
    and peremptory,

And majesty might never yet
    endure
The moody frontier of a servant
    brow.

King Henry in *Henry IV, Part 1*,
1.3.17–19

"Moody frontier" = angry frown; King Henry
is dismissing the rebellious Earl of Worcester.

6   *Kent.* You have that in your countenance which I would fain call
master.
Lear. What's that?
Kent. Authority.

King Lear, 1.4.27–30

7   *Lear.* Thou hast seen a farmer's
dog bark at a beggar?
Gloucester. Ay, sir.
Lear. And the creature run from
the cur? There thou mightst
behold the great image of authority: a dog's obeyed in office.

King Lear, 4.6.154–9

8   Thus can the demigod, Authority
Make us pay down for our offense,
    by weight,
The words of heaven: on whom it
    will, it will;
On whom it will not, so; yet still 'tis
    just.

Claudio in *Measure for Measure*,
1.2.120–3

On being committed to prison for getting
Juliet with child; the "words of heaven" are
from Romans 9:15–18, where God's pleasure
is to have mercy or otherwise as He pleases.

9   But man, proud man,
Dressed in a little brief authority,
Most ignorant of what he's most
    assured,

His glassy essence, like an angry ape
Plays such fantastic tricks before
    high heaven
As makes the angels weep.

Isabella in *Measure for Measure*,
2.2.117–22

Pleading with Angelo for her brother's life, she
reminds him of the pride that goes with
authority, and how ignorant men are of their
souls, the "essence" that like a glass or mirror
is reflected from God.

10   Authority, though it err like others,
Hath yet a kind of medicine in
    itself,
That skins the vice o' the top.

Isabella in *Measure for Measure*,
2.2.134–6

Reminding Angelo that men may use authority
to cover ("skin") their vices without remedying
them.

11   Though authority be a stubborn
bear, yet he is oft led by the nose
with gold. Show the inside of your
purse to the outside of his hand,
and no more ado.

Clown in *The Winter's Tale*, 4.4.801–4

Advising his father to bribe Autolycus, whom
he takes to be a great courtier.

Autumn, see Seasons

Avarice

1   How quickly nature falls into revolt
When gold becomes her object!

King Henry in *Henry IV*, Part 2,
4.5.65–6

"Nature" = human nature, or natural affection;
mistakenly thinking Prince Hal is greedy for
power.

2   Poorly rich so wanteth in his store
That, cloyed with much, he pineth
    still for more.

The Rape of Lucrece, 97–8

On the rich person who yet feels poor.

Banishment, see Exile

Bastardy

1   I grow, I prosper:
Now, gods, stand up for bastards!

Edmund in *King Lear*, 1.2.21–2

2   I am a bastard too. I love bastards.
I am bastard begot, bastard
instructed, bastard in mind,
bastard in valor, in every thing
illegitimate.

Thersites in *Troilus and Cressida*,
5.7.16–18

Encountering the bastard Margarelon on the
field of battle.

Beauty

1   For her own person,
It beggared all description: she did
    lie
In her pavilion—cloth of gold, of
    tissue—
O'er-picturing that Venus where we
    see
The fancy outwork nature.

Enobarbus in *Antony and Cleopatra*,
2.2.197–201

Cleopatra as she first appeared to Antony, out-
doing Venus, the goddess of love.

2   Alas, what danger will it be to us,
Maids as we are, to travel forth so
   far!
Beauty provoketh thieves sooner
   than gold.

Rosalind in *As You Like It*, 1.3.108–10

Commenting on Celia's suggestion that they
escape to the forest of Arden.

3   'Tis not your inky brows, your
   black silk hair,
Your bugle eyeballs, nor your cheek
   of cream
That can entame my spirits to your
   worship.

Rosalind in *As You Like It*, 3.5.46–8

Disguised as Ganymede, she rejects Phebe's
love; bugles were shiny black glass beads.

4   You are a thousand times a properer man
Than she a woman. 'Tis such fools
   as you
That makes the world full of ill-
   favored children.

Rosalind in *As You Like It*, 3.5.51–3

Disguised as a man, she advises Silvius, who
loves Phebe, who is in love with Rosalind;
"properer" = more handsome.

5   How bravely thou becom'st thy
   bed! fresh lily,
And whiter than the sheets!

Jachimo in *Cymbeline*, 2.2.15–16

Looking at Imogen asleep.

6   On her left breast
A mole cinque-spotted, like the
   crimson drops
I'the bottom of a cowslip.

Jachimo in *Cymbeline*, 2.2.37–9

Looking at Imogen asleep; "cinque-spotted" =
having five spots, an accurate description of
the cowslip flower.

7   See what a grace was seated on this
   brow:
Hyperion's curls, the front of Jove
   himself,
An eye like Mars, to threaten and
   command.

Hamlet in *Hamlet*, 3.4.55–7

To Gertrude, seeing his father in a picture as
like Hyperion, the ancient Greek sun-god, for
beauty; having a forehead (front) like Jupiter;
and an eye like the god of war.

8   'Tis beauty that doth oft make
   women proud.

York in *Henry VI, Part 3*, 1.4.128

9   The fairest hand I ever touched: O
   beauty,
Till now I never knew thee.

King Henry in *Henry VIII*, 1.4.75–6

On meeting Anne Boleyn.

10   Beauty and honor in her are so
   mingled
That they have caught the king.

Lord Chamberlain in *Henry VIII*,
2.3.76–7

On Anne Boleyn, soon to be queen.

11   Thou hast the sweetest face I ever
   looked on.
Sir, as I have a soul, she is an angel.

Second Gentleman in *Henry VIII*,
4.1.43–4

On seeing Anne Boleyn, now crowned as
queen.

12   My beauty, though but mean,
Needs not the painted flourish of
   your praise.
Beauty is bought by judgment of
   the eye.

Princess in *Love's Labor's Lost*, 2.1.13–15

Rejecting Boyet's flattery of her.

13 Beauty doth varnish age as if new
    born,
And gives the crutch the cradle's
    infancy.
O, 'tis the sun that maketh all
    things shine!

Berowne in *Love's Labor's Lost*,
4.3.240–2

In love with Rosaline, Berowne claims for her
a beauty that could restore youth to the aged.

14   Look on beauty,
And you shall see 'tis purchased by
    the weight,
Which therein works a miracle in
    nature,
Making them lightest that wear
    most of it.

Bassanio in *The Merchant of Venice*,
3.2.88–91

Referring to cosmetics as making the wearer
"light" or lascivious.

15   O happy fair!
Your eyes are lodestars, and your
    tongue's sweet air
More tuneable than lark to shep-
    herd's ear
When wheat is green, when
    hawthorn buds appear.

**Helena in *A Midsummer Night's
Dream*,** 1.1.182–5

To Hermia, whose eyes, she says, draw those
of Demetrius just as navigators fix their eyes
on a guiding star.

16   He hath achieved a maid
That paragons description and wild
    fame;
One that excels the quirks of bla-
    zoning pens.

Cassio in *Othello*, 2.1.61–3

The maid is Desdemona, who surpasses
("paragons") description, and goes beyond the
witty conceptions ("quirks") of those who

would proclaim her beauty; "blazon" is a term
from heraldry, meaning originally a shield or
badge.

17   O thou weed!
Who art so lovely fair and smell'st
    so sweet
That the sense aches at thee, would
    thou hadst ne'er been born!

Othello in *Othello*, 4.2.67–9

Thinking of Desdemona as false to him.

18   Yet I'll not shed her
    blood,
Nor scar that whiter skin of hers
    than snow,
And smooth as monumental
    alabaster.

Othello in *Othello*, 5.2.3–5

Seeing Desdemona as like an effigy in
alabaster on a tomb.

19 See where she comes, apparelled
    like the spring,
Graces her subjects, and her
    thoughts the king
Of every virtue gives renown to
    men.

Pericles in *Pericles*, 1.1.12–14

Admiring the approach of the daughter of
Antiochus.

20 *Simonides.* And she is fair too, is
    she not?
Pericles. As a fair day in summer,
    wondrous fair.

***Pericles*,** 2.5.35–6

They are speaking of Thaisa, the daughter of
Simonides.

21 O, she doth teach the torches to
    burn bright!

Romeo in *Romeo and Juliet*, 1.5.44

On first seeing Juliet.

22 Beauty too rich for use, for earth
too dear!

Romeo in *Romeo and Juliet*, 1.5.47

On Juliet; "dear" = precious.

23   But he's something stained
With grief, that's beauty's canker,
    thou mightst call him
A goodly person.

Prospero in *The Tempest*, 1.2.415–17

Describing Ferdinand; the cankerworm feeds
on buds.

24 Most radiant, exquisite, and
    unmatchable beauty.

Viola in *Twelfth Night*, 1.5.170–1

Addressing Olivia in Orsino's flowery style.

25 *Olivia.* Is't not well done?
Viola. Excellently done, if God did
    all.
Olivia. 'Tis in grain, sir, 'twill
    endure wind and weather.
Viola. 'Tis beauty truly blent,
    whose red and white
Nature's own sweet and cunning
    hand laid on.

Twelfth Night, 1.5.235–40

Viola admires the blending of colors in
Olivia's beauty, which is fast-dyed or natural
("in grain"), not contrived with cosmetics.

26 Who is Silvia? What is she,
That all our swains commend her?
Holy, fair, and wise is she.
The heaven such grace did lend her
That she might admirèd be.

**Song in *The Two Gentlemen of
Verona*, 4.2.39–43**

Sung under Sylvia's window at the instigation
of Thurio, who, like Proteus, is courting her.

27 Is she kind as she is fair?
For beauty lives with kindness.

**Song in *The Two Gentlemen of
Verona*, 4.2.44–5**

28   Black brows they say
Become some women best, so that
    there be not
Too much hair there, but in a semi-
    circle,
Or a half-moon made with a pen.

**Mamillius in *The Winter's Tale*,
2.1.8–11**

A precocious boy talking to the ladies who
attend his mother, Hermione.

29 Beauty itself doth of itself persuade
The eyes of men without an orator.

***The Rape of Lucrece*, 29–30**

Collatine has been boasting of the beauty of
his wife, Lucrece.

30 From fairest creatures we desire
    increase,
That thereby beauty's rose might
    never die.

Sonnet 1, 1–2

Urging his friend to perpetuate his beauty by
"increase," i.e., by having a child.

31 Shall I compare thee to a summer's
    day?
Thou art more lovely and more
    temperate:
Rough winds do shake the darling
    buds of May,
And summer's lease hath all too
    short a date.

Sonnet 18, 1–4

Addressed to his friend; "temperate" = moderate or even-tempered.

32 O how much more doth beauty
    beauteous seem
By that sweet ornament which
    truth doth give!

Sonnet 54, 1–2

The word "truth" means both fidelity ("troth")
and integrity.

33 My mistress' eyes are nothing like
    the sun;
Coral is far more red than her lips'
    red;
If snow be white, why then her
    breasts are dun;
If hairs be wires, black wires grow
    on her head . . .
And yet, by heaven, I think my
    love as rare
As any she belied with false com-
    pare.

Sonnet 130, 1–4, 13–14

Begging

1 I see, sir, you are liberal in offers.
You taught me first to beg, and now
    methinks
You teach me how a beggar should
    be answered.

Portia in *The Merchant of Venice*,
4.1.438–40

In disguise, she demands that Bassanio give
her the ring she gave him, and which he
swore should never leave his finger.

2 *Pericles.* He asks of you that never
    used to beg.
First Fisherman. No, friend, cannot
    you beg? Here's them in our

country of Greece gets more with
    begging than we can do with
    working.

Pericles, 2.1.62–5

Pericles, cast up on shore by a storm, is begging the fishermen to help him.

Belief

1 Before my God, I might not this
    believe
Without the sensible and true
    avouch
Of mine own eyes.

Horatio in *Hamlet*, 1.1.56–8

He is skeptical about the ghost until he sees it;
"sensible" = perceived by, or relating to, the
senses.

Bells

1 Go, bid thy mistress, when my
    drink is ready,
She strike upon the bell.

Macbeth in *Macbeth*, 2.1.31–2

To a servant.

2 I go, and it is done; the bell invites
    me.
Hear it not, Duncan, for it is a
    knell
That summons thee to heaven, or
    to hell.

Macbeth in *Macbeth*, 2.1.62–4

On his way to murder Duncan.

Betrayal

1 Where you are liberal of your loves
   and counsels,
   Be sure you be not loose; for those
   you make friends
   And give your hearts to, when they
   once perceive
   The least rub in your fortunes, fall
   away
   Like water from ye, never found
   again
   But where they mean to sink ye.

Buckingham in *Henry VIII*, 2.1.126–31

"Loose" = unrestrained; "rub" = check (from the game of bowls).

2   Yet I well remember
   The favors of these men. Were they
   not mine?
   Did they not sometimes cry "All
   hail!" to me?
   So Judas did to Christ; but He, in
   twelve,
   Found truth in all but one; I, in
   twelve thousand, none.

King Richard in *Richard II*, 4.1.167–71

Appearing, in effect, as Henry's prisoner; "favors" = looks as well as support. Judas Iscariot betrayed Christ; see Matthew 26:25.

Birds

1   When he had occasion to be
   seen
   He was but as the cuckoo is in June,
   Heard, not regarded.

King Henry in *Henry IV, Part 1*,
3.2.74–6

To the Prince, about Richard II.

2 Being fed by us you used us so
   As that ungentle gull, the cuckoo's
   bird,
   Useth the sparrow.

Worcester in *Henry IV, Part 1*, 5.1.59–61

The cuckoo lays its eggs in nests of other birds, such as the sparrow, which feeds the cuckoo's young at the expense of its own chicks.

3 O Westmorland, thou art a summer bird,
   Which ever in the haunch of winter
   sings
   The lifting up of day.

King Henry in *Henry IV, Part 2*,
4.4.91–3

"Haunch" = backside, latter part.

4 Like to a pair of loving turtle-doves
   That could not live asunder day or
   night.

Burgundy in *Henry VI, Part 1*, 2.2.30–1

Referring to the Dauphin and Joan of Arc.

5 So doth the swan her downy
   cygnets save,
   Keeping them prisoner underneath
   her wings.

Suffolk in *Henry VI, Part 1*, 5.3.56–7

Showing his affection for Margaret of France, taken prisoner by the English, and placed in his care.

6   This guest of summer,
   The temple-haunting martlet, does
   approve,
   By his loved mansionry, that the
   heaven's breath
   Smells wooingly here.

Banquo in *Macbeth*, 1.6.3–6

"Martlet" = house-martin, that migrates in winter, and builds nests under the eaves of houses.

7   No jutty, frieze,
Buttress, nor coign of vantage, but this bird
Hath made his pendant bed and procreant cradle;
Where they most breed and haunt, I have observed
The air is delicate.

Banquo in *Macbeth*, 1.6.6–10

Referring to the house-martin; "coign of vantage" = favorable corner.

8   It was the owl that shrieked, the fatal bellman,
Which gives the stern'st good night.

Lady Macbeth in *Macbeth*, 2.2.3–4

A duty of the "bellman" or town-crier was to announce deaths, and the owl was thought a bird of ill-omen.

9   A falcon, towering in her pride of place,
Was by a mousing owl hawked at and killed.

Old Man in *Macbeth*, 2.4.12–13

"Towering in her pride of place" = having risen to the point where it was ready to swoop down on its prey.

10   The crow doth sing as sweetly as the lark
When neither is attended.

Portia in *The Merchant of Venice*, 5.1.102–3

"When neither is attended" = when no one is listening.

11   I think
The nightingale, if she should sing by day
When every goose is cackling, would be thought
No better a musician than the wren.

Portia in *The Merchant of Venice*, 5.1.103–6

12   The ousel cock so black of hue,
With orange-tawny bill,
The throstle with his note so true,
The wren with little quill.

Bottom in *A Midsummer Night's Dream*, 3.1.125–8

Singing to cheer himself up; the "ousel cock" is the blackbird; the wren has only a small pipe ("little quill") or thin song.

13   The finch, the sparrow, and the lark,
The plainsong cuckoo grey,
Whose note full many a man doth mark
And dares not answer nay—

Bottom in *A Midsummer Night's Dream*, 3.1.130–3

The cuckoo invades the nests of other birds, and is associated with cuckoldry; Bottom sings because he is afraid.

14   The eagle suffers little birds to sing,
And is not careful what they mean thereby,
Knowing that with the shadow of his wings
He can at pleasure stint their melody.

Tamora in *Titus Andronicus*, 4.4.83–6

Tamora is trying to cheer up the Emperor Saturninus with this image of royal power.

Birth and Death

1 A terrible childbed hast thou had,
   my dear;
   No light, no fire: th'unfriendly elements
   Forgot thee utterly.

   Pericles in *Pericles*, 3.1.56–8

   He supposes Thaisa is dead, after giving birth
   to his daughter in a storm at sea.

2 Thou met'st with things dying, I
   with things new-born.

   Shepherd in *The Winter's Tale*,
   3.3.113–14

   His son has seen Antigonus die, while the
   Shepherd has found the baby, Perdita, left on
   the shore.

Birthdays

1 It is my birthday,
   I had thought t' have held it poor;
   but since my lord
   Is Antony again, I will be
   Cleopatra.

   Cleopatra in *Antony and Cleopatra*,
   3.13.184–6

   After her reconciliation with Antony.

Blessings

1 God's benison go with you, and
   with those
   That would make good of bad, and
   friends of foes!

   Old Man in *Macbeth*, 2.4.40–1

   "Benison" = blessing.

2 Heaven give thee joy!
   What cannot be eschewed must be
   embraced.

   Page in *The Merry Wives of Windsor*,
   5.5.236–7

   Discovering that Fenton has married his
   daughter.

3 Heaven give you many, many
   merry days!

   Mistress Page in *The Merry Wives of*
   ***Windsor*, 5.5.240**

   To Fenton on his marriage to Anne Page.

4 God keep your worship! I wish
   your worship well; God restore you
   to health! I humbly give you leave
   to depart; and if a merry meeting
   may be wished, God prohibit it!

   Dogberry in *Much Ado About*
   ***Nothing*, 5.1.323–6**

   Dogberry presumably means to ask leave to
   depart, and for God to permit a merry meeting.

5 Honor, riches, marriage-blessing,
   Long continuance, and increasing,
   Hourly joys be still upon you!

   Juno in *The Tempest*, 4.1.106–8

   The goddess of marriage sings a blessing on
   Ferdinand and Miranda.

6 Earth's increase, foison plenty,
   Barns and garners never empty,
   Vines with clustering bunches
   growing,
   Plants with goodly burden bowing;
   Spring come to you at the farthest
   In the very end of harvest.

   Ceres in *The Tempest*, 4.1.110–15

   Ceres, goddess of fertility, offers her blessing
   to Ferdinand and Miranda.

Body

1
        I will through and through
Cleanse the foul body of th'
   infected world,
If they will patiently receive my
   medicine.

Jaques in *As You Like It*, 2.7.60–1

Claiming a godlike ability to purge people of their sins.

2   Bear your body more seeming,
Audrey.

Touchstone in *As You Like It*, 5.4.68–9

"Seeming" = seemly, decorously.

3   When he was naked he was, for all
the world, like a forked radish, with
a head fantastically carved upon it
with a knife.

Falstaff in *Henry IV, Part 2*, 3.2.310–12

Falstaff describing Shallow as a young man.

4   What is the body when the head is
   off?

King Edward in *Henry VI, Part 3*, 5.1.41

Speaking to Warwick, he threatens to kill King Henry, who is his prisoner.

Books (see also Education, Learning, Study)

1   Whereas, before, our forefathers
had no other books but the score
and the tally, thou hast caused
printing to be used, and, contrary
to the king, his crown and dignity,
thou hast built a paper-mill.

Jack Cade in *Henry VI, Part 2*, 4.7.34–7

A peasant's idea of a treasonable offense; the score and tally were matching notched sticks used by creditor and debtor to keep primitive accounts.

2   All delights are vain, but that
   most vain
Which, with pain purchased, doth
   inherit pain,
As painfully to pore upon a book
To seek the light of truth.

Berowne in *Love's Labor's Lost*, 1.1.72–5

Berowne has in mind the "light" of love as found in a beautiful woman's eyes.

3
        My library
Was dukedom large enough.

Prospero in *The Tempest*, 1.2.109–10

Claiming he never cared for power as Duke of Milan.

4   Knowing I loved my books, he furnished me
From mine own library with vol-
   umes that
I prize above my dukedom.

Prospero in *The Tempest*, 1.2.166–8

On the loyal Gonzalo, who provided him with books in his exile.

5   Come and take choice of all my
   library,
And so beguile thy sorrow.

Titus in *Titus Andronicus*, 4.1.34–5

To Lavinia, who has no hands to cope with books.

Boys (see also Parents and Children, Youth)

1 Then the whining schoolboy, with his satchel
And shining morning face, creeping like snail
Unwillingly to school.

Jaques in *As You Like It*, 2.7.145–7

The second of the "seven ages" of man.

2   The boy disdains me,
He leaves me, scorns me. Briefly die their joys
That place them on the truth of girls and boys.

Lucius in *Cymbeline*, 5.5.105–7

His page Fidele (really Imogen in disguise) abandons Lucius on spying Jachimo wearing a ring stolen from her; "truth" = loyalty or trust.

3   O, 'tis a parlous boy,
Bold, quick, ingenious, forward, capable.
He is all the mother's, from the top to toe.

King Richard in *Richard III*, 3.1.154–6

Describing Prince Edward; "parlous" = dangerously clever.

4 When that I was and a little tiny boy,
With hey, ho, the wind and the rain,
A foolish thing was but a toy,
For the rain it raineth every day.

Feste in *Twelfth Night*, 5.1.389–92

A sobering thought at the end of the comedy, as the play may seem a "foolish thing," or trifle ("toy").

5 Two lads that thought there was no more behind

But such a day tomorrow as today,
And to be boy eternal.

Polixenes in *The Winter's Tale*, 1.2.63–5

Recalling his boyhood with Leontes.

Brevity

1 Brevity is the soul of wit.

Polonius in *Hamlet*, 2.2.90

2 *Brackenbury.* What, so brief?
Second Murderer. 'Tis better, sir, than to be tedious.

Richard III, 1.4.88–9

The murderer who has come for Clarence treats the Lieutenant of the Tower with scant respect.

Building

1   When we mean to build,
We first survey the plot, then draw the model,
And when we see the figure of the house,
Then must we rate the cost of the erection,
Which if we find outweighs ability,
What do we then but draw anew the model
In fewer offices, or at least desist
To build at all?

Lord Bardolph in *Henry IV, Part 2*, 1.3.41–8

On confining plans within the scope of available resources; "offices" = rooms.

2 The singing masons building roofs of gold.

Archbishop of Canterbury in *Henry V*, 1.2.198

The best-known line in his vision of bees as exemplifying an ordered society.

3   Having waste ground enough,
Shall we desire to raze the sanctuary,
And pitch our evils there?

Angelo in *Measure for Measure*, 2.2.169–71

The general idea is of destroying what is good in order to build (as in pitching a tent) something nasty; but "evils" is thought by some to mean privies or toilets. Angelo is brooding on his urge to violate the chastity of Isabella.

Burial (see also Epitaphs, Graves, Mourning)

1   *Rosencrantz.* What have you done, my lord, with the dead body?
Hamlet. Compounded it with dust, whereto 'tis kin.

Hamlet, 4.2.5–6

The body of Polonius, killed by Hamlet; "dust thou art, and unto dust shalt thou return," Genesis 3:19.

2   I cannot choose but weep to think they would lay him in the cold ground.

Ophelia in *Hamlet*, 4.5.69–70

Thinking of her father Polonius, killed by Hamlet.

3   Lay her i' th' earth,
And from her fair and unpolluted flesh
May violets spring.

Laertes in *Hamlet*, 5.1.238–40

On the burial of Ophelia.

4   According to his virtue let us use him,
With all respect and rites of burial.

Octavius in *Julius Caesar*, 5.5.76–7

On the death of Brutus.

Business (see also Money)

1   To business that we love we rise betime,
And go to't with delight.

Antony in *Antony and Cleopatra*, 4.4.20–21

Arming for a final battle; "betime" = early. The word "business" now suggests routines of the workplace so that these lines out of context take on quite a new meaning.

2   In the way of bargain, mark ye me, I'll cavil on the ninth part of a hair.

Hotspur in *Henry IV, Part 1*, 3.1.137–8

Talking with other rebels about the division of the spoils they hope to win.

3   Our hands are full of business, let's away,
Advantage feeds him fat while men delay.

King Henry in *Henry IV, Part 1*, 3.2.179–80

"Feeds him fat" = grows lazy, loses its edge.

4   A good wit will make use of anything. I will turn diseases to commodity.

Falstaff in *Henry IV, Part 2*, 1.2.247–8

Planning to claim he has been lamed in battle, not by gout brought on by drinking; "commodity" = profit.

5 Our bad neighbor makes us early
    stirrers,
Which is both healthful and good
    husbandry.

King Henry in *Henry V*, 4.1.6–7

"Husbandry" = management or thrift.

6   I thank my fortune for it,
My ventures are not in one bottom
    trusted,
Nor to one place.

**Antonio in *The Merchant of Venice*,
1.1.41–3**

He is glad that his merchandise is not
exported in a single ship ("bottom").

7 I will buy with you, sell with you,
talk with you, walk with you, and so
following; but I will not eat with
you, drink with you, nor pray with
you.

**Shylock in *The Merchant of Venice*,
1.3.35–8**

Speaking to the Christian Bassanio.

8 When rich villains have need of
poor ones, poor ones may make
what price they will.

**Borachio in *Much Ado About Nothing*,
3.3.113–4**

Reporting he has been well paid by Don John
to prevent the marriage of Claudio and Hero.

9 Let us, like merchants, show our
    foulest wares,
And think perchance they'll sell; if
    not,
The luster of the better yet to show
Shall show the better.

**Ulysses in *Troilus and Cressida*,
1.3.358–61**

Plotting with Nestor to ensure that Ajax, not
Achilles, meets Hector's challenge.

10   You do as chapmen do,
Dispraise the thing that they desire
    to buy.

Paris in *Troilus and Cressida*, 4.1.76–7

He is responding to the bitter criticism of
Helen by Diomedes; "chapmen" = merchants.
Compare Proverbs 20:14.

11 Let me have no lying. It becomes
none but tradesmen.

**Autolycus in *The Winter's Tale*,
4.4.722–3**

Addressing the old Shepherd and his son; the
comment is ironic since Autolycus is himself a
talented liar.

Caesar

1 I rather tell thee what is to be feared
Than what I fear; for always I am
    Caesar.

Caesar in *Julius Caesar*, 1.2.211–12

Caesar thinks of himself as an embodiment of
power, and his name has passed into dictionaries as such (compare the German
"Kaiser").

2 Know, Caesar doth not wrong, nor
    without cause
Will he be satisfied.

Caesar in *Julius Caesar*, 3.1.47–8

To Metellus, whose brother has been exiled.

3 As Caesar loved me, I weep for him;
as he was fortunate, I rejoice at it; as
he was valiant, I honor him; but as
he was ambitious, I slew him.
There is tears for his love; joy for

his fortune; honor for his valor; and
death for his ambition.

Brutus in *Julius Caesar*, 3.2.24–9

Defending the killing of Caesar.

4   Here was a Caesar! When comes
     such another?

Mark Antony in *Julius Caesar*, 3.2.252

The name "Caesar" already begins to take on
the meaning of "ruler" or "monarch."

5   O Julius Caesar, thou art mighty
     yet!
     Thy spirit walks abroad and turns
     our swords
     In our own proper entrails.

Brutus in *Julius Caesar*, 5.3.94–6

Brutus has just learned of the death of his
friend Cassius; "own proper" = very own.

Capriciousness

1   If you find him sad,
     Say I am dancing; if in mirth,
     report
     That I am sudden sick.

**Cleopatra in *Antony and Cleopatra*,
1.3.3–5**

Teasing Antony by being contrary.

2   The unruly waywardness that
     infirm and choleric years bring with
     them.

Goneril in *King Lear*, 1.1.298–9

On the behavior of her father, the old King
Lear.

Castles

1   This castle hath a pleasant seat; the
     air

Nimbly and sweetly recommends
     itself
Unto our gentle senses.

Duncan in *Macbeth*, 1.6.1–3

"Seat" = situation; "gentle senses" = sense
made gentle by the air or breeze.

2   There stands the castle, by yon tuft
     of trees.

Percy in *Richard II*, 2.3.53

Berkeley castle, defended by Richard.

Cause

1   I know no personal cause to spurn
     at him,
     But for the general: he would be
     crowned.
     How that might change his nature,
     there's the question.

Brutus in *Julius Caesar*, 2.1.11–13

Thinking about the conspiracy against Caesar.

2   The cause is in my will: I will not
     come.
     That is enough to satisfy the Senate.

Caesar in *Julius Caesar*, 2.2.71–2

Refusing to offer excuses for not going to the
Capitol.

3   You all did love him once, not
     without cause;
     What cause withholds you then to
     mourn for him?

Mark Antony in *Julius Caesar*, 3.2.102–3

Speaking to the people about Caesar.

4   Is there any cause in nature that
     make these hard hearts?

King Lear in *King Lear*, 3.6.77–8

5   It is the cause, it is the cause, my
     soul.
   Let me not name it to you, you
     chaste stars!
   It is the cause.

Othello in *Othello*, 5.2.1–3

Othello has no "cause," meaning both reason
and legal cause, to murder Desdemona other
than her imagined unchastity.

Celibacy

1   Shall I never see a bachelor of
   threescore again?

Benedick in *Much Ado About Nothing*,
1.1.199–200

Dismayed that his friend Claudio intends to
marry.

2   He that hath a beard is more than a
   youth, and he that hath no beard is
   less than a man; and he that is more
   than a youth is not for me, and he
   that is less than a man, I am not for
   him.

Beatrice in *Much Ado About Nothing*,
2.1.36–9

Rejecting the idea of marrying.

3   Good Lord, for alliance! Thus goes
   every one to the world but I, and I
   am sunburnt; I may sit in a corner
   and cry "Heigh-ho for a husband"!

Beatrice in *Much Ado About Nothing*,
2.1.318–20

To Claudio, who claims the privilege through
marriage of "alliance" in calling Beatrice
cousin; she feels left out, or "sunburnt" = dry
and withered.

Censorship

1   Art made tongue-tied by authority.

***Sonnet 66*, 9**

Censorship was one of the many evils in his
society listed by the narrator in this sonnet;
"art" = letters (literature) and learning rather
than fine art.

Ceremony

1   What infinite heart's ease
   Must kings neglect, that private
     men enjoy!
   And what have kings, that privates
     have not too,
   Save ceremony, save general cere-
     mony?

King Henry in *Henry V*, 4.1.236–9

On the burdens of responsibility; "ceremony"
suggests deference as well as the pomp and
display of majesty.

2   And what art thou, thou idol cere-
     mony?
   What kind of god art thou, that suf-
     fer'st more
   Of mortal griefs than do thy wor-
     shippers?
   What are thy rents? What are thy
     comings-in?

King Henry in *Henry V*, 4.1.240–3

Dismissing the pomp of majesty as worthless.

3   To my judgment your highness is
   not entertained with that ceremonious affection as you were wont.

Knight in *King Lear*, 1.4.58–9

On the treatment of King Lear by his daughter
Goneril.

4   To feed were best at home;
From thence, the sauce to meat is
    ceremony;
Meeting were bare without it.

Lady Macbeth in *Macbeth*, 3.4.34–6

"From thence" = away from home.

5   Ceremony was but devised at first
To set a gloss on faint deeds, hollow
    welcomes,
Recanting goodness, sorry e'er 'tis
    shown;
But where there is true friendship,
    there needs none.

Timon in *Timon of Athens*, 1.2.15–18

Timon claims true friendship needs no ceremony; "recanting goodness" = generosity
withdrawn even as it is offered.

Challenges

1   You are a villain. I jest not. I will
make it good how you dare, with
what you dare, and when you dare.

Benedick in *Much Ado About Nothing*,
5.1.145–7

Challenging Claudio to fight.

2   *Sir Andrew Aguecheek.* Here's the
challenge, read it. I warrant
there's vinegar and pepper in't.
Fabian. Is't so saucy?

Twelfth Night, 3.4.143–5

Sir Andrew is challenging Cesario (Viola in
disguise) to fight. "Saucy" = both spicy and
impertinent.

3   I will meditate the while upon some
horrid message for a challenge.

Sir Toby Belch in *Twelfth Night*,
3.4.199–200

In place of Sir Andrew's silly written challenge
to Cesario.

Chance (see also Fortune)

1   This is the night
That either makes me, or fordoes
    me quite.

Iago in *Othello*, 5.1.128–9

"Fordoes me quite" = destroys me utterly.

2   In the reproof of chance
Lies the true proof of men.

Nestor in *Troilus and Cressida*, 1.3.33–4

The true test of men, says Nestor, lies in the
way they cope with chance.

3   We profess
Ourselves to be the slaves of
    chance, and flies
Of every wind that blows.

Florizel in *The Winter's Tale*, 4.4.539–41

Having no idea where to take Perdita.

Change (see also Mutability)

1   When clouds are seen, wise men
    put on their cloaks;
When great leaves fall, then winter
    is at hand;
When the sun sets, who doth not
    look for night?

Third Citizen in *Richard III*, 2.3.32–4

Fearing the worst on learning of the death of
Edward IV.

Chaos (see also Anarchy, Confusion)

1 Men, wives, and children stare, cry
out, and run,
As it were doomsday.

Trebonius in *Julius Caesar*, 3.1.97–8

After the death of Caesar.

2 Though castles topple on their
warders' heads,
Though palaces and pyramids do
slope
Their heads to their foundations;
though the treasure
Of nature's germens tumble all
together,
Even till destruction sicken—
answer me
To what I ask you.

Macbeth in *Macbeth*, 4.1.56–61

A warder is a guardian; "nature's germens" =
the seeds or rudiments from which it was
thought all living organisms developed.

3   Nay, had I power, I should
Pour the sweet milk of concord
into hell,
Uproar the universal peace, con-
found
All unity on earth.

Malcolm in *Macbeth*, 4.3.97–100

"Uproar" = throw into confusion. Malcolm is
making out that he would be a worse king
than Macbeth.

Character

1   Along with them
They brought one Pinch, a hungry
lean-faced villain,
A mere anatomy, a mountebank,

A threadbare juggler and a fortune-
teller,
A needy, hollow-eyed, sharp looking wretch,
A living dead man.

**Antipholus of Ephesus in *The Comedy
of Errors*, 5.1.237–42**

Doctor Pinch, a schoolmaster and charlatan
("mountebank"), called in by Adriana to help
restore Antipholus when she supposed her
husband was mad; "anatomy" = skeleton.

2 You would play upon me, you
would seem to know my stops, you
would pluck out the heart of my
mystery, you would sound me from
my lowest note to the top of my
compass; and there is much music,
excellent voice, in this little organ.

Hamlet in *Hamlet*, 3.2.364–8

Hamlet shows Guildenstern he is more difficult to comprehend and play on than a
recorder.

3 Before I knew thee, Hal, I knew
nothing, and now am I, if a man
should speak truly, little better than
one of the wicked.

Falstaff in *Henry IV, Part 1*, 1.2.92–5

Blaming his faults on Prince Hal.

4 The Moor—howbeit that I endure
him not—
Is of a constant, loving, noble
nature,
And I dare think he'll prove to Desdemona
A most dear husband.

Iago in *Othello*, 2.1.288–91

Speaking to the audience about Othello.

5 He plays o'the viol-de-gamboys,
and speaks three or four languages

word for word without book, and hath all the good gifts of nature.

Sir Toby Belch in *Twelfth Night,*
1.3.25–8

Over-praising Sir Andrew Aguecheek; the viola da gamba, or bass viol, was held between the legs, and the image has sexual overtones; "without book" = by heart.

Charity

1   He hath a tear for pity, and a hand Open as day for melting charity.

King Henry in *Henry IV, Part 2,*
4.4.31–2

Praising Prince Hal.

2   For charity itself fulfills the law, And who can sever love from charity?

Berowne in *Love's Labor's Lost,*
4.3.361–2

Referring to the words of Saint Paul, Romans 13:8, "he that loveth another hath fulfilled the law"; "charity," from the Latin "caritas" = caring or compassion, love in the largest sense. Hence the last verse of I Corinthians 13, "And now abideth faith, hope and charity, these three; but the greatest of these is charity."

3   'Twere good you do so much for charity.

Portia in *The Merchant of Venice,*
4.1.261

Asking Shylock to allow a surgeon to be present when he takes his pound of flesh.

Charm

1   Fie, wrangling queen! Whom everything becomes—to chide, to laugh, To weep.

Antony in *Antony and Cleopatra,*
1.1.48–50

Cleopatra's "infinite variety" (see 3 below).

2   I saw her once Hop forty paces through the public street; And having lost her breath, she spoke, and panted, That she did make defect perfection.

Enobarbus in *Antony and Cleopatra,*
2.2.228–231

Cleopatra's charm in her less than queenly behavior.

3   Age cannot wither her, nor custom stale Her infinite variety.

Enobarbus in *Antony and Cleopatra,*
2.2.234–5

On Cleopatra's undying charm.

Chastity (see also Virginity)

1   Chaste as the icicle That's curdied by the frost from purest snow And hangs on Dian's temple.

Coriolanus in *Coriolanus,* 5.3.65–7

On Valeria, friend of his wife, Virgilia; "curdied" = congealed; Diana was goddess of the moon and of chastity.

2   The heavens hold firm The walls of thy dear honor; keep unshaked That temple, thy fair mind, that thou mayst stand T'enjoy thy banished lord, and this great land

Second Lord in *Cymbeline,* 2.1.62–5

Speaking of Imogen and her banished husband, Posthumus.

3   Me of my lawful pleasure she
    restrained,
    And prayed me oft forbearance; did
    it with
    A pudency so rosy the sweet view
    on't
    Might well have warmed old Sat-
    urn; that I thought her
    As chaste as unsunned snow.

Posthumus in *Cymbeline*, 2.5.9–13

Speaking of Imogen, when he believes,
falsely, that she has been unfaithful;
"pudency" = modesty. Saturn was one of the
ancient gods, father of Jupiter.

4   Weigh what loss your honor may
    sustain
    If with too credent ear you list his
    songs,
    Or lose your heart, or your chaste
    treasure open
    To his unmastered importunity.

Laertes in *Hamlet*, 1.3.29–32

Speaking to Ophelia of Hamlet's professions
of love to her; "credent" = credulous; "chaste
treasure" = virginity.

5   The chariest maid is prodigal
    enough
    If she unmask her beauty to the
    moon.

Laertes in *Hamlet*, 1.3.36–7

Warning Ophelia not to listen to Hamlet's
protestations of love; "chariest" = most modest.

6   In the morn and liquid dew of
    youth
    Contagious blastments are most
    imminent.

Laertes in *Hamlet*, 1.3.41–2

Warning his sister Ophelia against Hamlet's
advances; "contagious blastments" = disease-
bringing blights.

7   A virgin from her tender infancy,
    Chaste and immaculate in very
    thought.

**Joan la Pucelle in *Henry VI, Part 1*,
5.4.50–1**

Joan of Arc defending herself.

Cheerfulness

1   A light heart lives long.

Katherine in *Love's Labor's Lost*, 5.2.18

"Light" = merry, but could also mean
unchaste.

Chiding

1   Better a little chiding than a great
    deal of heart-break.

**Mistress Page in *The Merry Wives of
Windsor*, 5.3.9–10**

She expects to be rebuked by her husband for
encouraging their daughter Anne to marry a
man he despises.

Children (see also Boys, Girls, Parents and Children)

1   Barnes are blessings.

**Lavatch in *All's Well That Ends Well*,
1.3.25–6**

"Barnes" means bairns, or children.

2   He makes a July's day short as
    December,
    And with his varying childness
    cures in me
    Thoughts that would thick my
    blood.

Polixenes in *The Winter's Tale*,
1.2.169–71

On the pleasure his son gives him.

Chivalry

1   When first this order was ordained,
    my lords,
    Knights of the Garter were of noble
    birth,
    Valiant and virtuous, full of
    haughty courage.

    Talbot in *Henry VI, Part 1*, 4.1.33–5

    On the founding of the Order of the Garter,
    founded about 1344 by Edward III, who is
    said to have picked up the garter of a lady he
    was dancing with. It is a blue ribbon buckled
    with gold, worn on the left leg, and bears the
    inscription "*Honi soit qui mal y pense*," or
    curst be he who thinks evil of this.

Choice

1   To be, or not to be, that is the ques-
    tion:
    Whether 'tis nobler in the mind to
    suffer
    The slings and arrows of outra-
    geous fortune,
    Or to take arms against a sea of
    troubles,
    And by opposing, end them.

    Hamlet in *Hamlet*, 3.1.55–9

    His most famous soliloquy, much debated; the
    choice in context is between suffering in
    silence or taking action by fighting; but the
    first line is often associated with a death-wish.

2   "Who chooseth me shall get as
    much as he deserves."

    **Prince of Morocco in *The Merchant of
    Venice*, 2.7.23**

    Reading the message on the silver casket.

3   Here do I choose, and thrive I as I
    may!

    **Prince of Morocco in *The Merchant of
    Venice*, 2.7.60**

    Choosing the golden casket in the hope of
    winning Portia.

4   O, these deliberate fools, when they
    do choose,
    They have the wisdom by their wit
    to lose.

    **Portia in *The Merchant of Venice*,
    2.9.80–1**

    "Deliberate" = calculating; referring to the
    Prince of Aragon's mistaken choice of the sil-
    ver casket.

5   Let me choose,
    For as I am, I live upon the rack.

    **Bassanio in *The Merchant of Venice*,
    3.2.24–5**

    Facing the three caskets.

6   Here choose I. Joy be the conse-
    quence!

    **Bassanio in *The Merchant of Venice*,
    3.2.107**

    Choosing the leaden casket to win Portia.

7   "You that choose not by the view,
    Chance as fair, and choose as true:
    Since this fortune falls to you,
    Be content, and seek no new."

    **Bassanio in *The Merchant of Venice*,
    3.2.131–4**

    The message he finds in the leaden casket
    telling him he has won Portia.

8   There's small choice in rotten
    apples.

    **Hortensio in *The Taming of the
    Shrew*, 1.1.134–5**

    Shakespeare may have coined this proverb.

Cities

1   Sweep on, you fat and greasy citizens,
'Tis just the fashion.

First Lord in *As You Like It*, 2.1.55–6

Quoting Jaques, moralizing over the fate of a wounded stag, ignored by its fellows.

2   A city on whom plenty held full hand,
For riches strewed herself even in her streets;
Whose towers bore heads so high they kissed the clouds,
And strangers ne'er beheld but wondered at.

Cleon in *Pericles*, 1.4.22–5

On the former prosperity of Tarsus, now afflicted by famine.

3   This world's a city full of straying streets,
And death the market-place where each one meets.

Third Queen in *The Two Noble Kinsmen*, 1.5.15–16

Civil War

1   Civil dissension is a viperous worm
That gnaws the bowels of the commonwealth.

King Henry in *Henry VI, Part 1*, 3.1.72–3

2   'Tis much when scepters are in children's hands,
But more when envy breeds unkind division:
There comes the ruin, there begins confusion.

Exeter in *Henry VI, Part 1*, 4.1.192–4

While Henry was young the country was ruled by his uncle, Duke of Gloucester, the Lord Protector.

3   *First Plebeian.* Tear him to pieces, he's a conspirator!
Cinna. I am Cinna the poet! I am Cinna the poet!
Fourth Plebeian. Tear him for his bad verses, tear him for his bad verses.

Julius Caesar, 3.3.28–31

The angry plebeians are indiscriminate in their violence.

4   O, if you raise this house against this house
It will the woefullest division prove
That ever fell upon this cursèd earth.

Bishop of Carlisle in *Richard II*, 4.1.145–7

Prophesying civil war in England.

Cleverness

1   I know a trick worth two of that.

First Carrier in *Henry IV, Part 1*, 2.1.36–7

Varying a proverb; meaning "I'm too clever to be taken in by your trick."

Clothing (see also Fashion)

1   There can be no kernel in this light nut; the soul of this man is in his clothes.

Lafew in *All's Well That Ends Well*, 2.5.43–4

Referring to the extravagant dress of Parolles, the braggart soldier.

2　Good Hamlet, cast thy nighted
　　color off.

Gertrude in *Hamlet*, 1.2.68

Referring to Hamlet's black mourning dress
for his father's death.

3　Costly thy habit as thy purse can
　　buy,
　　But not expressed in fancy, rich,
　　not gaudy,
　　For the apparel oft proclaims the
　　man.

Polonius in *Hamlet*, 1.3.70–2

Advice to his son, going to live abroad;
"fancy" = ornamentation.

4　　　　Youth no less becomes
　　The light and careless livery that it
　　wears
　　Than settled age his sables and his
　　weeds,
　　Importing health and graveness.

Claudius in *Hamlet*, 4.7.78–81

"Sables" = dark robes trimmed with sable fur;
"weeds" = appropriate clothes.

5　There's not a shirt and a half in all
　　my company, and the half shirt is
　　two napkins tacked together and
　　thrown over the shoulders like a
　　herald's coat without sleeves.

Falstaff in *Henry IV, Part 1*, 4.2.42–5

Describing the men he has conscripted to
fight the rebels.

6　The naked truth of it is, I have no
　　shirt; I go woolward for penance.

**Armado in *Love's Labor's Lost*,
5.2.710–11**

He wears no linen beneath his outer woolen
clothes.

7　　　　Now does he feel his title

Hang loose about him like a giant's
　　robe
Upon a dwarfish thief.

Angus in *Macbeth*, 5.2.20–2

As if Macbeth has become too small for his
office as King of Scotland.

8　Rammed me in with foul shirts and
　　smocks, socks, foul stockings,
　　greasy napkins, that, Master Brook,
　　there was the rankest compound of
　　villainous smell that ever offended
　　nostril.

**Falstaff in *The Merry Wives of Wind-
sor*, 3.5.89–93**

On his experience of being hidden in a basket
of foul linen.

9　Ne'er ask me what raiment I'll
　　wear, for I have no more doublets
　　than backs, no more stockings than
　　legs, nor no more shoes than feet—
　　nay, sometime more feet than
　　shoes, or such shoes as my toes look
　　through the overleather.

**Sly in *The Taming of the Shrew*,
Induction, 2.8–12**

The drunkard, Sly, protests he has hardly any
clothes.

10　Our purses shall be proud, our gar-
　　ments poor,
　　For 'tis the mind that makes the
　　body rich,
　　And as the sun breaks through the
　　darkest clouds,
　　So honor peereth in the meanest
　　habit.

**Petruchio in *The Taming of the Shrew*,
4.3.171–4**

Proposing to take his wife, Katherine, to her
father's house in poor clothes; "peereth in" =
shows through.

11 *Trinculo.* O worthy Stephano!
   Look what a wardrobe here is for
   thee!
   Caliban. Let it alone, thou fool, it is
   but trash.

The Tempest, 4.1.222–4

Stephano and Trinculo are readily distracted
by gaudy clothes from their plot to kill Prospero.

12 These clothes are good enough to
   drink in, and so be these boots too.

Sir Toby Belch in *Twelfth Night*,
1.3.11–12

13   Sure this robe of mine
   Does change my disposition.

Perdita, *The Winter's Tale*, 4.4.133

She is dressed up as the goddess Flora.

14 He hath ribbons of all the colors
   i'the rainbow.

Servant in *The Winter's Tale*, 4.4.204–5

On Autolycus's stock of goods for sale.

15 Lawn as white as driven snow,
   Cyprus black as e'er was crow,
   Gloves as sweet as damask roses,
   Masks for faces and for noses.

Autolycus in *The Winter's Tale*,
4.4.218–21

Singing his catalogue of wares, linen ("lawn"),
crepe (imported from Cyprus), and masks used
by women to protect their faces.

Comfort

1 How mightily sometimes we make
   us comforts of our losses!

**First Lord in *All's Well That Ends
Well*,** 4.3.65–6

2   I will reward thee,
   Once for thy sprightly comfort, and
   tenfold
   For thy good valor.

Antony in *Antony and Cleopatra*,
4.7.14–16

To Eros or Scarus, on learning they have won
a battle against Caesar.

3 I must comfort the weaker vessel, as
   doublet and hose ought to show
   itself courageous to petticoat.

Rosalind in *As You Like It*, 2.4.5–7

In disguise as a boy; "the weaker vessel" is
woman, a biblical phrase (Paul's first epistle to
Peter 3:7).

4 I beg cold comfort, and you are so
   strait
   And so ingrateful, you deny me
   that.

King John in *King John*, 5.7.42–3

"Cold comfort" = empty consolation; "strait" =
severe.

5 Things at the worst will cease, or
   else climb upward
   To what they were before.

Ross in *Macbeth*, 4.2.24–5

Trying to comfort Lady Macduff in speaking of
the condition of Scotland under the tyranny of
Macbeth.

6 He receives comfort like cold porridge.

Sebastian in *The Tempest*, 2.1.10

On Alonso, who is sad supposing his son Ferdinand to be drowned.

Company, see Society

Comparisons

1   Now I perceive that she hath made
    compare
    Between our statures; she hath
    urged her height,
    And with her personage, her tall
    personage,
    Her height, forsooth, she hath pre-
    vailed with him.

**Hermia in *A Midsummer Night's
Dream*, 3.2.290–3**

Jealous of the taller Helena to whom her
former lover, Lysander, has switched his
affections.

2   So doth the greater glory dim the
    less:
    A substitute shines brightly as a
    king
    Until a king be by.

**Portia in *The Merchant of Venice*,
5.1.93–5**

On the way moonlight makes the light of a
candle seem faint.

Condescension

1   An honest soul, i'faith, sir, by my
    troth he is, as ever broke bread. But
    God is to be worshipped; all men
    are not alike.

**Dogberry in *Much Ado About
Nothing*, 3.5.38–40**

Dogberry, as Constable of the Watch, patron-
izes his assistant, Verges.

2   Your worship speaks like a most
    thankful and reverend youth, and I
    praise God for you.

**Dogberry in *Much Ado About
Nothing*, 5.1.315–16**

To old Leonato; Dogberry is comically muddled as ever.

Confidence

1   I am armed,
    And dangers are to me indifferent.

Cassius in *Julius Caesar*, 1.3.114–15

"Indifferent" = immaterial.

2   Nothing that can be can come
    between me and the full prospect of
    my hopes.

Malvolio in *Twelfth Night*, 3.4.81–2

Convinced that Olivia loves him.

Confusion (see also Chaos, Disorder)

1   My soul aches
    To know, when two authorities are
    up,
    Neither supreme, how soon confu-
    sion
    May enter 'twixt the gap of both
    and take
    The one by the other.

Coriolanus in *Coriolanus*, 3.1.108–12

The two authorities set up ("up") in the play
are the consuls and the tribunes of the people.

2   Fair is foul, and foul is fair;
    Hover through the fog and filthy
    air.

**The Witches (Weird Sisters) in *Mac-
beth*, 1.1.11–12**

3   So from that spring whence com-
    fort seemed to come,
    Discomfort swells.

Sergeant in *Macbeth*, 1.2.27–8

Reporting news that is at once good and bad.

4 My thought, whose murder yet is
    but fantastical,
Shakes so my single state of man,
That function is smothered in sur-
    mise,
And nothing is but what is not.

Macbeth in *Macbeth*, 1.3.139–42

What he imagines overwhelms his ability to
act ("function"), and nothing exists for him
but the thought of murder; "fantastical" =
imaginary.

5 Confusion now hath made his mas-
    terpiece!
Most sacrilegious murder hath
    broke ope
The Lord's anointed temple, and
    stole thence
The life o' the building.

Macduff in *Macbeth*, 2.3.66–9

Echoing biblical ideas of the king as the
"Lord's anointed" (anointed with holy oil; II
Samuel 1:16), and of the body as "the temple
of God" (I Corinthians 3:16).

6 But cruel are the times when we are
    traitors
And do not know ourselves, when
    we hold rumor
From what we fear, yet know not
    what we fear,
But float upon a wild and violent
    sea
Each way and move.

Ross in *Macbeth*, 4.2.18–22

"When we hold rumor/From what we fear" =
when we are led by fear to believe rumors;
"Each way and move" = this way and that,
making no headway.

7   All is uneven,
And everything is left at six and
    seven.

York in *Richard II*, 2.2.121–2

The phrase "six and seven," or more commonly in later usage "sixes and sevens" (= in
confusion) is derived from games with dice,
with the idea that all is at risk of being lost.

Conquest

1 Sir, you have wrestled well, and
    overthrown
More than your enemies.

Rosalind in *As You Like It*, 1.2.254–5

Orlando has defeated Charles the wrestler and
"overthrown" Rosalind, who has fallen in love
with him.

2 He saw me, and yielded, that I may
justly say, with the hook-nosed fellow of Rome, "I came, saw, and
overcame."

Falstaff in *Henry IV, Part 2*, 4.3.40–2

Ironically comparing himself with Julius Caesar, who is said to have announced a victory
with the words "*Veni, vidi, vici,*" I came, I
saw, I conquered.

Conscience (see also Guilt)

1 Taint not thy mind, nor let thy soul
    contrive
Against thy mother aught. Leave
    her to heaven,
And to those thorns that in her
    bosom lodge
To prick and sting her.

Ghost in *Hamlet*, 1.5.85–8

His father's ghost warning Hamlet.

2 Thus conscience does make cow-
    ards of us all,

And thus the native hue of resolution
Is sicklied o'er with the pale cast of thought.

Hamlet in *Hamlet*, 3.1.82–4

"Conscience" = consciousness, and also moral judgment.

3   Thus hulling in
The wild sea of my conscience, I did steer
Toward this remedy, whereupon we are
Now present here together.

King Henry in *Henry VIII*, 2.4.200–3

"Hulling" = drifting about; offering reasons for divorcing Katherine.

4   The worm of conscience still begnaw thy soul!

Queen Margaret in *Richard III*, 1.3.221

Addressing Richard; "still" = continually.

5   *First Murderer.* Where's thy conscience now?
. . .
Second Murderer. I'll not meddle with it. It makes a man a coward. . . . It fills a man full of obstacles. It made me once restore a purse of gold that by chance I found. It beggars any man that keeps it. It is turned out of towns and cities for a dangerous thing, and every man that means to live well endeavors to trust to himself and live without it.

Richard III, 1.4.127, 134–5, 139–44

Debating what they have been hired to do, i.e., murder Clarence.

6   O coward conscience, how dost thou afflict me!

King Richard in *Richard III*, 5.3.179

Starting out of a nightmare.

7   My conscience hath a thousand several tongues,
And every tongue brings in a several tale,
And every tale condemns me for a villain.

King Richard in *Richard III*, 5.3.193–5

For the first time Richard is afflicted with a sense of guilt.

8   Conscience is but a word that cowards use,
Devised at first to keep the strong in awe.

King Richard in *Richard III*, 5.3.309–10

Dismissing the conscience that had so troubled him in his dreams before the battle with Richmond.

9   I'll haunt thee like a wicked conscience still.

Troilus in *Troilus and Cressida*, 5.10.28

Speaking of Achilles, who has slain the unarmed Hector.

10   Love is too young to know what conscience is,
Yet who knows not conscience is born of love?

***Sonnet 151*, 1–2**

Cupid is suggested by "young," but also innocence; "conscience" may mean both knowledge, specifically carnal knowledge, and moral awareness, or sense of guilt.

Consideration

1   What you have said
       I will consider; what you have to
          say
       I will with patience hear, and find a
          time
       Both meet to hear and answer such
          high things.

Brutus in *Julius Caesar*, 1.2.167–70

"Meet" = fitting.

Conspiracy

1   I'll read you matter deep and dan-
        gerous,
     As full of peril and adventurous
        spirit
     As to o'erwalk a current roaring
        loud
     On the unsteadfast footing of a
        spear.

Worcester in *Henry IV, Part 1*, 1.3.190–3

Proposing rebellion against the king.

2   Be factious for redress of all these
        griefs,
     And I will set this foot of mine as
        far
     As who goes farthest.

Casca in *Julius Caesar*, 1.3.118–20

Speaking to Cassius; "factious" = actively par-
tisan; "griefs" = grievances.

3   The complexion of the element
     In favor's like the work we have in
        hand,
     Most bloody-fiery, and most terri-
        ble.

Cassius in *Julius Caesar*, 1.3.128–30

On the terrible storms that occur the night
before Caesar is assassinated.

4   Since the quarrel
       Will bear no color for the thing he
          is,
       Fashion it thus: that what he is,
          augmented,
       Would run to these and these
          extremities.

Brutus in *Julius Caesar*, 2.1.28–31

Finding specious reasons to join the conspiracy, and admitting it cannot be justified ("Will
bear no color") by what Caesar has done.

5   O conspiracy,
       Sham'st thou to show thy dan-
          g'rous brow by night,
       When evils are most free? O then,
          by day
       Where wilt thou find a cavern dark
          enough
       To mask thy monstrous visage?

Brutus in *Julius Caesar*, 2.1.77–81

On the arrival at his house of the conspirators,
hiding their faces in their cloaks.

6   Security gives way to conspiracy.

Artemidorus in *Julius Caesar*, 2.3.7–8

The soothsayer's message, but Caesar is too
busy to look at it.

7   I see your brows are full of discon-
        tent,
     Your hearts of sorrow, and your
        eyes of tears.

Abbot of Westminster in *Richard II*,
4.1.331–2

Speaking to the deposed King Richard's supporters.

8   O, heinous, strong, and bold con-
        spiracy!

King Henry IV in *Richard II*, 5.3.59

On learning of a plot to murder him;
"heinous" = abominable.

9   For conspiracy,
    I know not how it tastes, though it
        be dished
    For me to try how.

Hermione in *The Winter's Tale*,
3.2.71–3

Defending herself in court against accusations
that she conspired with Camillo.

Constancy

1   I am constant as the northern
        star,
    Of whose true-fixed and resting
        quality
    There is no fellow in the firma-
        ment.

Caesar in *Julius Caesar*, 3.1.60–2

The pole star thought of as constant and
immovable.

2   So in the world: 'tis furnished well
        with men,
    And men are flesh and blood, and
        apprehensive;
    Yet in the number I do know but
        one
    That unassailable holds on his rank,
    Unshaked of motion; and that I am
        he.

Caesar in *Julius Caesar*, 3.1.66–70

Boasting of his steadiness in holding his posi-
tion unshaken by movement around him, or
by "motions" = petitions; "apprehensive" =
capable of perception.

3   When this ring
    Parts from this finger, then parts
        life from hence.

Bassanio in *The Merchant of Venice*,
3.2.183–4

On the ring Portia has just given him; of
course he does part with it when she demands
it as her reward for defending his friend Antonio.

4   The sun was not so true unto the
        day
    As he to me.

Hermia in *A Midsummer Night's
Dream*, 3.2.50–1

Lamenting the disappearance of Lysander.

5   Nay, had she been true,
    If heaven would make me such
        another world
    Of one entire and perfect chrysolite,
    I'd not have sold her for it.

Othello in *Othello*, 5.2.143–6

Speaking of the now dead Desdemona;
"chrysolite" = topaz.

6   Our kindred, though they be long
    ere they be wooed, they are con-
    stant being won; they are burrs, I
    can tell you, they'll stick where they
    are thrown.

Pandarus in *Troilus and Cressida*,
3.2.109–12

Praising his niece, Cressida.

7   I am as true as truth's simplicity,
    And simpler than the infancy of
        truth.

Troilus in *Troilus and Cressida*,
3.2.169–70

Swearing eternal constancy in love to Cressida.

8   If I be false, or swerve a hair from
truth,
When time is old and hath forgot
itself,
When waterdrops have worn the
stones of Troy,
And blind oblivion swallowed cities
up,
And mighty states characterless are
grated
To dusty nothing, yet let memory
From false to false among false
maids in love
Upbraid my falsehood.

Cressida in *Troilus and Cressida*,
3.2.184–91

An oath she notoriously breaks when she is in
the Greek camp; "characterless are grated" =
reduced to ruins without written records.

9   If ever thou shalt love,
In the sweet pangs of it remember
me;
For such as I am, all true lovers are,
Unstaid and skittish in all motions
else
Save in the constant image of the
creature
That is beloved.

Orsino in *Twelfth Night*, 2.4.15–20

His constancy is indeed to the "image" of
Olivia, who refuses to see him; "motions" =
urges, feelings.

10   I cannot
Be mine own, nor anything to any,
if
I be not thine. To this I am most
constant,
Though destiny says no.

Florizel in *The Winter's Tale*, 4.4.43–6

He is saying he will be no use to himself or
anyone unless he can marry Perdita.

11   In all external grace you have some
part,
But you like none, none you, for
constant heart.

Sonnet 53, 13–14

12   Love's not Time's fool, though rosy
lips and cheeks
Within his bending sickle's compass come;
Love alters not with his brief hours
and weeks,
But bears it out even to the edge of
doom.
   If this be error, and upon me
proved,
   I never writ, nor no man ever
loved.

Sonnet 116, 9–14

Time is imaged as a reaper rapidly despoiling
human youth and beauty, but love is out of
his range ("compass"), and endures till the
brink of death (or perhaps doomsday).

13   If my dear love were but the child
of state,
It might for Fortune's bastard be
unfathered,
As subject to Time's love or to
Time's hate,
Weeds among weeds, or flowers
with flowers gathered.
No, it was builded far from acci-
dent;
It suffers not in smiling pomp, nor
falls
Under the blow of thrallèd discon-
tent,
Whereto th'inviting time our fash-
ion calls;
It fears not policy, that heretic,
Which works on leases of short-
numbered hours,

But all alone stands hugely politic,
That it nor grows with heat, nor
    drowns with showers.
    To this I witness call the Fools of
        Time,
    Which die for goodness, who have
        lived for crime.

Sonnet 124

The stability of the speaker's love is set against
the unstable world of "state" or politics, where
accident, changes of fashion with passing
time, discontent, and machination are all concerned with immediate change or advantage
("short-numbered hours"). "Fools of Time"
presumably waste their lives in pursuit of gain,
and claim "goodness" only when at death's
door; but see the quotation from *Sonnet* 116
(12 above).

Constraint

1   Nor stony tower, nor walls of
        beaten brass,
    Nor airless dungeon, nor strong
        links of iron,
    Can be retentive to the strength of
        spirit.

Cassius in *Julius Caesar*, 1.3.93–5

Trying to persuade Casca that they will have
no freedom under Caesar.

2   I am trusted with a muzzle and
    enfranchised with a clog; therefore I
    have decreed not to sing in my
    cage.

**Don John in *Much Ado About
Nothing*, 1.3.32–4**

Although treated generously by his brother
Don Pedro, after fighting as his enemy, Don
John grudgingly compares himself to a muz-
zled or hobbled animal, or a caged bird.

Contempt (see also Scorn)

1   How much methinks, I could
        despise this man,
    But that I am bound in charity
        against it.

**Cardinal Wolsey in *Henry VIII*,
3.2.297–8**

Speaking of the Earl of Surrey.

2   This is a slight unmeritable man,
    Meet to be sent on errands.

**Mark Antony in *Julius Caesar*,
4.1.12–13**

To Octavius, showing his contempt for the
third member of the triumvirate, Lepidus.

3   He must be taught, and trained and
        bid go forth;
    A barren-spirited fellow; one that
        feeds
    On objects, arts and imitations,
    Which, out of use and staled by
        other men,
    Begin his fashion.

**Mark Antony in *Julius Caesar*,
4.1.35–9**

On Lepidus, whose attention is taken by
curiosities, tricks, and copying fashions that
are already obsolete.

4   O, what a deal of scorn looks beau-
        tiful
    In the contempt and anger of his
        lip!

Olivia in *Twelfth Night*, 3.1.145–6

After an interview with Cesario, really Viola in
disguise.

Contentment (see also Happiness)

1   I earn that I eat, get that I wear, owe no man hate, envy no man's happiness, glad of other men's good, content with my harm.

Corin in *As You Like It*, 3.2.73–6

The shepherd's contentment with a pastoral life.

Conversation

1   More of your conversation would infect my brain.

Menenius in *Coriolanus*, 2.1.94

Speaking to the tribunes of the people.

2   Who can converse with a dumb show?

Portia in *The Merchant of Venice*, 1.2.73

Referring to her English suitor, who speaks no Italian.

Cooking (see also Food)

1   But his neat cookery! He cut our roots in characters,
And sauced our broths, as Juno had been sick
And he her dieter.

Guiderius in *Cymbeline*, 4.2.49–51

Speaking of Imogen, in disguise as a youth, making a meal fit for the gods; "characters" = letters.

2   'Tis an ill cook that cannot lick his own fingers.

Second Servingman in *Romeo and Juliet*, 4.2.6–7

Corruption

1   They say this town is full of cozenage:
As nimble jugglers that deceive the eye,
Dark-working sorcerers that change the mind,
Soul-killing witches that deform the body,
Disguisèd cheaters, prating mountebanks,
And many such-like liberties of sin.

Antipholus of Syracuse in *The Comedy of Errors*, 1.2.97–102

On the reputation of Ephesus, where Antipholus has just arrived; "mountebanks" were quack doctors or charlatans.

2   Something is rotten in the state of Denmark.

Marcellus in *Hamlet*, 1.4.90

Hamlet's general conclusion about the appearance of his father's ghost.

3   Lay not that flattering unction to your soul
That not your trespass but my madness speaks;
It will but skin and film the ulcerous place,
Whilst rank corruption, mining all within,
Infects unseen.

Hamlet in *Hamlet*, 3.4.145–9

Speaking to his mother, who thinks he is mad; "flattering unction" = soothing ointment of flattery.

4   Love thyself last, cherish those
     hearts that hate thee;
     Corruption wins not more than
     honesty.

Cardinal Wolsey in *Henry VIII*,
3.2.443–4

After his own downfall he advises Cromwell.

5   You yourself
     Are much condemned to have an
     itching palm,
     To sell and mart your offices for
     gold
     To undeservers.

Brutus in *Julius Caesar*, 4.3.9–12

Accusing his friend Cassius; "mart" = traffic
in.

6   Shall we now
     Contaminate our fingers with base
     bribes,
     And sell the mighty space of our
     large honors
     For so much trash as may be
     graspèd thus?
     I had rather be a dog and bay the
     moon
     Than such a Roman.

Brutus in *Julius Caesar*, 4.3.23–8

Reprimanding Cassius.

7   Who lives that's not depravèd or
     depraves?
     Who dies that bears not one spurn
     to their graves
     Of their friend's gift?

Apemantus in *Timon of Athens*,
1.2.140–1

A cynic's view of humanity; "spurn" = contemptuous rejection (literally, a kick).

Councils

1   Let us presently go sit in council,
     How covert matters may be best
     disclosed
     And open perils surest answerèd.

Mark Antony in *Julius Caesar*, 4.1.45–7

To Octavius, as they take power in Rome.

2   Now sit we close about this taper
     here,
     And call in question our necessities.

Brutus in *Julius Caesar*, 4.3.164–5

To Cassius, Titinius and Messala; "call in
question" = take stock of.

3   Words before blows; is it so, coun-
     trymen?

Brutus in *Julius Caesar*, 5.1.27

On meeting Octavius before the battle of
Philippi.

Countries

1   Hath Britain all the sun that shines?
     day? night?
     Are they not but in Britain?

Imogen in *Cymbeline*, 3.4.136–7

Alluding to the proverb, "The sun shines on
all alike."

2   I'the world's volume
     Our Britain seems as of it, but not
     in't;
     In a great pool a swan's nest.

Imogen in *Cymbeline*, 3.4.139

She thinks of going into exile abroad.

3 *Hamlet.* Why was he sent into England?

Grave-digger. Why, because 'a was mad. 'A shall recover his wits there; or if 'a do not, 'tis no great matter there.

Hamlet. Why?

Grave-digger. 'Twill not be seen in him there. There the men are as mad as he.

Hamlet, 5.1.149–55

The Grave-digger does not recognize Hamlet, who he supposes to be in England; "'a" = he.

4 But it was alway yet the trick of our English nation, if they have a good thing, to make it too common.

Falstaff in *Henry IV, Part 2*, 1.2.214–16

"Alway yet" = ever till now.

5 This royal throne of kings, this sceptered isle,

This earth of majesty, this seat of Mars,

This other Eden, demi-paradise.

John of Gaunt in *Richard II*, 2.1.40–2

His grand vision of England, as both warlike ("seat of Mars") and a garden of innocence ("Eden").

6 This happy breed of men, this little world,

This precious stone set in the silver sea,

Which serves it in the office of a wall,

Or as a moat defensive to a house,

Against the envy of less happier lands,

This blessèd plot, this earth, this realm, this England.

John of Gaunt in *Richard II*, 2.1.45–50

The dying Gaunt's vision of England.

7 That England, that was wont to conquer others,

Hath made a shameful conquest of itself.

John of Gaunt in *Richard II*, 2.1.65–6

Criticizing Richard's corrupt mode of governing.

8 *Viola.* What country, friends, is this?

Sea Captain. This is Illyria, lady.

Viola. And what should I do in Illyria? My brother he is in Elysium.

Twelfth Night, 1.2.1–4

Viola thinks her brother is dead and in heaven; "Elysium" parallels "Illyria," an area in the Balkans adjacent to the Adriatic sea.

Country Life and Countryside

1 They say he is already in the forest of Arden, and a many merry men with him; and there they live like the old Robin Hood of England.

Charles in *As You Like It*, 1.1.114–16

On the exiled Duke Senior; the Ardennes in Shakespeare's source becomes Arden, then a forest near Stratford-on-Avon.

2 This our life, exempt from public haunt,

Finds tongues in trees, books in the running brooks,

Sermons in stones, and good in everything.

Duke Senior in *As You Like It*, 2.1.15–17

Finding consolation in the forest.

3 Under the greenwood tree
Who loves to lie with me,
And turn his merry note
Unto the sweet bird's throat,
Come hither, come hither, come
    hither!
            Here shall he see
            No enemy
But winter and rough weather.

Amiens in *As You Like It*, 2.5.1–8

This picture of ideal pastoral life nevertheless
includes winter; "turn" means adapt or attune.

4 Who doth ambition shun,
And loves to live i' the sun,
Seeking the food he eats,
And pleased with what he gets,
Come hither, come hither, come
    hither!

Amiens in *As You Like It*, 2.5.38–42

Second stanza of a song praising the pastoral
life.

5 If it do come to pass
That any man turn ass,
Leaving his wealth and ease
A stubborn will to please,
Ducdame, ducdame, ducdame!
Here shall he see
Gross fools as he,
And if he will come to me.

Jaques in *As You Like It*, 2.5.50–7

His ridicule of the pastoral life so idealized by
the Duke and Amiens.

6 To get your living by the copulation
of cattle.

Touchstone in *As You Like It*, 3.2.79–80

Speaking to Corin the shepherd; Touchstone
remains unimpressed by life in the country.

7 In respect that it is solitary, I like it
very well; but in respect that it is
private, it is a very vile life. In
respect it is in the fields, it pleaseth
me well; but in respect it is not in
the court, it is tedious.

Touchstone in *As You Like It*, 3.2.15–19

On life in the forest of Arden as contrasted
with life at court.

8 West of this place, down in the
    neighbor bottom,
The rank of osiers by the murmur-
    ing stream
Left on your right hand brings you
    to the place.

Celia in *As You Like It*, 4.3.78–80

Directions to Oliver to the house Celia and
Rosalind live in; "left" = passed by.

9   O, this life
Is nobler than attending for a
    check;
Richer than doing nothing for a
    bauble;
Prouder than rustling in unpaid-for
    silk.

Belarius in *Cymbeline*, 3.3.21–4

Contrasting a simple country life with life at
the king's court; "attending for a check" =
doing service only for a rebuke.

10 What should we speak of
When we are old as you? When we
    shall hear
The rain and wind beat dark
    December, how,
In this our pinching cave, shall we
    discourse
The freezing hours away?

Arviragus in *Cymbeline*, 3.3.35–9

On growing up in remotest Wales.

11 Of all these bounds, even from this
line to this,
With shadowy forests and with
champains riched,
With plenteous rivers and wide-
skirted meads,
We make thee lady.

King Lear in *King Lear*, 1.1.63–6

Giving his daughter Goneril a third of the
kingdom; "champains" = open country;
"meads" = meadows.

Courage (see also Valor)

1   Husband, I come!
Now to that name my courage
prove my title!

**Cleopatra in *Antony and Cleopatra*,
5.2.287–8**

She welcomes death like a bride going to her
husband.

2   There's neither honesty, manhood,
nor good fellowship in thee, nor
thou cam'st not of the blood royal,
if thou darest not stand for ten
shillings.

Falstaff in *Henry IV, Part 1*, 1.2.139–41

"Stand" = stand and fight. The gold ten
shilling coin was called a "royal."

3   The smallest worm will turn being
trodden on,
And doves will peck in safeguard of
their brood.

Clifford in *Henry VI, Part 3*, 2.2.17–18

The first line is proverbial.

4   Why, courage then! what cannot be
avoided

'Twere childish weakness to lament
or fear.

**Queen Margaret in *Henry VI, Part 3*,
5.4.37–8**

Encouraging her army in their fight against
King Edward.

5   When the cross blue lightning
seemed to open
The breast of heaven, I did present
myself
Even in the aim and very flash of it.

Cassius in *Julius Caesar*, 1.3.50–2

Boasting to Casca that he is not afraid of ominous storms.

6   *Macbeth.* If we should fail?
Lady Macbeth.   We fail?
But screw your courage to the stick-
ing place,
And we'll not fail.

***Macbeth*, 1.7.59–61**

Plotting the murder of Duncan. The image
may relate to screwing the pegs of a musical
instrument to the point where the strings are
taut.

7   He hath borne himself beyond the
promise of his age, doing, in the
figure of a lamb, the feats of a lion.

**Messenger in *Much Ado About Noth-
ing*, 1.1.13–15**

On the feats of young Claudio in battle.

Court

1   I have trod a measure, I have flattered a lady, I have been politic
with my friend, smooth with mine
enemy.

Touchstone in *As You Like It*, 5.4.44–6

Part of Touchstone's claim to be a courtier.

Courtesy

1   I am the king of courtesy . . . a Corinthian, a lad of mettle, a good boy.

Prince Hal in *Henry IV, Part 1*, 2.4.10–11, 12

Terms of approval given to him by the bartenders of a tavern; Corinthians were noted as spendthrifts and profligates.

2   I am the very pink of courtesy.

Mercutio in *Romeo and Juliet*, 2.4.57

"Pink" = embodiment or perfection.

Courtship (see also Adoration, Devotion, Love)

1   *Orlando.* Fair youth, I would I could make thee believe I love.
    Rosalind. Me believe it? You may sooner make her that you love believe it, which I warrant she is apter to do than to confess she does.

As You Like It, 3.2.387–9

Orlando is trying to make her believe that he loves her.

2   Come, woo me, woo me; for now I am in a holiday humor, and like enough to consent.

Rosalind in *As You Like It*, 4.1.68–9

Pretending to be able to cure Orlando of his love-sickness.

3   *Rosalind.* I will be your Rosalind in a more coming-on disposition; and ask me what you will, I will grant it.

Orlando. Then love me, Rosalind.
Rosalind. Yes, faith, will I, Fridays and Saturdays and all.

As You Like It, 4.1.112–17

Orlando is practicing how to woo Rosalind, who is disguised as a youth.

4   Sing, siren, for thyself, and I will dote;
    Spread o'er the silver waves thy golden hairs,
    And as a bed I'll take them, and there lie.

Antipholus of Syracuse in *The Comedy of Errors*, 3.2.47–9

To Luciana, who has been pleading with him on her sister's behalf; "take" = make use of.

5   It is thyself, mine own self's better part:
    Mine eye's clear eye, my dear heart's dearer heart,
    My food, my fortune, and my sweet hope's aim,
    My sole earth's heaven, and my heaven's claim.

Antipholus of Syracuse in *The Comedy of Errors*, 3.2.61–4

Lovesick for Luciana.

6   *Adriana.* With what persuasion did he tempt thy love?
    Luciana. With words that in an honest suit might move. First he did praise my beauty, then my speech.

The Comedy of Errors, 4.2.13–15

They both suppose Adriana's husband has been making love to Luciana; they have mistaken his twin brother for him.

7 Will you vouchsafe to teach a soldier terms
Such as will enter at a lady's ear
And plead his love-suit to her gentle heart?

King Henry in *Henry V*, 5.2.99–101

Having defeated the French Henry tries to
make love to Katherine, daughter of the
French king.

8 An angel is like you, Kate, and you
are like an angel.

King Henry in *Henry V*, 5.2.109–10

Wooing Katherine of France.

9 I know no ways to mince it in love,
but directly to say, "I love you";
then if you urge me farther than to
say, "Do you in faith?," I wear out
my suit.

King Henry in *Henry V*, 5.2.126–9

"Wear out my suit" = use up all my words of
love; Henry presents himself as a plain man to
Katherine.

10 If thou canst love a fellow of this
temper, Kate, whose face is not
worth sunburning, that never looks
in his glass for love of anything he
sees there, let thine eyes be thy
cook.

King Henry in *Henry V*, 5.2.146–9

Henry presents himself as a plain soldier in
making love to Katherine; her eye will have to
dress him up to find beauty, as a cook embell-
ishes food.

11 A good leg will fall, a straight back
will stoop, a black beard will turn
white, a fair face will wither, a full

eye will wax hollow; but a good
heart, Kate, is the sun and the
moon—or rather the sun and not
the moon, for it shines bright and
never changes, but keeps his course
truly.

King Henry in *Henry V*, 5.2.159–64

Wooing the French Princess Katherine.

12 What other pleasure can the world
afford?
I'll make my heaven in a lady's lap,
And deck my body in gay orna-
ments,
And witch sweet ladies with my
words and looks.

**Richard of Gloucester in *Henry VI,
Part 3*, 3.2.147–50**

A lesser pleasure for the deformed Richard
than aiming to get the crown.

13 He capers, he dances, he has eyes of
youth; he writes verses, he speaks
holiday, he smells April and May.

**Host in *The Merry Wives of Windsor*,
3.2.67–9**

Recommending Fenton as a suitor for Anne
Page.

14 We cannot fight for love, as men
may do;
We should be wooed, and were not
made to woo.

**Helena in *A Midsummer Night's
Dream*, 2.1.241–2**

Following Demetrius who is trying to shake
her off.

15 Thou and I are too wise to woo
peaceably.

Benedick in *Much Ado About Nothing*,
5.2.72

To Beatrice; neither of them wants to admit to
passion.

Romeo in *Romeo and Juliet*,
1.1.212–14

Speaking of Rosaline, who rejects his
advances.

16   She thanked me,
And bade me, if I had a friend that
    loved her,
I should but teach him how to tell
    my story,
And that would woo her.

Othello in *Othello*, 1.3.163–6

Desdemona's indirect way of making known
her love for Othello.

17 Look how my ring encompasseth
    thy finger;
Even so thy breast encloseth my
    poor heart.
Wear both of them, for both of
    them are thine.

King Richard in *Richard III*, 1.2.203–5

Lady Anne succumbs to his wily courtship by
accepting the ring he gives her.

18 Was ever woman in this humor
    wooed?
Was ever woman in this humor
    won?

King Richard in *Richard III*, 1.2.227–8

Having successfully wooed the Lady Anne in
presence of her father-in-law's corpse.

19 She will not stay the siege of loving
    terms,
Nor bide the encounter of assailing
    eyes,
Nor ope her lap to saint-seducing
    gold.

20 Say that she rail, why then I'll tell
    her plain
She sings as sweetly as a nightin-
    gale.
Say that she frown, I'll say she looks
    as clear
As morning roses newly washed
    with dew.
Say she be mute, and will not speak
    a word,
Then I'll commend her volubility,
And say she uttereth piercing elo-
    quence.

Petruchio in *The Taming of the Shrew*,
2.1.170–6

Petruchio's plan for wooing Katherine.

21 She is a woman, therefore may be
    wooed;
She is a woman, therefore may be
    won.

Demetrius in *Titus Andronicus*,
2.1.82–3

Proposing to woo Lavinia, Titus's daughter.

22 But though I loved you well, I
    wooed you not;
And yet, good faith, I wished myself
    a man,
Or that we women had men's privi-
    lege
Of speaking first.

Cressida in *Troilus and Cressida*,
3.2.126–9

Confessing she has long desired Troilus.

23 Make me a willow cabin at your
gate,
And call upon my soul within the
house;
Write loyal cantons of contemnèd
love,
And sing them loud even in the
dead of night;
Halloo your name to the reverber-
ate hills,
And make the babbling gossip of
the air
Cry out "Olivia!" O, you should
not rest
Between the elements of air and
earth
But you should pity me.

Viola in *Twelfth Night*, 1.5.268–76

Her sentimental description of a devoted
lover; the willow was a symbol of unrequited
love; "my soul" = Olivia; "cantons" = songs.

24 That man that hath a tongue I say is
no man
If with his tongue he cannot win a
woman.

**Valentine in *The Two Gentlemen of
Verona*, 3.1.104–5**

Making it seem easy in advising the Duke,
who in fact knows that Valentine is aiming to
elope with his daughter Sylvia.

Cowardice

1 We'll have a swashing and a martial
outside,
As many other mannish cowards
have
That do outface it with their sem-
blances.

Rosalind in *As You Like It*, 1.3.118–22

Proposing a swashbuckling disguise as a fighting man.

2 I could brain him with his lady's
fan.

Hotspur in *Henry IV, Part 1*, 2.3.23

Exasperated by the writer of a letter criticizing
a plot, which Hotspur is involved in, against
the king.

3 A plague of all cowards, I say, and a
vengeance too!

Falstaff in *Henry IV, Part 1*, 2.4.114–15

Blustering after running away himself from
Hal and Poins; "of" = on.

4   Wouldst thou have that
Which thou esteem'st the orna-
ment of life,
And live a coward in thine own
esteem,
Letting "I dare not" wait upon "I
would,"
Like the poor cat i' th' adage?

Lady Macbeth in *Macbeth*, 1.7.41–5

Goading her husband, and alluding to the
proverb, "the cat would eat fish but she will
not wet her feet."

5 That which in mean men we entitle
patience
Is pale cold cowardice in noble
breasts.

**Duchess of Gloucester in *Richard II*,
1.2.33–4**

Accusing John of Gaunt of cowardice for taking no action about the murder of his brother.

6 A milksop, one that never in his life
Felt so much cold as over shoes in
snow.

King Richard in *Richard III*, 5.3.325–6

Trying to raise the spirits of his troops by abusing Richmond.

7 A coward, a most devout coward, religious in it.

Fabian in *Twelfth Night*, 3.4.389–90

Persuading Sir Andrew that Cesario is a coward.

8 If you had but looked big and spit at him, he'd have run.

Clown in *The Winter's Tale*, 4.3.105–6

To Autolycus, who claims to have been assaulted by a rogue.

Creatures (see also Animals, Birds, Dogs, Horses, Insects, Snakes)

1 *Lepidus.* What manner o' thing is your crocodile?
Antony. It is shaped, sir, like itself, and it is as broad as it hath breadth.

Antony and Cleopatra, 2.7.41–3

Antony mocks the drunken Lepidus, with whom he and Octavius share power.

2 'Tis a strange serpent.

Lepidus in *Antony and Cleopatra*, 2.7.48

The crocodile.

3 You spotted snakes with double tongue,
Thorny hedgehogs, be not seen.
Newts and blindworms, do no wrong,
Come not near our Fairy Queen.

First Fairy in *A Midsummer Night's Dream*, 2.2.9–12

Singing a charm to keep creatures thought to be poisonous away from the sleeping Titania;

"blindworms" are harmless snakes but sometimes confused with adders.

4 Weaving spiders, come not here;
Hence, you longlegged spinners, hence!
Beetles black approach not near;
Worm nor snail, do no offense.

First Fairy in *A Midsummer Night's Dream*, 2.2.20–3

A charm to protect the sleeping Titania from tiny creatures common in England, and all harmless, though once thought to be venomous.

5   Come on, poor babe,
Some powerful spirit instruct the kites and ravens
To be thy nurses. Wolves and bears, they say,
Casting their savageness aside, have done
Like offices of pity.

Antigonus in *The Winter's Tale*, 2.3.185–9

He obeys Leontes' command to deposit his baby daughter Perdita in a remote place.

Crime (see also Law, Murder, Punishment, Theft)

1 If little faults, proceeding on distemper,
Shall not be winked at, how shall we stretch our eye
When capital crimes, chewed, swallowed, and digested,
Appear before us?

King Henry in *Henry V*, 2.2.54–7

Forgiving the fault of a man who abused him as caused by drunkenness ("proceeding on distemper").

2   I am in blood
Stepped in so far, that should I
 wade nor more
Returning were as tedious as go
 o'er.

Macbeth in *Macbeth*, 3.4.135–7

The psychology of a serial killer?

Criticism

1 In such a time as this it is not meet
That every nice offense should bear
 his comment.

Cassius in *Julius Caesar*, 4.3.7–8

To Brutus; "nice" = trivial; "bear his comment" = be subject to criticism.

2   Cassius is aweary of the world;
Hated by one he loves; braved by
 his brother;
Checked like a bondman; all his
 faults observed,
Set in a notebook, learned and
 conned by rote
To cast into my teeth.

Cassius in *Julius Caesar*, 4.3.95–9

Quarreling with Brutus: "braved" = defied;
"Checked" = rebuked; "conned by rote" =
learned by heart.

3 So turns she every man the wrong
 side out,
And never gives to truth and virtue
 that
Which simpleness and merit purchaseth.

**Hero in *Much Ado About Nothing*,
3.1.68–70**

Making sure that Beatrice hears this criticism
of her as too judgmental, and as denying
integrity ("simpleness") and merit what they
deserve ("purchaseth").

4 O gentle lady, do not put me to't,
For I am nothing if not critical.

Iago in *Othello*, 2.1.118–19

Desdemona has invited him to praise her.

Cruelty (see also Ruthlessness)

1 O tiger's heart wrapped in a
 woman's hide!

York in *Henry VI, Part 3*, 1.4.137

To Queen Margaret, who is gloating over the
murder of his son.

2 All pity choked with custom of fell
 deeds.

Mark Antony in *Julius Caesar*, 3.1.269

In the wake of Caesar's death, cruel ("fell")
deeds will become so familiar ("choked with
custom") that no-one will feel pity.

3   Come, you spirits
That tend on mortal thoughts,
 unsex me here,
And fill me from the crown to the
 toe, top-full
Of direst cruelty!

Lady Macbeth in *Macbeth*, 1.5.40–3

Summoning evil spirits that attend on murderous ("mortal") thoughts.

4 Did you say all? O hell-kite! All?
What, all my pretty chickens and
 their dam
At one fell swoop?

Macduff in *Macbeth*, 4.3.217–19

On learning that his wife and children have
been murdered by Macbeth.

5   Thou art come to answer
A stony adversary, an inhuman
    wretch,
Uncapable of pity, void and empty
From any dram of mercy.
Duke in *The Merchant of Venice*,
4.1.3–6

To Antonio, about Shylock; "answer" =
defend yourself; "dram" = minute amount.

6   The pound of flesh which I demand
    of him
Is dearly bought as mine, and I will
    have it.
Shylock in *The Merchant of Venice*,
4.1.99–100

Insisting on having a pound of Antonio's flesh.

7   For thy desires
Are wolvish, bloody, starved, and
    ravenous.
Gratiano in *The Merchant of Venice*,
4.1.137–8

On Shylock demanding his pound of flesh.

Curses

1   What, shall we curse the planets of
    mishap
That plotted thus our glory's over-
    throw?
Exeter in *Henry VI, Part 1*, 1.1.23–4

Attributing the early death of Henry V to the
influence of the planets.

2   Let this pernicious hour
Stand aye accursèd in the calendar!
Macbeth in *Macbeth*, 4.1.133–4

He has just seen the apparitions that show the
descendants of Banquo ruling in Scotland, not
his own; "aye" = forever.

3   Infected be the air whereon they
    ride,
And damned all those that trust
    them!
Macbeth in *Macbeth*, 4.1.138–9

Cursing the Witches.

4   The devil damn thee black, thou
    cream-faced loon!
Macbeth in *Macbeth*, 5.3.11

The stupid servant ("loon") is white with fear.

5   Curses, not loud but deep, mouth-
    honor, breath
Which the poor heart would fain
    deny, and dare not.
Macbeth in *Macbeth*, 5.3.27–8

"Mouth-honor" = merely superficial respect,
which is all Macbeth's achievement of the
crown of Scotland has brought him.

6   The devil take one party and his
    dam the other!
**Falstaff in *The Merry Wives of Wind-
sor*, 4.5.106–7**

On being tricked by Mrs. Ford and Mistress
Page; "dam" = dame or woman.

7   The day will come when thou shalt
    wish for me
To help thee curse this poisonous
    bunch-backed toad.
Queen Margaret in *Richard III*,
1.3.244–5

Foreshadowing the misery Richard (the
"toad") will inflict on Edward's Queen, Elizabeth.

8   A plague o' both your houses!
Mercutio in *Romeo and Juliet*, 3.1.99

As he is dying in their quarrel, Mercutio
curses both Capulets and Montagues.

9   The common curse of mankind,
folly and ignorance, be thine in
great revenue!

Thersites in *Troilus and Cressida*,
2.3.27–9

Cursing Patroclus.

Custom

1   Custom calls me to't.
What custom wills, in all things
   should we do't,
The dust on antique time would lie
   unswept,
And mountainous error be too
   highly heaped
For truth to o'erpeer.

Coriolanus in *Coriolanus*, 2.3.117–121

Coriolanus hates following the custom that
requires him to solicit votes from the citizens
of Rome for election as consul; if we obey
custom, he says ("should we do't"), nothing
would ever change.

2   But to my mind, though I am
   native here
And to the manner born, it is a custom
More honored in the breach than
   the observance.

Hamlet in *Hamlet*, 1.4.14–16

Commenting on the music accompanying the
king's carousing and revelry by night; "manner" = custom; "more honored in the breach
than the observance" = which it is more honorable to break than to observe.

3   Use almost can change the stamp of
   nature.

Hamlet in *Hamlet*, 3.4.168

Proverbial; "stamp of nature" = innate charac-
teristics.

4   O Kate, nice customs curtsy to
great kings. Dear Kate, you and I
cannot be confined within the weak
list of a country's fashion. We are
the makers of manners, Kate.

King Henry in *Henry V*, 5.2.268–71

"Nice" = punctilious or particular; "weak list"
= feeble bounds or barriers.

5   How use doth breed a habit in a
   man!

**Valentine in *The Two Gentlemen of
Verona*,** 5.4.1

"Use" = continual usage or practice.

Damnation

1   For Banquo's issue have I filed my
   mind;
For them the gracious Duncan have
   I murdered;
Put rancors in the vessel of my
   peace
Only for them; and mine eternal
   jewel
Given to the common enemy of
   man,
To make them kings, the seeds of
   Banquo kings!

Macbeth in *Macbeth*, 3.1.64–9

He has defiled ("filed") his mind, filled the
cup of his peace with enmity, and given his
soul ("eternal jewel") to the devil; "seeds" =
descendants.

Dancing

1   If you will patiently dance in our
   round,
And see our moonlight revels, go
   with us.

Titania in *A Midsummer Night's Dream*, 2.1.140–1

Titania inviting Oberon to join in the fairy dance or "round."

2 He capers nimbly in a lady's chamber
To the lascivious pleasing of a lute.

King Richard in *Richard III*, 1.1.12–13

The warrior has become the courtier in peacetime.

3 You and I are past our dancing days.

Capulet in *Romeo and Juliet*, 1.5.31

Old Capulet talks with his cousin while watching the dance.

4 When you do dance, I wish you
A wave o'the sea, that you might ever do
Nothing but that, move still, still so,
And own no other function.

Florizel in *The Winter's Tale*, 4.4.140–3

Describing Perdita, with whom he is in love.

Danger

1 Out of this nettle, danger, we pluck this flower, safety.

Hotspur in *Henry IV, Part 1*, 2.3.9–10

On a lord who has refused out of fear to join his rebellion.

2 I must go and meet with danger there,
Or it will seek me in another place,
And find me worse provided.

Northumberland in *Henry IV, Part 2*, 2.3.48–50

He is wondering whether to join with other rebels to fight King Henry; "provided" = prepared.

3 Gloucester, 'tis true that we are in great danger;
The greater therefore should our courage be.

King Henry in *Henry V*, 4.1.1–2

Preparing to fight the French army.

4 *Williams.* I pray you, what thinks he of our estate?
King Henry. Even as men wrecked upon a sand, that look to be washed off the next tide.

Henry V, 4.1.96–8

"Estate" = state of affairs, condition; the disguised king can say what he really thinks.

5 *Soothsayer.* Beware the Ides of March.
Caesar. He is a dreamer. Let us leave him. Pass.

Julius Caesar, 1.2.23–4

Caesar was assassinated on the Ides (15th) of March.

6 It is the bright day that brings forth the adder,
And that craves wary walking.

Brutus in *Julius Caesar*, 2.1.14–15

"Craves" = requires.

7 Think him as a serpent's egg,
Which, hatched, would as his kind grow mischievous,
And kill him in the shell.

Brutus in *Julius Caesar*, 2.1.32–4

The snake (Caesar) will behave according to its nature ("as his kind").

8   Danger knows full well
That Caesar is more dangerous
  than he.
We are two lions littered in one day,
And I the elder and more terrible,
And Caesar shall go forth.

Caesar in *Julius Caesar*, 2.2.44–8

He feels he has to live up to his name.

9   We are at the stake
And bayed about with many ene-
  mies;
And some that smile have in their
  hearts, I fear,
Millions of mischiefs.

Octavius in *Julius Caesar*, 4.1.48–51

To Antony; the image is from bear-baiting;
bears were tied to a stake and mastiff dogs set
on them.

10 I am amazed, methinks, and lose
  my way
Among the thorns and dangers of
  this world.

**The Bastard Falconbridge in *King
John*, 4.3.140–1**

On finding the young prince Arthur murdered;
"amazed" = astonished, but also carries the
sense "lost as in a maze."

11 The bow is bent and drawn; make
  from the shaft.

King Lear in *King Lear*, 1.1.143

Threatening Kent; "make" = get away.

12 There's daggers in men's smiles.

Donalbain in *Macbeth*, 2.3.140

Feeling unsafe after the murder of his father,
Duncan.

13 We have scorched the snake, not
  killed it:

She'll close and be herself.

Macbeth in *Macbeth*, 3.2.13–14

Macbeth fails to find the security he thought
the death of Duncan would bring him;
"scorched" = slashed, scored; "close" = heal
up.

14 Why strew'st thou sugar on that
  bottled spider
Whose deadly web ensnareth thee
  about?

**Queen Margaret in *Richard III*,
1.3.241–2**

Speaking to Edward's Queen, Elizabeth, who
does not join her in her denunciation of
Richard.

15 Thus have I shunned the fire for
  fear of burning,
And drenched me in the sea, where
  I am drowned.

**Proteus in *The Two Gentlemen of
Verona*, 1.3.78–9**

Having concealed his love for Julia, his reason
for staying at home in Verona, Proteus now
finds he is sent off by his father to further his
education in Milan.

Darkness (see also Night)

1   O sun,
Burn the great sphere thou mov'st
  in! darkling stand
The varying shore o' the world!

**Cleopatra in *Antony and Cleopatra*,
4.15.9–11**

Calling for universal darkness to mark the
death of Antony.

2   There's husbandry in heaven,
Their candles are all out.

Banquo in *Macbeth*, 2.1.4–5

"Husbandry" = thrift, meaning the stars are
not visible.

3   This thing of darkness I
Acknowledge mine.

Prospero in *The Tempest*, 5.1.275–6

Owning that he is responsible for Caliban;
"darkness" suggests both ignorance and evil
(as commonly in the Bible).

Dawn (see also Sunrise)

1   But look, the morn in russet mantle
clad
Walks o'er the dew of yon high
eastward hill.

Horatio in *Hamlet*, 1.1.166–7

2   But soft, methinks I scent the
morning air,
Brief let me be.

Ghost in *Hamlet*, 1.5.58–9

3   The glow-worm shows the matin to
be near,
And 'gins to pale his ineffectual fire.

Ghost in *Hamlet*, 1.5.89–90

Signaling the end of his interview with Hamlet
as day approaches.

4   Yonder shines Aurora's harbinger.

**Puck in *A Midsummer Night's Dream*,
3.2.380**

The morning star, or Venus, precursor of
dawn; Venus is also goddess of love, and here
heralds the reconciliation of the lovers in the
play.

5   The grey-eyed morn smiles on the
frowning night,
Checkering the eastern clouds with
streaks of light.

**Friar Lawrence in *Romeo and Juliet*,
2.3.1–2**

6   It was the lark, the herald of the
morn,
No nightingale. Look, love, what
envious streaks
Do lace the severing clouds in yonder east.

Romeo in *Romeo and Juliet*, 3.5.6–8

To Juliet; their wedding night has ended all
too soon.

7   Night's candles are burnt out, and
jocund day
Stands tiptoe on the misty mountain tops.
I must be gone and live, or stay and
die.

Romeo in *Romeo and Juliet*, 3.5.9–11

The exiled Romeo parts from Juliet after their
wedding night.

8   O Cressida! But that the busy day,
Waked by the lark, hath roused the
ribald crows,
And dreaming night will hide our
joys no longer,
I would not from thee.

**Troilus in *Troilus and Cressida*,
4.2.8–11**

The morning after their first night together.

Death (see also Death-Wish, Dying, Mortality)

1   There's a great spirit gone!

**Antony in *Antony and Cleopatra*,
1.2.122**

Antony has just learned of the death of his
wife, Fulvia.

2   I will be
A bridegroom in my death, and run
   into't
As to a lover's bed.

Antony in *Antony and Cleopatra*,
4.14.99–101

Only in dying does he think of Cleopatra in
terms of marriage.

3   Where art thou, death?
Come hither, come! Come, come,
   and take a queen
Worth many babes and beggars!

Cleopatra in *Antony and Cleopatra*,
5.2.46–8

Preferring death to being a captive.

4   His biting is immortal; those that
do die of it do seldom or never
recover.

Clown in *Antony and Cleopatra*,
5.2.246–8

Referring to the asp or snake he brings to
Cleopatra.

5   Now boast thee, death, in thy possession lies
A lass unparalleled! Downy windows, close,
And golden Phoebus never be
beheld
Of eyes again so royal!

Charmian in *Antony and Cleopatra*,
5.2.315–18

Closing Cleopatra's eyes after her death.

6   She looks like sleep,
As she would catch another Antony
In her strong toil of grace.

**Octavius Caesar in *Antony and
Cleopatra*,** 5.2.346–8

Looking at the dead Cleopatra; a "toil" is a net
or snare.

7   To die, to sleep—
To sleep, perchance to dream—ay,
   there's the rub,
For in that sleep of death what
   dreams may come,
When we have shuffled off this
   mortal coil,
Must give us pause.

Hamlet in *Hamlet*, 3.1.63–7

Sleep was proverbially the image of death;
"rub" = snag (a term from the game of bowls);
"coil" = turmoil.

8   He is dead and gone, lady,
   He is dead and gone;
At his head a grass-green turf,
   At his heels a stone.

Ophelia in *Hamlet*, 4.5.29–32

Singing in her madness, after her father's
death.

9   Had I but time—as this fell
   sergeant, Death,
Is strict in his arrest—O, I could tell
   you—
But let it be.

Hamlet in *Hamlet*, 5.2.336–8

As he lies dying, to Horatio; "fell" = fierce;
"sergeant" = officer of the law-courts.

10   O proud death,
What feast is toward in thine eter-
nal cell,
That thou so many princes at a shot
So bloodily hast struck?

Fortinbras in *Hamlet*, 5.2.364–7

Arriving after the deaths of Hamlet, Laertes,
Claudius and Gertrude; "toward" = in prepa-
ration; "eternal cell" = the grave.

11 Doomsday is near, die all, die merrily.

Hotspur in *Henry IV, Part 1*, 4.1.134

A rallying call to his fellow rebels as they face a battle against the king's forces.

12 *Prince Hal.* Why, thou owest God a death.
Falstaff. 'Tis not due yet, I would be loath to pay him before his day.

Henry IV, Part 1, 5.1.126–8

Hal's phrase is proverbial, and true for everyone.

13 Death, as the Psalmist saith, is certain to all, all shall die.

Shallow in *Henry IV, Part 2*, 3.2.37–8

Psalms 89:48.

14 A man can die but once, we owe God a death.

Feeble in *Henry IV, Part 2*, 3.2.234–5

Proverbial (see also 12 above); Feeble shows his courage.

15 This sleep is sound indeed, this is a sleep
That from this golden rigol hath divorced
So many English kings.

Prince Hal in *Henry IV, Part 2*, 4.5.35–7

Sitting by his father's bedside, he thinks his father is dead; "rigol" = circle (compare "regal").

16 Here was a royal fellowship of death.

King Henry in *Henry V*, 4.8.101

On hearing of the 126 French princes and nobles killed in the battle of Agincourt.

17 Cowards die many times before their deaths;
The valiant never taste of death but once.

Caesar in *Julius Caesar*, 2.2.32–3

18 It seems to me most strange that men should fear,
Seeing that death, a necessary end,
Will come when it will come.

Caesar in *Julius Caesar*, 2.2.35–7

The idea that nothing is more certain than death, and nothing more uncertain than the time it will come, is proverbial.

19 That we shall die we know, 'tis but the time
And drawing days out that men stand upon.

Brutus in *Julius Caesar*, 3.1.99–100

"Drawing days out" = prolonging their lives.

20 She's gone for ever.
I know when one is dead, and when one lives;
She's dead as earth.

King Lear in *King Lear*, 5.3.260–2

Looking at his dead or dying daughter Cordelia.

21 And my poor fool is hanged! No, no, no life!
Why should a dog, a horse, a rat have life,
And thou no breath at all? Thou'lt come no more,
Never, never, never, never, never.

King Lear in *King Lear*, 5.3.306–9

"Poor fool" affectionately refers to his daughter Cordelia, whose body he is looking at (but may recall the Fool, who has not been seen since Act 3).

22   The sleeping and the dead
Are but as pictures; 'tis the eye of
  childhood
That fears a painted devil.

Lady Macbeth in *Macbeth*, 2.2.50–2

To Macbeth, who cannot face looking on the
scene of the murder he has carried out.

23 Shake off this downy sleep, death's
  counterfeit,
And look on death itself!

Macduff in *Macbeth*, 2.3.76–7

On the death of Duncan; varying the proverb,
"sleep is the image of death."

24 Banquo, thy soul's flight,
If it find heaven, must find it out
  tonight.

Macbeth in *Macbeth*, 3.1.140–1

Having arranged the murder of Banquo.

25   Duncan is in his grave;
After life's fitful fever he sleeps well.

Macbeth in *Macbeth*, 3.2.22–3

The murder of Duncan has not cured Macbeth's "fitful fever."

26 Be absolute for death. Either death
  or life
Shall thereby be the sweeter. Rea-
  son thus with life:
If I do lose thee I do lose a thing
That none but fools would keep.

Duke in *Measure for Measure*, 3.1.5–8

Preparing Claudio to face the death penalty.

27 The sense of death is most in apprehension,
And the poor beetle that we tread
  upon
In corporal sufferance finds a pang
  as great

As when a giant dies.

Isabella in *Measure for Measure*,
3.1.77–80

Trying to reconcile Claudio, her brother, to
the idea that he must die; "apprehension" =
anticipation.

28   If I must die,
I will encounter darkness as a bride,
And hug it in mine arms.

Claudio in *Measure for Measure*,
3.1.83–5

Claudio has been sentenced to death for getting Juliet with child.

29 Death is a fearful thing.

Claudio in *Measure for Measure*,
3.1.115

He is in prison, and sentenced to death.

30 The weariest and most loathèd
  worldly life
That age, ache, penury, and
  imprisonment
Can lay on nature is a paradise
To what we fear of death.

Claudio in *Measure for Measure*,
3.1.128–31

He is in prison, and sentenced to death; "To"
= compared to.

31 A man that apprehends death no
more dreadfully but as a drunken
sleep, careless, reckless, and fearless
of what's past, present, or to come;
insensible of mortality, and desperately mortal.

Provost in *Measure for Measure*,
4.2.142–5

On Barnardine, long since sentenced to die,
and who has no fear of death, and no hope of
escaping it ("desperately mortal").

32 Death may usurp on nature many
        hours,
    And yet the fire of life kindle again
    The o'erpressed spirits.

    Cerimon in *Pericles*, 3.2.82–4

    He restores to life the shipwrecked and almost
    dead Thaisa.

33 Cry woe, destruction, ruin, and
        decay:
    The worst is death, and death will
        have his day.

    King Richard in *Richard II*, 3.2.102–3

    Despairing at ever more bad news.

34 Nothing can we call our own but
        death,
    And that small model of the barren
        earth
    Which serves as paste and cover to
        our bones.

    King Richard in *Richard II*, 3.2.152–4

    The "model" is the body, made of earth (Genesis 3:19).

35   Within the hollow crown
    That rounds the mortal temples of
        a king
    Keeps Death his court, and there
        the antic sits,
    Scoffing his state and grinning at
        his pomp,
    Allowing him a breath, a little
        scene,
    To monarchize, be feared, and kill
        with looks.

    King Richard in *Richard II*, 3.2.160–5

    Death was often personified as a grinning
    skeleton, as in the common images of the
    Dance of Death; "antic" = grotesque clown.

36 'Tis a vile thing to die, my gracious
        lord,

When men are unprepared, and
    look not for it.

Catesby in *Richard III*, 3.2.62–3

Speaking to Hastings, who is unaware that
Richard will shortly have him executed.

37 Death lies on her like an untimely
        frost
    Upon the sweetest flower of all the
        field.

    Capulet in *Romeo and Juliet*, 4.5.28–9

    Old Capulet thinks Juliet is dead.

38 Death, that hath sucked the honey
        of thy breath,
    Hath had no power yet upon thy
        beauty.
    Thou art not conquered. Beauty's
        ensign yet
    Is crimson in thy lips and in thy
        cheeks,
    And death's pale flag is not
        advanced there.

    Romeo in *Romeo and Juliet*, 5.3.92–6

    He has opened the tomb where Juliet lies,
    thought to be dead, but really unconscious
    and still alive.   . . . .

39 Grim death, how foul and loath-
        some is thine image.

    **Lord in *The Taming of the Shrew*,
    Induction, 1.35**

    The "image" is that of a drunken man.

40 Come away, come away, death,
        And in sad cypress let me be laid.
    Fly away, fly away, breath,
        I am slain by a fair cruel maid.

    Feste in *Twelfth Night*, 2.4.51–4

    A song for Orsino; a reminder of mortality, as
    cypress was an emblem of mourning; the
    image is of the lover slain by the power of a
    maid's beauty, suggesting also Cupid's arrow.

Death-Wish

1 Unarm, Eros, the long day's task is
done,
And we must sleep.

Antony in *Antony and Cleopatra*,
4.14.35–6

To his servant, Eros, preparing for death.

2 Finish, good lady, the bright day is
done,
And we are for the dark.

Iras in *Antony and Cleopatra*, 5.2.193–4

Encouraging Cleopatra to take her own life.

3 Give me my robe, put on my
crown, I have
Immortal longings in me.

Cleopatra in *Antony and Cleopatra*,
5.2.280–1

To Iras; Cleopatra is preparing her death
scene.

4   Look,
I draw the sword myself; take it and
hit
The innocent mansion of my love,
my heart.
Fear not, 'tis empty of all things but
grief.

Imogen in *Cymbeline*, 3.4.66–9

She draws Pisanio's sword on learning he has
been ordered by her husband Posthumus to
kill her.

5   'Tis a consummation
Devoutly to be wished.

Hamlet in *Hamlet*, 3.1.62–3

"Consummation" = final completion of this
life.

6 Live a thousand years,
I shall not find myself so apt to die.
No place will please me so, no
mean of death,
As here by Caesar, and by you cut
off,
The choice and master spirits of
this age.

Mark Antony in *Julius Caesar*,
3.1.159–63

To Brutus and the conspirators who assassinated Caesar.

7 Death, death! O amiable, lovely
Death!
Thou odoriferous stench, sound
rottenness!
Arise forth from the couch of last-
ing night,
Thou hate and terror to prosperity,
And I will kiss thy detestable bones.

Constance in *King John*, 3.4.25–9

Behind these lines lies the image of Death as
often depicted in drawings of the "Dance of
Death," a skeleton seizing victims at random.
Her son, Arthur, is imprisoned, and she fears
for his life.

8 Hath no man's dagger here a point
for me?

Leonato in *Much Ado About Nothing*,
4.1.109

Reacting to the public defamation of his
daughter Hero.

9 O that I were a mockery king of
snow,
Standing before the sun of Bolingbroke,
To melt myself away in water
drops!

King Richard in *Richard II*, 4.1.260–2

Humiliated in front of the whole court.

10   O, here
Will I set up my everlasting rest,
And shake the yoke of inauspicious
    stars
From this world-wearied flesh.

Romeo in *Romeo and Juliet*, 5.3.109–12

He supposes Juliet is dead, and resolves (sets
up his rest) to seek everlasting repose and die
himself.

11   Sir, spare your
    threats;
The bug that you would fright me
    with, I seek.
To me life can be no commodity.

**Hermione in *The Winter's Tale*,
3.2.92–4**

She is threatened with death by Leontes;
"bug" = bugbear, terror; "commodity" = benefit.

12   Tired with all these, for restful
    death I cry.

***Sonnet* 66, 1**

"All these" are the wrongs and corruption the
narrator finds widespread in society.

Deceit/Deception (see also Duplicity, Hypocrisy)

1   Apparel vice like virtue's harbinger;
   Bear a fair presence, though your
     heart be tainted;
   Teach sin the carriage of a holy
     saint;
   Be secret-false.

**Luciana in *The Comedy of Errors*,
3.2.12–15**

Her advice is wasted on the twin brother of
her sister's husband.

2   O,
Dissembling courtesy! How fine
    this tyrant
Can tickle where she wounds!

Imogen in *Cymbeline*, 1.1.83–5

On her step-mother, the Queen, as pretending
to care for her.

3   What says she, fair one? That the
   tongues of men are full of deceits?

King Henry in *Henry V*, 5.2.117–8

Discovering that Katherine understands his
English flattery.

4   To beguile the time,
Look like the time, bear welcome in
    your eye,
Your hand, your tongue; look like
    the innocent flower,
But be the serpent under't.

Lady Macbeth in *Macbeth*, 1.5.63–6

"To beguile the time, Look like the time" = to
deceive people, behave as they do ("time" =
society at large); the idea of the snake in the
grass is proverbial.

5   Away, and mock the time with
    fairest show;
False face must hide what the false
    heart doth know.

Macbeth in *Macbeth*, 1.7.81–2

Recalling the proverb, "false face, foul heart."

6   So may the outward shows be least
    themselves—
The world is still deceived with
    ornament.

**Bassanio in *The Merchant of Venice*,
3.2.73–4**

Thinking about his choice of caskets; outward
appearance may conceal inner reality.

7 There is no vice so simple but assumes
Some mark of virtue on his outward parts.

Bassanio in *The Merchant of Venice*, 3.2.81–2

"Simple" = plain or unadulterated.

8 Thus ornament is but the guilèd shore
To a most dangerous sea; the beauteous scarf
Veiling an Indian beauty; in a word,
The seeming truth which cunning times put on
To entrap the wisest.

Bassanio in *The Merchant of Venice*, 3.2.97–101

Rejecting the silver and gold caskets; "guiled" = treacherous.

9 O, what authority and show of truth
Can cunning sin cover itself withal!

Claudio in *Much Ado About Nothing*, 4.1.35–6

To Leonato, who, he thinks, is deceiving him; "authority" = assurance.

10 When my outward action doth demonstrate
The native act and figure of my heart
In compliment extern, 'tis not long after
But I will wear my heart upon my sleeve
For daws to peck at: I am not what I am.

Iago in *Othello*, 1.1.61–5

Boasting of concealing his true feelings; "compliment extern" = external show or behavior to others; "daws" = jackdaws, i.e., fools.

11 Look to her, Moor, if thou hast eyes to see;
She has deceived her father, and may thee.

Brabantio in *Othello*, 1.3.292–3

Brabantio's last words to Othello about his daughter, Desdemona.

12 The Moor is of a free and open nature,
That thinks men honest that but seem to be so,
And will as tenderly be led by the nose
As asses are.

Iago in *Othello*, 1.3.399–402

Speaking of Othello as artless ("free and open") and easily ("tenderly") deceived.

13 'Tis here, but yet confused.
Knavery's plain face is never seen till used.

Iago in *Othello*, 2.1.311–12

Scheming against Othello.

14 I know our country disposition well;
In Venice they do let God see the pranks
They dare not show their husbands; their best conscience
Is not to leave't undone, but keep't unknown.

Iago in *Othello*, 3.3.201–4

Cynically suggesting Venetian women are all covert adulterers.

15 Who makes the fairest show means most deceit.

Cleon in *Pericles*, 1.4.75

Misinterpreting the arrival of the fleet of Pericles that is bringing aid to Tarsus; proverbial.

16 Ah, that deceit should steal such
 gentle shape,
And with a virtuous visor hide deep
 vice!

Duchess of York in *Richard III*,
2.2.27–8

On Richard, who wears a mask ("visor") of
virtue.

17 We know each other's faces; for our
 hearts,
He knows no more of mine than I
 of yours,
Or I of his, my lord, than you of
 mine.

Buckingham in *Richard III*, 3.4.10–12

Deceiving the Bishop of Ely; Buckingham is
conspiring with Richard.

18 Here's a good world the while!
 Who is so gross
That cannot see this palpable
 device?
Yet who's so bold but says he sees it
 not.

Scrivener in *Richard III*, 3.6.10–12

On an indictment written after the execution
of Hastings.

19 Be not easily won to our requests;
Play the maid's part: still answer
 nay, and take it.

Buckingham in *Richard III*, 3.7.50–1

Advising Richard on how to behave when he
is offered the crown; it was proverbial that
maids said no when they meant yes.

20 For God doth know, and you may
 partly see,

How far I am from the desire of
 this.

King Richard in *Richard III*, 3.7.235–6

Pretending he does not want power and the
throne.

21 If ye should lead her in a fool's paradise, as they say, it were a very
 gross kind of behavior.

Nurse in *Romeo and Juliet*, 2.4.165–7

Speaking to Romeo about Juliet; "a fool's
paradise" = a state of delusory happiness;
proverbial.

22 O serpent heart, hid with a
 flow'ring face!

Juliet in *Romeo and Juliet*, 3.2.73

On learning that Romeo has killed Tybalt;
varying the idea of the proverbial "snake in
the grass."

23 Was ever book containing such vile
 matter
So fairly bound? O that deceit
 should dwell
In such a gorgeous palace!

Juliet in *Romeo and Juliet*, 3.2.83–5

Thinking Romeo has deceived her.

24 So shall I live, supposing thou art
 true,
Like a deceivèd husband, so love's
 face
May still seem love to me, though
 altered new,
Thy looks with me, thy heart in
 other place.

***Sonnet 93*, 1–4**

Fearing his lover is deceiving him, he will be
content with the appearance of love ("love's
face").

Decline (see also Downfall)

1   O Hamlet, what a falling off was
    there!

Ghost in *Hamlet*, 1.5.45–7

On the part of his widow, Gertrude, who has
married his brother Claudius.

2   So now prosperity begins to mellow
    And drop into the rotten mouth of
    death.

Queen Margaret in *Richard III*, 4.4.1–2

Happy to see Richard's fortunes declining and
her enemies being destroyed.

3   'Tis certain, greatness, once fallen
    out with fortune,
    Must fall out with men too. What
    the declined is,
    He shall as soon read in the eyes of
    others
    As feel in his own fall.

**Achilles in *Troilus and Cressida*,
3.3.75–8**

On finding he is ignored by the other Greek
generals.

Defeat

1   Our enemies have beat us to the pit.
    It is more worthy to leap in our-
    selves
    Than tarry till they push us.

Brutus in *Julius Caesar*, 5.5.23–5

Accepting defeat; the "pit" could be a trap for
wild animals.

Dejection

1   How weary, stale, flat, and unprof-
    itable

    Seem to me all the uses of this
    world!
    Fie on't, ah fie! 'tis an unweeded
    garden
    That grows to seed, things rank and
    gross in nature
    Possess it merely.

Hamlet in *Hamlet*, 1.2.133–7

Expressing his world-weariness after his
mother's remarriage.

2   I have of late—but wherefore I
    know not—lost all my mirth, for-
    gone all custom of exercise.

Hamlet in *Hamlet*, 2.2.295–7

To Rosencrantz and Guildenstern, on his
melancholy.

3   I, of ladies most deject and
    wretched,
    That sucked the honey of his music
    vows,
    Now see that noble and most sover-
    eign reason
    Like sweet bells jangled out of tune
    and harsh.

Ophelia in *Hamlet*, 3.1.155–8

On Hamlet's supposed madness.

4   I have not that alacrity of spirit
    Nor cheer of mind that I was wont
    to have.

King Richard in *Richard III*, 5.3.73–4

A premonition of his defeat to come.

Delay

1   I do not know
    Why yet I live to say, "This thing's
    to do,"
    Since I have cause, and will, and
    strength, and means
    To do't.

Hamlet in *Hamlet*, 4.4.43–6

On his failure to carry out his revenge on Claudius.

2   That we would do
We should do when we would, for this "would" changes,
And hath abatements and delays as many
As there are tongues, are hands, are accidents.

Claudius in *Hamlet*, 4.7.118–21

"Abatements" = loss of momentum; what people do or say, and mere chance, may cause us to delay doing what we should.

3   Defer no time; delays have dangerous ends.

Reignier in *Henry VI, Part 1*, 3.2.33

Urging immediate assault by the French on Rouen, held by the English.

Demons

1   As I stood here below, methought his eyes
Were two full moons; he had a thousand noses,
Horns whelked and waved like the enridgèd sea.
It was some fiend.

Edgar in *King Lear*, 4.6.69–72

Deceiving his father into thinking he has been led by a fiend; "whelked" = twisted.

Deserving (see also Merit)

1   We wound our modesty, and make foul the clearness of our deservings, when of ourselves we publish them.

Steward in *All's Well That Ends Well*, 1.3.5–7

"Make foul" = obscure or sully; "publish" = boast of.

2   Use every man after your own desert, and who should scape whipping? Use them after your own honor and dignity—the less they deserve, the more merit is in your bounty.

Hamlet in *Hamlet*, 2.2.529–32

Speaking to Polonius about the actors who have come to court.

3   Well you deserve. They well deserve to have
That know the strong'st and surest way to get.

King Richard in *Richard II*, 3.3.200–1

To Bolingbroke, who has seized power.

4   Plead what I will be, not what I have been;
Not my deserts, but what I will deserve.

King Richard in *Richard III*, 4.4.414–15

Begging Queen Elizabeth to plead on his behalf with her daughter for her hand in marriage.

Desire (see also Lust)

1   Yet have I fierce affections, and think
What Venus did with Mars.

Mardian in *Antony and Cleopatra*, 1.5.17–18

A eunuch speaks of his desires.

2   He will to his Egyptian dish again.

Enobarbus in *Antony and Cleopatra*,
2.6.126

Forseeing that Antony, though married and in
Rome, will not stay away from Cleopatra.

3   Your heart's desires be with you!

Celia in *As You Like It*, 1.2.199

To Orlando as he is about to fight with
Charles, the wrestler.

4   *Phebe*. Thou hast my love; is not
         that neighborly?
     Silvius. I would have you.
     Phebe.   Why, that were
         covetousness.

***As You Like It*, 3.5.90–1**

"Thou shalt not covet . . . any thing that is thy
neighbor's" is God's commandment, Exodus
20:17.

5   Can one desire too much of a good
     thing?

Rosalind in *As You Like It*, 4.1.123–4

An ambiguous question; proverbially "The
more common a good thing is the better," and
also "Too much of one thing is good for nothing."

6   I hope it is no dishonest desire to
     desire to be a woman of the world.

Audrey in *As You Like It*, 5.3.3–5

"A woman of the world" = married woman;
"dishonest" = dishonorable.

7   Is it not strange that desire should
     so many years outlive performance?

Poins in *Henry IV, Part 2*, 2.4.260–1

Commenting on old Falstaff with Doll
Tearsheet sitting on his lap.

8   O, the difference of man and man!
     To thee a woman's services are due.

Goneril in *King Lear*, 4.2.26–7

Making love to Edmund, so different from her
husband, Albany.

9   Stars, hide your fires;
     Let not light see my black and deep
         desires!
     The eye wink at the hand; yet let
         that be
     Which the eye fears, when it is
         done, to see.

Macbeth in *Macbeth*, 1.4.50–3

Contemplating murder; "wink at" = overlook,
or connive at what the hand does.

10   Nought's had, all's spent,
     Where our desire is got without
         content.

Lady Macbeth in *Macbeth*, 3.2.4–5

"Content" = contentment.

11   It oft falls out,
     To have what we would have, we
         speak not what we mean.

Isabella in *Measure for Measure*,
2.4.117–18

To Angelo; she has overpitched her pleading
for the life of her brother.

12   "Who chooseth me shall gain what
         many men desire."
     Why, that's the lady, all the world
         desires her.

**Prince of Morocco in *The Merchant of
Venice*, 2.7.37–8**

Reading the message on the golden casket.

13   "Who chooseth me shall gain what
         many men desire."
     What many men desire! That
         many may be meant

By the fool multitude that choose
by show.

Prince of Aragon in *The Merchant of*
Venice, 2.9.24–6

He starts by examining the golden casket.

14 I know a lady in Venice would have
walked barefoot to Palestine for a
touch of his nether lip.

Emilia in *Othello,* 4.3.38–9

15 That she was never yet that ever
knew
Love got so sweet as when desire
did sue.
Therefore this maxim out of love I
teach:
Achievement is command;
ungained, beseech.

Cressida in *Troilus and Cressida,*
1.2.290–3

Realizing that once she has yielded to a man
she will be subject to his whims ("command"), but if she holds off he will remain a
suitor.

16 O, when mine eyes did see Olivia
first,
Methought she purged the air of
pestilence;
That instant was I turned into a
hart,
And my desires, like fell and cruel
hounds,
E'er since pursue me.

Orsino in *Twelfth Night,* 1.1.18–22

The image of Actaeon, transformed into a stag
by Diana, lies behind these lines.

17 The trustless wings of false desire.

The Rape of Lucrece, 2

"Trustless" = not to be trusted.

18 What win I if I gain the thing I
seek?
A dream, a breath, a froth of fleeting joy.
Who buys a minute's worth to wail
a week?
Or sells eternity to gain a toy?

The Rape of Lucrece, 211–4

Tarquin struggles with his conscience about
the rape; "toy" = a trivial thing.

19 Desire my pilot is, beauty my prize,
Then who fears sinking where such
treasure lies?

Tarquin in *The Rape of Lucrece,* 279–80

Inventing reasons to pursue the rape of the
chaste Lucrece.

20 The sweets we wish for turn to
loathèd sours
Even in the moment that we call
them ours.

The Rape of Lucrece, 867–8

Lucrece reflects on the rape she has suffered.

21 "In night," quoth she, "desire sees
best of all."

Venus and Adonis, 720

Venus is trying to seduce Adonis.

Despair

1 I am so lated in this world, that I
Have lost my way for ever.

Antony in *Antony and Cleopatra,*
3.11.3–4

Despairing after losing the Battle of Actium;
"lated" means belated, or benighted as if
obscured in darkness.

2 The happiest youth, viewing his
   progress through,
   What perils past, what crosses to
   ensue,
   Would shut the book, and sit him
   down and die.

King Henry in *Henry IV, Part 2*,
3.1.54–6

If the happiest youth could foresee his life's
passage ("progress through"), and what afflictions ("crosses") he would have to face, he
might be content to die rather than live.

3 I 'gin to be aweary of the sun,
   And wish th' estate o' the world
   were now undone.

Macbeth in *Macbeth*, 5.5.48–9

At the end of his tether; " 'gin" = begin; "th'
estate o' the world" = the condition or fixed
order of the universe.

4 I will despair, and be at enmity
   With cozening hope.

Queen in *Richard II*, 2.2.68–9

On learning that Henry Bolingbroke makes
war against Richard; "cozening" = deceiving.

5   Of comfort no man speak.
   Let's talk of graves, of worms and
   epitaphs,
   Make dust our paper, and with
   rainy eyes
   Write sorrow on the bosom of the
   earth.
   Let's choose executors and talk of
   wills.

King Richard in *Richard II*, 3.2.144–8

In despair as he realizes all is lost.

6   What comfort have we now?
   By heaven, I'll hate him everlast-
   ingly

That bids me be of comfort any
   more.

King Richard in *Richard II*, 3.2.206–8

Rejecting comfort in favor of despair.

7 I shall despair. There is no creature
   loves me,
   And if I die no soul will pity me.
   And wherefore should they, since
   that I myself
   Find in myself no pity to myself?

King Richard in *Richard III*, 5.3.200–3

Realizing that he has cut himself off from
everyone.

8 Come weep with me, past hope,
   past cure, past help!

Juliet in *Romeo and Juliet*, 4.1.45

Unable to see a way out of being forced to
marry Paris, she turns to Friar Lawrence.

Desperation

1 A horse! A horse! My kingdom for
   a horse!

King Richard in *Richard III*, 5.4.7

His famous line in the heat of battle; the kingdom he so ruthlessly sought has become
worthless.

Determination (see also Resolution)

1   Unhand me, gentlemen.
   By heaven, I'll make a ghost of him
   that lets me!

Hamlet in *Hamlet*, 1.4.84–5

To his companions who try to stop Hamlet
following his father's ghost; "lets" = hinders.

2   I'll have my bond, speak not against
     my bond,
     I have sworn an oath that I will
     have my bond.

     Shylock in *The Merchant of Venice*,
     3.3.4–5

     The bond demands a pound of Antonio's
     flesh.

3   By my soul I swear
     There is no power in the tongue of
     man
     To alter me.

     Shylock in *The Merchant of Venice*,
     4.1.240–2

     Standing on his legal right to cut flesh from
     Antonio.

4   He's fortified against any denial.

     Malvolio in *Twelfth Night*, 1.5.145

     On Cesario (Viola in disguise), who is deter-
     mined to speak with Olivia.

The Devil (see also Hell)

1   He must needs go that the devil
     drives.

     Lavatch in *All's Well That Ends Well*,
     1.3.29–30

     Proverbial.

2   The spirit that I have seen
     May be the devil, and the devil hath
     power
     T'assume a pleasing shape.

     Hamlet in *Hamlet*, 2.2.598–600

     Reflecting on his father's ghost.

3   Now I perceive the devil under-
     stands Welsh.

     Hotspur in *Henry IV, Part 1*, 3.1.229

     Alluding to Glendower's claim to supernatural
     powers.

4   Give the devil his due.

     Orleans in *Henry V*, 3.7.116–17

     Orleans and the Constable of France swap
     proverbs; even the devil may deserve some
     credit.

5   The prince of darkness is a gentle-
     man.

     Edgar in *King Lear*, 3.4.143

     Referring to Ephesians 6:12, "we wrestle not
     against flesh and blood, but against principali-
     ties, against powers, against the rulers of the
     darkness of this world"; the Geneva Bible,
     used by Shakespeare, has "princes" for
     "rulers."

6   Devils soonest tempt, resembling
     spirits of light.

     Berowne in *Love's Labor's Lost*, 4.3.253

     Referring to the black-eyed Rosaline.

7   What, can the devil speak true?

     Banquo in *Macbeth*, 1.3.107

     On one of the Witches' prophecies being ful-
     filled; varying the proverb, "the devil some-
     times speaks the truth."

8   The devil can cite scripture for his
     purpose.

     Antonio in *The Merchant of Venice*,
     1.3.98

     Proverbial, alluding to Matthew 4:6, where
     the devil tempts Jesus.

9 Naked in bed, Iago, and not mean
   harm?
   It is hypocrisy against the devil.
   They that mean virtuously and yet
   do so,
   The devil their virtue tempts, and
   they tempt heaven.

   Othello in *Othello*, 4.1.5–8

   Imagining Cassio in bed with Desdemona; as
   good covering up evil is hypocrisy against
   God, so evil actions that claim to be virtuous
   constitute hypocrisy against the devil.

10 Now the devil that told me I did
   well
   Says that this deed is chronicled in
   hell.

   Sir Pierce of Exton in *Richard II*,
   5.5.115–16

   He has just killed Richard in prison.

11 What, man, defy the devil. Consider, he's an enemy to mankind.

   Sir Toby Belch in *Twelfth Night*,
   3.4.97–8

   Treating Malvolio as if he is mad.

Deviousness

1 Your bait of falsehood takes this
   carp of truth,
   And this do we of wisdom and of
   reach,
   With windlasses and with assays of
   bias,
   By indirections find directions out.

   Polonius in *Hamlet*, 2.1.60–3

   Sending Reynaldo to spy on his son Laertes,
   and spread a few lies about him; "windlasses"
   = roundabout methods; "assays of bias" =
   indirect attempts, "bias" referring to the curv-
   ing line in which a bowl runs.

2 I am well acquainted with your
   manner of wrenching the true
   cause the false way.

   Chief Justice in *Henry IV, Part 2*,
   2.1.109–11

   On Falstaff's deviousness.

3   God knows, my son,
   By what by-paths and indirect
   crooked ways
   I met this crown.

   King Henry in *Henry IV, Part 2*,
   4.5.183–5

   On the devious means by which he came to
   power.

Devotion (see also Infatuation, Love)

1 He has my heart yet, and shall have
   my prayers
   While I shall have my life.

   Queen Katherine in *Henry VIII*,
   3.1.180–1

   Speaking about Henry, who has just divorced
   her.

2 All the faith, the virtue of my heart,
   The object and the pleasure of mine
   eye,
   Is only Helena.

   Demetrius in *A Midsummer Night's
   Dream*, 4.1.169–71

   Though he had been in love with Hermia until
   Puck made him see differently.

3   To her, my lord,
   Was I betrothed ere I saw Hermia;
   But like a sickness did I loathe this
   food.

But, as in health come to my nat-
ural taste,
Now I do wish it, love it, long for it,
And will for evermore be true to it.

Demetrius in *A Midsummer Night's*
Dream, 4.1.171–6

Protesting his eternal loyalty to Helena.

4   My heart's subdued
Even to the very quality of my lord.
I saw Othello's visage in his mind,
And to his honors and his valiant
    parts
Did I my soul and fortunes conse-
    crate.

Desdemona in *Othello*, 1.3.250–4

Rejecting her father's assumption that she
could not love a black man.

5   My love doth so approve
    him,
That even his stubbornness, his
    checks, his frowns—
Prithee unpin me—have grace and
    favor in them.

Desdemona in *Othello*, 4.3.19–21

To Emilia, about Othello's harsh behavior.

6   All my fortunes at thy foot I'll lay,
And follow thee my lord through-
    out the world.

Juliet in *Romeo and Juliet*, 2.2.147–8

Offering to marry Romeo.

7   Being your slave, what should I do
    but tend
Upon the hours and times of your
    desire?
I have no precious time at all to
    spend,

Nor services to do, till you require.

Sonnet 57, 1–4

The narrator's total devotion to his friend is
imaged as slavery; "tend" = attend.

Dignity

1   I am a wise fellow, and, which is
more, an officer; and, which is
more, a householder; and, which is
more, as pretty a piece of flesh as
any is in Messina; and one that
knows the law, go to; and a rich fellow enough, go to; and a fellow that
hath had losses; and one that hath
two gowns and everything handsome about him.

Dogberry in *Much Ado About*
Nothing, 4.2.80–6

Priding himself on his modest wealth and
status.

Disappointment

1   Thus do the hopes we have in him
    touch ground
And dash themselves to pieces.

Mowbray in *Henry IV, Part 2*, 4.1.17–18

On Northumberland's failure to support the
rebels.

2   Thus hath the candle singed the
    moth.

Portia in *The Merchant of Venice*,
2.9.79

On the Prince of Aragon's disappointment in
choosing the wrong casket.

Discontent

1   But whate'er I be,
Nor I, nor any man that but man is,
With nothing shall be pleased till he
be eased
With being nothing.

King Richard in *Richard II*, 5.5.38–41

Brooding in prison that he cannot be content
with having nothing until he is nothing, i.e.,
dead.

Disease, see Sickness

Disillusion

1   Heigh-ho, sing heigh-ho! unto the
green holly,
Most friendship is feigning, most
loving mere folly.

Amiens in *As You Like It*, 2.7.180–1

Sung by a follower of the banished rightful
Duke Senior.

Dismissal

1   Get you hence, sirrah! Saucy fellow, hence!

Brutus in *Julius Caesar*, 4.3.134

Dismissing a poet who seeks to reconcile him
with Cassius.

Disorder (see also Anarchy, Chaos, Confusion)

1   Love cools, friendship falls off,
brothers divide: in cities, mutinies;
in countries, discord; in palaces,
treason; and the bond cracked
'twixt son and father.

Gloucester in *King Lear*, 1.2.106–9

Thinking of King Lear's banishment of Kent,
and believing his own son Edgar seeks his life.

2   We have seen the best of our time.
Machinations, hollowness, treachery, and all ruinous disorders follow us disquietly to our graves.

Gloucester in *King Lear*, 1.2.112–14

3   Our sea-walled garden, the whole
land,
Is full of weeds, her fairest flowers
choked up,
Her fruit-trees all unpruned, her
hedges ruined,
Her knots disordered, and her
wholesome herbs
Swarming with caterpillars.

Gardener's Man in *Richard II*, 3.4.43–7

Recalling the image of King Richard's favorites
as "caterpillars of the commonwealth";
"knots" were patterned beds of flowers.

4   Have you no wit, manners nor
modesty, to gabble like tinkers at
this time of night?

Malvolio in *Twelfth Night*, 2.3.87–8

Olivia's steward rebukes Sir Toby Belch, Feste
and Sir Andrew Aguecheek for making merry
late at night in her house.

5   Is there no respect of place, persons, nor time in you?

Malvolio in *Twelfth Night*, 2.3.91–2

Reprimanding Sir Toby and his companions
for their rowdiness at night.

Dogs

1   As familiar with me as my dog.
    Prince Hal in *Henry IV, Part 2,*
    2.2.106–7

2   That island of England breeds very
    valiant creatures; their mastiffs are
    of unmatchable courage.
    Rambures in *Henry V,* 3.7.140–2

3   The little dogs and all,
    Trey, Blanch and Sweetheart, see,
       they bark at me.
    King Lear in *King Lear,* 3.6.62–3

    The mad old king's imaginary dogs might sug-
    gest his three daughters, Goneril, Regan
    (betrayal and fear), and "blanch" = make pale with
    fear), and Cordelia, his favorite.

4   Ay, in the catalogue ye go for men,
    As hounds and greyhounds, mon-
       grels, spaniels, curs,
    Shoughs, water-rugs, and demi-
       wolves, are clept
    All by the name of dogs.
    Macbeth in *Macbeth,* 3.1.91–4

    Speaking to the murderers he has hired;
    "shoughs" are rough mongrels, and "water-
    rugs" dogs used for fowling; "clept" = called.

5   My love shall hear the music of my
    hounds.
    Theseus in *A Midsummer Night's*
    Dream, 4.1.106

    Speaking to Hippolyta.

6   My hounds are bred out of the
       Spartan kind,
    So flewed, so sanded; and their
    heads are hung

With ears that sweep away the
    morning dew;
Crook-kneed, and dewlapped like
    Thessalian bulls;
Slow in pursuit, but matched in
    mouth like bells,
Each under each.
Theseus in *A Midsummer Night's*
Dream, 4.1.119–24

Praising sand-colored ("sanded") hunting
dogs; "flews" are the large hanging chaps of a
hound; Thessaly was in ancient Greece.

7   I think Crab, my dog, be the
    sourest-natured dog that lives: my
    mother weeping, my father wailing,
    my sister crying, our maid howling,
    our cat wringing her hands, and all
    our house in a great perplexity, yet
    did not this cruel-hearted cur shed
    one tear. He is a stone, a very peb-
    ble-stone, and has no more pity in
    him than a dog.
    Launce in *The Two Gentlemen of*
    Verona, 2.3.5–11

Doomsday

1   Doomsday is near; die all, die mer-
    rily.
    Hotspur in *Henry IV, Part 1,* 4.1.134

    Spoken as he prepares for battle.

2   *Kent.*   Is this the promised
       end?
    Edgar. Or image of that horror?
    Albany.   Fall and
       cease.
    King Lear, 5.3.264–5

    Imagining doomsday on seeing King Lear
    enter carrying his dying or dead daughter
    Cordelia.

3 What, will the line stretch out to
   the crack of doom?

Macbeth in *Macbeth*, 4.1.117

Referring to the line of Banquo's descendants;
"crack of doom" = the peal of thunder on
Judgment Day.

Doubt

1 Doubting things go ill often hurts
   more
   Than to be sure they do; for cer-
   tainties
   Either are past remedies, or, timely
   knowing,
   The remedy then born.

Imogen in *Cymbeline*, 1.6.95–8

To Jachimo, who has hinted that all is not well
with her; "Doubting" = suspecting; "timely
knowing" = knowing in time.

2 Our doubts are traitors,
   And makes us lose the good we oft
   might win,
   By fearing to attempt.

Lucio in *Measure for Measure*, 1.4.77–9

Urging Isabella to plead for her brother with
Angelo.

Downfall (see also Decline)

1 I have touched the highest point of
   all my greatness,
   And from that full meridian of my
   glory
   I haste now to my setting. I shall
   fall
   Like a bright exhalation in the
   evening,
   And no man see me more.

**Cardinal Wolsey in *Henry VIII*,
3.2.223–7**

Cardinal Wolsey contemplates his downfall.

2   O how wretched
   Is that poor man that hangs on
   princes' favors!
   There is betwixt that smile we
   would aspire to,
   More pangs and fears than wars or
   women have;
   And when he falls, he falls like
   Lucifer,
   Never to hope again.

**Cardinal Wolsey in *Henry VIII*,
3.2.366–72**

Comparing himself to Lucifer, the brightest
angel, who fell from heaven to hell (Isaiah
14:12).

3   Men so noble,
   However faulty, yet should find
   respect
   For what they have been. 'Tis a
   cruelty
   To load a falling man.

Cromwell in *Henry VIII*, 5.2.109–12

Speaking on behalf of Archbishop Cranmer.

4 Men shut their doors against a setting sun.

Apemantus in *Timon of Athens*, 1.2.145

Foreshadowing the fall of Timon.

Dreams (see also Sleep)

1 I dreamt there was an Emperor
   Antony.
   O, such another sleep, that I might
   see
   But such another man!

Cleopatra in *Antony and Cleopatra*,
5.2.76–8

After Antony's death.

2 *Cleopatra.* Think you there was or
     might be such a man
  As this I dreamt of?
  Dolabella.   Gentle madam, no.

Antony and Cleopatra, 5.2.93–4

Dolabella punctures Cleopatra's fantasy of
Antony as superman.

3 I could be bounded in a nutshell
  and count myself a king of infinite
  space, were it not that I have bad
  dreams.

Hamlet in *Hamlet*, 2.2.254–6

To his college friends Rosencrantz and
Guildenstern.

4 *Guildenstern.* The very substance of
     the ambitious is merely the
     shadow of a dream.
  Hamlet. A dream itself is but a
     shadow.

Hamlet, 2.2.257–60

Guildenstern thinks Hamlet's problem may be
ambition.

5 That, he awaking when the other
     do,
  May all to Athens back again repair,
  And think no more of this night's
     accidents
  But as the fierce vexation of a
     dream.

Oberon in *A Midsummer Night's
Dream*, 4.1.66–9

Planning to release the lovers and Bottom
from the magic spell; "other" = others; "vexation" = affliction.

6 I have had a most rare vision. I
  have had a dream, past the wit of
  man to say what dream it was.
  Man is but an ass if he go about to
  expound this dream.

Bottom in *A Midsummer Night's
Dream*, 4.1.204–7

7 The eye of man hath not heard, the
  ear of man hath not seen, man's
  hand is not able to taste, his tongue
  to conceive, nor his heart to report
  what my dream was!

Bottom in *A Midsummer Night's
Dream*, 4.1.211–14

Bottom confuses the senses, in a garbled recollection of I Corinthians 2:9–10, just as his
dream is confused in recollection.

8 O, I have passed a miserable night,
  So full of fearful dreams, of ugly
     sights,
  That, as I am a Christian faithful
     man,
  I would not spend another such a
     night
  Though 'twere to buy a world of
     happy days,
  So full of dismal terror was the
     time.

Clarence in *Richard III*, 1.4.2–7

In prison, his dream foreshadows his death.

9 O Lord, methought what pain it
     was to drown,
  What dreadful noise of waters in
     my ears!
  What sights of ugly death within
     my eyes!

Clarence in *Richard III*, 1.4.21–3

Describing a fearful dream; anticipating his
own death.

10 Methought I saw a thousand fearful
wrecks,
A thousand men that fishes gnawed
upon,
Wedges of gold, great anchors,
heaps of pearl,
Inestimable stones, unvalued jewels,
All scattered in the bottom of the
sea.

Clarence in *Richard III*, 1.4.24–8

Describing his dream of wealth scattered
among dead bodies.

11　　　　　Methought a legion of foul
fiends
Environed me, and howlèd in mine
ears
Such hideous cries that with the
very noise
I trembling waked, and for a season
after
Could not believe but that I was in
hell,
Such terrible impression made my
dream.

Clarence in *Richard III*, 1.4.58–63

His fearful dream, anticipating his own death.

12　*Romeo.* I dreamt a dream tonight.
Mercutio. And so did I.
Romeo. Well, what was yours?
Mercutio. That dreamers often lie.
Romeo. In bed asleep, while they
do dream things true.
Mercutio. O then I see Queen Mab
hath been with you.
She is the fairies' midwife, and she
comes
In shape no bigger than an agate
stone
On the forefinger of an alderman,
Drawn with a team of little atomi
Over men's noses as they lie asleep.

Romeo and Juliet, 1.4.50–8

Mercutio's fairy-tale seems meant to divert
Romeo from his preoccupation with Rosaline;
agates were carved with tiny figures (like
"atomi") and used as seal-rings by town offi-
cials ("aldermen").

13　*Romeo.* Peace, peace, Mercutio,
peace!
Thou talk'st of nothing.
Mercutio.　　　　True, I talk of
dreams,
Which are the children of an idle
brain,
Begot of nothing but vain fantasy,
Which is as thin of substance as the
air,
And more inconstant than the
wind.

Romeo and Juliet, 1.4.95–100

Mercutio implies that Romeo's love for Rosaline is as much a vain fantasy as a dream.

14　If I may trust the flattering truth of
sleep,
My dreams presage some joyful
news at hand.

Romeo in *Romeo and Juliet*, 5.1.1–2

In exile, Romeo hopes for good news from
Verona.

15　　　　　In dreaming,
The clouds methought would open,
and show riches
Ready to drop upon me; that, when
I waked,
I cried to dream again.

Caliban in *The Tempest*, 3.2.140–3

16　　　　　Dreams are toys.
Yet for this once, yea, supersti-
tiously,
I will be squared by this.

Antigonus in *The Winter's Tale*,
3.3.39–41

Dreams are trifles ("toys"), yet Antigonus
allows himself to be directed ("squared") in
his course of action by his dream of
Hermione.

17 Thus have I had thee as a dream
doth flatter,
In sleep a king, but waking no such
matter.

Sonnet 87, 13–14

From a sonnet that relates to a quarrel with his
friend.

Drinking

1 Come, thou monarch of the vine.

Song in *Antony and Cleopatra*, 2.7.113

Song to Bacchus, god of wine.

2 In my youth I never did apply
Hot and rebellious liquors in my
blood.

Adam in *As You Like It*, 2.3.48–9

Adam's recipe for a healthy old age.

3 One that loves a cup of hot wine
with not a drop of allaying Tiber
in't.

Menenius in *Coriolanus*, 2.1.48–9

Portraying himself as a drinker, who prefers
his wine undiluted; the Tiber is the river that
flows through Rome.

4 One that converses more with the
buttock of the night than with the
forehead of the morning.

Menenius in *Coriolanus*, 2.1.51–3

Presenting himself as liking to carouse at night
rather than rise early.

5 We'll teach you to drink deep ere
you depart.

Hamlet in *Hamlet*, 1.2.175

To his friend, Horatio, visiting him in Denmark.

6 These mad mustachio purple-hued
maltworms.

Gadshill in *Henry IV, Part 1*, 2.1.74–5

Beer-drinkers whose moustaches are stained
with drink.

7 O monstrous! but one half-penny-
worth of bread to this intolerable
deal of sack!

**Prince Hal in *Henry IV, Part 1*,
2.4.540–1**

Reading the tavern bill found in Falstaff's
pocket.

8 Doth it not show vilely in me to
desire small beer?

Prince Hal in *Henry IV, Part 2*, 2.2.5–6

Implying that a prince should want strong
drink, not weak ("small") beer.

9 A good sherris-sack hath a twofold
operation in it. It ascends me into
the brain, . . . makes it apprehensive, quick, forgetive, full of nimble,
fiery, and delectable shapes.

**Falstaff in *Henry IV, Part 2*, 4.3.96–7,
99–100**

Praising the effects of drinking sherry ("sherris-
sack," from "Xeres" in Spain and "seco" =
dry), that stimulates the imagination to be cre-
ative ("forgetive," from the verb to forge).

10 The second property of your excellent sherris is the warming of the
blood.

Falstaff in *Henry IV, Part 2*, 4.3.102–3

Drinking wine or sherry was thought to heat
the blood.

11 It illumineth the face, which as a beacon gives warning to all the rest of this little kingdom, man, to arm . . . this valor comes of sherris.

Falstaff in *Henry IV, Part 2*, 4.3.107–9, 112–13

On drinking wine or sherry as promoting courage.

12 If I had a thousand sons, the first humane principle I would teach them should be, to forswear thin potations and to addict themselves to sack.

Falstaff in *Henry IV, Part 2*, 4.3.122–5

"Sack" = sherry; see 9 above.

13 That which hath made them drunk hath made me bold;
What hath quenched them hath given me fire.

Lady Macbeth in *Macbeth*, 2.2.1–2

Referring to the wine she has given Duncan's attendants.

14 *Macduff.* What three things does drink especially provoke?
Porter. Marry, sir, nose-painting, sleep, and urine. Lechery, sir, it provokes, and unprovokes: it provokes the desire, but it takes away the performance.

Macbeth, 2.3.26–30

"Marry" = by the Virgin Mary (an oath); "nose-painting" = red noses.

15 When he is best, he is a little worse than a man, and when he is worst, he is little better than a beast.

Portia in *The Merchant of Venice*, 1.2.88–9

Describing her German suitor, who is often drunk.

16 I'll ne'er be drunk, whilst I live, again, but in honest, civil, godly company.

Slender in *The Merry Wives of Windsor*, 1.1.181–2

17 Come, gentlemen, I hope we shall drink down all unkindness.

Page in *The Merry Wives of Windsor*, 1.1.196–7

18 You love sack, and so do I; would you desire better sympathy?

Mistress Page in *The Merry Wives of Windsor*, 2.1.8–10

Mistress Page is reading Falstaff's letter, which shows his peculiar way of making love to her.

19 *Falstaff.* Go, brew me a pottle of sack, finely.
Bardolph. With eggs, sir?
Falstaff. Simple of itself; I'll no pullet-sperm in my brewage.

The Merry Wives of Windsor, 3.5.28–32

Falstaff asks for two quarts of sherry to be heated.

20 I have very poor and unhappy brains for drinking. I could well wish courtesy would invent some other custom of entertainment.

Cassio in *Othello*, 2.3.33–6

21 O thou invisible spirit of wine, if thou hast no name to be known by, let us call thee devil!

Cassio in *Othello*, 2.3.281–3

His drunkenness has cost him his office.

22 O God, that men should put an enemy into their mouths to steal away their brains!

Cassio in *Othello*, 2.3.289–91

On losing his office because of drunkenness.

23 Good wine is a good familiar creature, if it be well used.

Iago in *Othello*, 2.3.309–10

Iago seems to praise wine as friendly, but a "familiar" was also the name for demons thought to attend on witches in the shape of creatures.

24 Prithee do not turn me about, my stomach is not constant.

Stephano in *The Tempest*, 2.2.114–15

The butler is drunk, having found a cask of wine driven ashore on the island where they have been shipwrecked.

25 *Sebastian.* He is drunk now. Where had he wine?
   Alonso. And Trinculo is reeling ripe. Where should they Find this grand liquor that hath gilded 'em?

The Tempest, 5.1.278–80

On the arrival of the drunken butler Stephano and his companion Trinculo; "gilded" = flushed, made them red-faced.

26 Here's that which is too weak to be a sinner,
   Honest water, which ne'er left man i' the mire.

Apemantus in *Timon of Athens*, 1.2.58–9

As opposed to the wine that flows in Timon's house.

27 *Maria.* He's drunk nightly in your company.
   Sir Toby Belch. With drinking healths to my niece. I'll drink to her as long as there is a passage in my throat, and drink in Illyria.

Twelfth Night, 1.3.36–40

Referring to Sir Andrew Aguecheek.

28 O, he's drunk, Sir Toby, an hour agone; his eyes were set at eight i' the morning.

Feste in *Twelfth Night*, 5.1.198–9

Referring to the surgeon who should attend to the injured Sir Toby.

Duplicity (see also Deceit/Deception, Hypocrisy)

1 Why, I can smile, and murder whiles I smile,
   And cry "Content!" to that which grieves my heart,
   And wet my cheeks with artificial tears,
   And frame my face to all occasions.

Richard of Gloucester in *Henry VI, Part 3*, 3.2.182–5

Boasting to the audience in soliloquy.

2 I can add colors to the chameleon, Change shapes with Proteus for advantages,
   And set the murderous Machiavel to school.

Richard of Gloucester in *Henry VI, Part 3*, 3.2.191–3

Proteus, the old man of the sea, could change himself into any shape. Machiavelli was identified with ruthless political cunning.

3 And that I love the tree from
   whence thou sprang'st,
   Witness the loving kiss I give the
   fruit.
   He kisses the infant prince
   [*Aside*] To say the truth, so Judas
   kissed his master,
   And cried "All hail!" whenas he
   meant all harm.

**Richard of Gloucester in *Henry VI,
Part 3*, 5.7.31–4**

Richard of Gloucester, later Richard III,
already has in mind getting rid of the prince
he has just kissed, son of Edward IV. It was
the kiss Judas Iscariot gave to Christ that
betrayed him to the chief priests (Mark
14:44–6).

4 An evil soul producing holy witness
   Is like a villain with a smiling cheek,
   A goodly apple rotten at the heart.

**Antonio in *The Merchant of Venice*,
1.3.99–101**

Referring to Shylock.

5 O, what a goodly outside falsehood
   hath!

**Antonio in *The Merchant of Venice*,
1.3.102**

Referring to Shylock, from whom he wants to
borrow money.

6 Cannot a plain man live and think
   no harm,
   But that his simple truth must be
   abused
   With silken, sly, insinuating Jacks?

King Richard in *Richard III*, 1.3.51–3

Falsely protesting his honest simplicity;
"Jacks" is a scornful term for people of lower
rank or low breeding.

7 I do the wrong, and first begin to
   brawl.

The secret mischiefs that I set
   abroach
I lay unto the grievous charge of
   others.

King Richard in *Richard III*, 1.3.323–5

Laying the responsibility for his own wicked
schemes on others; "set abroach" = initiate,
set going.

Duty

1 He was disposed to mirth, but on
   the sudden
   A Roman thought hath struck him.

**Cleopatra in *Antony and Cleopatra*,
1.2.82–3**

In Alexandria, Antony occasionally remembers his duties as a ruler and his wife in Rome.

2 Every subject's duty is the King's,
   but every subject's soul is his own.

King Henry in *Henry V*, 4.1.176–7

The king, disguised, speaks with common soldiers.

3 I owe him little duty and less love.

Somerset in *Henry VI, Part 1*, 4.4.34

Referring to Richard, Duke of York; they are
supposed to be supporting one another in
fighting the French.

4   What wouldst thou do, old
      man?
   Think'st thou that duty shall have
      dread to speak
   When power to flattery bows?

Kent in *King Lear*, 1.1.146–8

Reminding the king of his age ("fourscore and
upward" as we learn later).

5 I do perceive here a divided duty.

Desdemona in _Othello_, 1.3.181

To her father, Brabantio, and her husband,
Othello.

6 Duty never yet did want his meed.

**Silvia in _The Two Gentlemen of
Verona_,** 1.4.112

To Proteus, who is offering his service to her;
"want his meed" = lack his reward.

Dying (see also Death, Mortality)

1 I am dying, Egypt, dying.

Antony in _Antony and Cleopatra_,
4.15.18, 41

Antony's only reference to Cleopatra's title as
Queen of Egypt.

2 I am fire and air; my other elements
I give to baser life.

Cleopatra in _Antony and Cleopatra_,
5.2.289–90

Earth and water were the heavier of the four
elements of which it was thought life was
composed.

3 If thou and nature can so gently
  part,
The stroke of death is as a lover's
  pinch,
Which hurts, and is desired.

Cleopatra in _Antony and Cleopatra_,
5.2.294–6

Addressing Iras, one of her attendants, who
dies just before Cleopatra herself.

4 The poor world is almost six thousand years old, and in all this time

there was not any man died in his
own person, videlicet, in a love-
cause.

Rosalind in _As You Like It_, 4.1.94–7

"Videlicet" = namely; calculating from the
Bible, it was thought that the world was created about 4000 B.C.

5 Men have died from time to time,
and worms have eaten them, but
not for love.

Rosalind in _As You Like It_, 4.1.106–8

6 'A parted even just between twelve
and one, even at the turning o' the
tide; for after I saw him fumble
with the sheets, and play with flowers, and smile upon his finger's end,
I knew there was but one way; for
his nose was as sharp as a pen, and
'a babbled of green fields.

Mistress Quickly in _Henry V_, 2.3.12–17

On the death of Falstaff; " 'A parted" = he
departed.

7 So 'a bade me lay more clothes on
his feet. I put my hand into the bed
and felt them, and they were as cold
as any stone; then I felt to his knees,
and so upward and upward, and all
was as cold as any stone.

Mistress Quickly in _Henry V_, 2.3.22–6

On the death of Falstaff.

8 The sands are numbered that
  makes up my life,
Here must I stay, and here my life
  must end.

York in _Henry VI, Part 3_, 1.4.25–6

He is defeated and alone on the field of battle.

9   Why, what is pomp, rule, reign, but
    earth and dust?
    And live we how we can, yet die we
    must.

Warwick in *Henry VI, Part 3*, 5.2.27–8

He is wounded and near death; "die we must"
is proverbial.

10 He gave his honors to the world
    again,
    His blessèd part to heaven, and
    slept in peace.

Griffith in *Henry VIII*, 4.2.29–30

Reporting the death of Cardinal Wolsey.

11 My heart hath one poor string to
    stay it by.

King John in *King John*, 5.7.55

12   But his flawed heart
    (Alack, too weak the conflict to
    support!)
    'Twixt two extremes of passion, joy
    and grief,
    Burst smilingly.

Edgar in *King Lear*, 5.3.197–200

On the death of his father, Gloucester;
"flawed" = cracked.

13   Nothing in his life
    Became him like the leaving it. He
    died
    As one that had been studied in his
    death,
    To throw away the dearest thing he
    owed
    As 'twere a careless trifle.

Malcolm in *Macbeth*, 1.4.7–11

On the execution of the traitor Cawdor.

14   I will play the swan,
    And die in music.

Emilia in *Othello*, 5.2.247–8

Proverbially the swan sang before it died
(hence the term "swan song").

15 *Romeo.* Courage, man, the hurt
    cannot be much.
    Mercutio. No, 'tis not so deep as a
    well, nor so wide as a church
    door, but 'tis enough, 'twill serve.
    Ask for me tomorrow, and you
    shall find me a grave man.

Romeo and Juliet, 3.1.95–8

Even as he is dying, stabbed by Tybalt, Mercutio jests with a pun on the word "grave."

16   My long sickness
    Of health and living now begins to
    mend,
    And nothing brings me all things.

Timon in *Timon of Athens*, 5.1.186–8

Foreseeing his death.

Earthquakes

1   Diseasèd nature oftentimes breaks
    forth
    In strange eruptions; oft the teem-
    ing earth
    Is with a kind of colic pinched and
    vexed
    By the imprisoning of unruly wind
    Within her womb, which, for
    enlargement striving,
    Shakes the old beldame earth, and
    topples down
    Steeples and moss-grown towers.

Hotspur in *Henry IV, Part 1*, 3.1.26–32

Rejecting Glendower's claim that extraordinary events in nature at his birth were signs
that he was to be remarkable; "beldame" =
grandmother.

Eating (see also Food)

1   On the Alps
It is reported thou didst eat strange
flesh,
Which some did die to look on.

Octavius Caesar in *Antony and Cleopatra*, 1.4.66–8

Hardships endured by Antony as a soldier.

2   Unquiet meals make ill digestions.

The Abbess in *The Comedy of Errors*, 5.1.74

To Adriana, who has been criticizing her husband.

3   They surfeited with honey and
began
To loathe the taste of sweetness,
whereof a little
More than a little is by much too
much.

King Henry in *Henry IV, Part 1*, 3.2.71–3

Describing how the people became tired of seeing Richard II.

4   He hath eaten me out of house and
home, he hath put all my substance
into that fat belly of his.

Mistress Quickly in *Henry IV, Part 2*, 2.1.74–5

On Falstaff's gargantuan appetite.

5   We will eat a last year's pippin of
mine own grafting, with a dish of
caraways, and so forth.

Shallow in *Henry IV, Part 2*, 5.3.2–3

Apples were often eaten with caraway seeds.

6   Read o'er this,
And after this, and then to breakfast
with
What appetite you have.

King Henry in *Henry VIII*, 3.2.201–3

Henry hands Cardinal Wolsey documents proving his disloyalty to the King.

7   Now good digestion wait on
appetite,
And health on both!

Macbeth in *Macbeth*, 3.4.37–8

Welcoming his guests to a banquet.

8   Who riseth from a feast
With that keen appetite that he sits
down?

Gratiano in *The Merchant of Venice*, 2.6.8–9

9   Truly, a peck of provender, I could
munch your good dry oats.
Methinks I have a great desire to a
bottle of hay. Good hay, sweet hay
hath no fellow.

Bottom in *A Midsummer Night's Dream*, 4.1.31–4

Bottom when transformed into an ass; a "bottle" is a truss.

10   Eat no onions nor garlic, for we are
to utter sweet breath.

Bottom in *A Midsummer Night's Dream*, 4.2.42–3

Advising the actors who are to perform "Pyramus and Thisbe."

11   Things sweet to taste prove in
digestion sour.

John of Gaunt in *Richard II*, 1.3.236

Proverbial; compare Revelation 10:9–10.

12 Nothing but sit and sit, and eat and eat!

Petruchio in *The Taming of the Shrew*, 5.2.12

At Lucentio's banquet to celebrate his marriage.

13 I am a great eater of beef, and I believe that does harm to my wit.

Sir Andrew Aguecheek in *Twelfth Night*, 1.3.85–6

Eating beef was proverbially linked to being stupid or "beef-witted."

14 A plague o' these pickle herring!

Sir Toby Belch in *Twelfth Night*, 1.5.120–1

Excusing a drunken belch.

15 Though the chameleon love can feed on the air, I am one that am nourished by my victuals, and would fain have meat.

Speed in *The Two Gentlemen of Verona*, 2.1.172–4

The chameleon, once supposed to live on air, changes its color, just as the lover varies in mood.

Education (see also Books, Learning, Study)

1 Thou hast most traitorously corrupted the youth of the realm in erecting a grammar school.

Jack Cade in *Henry VI, Part 2*, 4.7.32–4

The peasants' accusations against Lord Saye.

2 Ignorance is the curse of God,

Knowledge the wing wherewith we fly to heaven.

Lord Saye in *Henry VI, Part 2*, 4.7.73–4

3 He must be taught, and trained, and bid go forth:
A barren-spirited fellow; one that feeds
On objects, arts, and imitations,
Which, out of use and staled by other men,
Begin his fashion.

Mark Antony in *Julius Caesar*, 4.1.35–9

On Lepidus, the third member of the triumvirate ruling Rome as one whose attention is taken by curiosities, tricks and copying fashions that are already obsolete.

4 Those that do teach young babes
Do it with gentle means and easy tasks.

Desdemona in *Othello*, 4.2.111–12

5 While I play the good husband at home, my son and his servant spend all at the university.

Vincentio in *The Taming of the Shrew*, 5.1.68–70

Mistakenly thinking his son Lucentio is a spendthrift; "good husband" = careful manager.

6 I prithee let me bring thee where crabs grow,
And I with my long nails will dig thee pig-nuts,
Show thee a jay's nest, and instruct thee how
To snare the nimble marmoset.

Caliban in *The Tempest*, 2.2.267–70

Offering to educate Stephano and Trinculo in what the island has to offer in the way of interest and food, crab-apples, tubers ("pig-nuts").

7   A devil, a born devil, on whose
    nature
    Nurture can never stick; on whom
      my pains
    Humanely taken, all, all quite lost.

Prospero in *The Tempest*, 4.1.188–90

Complaining that a European mode of moral education is wasted on the native of the island, Caliban.

Effeminacy

1   He was perfumèd like a milliner.

Hotspur in *Henry IV, Part 1*, 1.3.36

Describing an effeminate courtier who appeared thus inappropriately on a battlefield.

2   A woman impudent and mannish
      grown
    Is not more loathed than an effemi-
    nate man
    In time of action.

Patroclus in *Troilus and Cressida*, 3.3.217–19

Speaking of his own reluctance to fight; Thersites calls Patroclus Achilles's "masculine whore."

Eloquence (see also Speech, Speechmaking)

1   Very good orators, when they are
      out, they will spit.

Rosalind in *As You Like It*, 4.1.75–6

"Out" = lost for words.

2   More matter with less art.

Gertrude in *Hamlet*, 2.2.95

To Polonius, who claims to know the cause of Hamlet's madness but is being longwinded in coming to the point; "art" = rhetorical decoration.

3   When he speaks,
    The air, a chartered libertine, is still.

Archbishop of Canterbury in *Henry V*, 1.1.47–8

On King Henry's eloquence in stilling the air, which has license to move freely (as a "chartered libertine").

4   You have witchcraft in your lips,
    Kate. There is more eloquence in a
    sugar touch of them than in the
    tongues of the French council.

King Henry in *Henry V*, 5.2.275–7

The French council negotiates for peace while Henry makes love.

5   The gentleman is learned, and a
      most rare speaker.

King Henry in *Henry VIII*, 1.2.111

On Buckingham, arrested as a traitor.

6   With all the gracious utterance
      thou hast
    Speak to his gentle hearing kind
      commends.

King Richard in *Richard II*, 3.3.125–6

Flattering Henry Bolingbroke, who has control of the kingdom.

7   Doubt not, my lord, I'll play the
      orator
    As if the golden fee for which I
      plead
    Were for myself.

Buckingham in *Richard III*, 3.5.95–7

Promising to persuade the people to acclaim Richard as king.

8   All orators are dumb when beauty
    pleadeth.

The Rape of Lucrece, 268

Tarquin is finding excuses to pursue the rape
of the chaste Lucrece; her beauty, he claims,
silences objections.

Empire

1   Let Rome in Tiber melt, and the
    wide arch
    Of the ranged empire fall! Here is
    my space.

Antony in Antony and Cleopatra,
1.1.33–4

Putting love before empire; already signaling
what leads to Antony's downfall.

2   The greater cantle of the world is
    lost
    With very ignorance, we have
    kissed away
    Kingdoms and provinces.

Scarus in Antony and Cleopatra,
3.10.6–8

After Antony has lost the Battle of Actium
against Caesar; "cantle" = portion.

Encouragement

1   Wise men ne'er sit and wail their
    loss,
    But cheerly seek how to redress
    their harms.

Queen Margaret in Henry VI, Part 3,
5.4.1–2

Encouraging her allies after the death of their
leader, Warwick.

2   But wherefore do you droop? Why
    look you sad?

Be great in act as you have been in
    thought.

**The Bastard Falconbridge in King
John, 5.1.44–5**

Comforting the king.

3   What, courage, man! What though
    care killed a cat, thou hast mettle
    enough in thee to kill care.

Claudio in Much Ado About Nothing,
5.1.132–4

To Benedick, who is unusually serious and
full of care; "care will kill a cat" is proverbial.

Endings

1   All's well that ends well yet,
    Though time seem so adverse and
        means unfit.

Helena in All's Well That Ends Well,
5.1.25–6

2   Our wooing doth not end like an
        old play.
    Jack hath not Jill.

Berowne in Love's Labor's Lost,
5.2.874–5

The courtiers have to practice austerity for a
year before the ladies will have them.

3   O most lame and impotent conclu-
    sion!

Desdemona in Othello, 2.1.161

On Iago's anticlimactic winding-up of his
praise of women.

4   More are men's ends marked than
        their lives before.
    The setting sun, and music at the
        close,

As the last taste of sweets, is sweetest last,
Writ in remembrance more than
things long past.

John of Gaunt in *Richard II*, 2.1.11–14

Spoken as he anticipates his death; "marked"
= noticed.

Endurance

1   Thou didst drink
The stale of horses and the gilded
puddle
That beasts would cough at.

Octavius Caesar in *Antony and Cleopatra*, 1.4.61–3

Hardships that Antony suffered as a soldier;
"stale" is urine.

2   Bid that welcome
Which comes to punish us, and we
punish it
Seeming to bear it lightly.

Antony in *Antony and Cleopatra*, 4.14.136–8

The dying Antony asks his guard to carry him
to Cleopatra.

3   *Gloucester.* No further, sir, a man
may rot even here.
Edgar. What, in ill thoughts again?
Men must endure
Their going hence, even as their
coming hither;
Ripeness is all.

King Lear, 5.2.8–11

"Ripeness is all" may mean the gods deter-
mine when we die, or that we must await the
time of ripeness when we are ready for death.

4   He's truly valiant that can wisely
suffer

The worst that man can breathe,
and make his wrongs
His outsides, to wear them like his
raiment carelessly,
And ne'er prefer his injuries to his
heart,
To bring it into danger.

First Senator in *Timon of Athens*, 3.5.31–5

The idea is of enduring wrongs as merely
external ("outsides"), like clothes ("raiment"),
not taking them to heart (and seeking
revenge).

5   Jog on, jog on, the footpath way,
And merrily hent the stile-a.
A merry heart goes all the day,
Your sad tires in a mile-a.

Autolycus in *The Winter's Tale*, 4.3.123–6

Having tricked the shepherd's son, Autolycus
goes off with a song; "hent" = take hold of.

Enemies

1   Why, Harry, do I tell thee of my
foes,
Which art my nearest and dearest
enemy?

King Henry in *Henry IV, Part 1*, 3.2.122–3

To Prince Hal, reproaching him for failing to
support his father.

2   If the enemy is an ass and a fool
and a prating coxcomb, is it meet,
think you, that we should also, look
you, be an ass and a fool and a prating coxcomb, in your own conscience now?

Fluellen in *Henry V*, 4.1.77–80

Fluellen's quaint way of cautioning the army
against being noisy.

3   You have many enemies that
know not
Why they are so, but like to village
curs
Bark when their fellows do.

King Henry in *Henry VIII*, 2.4.159–61

To Cardinal Wolsey.

4   Keep this man safe;
Give him all kindness. I had rather
have
Such men my friends than enemies.

Mark Antony in *Julius Caesar*, 5.4.27–9

On the capture of Lucilius.

Envy

1   Men that make
Envy and crooked malice nourish-
ment
Dare bite the best.

**Archbishop Cranmer in *King Henry
VIII*, 5.2.78–80**

Defending himself against the malice of Gardiner, Bishop of Winchester.

Epitaphs (see also Burial, Graves, Mourning)

1   O, withered is the garland of the
war,
The soldier's pole is fallen!

**Cleopatra in *Antony and Cleopatra*,
4.15.64–5**

"Garland" suggests the wreath of victory, and
"pole" the standard-bearer, and also a phallus,
reminding us of the dead Antony's sexuality.

2   Now boast thee, death, in thy possession lies
A lass unparalleled.

**Charmian in *Antony and Cleopatra*,
5.2.315–16**

The "lass" is Cleopatra, Queen of Egypt.

3   She shall be buried by her Antony;
No grave upon the earth shall clip
in it
A pair so famous.

**Octavius Caesar in *Antony and
Cleopatra*, 5.2.358–60**

He is speaking about Cleopatra.

4   Alas, poor Yorick! I knew him,
Horatio, a fellow of infinite jest, of
most excellent fancy.

Hamlet in *Hamlet*, 5.1.184–5

The grave-digger has turned up the skull of
Yorick, the king's jester; on stage Hamlet usually holds the skull while he says this; "fancy"
= imagination.

5   Now cracks a noble heart. Good
night, sweet prince,
And flights of angels sing thee to
thy rest!

Horatio in *Hamlet*, 5.2.359–60

On Hamlet's death; "flights of angels sing" =
may flights of angels sing.

6   Adieu, and take thy praise with thee
to heaven!

Prince Hal in *Henry IV, Part 1*, 5.4.99

Bidding farewell to the dead Hotspur.

7   Thy ignominy sleep with thee in the
grave,

But not remembered in thy epitaph!

Prince Hal in *Henry IV, Part 1,*
5.4.100–1

On the rebel Hotspur, killed by Hal.

8 O mighty Caesar! Dost thou lie so
low?
Are all thy conquests, glories, tri-
umphs, spoils,
Shrunk to this little measure? Fare
thee well.

Mark Antony in *Julius Caesar,*
3.1.148–50

Seeing the dead body of Caesar.

9 Thou art the ruins of the noblest
man
That ever livèd in the tide of times.

Mark Antony in *Julius Caesar,* 3.1.256–7

Mourning Caesar; "tide of times" = course of
history.

10 Friends, Romans, countrymen, lend
me your ears.
I come to bury Caesar, not to praise
him.
The evil that men do lives after
them;
The good is oft interrèd with their
bones—
So let it be with Caesar.

Mark Antony in *Julius Caesar,* 3.2.73–7

11 The last of all the Romans, fare thee
well.
It is impossible that ever Rome
Should breed thy fellow.

Brutus in *Julius Caesar,* 5.3.99–101

On the death of Cassius.

12 His life was gentle, and the elements
So mixed in him that Nature might
stand up
And say to all the world, "This was
a man!"

Mark Antony in *Julius Caesar,* 5.5.73–5

On Brutus; human beings were thought to be
composed of the four elements, fire, air, earth
and water.

13 The ripest fruit first falls, and so
doth he.
His time is spent; our pilgrimage
must be.

King Richard in *Richard II,* 2.1.153–4

Referring to the death of his uncle John of
Gaunt; "pilgrimage" = journey through life.

14 Sweet peace conduct his sweet soul
to the bosom
Of good old Abraham!

Bolingbroke in *Richard II,* 4.1.103–4

On news of the death of his enemy Mowbray;
"Abraham's bosom" = heaven, from Luke
16:22.

15 Timon hath made his everlasting
mansion
Upon the beachèd verge of the salt
flood,
Who once a day with his embossèd
froth
The turbulent surge shall cover;
thither come,
And let my grave-stone be your
oracle.

Timon in *Timon of Athens,* 5.1.215–19

"Embossed" = foaming; "oracle" = source of
wisdom.

16   Repose you here in rest,
Secure from worldly chances and
   mishaps.
Here lurks no treason, here no envy
   swells,
Here grow no damnèd drugs, here
   are no storms,
No noise, but silence and eternal
   sleep.

Titus in *Titus Andronicus*, 1.1.151–5

Burying his sons, slain in war.

17 His part is played, and though it
   were too short,
He did it well.

Theseus in *The Two Noble Kinsmen*,
5.4.102–3

On the death of young Arcite, thrown acci-
dentally from his horse.

Eternity

1   When you sued staying,
Then was the time for words; no
   going then;
Eternity was in our lips and eyes.

Cleopatra in *Antony and Cleopatra*,
1.3.33–5

"Sued staying" = begged to stay; Antony is setting off for Rome.

2 But this eternal blazon must not be
To ears of flesh and blood.

Ghost in *Hamlet*, 1.5.21–2

Refusing to describe his afterlife to Hamlet;
"eternal blazon" = revelation of eternal things.

3 But thy eternal summer shall not
   fade,

Nor lose possession of that fair
   thou owest,
Nor shall Death brag thou wander-
   est in his shade,
When in eternal lines to time thou
   growest.
   So long as men can breathe or
      eyes can see,
   So long lives this, and this gives
      life to thee.

Sonnet 18, 9–14

On the poet's lines as conferring eternity on
the transient beauty of his friend.

4 Poor soul, the center of my sinful
   earth,
[Slave to] these rebel powers that
   thee array,
Why dost thou pine within and suf-
   fer dearth,
Painting thy outward walls so costly
   gay?
Why so large cost, having so short a
   lease,
Dost thou upon thy fading mansion
   spend?
Shall worms, inheritors of this
   excess,
Eat up thy charge? Is this thy
   body's end?
Then, soul, live thou upon thy ser-
   vant's loss,
And let that pine to aggravate thy
   store;
Buy terms divine in selling hours of
   dross,
Within be fed, without be rich no
   more:
   So shalt thou feed on Death, that
      feeds on men,
   And Death once dead, there's no
      more dying then.

Sonnet 146

A powerful sonnet that sets enriching the soul
("aggravate thy store" = increase your wealth)

against enriching the body, and the brevity of the "short lease" of this world's existence against eternal life ("terms divine"). "Slave to" in the second line is a guess; the first edition repeats "My sinful earth."

Evening

1   How still the evening is,
     As hushed on purpose to grace har-
     mony!

     Claudio in *Much Ado About Nothing*,
     2.3.38–9

Evil (see also Wrongdoing)

1   A very tainted fellow, and full of
     wickedness.

     **Countess of Rossillion in *All's Well
     That Ends Well*, 3.2.87**

     Describing Parolles.

2   What rein can hold licentious
     wickedness
     When down the hill he holds his
     fierce career?

     King Henry in *Henry V*, 3.3.22–3

     Suggesting a victorious army, like a horse in full gallop ("career"), cannot be restrained from rape and pillage.

3   Now let it work! Mischief, thou art
     afoot,
     Take thou what course thou wilt.

     Mark Antony in *Julius Caesar*, 3.2.260–1

     He has achieved his aim, as the people rush off to burn and destroy.

4   Those wicked creatures yet do look
     well-favored
     When others are more wicked; not
     being the worst
     Stands in some rank of praise.

     King Lear in *King Lear*, 2.4.255–7

     The "wicked creatures" are his two elder daughters; he hopes Goneril will treat him better than Regan.

5   Oftentimes, to win us to our
     harm,
     The instruments of darkness tell us
     truths,
     Win us with honest trifles, to
     betray 's
     In deepest consequence.

     Banquo in *Macbeth*, 1.3.123–6

     The Weird Sisters are the "instruments of darkness," or agents of evil; "in deepest consequence" = in matters of greatest importance.

6   Come to my woman's breasts,
     And take my milk for gall, you
     murdering ministers,
     Wherever in your sightless sub-
     stances
     You wait on nature's mischief!

     Lady Macbeth in *Macbeth*, 1.5.47–50

     Summoning spirits ("ministers") to make her ruthless; "sightless" = invisible.

7   Ere the bat hath flown
     His cloistered flight, ere to black
     Hecate's summons
     The shard-borne beetle with his
     drowsy hums
     Hath rung night's yawning peal,
     there shall be done
     A deed of dreadful note.

     Macbeth in *Macbeth*, 3.2.40–4

     Bats and dung-beetles ("shard-borne") were associated with darkness, and here with Hecate, goddess of witchcraft.

8   Come, seeling night,
Scarf up the tender eye of pitiful
    day,
And with thy bloody and invisible
    hand
Cancel and tear to pieces that great
    bond
Which keeps me pale.

Macbeth in *Macbeth*, 3.2.46–50

Night that "seels" or covers up (like stitching
the eyelids of a hawk in order to tame it) is
"bloody" because it provides concealment for
murder; the "bond" is the obligation of love to
all, as in Matthew 5:43–4, "Do good to them
which hate you."

9   By the pricking of my thumbs,
Something wicked this way comes.

Second Witch in *Macbeth*, 4.1.44–5

Announcing the arrival of Macbeth.

10   I have't. It is engendered. Hell and
    night
Must bring this monstrous birth to
    the world's light.

Iago in *Othello*, 1.3.403–4

Exactly what evil Iago has in mind is not yet
clear.

11   O mischief, thou art swift
To enter in the thoughts of desper-
    ate men!

Romeo in *Romeo and Juliet*, 5.1.35–6

On hearing news of Juliet's death, he thinks of
suicide, regarded as wicked because of he
biblical injunction against taking life, as at
Matthew 5:21.

Exaggeration

1   Well said—that was laid on with a
    trowel.

Celia in *As You Like It*, 1.2.105–6

Meaning something stated with exaggerated
force.

Excellence

1   So excellent a king that was to this
Hyperion to a satyr, so loving to my
    mother
That he might not beteem the
    winds of heaven
Visit her face too roughly.

Hamlet in *Hamlet*, 1.2.139–42

Remembering his father as a sun-god compared to Claudius, the satyr, half-goat, half-
man; "beteem" = permit.

Excuses (see also Apologies)

1   I would I could
Quit all offences with as clear
    excuse
As well as I am doubtless I can
    purge
Myself of many I am charged
    withal.

Prince Hal in *Henry IV, Part 1*,
3.2.18–21

Apologizing to the king, his father; "quit" = be
clear of.

2   Thou knowest in the state of inno-
cency Adam fell, and what should
poor Jack Falstaff do in the days of
villainy?

Falstaff in *Henry IV, Part 1*, 3.3.164–6

To Prince Hal, who has exposed Falstaff's lies
about what was stolen from his pocket.

3 Thou seest I have more flesh than
   another man, and therefore more
   frailty.
   Falstaff in *Henry IV, Part 1*, 3.3.166–8

4 Look what is done cannot be now
   amended:
   Men shall deal unadvisedly sometimes,
   Which after-hours gives leisure to
   repent.
   King Richard in *Richard III*, 4.4.291–3

   Trying to excuse his murder of Queen Elizabeth's relatives; proverbial (what's done cannot be undone).

Execution

1   Thou art a traitor.
   Off with his head!
   King Richard in *Richard III*, 3.4.75–6

   Accusing and sentencing Hastings at the same
   time.

Exercise

1   A turn or two I'll walk
   To still my beating mind.
   Prospero in *The Tempest*, 4.1.162–3

   He becomes angry as he recalls the "foul conspiracy" by Stephano, Trinculo and Caliban,
   who plot to kill him.

2   He hopes it is no other
   But for your health and your diges-
   tion sake,
   An after-dinner's breath.
   Patroclus in *Troilus and Cressida*,
   2.3.110–12

   The Greek leaders, calling on Achilles, meet
   with this rebuff.

Exile

1 Now, my co-mates and brothers in
   exile,
   Hath not old custom made this life
   more sweet
   Than that of painted pomp?
   Duke Senior in *As You Like It*, 2.1.1–3

   The banished Duke moralizing in the forest of
   Arden.

2   Despising,
   For you, the city, thus I turn my
   back;
   There is a world elsewhere.
   Coriolanus in *Coriolanus*, 3.3.133–5

   Coriolanus is banished by the people of
   Rome.

3 This must my comfort be:
   That sun that warms you here shall
   shine on me.
   Bolingbroke in *Richard II*, 1.3.144–5

   On being banished by King Richard.

4 Then thus I turn me from my
   country's light,
   To dwell in solemn shades of endless night.
   Mowbray in *Richard II*, 1.3.176–7

   Seeing his exile as a kind of death.

5   Now no way can I stray;
   Save back to England, all the
   world's my way.
   Mowbray in *Richard II*, 1.3.206–7

   "Stray" = take a wrong turn.

6   Then England's ground, farewell.
    Sweet soil, adieu,
    My mother and my nurse that bears
    me yet!
    Where e'er I wander, boast of this I
    can:
    Though banished, yet a true-born
    Englishman.

Bolingbroke in *Richard II*, 1.3.306–9

Spoken as he goes off to exile.

7   Eating the bitter bread of banish-
    ment.

Bolingbroke in *Richard II*, 3.1.21

Recalling his years in exile.

8   Ha, banishment? Be merciful, say
    "death";
    For exile hath more terror in his
    look,
    Much more than death. Do not say
    "banishment"!

Romeo in *Romeo and Juliet*, 3.3.12–14

On hearing from Friar Lawrence that he is
banished from Verona, and hence from Juliet.

9   There is no world without Verona
    walls
    But purgatory, torture, hell itself.
    Hence "banishèd" is banished from
    the world.

Romeo in *Romeo and Juliet*, 3.3.17–19

His "world" being Juliet.

Exorcism

1   I charge thee, Satan, housed within
    this man,
    To yield possession to my holy
    prayers.

**Doctor Pinch in *The Comedy of
Errors*, 4.4.54–5**

Treating the supposedly mad Antipholus of
Ephesus.

Expectation

1   Oft expectation fails, and most oft
    there
    Where most it promises; and oft it
    hits
    Where hope is coldest, and despair
    most fits.

**Helena in *All's Well That Ends Well*,
2.1.142–4**

"Hits" = is fulfilled.

Experience

1   The oldest hath borne most; we
    that are young
    Shall never see so much, nor live so
    long.

Edgar in *King Lear*, 5.3.326–7

These are the final lines of the play, referring
to the sufferings of the "oldest," King Lear and
Gloucester. The lines are assigned to Edgar in
the Folio text (1623), and to Albany in the
Quarto (1608).

2   A man loves the meat in his youth
    that he cannot endure in his age.

**Benedick in *Much Ado About Nothing*,
2.3.238–40**

Justifying his sudden love for Beatrice.

3   Men
    Can counsel and speak comfort to
    that grief

Which they themselves not feel;
but, tasting it,
Their counsel turns to passion.

Leonato in *Much Ado About Nothing,*
5.1.20–3

Proverbial; it is easy to advise others who are
suffering, but hard for those in pain to accept
counsel.

4   Experience is by industry achieved,
And perfected by the swift course of
time.

Antonio in *The Two Gentlemen of*
Verona, 1.3.22–3

He is thinking of sending his son off to court
to complete his education.

5   His years but young, but his experience old;
His head unmellowed, but his judgment ripe.

Valentine in *Two Gentlemen of*
Verona, 2.4.69–70

Praising his friend Proteus.

Extravagance

1   *Chief Justice.* Your means are very
slender, and your waste is great.
Falstaff. I would it were otherwise.
I would my means were greater,
and my waist slenderer.

Henry IV, Part 2, 1.2.140–3

"Waste" = expense; Falstaff lives beyond his
means.

2   To gild refinèd gold, to paint the
lily,
To throw a perfume on the violet,

To smooth the ice, or add another
hue
Unto the rainbow, or with taper-
light
To seek the beauteous eye of
heaven to garnish,
Is wasteful and ridiculous excess.

Salisbury in *King John,* 4.2.11–16

"The beauteous eye of heaven" is the sun.

3   No care, no stop; so senseless of
expense
That he will neither know how to
maintain it
Nor cease his flow of riot, takes no
account
How things go from him, nor
resumes no care
Of what is to continue.

Flavius in *Timon of Athens,* 2.2.1–5

On Timon's reckless spending on feasting his
friends.

Eyes

1   Eyes, that are the frail'st and softest
things,
Who shut their coward gates on
atomies.

Phebe in *As You Like It,* 3.5.12–13

"Atomies" are atoms or motes.

2   I think she means to tangle my eyes
too!

Rosalind in *As You Like It,* 3.5.44

Phebe begins to fall in love with Rosalind,
who is disguised as a boy.

3   The flame o'the taper
Bows toward her, and would
   under-peep her lids,
To see th'enclosèd lights, now
   canopied
Under these windows, white and
   azure laced
With blue of heaven's own tinct.

Jachimo in *Cymbeline*, 2.2.19–23

Looking at the eyes of the sleeping Imogen.

4   I see before me, man; nor here,
   nor here,
Nor what ensues, but have a fog in
   them
That I cannot look through.

Imogen in *Cymbeline*, 3.2.78–80

On Pisanio advising her to think about what
she is doing.

5   Our very eyes
Are sometimes, like our judgments,
   blind.

Imogen in *Cymbeline*, 4.2.301–2

Not knowing whether she is dreaming or
awake.

6   With his head over his shoulder
   turned,
He seemed to find his way without
   his eyes,
For out o' doors he went without
   their help,
And to the last bended their light
   on me.

Ophelia in *Hamlet*, 2.1.94–7

Hamlet has appeared like a ghost or madman
to Ophelia.

7   The eye sees not itself
But by reflection.

Brutus in *Julius Caesar*, 1.2.52–3

8   *Old Man.*   You cannot see your
   way.
   Gloucester. I have no way, and
      therefore want no eyes;
   I stumbled when I saw.

King Lear, 4.1.17–19

Gloucester has been blinded by Regan and
Cornwall, and turned out of doors; he "stumbled" in misjudging his son Edgar.

9   *Macbeth.*   This is a sorry
   sight.
   Lady Macbeth. A foolish thought,
      to say "A sorry sight."

Macbeth, 2.2.18–19

Referring to the blood on Macbeth's hands
after he has killed Duncan.

10   Show his eyes and grieve his heart.

**Witches (Weird Sisters) in *Macbeth*,
4.1.110**

What Macbeth sees is the line of Banquo's
descendants as kings.

11   *Claudio.* In mine eye she is the
   sweetest lady that ever I looked
   on.
   Benedick. I can see yet without
      spectacles, and I see no such mat-
      ter.

Much Ado About Nothing, 1.1.187–90

Claudio has fallen in love with Hero.

12   I have a good eye, uncle; I can see a
   church by daylight.

**Beatrice in *Much Ado About Nothing*,
2.1.82–3**

On her clear-sighted view of marriage.

13   He that is strucken blind cannot
   forget

The precious treasure of his eyesight lost.

Romeo in *Romeo and Juliet*, 1.1.232–3

14 The fringèd curtains of thine eye
advance,
And say what thou seest yond.

Prospero in *The Tempest*, 1.2.409–10

"Advance" = lift up, implying Miranda has
been demurely looking down; she now sees
young Ferdinand.

15   At the first sight
They have changed eyes.

Prospero in *The Tempest*, 1.2.441–2

Watching Ferdinand and Miranda fall in love
at first sight.

16 What a pair of spectacles is here!

Pandarus in *Troilus and Cressida*,
4.4.14

Looking at Troilus and Cressida embracing,
and quibbling on "spectacles" = eyeglasses.

Faces

1 He'll make a proper man. The best
thing in him
Is his complexion.

Phebe in *As You Like It*, 3.5.115–16

On Rosalind disguised as a youth.

2 *Hamlet.* What, looked he frowningly?
Horatio. A countenance more in
sorrow than in anger.

***Hamlet*, 1.2.231–2**

Describing the expression of the ghost of old
Hamlet.

3 Do thou amend thy face, and I'll
amend my life.

Falstaff in *Henry IV, Part 1*, 3.3.24

Bardolph's face is inflamed with drinking.

4 I never see thy face but I think
upon hell-fire.

Falstaff in *Henry IV, Part 1*, 3.3.31

To Bardolph, whose nose is red.

5 His face is all bubukles and whelks,
and knobs, and flames of fire.

Fluellen in *Henry V*, 3.6.102–3

On Bardolph; "bubukles and whelks" = car-
buncles and pimples.

6 Your face, my thane, is as a book,
where men
May read strange matters.

Lady Macbeth in *Macbeth*, 1.5.62–3

Speaking to her husband; thanes were Scottish
noblemen.

7 He does smile his face into more
lines than is in the new map with
the augmentation of the Indies.

Maria in *Twelfth Night*, 3.2.78–80

On Malvolio, referring to the new Mercator
map showing the East Indies in full.

8   I do believe thee;
I saw his heart in's face.

Polixenes in *The Winter's Tale*,
1.2.446–7

Leontes has shown in his expression his
hatred of Polixenes.

Fairies

1 Over hill, over dale,
  Thorough bush, thorough briar,
  Over park, over pale,
  Thorough flood, thorough fire;
  I do wander everywhere
  Swifter than the moon's sphere.

  Fairy in *A Midsummer Night's Dream*,
  2.1.2–7

  "Thorough" = through (as in the modern
  "thoroughfare"); a pale is a fence, which
  would not stop fairies.

2 I must go seek some dewdrops
  here,
  And hang a pearl in every cowslip's
  ear.

  Fairy in *A Midsummer Night's Dream*,
  2.1.14–15

  A charming image of fairies as responsible for
  scattering dew.

3 Either I mistake your shape and
  making quite,
  Or else you are that shrewd and
  knavish sprite
  Called Robin Goodfellow.

  Fairy in *A Midsummer Night's Dream*,
  2.1.32–4

  Robin is better known as Puck, the mischievous ("shrewd") servant of Oberon, King of
  the Fairies.

4 *Fairy.* Those that "Hobgoblin" call
  you, and "Sweet Puck,"
  You do their work, and they shall
  have good luck.
  Are not you he?
  Puck.   Thou speakest aright;
  I am that merry wanderer of the
  night.

  A Midsummer Night's Dream, 2.1.40–3

5 Peaseblossom, Cobweb, Moth, and
  Mustardseed!

  **Titania in *A Midsummer Night's
  Dream*, 3.1.162**

  The charming names of Titania's diminutive
  fairy servants; "Moth" sounded like "mote" or
  speck.

6 And we fairies, that do run
  By the triple Hecate's team
  From the presence of the sun,
  Following darkness like a dream,
  Now are frolic. Not a mouse
  Shall disturb this hallowed house.

  Puck in *A Midsummer Night's Dream*,
  5.1.383–8

  The goddess of the moon ruled under three
  names, Hecate in the underworld, Diana on
  earth, and Phoebe or Cynthia in the heavens;
  her chariot was supposed to be drawn across
  the sky by a team of dragons.

7 Hand in hand, with fairy grace,
  Will we sing, and bless this place.

  **Titania in *A Midsummer Night's
  Dream*, 5.1.399–400**

  Blessing the bridal chamber of Theseus and
  Hippolyta.

8 Ye elves of hills, brooks, standing
  lakes, and groves,
  And ye that on the sands with
  printless foot
  Do chase the ebbing Neptune, and
  do fly him
  When he comes back. . . .

  Prospero in *The Tempest*, 5.1.33–6

  The beginning of the speech in which Prospero renounces his magic powers.

9 Where the bee sucks, there suck I,
  In a cowslip's bell I lie;
  There I couch when owls do cry.
  On the bat's back I do fly

After summer merrily.
Merrily, merrily shall I live now,
Under the blossom that hangs on
the bough.

Ariel in *The Tempest*, 5.1.88–94

Celebrating his freedom, Ariel dwindles into a
delicate fairy.

Falconry

1   My falcon now is sharp and passing
empty,
And till she stoop she must not be
full-gorged,
For then she never looks upon her
lure.

**Petruchio in *The Taming of the Shrew*,
4.1.190–2**

Like a falcon, Katherine has been starved in
order to tame her; the "lure," baited with
pieces of meat, was used by falconers to recall
the bird.

Fall, see Seasons

Fame (see also Reputation)

1   By being seldom seen, I could not
stir
But like a comet I was wondered at.

**King Henry in *Henry IV, Part 1*,
3.2.46–7**

Describing his own youthful renown to his
son.

2   Let fame, that all hunt after in their
lives,
Live registered upon our brazen
tombs,
And then grace us in the disgrace of
death;

When spite of cormorant devouring Time,
Th'endeavor of this present breath
may buy
That honor which shall bate his
scythe's keen edge,
And make us heirs of all eternity.

**King of Navarre in *Love's Labor's Lost*,
1.1.1–7**

The King of Navarre's lofty idea of gaining
eternal fame through the "breath" or breathing-space of three years of hermit-like study.

3   From the four corners of the earth
they come
To kiss this shrine, this mortal-
breathing saint.

**Prince of Morocco in *The Merchant of
Venice*, 2.7.39–40**

In adoration of Portia.

4   Death makes no conquest of this
conqueror,
For now he lives in fame though
not in life.

Prince Edward in *Richard III*, 3.1.87–8

Commenting on Julius Caesar.

5   Much attribute he hath, and much
the reason
Why we ascribe it to him; yet all his
virtues,
Not virtuously of his own part
beheld,
Do in our eyes begin to lose their
gloss,
Yea, like fair fruit in an unwhole-
some dish,
Are like to rot untasted.

**Agamemnon in *Troilus and Cressida*,
2.3.116–21**

Commenting on the scornful behavior of
Achilles; "attribute" = distinction, fame.

Familiarity

1   *Aeneas.* We know each other well.
    Diomedes. We do, and long to
    know each other worse.

Troilus and Cressida, 4.1.31–2

A Trojan and a Greek meeting during a truce; they will know each other "worse" on the field of battle.

Farewells (see also Parting)

1   Fare thee well, dame. Whate'er
    becomes of me,
    This is a soldier's kiss.

Antony in *Antony and Cleopatra*, 4.4.29–30

Renewing his role as a soldier, and bidding farewell to Cleopatra as if she were a house-wife.

2   Hereafter, in a better world than
    this,
    I shall desire more love and knowl-
    edge of you.

Le Beau in *As You Like It*, 1.2.284–5

Addressing Orlando; "better world" may mean better conditions than under the Duke's tyranny, or the next world, heaven.

3   Adieu, adieu, adieu! Remember
    me.

Ghost in *Hamlet*, 1.5.91

His father's ghost gives a final command to Hamlet.

4   Come, my coach. Good night,
    ladies, good night, sweet ladies,
    good night, good night.

Ophelia in *Hamlet*, 4.5.71–3

In her madness Ophelia makes a grand exit; her words are quoted in a well-known passage in T.S. Eliot's *The Waste Land.*

5   Sweets to the sweet, farewell!

Gertrude in *Hamlet*, 5.1.243

Scattering flowers on the corpse of Ophelia.

6   Fare thee well, great heart!

Prince Hal in *Henry IV, Part 1*, 5.4.87

His farewell to the dead Hotspur.

7   What, old acquaintance! could not
    all this flesh
    Keep in a little life? Poor Jack,
    farewell!
    I could have better spared a better
    man.

Prince Hal in *Henry IV, Part 1*, 5.4.102–4

He finds Falstaff pretending to be dead.

8   Well, fare thee well. I have known
    thee these twenty-nine years, come
    peascod-time, but an honester and
    truer-hearted man—well, fare thee
    well.

Mistress Quickly in *Henry IV, Part 2*, 2.4.382–4

"Peascod-time" is in summer, when pea-pods are harvested.

9   Yet now farewell, and farewell life
    with thee!

Queen Margaret in *Henry VI, Part 2*, 3.2.356

Bidding farewell to her banished lover, the Duke of Suffolk.

10   Farewell? A long farewell to all my
    greatness.
    This is the state of man; today he
    puts forth
    The tender leaves of hopes, tomor-
    row blossoms,

And bears his blushing honors
thick upon him:
The third day comes a frost, a
killing frost,
And when he thinks, good easy
man, full surely
His greatness is a-ripening, nips his
root,
And then he falls as I do.

Cardinal Wolsey in *Henry VIII*,
3.2.351–8

Wolsey's famous soliloquy, bidding farewell
to his power.

11 Whether we shall meet again I
know not.
Therefore our everlasting farewell
take.

Brutus in *Julius Caesar*, 5.1.114–15

Saying farewell to Cassius.

12 Thus Kent, O princes, bids you all
adieu;
He'll shape his old course in a
country new.

Kent in *King Lear*, 1.1.186–7

13 Fair thoughts and happy hours
attend on you!

Lorenzo in *The Merchant of Venice*,
3.4.41

Saying farewell to Portia as she sets off for
Venice.

14   O, now for ever
Farewell the tranquil mind, farewell
content,
Farewell the plumèd troops and the
big wars
That makes ambition virtue! O,
farewell!

Othello in *Othello*, 3.3.347–50

Jealousy in love destroys Othello as a soldier.

15 Once more, adieu. The rest let sorrow say.

King Richard in *Richard II*, 5.1.102

Bidding farewell to his Queen as they are separated.

16 Sleep dwell upon thine eyes, peace
in thy breast.

Romeo in *Romeo and Juliet*, 2.2.186

To Juliet as she goes in from her window.

17 But that a joy past joy calls out on
me,
It were a grief, so brief to part with
thee.

Romeo in *Romeo and Juliet*, 3.3.173–4

On leaving Friar Lawrence to go to Juliet.

18   It is so very late that we
May call it early by and by. Good
night.

Capulet in *Romeo and Juliet*, 3.4.34–5

Dismissing Paris, who has been waiting in
hopes of seeing Juliet.

19   Eyes, look your last.
Arms, take your last embrace, and
lips, O you
The doors of breath, seal with a
righteous kiss
A dateless bargain to engrossing
death.

Romeo in *Romeo and Juliet*, 5.3.112–15

Kissing Juliet before drinking the apothecary's
poison; "engrossing" = 1. taking all; 2. preparing the contract or "bargain."

20 The gentleness of all the gods go
with thee!

Antonio in *Twelfth Night*, 2.1.44

Bidding farewell to his friend Sebastian.

21 Farewell, thou art too dear for my
    possessing,
And like enough thou know'st thy
    estimate;
The charter of thy worth gives thee
    releasing;
My bonds in thee are all determi-
    nate.

Sonnet 87, 1–4

On the superior wealth and status of the loved
one, who knows his worth ("estimate"), and
through the privilege ("charter") of his standing is released from the obligations ("bonds")
of love, which have expired; the imagery is
drawn from legal terms.

Farming

1 All her husbandry doth lie on
    heaps,
Corrupting in its own fertility.

Burgundy in *Henry V*, 5.2.39–40

"Husbandry" = cultivation; French farms are
overgrown with noxious weeds because of
war.

2 The even mead, that erst brought
    sweetly forth
The freckled cowslip, burnet, and
    green clover,
Wanting the scythe, all uncor-
    rected, rank,
Conceives by idleness, and nothing
    teems
But hateful docks, rough thistles,
    kecksies, burrs,
Losing both beauty and utility.

Burgundy in *Henry V*, 5.2.48–53

Describing France as overgrown with weeds
instead of flowers, as a result of war.

Fashion (see also Clothing)

1 Thou art not for the fashion of
    these times,
When none will sweat but for pro-
    motion.

Orlando in *As You Like It*, 2.3.59–62

2 The glass of fashion and the mold
    of form,
Th' observed of all observers.

Ophelia in *Hamlet*, 3.1.153–4

Seeing Hamlet as a mirror ("glass") by which
fashion is measured, and a pattern ("mold") of
the perfect courtier.

3   He was indeed the glass
Wherein the noble youth did dress
    themselves.

Lady Percy in *Henry IV, Part 2*, 2.3.21–2

"Glass" = mirror; everyone imitated the fashion of Hotspur.

4 He was the mark and glass, copy
    and book,
That fashioned others.

Lady Percy in *Henry IV, Part 2*, 2.3.31–2

On Hotspur as the ideal others sought to imitate; "mark" = target, aim; "glass" = mirror.

5   New customs,
Though they be never so ridiculous
(Nay, let 'em be unmanly) yet are
    followed.

Lord Sands in *Henry VIII*, 1.3.2–4

On new fashions imported from France.

6   Thou art a lady;
If only to go warm were gorgeous,

Why, nature needs not what thou
  gorgeous wear'st,
Which scarcely keeps thee warm.

King Lear in *King Lear*, 2.4.267–70

Speaking to his daughter Regan.

7   A man in all the world's new fash-
      ion planted,
    That hath a mint of phrases in his
      brain.
    One who the music of his own vain
      tongue
    Doth ravish like enchanting har-
      mony.

**King of Navarre in *Love's Labor's Lost*,
1.1.164–7**

Commenting on Armado and his extravagant
language.

8   I see that the fashion wears out
    more apparel than the man.

**Conrade in *Much Ado About Nothing*,
3.3.139–40**

Changes in fashion often cause people to dis-
card clothing before it is worn out.

9   Report of fashions in proud Italy,
    Whose manners still our tardy,
      apish nation
    Limps after in base imitation.

York in *Richard II*, 22.21–3

Accusing the English of being belatedly imita-
tive ("apish") of Italian fashions.

10   Old fashions please me best.

**Bianca in *The Taming of the Shrew*,
3.1.80**

11   One touch of nature makes the
      whole world kin,
    That all, with one consent, praise
      new-born gauds,

Though they are made and molded
  of things past,
And give to dust that is a little gilt
More laud than gilt o'erdusted;
The present eye praises the present
  object.

**Ulysses in *Troilus and Cressida*,
3.3.175–80**

Appealing to the way human nature makes
everyone eager to follow new fashions; he is
trying to persuade Achilles to return to the
battlefield; "gauds" = trifles; "laud" = praise.

Fate (see also Necessity)

1   My fate cries out,
    And makes each petty artery in this
      body
    As hardy as the Nemean lion's
      nerve.

Hamlet in *Hamlet*, 1.4.81–3

Desperately trying, against his companions'
persuasion, to follow his father's ghost;
"Nemean lion" = slain by Hercules as one of
his twelve labors; "nerve" = sinew.

2   Our wills and fates do so contrary
      run
    That our devices still are over-
      thrown.

Player King in *Hamlet*, 3.2.211–2

3   O God, that one might read the
      book of fate,
    And see the revolution of the times
    Make mountains level, and the con-
      tinent,
    Weary of solid firmness, melt itself
    Into the sea.

**King Henry in *Henry IV, Part 2*,
3.1.45–9**

Gloomily expecting one calamity after
another.

4   What fates impose, that men must
     needs abide;
    It boots not to resist both wind and
     tide.

King Edward in *Henry VI, Part 3*,
4.3.58–9

He has been taken prisoner by Warwick and
Somerset; "boots" = helps.

5   Men at some time are masters of
     their fates.

Cassius in *Julius Caesar*, 1.2.139

Urging Brutus to take action against Caesar.

6   What can be avoided
    Whose end is purposed by the
     mighty gods?

Caesar in *Julius Caesar*, 2.2.26–7

He refuses to be swayed by his wife's fears of
portents and predictions.

7   Who can control his fate?

Othello in *Othello*, 5.2.265

Accepting that he must die, though he has
made his own "fate" in murdering Desdemona.

Fatness

1   Falstaff sweats to death,
  And lards the lean earth as he walks
     along.

Prince Hal in *Henry IV, Part 1*,
2.2.108–9

"Lards" = covers in grease.

2   How now, my sweet creature of
  bombast, how long is't ago, Jack,
  since thou sawest thine own knee?

Prince Hal in *Henry IV, Part 1*,
2.4.326–8

To Falstaff; "bombast" = cotton padding.

3   A goodly portly man, i'faith, and a
  corpulent, of a cheerful look, a
  pleasing eye, and a most noble carriage.

Falstaff in *Henry IV, Part 1*, 2.4.422–4

Under cover of playing King Henry IV, he
describes himself in flattering terms; "portly" =
stately; "carriage" = bearing.

4   That trunk of humors, that bolting-
  hutch of beastliness, that swollen
  parcel of dropsies, that huge bombard of sack, that stuffed cloak-bag
  of guts, that roasted Manningtree
  ox with the pudding in his belly.

Prince Hal in *Henry IV, Part 1*,
2.4.449–53

Describing Falstaff; "bolting-hutch" = flour
bin; "bombard" = leather wine vessel; "Manningtree" = a town in Essex.

5   There's no room for faith, truth,
  nor honesty in this bosom of thine;
  it is all filled up with guts and
  midriff.

Prince Hal in *Henry IV, Part 1*,
3.3.153–5

Another comment on Falstaff.

Faults

1   A man who is the abstract of all
    faults
  That all men follow.

**Octavius Caesar in *Antony and
Cleopatra*,** 1.4.9–10

Commenting on Antony.

2 His taints and honors
Waged equal with him.

Maecenas in *Antony and Cleopatra*,
5.1.30–1

Another, more fair, assessment of Antony;
"taints" = faults.

3 A rarer spirit never
Did steer humanity; but you gods
will give us
Some faults to make us men.

Agrippa in *Antony and Cleopatra*,
5.1.31–3

A kinder comment on Antony, after his death.

4 *Jaques.* The worst fault you have is
to be in love.
Orlando. 'Tis a fault I will not
change for your best virtue.

As You Like It, 3.2.282–4

5 Fie, 'tis a fault to heaven,
A fault against the dead, a fault to
nature,
To reason most absurd, whose
common theme
Is death of fathers, and who still
hath cried,
From the first corse till he that died
today,
"This must be so."

Claudius in *Hamlet*, 1.2.101–6

Trying to persuade Hamlet against persisting
in mourning for his father's death; "first corse"
= first corpse, Abel, murdered by his brother
Cain (Genesis 4).

6 The fault, dear Brutus, is not in our
stars,
But in ourselves, that we are underlings.

Cassius in *Julius Caesar*, 1.2.140–1

7 *Brutus.* I do not like your
faults.
Cassius. A friendly eye could never
see such faults

Julius Caesar, 4.3.89–90

8 They say best men are molded out
of faults,
And for the most, become much
more the better
For being a little bad.

Mariana in *Measure for Measure*,
5.1.439–41

Speaking about Angelo, now her husband.

Fear

1 How now, Horatio? You tremble
and look pale.
Is not this something more than
fantasy?

Barnardo in *Hamlet*, 1.1.53–4

The skeptical Horatio has seen the ghost; "fantasy" = imagination.

2 What, frighted with false fire?

Hamlet in *Hamlet*, 3.2.266

He thinks Claudius has taken fright at the play
they have been watching; "false fire" is the
flash produced by a blank shot or cartridge.

3 He that but fears the thing he
would not know
Hath by instinct knowledge from
others' eyes
That what he feared is chanced.

Northumberland in *Henry IV, Part 2*,
1.1.85–7

He is anticipating the news that his son, Hotspur, is dead; "is chanced" = has happened.

4   Of all base passions, fear is the most
     accursed.

Joan la Pucelle in *Henry VI, Part 1*,
5.2.18

5   True nobility is exempt from fear:
     More can I bear than you can exe-
     cute.

Suffolk in *Henry VI, Part 2*, 4.1.129–30

Spoken as he is about to be beheaded.

6   Suspicion always haunts the guilty
     mind;
     The thief doth fear each bush an
     officer.

**Richard of Gloucester in *Henry VI,
Part 3*, 5.6.11–12**

To Henry VI, who rightly fears Richard intends
to kill him.

7   Would he were fatter! But I fear
     him not.
     Yet if my name were liable to fear,
     I do not know the man I should
     avoid
     So soon as that spare Cassius.

Caesar in *Julius Caesar*, 1.2.198–201

Caesar's name has become a symbol of domi-
nation, and seems to exist separately from the
man.

8   Caesar should be a beast without a
     heart
     If he should stay at home today for
     fear.

Caesar in *Julius Caesar*, 2.2.42–3

In spite of bad omens, he is determined to go
to the Capitol.

9   Who dares not stir by day must
     walk by night.

**The Bastard Falconbridge in *King
John*, 1.1.172**

Suggesting that his unknown father begot him
obscurely; he claims to be the bastard son of
King Richard I, Richard Lionheart.

10   I find the people strangely fan-
     tasied,
     Possessed with rumors, full of idle
     dreams,
     Not knowing what they fear, but
     full of fear.

**The Bastard Falconbridge in *King
John*, 4.2.144–6**

Reporting that people are full of strange fancies and pre-occupied with fearful rumors.

11   *Albany*. Well, you may fear too far.
     Goneril. Safer than trust too far.

***King Lear*, 1.4.328**

12   Present fears
     Are less than horrible imaginings.

Macbeth in *Macbeth*, 1.3.137–8

"Present" as contrasted with what may happen in the future.

13   When our actions do not,
     Our fears do make us traitors.

Lady Macduff in *Macbeth*, 4.2.3–4

She refers to her husband, who has fled to
England.

14   I have almost forgot the taste of
     fears.
     The time has been, my senses
     would have cooled
     To hear a night-shriek, and my fell
     of hair
     Would at a dismal treatise rouse
     and stir

As life were in't. I have supped full
  with horrors;
Direness, familiar to my slaughter-
  ous thoughts,
Cannot once start me.

Macbeth in *Macbeth*, 5.5.9–15

Macbeth has destroyed his capacity to feel
emotion; "my fell" = my skin covered in hair,
or all my hair; "dismal treatise" = horror story.

15 I have a faint cold fear thrills
      through my veins,
    That almost freezes up the heat of
      life.

Juliet in *Romeo and Juliet*, 4.3.15–16

She is afraid to drink the opiate Friar
Lawrence has given her.

16 Blind fear that seeing reason leads
    finds safer footing than blind rea-
    son stumbling without fear. To
    fear the worst oft cures the worst.

**Cressida in *Troilus and Cressida*,
3.2.71–3**

The last phrase is proverbial. She is expressing anxiety about accepting Troilus as her
lover.

Feasts

1   This is not yet an Alexandrian feast.

**Pompey in *Antony and Cleopatra*,
2.7.96**

A Roman feast proves less of an orgy than one
in Alexandria, Egypt.

2   Come,
    Let's have one other gaudy night.

**Antony in *Antony and Cleopatra*,
3.13.181–2**

Calling, in defeat, for one more night of feasting (certain college feasts in Oxford and Cambridge are still called a "gaudy").

3   Small cheer and great welcome
      makes a merry feast.

**Balthazar in *The Comedy of Errors*,
3.1.26**

Proverbial.

4   Let me see, what am I to buy for
    our sheep-shearing feast? Three
    pound of sugar, five pound of cur-
    rants, rice—what will this sister of
    mine do with rice? But my father
    hath made her mistress of the feast,
    and she lays it on.

Clown in *The Winter's Tale*, 4.3.36–40

"Lays it on" = does it thoroughly; the midsummer sheep-shearing feast celebrated country-
wide with festivity.

Fellowship (see also Society)

1   Watch tonight, pray tomorrow.
    Gallants, lads, boys, hearts of gold,
    all the titles of good fellowship
    come to you!

Falstaff in *Henry IV, Part 1*, 2.4.277–9

Happy in the prospect of a night's festivity
("watch" = stay awake).

2   We few, we happy few, we band of
      brothers.
    For he today that sheds his blood
      with me
    Shall be my brother.

King Henry in *Henry V*, 4.3.60–2

Encouraging his soldiers before the battle of
Agincourt.

3 Misery acquaints a man with strange bedfellows.

Trinculo in _The Tempest_, 2.2.39–40

Creeping under Caliban's cloak to shelter from a storm.

4 Fellowship in woe doth woe assuage.

The Rape of Lucrece, 790

Lucrece broods alone after being raped by Tarquin.

Festivals

1 Some say that ever 'gainst that season comes
Wherein our Savior's birth is celebrated,
This bird of dawning singeth all night long,
And then they say no spirit dare stir abroad,
The nights are wholesome, then no planets strike,
No fairy takes, nor witch hath power to charm,
So hallowed, and so gracious, is that time.

Marcellus in _Hamlet_, 1.1.158–64

The bird of dawning is the cock; planets were thought to exert malign influence, and fairies to bewitch people.

2 Tomorrow is Saint Valentine's Day,
All in the morning betime,
And I a maid at your window,
To be your Valentine.

Ophelia in _Hamlet_, 4.5.48–51

Singing in her madness after her father's death.

3 This day is called the Feast of Crispian.
He that outlives this day and comes safe home
Will stand a-tiptoe when this day is named
And rouse him at the name of Crispian.

King Henry in _Henry V_, 4.3.40–3

October 25th was the feast of St. Crispian, a legendary Roman martyr, and patron saint of shoemakers; "safe home" = to England.

4 He that shall see this day and live old age
Will yearly on the vigil feast his neighbors
And say, "Tomorrow is Saint Crispian."

King Henry in _Henry V_, 4.3.44–6

October 25th, the day the battle of Agincourt was fought.

5 No doubt they rose up early to observe
The rite of May.

Theseus in _A Midsummer Night's Dream_, 4.1.132–3

May Day festivities in England involved going to woods to gather flowers and bring them, as symbolic of new life, into towns and villages (the play is nominally set in Greece).

Fighting (see also Soldiers, War)

1 To the latter end of a fray and the beginning of a feast
Fits a dull fighter and a keen guest.

Falstaff in _Henry IV, Part 1_, 4.2.79–80

He prefers feasting to fighting; "fray" = battle.

2   Lay on, Macduff,
And damned be him that first cries,
   "Hold, enough!"

Macbeth in *Macbeth*, 5.8.33–4

Macbeth's last words, as Macduff kills him in
their fight.

3   You dare easier be friends with me
than fight with mine enemy.

Beatrice in *Much Ado About Nothing*,
4.1.298–9

To Benedick, who hesitates at the idea of
killing his friend Claudio.

4   Keep up your bright swords, for the
dew will rust them.

Othello in *Othello*, 1.2.59

Preventing by his calm authority a fight
between his supporters and those of Brabantio, who thinks Othello has stolen away his
daughter Desdemona.

5   Were it my cue to fight, I should
have known it
Without a prompter.

Othello in *Othello*, 1.2.83–4

Speaking as a soldier.

Fire

1   A little fire is quickly trodden out,
Which, being suffered, rivers cannot quench.

Clarence in *Henry VI, Part 3*, 4.8.7–8

"Being suffered" = being unchecked, allowed
to grow.

2   Those that with haste will make a
mighty fire
Begin it with weak straws.

Cassius in *Julius Caesar*, 1.3.107–8

Meaning that a huge conflagration can
quickly be started with a few worthless straws
(and so may a revolution be begun from
nothing).

3   Tut, man, one fire burns out
another's burning,
One pain is lessened by another's
anguish.

Benvolio in *Romeo and Juliet*, 1.2.45–6

On Romeo's unrequited love for Rosaline;
varying the proverb, "one fire drives out
another."

4   Where two raging fires meet
together,
They do consume the thing that
feeds their fury.
Though little fire grows great with
little wind,
Yet extreme gusts will blow out fire
and all.

Petruchio in *The Taming of the Shrew*,
2.1.132–5

This is how he sees his relationship with
Katherine, the shrew.

5   The fire i'the flint
Shows not till it be struck.

Poet in *Timon of Athens*, 1.1.22–3

Fish

1   *Third Fisherman.* I marvel how the
fishes live in the sea.
First Fisherman. Why, as men do a-
land: the great ones eat up the little ones.

Pericles, 2.1.26–9

2 A fish, he smells like a fish; a very
   ancient and fish-like smell.

Trinculo in *The Tempest*, 2.2.25–6

Finding a strange creature (Caliban) on Prospero's island.

Fishing

1 Give me mine angle, we'll to the
   river; there,
   My music playing far off, I will
   betray
   Tawny-finned fishes; my bended
   hook shall pierce
   Their slimy jaws; and as I draw
   them up,
   I'll think them every one an
   Antony,
   And say, "Ah, ha! y'are caught."

**Cleopatra in *Antony and Cleopatra*,
2.5.10–15**

Imagining getting her hooks into Antony, as
we now say; an "angle" is a fishing rod and
line.

2 The pleasant'st angling is to see the
   fish
   Cut with her golden oars the silver
   stream,
   And greedily devour the treacherous bait.

**Ursula in *Much Ado About Nothing*,
3.1.26–8**

"Oars" = fins.

3 Here's a fish hangs in the net like a
   poor man's right in the law; 'twill
   hardly come out.

**Second Fisherman in *Pericles*,
2.1.116–18**

Fitness

1 　　　Now bid me run,
   And I will strive with things impos-
   sible,
   Yea, get the better of them.

Ligarius in *Julius Caesar*, 2.1.324–6

Though sick, Ligarius joins the conspirators
against Caesar.

Flattery

1 　　　Why should the poor be
   flattered?
   No, let the candied tongue lick
   absurd pomp,
   And crook the pregnant hinges of
   the knee
   Where thrift may follow fawning.

Hamlet in *Hamlet*, 3.2 59–60

Praising Horatio: "pregnant" = pliant, readily
bending; "thrift" = profit.

2 Why, what a candy deal of courtesy
   This fawning greyhound then did
   proffer me!

Hotspur in *Henry IV, Part 1*, 1.3.251–2

Henry IV once needed the help of Hotspur to
regain his rights; "candy deal" = sugary quantity.

3 There is flattery in friendship.

Constable in *Henry V*, 3.7.114–15

4 　　　When I tell him he hates flatterers,
   He says he does, being then most
   flattered.

Decius in *Julius Caesar*, 2.1.207–8

Speaking of Julius Caesar.

5 They told me I was everything. 'Tis a lie, I am not ague-proof.

King Lear in *King Lear*, 4.6.104–5

"They" are flattering courtiers; "ague-proof" = immune to fever.

6 He does me double wrong
That wounds me with the flatteries of his tongue.

King Richard in *Richard II*, 3.2.215–6

"Double wrong" in deceiving and in raising false hopes.

7 He that loves to be flattered is worthy o'the flatterer.

Apemantus in *Timon of Athens*, 1.1.226–7

8 O that men's ears should be
To counsel deaf, but not to flattery!

Apemantus in *Timon of Athens*, 1.2.249–50

On Timon, who refuses to listen to his good advice.

9 Most smiling, smooth, detested parasites,
Courteous destroyers, affable wolves, meek bears,
You fools of fortune, trencher-friends, time's flies.

Timon in *Timon of Athens*, 3.6.94–6

Cursing his former friends; "fools of fortune" = playthings at the mercy of fortune; "flies" come in summer and disappear in winter.

Flowers

1 A violet in the youth of primy nature,

Forward, not permanent, sweet, not lasting.

Laertes in *Hamlet*, 1.3.7–8

Describing Hamlet's love as expressed to Ophelia; "primy" = in its prime, in the spring.

2 There's rosemary, that's for remembrance; pray you, love, remember. And there is pansies, that's for thoughts.

Ophelia in *Hamlet*, 4.5.175–7

In her madness, handing out flowers; these meanings are traditional.

3 O that this blossom could be kept from cankers!

Poins in *Henry IV, Part 2*, 2.2.94–5

Referring to Falstaff's boy; "cankers" = corruption, from canker-worms that eat into blossoms.

4 I pluck this pale and maiden blossom here.

Vernon in *Henry VI, Part 1*, 2.4.47

Plucking a white rose, the badge of the faction of York.

5 Yet marked I where the bolt of Cupid fell:
It fell upon a little western flower,
Before, milk-white; now purple with love's wound:
And maidens call it "love-in-idleness."

Oberon in *A Midsummer Night's Dream*, 2.1.165–8

Describing how the arrow ("bolt") of Cupid falls on the pansy, and stains it the color of blood.

6   I know a bank where the wild
     thyme blows,
     Where oxlips and the nodding vio-
     let grows,
     Quite overcanopied with luscious
     woodbine,
     With sweet musk-roses, and with
     eglantine:
     There sleeps Titania sometime of
     the night,
     Lulled in these flowers with dances
     and delight.

**Oberon in *A Midsummer Night's
Dream*, 2.1.249–54**

Describing the nighttime bower of the Queen
of the Fairies; the flowers include scented wild
roses and sweet-briar ("eglantine"), and all
grow wild in the English countryside.

7   Who are the violets now
     That strew the green lap of the new-
     come spring?

Duchess of York in *Richard II*, 5.2.46–7

Asking her son Aumerle to tell her who is in
favor with the new king, Henry IV.

8   Away before me to sweet beds of
     flowers.
     Love-thoughts lie rich when
     canopied with bowers.

Orsino in *Twelfth Night*, 1.1.39–40

Lovesick for Olivia, who has no interest in
him.

9   There's rosemary and rue. These
     keep
     Seeming and savor all the winter
     long.
     Grace and remembrance be to you.

Perdita in *The Winter's Tale*, 4.4.74–6

Rosemary was an emblem of remembrance,
and rue, or "herb grace," of repentance; she
gives them to Polixenes and Camillo.

10   The year growing ancient,
      Not yet on summer's death, nor on
      the birth
      Of trembling winter, the fairest
      flowers o'the season
      Are our carnations and streaked
      gillyvors.

Perdita in *The Winter's Tale*, 4.4.79–82

"Gillyvors" are a kind of carnation or pink.

11   Here's flowers for you:
      Hot lavender, mints, savory, marjo-
      ram,
      The marigold, that goes to bed
      wi'the sun,
      And with him rises, weeping.

Perdita in *The Winter's Tale*, 4.4.103–6

Giving "hot" flowers to Polixenes and Camillo
as appropriate to older men, perhaps as
restorative in some way.

12   Daffodils,
      That come before the swallow
      dares, and take
      The winds of March with beauty.

Perdita in *The Winter's Tale*, 4.4.118–20

Perdita wishes for flowers to express her love
for Florizel.

13   Pale primroses,
      That die unmarried ere they can
      behold
      Bright Phoebus in his strength.

Perdita in *The Winter's Tale*, 4.4.122–4

Spring flowers that do not live to see the sun
("Phoebus") at full strength in the summer.

14   The summer's flower is to the sum-
      mer sweet
      Though to itself it only live and die,
      But if that flower with base infec-
      tion meet,

The basest weed outbraves his dignity:
For sweetest things turn sourest
   by their deeds;
Lilies that fester smell far worse
   than weeds.

Sonnet 94, 9–14

The last line has become proverbial; "it only live and die" = it lives and dies alone; "outbraves his dignity" = exceeds its worth (though "his" points to the real subject, the unfaithful lover).

Folly

1   The triple pillar of the world transformed
Into a strumpet's fool.

Philo in *Antony and Cleopatra*,
1.1.12–13

Antony, one of the three rulers of the Roman Empire, unflatteringly described before we meet him and Cleopatra.

2   I see still
A diminution in our captain's brain
Restores his heart.

Enobarbus in *Antony and Cleopatra*,
3.13.196–8

Pointing to Antony's folly thinking he can still beat Octavius; "heart" = courage.

3   In everything the purpose must
weigh with the folly.

Prince Hal in *Henry IV, Part 2*,
2.2.175–6

Meaning that folly may be justified if the purpose is good.

4   I will keep where there is wit stirring, and leave the faction of fools.

Thersites in *Troilus and Cressida*,
2.1.118–19

Parting from Achilles and Ajax.

5   Alas, 'tis true, I have gone here and
   there,
And made myself a motley to the
   view,
Gored mine own thoughts, sold
   cheap what is most dear,
Made old affections of offenses
   new.

Sonnet 110, 1–4

The speaker has made a fool of himself (a motley coat was the dress of the professional fool), wounded ("gored") his own self-esteem, and offended against old friendships by his choice of new ones.

Food (see also Cooking, Eating)

1   Now I feed myself
With most delicious poison.

Cleopatra in *Antony and Cleopatra*,
1.5.26–7

Imagining the absent Antony.

2   Epicurean cooks
Sharpen with cloyless sauce his
   appetite.

Pompey in *Antony and Cleopatra*,
2.1.24–5

Imagining Antony's luxurious idling in Egypt.

3   I found you as a morsel, cold upon
Dead Caesar's trencher.

Antony in *Antony and Cleopatra*,
3.13.116–17

Referring to Cleopatra's past affair with Julius Caesar.

4 Truly, thou art damned, like an ill-roasted egg, all on one side.

Touchstone in *As You Like It*, 3.2.37–8

Part of a sophistical argument that Corin is damned for not being at court.

5 Sweetest nut hath sourest rind.

Touchstone in *As You Like It*, 3.2.155–7

Mocking Rosalind as sweet and sour.

6 Thrift, thrift, Horatio, the funeral baked meats
Did coldly furnish forth the marriage tables.

Hamlet in *Hamlet*, 1.2.180–1

In reply to Horatio's acknowledgment that Hamlet's mother's marriage took place very soon after her first husband's death; "coldly" = when cold.

7 What's a joint of mutton or two in a whole Lent?

Mistress Quickly in *Henry IV, Part 2*, 2.4.346–7

No meat was supposed to be eaten in the whole six weeks of Lent before Easter.

8 This making of Christians will raise the price of hogs. If we grow all to be pork-eaters, we shall not shortly have a rasher on the coals for money.

Launcelot Gobbo in *The Merchant of Venice*, 3.5.23–6

Referring to the conversion of Jessica, Shylock's daughter, to Christianity.

9 I will make an end of my dinner; there's pippins and cheese to come.

Evans in *The Merry Wives of Windsor*, 1.2.11–13

Apples and cheese round off the meal.

10 A surfeit of the sweetest things
The deepest loathing to the stomach brings.

Lysander in *A Midsummer Night's Dream*, 2.2.137–8

Finding he now hates his earlier love, Hermia.

11 Feed him with apricots and dewberries,
With purple grapes, green figs, and mulberries.

Titania in *A Midsummer Night's Dream*, 3.1.166–7

Infatuated with Bottom, she tells her fairies to indulge him.

12 Good Master Mustardseed, I know your patience well. That same cowardly, giant-like ox-beef hath devoured many a gentleman of your house. I promise you, your kindred hath made my eyes water ere now.

Bottom in *A Midsummer Night's Dream*, 3.1.191–5

Addressing one of Titania's fairies.

13 Come, thou shalt go home, and we'll have flesh for holidays, fish for fasting-days, and moreover puddings and flap-jacks, and thou shalt be welcome.

First Fisherman in *Pericles*, 2.1.80–3

The fisherman takes pity on the shipwrecked Pericles; "flap-jacks" = pancakes.

14 What say you to a piece of beef and mustard?

Grumio in *The Taming of the Shrew*, 4.3.23

Teasing Katherine, who is being denied anything to eat.

15 Though the chameleon love can feed on the air, I am one that am nourished by my victuals, and would fain have meat.

Speed in *Two Gentlemen of Verona*, 2.1.172–4

"Fain" = gladly.

Foolery

1   Being fooled, by foolery thrive;
There's place and means for every man alive.

Parolles in *All's Well That Ends Well*, 4.3.339

Shown up as a fool, he hopes to live by fooling others.

2 There was more foolery yet, if I could remember it.

Casca in *Julius Caesar*, 1.2.287

Reporting to Cassius what happened when Caesar addressed the people of Rome.

3 Foolery, sir, does walk about the orb like the sun, it shines everywhere.

Feste in *Twelfth Night*, 3.1.38–9

To Cesario (Viola in disguise), varying the proverb, "the sun shines on all alike"; "foolery" is Feste's profession, but also = foolish behavior.

4 More matter for a May morning.

Fabian in *Twelfth Night*, 3.4.142

That is, fit for May Day sports; Sir Andrew has arrived with his absurd challenge to Cesario.

Fools

1 A fool, a fool! I met a fool i' the forest,
A motley fool.

Jaques in *As You Like It*, 2.7.12–13

Delighted to encounter Touchstone, the professional fool.

2 Motley's the only wear.

Jaques in *As You Like It*, 2.7.34

"Motley" was the costume of a professional fool.

3   O that I were a fool!
I am ambitious for a motley coat.

Jaques in *As You Like It*, 2.7.42–3

"Motley," usually a parti-colored coat, was worn by the professional fool.

4 *Jaques.* I was seeking for a fool when I found you.
Orlando. He is drowned in the brook; look but in, and you shall see him.

***As You Like It*,** 3.2.285–8

The lover Orlando wittily puts down the melancholy Jaques.

5 The fool doth think he is wise, but the wise man knows himself to be a fool.

Touchstone in *As You Like It*, 5.1.31–2

Echoing such biblical injunctions as that at I Corinthians 3:18, "If any man among you seemeth to be wise in this world, let him become a fool, that he may be wise."

6 Here comes a pair of very strange beasts, which in all tongues are called fools.

Jaques in *As You Like It*, 5.4.36–8

Referring to Touchstone and Audrey.

7 A fool's bolt is soon shot.

Orleans in *Henry V*, 3.7.122

Proverbial; a fool lets fly with his arrow ("bolt") too soon.

8 *Lear.* Dost thou call me fool, boy?
Fool. All thy other titles thou hast given away; that thou wast born with.

King Lear, 1.4.148–50

On King Lear, who has given away his kingdom to his daughters.

9 Shall we their fond pageant see?
Lord, what fools these mortals be!

Puck in *A Midsummer Night's Dream*, 3.2.114–5

Watching the quarrels of the lovers; "fond" = both foolish and affectionate.

10 Why, my cheese, my digestion, why hast thou not served thyself in to my table, so many meals?

Achilles in *Troilus and Cressida*, 2.3.41–2

Pleased to have Thersites attending on him as a scurrilous jester.

11 Better a witty fool than a foolish wit.

Feste in *Twelfth Night*, 1.5.36

Feste is a witty professional fool; "wit" = understanding or intelligence.

12 *Feste.* Beshrew me, the knight's in admirable fooling.
Sir Andrew Aguecheek. Ay, he does well enough if he be disposed, and so do I, too. He does it with a better grace, but I do it more natural.

Twelfth Night, 2.3.80–3

The "knight" is the witty Sir Toby Belch; Sir Andrew does it more naturally because he is a "natural," a born fool.

13 She will keep no fool, sir, till she be married, and fools are as like husbands as pilchards are to herrings— the husband's the bigger.

Feste in *Twelfth Night*, 3.1.33–5

Referring to Olivia; "pilchards," small fish, are common off European coasts.

14 I am indeed not her fool, but her corrupter of words.

Feste in *Twelfth Night*, 3.1.35–6

Referring to his function in relation to the Lady Olivia.

15 This fellow is wise enough to play the fool,
And to do that well craves a kind of wit.
He must observe their mood on whom he jests,
The quality of persons, and the time,
Not, like the haggard, check at every feather
That comes before his eye. This is a practice
As full of labor as a wise man's art.

Viola in *Twelfth Night*, 3.1.60–6

Recognizing that the Fool (Feste) may be wise; "quality" = rank or nature; a "haggard" was an untrained hawk.

Forbearance

1   Be angry when you will, it shall
    have scope.
  Do what you will, dishonor shall be
    humor.

Brutus in *Julius Caesar*, 4.3.108–9

To Cassius, patching their quarrel by giving
his anger free rein ("scope"), and humoring
his questionable conduct.

2   Have you not love enough to bear
    with me,
  When that rash humor which my
    mother gave me
  Makes me forgetful?

Cassius in *Julius Caesar*, 4.3.119–21

To Brutus; "rash humor" = hasty temper.

3   Bear with me, good boy, I am much
    forgetful.

Brutus in *Julius Caesar*, 4.3.255

To his servant Lucius.

Foreboding (see also Portents)

1   *Messenger.*   But yet, madam—
  Cleopatra. I do not like "but yet."

***Antony and Cleopatra*,** 2.5.49–50

Heralding unwelcome news that Antony is
married.

2   *Francisco.* For this relief much
    thanks. 'Tis bitter cold,
  And I am sick at heart.

  Barnardo. Have you had quiet
    guard?
  Francisco. Not a mouse stirring.

***Hamlet*,** 1.1.8–10

Francisco's sense of foreboding ("I am sick at
heart") establishes right away the atmosphere
of the play.

3   In the gross and scope of mine
    opinion,
  This bodes some strange eruption
    to our state.

Horatio in *Hamlet*, 1.1.68–9

This appearance of the ghost foretells some
political upheaval; "gross and scope" = general drift.

4   A mote it is to trouble the mind's
    eye.

Horatio in *Hamlet*, 1.1.112

On the disturbing appearance of the ghost of
Hamlet's father.

5   My father's spirit in arms! All is
    not well.
  I doubt some foul play. Would the
    night were come!
  Till then sit still, my soul. Foul
    deeds will rise,
  Though all the earth o'erwhelm
    them, to men's eyes.

Hamlet in *Hamlet*, 1.2.254–7

Left alone now he knows about the ghost,
Hamlet plans to watch for it that night; compare the proverb, "murder will out."

6   Thou wouldst not think how ill all's
    here about my heart—but it is no
    matter.

Hamlet in *Hamlet*, 5.2.212–13

Just before the fencing-match with Laertes.

7 *Portia.* Why, know'st thou any
harm's intended towards him?
Soothsayer. None that I know will
be, much that I fear may chance.
Julius Caesar, 2.4.31–2

The soothsayer fears for Caesar.

8   O that a man might know
The end of this day's business ere it
come!
Brutus in Julius Caesar, 5.1.122–3

Before the battle of Philippi.

9   The raven himself is hoarse
That croaks the fatal entrance of
Duncan
Under my battlements.
Lady Macbeth in Macbeth, 1.5.38–40

The croaking of the raven proverbially fore-
shadowed misfortune or death.

10 There is some ill a-brewing towards
my rest,
For I did dream of money-bags
tonight.
Shylock in The Merchant of Venice,
2.5.17–18

11   O, it comes o'er my memory
As doth the raven o'er the infected
house,
Boding to all!
Othello in Othello, 4.1.20–2

Recalling the handkerchief he thinks Desdemona gave Cassio; the raven proverbially
foreboded bad luck or death.

12   Methinks
Some unborn sorrow, ripe in fortune's womb,

Is coming towards me, and my
inward soul
With nothing trembles.
Queen in Richard II, 2.2.9–12

Anticipating the fall of Richard.

13 *Richard.*   Give me a calendar.
Who saw the sun today?
Ratcliffe.   Not I, my lord.
Richard. Then he disdains to shine,
for by the book
He should have braved the east an
hour ago.
A black day will it be to somebody.
Richard III, 5.3.276–80

Before the Battle of Bosworth; it turns out to
be a black day for Richard, who is killed by
Richmond.

Forgetfulness

1 O, my oblivion is a very Antony,
And I am all forgotten.
Cleopatra in Antony and Cleopatra,
1.3.90–1

Her forgetfulness (oblivion) is due to her preoccupation with Antony, so that she forgets
herself, and at the same time implies that he
forgets her in going to Rome.

2 Give me to drink mandragora. . . .
That I might sleep out this great
gap of time
My Antony is away.
Cleopatra in Antony and Cleopatra,
1.5.4, 5–6

An opiate Cleopatra desires to pass the time
while Antony is away.

3 Great thing of us forgot!
Albany in King Lear, 5.3.237

In the excitement of other events, he has forgotten to find out what has happened to Lear and Cordelia.

Forgiveness (see also Mercy)

1 Far from her nest the lapwing cries away;
My heart prays for him, though my tongue do curse.

Adriana in *The Comedy of Errors*, 4.2.27–8

On her husband, who, she thinks, is making love to her sister; the lapwing proverbially cries most when far from the nest.

2 The power that I have on you is to spare you;
The malice towards you, to forgive you. Live,
And deal with others better.

Posthumus in *Cymbeline*, 5.5.418–20

To Jachimo, after Jachimo's explanation of the way he deceived Posthumus.

3   What if this cursèd hand
Were thicker than itself with brother's blood,
Is there not rain enough in the sweet heavens
To wash it white as snow?

Claudius in *Hamlet*, 3.3.43–6

Claudius wishes he could be forgiven.

4   I as free forgive you
As I would be forgiven: I forgive all.

Buckingham in *Henry VIII*, 2.1.82–3

Speaking on his way to be executed.

5 Though with their high wrongs I am struck to the quick,
Yet with my nobler reason 'gainst my fury
Do I take part. The rarer action is
In virtue than in vengeance.

Prospero in *The Tempest*, 5.1.25–8

Abandoning thoughts of revenging himself on his enemies.

6 Do as the heavens have done, forget your evil;
With them, forgive yourself.

Cleomenes in *The Winter's Tale*, 5.1.5–6

Begging Leontes to forgive himself for causing, as he thinks, the death of his wife, Hermione.

Fortune (see also Chance)

1 I am a man whom Fortune hath cruelly scratched.

Parolles in *All's Well That Ends Well*, 5.2.26–7

Appealing for pity after being exposed as a liar and braggart.

2   Fortune knows
We scorn her most when most she offers blows.

Antony in *Antony and Cleopatra*, 3.11.73–4

3 Let us sit and mock the good huswife Fortune from her wheel, that her gifts may henceforth be bestowed equally.

Celia in *As You Like It*, 1.2.31–3

The goddess Fortune turns her wheel bringing both good and bad luck; Celia playfully refers to her as a housewife at a spinning wheel.

4 Fortune reigns in the gifts of the
   world, not in the lineaments of
   nature.
   Rosalind in *As You Like It*, 1.2.41–2

   Expressing the common idea that beauty and
   cleverness were thought of as given by nature,
   wealth and status by fortune.

5 Wear this for me: one out of suits
     with Fortune,
   That could give more, but that her
     hand lacks means.
   Rosalind in *As You Like It*, 1.2.246–7

   Giving Orlando a chain; she is out of Fortune's favor because her father has been driven into exile.

6 Fortune brings in some boats that
     are not steered.
   Pisanio in *Cymbeline*, 4.3.46

   Putting his trust in chance.

7 A man that Fortune's buffets and
     rewards
   Hast ta'en with equal thanks.
   Hamlet in *Hamlet*, 3.2.67–8

   Describing his friend Horatio.

8 Will Fortune never come with both
     hands full,
   But write her fair words still in
     foulest terms?
   She either gives a stomach and no
     food—
   Such are the poor, in health; or else
     a feast
   And takes away the stomach—such
     are the rich,
   That have abundance and enjoy it
     not.
   **King Henry in *Henry IV, Part 2*,
   4.4.105–8**

   Henry feels ill even as he receives good news.

9 Fortune is painted blind, with a
   muffler afore his eyes, to signify to
   you that Fortune is blind; and she is
   painted also with a wheel, to signify
   to you, which is the moral of it, that
   she is turning, and inconstant, and
   mutability, and variation; and her
   foot, look you, is fixed upon a
   spherical stone, which rolls and
   rolls and rolls.
   Fluellen in *Henry V*, 3.6.30–6

   Fluellen quaintly describes Fortune as the
   goddess was often represented, notably in
   emblem books.

10 Doth Fortune play the huswife with
    me now?
    Pistol in *Henry V*, 5.1.80

    "Huswife" = hussy; he complains that fortune
    is being fickle; proverbial.

11   Fortune is merry,
    And in this mood will give us any-
      thing.
    Mark Antony in *Julius Caesar*, 3.2.266–7

    He has achieved his aim, to launch a civil
    war.

12   When Fortune means to men
      most good,
    She looks upon them with a threat-
      ening eye.
    **Cardinal Pandulph in *King John*,
    4.3.119–20**

    The French have been defeated, and the slip-
    pery Cardinal is encouraging the Dauphin to
    attack England.

13 A good man's fortune may grow
      out at heels.
    Kent in *King Lear*, 2.2.157

"Out at heels" literally = threadbare, worn
out; Kent is sitting in the stocks, so there's a
bitter humor in his remark.

He means he will be blessed if he chooses the
right casket and wins Portia.

14 Fortune, good night; smile once
more, turn thy wheel.

Kent in *King Lear*, 2.2.173

Recalling the proverbs, "Fortune's wheel is
ever turning," and "Fortune can both smile
and frown."

19 Well, if Fortune be a woman, she's
a good wench for this gear.

**Launcelot Gobbo in *The Merchant of
Venice*, 2.2.166–7**

Fortune was depicted as a goddess; "gear" =
business; Launcelot has the good fortune to be
taken on as a servant by Bassanio.

15 He that has and a little tiny wit—
With heigh-ho, the wind and the
rain—
Must make content with his fortunes fit,
Though the rain it raineth every
day.

Fool in *King Lear*, 3.2.74–7

"Wit" = brain or intelligence; a spin-off from a
song sung by Feste in *Twelfth Night*.

20 Fortune now
To my heart's hope!

**Prince of Aragon in *The Merchant of
Venice*, 2.9.19–20**

Hoping for good luck in choosing the right
casket.

16 The wheel is come full circle.

Edmund in *King Lear*, 5.3.175

That is, fortune's wheel, ever turning.

21 Herein Fortune shows herself more
kind
Than is her custom. It is still her
use
To let the wretched man outlive his
wealth,
To view with hollow eye and wrinkled brow
An age of poverty; from which lin-
gering penance
Of such misery doth she cut me off.

**Antonio in *The Merchant of Venice*,
4.1.267–72**

Finding reasons to welcome the prospect of
death.

17 So may I, blind fortune leading me,
Miss that which one unworthier
may attain,
And die with grieving.

**Prince of Morocco in *The Merchant of
Venice*, 2.1.36–8**

Determined to take his chance in choosing
among the caskets that will show whether he
is to be Portia's husband; Fortune is proverbially blind.

22 If it be my luck, so; if not, happy
man be his dole.

**Slender in *The Merry Wives of Wind-
sor*, 3.4.64–5**

On the possibility of marrying Anne Page;
"dole" literally = lot; in effect he is saying,
"good luck to him who wins her." The phrase
is proverbial, and occurs also in *The Winter's
Tale*, 1.2.163.

18 Good fortune then!
To make me blest or cursed'st
among men.

**Prince of Morocco in *The Merchant of
Venice*, 2.1.45–6**

23   O Lady Fortune,
Stand you auspicious!

Perdita in *The Winter's Tale,* 4.4.51–2

Hoping nothing will prevent her marriage to
the prince, Florizel.

24 If I had a mind to be honest, I see
Fortune would not suffer me: she
drops booties in my mouth.

Autolycus in *The Winter's Tale,*
4.4.831–2

Thinking him a courtier, the Shepherds have
given him gold to conduct their business at
court.

Freedom

1   The fated sky
Gives us free scope, only doth backward pull
Our slow designs when we ourselves are dull.

Helena in *All's Well That Ends Well,*
1.1.217–9

Claiming, in effect, that she will have God on
her side in actively seeking a way to win
Bertram as a husband.

2   I must have liberty
Withal, as large a charter as the
wind,
To blow on whom I please.

Jaques in *As You Like It,* 2.7.47–8

He wants to be free to satirize everyone.

3 I had as lief not be as live to be
In awe of such a thing as I myself.

Cassius in *Julius Caesar,* 1.2.95–6

"As lief not be" = as soon not exist; he is
thinking of Caesar.

4 Liberty! Freedom! Tyranny is
dead!
Run hence, proclaim, cry it about
the streets!

Cinna in *Julius Caesar,* 3.1.78–9

After the assassination of Caesar.

5 Had you rather Caesar were living,
and die all slaves, than that Caesar
were dead, to live all free men?

Brutus in *Julius Caesar,* 3.2.22–24

Addressing the people after the death of
Caesar.

6 Liberty plucks justice by the nose.

Duke in *Measure for Measure,* 1.3.29

He means license, or too much freedom.

7 Thou shalt be as free
As mountain winds; but then
exactly do
All points of my command.

Prospero in *The Tempest,* 1.2.499–501

Promising Ariel his liberty, but demanding
obedience.

8 Freedom, high-day! high-day, freedom! freedom, high-day, freedom!

Caliban in *The Tempest,* 2.2.186–7

In fact Caliban is only exchanging one kind of
servitude, under Prospero, for another, under
Stephano and Trinculo.

9   Then to the elements
Be free, and fare thou well!

Prospero in *The Tempest,* 5.1.318–19

His final parting from his devoted spirit, Ariel.

Friendship

1   I cannot live out of her company.

Celia in *As You Like It*, 1.3.86

Referring to herself and her cousin Rosalind.

2   O! let me clip ye
In arms as sound as when I wooed, in heart
As merry as when our nuptial day was done
And tapers burnt to bedward!

Caius Martius, later Coriolanus, in *Coriolanus*, 1.6.29–32

Coriolanus seems happier embracing Cominius, his fellow commander, than his wife Virgilia.

3   Those friends thou hast, and their adoption tried,
Grapple them to thy soul with hoops of steel.

Polonius in *Hamlet*, 1.3.62–3

Advice to his son as he goes to live abroad; "their adoption tried" = their association with you tested.

4   In the beaten way of friendship, what make you at Elsinore?

Hamlet in *Hamlet*, 2.2.269–70

Questioning Rosencrantz and Guildenstern, his old school fellows, as to why they have come to Denmark; "beaten way" = well-trodden track, i.e., be honest with me.

5   Give me that man
That is not passion's slave, and I will wear him
In my heart's core, ay, in my heart of heart,
As I do thee.

Hamlet in *Hamlet*, 3.2.71–4

Praising the stoical Horatio.

6   I cannot flatter; I do defy
The tongues of soothers, but a braver place
In my heart's love hath no man than yourself.

Hotspur in *Henry IV, Part 1*, 4.1.6–8

To Douglas; they are joining forces with other nobles against King Henry; "soothers" = flatterers.

7   We were the first and dearest of your friends.

Worcester in *Henry IV, Part 1*, 5.1.33

Referring to the support Worcester and his allies gave to Bolingbroke before he became king.

8   Come, I'll be friends with thee, Jack. Thou art going to the wars, and whether I shall ever see thee again or no, there is nobody cares.

Doll Tearsheet in *Henry IV, Part 2*, 2.4.65–8

Bidding goodbye to Falstaff.

9   The man nearest my soul,
Who like a brother toiled in my affairs,
And laid his love and life under my foot.

King Henry in *Henry IV, Part 2*, 3.1.61–3

On Northumberland, once his friend, now his enemy.

10   At your return visit our house; let our old acquaintance be renewed.

Shallow in *Henry IV, Part 2*, 3.2.293–4

Inviting Falstaff to return.

11 A friend i'the court is better than a
penny in purse.

Shallow in *Henry IV, Part 2*, 5.1.30–1

12 I have not from your eyes that gentleness
And show of love as I was wont to
have.

Cassius in *Julius Caesar*, 1.2.33–4

To his friend Brutus, who is troubled in mind.

13 Good friends, go in, and taste some
wine with me,
And we, like friends, will straight-
way go together.

Caesar in *Julius Caesar*, 2.2.126–7

14 What compact mean you to have
with us?
Will you be pricked in number of
our friends,
Or shall we on, and not depend on
you?

Cassius in *Julius Caesar*, 3.1.215–17

To Mark Antony; "compact" = agreement;
"pricked" = marked down.

15 Friends am I with you all, and love
you all.

Mark Antony in *Julius Caesar*, 3.1.220

To Cassius and the conspirators who killed
Caesar; Antony is being disingenuous.

16 He was my friend, faithful and just
to me.

Mark Antony in *Julius Caesar*, 3.2.85

Praising the dead Caesar.

17 A friend should bear his friend's
infirmities,

But Brutus makes mine greater
than they are.

Cassius in *Julius Caesar*, 4.3.86–7

18 I think he only loves the world for
him.

Solanio in *The Merchant of Venice*,
2.8.50

On Antonio's affection for Bassanio.

19   In companions
That do converse and waste the
time together,
Whose souls do bear an equal yoke
of love,
There must be needs a like proportion
Of lineaments, of manners, and of
spirit.

Portia in *The Merchant of Venice*,
3.4.11–15

Arguing that Bassanio and his friend Antonio,
who spend ("waste") so much time together,
must be alike.

20 Life itself, my wife, and all the
world,
Are not with me esteemed above
thy life.
I would lose all, ay, sacrifice them
all
Here to this devil, to deliver you.

Bassanio in *The Merchant of Venice*,
4.1.284–7

To his friend Antonio; the devil is Shylock,
demanding his pound of flesh.

21 Is all the counsel that we two have
shared,
The sisters' vows, the hours that we
have spent

When we have chid the hasty-footed time
For parting us—O, is all forgot?
All schooldays' friendship, child-hood innocence?

Helena in *A Midsummer Night's Dream*, 3.2.198–202

On finding her school-friend Hermia hostile to her.

22 My love is thine to teach; teach it but how,
And thou shalt see how apt it is to learn
Any hard lesson that may do thee good.

Don Pedro in *Much Ado About Nothing*, 1.1.291–3

Offering to help Claudio in any way to woo Hero.

23 Friendship is constant in all other things
Save in the office and affairs of love.

Claudio in *Much Ado About Nothing*, 2.1.175–6

Thinking he has been betrayed by his friend Don Pedro; "office" = business.

24 If I do vow a friendship, I'll perform it
To the last article.

Desdemona in *Othello*, 3.3.21–2

Going out of her way to help Cassio.

25 I count myself in nothing else so happy
As in a soul remembering my good friends.

Bolingbroke in *Richard II*, 2.3.46–7

He quarrels with them, however, once he becomes King Henry IV.

26 'Twixt such friends as we
Few words suffice.

Petruchio in *The Taming of the Shrew*, 1.2.65–6

To his good friend Hortensio.

27 Do as adversaries do in law,
Strive mightily, but eat and drink as friends.

Tranio in *The Taming of the Shrew*, 1.2.276–7

Speaking to the other suitors for Baptista's daughters.

28 What need we have any friends, if we should ne'er have need of 'em?
They were the most needless creatures living, if we should ne'er have use for 'em.

Timon in *Timon of Athens*, 1.2.95–8

Believing his friends will help him if need be.

29 We are born to do benefits; and what better or properer can we call our own than the riches of our friends? O, what a precious comfort 'tis to have so many like brothers commanding one another's fortunes!

Timon in *Timon of Athens*, 1.2.101–5

Timon's naive and misplaced trust in his friends.

30 I weigh my friend's affection with mine own.

Timon in *Timon of Athens*, 1.2.216

Assuming his friends are like himself.

31 The amity that wisdom knits not,
folly may easily untie.

Ulysses in *Troilus and Cressida*,
2.3.101–2

Referring to the friendship of Ajax and
Achilles.

32 'Twere pity two such friends should
be long foes.

**Valentine in *The Two Gentlemen of
Verona*, 5.4.118**

Reconciled at last with his old friend Proteus

33 They have seemed to be together,
though absent; shook hands as over
a vast; and embraced as it were
from the ends of opposed winds.

Camillo in *The Winter's Tale*, 1.1.29–31

Describing the long friendship of Leontes of
Sicily and Polixenes of Bohemia.

Futility

1   The task he undertakes
Is numbering sands and drinking
oceans dry.

Green in *Richard II*, 2.2.145–6

Seeing it is impossible for the old Duke of
York to hold back the rebels led by Henry
Bolingbroke.

2 Nay, if our wits run the wild-goose
chase, I am done.

Mercutio in *Romeo and Juliet*, 2.4.71–2

To Romeo, giving up a futile argument.

Gardens and Gardening

1 Most subject is the fattest soil to
weeds.

King Henry in *Henry IV*, *Part 2*, 4.4.54

"Fattest" = richest, best; the "weeds" refer to
Prince Hal's base companions.

2 The strawberry grows underneath
the nettle,
And wholesome berries thrive and
ripen best
Neighbored by fruit of baser quality.

Bishop of Ely in *Henry V*, 1.1.60–2

Prince Hal was the strawberry growing under
the shade of base companions like Falstaff.

3 Now 'tis the spring, and weeds are
shallow-rooted;
Suffer them now, and they'll out-
grow the garden,
And choke the herbs for want of
husbandry.

**Queen Margaret in *Henry VI*, *Part 2*,
3.1.31–3**

She is speaking to the king about noblemen
who may challenge his power; "want of husbandry" = lack of proper cultivation.

4 Adam was a gardener.

Jack Cade in *Henry VI*, *Part 2*, 4.2.134

A peasant claiming all men are descended
from a working man, though Adam did not
have to work in the Garden of Eden.

5 Go bind thou up yon dangling apricots,
Which, like unruly children, make
their sire
Stoop with oppression of their
prodigal weight.

Gardener in *Richard II*, 3.4.29–31

Giving instructions to his assistant; "prodigal"
= excessive.

6   I will go root away
The noisome weeds which without
   profit suck
The soil's fertility from wholesome
   flowers.

Gardener in *Richard II*, 3.4.37–9

The gardener's care contrasts with King
Richard's failure to rid himself of parasites and
look after his kingdom.

7   Superfluous branches
We lop away, that bearing boughs
   may live.

Gardener in *Richard II*, 3.4.63–4

8   Thou, old Adam's likeness, set to
   dress this garden.

Queen in *Richard II*, 3.4.73

Speaking to the gardener as if he were the first
gardener, Adam.

9   Here did she fall a tear. Here in this
   place
I'll set a bank of rue, sour herb-of-
   grace.
Rue even for ruth here shortly shall
   be seen
In the remembrance of a weeping
   queen.

Gardener in *Richard II*, 3.4.104–7

Speaking of the distressed Queen; "fall" = let
fall; rue was a herb symbolic of repentance,
and signifying sorrow; "ruth" = pity.

10   How lush and lusty the grass looks!
   How green!

Gonzalo in *The Tempest*, 2.1.53–4

The good Gonzalo sees the island on which
he has been shipwrecked in the best light.

Generosity

1   For his bounty,
There was no winter in't; an
   autumn it was
That grew the more by reaping.

**Cleopatra in *Antony and Cleopatra*,
5.2.86–8**

Exaggerating Antony's generosity, after his
death.

2   Use every man after his desert, and
who should scape whipping? Use
them after your own honor and
dignity—the less they deserve, the
more merit is in your bounty.

Hamlet in *Hamlet*, 2.2.529–32

Asking Polonius to deal well with the actors.

3   A largess universal, like the sun,
His liberal eye doth give to every-
   one,
Thawing cold fear.

Chorus in *Henry V*, 4.Prologue, 43–5

On the influence of the King on his army;
"largess" = bounty.

4   The fashion of the world is to avoid
cost, and you encounter it.

Don Pedro in *Much Ado About Nothing*, 1.1.97–8

To Leonato, who offers hospitality to Don
Pedro and his companions.

5   There's none
Can truly say he gives if he receives.
If our betters play at that game, we
   must not dare
To imitate them; faults that are rich
   are fair.

Timon in *Timon of Athens*, 1.2.10–13

The "fault" is to expect something in return for
a gift.

6 No villainous bounty yet hath
  passed my heart;
  Unwisely, not ignobly, have I given.

Timon in *Timon of Athens*, 2.2.173–4

On being upbraided by his steward, Flavius.

7   At your request
  My father will grant precious things
  as trifles.

Florizel in *The Winter's Tale*, 5.1.221–2

To Perdita; "as" = as if they were.

Ghosts (see also Apparitions)

1 Such was the very armor he had on
  When he the ambitious Norway
  combated.

Horatio in *Hamlet*, 1.1.60–1

Speaking of the ghost which has just appeared
in the likeness of the dead King of Denmark;
"Norway" = King of Norway.

2 Thus twice before, and jump at this
  dead hour,
  With martial stalk hath he gone by
  our watch.

Marcellus in *Hamlet*, 1.1.65–6

Telling of earlier appearances of the ghost of
Hamlet's father, always exactly at midnight
("jump at this dead hour").

3 But soft, behold! lo where it comes
  again!
  I'll cross it though it blast me. Stay,
  illusion!

Horatio in *Hamlet*, 1.1.126–7

Seeing the ghost of Hamlet's father again;
"cross" = confront, and perhaps make the sign
of the cross; "blast" = wither or destroy.

4 We do it wrong, being so majesti-
  cal,
  To offer it the show of violence,
  For it is as the air, invulnerable,
  And our vain blows malicious
  mockery.

Marcellus in *Hamlet*, 1.1.143–6

On the apparition of the dead King Hamlet of
Denmark.

5 *Barnardo.* It was about to speak
  when the cock crew.
  Horatio. And then it started like a
  guilty thing
  Upon a fearful summons.

Hamlet, 1.1.147–9

Describing the ghost of Hamlet's father; "fearful" = terrifying.

6 The cock, that is the trumpet to the
  morn,
  Doth with his lofty and shrill-
  sounding throat
  Awake the god of day, and at his
  warning,
  Whether in sea or fire, in earth or
  air,
  Th' extravagant and erring spirit
  hies
  To his confine.

Horatio in *Hamlet*, 1.1.150–5

Wandering ("extravagant") spirits return to
where they came from in daylight.

7 Be thou a spirit of health, or goblin
  damned,
  Bring with thee airs from heaven,
  or blasts from hell,
  Be thy intents wicked or charitable,
  Thou com'st in such a questionable
  shape
  That I will speak to thee.

Hamlet in *Hamlet*, 1.4.40–4

Addressing the ghost as a spirit that appears in his father's shape; "questionable" = which invites questions.

8   What if it tempt you toward the
     flood, my lord,
  Or to the dreadful summit of the
     cliff
  That beetles o'er his base into the
     sea,
  And there assume some other hor-
     rible form
  Which might deprive your sover-
     eignty of reason,
  And draw you into madness?

Horatio in *Hamlet*, 1.4.69–74

Trying to persuade Hamlet not to follow his father's ghost, uncertain whether the spirit is good or evil; "deprive your sovereignty of reason" = make you lose control of your mind.

9   I am thy father's spirit,
  Doomed for a certain term to walk
     the night,
  And for the day confined to fast in
     fires,
  Till the foul crimes done in my days
     of nature
  Are burnt and purged away.

Ghost in *Hamlet*, 1.5.9–13

The ghost, alone with Hamlet, describes his fate; it seems his days are spent in purgatory.

10   Art thou there, truepenny?
  You hear this fellow in the cel-
     larage,
  Consent to swear.

Hamlet in *Hamlet*, 1.5.151–2

His father's honest ghost ("truepenny") speaks from under the stage ("the cellarage"), urging Hamlet's friends to swear secrecy.

11   Well said, old mole, canst work i'th'
     earth so fast?

Hamlet in *Hamlet*, 1.5.162

To the ghost, who seems to be moving about under the stage as it calls on Hamlet's friends to swear secrecy.

12   Rest, rest, perturbèd spirit!

Hamlet in *Hamlet*, 1.5.182

To his father's ghost, who has spoken from under the stage.

13   Thou canst not say I did it; never
     shake
  Thy gory locks at me.

Macbeth in *Macbeth*, 3.4.49–50

On seeing the ghost of the murdered Banquo.

14   Now it is the time of night
  That the graves, all gaping wide,
  Every one lets forth his sprite
  In the church-way paths to glide.

**Puck in *A Midsummer Night's Dream*,
5.1.379–82**

Ghosts were thought to wander abroad at midnight, returning to their graves at dawn.

15   I have heard, but not believed, the
     spirits o'the dead
  May walk again.

**Antigonus in *The Winter's Tale*,
3.3.16–17**

After dreaming that he saw Hermione, whom he believes to be dead.

Giddiness

1   He that is giddy thinks the world
     turns round.

**Widow in *The Taming of the Shrew*,
5.2.20**

Proverbial; meaning her husband, Hortensio, who finds his wife domineering, and not at all what he expected.

Gifts

1 What have I to give you back,
whose worth
May counterpoise this rich and precious gift?

Claudio in *Much Ado About Nothing*,
4.1.27–8

The "gift" is Leonato's daughter, Hero.

2   O you gods!
Why do you make us love your
goodly gifts,
And snatch them straight away?

Pericles in *Pericles*, 3.1.22–4

Thinking his wife Thaisa has died in giving
birth to their daughter.

3 Yet my good will is great, though
the gift small.

Thaisa in *Pericles*, 3.4.18

4 I am not in the giving vein today.

King Richard in *Richard III*, 4.2.116

Refusing to give Buckingham the reward he
promised.

5 Win her with gifts if she respect not
words.
Dumb jewels often in their silent
kind
More than quick words do move a
woman's mind.

**Valentine in *The Two Gentlemen of
Verona*, 3.1.89–91**

6 She prizes not such trifles as these
are.
The gifts she looks from me are
packed and locked

Up in my heart, which I have given
already,
But not delivered.

Florizel in *The Winter's Tale*, 4.4.357–60

Speaking to his disguised father, Polixenes,
about Perdita; his gifts are love and marriage.

Girls (see also Parents and Children, Youth)

1 Those girls of Italy, take heed of
them.

**King of France in *All's Well That Ends
Well*, 2.1.19**

2   Briefly die their joys
That place them on the truth of
girls and boys.

Lucius in *Cymbeline*, 5.5.106–5

Imogen, disguised as Fidele, a faithful page in
his service, loses interest in him in concern for
her husband, Posthumus, who is on stage as a
prisoner of the Romans.

3 An unlessoned girl, unschooled,
unpracticed;
Happy in this, she is not yet so old
But she may learn; happier in this,
She is not bred so dull but she can
learn.

**Portia in *The Merchant of Venice*,
3.2.159–62**

Describing herself to Bassanio, who is to be
her husband.

Glory

1 Glory is like a circle in the water,
Which never ceaseth to enlarge
itself,

Till by broad spreading it disperse
to nought.

Joan la Pucelle (Joan of Arc) in *Henry*
VI, Part 1, 1.2.133–5

The "glory" is that brought to England by
Henry V, now dead.

God

1   He that of greatest works is finisher
Oft does them by the weakest minister.

Helena in *All's Well That Ends Well,*
2.1.136–7

Hoping that God will work through her as
agent to cure the French king's disease.

2   *Gloucester.* I hope they will not
come upon us now.
King Henry. We are in God's
hands, brother, not in theirs.

Henry V, 3.6.168–9

Henry soothes Gloucester's anxiety that the
French might attack.

3   O God, thy arm was here,
And not to us, but to thy arm alone
Ascribe we all.

King Henry in *Henry V,* 4.8.106–8

Ascribing his victory to God's help.

4   God is our fortress.

Talbot in *Henry VI, Part 1,* 2.1.26

Claiming God's protection as he attacks the
French at Orleans.

5   Now God be praised, that to believing souls

Gives light in darkness, comfort in
despair!

King Henry in *Henry VI, Part 2,*
2.1.64–5

On the miracle of a blind man recovering his
sight.

6   Let never day nor night unhallowed
pass,
But still remember what the Lord
hath done.

King Henry in *Henry VI, Part 2,*
2.1.83–4

To a blind man who recovered his sight;
"unhallowed" = unblessed by prayers.

7   God shall be my hope,
My stay, my guide, and lantern to
my feet.

King Henry in *Henry VI, Part 2,*
2.3.24–5

8   Heaven is above all yet; there sits a
judge
That no king can corrupt.

Queen Katherine in *Henry VIII,*
3.1.100–1

Rejecting the corrupt advice of Wolsey and
Campeius.

Gods and Goddesses

1   As flies to wanton boys are we to
the gods,
They kill us for their sport.

Gloucester in *King Lear,* 4.1.36–7

A cynical or despairing view; "wanton" =
playful.

2   That very time I saw (but thou
        couldst not)
    Flying between the cold moon and
        the earth
    Cupid all armed.

Oberon in *A Midsummer Night's Dream,* 2.1.155–7

Speaking to Puck; the cold moon symbolizes chastity (the goddess Diana).

3   Here she comes, curst and sad.
    Cupid is a knavish lad
    Thus to make poor females mad.

Puck in *A Midsummer Night's Dream,* 3.2.439–41

On Hermia, ill-tempered ("curst"), and thinking she is abandoned in the woods by night.

4   O you heavenly charmers,
    What things you make of us! For
        what we lack
    We laugh, for what we have are
        sorry, still
    Are children in some kind.

Theseus in *The Two Noble Kinsmen,* 5.4.131–4

"For what we lack we laugh" = we happily anticipate getting what we desire.

5   The gods themselves,
    Humbling their deities to love, have
        taken
    The shapes of beasts upon them.
        Jupiter
    Became a bull, and bellowed; the
        green Neptune
    A ram, and bleated; and the fire-
        robed god,
    Golden Apollo, a poor humble
        swain.

Florizel in *The Winter's Tale,* 4.4.25–30

What Florizel does not say to Perdita is that the aim of all these gods was to seduce a mortal girl; Apollo was god of the sun.

Gold (see also Money)

1   I see the jewel best enamelèd
    Will lose his beauty; yet the gold
        bides still
    That others touch, and often touch-
        ing will
    Wear gold.

Adriana in *The Comedy of Errors,* 2.1.109–12

The sense is that jewels tarnish, while gold retains its luster.

2   'Tis gold
    Which makes the true man killed
        and saves the thief;
    Nay, sometimes hangs both thief
        and true man. What
    Can it not do and undo?

Cloten in *Cymbeline,* 2.3.70–3

3   How quickly nature falls into revolt
    When gold becomes her object!

King Henry in *Henry IV, Part 2,* 4.5.65–67

He thinks his son, Prince Hal, has stolen his golden crown.

4   Plate sin with gold
    And the strong lance of justice
        hurtless breaks.

King Lear in *King Lear,* 4.6.165–6

The image is of plate armor, and suggests how wealth can buy out the law.

5   "All that glisters is not gold,
Often have you heard that told;
Many a man his life hath sold
But my outside to behold.
Gilded tombs do worms infold.
Had you been as wise as bold,
Young in limbs, in judgment old,
Your answer had not been
    inscrolled.
Fare you well, your suit is cold."

Prince of Morocco in *The Merchant of Venice*, 2.7.65–73

The message set down ("inscrolled") in the golden casket, beginning with a well-known proverb.

6   Gold? Yellow, glittering, precious
    gold?
  . . .
This yellow slave
Will knit and break religions, bless
    th' accursed,
Make the hoar leprosy adored,
    place thieves,
And give them title, knee and
    approbation
With senators on the bench.

Timon in *Timon of Athens*, 4.3.26, 34–8

Digging for roots to eat, Timon finds buried gold; "place" = place in office. The idea of a leper as white (hoary) may be derived from I Kings 5:27, "a leper white as snow."

Golden Age

1   They . . . fleet the time carelessly, as
they did in the golden world.

Charles in *As You Like It*, 1.1.118–19

The exiled Duke and his followers pass their time free from care, recalling the mythical golden age of man.

Goodness (see also Virtue)

1   They should be good men, their
    affairs as righteous,
But all hoods make not monks.

Queen Katherine in *Henry VIII*, 3.1.22–3

Referring to the two Cardinals, Wolsey and Campeius; it was proverbial that a monk's hood did not guarantee holiness.

2   I never did repent for doing good,
Nor shall not now.

Portia in *The Merchant of Venice*, 3.4.10–11

On setting off to help Antonio.

3   How far that little candle throws his
    beams!
So shines a good deed in a naughty
    world.

Portia in *The Merchant of Venice*, 5.1.90–1

Seeing a light in her house as she arrives back from Venice; "naughty" = wicked.

4   There's nothing ill can dwell in
    such a temple.
If the ill spirit have so fair a house,
Good things will strive to dwell
    with 't.

Miranda in *The Tempest*, 1.2.458–60

Her first impression of Ferdinand.

Gossip

1   What great ones do, the less will
    prattle of.

Sea Captain in *Twelfth Night*, 1.2.33

"Less" = social inferiors.

Government

1 Let men say we be men of good
government, being governed, as the
sea is, by our noble and chaste mistress the moon, under whose countenance we steal.

Falstaff in *Henry IV, Part 1*, 1.2.27–9

Wittily claiming to be well-behaved ("of good
government"), under Diana, goddess of
chastity and the moon, while planning a robbery by night.

2 For government, though high, and
low, and lower,
Put into parts, doth keep in one
consent,
Congreeing in a full and natural
close,
Like music.

Exeter in *Henry V*, 1.2.180–3

Though divided among social groups, and
into various functions ("parts"), the aspects of
government agree together ("congreeing") in a
final harmony "close"; "parts" quibbles on the
parts in a musical score.

3 So work the honey-bees,
Creatures that by a rule in nature
teach
The act of order to a peopled kingdom.

**Archbishop of Canterbury in *Henry
V*, 1.2.187–9**

4 Woe to that land that's governed by
a child.

Third Citizen in *Richard III*, 2.3.11

Hearing news of the death of King Edward IV;
proverbial, from the Bible (Ecclesiastes 10:16).

5 I would with such perfection govern, sir,

T'excel the golden age.

Gonzalo in *The Tempest*, 2.1.168–9

The climax of his vision of a utopian society;
the mythical golden age of antiquity was an
age of innocence and plenty.

6 There is a mystery (with whom
relation
Durst never meddle) in the soul of
state,
Which hath an operation more
divine
Than breath or pen can give expressure to.

**Ulysses in *Troilus and Cressida*,
3.3.201–5**

He is mystifying the idea of government in
talking to Achilles; "relation" = report;
"expressure" = expression.

Grace

1 Grace me no grace, nor uncle me
no uncle;
I am no traitor's uncle, and that
word "grace"
In an ungracious mouth is but profane.

York in *Richard II*, 2.3.87–9

On being greeted as "gracious uncle" by
Henry Bolingbroke, who has invaded England.

2 O momentary grace of mortal men,
Which we more hunt for than the
grace of God!

Hastings in *Richard III*, 3.4.96–7

Sentenced to death, he realizes how uncertain
the favor ("grace") of Richard is.

Gratitude, see Thanks

Graves (see also Burial, Epitaphs, Mourning)

1   Ay, but to die, and go we know
    not where;
    To lie in cold obstruction and to
    rot.

Claudio in *Measure for Measure*,
3.1.117–18

Expressing his fear of death.

2   Not a flower, not a flower sweet
    On my black coffin let there be
        strewn.
    Not a friend, not a friend greet
    My poor corpse, where my bones
        shall be thrown.
    A thousand thousand sighs to save,
    Lay me, O, where
    Sad true lover never find my grave,
    To weep there.

Feste in *Twelfth Night*, 2.4.59–66

The image of sexual consummation as "dying"
here passes into a reminder of death indeed.

Greatness (see also Politics, Power)

1   The soul and body rive not more in
        parting
    Than greatness going off.

Charmian in *Antony and Cleopatra*,
4.13.5–6

On Antony's wild behavior in defeat.

2   Rightly to be great
    Is not to stir without great argu-
        ment,
    But greatly to find quarrel in a
        straw

When honor's at the stake.

Hamlet in *Hamlet*, 4.4.53–6

True greatness consists not in fighting for any
trivial cause, unless honor is involved, when it
is noble to act.

3   All the courses of my life do show
    I am not in the roll of common
        men.

Glendower in *Henry IV, Part 1*, 3.1.41–2

Boasting of his greatness.

4   Thus did I keep my person fresh
        and new,
    My presence, like a robe pontifical,
    Ne'er seen but wondered at, and so
        my state,
    Seldom but sumptuous, showed
        like a feast.

King Henry in *Henry IV, Part 1*,
3.2.55–8

Recalling his former renown when he was
able to appear more important than Richard II,
king at the time; "state" = greatness, pomp.

5   Greatness knows itself.

Hotspur in *Henry IV, Part 1*, 4.3.74

Implying that great men take power for
granted.

6   Th' abuse of greatness is when it
        disjoins
    Remorse from power.

Brutus in *Julius Caesar*, 2.1.18–19

Thinking of Caesar; "Remorse" = mercy.

7   Think not, thou noble Roman,
    That ever Brutus will go bound to
        Rome.
    He bears too great a mind.

Brutus in *Julius Caesar*, 5.1.110–12

To Cassius, anticipating what may happen if
they lose the battle with Octavius.

8   Spirits are not finely touched
    But to fine issues.

Duke in *Measure for Measure*, 1.1.35–6

Arguing that souls are given greatness (and put to the test, as gold by a touchstone) for noble purposes.

9   This did I fear, but thought he had no weapon;
    For he was great of heart.

Cassio in *Othello*, 5.2.360–1

On Othello killing himself.

10   They that stand high have many blasts to shake them,
    And if they fall, they dash themselves to pieces.

Queen Margaret in *Richard III*, 1.3.258–9

As she, the widow of Henry VI, has become an object of scorn in the court of Edward IV.

11   Some are born great, some achieve greatness, and some have greatness thrust upon 'em.

Malvolio in *Twelfth Night*, 2.5.145–6

Reading Maria's letter that feeds his self-importance.

12   The mightier man, the mightier is the thing
    That makes him honored or begets him hate;
    For greatest scandal waits on greatest state.

The Rape of Lucrece, 1004–6

"Waits on greatest state" = attends on men of the highest rank.

Greed (see also Avarice)

1   My more-having would be as a sauce
    To make me hunger more.

Malcolm in *Macbeth*, 4.3.81–2

Greetings (see also Welcome)

1   Health and fair time of day!

King Henry in *Henry V*, 5.2.3

Greeting the King of France and his nobility.

2   Give me your hands all over, one by one.

Brutus in *Julius Caesar*, 2.1.112

3   You are come in very happy time
    To bear my greeting to the senators
    And tell them that I will not come today.

Caesar in *Julius Caesar*, 2.2.60–2

To Decius, who has come to fetch him to the senate chamber.

4   Let each man render me his bloody hand.

Mark Antony in *Julius Caesar*, 3.1.184

Shaking hands with the murderers of Caesar, and seeming to make peace with them.

5   Ill met by moonlight, proud Titania!

Oberon in *A Midsummer Night's Dream*, 2.1.60

The first meeting between the King and Queen of the Fairies.

6   Good morrow, friends. Saint
    Valentine is past;
    Begin these woodbirds but to cou-
    ple now?

**Theseus in *A Midsummer Night's
Dream*, 4.1.139–40**

Birds were proverbially supposed to choose
their mates on St. Valentine's Day, 14th February.

7   Joy, gentle friends, joy and fresh
    days of love
    Accompany your hearts!

**Theseus in *A Midsummer Night's
Dream*, 5.1.29–30**

Addressing the reconciled lovers.

8   What, my dear Lady Disdain! Are
    you yet living?

**Benedick in *Much Ado About Nothing*,
1.1.118–19**

His first, mocking words to Beatrice.

9   Most potent, grave, and reverend
    signiors,
    My very noble and approved good
    masters.

Othello in *Othello*, 1.3.76–7

Addressing the senate of Venice; "potent" =
powerful; "approved" = tested by experience.

10 Hail to thee, lady! and the grace of
    heaven,
    Before, behind thee, and on every
    hand,
    Enwheel thee round!

Cassio in *Othello*, 2.1.85–7

On Desdemona's arrival in Cyprus.

11 As a long-parted mother with her
    child
    Plays fondly with her tears and
    smiles in meeting,
    So weeping, smiling, greet I thee,
    my earth.

King Richard in *Richard II*, 3.2.8–10

Returning from Ireland, he greets the soil of
England.

Grief (see also Affliction, Mourning, Sorrow)

1   Moderate lamentation is the right
    of the dead, excessive grief the
    enemy to the living.

**Lafew, *All's Well That Ends Well*,
1.1.55–6**

Referring to the Countess of Rossillion, whose
husband has died, and Helena, who has lost
her father.

2   A heavier task could not have been
       imposed
    Than I to speak my griefs unspeak-
    able.

Egeon in *The Comedy of Errors*, 1.1.31–2

Beginning the story of how he was separated
from his wife and one of their twin sons.

3   O! grief hath changed me since you
       saw me last,
    And careful hours with time's
       deformèd hand
    Have written strange defeatures in
       my face.

**Egeon in *The Comedy of Errors*,
5.1.298–300**

Meeting Antipholus and Dromio of Ephesus,
who do not recognize him; "defeatures" = dis-
figurement.

4   Great griefs, I see, medicine the less.

Belarius in *Cymbeline*, 4.2.243

Alluding to the proverb, a greater sorrow (for the supposed death of Imogen) drives out a lesser one (for the death of Cloten).

5   *Claudius.* How is it that the clouds still hang on you?
    Hamlet. Not so, my lord, I am too much in the sun.

Hamlet, 1.2.66–7

Claudius probes Hamlet's grief at his father's death, while Hamlet resists Claudius's attempts to treat him as a son in the quibble on "sun."

6   It is not, nor it cannot come to good.
    But break, my heart, for I must hold my tongue.

Hamlet in *Hamlet*, 1.2.158–9

Expressing his grief and dismay at his mother's hasty marriage to his uncle after his father's death.

7   Mine eyes are full of tears, my heart of grief.

Gloucester in *Henry VI, Part 2*, 2.3.17

On the banishment of his wife.

8   My grief's so great
    That no supporter but the huge firm earth
    Can hold it up.

Constance in *King John*, 3.1.71–3

The widow of John's elder brother, she fears for the life of her young son Arthur.

9   Grief fills the room up of my absent child,
    Lies in his bed, walks up and down with me,
    Puts on his pretty looks, repeats his words,

Remembers me of all his gracious parts,
Stuffs out his vacant garments with his form;
Then have I reason to be fond of grief?

Constance in *King John*, 3.4.93–8

Lamenting for her son, Arthur, who is imprisoned; "remembers" = reminds.

10 Give sorrow words; the grief that does not speak
    Whispers the o'er-fraught heart and bids it break.

Malcolm in *Macbeth*, 4.3.209–10

Addressing Macduff, who has just learned that his wife and children have been slaughtered; "whispers" = whispers to the overburdened heart.

11 *Malcolm.* Dispute it like a man.
    Macduff.   I shall do so;
    But I must also feel it as a man.
    I cannot but remember such things were
    That were most precious to me.

Macbeth, 4.3.220–3

"Dispute it" = struggle against your grief.

12 Poor Desdemona! I am glad thy father's dead.
    Thy match was mortal to him, and pure grief
    Shore his old thread in twain.

Gratiano in *Othello*, 5.2.204–6

Cutting the thread of life alludes to the Fates who in ancient mythology spun the thread (Clotho) and cut it at death (Atropos); the phrase became proverbial; "shore" = sheared.

13 Shorten my days thou canst with sullen sorrow,

And pluck nights from me, but not
  lend a morrow;
Thou canst help time to furrow me
  with age,
But stop no wrinkle in his pilgrimage.

John of Gaunt in *Richard II*, 1.3.227–30

To King Richard, who has just banished his
son, Bolingbroke.

14   My grief lies all within,
And these external manners of
  laments
Are merely shadows to the unseen
  grief
That swells with silence in the tor-
  tured soul.
There lies the substance.

King Richard in *Richard II*, 4.1.295–9

Lamenting his fall; "manners" = shows or
forms.

15 I am not prone to weeping, as our
  sex
Commonly are, the want of which
  vain dew
Perchance shall dry your pities; but
  I have
That honorable grief lodged here
  which burns
Worse than tears drown.

Hermione in *The Winter's Tale*,
2.1.108–12

On being accused of adultery and sent to
prison.

Guilt (see also Conscience)

1 O, my offense is rank, it smells to
  heaven,
It hath the primal eldest curse
  upon't,

A brother's murder.

Claudius in *Hamlet*, 3.3.36–8

Left alone, Claudius confesses to his crime,
alluding to Cain's slaughter of Abel (Genesis
4).

2 O limèd soul, that struggling to be
  free
Art more engaged!

Claudius in *Hamlet*, 3.3.68–9

Attempting to pray for forgiveness, he
becomes more conscious of his guilt; "limed"
= caught in birdlime, a sticky substance
smeared on twigs to catch birds.

3 Thou turn'st my eyes into my very
  soul,
And there I see such black and
  grainèd spots
As will not leave their tinct.

Gertrude in *Hamlet*, 3.4.89–91

Hamlet has made her conscious of her guilt in
marrying Claudius; "grained" = ingrained,
fast-dyed.

4 To my sick soul, as sin's true nature
  is,
Each toy seems prologue to some
  great amiss.
So full of artless jealousy is guilt,
It spills itself in fearing to be spilt.

Gertrude in *Hamlet*, 4.5.17–20

"Toy" = trifle; "jealousy" = suspicion; "spills"
= reveals and destroys.

5 Will all great Neptune's ocean wash
  this blood
Clean from my hand? No. This my
  hand will rather
The multitudinous seas incarnadine,
Making the green one red.

Macbeth in *Macbeth*, 2.2.57–60

"Incarnadine" = turn red.

6 A little water clears us of this deed. How easy is it then!

Lady Macbeth in _Macbeth_, 2.2.64–5

Referring to the blood on their hands after the murder of Duncan.

7 Out, damned spot! Out, I say!

Lady Macbeth in _Macbeth_, 5.1.35

Sleepwalking, she imagines Duncan's blood is still on her hands.

8 Here's the smell of the blood still: all the perfumes ofArabia will not sweeten this little hand.

Lady Macbeth in _Macbeth_, 5.1.50–1

Imagining in her sleepwalking that she can smell Duncan's blood on her hands.

9 Foul whisp'rings are abroad.
   Unnatural deeds
Do breed unnatural troubles.
   Infected minds
To their deaf pillows will discharge their secrets.
More needs she the divine than the physician.

Doctor in _Macbeth_, 5.1.71–4

Unable to cure Lady Macbeth's disease of the mind, the guilt confessed in her sleepwalking.

10   She, O, she is fallen
Into a pit of ink, that the wide sea
Hath drops too few to wash her clean again
And salt too little which may season give
To her foul tainted flesh!

Leonato in _Much Ado About Nothing_, 4.1.139–43

Believing his daughter to have been unchaste; "season give" = make sound again (literally, give relish to, like salt).

11 They whose guilt within their bosoms lie
Imagine every eye beholds their blame.

The Rape of Lucrece, 1342–3

Lucrece imagines everyone can see that she has been raped.

Habit, see Custom

Hair

1 _Rosalind._ His very hair is of the dissembling color. . . .
Celia. An excellent color. Your chestnut was ever the only color.

As You Like It, 3.4.10–12

Rosalind disparages Orlando (tawny or chestnut was said to be the color of Judas's hair), in order to hear Celia praise him.

2 There's many a man has more hair than wit.

Antipholus of Syracuse in _The Comedy of Errors_, 2.2.82–3

"Wit" = intelligence or sense.

3 I must to the barber's, monsieur, for methinks I am marvellous hairy about the face; and I am such a tender ass, if my hair do but tickle me, I must scratch.

Bottom in _A Midsummer Night's Dream_, 4.1.23–6

Bottom, who does not realize Puck has given him an ass's head, addresses the fairy, Cobweb.

Happiness (see also Contentment, Joy)

1   O, how bitter a thing it is to look into happiness through another man's eyes!

Orlando in *As You Like It*, 5.2.43–5

The happiness is that of his brother Oliver, who is to marry Celia.

2   Believe me, I am passing light in spirit.

Archbishop of York in *Henry IV*, Part 2, 4.2.85

"Passing" = exceedingly.

3   O God! methinks it were a happy life
    To be no better than a homely swain.

King Henry in *Henry VI*, Part 3, 2.5.21–2

Caught in a brutal civil war, the king wishes he were a shepherd.

4   Our content is our best having.

Old Lady in *Henry VIII*, 2.3.22–3

She would like to be rich all the same; "having" = possession.

5   Happy thou art not,
    For what thou hast not, still thou striv'st to get,
    And what thou hast, forget'st.

Duke in *Measure for Measure*, 3.1.21–3

Depicting life as an unrewarding struggle in order to prepare Claudio to face death.

6   If it were now to die,
    'Twere now to be most happy; for I fear

My soul hath her content so absolute
That not another comfort like to this
Succeeds in unknown fate.

Othello in *Othello*, 2.1.189–93

This ironically does turn out to be Othello's happiest moment.

7   One feast, one house, one mutual happiness.

Valentine in *The Two Gentlemen of Verona*, 5.4.173

Marking the marriages promised at the end of the play.

Haste

1   To climb steep hills
        Requires slow pace at first.

Norfolk in *Henry VIII*, 1.1.131–2

Advising the hasty Buckingham to act with caution.

2   Wisely and slow. They stumble that run fast.

Friar Lawrence in *Romeo and Juliet*, 2.3.94

Cautioning Romeo against marrying too hastily; varying the proverb "more haste, less speed."

Hate (see also Malice)

1   I care not for you,
        And am so near the lack of charity
        To accuse myself I hate you; which I had rather
        You felt than make't my boast.

Imogen in *Cymbeline*, 2.3.108–11

To the stupid Cloten, whom she detests.

2 If I can cross him any way, I bless
myself every way.

Don John in *Much Ado About Nothing*, 1.3.67–8

Referring to Claudio, whom he hates; "cross" = thwart, quibbling also on making the sign of the cross, so leading into "bless."

Health

1 *Ligarius.* What's to do?
Brutus. A piece of work that will make sick men whole.

Julius Caesar, 2.1.326–7

The "work" is the planned killing of Caesar.

Heaven

1 Where souls do couch on flowers, we'll hand in hand,
And with our sprightly port make the ghosts gaze.

Antony in *Antony and Cleopatra*, 4.14.51–2

Imagining a blissful afterlife united with Cleopatra.

2 The treasury of everlasting joy.

King Henry in *Henry VI, Part 2*, 2.1.18

Henry's formula for heaven.

3 There's not the smallest orb which thou behold'st
But in his motion like an angel sings,
Still quiring to the young-eyed cherubins;
Such harmony is in immortal souls,
But whilst this muddy vesture of decay
Doth grossly close it in, we cannot hear it.

Lorenzo in *The Merchant of Venice*, 5.1.60–5

It was thought that the soul liberated from the body ("vesture of decay") might hear the music made by the stars in their motions; cherubim were covered with eyes, according to Ezekiel 10:12.

Hedonism

1 I am sure care's an enemy to life.

Sir Toby Belch in *Twelfth Night*, 1.3.2–3

2 *Sir Toby Belch.* Does not our life consist of the four elements?
Sir Andrew Aguecheek. Faith, so they say, but I think it rather consists of eating and drinking.
Sir Toby Belch. Thou'rt a scholar; therefore let us eat and drink.

Twelfth Night, 2.3.9–14

All matter was thought to be composed of the four elements, earth, water, air, and fire.

Height

1 *Jaques.* What stature is she of?
Orlando. Just as high as my heart.

As You Like It, 3.2.268–9

A lover's answer to a pointless question.

2 He is not very tall—yet for his years he's tall.

Phebe in *As You Like It*, 3.5.118

Fondly describing Rosalind, who is disguised as a youth.

Hell (see also The Devil)

1   All hell shall stir for this.

Pistol in *Henry V*, 5.1.68

On being forced by Fluellen to eat a leek.

2   But this place is too cold for hell.
I'll devil-porter it no further; I had
thought to have let in some of all
professions that go the primrose
way to th' everlasting bonfire.

Porter in *Macbeth*, 2.3.16–19

The porter imagines Macbeth's castle as hell:
the flowery path to hell is derived from
Matthew 7:13, "broad is the way that leadeth
to destruction."

3   Not in the legions
Of horrid hell can come a devil
    more damned
To top Macbeth.

Malcolm in *Macbeth*, 4.3.55–7

4   Hell is murky.

Lady Macbeth in *Macbeth*, 5.1.36

Speaking in her sleepwalking as if she is in
hell.

5   You, mistress,
That have the office opposite to
    Saint Peter,
And keep the gate of hell!

Othello in *Othello*, 4.2.90–2

To Emilia, Desdemona's attendant, treating
her as a bawd; the "harlot's house is the way
to hell" in Proverbs 7:27.

6   Whip me, ye devils,
From the possession of this heav-
    enly sight!
Blow me about in winds! Roast me
    in sulphur!

Wash me in steep-down gulfs of
    liquid fire!

Othello in *Othello*, 5.2.277–80

His vision, as he realizes the horror of his
murder of Desdemona, of the torments of hell.

Helping

1   Well then, it now appears you need
my help.

Shylock in *The Merchant of Venice*,
1.3.114

To Antonio, who has reviled him.

2   'Tis not enough to help the feeble
up,
But to support him after.

Timon in *Timon of Athens*, 1.1.107–8

On Ventidius, imprisoned for debt.

Hindrance

1   Any bar, any cross, any impediment
will be medicinable to me.

Don John in *Much Ado About
Nothing*, 2.2.4–5

Hoping to prevent by any means the marriage
of Claudio and Hero; any obstacle will do him
good ("be medicinable").

History

1   'Tis no sinister nor awkward claim
Picked from the wormholes of
    long-vanished days,
Nor from the dust of old oblivion
    raked.

Exeter in *Henry V*, 2.4.85–7

On Henry's claim to France; "sinister" = erro-
neous or underhand.

2   When went there by an age, since
the great Flood,
But it was famed with more than
with one man?

Cassius in *Julius Caesar*, 1.2.152–3

Greek mythology and the Bible both describe
a great flood; in the first Zeus spared Deu-
calion, and in the second God spared Noah.

Holidays

1   If all the year were playing holidays,
To sport would be as tedious as to
work;
But when they seldom come, they
wished for come,
And nothing pleaseth but rare accidents.

**Prince Hal in *Henry IV*, *Part 1*,
1.2.204–7**

"Rare accidents" = unusual events.

2   A while to work, and after, holiday.

Bolingbroke in *Richard II*, 3.1.44

Seeing he needs only to defeat the Welsh to
gain the kingdom.

Home

1   East, west, north, south, or like a
school broke up,
Each hurries toward his home and
sporting-place.

Hastings in *Henry IV*, *Part 2*, 4.2.104–5

On an army dispersing for home.

Homelessness

1   Return to her? And fifty men dismissed?

No, rather I abjure all roofs, and
choose
To wage against the enmity o' th'
air,
To be a comrade with the wolf and
owl—
Necessity's sharp pinch.

King Lear in *King Lear*, 2.4.207–11

Preferring to struggle against storms and winds
("the enmity o' th' air"), and live with wild
beasts, than stay with his ungrateful daughters.

2   Poor naked wretches, wheresoe'er
you are,
That bide the pelting of this pitiless
storm,
How shall your houseless heads and
unfed sides,
Your looped and windowed
raggedness, defend you
From seasons such as these?

King Lear in *King Lear*, 3.4.28–32

"Bide" = endure; "looped and windowed
raggedness" = ragged clothes full of holes and
tatters.

3   Who can speak broader than he
that has no house to put his head
in? Such may rail against great
buildings.

**Varro's Second Servant in *Timon of
Athens*, 3.4.63–5**

"Broader" = more freely.

Honesty (see also Integrity, Truth)

1   Rich honesty dwells like a miser, sir,
in a poor house, as your pearl in
your foul oyster.

Touchstone in *As You Like It*, 5.4.59–61

Speaking of the sluttish Audrey.

2   To be honest, as this world goes, is to be one man picked out of ten thousand.

Hamlet in *Hamlet*, 2.2.178–9

Speaking to Polonius in real or pretended cynicism.

3   Where I could not be honest, I never yet was valiant.

Albany in *King Lear*, 5.1.23–4

He is unwilling to fight except in a good cause; "honest" = honorable.

4   An old man, sir, and his wits are not so blunt as, God help, I would desire they were; but, in faith, honest as the skin between his brows.

Dogberry in *Much Ado About Nothing*, 3.5.10–12

Commenting on his assistant, Verges, and, as often, in the word "blunt" (= sharp) saying the opposite of what he means; "honest as the skin between his brows" is proverbial.

5   I know thou'rt full of love and honesty,
And weigh'st thy words before thou giv'st them breath.

Othello in *Othello*, 3.3.118–19

Iago has convinced everyone of his honesty.

6   This fellow's of exceeding honesty,
And knows all qualities, with a learnèd spirit,
Of human dealings.

Othello in *Othello*, 3.3.258–60

Trusting Iago as one who knows all types of characters ("qualities").

7   O wretched fool,
That lov'st to make thine honesty a vice!
O monstrous world! Take note, take note, O world,
To be direct and honest is not safe.

Iago in *Othello*, 3.3.375–8

The "wretched fool" is Iago himself, hypocritically protesting his honesty to Othello.

8   What a fool Honesty is! and Trust, his sworn brother, a very simple gentleman!

Autolycus in *The Winter's Tale*, 4.4.595–6

Proverbial; he finds it easy to cheat the honest shepherds.

9   Though I am not naturally honest, I am so sometimes by chance.

Autolycus in *The Winter's Tale*, 4.4.712–13

The rogue finds it useful sometimes to tell the truth.

Honor

1   Honors thrive
When rather from our acts we them derive
Than our foregoers.

King of France in *All's Well That Ends Well*, 2.3.135–7

2   The honor of a maid is her name, and no legacy is so rich as honesty.

Mariana in *All's Well That Ends Well*, 3.5.12–13

3   By heaven, methinks it were an easy
      leap
     To pluck bright honor from the
      pale-faced moon,
     Or dive into the bottom of the
      deep,
     Where fathom-line could never
      touch the ground,
     And pluck up drownèd honor by
      the locks.

     Hotspur in *Henry IV, Part 1*, 1.3.201–5

     For Hotspur "honor" means fame or glory
     gained in battle; "locks" = hair.

4   Thou art the king of honor.

     Douglas in *Henry IV, Part 1*, 4.1.10

     To Hotspur, who has gained honor or fame on
     the battlefield.

5   Well, 'tis no matter, honor pricks
     me on. Yes, but how if honor prick
     me off when I come on? How
     then?

     Falstaff in *Henry IV, Part 1*, 5.1.129–31

     Quibbling on meanings of "honor" = moral
     obligation and fame; and "prick" = spur on
     and mark down as dead.

6   What is honor? A word. What is in
     that word honor? What is that
     honor? Air. A trim reckoning!
     Who hath it? He that died o'
     Wednesday.

     Falstaff in *Henry IV, Part 1*, 5.1.133–6

     Reducing fame and moral obligation to mere
     noise.

7   Honor's thought
     Reigns solely in the breast of every
      man.

     Chorus in *Henry V*, 2.Prologue, 3–4

8   The fewer men, the greater share of
     honor.

     King Henry in *Henry V*, 4.3.22

     In fighting against the French.

9   By Jove, I am not covetous for gold,
     . . .
     But if it be a sin to covet honor
     I am the most offending soul alive.

     King Henry in *Henry V*, 4.3.24, 28–9

     Before the battle of Agincourt.

10   I would not lose so great an honor
     As one man more methinks would
      share with me
     For the best hope I have.

     King Henry in *Henry V*, 4.3.31–3

     Rejecting Westmorland's wish for a larger
     army to fight the French.

11   In thy face I see
     The map of honor, truth, and loy-
      alty.

     King Henry in *Henry VI, Part 2*,
     3.1.202–3

     On his uncle, the Duke of Gloucester,
     arrested for treason.

12   If it be aught toward the general
      good,
     Set honor in one eye, and death
      i'th' other,
     And I will look on both indiffer-
      ently;
     For let the gods so speed me as I
      love
     The name of honor more than I
      fear death.

     Brutus in *Julius Caesar*, 1.2.85–9

     Proclaiming his integrity.

13 Well, honor is the subject of my story.

Cassius in *Julius Caesar*, 1.2.92

For Brutus honor concerns the general good, but for Cassius it concerns his personal status.

14 Believe me for mine honor, and have respect to mine honor, that you may believe.

Brutus in *Julius Caesar*, 3.2.14–16

Speaking to the people.

15 Here, under leave of Brutus and the rest—
For Brutus is an honorable man;
So are they all, all honorable men—
Come I to speak in Caesar's funeral.

Mark Antony in *Julius Caesar*, 3.2.81–4

Beginning to make the people question the notion of "honor."

16 O, if thou wert the noblest of thy strain,
Young man, thou couldst not die more honorable.

Brutus in *Julius Caesar*, 5.1.59–60

That is, if he were to die on the sword of Brutus.

17 Thou art a fellow of a good respect;
Thy life hath had some smatch of honor in it.

Brutus in *Julius Caesar*, 5.5.45–6

Asking Strato to kill him; "respect" = reputation; "smatch" = touch, smack.

18 If you were born to honor, show it now;
If put upon you, make the judgment good
That thought you worthy of it.

Marina in *Pericles*, 4.6.92–4

Held in a brothel, she appeals to Lysimachus not to attempt sex with her.

19 Mine honor is my life, both grow in one,
Take honor from me, and my life is done.

Mowbray in *Richard II*, 1.1.182–3

"Honor" is a complex word; Mowbray seems to mean by it both fame or reputation, and moral probity.

20 Though mine enemy thou hast ever been,
High sparks of honor in thee have I seen.

King Henry IV in *Richard II*, 5.6.28–9

Speaking to the Bishop of Carlisle, a supporter of the dead Richard II; here "honor" = probity or virtue.

21 Not a man, for being simply man,
Hath any honor, but honor for those honors
That are without him, as place, riches and favor—
Prizes of accident as oft as merit.

Achilles in *Troilus and Cressida*, 3.3.83–6

Reducing "honor" to mere fame or dignity; "without" = external to; "place" = office or status.

22 Life every man holds dear, but the dear man
Holds honor far more precious-dear than life.

Hector in *Troilus and Cressida*, 5.3.27–8

Refusing to be dissuaded from fighting by pressure from his wife Andromache and Cassandra; "dear man" = man of worth, noble man.

23   The painful warrior famousèd for
         fight,
      After a thousand victories once
         foiled
      Is from the book of honor rasèd
         quite,
      And all the rest forgot for which he
         toiled.

Sonnet 25, 9–12

Once defeated ("foiled"), the toil and pain
endured by a fighter in a thousand victories is
blotted out or erased.

Hope

1   It never yet did hurt
      To lay down likelihoods and forms
         of hope.

Hastings in *Henry IV, Part 2*, 1.3.34–5

To his fellow-conspirators, plotting rebellion.

2   To be worst,
      The lowest and most dejected thing
         of fortune,
      Stands still in esperance, lives not in
         fear.
      The lamentable change is from the
         best,
      The worst returns to laughter.

Edgar in *King Lear*, 4.1.2–6

"Esperance" = hope; alluding to the proverb,
"when things are at the worst they will mend."

3   The miserable have no other medi-
      cine
      But only hope.

Claudio in *Measure for Measure*,
3.1.2–3

He is in prison, hoping to be pardoned for getting Juliet with child.

4   True hope is swift, and flies with
      swallow's wings:

Kings it makes gods, and meaner
   creatures kings.

Richmond in *Richard III*, 5.2.23–4

Encouraging his supporters in their drive
against Richard.

Horror

1   But that I am forbid
      To tell the secrets of my prison-
         house,
      I could a tale unfold whose lightest
         word
      Would harrow up thy soul, freeze
         thy young blood,
      Thy knotted and combinèd locks to
         part,
      And each particular hair to stand
         on end,
      Like quills upon the fretful porpen-
         tine.

Ghost in *Hamlet*, 1.5.14–20

Hinting at horrors he will not describe to
Hamlet; "harrow up" means lacerate; "porpentine" = porcupine.

Horses

1   O happy horse, to bear the weight
      of Antony!

Cleopatra in *Antony and Cleopatra*,
1.5.21

Thinking, with a sexual suggestiveness, of the
absent Antony.

2   I will not change my horse with any
      that treads but on four pasterns. . . .
      When I bestride him, I soar, I am a
      hawk; he trots the air.

Dauphin in *Henry V*, 3.7.11–12, 15–16

"Pasterns" = hooves.

Hospitality

1   I have heard it said unbidden
    guests
    Are often welcomest when they are
    gone.
    Bedford in *Henry VI, Part 1*, 2.2.55–6

2   Ourself will mingle with society
    And play the humble host.
    Macbeth in *Macbeth*, 3.4.3–4

"Society" = the guests at his feast.

3   When my old wife lived,
         upon
    This day she was both pantler, but-
    ler, cook,
    Both dame and servant, welcomed
    all, served all,
    Would sing her song and dance her
    turn, now here
    At upper end o'the table, now i'the
    middle,
    On his shoulder, and his, her face
    afire
    With labor, and the thing she took
    to quench it
    She would to each one sip.
    Shepherd in *The Winter's Tale*,
    4.4.55–62

Urging his (supposed) daughter Perdita to play
the hostess; "pantler" = pantry server; "On his
shoulder" = at his shoulder, i.e., to serve food
or drink.

4   You are retired
    As if you were a feasted one and not
    The hostess of the meeting.

Shepherd in *The Winter's Tale*, 4.4.62–4

Perdita is behaving as a guest rather than as
the hostess.

Humanity

1   Yet to me what is this quintessence
    of dust? Man delights not me—nor
    woman neither, though by your
    smiling you seem to say so.
    Hamlet in *Hamlet*, 2.2.308–10

Referring to Genesis 3:19, "For dust thou art,
and to dust shalt thou return."

2   What should such fellows as I do
    crawling between earth and heaven?
    Hamlet in *Hamlet*, 3.1.126–8

To Ophelia, accusing himself of many faults.

3   When we are born, we cry that we
        are come
    To this great stage of fools.
    King Lear in *King Lear*, 4.6.182–3

Shakespeare often compares the world to a
theater in which everyone plays a part; the
idea became proverbial.

4   Nature hath framed strange fellows
        in her time.
    Antonio in *The Merchant of Venice*,
    1.1.51

On the strange eccentricities of human
behavior.

5   Lord, what fools these mortals be!
    Puck in *A Midsummer Night's Dream*,
    3.2.115

He is enjoying the confusions of the lovers,
which he has brought about.

6   Throw away respect,
Tradition, form, and ceremonious
  duty,
For you have but mistook me all
  this while.
I live with bread like you, feel want,
Taste grief, need friends.

King Richard in *Richard II*, 3.2.172–6

Acknowledging his common humanity.

7   O wonder!
How many goodly creatures are
  there here!
How beauteous mankind is! O
  brave new world
That has such people in't!

Miranda in *The Tempest*, 5.1.181–4

Her first sight of a group of courtiers from
Italy, some of them in fact anything but
"goodly."

8 Who lives that's not depravèd or
  depraves?
Who dies that bears not one spurn
  to their graves
Of their friend's gift?

Apemantus in *Timon of Athens*,
1.2.140–2

A cynic's view of humanity; "spurn" = kick or
rejection.

9 The middle of humanity thou never
knewest, but the extremity of both
ends. When thou wast in thy gilt
and perfume, they mocked thee for
too much curiosity; in thy rags thou
know'st none, but art despised for
the contrary.

Apemantus in *Timon of Athens*,
4.3.300–4

Apemantus describes the once wealthy Timon,
now penniless, who has become a misan-
thropic outcast; "curiosity" = refinement.

Humility

1 Humble as the ripest mulberry
That will not hold the handling.

Volumnia in *Coriolanus*, 3.2.79–80

Advising Coriolanus how to appear to the
people.

2 I have sounded the very base string
of humility.

Prince Hal in *Henry IV, Part 1*, 2.4.5

He has been mixing with servants in an inn;
he is quibbling on "base" and "bass."

3 Then I stole all courtesy from
  heaven
And dressed my self in such humility
That I did pluck allegiance from
  men's hearts,
Loud shouts and salutations from
  their mouths,
Even in the presence of the
  crownèd king.

King Henry in *Henry IV, Part 1*,
3.2.50–4

Recalling his popularity before he became
king.

4 How like a fawning publican he
  looks!

Shylock in *The Merchant of Venice*,
1.3.41

Referring to Antonio as if he were a tax-col-
lector for the ancient Romans; an allusion to
Luke 18:10–14, where the publican looks
down humbly in contrast to the Pharisee,
showing that "everyone that exalteth himself
shall be abased; and he that humbleth himself
shall be exalted."

Hunger

1 They said they were an-hungry;
  sighed forth proverbs—

That hunger broke stone walls, that
    dogs must eat,
That meat was made for mouths,
    that the gods sent not
Corn for the rich men only.

Caius Martius, later Coriolanus, in
Coriolanus, 1.1.205–8

A patrician's contempt for the starving populace of Rome.

Hunting

1   What shall he have that killed the
      deer?
    His leather skin and horns to wear.
    Then sing him home.
    Take thou no scorn to wear the
      horn,
    It was a crest ere thou wast born;
    Thy father's father wore it,
    And thy father bore it.
    The horn, the horn, the lusty horn
    Is not a thing to laugh to scorn.

Second Lord in *As You Like It*, 4.2.10–18

A hunting song; also an elaborate play on the
horns of a cuckold, a husband whose wife is
unfaithful.

2   As wild geese that the creeping
      fowler eye,
    Or russet-pated choughs, many in
      sort,
    Rising and cawing at the gun's
      report,
    Sever themselves and madly sweep
      the sky—
    So at his sight away his fellows fly.

Puck in *A Midsummer Night's Dream*,
3.2.20–4

"Russet-pated choughs, many in sort" = jackdaws with dun-colored heads in a large flock;
"sever themselves" = scatter, as Bottom's
friends scattered when they saw his ass's
head.

3   I was with Hercules and Cadmus
      once,
    When in a wood of Crete they
      bayed the bear
    With hounds of Sparta: never did I
      hear
    Such gallant chiding; for besides the
      groves,
    The skies, the fountains, every
      region near
    Seemed all one mutual cry. I never
      heard
    So musical a discord, such sweet
      thunder.

Hippolyta in *A Midsummer Night's*
***Dream*, 4.1.112–18**

Theseus is here associated with classical legends in praise of hunting with a pack of
hounds; "bayed" = brought to bay.

4   The hunt is up, the morn is bright
      and grey,
    The fields are fragrant and the
      woods are green.

Titus in *Titus Andronicus*, 2.2.1–2

Titus and his sons, "making a noise with
hounds and horns" (stage direction), set off to
hunt.

Hypocrisy (see also Deceit, Duplicity)

1   We are oft to blame in
    this,
    'Tis too much proved, that with
      devotion's visage
    And pious action we do sugar o'er
    The devil himself.

Polonius in *Hamlet*, 3.1.45–8

Using Ophelia, made to hold a prayer-book,
to spy on Hamlet; for the moment he realizes
what he is doing is wrong.

2   The lady doth protest too much,
     methinks.

Gertrude in *Hamlet*, 3.2.230

Reacting to a speech by the Player Queen,
who swears she will never remarry if left a
widow, as Gertrude herself has done.

3   Why, I can smile, and murder
       whiles I smile,
     And cry "Content!" to that which
       grieves my heart,
     And wet my cheeks with artificial
       tears,
     And frame my face to all occasions.

**Richard of Gloucester (later Richard
III) in *Henry VI, Part 3*, 3.2.182–5**

4   Would I had never trod this English
       earth!
     Or felt the flatteries that grow upon
       it;
     Ye have angels' faces, but heaven
       knows your hearts.

**Queen Katherine in *Henry VIII*,
3.1.143–5**

Distrusting the crafty Cardinal Wolsey, who
says he has come to counsel her.

5   When love begins to sicken and
       decay
     It useth an enforcèd ceremony.
     There are no tricks in plain and
       simple faith.

Brutus in *Julius Caesar*, 4.2.20–2

To Lucilius, who reports that Cassius appears
unfriendly.

6   Well, whiles I am a beggar, I will
       rail
     And say there is no sin but to be
       rich;
     And being rich, my virtue then shall
       be

To say there is no sin but beggary.

**The Bastard Falconbridge in *King
John*, 2.1.593–6**

The hypocrisy of the politicians provokes him
into cynicism.

7   I want that glib and oily art
     To speak and purpose not, since
       what I well intend,
     I'll do't before I speak.

Cordelia in *King Lear*, 1.1.224–6

Alluding to the flattering words of her sisters.

8   To show an unfelt sorrow is an
       office
     Which the false man does easy.

Malcolm in *Macbeth*, 2.3.136–7

"Easy" = easily.

9   O, what may man within him hide,
     Though angel on the outward side!

Duke in *Measure for Measure*, 3.2.271–2

Alluding to the hypocrisy of Angelo, and also
to the coin that had the figure of an angel on
its face.

10   In law, what plea so tainted and
       corrupt
     But, being seasoned with a gracious
       voice,
     Obscures the show of evil?

**Bassanio in *The Merchant of Venice*,
3.2.75–7**

11   Though I do hate him as I do hell
       pains,
     Yet, for necessity of present life,
     I must show out a flag and sign of
       love,
     Which is indeed but sign.

Iago in *Othello,* 1.1.154–7

Telling Roderigo his true attitude to Othello.

12   Divinity of hell!
When devils will the blackest sins
    put on,
They do suggest at first with heav-
    enly shows,
As I do now.

Iago in *Othello,* 2.3.350–3

The divinity of hell is the inverted theology
that leads people to damnation; "put on" =
encourage; "suggest" = tempt.

13   Though some of you, with Pilate,
    wash your hands,
Showing an outward pity, yet you
    Pilates
Have here delivered me to my sour
    cross.

King Richard in *Richard II,* 4.1.120–1

Referring to his nobles, who have gone over
to his rival, Bolingbroke: the biblical allusion
is to Matthew 27:24.

14   Thus I clothe my naked villainy
With odd old ends stolen forth of
    holy writ,
And seem a saint, when most I play
    the devil.

King Richard in *Richard III,* 1.3.335–7

Taking the audience into his confidence.

15   I thank my God for my humility.

King Richard in *Richard III,* 2.1.73

Speaking to all at court, after he has just
arranged the murder of his own brother,
Clarence.

16   Alas, why would you heap this care
    on me?
I am unfit for state and majesty.

I do beseech you take it not amiss,
I cannot nor I will not yield to you.

King Richard in *Richard III,* 3.7.204–7

Pretending he does not want the crown.

Identity (see also Self-Knowledge)

1   I to the world am like a drop of
    water
That in the ocean seeks another
    drop,
Who, falling there to find his fellow
    forth,
(Unseen, inquisitive) confounds
    himself.
So I, to find a mother and a
    brother,
In quest of them, unhappy, lose
    myself.

Antipholus of Syracuse in *The Com-edy of Errors,* 1.2.35–40

"To the world" = in relation to the world;
"confounds himself" = mingles and loses its
identity.

2   Would you have me
False to my nature? Rather say, I
    play
The man I am.

Coriolanus in *Coriolanus,* 3.2.14–16

His mother is trying to persuade him to be
show humility.

3   Does any here know me? This is
    not Lear.
Does Lear walk thus? Speak thus?
    Where are his eyes?

King Lear in *King Lear,* 1.4.226–7

The old king cannot believe his daughter
Goneril would stand up against him.

4 *Lear.* Who is it that can tell me
who I am?
Fool. Lear's shadow.
King Lear, 1.4.230–1

Lear has given away his power to his daughters, hence the Fool's reply.

5 Thus play I in one person many
people,
And none contented.
King Richard in *Richard II*, 5.5.31–2

Humiliated and imprisoned, Richard tries to escape from the crushing sense of his own identity.

6 I am myself alone.
**Richard of Gloucester in *Henry VI*,
Part 3,** 5.6.83

The future Richard III prides himself on his own uniqueness.

Idleness

1 Hence! Home, you idle creatures,
get you home!
Is this a holiday?
Flavius in *Julius Caesar*, 1.1.1–2

One of the tribunes orders people who have come to see Caesar to get off the streets.

Idolatry

1 'Tis mad idolatry
To make the service greater than
the god.
Hector in *Troilus and Cressida*, 2.2.56–7

To offer more devotion than the "god" is worth seems mad to Hector, who is thinking of Helen.

Ignorance

1 O thou monster ignorance, how
deformed dost thou look!
Holofernes in *Love's Labor's Lost*,
4.2.23

On Dull's inability to understand Latin.

2 I say there is no darkness but ignorance.
Feste in *Twelfth Night*, 4.2.42–3

Pretending to be a priest, Sir Topas, he preaches to the imprisoned Malvolio.

Imagination

1 To imagine
An Antony were nature's piece
'gainst fancy,
Condemning shadows quite.
Cleopatra in *Antony and Cleopatra*,
5.2.98–100

Claiming her dream of Antony as superman is nature's masterpiece, more valid than the "shadows" created by fancy, which have no substance.

2 Piece out our imperfections with
your thoughts.
Chorus in *Henry V*, Prologue, 23

"Piece out" = make good.

3 Think, when we talk of horses, that
you see them
Printing their proud hooves i' the
receiving earth;
For 'tis your thoughts that now
must deck our kings.
Chorus in *Henry V*, Prologue, 26–8

Calling on the spectators to use their imagination.

4 Lovers and madmen have such
   seething brains,
   Such shaping fantasies, that appre-
   hend
   More than cool reason ever com-
   prehends.
   The lunatic, the lover, and the poet
   Are of imagination all compact.
   Theseus in *A Midsummer Night's*
   Dream, 5.1.4–8

   In their shaping visions lovers and madmen
   conceive ("apprehend") more than cool reason understands; "compact" = composed.

5 Such tricks hath strong imagina-
   tion
   That, if it would but apprehend
   some joy,
   It comprehends some bringer of
   that joy;
   Or in the night, imagining some
   fear,
   How easy is a bush supposed a
   bear?
   Theseus in *A Midsummer Night's*
   Dream, 5.1.18–22

   The last line is proverbial ("bear" may = "bugbear" or hobgoblin).

6 O, who can hold a fire in his hand
   By thinking on the frosty Caucasus?
   Or cloy the hungry edge of appetite
   By bare imagination of a feast?
   Or wallow naked in December
   snow
   By thinking on fantastic summer's
   heat?
   O no, the apprehension of the good
   Gives but the greater feeling to the
   worse.
   Bolingbroke in *Richard II*, 1.3.294–301

   Rejecting his father's attempt to console him
   in his banishment; "fantastic" = imagined.

Impatience

1 Why, what a wasp-stung and impatient fool
   Art thou to break into this woman's
   mood,
   Tying thine ear to no tongue but
   thine own!
   Northumberland in *Henry IV, Part 1,*
   1.3.236–8

   To Hotspur, who keeps talking, too enraged to
   listen to anyone.

2 I am as poor as Job, my lord, but
   not so patient.
   Falstaff in *Henry IV, Part 2*, 1.2.126–7

   Various calamities reduce Job to poverty, but
   he does not complain (Job 1:13–22).

3   So tedious is this day
   As is the night before some festival
   To an impatient child that hath
      new robes
   And may not wear them.
   Juliet in *Romeo and Juliet*, 3.2.28–31

   Waiting impatiently for Romeo to come to her
   on her wedding night.

Improvement

1 Do thou amend thy face, and I'll
   amend my life.
   Falstaff in *Henry IV, Part 1*, 3.3.24–5

   To Bardolph, whose nose is inflamed with
   drinking.

2 Mend when thou canst, be better at
      thy leisure.
   King Lear in *King Lear*, 2.4.229

   Speaking to his daughter Goneril; "mend" =
   improve.

3   Now is the winter of our discontent
    Made glorious summer by this son
    of York.

King Richard in *Richard III*, 1.1.1–2

The "son of York" is King Edward IV, now ruling England from 1471.

Inconstancy

1   Take, O, take those lips away,
    That so sweetly were forsworn,
    And those eyes, the break of day,
    Lights that do mislead the morn;
    But my kisses bring again, bring
    again,
    Seals of love, but sealed in vain,
    sealed in vain.

Song in *Measure for Measure*, 4.1.1–6

A well-known song; the eyes are lights that
"mislead the morn" by suggesting sunrise and
happiness rather than being betrayed ("for-
sworn").

2   Not Hermia but Helena I love.
    Who will not change a raven for a
    dove?

**Lysander in *A Midsummer Night's
Dream*, 2.2.113–14**

Puck's magic juice has made Lysander switch
his affections to Helena.

3   He wears his faith but as the fash-
    ion of his hat; it ever changes with
    the next block.

**Beatrice in *Much Ado About Nothing*,
1.1.75–7**

Mocking Benedick as one who changes loyalty to friends (and perhaps religious faith) as
often as he changes the fashion of his hat;
"block" = mold.

4   Sigh no more, ladies, sigh no more,
    Men were deceivers ever,
    One foot in sea and one on shore,
    To one thing constant never:
    Then sigh not so, but let them go,
    And be you blithe and bonny,
    Converting all your sounds of woe
    Into Hey nonny, nonny.

**Balthasar in *Much Ado About
Nothing*, 2.3.62–9**

One of Shakespeare's best-known songs.

5   If she be false, O then heaven
    mocks itself!
    I'll not believe't.

Othello in *Othello*, 3.3.278–9

On seeing Desdemona approaching him.

6   Ah, poor our sex! This fault in us I
    find,
    The error of our eye directs our
    mind.
    What error leads must err; O then
    conclude,
    Minds swayed by eyes are full of
    turpitude.

**Cressida in *Troilus and Cressida*,
5.2.109–12**

On abandoning Troilus for Diomedes.

7   Were man
    But constant, he were perfect. That
    one error
    Fills him with faults, makes him
    run through all the sins;
    Inconstancy falls off ere it begins.

**Proteus in *The Two Gentlemen of
Verona*, 5.4.110–13**

He switched his affections from Julia to Sylvia,
and now returns to Julia; "falls off ere it
begins" = is unfaithful, or is a falling off from
virtue, before the lover is aware of it.

Indecision

1   The swan's down feather,
That stands upon the swell at the
   full of tide,
And neither way inclines.

Antony in *Antony and Cleopatra*,
3.2.48–50

His image of Octavia's state of mind as she
goes to Greece with him, and leaves her
brother Octavius in Rome.

2   Like a man to double business
         bound,
I stand in pause where I shall first
   begin,
And both neglect.

Claudius in *Hamlet*, 3.3.41–3

He wants to pray, but cannot because of his
sense of guilt.

3   'Tis with my mind
As with the tide swelled up unto his
   height,
That makes a still-stand, running
   neither way.

Northumberland in *Henry IV, Part 2*,
2.3.62–4

"Still-stand" suggests the moment at which the
tide is about to turn.

4   I am a feather for each wind that
         blows.

Leontes in *The Winter's Tale*, 2.3.154

Inevitability (see also Fate)

1   What cannot be eschewed must be
         embraced.

Page in *The Merry Wives of Windsor*,
5.5.237

Accepting his daughter's marriage to Fenton.

2   *Juliet.* What must be shall be.
     Friar Lawrence.   That's a
        certain text.

Romeo and Juliet, 4.1.21

Proverbial.

3   There is no help.
The bitter disposition of the time
Will have it so.

Paris in *Troilus and Cressida*, 4.1.48–50

On Cressida being sent to the Greek camp in
exchange for Antenor.

Infancy (see also Children)

1   Peace, peace!
Dost thou not see my baby at my
   breast
That sucks the nurse asleep?

Cleopatra in *Antony and Cleopatra*,
5.2.308–10

Her "baby" in this beautiful image is the asp
that is poisoning her.

2   At first the infant,
Mewling and puking in the nurse's
   arms.

Jaques in *As You Like It*, 2.7.143–4

The first of the "seven ages" of man, that of
the infant crying and being sick.

3   I have given suck, and
   know
How tender 'tis to love the babe
   that milks me.

Lady Macbeth in *Macbeth*, 1.7.54–5

Infatuation (see also Adoration, Devotion, Love)

1   There is no living, none,
If Bertram be away. 'Twere all one
That I should love a bright particu-
lar star
And think to wed it, he is so above
me.

Helena in *All's Well That Ends Well*,
1.1.84–5

Expressing her unrequited adoration for a
social superior (" 'Twere all one That" = it is
as if).

2   But now he's gone, and my idola-
trous fancy
Must sanctify his relics.

Helena in *All's Well That Ends Well*,
1.1.97–8

Love ("fancy") turns into quasi-religious worship.

3   These strong Egyptian fetters I
must break,
Or lose myself in dotage.

Antony in *Antony and Cleopatra*,
1.2.116–17

The fetters are those of his love for Cleopatra.

4   I must from this enchanting queen
break off.

Antony in *Antony and Cleopatra*,
1.2.128

Recalling his responsibilities; "queen" puns on
"quean," or whore.

5   Run, run, Orlando, carve on every
tree
The fair, the chaste, the unexpressive she.

Orlando in *As You Like It*, 3.2.10

"Unexpressive" = inexpressible.

6   Loose now and then
A scattered smile, and that I'll live
upon.

Silvius in *As You Like It*, 3.5.103–4

Infatuated with Phebe.

7   Ever till now,
When men were fond, I smiled and
wondered how.

Angelo in *Measure for Measure*,
2.2.185–6

Admitting he is sexually attracted by Isabella;
"fond" = infatuated and foolish.

8   So doth the woodbine the sweet
honeysuckle
Gently entwist; the female ivy so
Enrings the barky fingers of the
elm.
O how I love thee! How I dote on
thee!

**Titania in *A Midsummer Night's
Dream*, 4.1.42–5**

Puck's magic juice has made her fall in love
with Bottom; "woodbine" is convolvulus.

9   One fairer than my love! The all-
seeing sun
Ne'er saw her match since first the
world begun.

Romeo in *Romeo and Juliet*, 1.2.92–3

He is infatuated with Rosaline.

10   Cesario, by the roses of the spring,
By maidhood, honor, truth, and
everything,

I love thee so, that maugre all thy
pride,
Nor wit nor reason can my passion
hide.

Olivia in *Twelfth Night*, 3.1.149–52

She doesn't yet know that Cesario is Viola in
disguise; "maugre" = in spite of.

Infidelity

1 She was false as water.

Othello in *Othello*, 5.2.134

Proverbial; "false" = unstable, unreliable.

Inflexibility

1 I'll not be made a soft and dull-eyed
fool
To shake the head, relent, and sigh,
and yield
To Christian intercessors.

**Shylock in *The Merchant of Venice*,
3.3.14–16**

Ingratitude

1 Blow, blow thou winter wind,
Thou art not so unkind
As man's ingratitude.

Amiens in *As You Like It*, 2.7.174–7

Setting a winter scene in the forest of Arden.

2 Ingratitude is monstrous, and for
the multitude to be ingrateful were
to make a monster of the multitude.

Third Citizen in *Coriolanus*, 2.3.9–11

Arguing that the people should be grateful to
Caius Martius for defeating the Volsces.

3 Run to your houses, fall upon your
knees,
Pray to the gods to intermit the
plague
That needs must light on this
ingratitude.

Marullus in *Julius Caesar*, 1.1.53–5

Addressing working men who have come to
see Caesar, and have forgotten Pompey
(hence their "ingratitude").

4 This was the most unkindest cut of
all;
For when the noble Caesar saw him
stab,
Ingratitude, more strong than traitors' arms,
Quite vanquished him.

Mark Antony in *Julius Caesar*, 3.2.183–6

Pointing to the wound Brutus made.

5 The hedge-sparrow fed the cuckoo
so long
That it had its head bit off by its
young.

Fool in *King Lear*, 1.4.215–6

The cuckoo lays its eggs in another bird's nest,
and so is an emblem of ingratitude; Lear is the
sparrow and Goneril, his daughter, the
cuckoo.

6 Ingratitude, thou marble-hearted
fiend,
More hideous when thou show'st
thee in a child
Than the sea-monster.

King Lear in *King Lear*, 1.4.259–61

Reacting to Goneril's demand that he send
away half his train of followers.

7   Turn all her mother's pains and
        benefits
    To laughter and contempt, that she
        may feel
    How sharper than a serpent's tooth
        it is
    To have a thankless child!

    King Lear in *King Lear*, 1.4.286–9

    Cursing his daughter Goneril.

8   When the mind's free,
    The body's delicate; this tempest in
        my mind
    Doth from my senses take all feel-
        ing else,
    Save what beats there—filial ingrat-
        itude!

    King Lear in *King Lear*, 3.4.11–14

    He is wandering bareheaded in a "contentious
    storm" of rain and wind.

9   O, see the monstrousness of
        man
    When he looks out in an ungrateful
        shape!

    **First Stranger in *Timon of Athens*,
    3.2.72–3**

    Commenting on those who benefited from
    Timon's generosity, and refuse to help him in
    his need.

10 I hate ingratitude more in a man
    Than lying, vainness, babbling,
        drunkenness,
    Or any taint of vice whose strong
        corruption
    Inhabits our frail blood.

    Viola in *Twelfth Night*, 3.4.354–7

    To Antonio, who mistakes her, in her disguise
    as Cesario, for her brother Sebastian.

Injustice

1   Some rise by sin, and some by
        virtue fall.

    Escalus in *Measure for Measure*, 2.1.38

    Thinking of the generally virtuous Claudio,
    sentenced to death by Angelo.

Innocence

1   Some innocents 'scape not the
        thunderbolt.

    **Cleopatra in *Antony and Cleopatra*,
    2.5.77**

    Attacking the messenger who has brought bad
    news.

2   Never so much as in a thought
        unborn
    Did I offend your Highness.

    Rosalind in *As You Like It*, 1.3.51–2

    Accused of treason by her uncle, Rosalind
    protests her innocence.

3   Our kinsman Gloucester is as inno-
        cent
    From meaning treason to our royal
        person
    As is the sucking lamb or harmless
        dove.

    **King Henry in *Henry VI, Part 2*,
    3.1.69–71**

    The comparisons are proverbial.

4   It will help me nothing
    To plead mine innocence, for that
        dye is on me
    Which makes my whit'st part black.

Buckingham in *Henry VIII*, 1.1.207–9

On being arrested as a traitor; "nothing" = not at all.

5   I have done no harm. But I
        remember now
    I am in this earthly world, where to
        do harm
    Is often laudable, to do good some-
        time
    Accounted dangerous folly.
    Lady Macduff in *Macbeth*, 4.2.74–7

6   We were as twinned lambs that did
        frisk i'the sun,
    And bleat the one at th'other.
        What we changed
    Was innocence for innocence. We
        knew not
    The doctrine of ill-doing, nor
        dreamed
    That any did.
    **Polixenes in *The Winter's Tale*,
    1.2.67–71**

    On his childhood friendship with Leontes;
    "changed" = exchanged.

7   The silence often of pure innocence
    Persuades when speaking fails.
    Paulina in *The Winter's Tale*, 2.2.39–40

    Proposing to present Hermione's baby to the
    king, Leontes.

8   If powers divine
    Behold our human actions—as
        they do—
    I doubt not then but innocence
        shall make
    False accusation blush.
    **Hermione in *The Winter's Tale*,
    3.2.28–31**

Innovation

1   Things done without example in
        their issue
    Are to be feared.
    King Henry in *Henry VIII*, 1.2.90–1

    On learning that Cardinal Wolsey has
    imposed a tax without precedent.

2   Who are the violets now
    That strew the green lap of the new-
        come spring?
    Duchess of York in *Richard II*, 5.2.46–7

    Asking her son Aumerle to tell her who is in
    favor with the new King Henry IV.

Insects (see also Creatures)

1   When the sun shines, let foolish
        gnats make sport,
    But creep in crannies, when he
        hides his beams.
    **Antipholus of Syracuse in *The Com-
    edy of Errors*, 2.2.30–1**

2   I think this be the most villainous
    house in all London road for fleas.
    **Second Carrier in *Henry IV, Part 1*,
    2.1.14–15**

    "House" = inn.

3   Poor harmless fly,
    That with his pretty buzzing
        melody
    Came here to make us merry. And
        thou hast killed him!
    Titus in *Titus Andronicus*, 3.2.63–5

    To his brother Marcus; Titus is going mad.

Instinct

1   Beware instinct—the lion will not
    touch the true prince.
    Instinct is a great matter.
    Falstaff in *Henry IV, Part 1*, 2.4.271–2

    Justifying as instinct his failure to fight the dis-
    guised Hal; "the lion will not touch the true
    prince" is an ancient belief.

Insults

1   I saw her hand, she has a leathern
    hand,
    A freestone-colored hand. I verily
    did think
    That her old gloves were on, but
    'twas her hands.
    Rosalind in *As You Like It*, 4.3.24–6

    Making Phebe out to be ugly; "freestone" =
    sandstone.

2   He is deformèd, crooked, old and
    sere,
    Ill-faced, worse bodied, shapeless
    everywhere;
    Vicious, ungentle, foolish, blunt,
    unkind,
    Stigmatical in making, worse in
    mind.
    Adriana in *The Comedy of Errors*,
    4.2.19–22

    On her husband, who, she thinks, has been
    wooing her sister Luciana; "stigmatical" =
    deformed.

3   Hang thyself in thine own heir-
    apparent garters!
    Falstaff in *Henry IV, Part 1*, 2.2.43–4

    A friendly insult to Prince Hal, heir to the
    throne.

4   Thou clay-brained guts, thou
    knotty-pated fool, thou whoreson,
    obscene, greasy tallow-catch.
    Prince Hal in *Henry IV, Part 1*,
    2.4.226–8

    Abusing the notoriously fat Falstaff for his lies;
    "knotty-pated" = blockheaded; "tallow-catch"
    = vessel to catch fat drippings.

5   This sanguine coward, this bed-
    presser, this horse-back-breaker,
    this huge hill of flesh.
    Prince Hal in *Henry IV, Part 1*,
    2.4.241–3

    Insulting Falstaff.

6   You starveling, you eel-skin, you
    dried neat's tongue, you bull's piz-
    zle, you stock-fish!
    Falstaff in *Henry IV, Part 1*, 2.4.244–5

    Getting his own back by insulting Hal; "neat's
    tongue" = ox tongue; "stock-fish" was dried
    cod.

7   O for breath to utter what is like
    thee! You tailor's yard, you sheath,
    you bowcase, you vile standing
    tuck.
    Falstaff in *Henry IV, Part 1*, 2.4.246–8

    Insulting Hal; "tuck" = rapier.

8   I scorn you, scurvy companion.
    What, you poor, base, rascally,
    cheating, lack-linen mate! Away,
    you moldy rogue, away! I am meat
    for your master.
    Doll Tearsheet in *Henry IV, Part 2*,
    2.4.123–6

    Dismissing Pistol; "lack-linen mate" = fellow
    without a shirt.

9   His wit's as thick as Tewkesbury
    mustard, there's no more conceit in
    him than is in a mallet.

Falstaff in *Henry IV, Part 2*, 2.4.240–2

Tewkesbury is a small town in Gloucestershire; "conceit" = imagination. He is speaking of Poins, who overhears his insult.

10 You blocks, you stones, you worse than senseless things!

Marullus in *Julius Caesar*, 1.1.35

To the working men who have forgotten Pompey and come out to greet Caesar.

11 Thou whoreson zed, thou unnecessary letter!

Kent in *King Lear*, 2.2.64

Expressing his contempt for Oswald, Goneril's steward.

12 A very superficial, ignorant, unweighing fellow.

Lucio in *Measure for Measure*, 3.2.139–40

Abusing the Duke to a Friar (the Duke in disguise); "unweighing" = injudicious.

13 Thou call'st me dog before thou hadst a cause,
But since I am a dog, beware my fangs.

Shylock in *The Merchant of Venice*, 3.3.6–7

Threatening Antonio.

14 Old, cold, withered, and of intolerable entrails.

Page in *The Merry Wives of Windsor*, 5.5.153–4

Page's description of Falstaff and his great belly.

15 How low am I, thou painted maypole? Speak!

Hermia in *A Midsummer Night's Dream*, 3.2.296

Angry with the taller Helena.

16 *Conrade.* Here, man, I am at thy elbow.
Borachio. Mass, and my elbow itched; I thought there would a scab follow.

Much Ado About Nothing, 3.3.98–100

"Scab" = scoundrel, as well as the literal meaning.

17 *Conrade.* Away! You are an ass, you are an ass.
Dogberry. Dost thou not suspect my place? Dost thou not suspect my years?

Much Ado About Nothing, 4.2.73–5

As usual getting the word wrong; Dogberry means "respect," not "suspect."

18 That bottled spider, that foul bunch-backed toad.

Queen Elizabeth in *Richard III*, 4.4.81

Referring to Richard; spiders and toads were thought to be venomous.

19 Thou flea, thou nit, thou winter-cricket thou.

Petruchio in *The Taming of the Shrew*, 4.3.109

An example of Petruchio's insults, here directed at a tailor; a "nit" is the egg of a louse.

Integrity (see also Honesty, Truth)

1 The good I stand on is my truth and honesty.

Archbishop Cranmer in *Henry VIII*, 5.1.122

He is about to face a hostile council.

2   When you do find him, or alive or
     dead,
     He will be found like Brutus, like
     himself.
     Lucilius in *Julius Caesar*, 5.4.24–5

To Antony, searching for Brutus now that he
and Octavius have won the battle of Philippi.

3   Truth hath a quiet breast.
     Mowbray in *Richard II*, 1.3.96

Protesting his loyalty as he is about to fight
Henry Bolingbroke.

Investment

1   *Douglas.* Now remains a sweet
     reversion—
     We may boldly spend, upon the
     hope
     Of what is to come in.
     A comfort of retirement lives in
     this.
     Hotspur. A rendezvous, a home to
     fly unto.
     Henry IV, Part 1, 4.1.53–7

Thinking of Northumberland and his army,
not with them now, as a reserve for the future;
taken in their modern sense, the lines suggest
an investment plan; "reversion" = inheritance.

Invitations

1   *Cassius.* Will you dine with me
     tomorrow?
     Casca. Ay, if I be alive, and your
     mind hold, and your dinner be
     worth the eating.
     Julius Caesar, 1.2.290–2

2   I am not bid for love, they flatter
     me.
     **Shylock in *The Merchant of Venice*,
     2.5.13**

On being invited to eat supper with Christians.

Isolation (see also Solitude)

1   Now I stand as one upon a rock,
     Environed with a wilderness of sea,
     Who marks the waxing tide grow
     wave by wave,
     Expecting ever when some envious
     surge
     Will in his brinish bowels swallow
     him.
     Titus in *Titus Andronicus*, 3.1.93–7

On finding his daughter Lavinia "ravished,"
and with her hands cut off and tongue cut out;
"his" = its.

Jealousy

1   How many fond fools serve mad
     jealousy?
     **Luciana in *The Comedy of Errors*,
     2.1.116**

2   The venom clamors of a jealous
     woman
     Poisons more deadly than a mad
     dog's tooth.
     **The Abbess in *The Comedy of Errors*,
     5.1.69–70**

The Abbess has drawn from Adriana the con-
fession that she constantly reproached her
husband about his unfaithfulness and supposedly drove him mad.

3   Thy jealous fits
     Have scared thy husband from the
     use of wits.
     **The Abbess in *The Comedy of Errors*,
     5.1.85–6**

To Adriana, whose reproaches have supposedly driven her husband Antipholus mad.

4 The Count is neither sad, nor sick,
nor merry, nor well; but civil count,
civil as an orange, and something of
that jealous complexion.

Beatrice in Much Ado About Nothing,
2.1.293–5

Referring to the jealous Claudio; "civil" puns
on "Seville," where the bitter-sweet oranges
used to make marmalade are grown.

5 I do suspect the lusty Moor
Hath leaped into my seat; the
thought whereof
Doth, like a poisonous mineral,
gnaw my inwards.

Iago in Othello, 2.1.295–7

"Leaped into my seat" = made love to my
wife, Emilia.

6 O, beware, my lord, of jealousy!
It is the green-eyed monster which
doth mock
The meat it feeds on.

Iago in Othello, 3.3.165–7

Iago here plants the idea of jealousy in Othello; "mocks the meat it feeds on" = torments
the victim who suffers jealousy.

7 O, what damnèd minutes tells he
o'er
Who dotes, yet doubts; suspects, yet
strongly loves!

Iago in Othello, 3.3.169–70

The clash of love and suspicion in Othello.

8 Good God, the souls of all my tribe
defend
From jealousy!

Iago in Othello, 3.3.175–6

9 Trifles light as air
Are to the jealous confirmation
strong

As proofs of holy writ.

Iago in Othello, 3.3.322–4

So he works to make Othello jealous; "holy
writ" = scripture.

10 Dangerous conceits are in their
natures poisons,
Which at the first are scarce found
to distaste,
But with a little act upon the blood
Burn like the mines of sulphur.

Iago in Othello, 3.3.326–9

"Conceits" = fancies; mines of sulphur were
associated with the areas around Sicily and
the ever-burning volcano, Mount Etna.

11 But jealous souls will not be
answered so;
They are not ever jealous for the
cause,
But jealous for they're jealous. It is
a monster
Begot upon itself, born on itself.

Emilia in Othello, 3.4.159–62

Responding to Desdemona's consciousness
that she has given Othello no cause for jealousy.

12 Then must you speak
Of one that loved not wisely but too
well;
Of one not easily jealous, but being
wrought,
Perplexed in the extreme; of one
whose hand,
Like the base Judean threw a pearl
away
Richer than all his tribe.

Othello in Othello, 5.2.343–8

"Judean" may refer to the betrayal of Christ by
Judas, who threw away the "pearl of great
price" (Matthew 13:46) which is heaven; but
the earliest text reads "Indian," suggesting an
ignorant East or West Indian who does not
know the value of a precious stone.

Jewels

1   The jewel that we find, we stoop
     and take't
     Because we see it; but what we do
     not see
     We tread upon and never think of
     it.

     Angelo in *Measure for Measure*,
     2.1.24–6

2   Never so rich a gem
     Was set in worse than gold.

     Prince of Morocco in *The Merchant of*
     Venice, 2.7.54–5

     Convincing himself that Portia's image will be
     in the golden casket.

Jokes (see also Laughter, Merriment)

1   His eye begets occasion for his wit,
     For every object that the one doth
     catch
     The other turns to a mirth-moving
     jest.

     Rosaline in *Love's Labor's Lost*,
     2.1.69–71

     Describing Berowne.

2   *Maria.* Not a word with him but a
     jest.
     Boyet. And every jest but a word.

     Love's Labor's Lost, 2.1.216

     Speaking of the witty Berowne.

3   A jest's prosperity lies in the ear
     Of him that hears it, never in the
     tongue

Of him that makes it.

Rosaline in *Love's Labor's Lost*,
5.2.861–3

4   He jests at scars that never felt a
     wound.

     Romeo in *Romeo and Juliet*, 2.2.1

     Referring to Mercutio, who has been teasing
     him for being lovesick.

Joy (see also Happiness)

1   I wish you all joy of the worm.

     Clown in *Antony and Cleopatra*, 5.2.260

     His parting words to Cleopatra as he leaves
     her the asps or snakes she uses to kill herself.

2   If he be sick with joy, he'll recover
     without physic.

     Prince Hal in *Henry IV, Part 2*, 4.5.15

     Misunderstanding the nature of his father's ill-
     ness.

3   Silence is the perfectest herald of
     joy.

     Claudio in *Much Ado About Nothing*,
     2.1.306

     Unable to express his happiness on being
     offered Hero in marriage.

4   It gives me wonder great as my
     content
     To see you here before me.

     Othello in *Othello*, 2.1.183–4

     Greeting Desdemona on his safe arrival in
     Cyprus.

5   Beseech you, sir, be merry; you
     have cause,

So have we all, of joy.

Gonzalo in *The Tempest*, 2.1.1–2

Appealing to Alonso to be joyful after coming safely ashore.

6 There might you have beheld one joy crown another, so and in such manner that it seemed sorrow wept to take leave of them, for their joy waded in tears.

Third Gentleman in *The Winter's Tale*, 5.2.43–6

On the reconciliation of Leontes and Polixenes.

Judgment (see also Justice, Law)

1 Censure me in your wisdom, and awake your senses, that you may the better judge.

Brutus in *Julius Caesar*, 3.2.16–17

To the people; "censure" = judge.

2 To offend and judge are distinct offices,
And of opposèd natures.

Portia in *The Merchant of Venice*, 2.9.61–2

To the Prince of Aragon, who has judged badly in choosing the silver casket, and is offended because he feels he deserves better.

3 Seven times tried that judgment is That did never choose amiss.
Some there be that shadows kiss, Such have but a shadow's bliss.

Prince of Aragon in *The Merchant of Venice*, 2.9.64–7

The message in the silver casket telling him his hopes are illusory.

4 What judgment shall I dread, doing no wrong?

Shylock in *The Merchant of Venice*, 4.1.89

Going by the letter of the law.

5 A Daniel come to judgment! Yea, a Daniel!
O wise young judge, how I do honor thee!

Shylock in *The Merchant of Venice*, 4.1.223–4

On Portia, who argues the law must take its course. In the Apocrypha, Daniel rescues Susannah from her accusers, as Portia will rescue Antonio from Shylock's cruelty.

6 The urging of that word "judgment" hath bred a kind of remorse in me.

Second Murderer in *Richard III*, 1.4.107–8

Commissioned to murder Clarence, he hesitates at the thought of doomsday, or the Day of Judgment (see Matthew 10:15, etc.).

Justice (see also Judgment, Law, Punishment)

1 'Tis the sport to have the enginer Hoist with his own petard.

Hamlet in *Hamlet*, 3.4.206–7

"Enginer" = maker of military "engines" or devices; "hoist" = blown up by; "petard" = explosive device.

2 As a woodcock to mine own springe, Osric:
I am justly killed with mine own treachery.

Laertes in *Hamlet*, 5.2.306–7

He is wounded by the poisoned rapier he intended for Hamlet; "springe" = snare.

3 Sir, I desire you do me right and
   justice,
   And to bestow your pity on me; for
   I am a most poor woman, and a
   stranger,
   Born out of your dominions.
   Queen Katherine in *Henry VIII*,
   2.4.13–16

At the divorce proceedings, she appeals to her
husband, Henry VIII.

4 Remember March, the Ides of
   March remember.
   Did not great Julius bleed for jus-
   tice' sake?
   What villain touched his body, that
   did stab
   And not for justice?
   Brutus in *Julius Caesar*, 4.3.18–21

5   Take physic, pomp,
   Expose thyself to feel what wretches
   feel,
   That thou mayst shake the super-
   flux to them
   And show the heavens more just.
   King Lear in *King Lear*, 3.4.33–6

"Superflux" = superfluous possessions.

6 A man may see how this world goes
   with no eyes. Look with thine ears;
   see how yond justice rails upon
   yond simple thief. Hark in thine
   ear: change places, and handy-
   dandy, which is the justice, which is
   the thief?
   King Lear in *King Lear*, 4.6.150–4

Addressing the blind Gloucester.

7 Through tattered clothes great vices
   do appear;
   Robes and furred gowns hide all.
   Plate sin with gold,

And the strong lance of justice
   hurtless breaks:
   Arm it in rags, a pigmy's straw does
   pierce it.
   King Lear in *King Lear*, 4.6.164–7

Or, it is often said now, there is one justice for
the rich, and another for the poor.

8 The gods are just, and of our pleas-
   ant vices
   Make instruments to plague us.
   Edgar in *King Lear*, 5.3.171–2

Speaking to his half-brother, the dying
Edmund, whose vices have led to his death,
just as their father Gloucester's vices have
brought about his blinding.

9   This even-handed justice
   Commends the ingredients of our
   poisoned chalice
   To our own lips.
   Macbeth in *Macbeth*, 1.7.10–12

Contemplating murdering Duncan; "even-
handed" = impartial.

10 Liberty plucks justice by the nose.
   Duke in *Measure for Measure*, 1.3.29

"Liberty" = license, or excessive freedom.

11   I not deny
   The jury, passing on the prisoner's
   life,
   May in the sworn twelve have a
   thief or two
   Guiltier than him they try. What's
   open made to justice,
   That justice seizes.
   Angelo in *Measure for Measure*,
   2.1.18–22

To Escalus, who has been pleading to save
Claudio from a sentence of death.

12 Under your good correction, I have
seen
When, after execution, judgment
hath
Repented o'er his doom.

Provost in *Measure for Measure,*
2.2.10–12

Cautioning Angelo against the too hasty execution of Claudio; "doom" = sentence.

13 He who the sword of heaven would
bear
Must be as holy as severe,
Pattern in himself to know,
Grace to stand and virtue go.

Duke in *Measure for Measure,* 3.2.261–4

On the need for the judge to be a model of
virtue, and have grace to be upright, as well
as virtue to lead.

14 Haste still pays haste, and leisure
answers leisure;
Like doth quit like, and measure
still for measure.

Duke in *Measure for Measure,*
5.1.410–11

Alluding to Matthew 7:2, "with what measure
ye mete, it shall be measured unto you again."

15 As thou urgest justice, be assured
Thou shalt have justice more than
thou desirest.

Portia in *The Merchant of Venice,*
4.1.315–6

The law says that Shylock must not shed the
blood of a Christian.

16 Justice is feasting while the widow
weeps.

The Rape of Lucrece, 906

Lamenting after being raped, Lucrece
becomes bitter.

Kindness

1 Kindness, nobler ever than revenge.

Oliver in *As You Like It,* 4.1.128

Speaking of Orlando's resolve to rescue his
brother from danger.

2 Yet I do fear thy nature;
It is too full o' the milk of human
kindness
To catch the nearest way.

Lady Macbeth in *Macbeth,* 1.5.16–18

Fearing Macbeth is too gentle to murder the
king ("catch the nearest way").

3 A kind heart he hath. A woman
would run through fire and water
for such a kind heart.

Mistress Quickly in *The Merry Wives
of Windsor,* 3.4.102–4

Speaking of Fenton, one of the suitors for the
hand of Anne Page.

4 Timon will to the woods, where he
shall find
Th'unkindest beast more kinder
than mankind.

Timon in *Timon of Athens,* 4.1.35–6

The beginning of his misanthropy.

Kings, see Royalty

Kinship

1   *Claudius.* But now, my cousin
     Hamlet, and my son—
     Hamlet. [Aside] A little more than
     kin, and less than kind.

     Hamlet, 1.2.64–5

     "Cousin" = kinsman, here a nephew; Hamlet
     is more closely related than a nephew, since
     his uncle has married his mother, yet less close
     than a son, and not well disposed to Claudius.

Kissing (see also Love)

1   Kingdoms are clay; our dungy earth
     alike
     Feeds beast as man; the nobleness
     of life
     Is to do thus—when such a mutual
     pair
     And such a twain can do't.

     Antony in *Antony and Cleopatra*,
     1.1.35–8

     Rating an embrace with Cleopatra as worth
     more than empire.

2   If she first meet the curlèd Antony,
     He'll make demand of her, and
     spend that kiss
     Which is my heaven to have.

     Cleopatra in *Antony and Cleopatra*,
     5.2.301–2

     Referring to her servant Iras, who has just
     died; Cleopatra expects to meet Antony in
     death.

3   O, a kiss
     Long as my exile, sweet as my
     revenge!

     Coriolanus in *Coriolanus*, 5.3.44–5

Greeting his wife, Virgilia, who comes with
his son and mother to plead with him not to
make war on Rome.

4   Ere I could
     Give him that parting kiss which I
     had set
     Betwixt two charming words,
     comes in my father,
     And like the tyrannous breathing of
     the north
     Shakes all our buds from growing.

     Imogen in *Cymbeline*, 1.3.33–7

     Recalling her parting from Posthumus, her
     husband, who is banished; "charming words"
     = words which may protect him from evil;
     "north" = north wind.

5   I understand thy kisses, and thou
     mine,
     And that's a feeling disputation.

     Mortimer in *Henry IV, Part 1*, 3.1.202–3

     An Englishman speaking to his Welsh wife;
     they do not speak each other's languages;
     "feeling disputation" = exchange of feelings.

6   By my troth, I kiss thee with a most
     constant heart.

     Doll Tearsheet in *Henry IV, Part 2*,
     2.4.269–70

     The old whore speaking to old Falstaff.

7   I can express no kinder sign of love
     Than this kind kiss.

     King Henry in *Henry VI, Part 2*,
     1.1.18–19

     Welcoming his French queen to England.

8   *Beatrice.* Let me go with that I
     came, which is, with knowing
     what hath passed between you
     and Claudio.

Benedick. Only foul words; and thereupon I will kiss thee.

Beatrice. Foul words is but foul wind, and foul wind is but foul breath, and foul breath is noisome; therefore I will depart unkissed.

Much Ado About Nothing, 5.2.47–54

Benedick reports he has not fought with Claudio, and Beatrice plays on the idea of the proverb, "words are but wind."

9 Kiss me, Kate; we will be married o'Sunday.

Petruchio in The Taming of the Shrew, 2.1.324

Speaking to the shrew, Katherine; the well-known musical, based on the play, is called "Kiss Me Kate."

Lament

1 The poor soul sat sighing by a sycamore tree,
Sing all a green willow;
Her hand on her bosom, her head on her knee,
Sing willow, willow, willow.

Desdemona in Othello, 4.3.40–3

Reworking an old song, Shakespeare changed the sex of the lover to suit Desdemona's sense of being forsaken.

Language (see also Solecisms, Speech, Words)

1   Thy tongue
Makes Welsh as sweet as ditties highly penned,

Sung by a fair queen in a summer's bower,
With ravishing division, to her lute.

Mortimer in Henry IV, Part 1, 3.1.205–8

To his wife, whose speech in Welsh he does not understand.

2 The Prince but studies his companions
Like a strange tongue, wherein, to gain the language,
'Tis needful that the most immodest word
Be looked upon and learnt, which once attained,
Your highness knows, comes to no further use
But to be known and hated.

Warwick in Henry IV, Part 2, 4.4.68–73

On Prince Hal as using Falstaff and others for his education.

3 I will tell thee in French—which I am sure will hang upon my tongue like a new-married wife about her husband's neck, hardly to be shook off.

King Henry in Henry V, 5.2.178–81

On his difficulty in finding French words in which to make love to Katherine.

4 It will be proved to thy face that thou hast men about thee that usually talk of a noun and a verb and such abominable words as no Christian ear can endure to hear.

Jack Cade in Henry VI, Part 2, 4.7.37–41

An illiterate peasant accusing Lord Saye of treason.

5 Those that understood him smiled
at one another and shook their
heads; but for mine own part, it was
Greek to me.

Casca in *Julius Caesar*, 1.2.282–4

Reporting Caesar's speech to the people.

6 They have been at a great feast of
languages and stolen the scraps.

Moth in *Love's Labor's Lost*, 5.1.36–7

Moth is looking at Armado, Holofernes and
Nathaniel, all lovers of wordiness.

7 The language I have learnt these
forty years,
My native English, now I must
forgo,
And now my tongue's use is to me
no more
Than an unstringèd viol or a harp.

Mowbray in *Richard II*, 1.3.159–62

On being banished to foreign parts; a "viol"
was the forerunner of the modern violin.

8 You taught me language, and my
profit on't
Is, I know how to curse. The red
plague rid you
For learning me your language!

Caliban in *The Tempest*, 1.2.363–5

To Prospero; "red" refers to red sores caused
by plague.

9 *Sir Toby Belch. Pourquoi*, my dear
knight?
Sir Andrew Aguecheek. What is
"*pourquoi*"? Do, or not do? I
would I had bestowed that time in
the tongues that I have in fencing,
dancing, and bear-baiting. O had
I but followed the arts!

Twelfth Night, 1.3.90–4

"Tongues" = languages; Sir Andrew does not
understand the simplest French, "pourquoi" =
why; setting dogs to bait bears was a popular
sport in Shakespeare's day.

Last Words

1 The rest is silence.

Hamlet in *Hamlet*, 5.2.358

2 *Et tu, Brute?*—Then fall, Caesar!

Caesar in *Julius Caesar*, 3.1.77

There is no classical source for Caesar's
famous last words, which seem to have
become well-known in Shakespeare's age,
though he did not invent them.

3 They say the tongues of dying men
Enforce attention like deep harmony.
Where words are scarce, they are
seldom spent in vain,
For they breathe truth that breathe
their words in pain.

John of Gaunt in *Richard II*, 2.1.5–8

Speaking on his deathbed.

4 Mount, mount, my soul! thy seat is
up on high,
Whilst my gross flesh sinks down-
ward, here to die.

King Richard in *Richard II*, 5.5. 111–2

It was proverbial that "dying men speak true."

5 A horse, a horse, my kingdom for a
horse!

King Richard in *Richard III*, 5.4.13

His last desperate cry on the field of battle
before he is killed.

6 O true apothecary!
Thy drugs are quick. Thus with a
kiss I die.

Romeo in *Romeo and Juliet*, 5.3.119–20

He kisses Juliet, supposing her to be dead.

7 This is the chase;
I am gone for ever.

**Antigonus in *The Winter's Tale*,
3.3.57–8**

He runs off "pursued by a bear" (stage direction).

Lateness

1 I am glad I was up so late, for that's
the reason I was up so early.

Cloten in *Cymbeline*, 2.3.33–4

He has been gaming all night, and so was
early enough to fee musicians to sing at sunrise to wake Imogen.

2 Better three hours too soon than a
minute too late.

**Ford in *The Merry Wives of Windsor*,
2.2.312–3**

3 Pray God we may make haste and
come too late!

King Richard in *Richard II*, 1.4.64

On his way to the dying John of Gaunt,
Richard hopes to find his uncle dead.

4 Better once than never, for never
too late.

**Petruchio in *The Taming of the Shrew*,
5.1.150**

To Katherine, on her agreeing to kiss him in
the street; proverbial: "better late than never"
and "it is never too late to mend."

5 *Sir Andrew Aguecheek.* I know, to
be up late is to be up late.

Sir Toby Belch. A false conclusion.
I hate it as an unfilled can. To be
up after midnight and to go to
bed then, is early; so that to go to
bed after midnight is to go to·bed
betimes.

***Twelfth Night*, 2.3.4–9**

Sir Toby's excuse for staying up drinking.

Laughter (see also Jokes, Merriment)

1 O, you shall see him laugh till his
face be like a wet cloak ill laid up.

Falstaff in *Henry IV, Part 2*, 5.1.84–5

2 The lamentable change is from the
best,
The worst returns to laughter.

Edgar in *King Lear*, 4.1.5–6

An outcast, and disguised as a beggar Edgar
reflects on his state. The idea that at the worst
things can only get better was proverbial.

Law (see also Judgment, Justice, Punishment)

1 In the corrupted currents of this
world
Offense's gilded hand may shove by
justice,
And oft 'tis seen the wicked prize
itself
Buys out the law; but 'tis not so
above:
There is no shuffling.

Claudius in *Hamlet*, 3.3.57–61

As king, Claudius is the law in Denmark; "currents" = transactions; "gilded" = bribing;
"shove by" = push aside; "shuffling" = evasion.

2   Resolution thus fubbed as it is with
     the rusty curb of old father antic
     the law.

Falstaff in *Henry IV, Part 1*, 1.2.60–1

Falstaff's "resolution" has to do with robbery,
thwarted ("fubbed") by the law.

3   Faith, I have been a truant in the
     law,
     And never yet could frame my will
     to it,
     And therefore frame the law unto
     my will.

Suffolk in *Henry VI, Part 1*, 2.4.7–9

Having neglected study of the law ("been a
truant"), he makes his own, since he cannot
adapt or bend ("frame") his will to it.

4   I have perhaps some shallow spirit
     of judgment,
     But in these nice sharp quillets of
     the law,
     Good faith, I am no wiser than a
     daw.

Warwick in *Henry VI, Part 1*, 2.4.16–18

"Sharp quillets" = nice distinctions; a "daw" is
a jackdaw, proverbial for foolishness.

5   And what makes robbers bold but
     too much lenity?

Clifford in *Henry VI, Part 3*, 2.6.22

6   The law I bear no malice for my
     death;
     'T has done upon the premises but
     justice;
     But those that sought it I would
     wish more Christians.

Buckingham in *Henry VIII*, 2.1.62–4

7   We must not make a scarecrow of
     the law,

Setting it up to fear the birds of
     prey,
     And let it keep one shape, till cus-
     tom make it
     Their perch and not their terror.

Angelo in *Measure for Measure*, 2.1.1–4

Angelo favors harsh sentencing; "fear" =
frighten.

8   The law hath not been dead,
        though it hath slept.

Angelo in *Measure for Measure*, 2.2.90

Reminding Isabella that the laws have existed
even though they have not been enforced for
some time.

9   Wrest once the law to your author-
     ity:
     To do a great right, do a little
     wrong.

**Bassanio in *The Merchant of Venice*,
4.1.215–6**

Asking the Duke to bend the law in order to
curb Shylock.

10   I am a humble suitor to your
     virtues;
     For pity is the virtue of the law,
     And none but tyrants use it cruelly.

Alcibiades in *Timon of Athens*, 3.5.7–9

Begging the senators of Athens for the life of a
friend who has killed a man in a duel.

11   There is a law in each well-ordered
     nation
     To curb those raging appetites that
     are
     Most disobedient and refractory.

**Hector in *Troilus and Cressida*,
2.2.180–2**

"Refractory" = willful, stubborn.

Lawyers

1 The first thing we do, let's kill all
the lawyers.

Dick the Butcher in _Henry VI, Part 2_,
4.2.76–7

The first aim of the rebels (Shakespeare's version of the Peasants' Revolt of 1381).

2 _Kent._ This is nothing, Fool.
Fool. Then 'tis like the breath of an
unfeed lawyer, you gave me nothing for't.

King Lear, 1.4.128–30

Kent comments on the Fool's rhymes.

Learning (see also Books, Education, Study)

1 He was a scholar, and a ripe and
good one,
Exceeding wise, fair-spoken and
persuading.

Griffith in _Henry VIII_, 4.2.51–2

Speaking of Wolsey's good qualities.

23 To be a well-favored man is the gift
of fortune; but to write and read
comes by nature.

**Dogberry in _Much Ado About
Nothing_, 3.3.14–16**

The comic constable, splendidly muddled as
usual, has a low opinion of reading and writing; "well-favored" = good-looking.

3 For your writing and reading, let
that appear when there is no need
of such vanity.

**Dogberry in _Much Ado About
Nothing_, 3.3.20–2**

Priding himself on his own illiteracy.

4 O this learning, what a thing it is!

Gremio in _The Taming of the Shrew_,
1.2.159

The foolish Gremio admires learning.

Lechery (see also Lust, Sex)

1 Sparrows must not build in his
house-eaves, because they are lecherous.

Lucio in _Measure for Measure_, 3.2.175–6

Criticizing the puritanical Angelo.

2 An honest woman's son, for indeed
my father did something smack,
something grow to, he had a kind
of taste.

**Launcelot Gobbo in _The Merchant of
Venice_, 2.2.16–18**

Meaning that his father was known for lechery, and so was not "honest" = honorable.

3 It is impossible you should see this,
Were they as prime as goats, as hot
as monkeys,
As salt as wolves in pride, and fools
as gross
As ignorance made drunk.

Iago in _Othello_, 3.3.402–5

Goats were proverbially lecherous, and monkeys noted for lust, as were wolves in heat;
"salt" = lustful; Iago protests that Othello cannot see Cassio and Desdemona in the act of
lust.

4   There's language in her eye, her
      cheek, her lip,
    Nay, her foot speaks; her wanton
      spirits look out
    At every joint and motive of her
      body.

Ulysses in *Troilus and Cressida*,
4.5.55–7

Condemning Cressida, who has been kissed in
turn by all the Greek leaders.

5   O these encounterers, so glib of
      tongue,
    That give a coasting welcome ere it
      comes,
    And wide unclasp the tables of their
      thoughts
    To every ticklish reader! Set them
      down
    For sluttish spoils of opportunity
    And daughters of the game.

Ulysses in *Troilus and Cressida*,
4.5.58–63

His scornful assessment of Cressida, as she
arrives in the Grecian camp; "ticklish" = lustful.

6   Lechery, lechery, still wars and lech-
      ery. Nothing else holds fashion.

Thersites in *Troilus and Cressida*,
5.2.194–5

After watching Cressida making love to
Diomedes.

Leisure

1   When thou hast leisure, say thy
      prayers; when thou hast none,
    remember thy friends.

Parolles, *All's Well That Ends Well*,
1.1.212–3

His parting advice to Helena at the end of the
first scene.

2   Shall I not take mine ease in mine
      inn?

Falstaff in *Henry IV, Part 1*, 3.3.80–1

Falstaff's way of avoiding paying what he
owes.

Letters

1   Who's born that day
    When I forget to send to Antony,
    Shall die a beggar.

Cleopatra in *Antony and Cleopatra*,
1.5.63–5

Messages of love to the absent Antony.

2   Get posts and letters, and make
      friends with speed;
    Never so few, and never yet more
      need.

Northumberland in *Henry IV, Part 2*,
1.1.214–15

"Posts" were messengers who rode by stages
where they changed horses.

3   What presence must not know,
    From where you do remain let
      paper show.

Aumerle in *Richard II*, 1.3.249–50

To the exiled Bolingbroke: "presence" = royal
presence, King Richard; and also, our inability
to talk face to face.

Liberality

1   Since he hath got the jewel that I
      loved,

And that which you did swear to
   keep for me,
I will become as liberal as you,
I'll not deny him anything I have,
No, not my body nor my husband's
   bed.

Portia in *The Merchant of Venice*,
5.1.224–8

Teasing Bassanio, who has given Portia's ring
to the lawyer Balthasar, not knowing that
Balthasar was his wife in disguise.

Liberty, see Freedom

Lies, see Deceit, Lying

Life

1   The web of our life is of a mingled
   yarn, good and ill together.

   **First Lord in *All's Well That Ends
   Well*,** 4.3.71–2

2   I love long life better than figs.

   Charmian in *Antony and Cleopatra*,
   1.2.32

   Figs were associated with sexual activity.

3   For some must watch while some
     must sleep,
   Thus runs the world away.

   Hamlet in *Hamlet*, 3.2.273–4

   Hamlet has been watching Claudius, who has
   just hurried away from the play within the
   play; "watch" = stay awake, or work.

4   O gentlemen, the time of life is
     short!

To spend that shortness basely were
   too long.

Hotspur in *Henry IV, Part 1*, 5.2.81–2

5   There is a history in all men's lives,
   Figuring the natures of the times
     deceased,
   The which observed, a man may
     prophesy,
   With a near aim, of the main
     chance of things
   As yet not come to life.

   Warwick in *Henry IV, Part 2*, 3.1.80–4

   A chain of events ("history") in everyone's
   past life may indicate pretty well ("with a near
   aim") the likely shape of things to come.

6   This day I breathèd first—time is
     come round,
   And where I did begin, there shall I
     end.
   My life is run his compass.

   Cassius in *Julius Caesar*, 5.3.23–5

   Believing the battle is lost; "compass" = full
   circle.

7   Out, out, brief candle!
   Life's but a walking shadow, a poor
     player
   That struts and frets his hour upon
     the stage
   And then is heard no more. It is a
     tale
   Told by an idiot, full of sound and
     fury,
   Signifying nothing.

   Macbeth in *Macbeth*, 5.5.23–8

   The idea of life as fleeting and as a light or
   candle is common in the Bible, as at Job 18:6,
   "The light shall be dark in his dwelling, and
   his candle shall be put out with him," and Job
   14:1–2, "Man . . . fleeth as it were a shadow,
   and never continueth in one state."

8 You take my house when you do
   take the prop
   That doth sustain my house; you
   take my life
   When you do take the means
   whereby I live.

Shylock in *The Merchant of Venice*,
4.1.375–7

To the Duke, whose judgment is to pardon
Shylock his life, but seize all his wealth.

9 This queen will live. Nature
   awakes,
   A warmth breathes out of her. She
   hath not been
   Entranced above five hours. See
   how she 'gins
   To blow into life's flower again.

Cerimon in *Pericles*, 3.2.92–5

Thaisa, found unconscious and coffined as if
dead, revives; " 'gins" = begins.

10 Even through the hollow eyes of
    death
    I spy life peering.

Northumberland in *Richard II*,
2.1.270–1

Even as John of Gaunt dies, word comes that
Henry Bolingbroke is ready to make war on
Richard.

11 *Gonzalo.* Here is everything advan-
    tageous to life.
    Antonio. True, save means to live.

The Tempest, 2.1.50

On Prospero's island.

12 Life's uncertain voyage.

Timon in *Timon of Athens*, 5.1.202

Light

1 Light, seeking light, doth light of
   light beguile;
   So ere you find where light in darkness lies,
   Your light grows dark by losing of
   your eyes.

Berowne in *Love's Labor's Lost*, 1.1.77–9

Arguing that as too much light dazzles and
makes the eye unable to see, so too much
study only confuses the student.

2 Put out the light, and then put out
   the light.
   If I quench thee, thou flaming min-
   ister,
   I can again thy former light restore
   Should I repent me; but once put
   out thy light,
   Thou cunning'st pattern of
   excelling nature,
   I know not where is that
   Promethean heat
   That can thy light relume.

Othello in *Othello*, 5.2.7–13

The "light" is both that of the candle ("flaming
minister") he carries, and that of Desdemona;
Prometheus in Greek legend stole fire from
the gods to give it to human beings; "relume"
= light again.

Loss

1   Love that comes too late,
   Like a remorseful pardon slowly
      carried,
   To the great sender turns a sour
      offense,
   Crying, "That's good that's gone."

King of France in *All's Well That Ends Well,* 5.3.57–60

Expressing the familiar feeling of realizing that we value a thing only when it is lost.

2   I can give the loser leave to chide.

Queen Margaret in *Henry VI, Part 2,* 3.1.182

The loser is the Duke of Gloucester, arrested at her instigation.

3   O insupportable and touching loss!

Cassius in *Julius Caesar,* 4.3.151

On the news of the death of Portia, Brutus's wife.

4   "My daughter! O my ducats! O my daughter!
     Fled with a Christian! O my Christian ducats!
     Justice! The law! My ducats, and my daughter!"

Solanio in *The Merchant of Venice,* 2.8.15–17

Mockingly imitating Shylock's outcry on finding his daughter has stolen away with bags of ducats.

5   Thou torturest me, Tubal. It was my turquoise; I had it of Leah when I was a bachelor. I would not have given it for a wilderness of monkeys.

Shylock in *The Merchant of Venice,* 3.1.120–3

On hearing that his daughter Jessica has traded his jewel for a monkey; he refers to his dead wife, Leah.

6   But there, where I have garnered up my heart,
     Where either I must live or bear no life;

The fountain from the which my current runs
Or else dries up: to be discarded thence,
Or keep it as a cistern for foul toads
To knot and gender in!

Othello in *Othello,* 4.2.57–62

"Knot and gender" = copulate and breed; the foulness is all in Othello's imagination.

7   My wife, my wife! What wife? I have no wife.
     O insupportable! O heavy hour!
     Methinks it should be now a huge eclipse
     Of sun and moon, and that th' affrighted globe
     Should yawn at alteration.

Othello in *Othello,* 5.2.97–101

That the earth ("globe") should gape wide ("yawn") at the change brought by Desdemona's death suggests an earthquake.

8   Say, is my kingdom lost? Why, 'twas my care,
     And what loss is it to be rid of care?

King Richard in *Richard II,* 3.2.95–6

Anticipating the takeover by Bolingbroke (later Henry IV).

Love (see also Adoration, Courtship, Devotion, Kissing)

1   The hind that would be mated by the lion
     Must die for love.

Helena in *All's Well That Ends Well,* 1.1.91–2

On the unbridgeable gulf between herself ("hind" = deer) and Count Bertram.

2   My friends were poor, but honest,
    so's my love.

Helena in *All's Well That Ends Well,*
1.3.195

On her love for Bertram, nobly born; "friends"
here means relations.

3   Love is holy.

Bertram in *All's Well That Ends Well,*
4.2.32

Said as he is trying to seduce Diana.

4   All impediments in fancy's
    course
    Are motives of more fancy.

Bertram in *All's Well That Ends Well,*
5.3.214–5

"Fancy," as commonly, = love; "motives of" =
incitements to.

5   *Cleopatra.* If it be love indeed, tell
    me how much.
    Antony. There's beggary in the love
    that can be reckoned.

Antony and Cleopatra, 1.1.14–15

A grand conception of love as beyond measure.

6   But you are come
    A market-maid to Rome, and have
    prevented
    The ostentation of our love.

Octavius Caesar in *Antony and*
Cleopatra, 3.6.50–2

Octavius sees his sister returning to Rome
with a smaller train than he thinks appropriate.

7   O thou day o' the world,
    Chain mine armed neck, leap thou,
    attire and all,

Through proof of harness to my
    heart, and there
Ride on the pants triumphing!

Antony in *Antony and Cleopatra,*
4.8.13–16

In victory he invites Cleopatra to bind
("chain") him, and leap through his strong
armor to her sexual embrace.

8   Love no man in good earnest, nor
    no further in sport neither, than
    with safety of a pure blush thou
    mayst in honor come off again.

Celia in *As You Like It,* 1.2.27–9

Advice to Rosalind on avoiding commitment
in love.

9   Whose loves
    Are dearer than the natural bond of
    sisters.

Le Beau in *As You Like It,* 1.2.275–6

Speaking of the cousins, Rosalind and Celia.

10   As true a lover
    As ever sighed upon a midnight pil-
    low.

Silvius in *As You Like It,* 2.4.26–7

On the absurdity of unrequited love.

11 Alas, poor shepherd, searching of
    thy wound,
    I have by hard adventure found
    mine own.

Rosalind in *As You Like It,* 2.4.44–5

Examining (searching) Silvius's wound of love,
Rosalind recognizes her own complaint.

12 We that are true lovers run into
    strange capers.

Touchstone in *As You Like It,* 2.4.54–5

On the folly of love.

13   Then the lover,
Sighing like furnace, with a woeful
  ballad
Made to his mistress' eyebrow.

Jaques in *As You Like It*, 2.7.147–9

The third of the "seven ages" of man.

14 From the east to western Inde,
    No jewel is like Rosalind.

Rosalind in *As You Like It*, 3.2.88–9

Reading one of Orlando's love poems, with its
poor rhyme ("Inde" = the Indies).

15 Your hose should be ungartered,
    your bonnet unbanded, your sleeve
    unbuttoned, your shoe untied, and
    everything about you demonstrat-
    ing a careless desolation.

Rosalind in *As You Like It*, 3.2.378–81

How the melancholy lover should look.

16 Love is merely a madness.

Rosalind in *As You Like It*, 3.2.400

17 I think he is not a pick-purse nor a
    horse-stealer, but for his verity in
    love, I do think him as concave as a
    covered goblet or a worm-eaten
    nut.

Celia in *As You Like It*, 3.4.22–5

18 The sight of lovers feedeth those in
    love.

Rosalind in *As You Like It*, 3.4.57

Going to see Silvius wooing Phebe.

19 If ever (as that ever may be near)
    You meet in some fresh cheek the
      power of fancy,

Then shall you know the wounds
  invisible
That love's keen arrows make.

Silvius in *As You Like It*, 3.5.28–31

On the power of love to hurt; the image of
Cupid shooting love's darts at random underlies these lines.

20 I pray you do not fall in love with
    me,
For I am falser than vows made in
  wine.
Besides, I like you not.

Rosalind in *As You Like It*, 3.5.72–4

To Phebe, while Rosalind is in disguise as a
man.

21 Dead shepherd, now I find thy saw
    of might,
"Who ever loved that loved not at
    first sight?"

Phebe in *As You Like It*, 3.5.81–2

The quotation from Christopher Marlowe's
poem *Hero and Leander* (published 1598),
l.176, has passed into proverb lore. Marlowe
died in 1593. Phebe, a shepherdess, calls
Marlowe a shepherd.

22 O coz, coz, coz, my pretty little coz,
    that thou didst know how many
    fathom deep I am in love!

Rosalind in *As You Like It*, 4.1.205–7

Addressing Celia.

23 That same wicked bastard of Venus
    that was begot of thought, con-
    ceived of spleen, and born of mad-
    ness, that blind rascally boy that
    abuses everyone's eyes because his
    own are out, let him be judge how
    deep I am in love.

Rosalind in *As You Like It*, 4.1.211–15

"Bastard of Venus" = Cupid.

24   She could not love me
Were man as rare as phoenix.

Rosalind in *As You Like It*, 4.3.16–17

Misrepresenting Phebe's letter protesting love;
"phoenix" = a mythical bird, only one of
which lived at a time.

25   Pacing through the forest,
Chewing the food of sweet and bitter fancy.

Oliver in *As You Like It*, 4.3.100–1

Oliver's image of the love-sick Orlando.

26 Your brother and my sister no
sooner met but they looked; no
sooner looked but they loved; no
sooner loved but they sighed; no
sooner sighed but they asked one
another the reason; no sooner knew
the reason but they sought the remedy.

Rosalind in *As You Like It*, 5.2.32–7

Describing the sudden passion of Oliver and
Celia for one another.

27 *Phebe.* Good shepherd, tell this
youth what 'tis to love.
Silvius. It is to be all made of sighs
and tears.
   . . .
It is to be all made of faith and ser-
vice.
   . . .
It is to be all made of fantasy,
All made of passion, and all made
of wishes,
All adoration, duty, and obser-
vance,
All humbleness, all patience, and
impatience,
All purity, all trial, all observance.

***As You Like It*, 5.2.83–4,89,94–8**

A definition of love by the infatuated Silvius;
"fantasy" = imagination.

28 Hang there like fruit, my soul,
Till the tree die!

Posthumus in *Cymbeline*, 5.5.263–4

Embracing Imogen, as all deceptions and mistakes in the story are revealed.

29 This is the very ecstasy of love.

Polonius in *Hamlet*, 2.1.99

Interpreting Hamlet's strange behavior to
Ophelia as the "ecstasy" or madness of love
for her.

30 Doubt thou the stars are fire,
Doubt that the sun doth move,
Doubt truth to be a liar,
But never doubt I love.

Polonius in *Hamlet*, 2.2.116–19

Quoting from Hamlet's letter to Ophelia, who
has given it to him; "doubt" = suspect.
(According to the Ptolemaic idea of the universe, the sun moved round the earth).

31 *Hamlet.* Is this a prologue, or the
posy of a ring?
Ophelia. 'Tis brief, my lord.
Hamlet. As woman's love.

***Hamlet*, 3.2.152–4**

After the three-line prologue to the play within
the play; "posy of a ring" = short motto
engraved in a ring.

32 How should I your true love know
From another one?
By his cockle hat and staff,
And his sandal shoon.

Ophelia in *Hamlet*, 4.5.23–6

Singing old songs in her madness after her
father's death; "cockle hat" = hat bearing a
cockle-shell, the sign, with the sandals, of a
pilgrim; "shoon" = shoes.

33 Not that I think you did not love
your father,
But that I know love is begun by
time,

And that I see, in passages of proof,
Time qualifies the spark and fire of
    it.

Claudius in *Hamlet*, 4.7.110–13

To Laertes, about his love for his father, now
dead; "passages of proof" = examples that
prove what I am saying.

34 There lives within the very flame of
    love
A kind of wick or snuff that will
    abate it.

Claudius in *Hamlet*, 4.7.114–15

"Snuff" = charred portion of the wick.

35 Do you not love me? Do you not
    indeed?
Well, do not then, for since you
    love me not,
I will not love myself.

Lady Percy in *Henry IV, Part 1*, 2.3.96–8

To her husband; she is trying to get information out of him, and he says jokingly that he
does not love her.

36 *Falstaff.* I am old, I am old.
   Doll Tearsheet. I love thee better
      than I love e'er a scurvy young
      boy of them all.

Henry IV, Part 2, 2.4.271–3

"Scurvy" = contemptible; a term of abuse.

37 When love begins to sicken and
    decay,
It useth an enforcèd ceremony.
There are no tricks in plain and
    simple faith.

Brutus in *Julius Caesar*, 4.2.20–2

To Lucilius, who reports that Cassius is
unfriendly.

38 What shall Cordelia speak? Love,
    and be silent.

Cordelia in *King Lear*, 1.1.62

On being asked to spell out how much she
loves her father.

39   I am sure my love's
More ponderous than my tongue.

Cordelia in *King Lear*, 1.1.77–8

Her love is weightier than she can put into
words.

40   Love's not love
When it is mingled with regards
    that stand
Aloof from th'entire point.

King of France in *King Lear*, 1.1.238–40

"Regards" = considerations; his rival for the
hand of Cordelia has been setting conditions
for marrying her.

41 On a day—alack the day—
Love, whose month is ever May,
Spied a blossom passing fair
Playing in the wanton air.

Dumaine in *Love's Labor's Lost*,
4.3.99–102

Expressing his love for Katherine.

42 A lover's eyes will gaze an eagle
    blind.
A lover's ear will hear the lowest
    sound.

Berowne in *Love's Labor's Lost*,
4.3.331–2

In a speech in praise of love.

43 Love's feeling is more soft and sen-
    sible
Than are the tender horns of cock-
    led snails.

Berowne in *Love's Labor's Lost*,
4.3.334–5

"Cockled" = possessing a shell.

44   When love speaks, the voice of all
        the gods
        Make heaven drowsy with the har-
        mony.

        Berowne in *Love's Labor's Lost*,
        4.3.341–2

        As if the gods sing in response to human love.

45   Believe not that the dribbling dart
        of love
        Can pierce a complete bosom.

        Duke in *Measure for Measure*, 1.3.2–3

        The Duke does in the end succumb to the
        attractions of Isabella; the "dart" suggests
        Cupid's arrow.

46   But love is blind, and lovers cannot
        see
        The pretty follies that themselves
        commit,
        For if they could, Cupid himself
        would blush
        To see me thus transformèd to a
        boy.

        Jessica in *The Merchant of Venice*,
        2.6.36–9

        She is disguised to elope with Lorenzo; "love
        is blind" is proverbial.

47   Beshrew me but I love her heartily,
        For she is wise, if I can judge of her,
        And fair she is, if that mine eyes be
        true,
        And true she is, as she hath proved
        herself;
        And therefore, like herself, wise,
        fair, and true,
        Shall she be placèd in my constant
        soul.

        Lorenzo in *The Merchant of Venice*,
        2.6.52–7

        On his love for Jessica.

48   One half of me is yours, the other
        half yours—
        Mine own, I would say; but if mine,
        then yours,
        And so all yours.

        Portia in *The Merchant of Venice*,
        3.2.16–18

        Confessing her love to Bassanio.

49   If you do love me, you will find me
        out.

        Portia in *The Merchant of Venice*,
        3.2.41

        Meaning that Bassanio will choose the right
        casket.

50   Tell me where is fancy bred,
        Or in the heart or in the head?
        How begot, how nourishèd?
        Reply, reply.
        It is engendered in the eyes,
        With gazing fed, and fancy dies
        In the cradle where it lies.
        Let us all ring fancy's knell.
        I'll begin it. Ding, dong, bell.

        Song in *The Merchant of Venice*,
        3.2.63–71

        The rhymes and the idea of dying help to
        guide Bassanio to choose the leaden casket;
        love ("fancy") was supposed to enter the heart
        through the eyes.

51   O love, be moderate, allay thy
        ecstasy,
        In measure rain thy joy, scant this
        excess!
        I feel too much thy blessing; make
        it less,
        For fear I surfeit.

        Portia in *The Merchant of Venice*,
        3.2.111–14

        Overjoyed on seeing Bassanio choose the
        right casket to win her; "scant" = moderate.

52   The course of true love never did run smooth.

Lysander in *A Midsummer Night's Dream*, 1.1.134

To Hermia, whose father has forbidden her to have anything to do with Lysander.

53   Before the time I did Lysander see,
Seemed Athens as a paradise to me.
O then, what graces in my love do dwell,
That he hath turned a heaven unto a hell?

Hermia in *A Midsummer Night's Dream*, 1.1.204–7

Her "love" is Lysander, who has provoked the anger of her father and jealousy of Demetrius, and so made Athens hell for her.

54   Things base and vile, holding no quantity,
Love can transpose to form and dignity.
Love looks not with the eyes, but with the mind,
And therefore is winged Cupid painted blind.

Helena in *A Midsummer Night's Dream*, 1.1.232–5

Love is conventionally roused through sight, but the lover also lacks judgment in seeing beauty where others do not, hence the proverb, "Love is without reason." Cupid was often represented as blind or blindfolded, since his arrows were supposed to be fired at random.

55   Therefore is love said to be a child
Because in choice he is so oft beguiled.

Helena in *A Midsummer Night's Dream*, 1.1.238–9

"Child" = both Cupid, and lovers who are so often deluded ("beguiled").

56   It is not night when I do see your face,
Therefore I think I am not in the night;
Nor doth this wood lack worlds of company,
For you, in my respect, are all the world.

Helena in *A Midsummer Night's Dream*, 2.1.221–4

Helena's infatuation with Demetrius; "in my respect" = esteem.

57   One turf shall serve as pillow for us both;
One heart, one bed, two bosoms, and one troth.

Lysander in *A Midsummer Night's Dream*, 2.2.41–2

Lysander trying to persuade Hermia to sleep by him.

58   I mean that my heart unto yours is knit,
So that but one heart we can make of it:
Two bosoms interchainèd with an oath,
So then two bosoms and a single troth.

Lysander in *A Midsummer Night's Dream*, 2.2.47–50

A pretty idea of the union of lovers, but a bit premature for Hermia.

59   Thy fair virtue's force perforce doth move me
On the first view to say, to swear, I love thee.

Titania in *A Midsummer Night's Dream*, 3.1.140–1

To Bottom, transformed by Oberon's magic into an ass; "fair virtue's force" = power of your unblemished excellence.

60 Prove that ever I lose more blood
with love than I will get again with
drinking, pick out mine eyes with a
ballad-maker's pen and hang me up
at the door of a brothel-house for
the sign of blind Cupid.

Benedick in *Much Ado About Nothing*,
1.1.250–4

Sighing was thought to dry up the blood, and
drinking wine to produce new blood;
Benedick scorns the very idea of love by asso-
ciating it with sentimental ballads and the
brothel-house. Cupid was often depicted with
blindfold eyes, since his arrows were shot at
random.

61 How sweetly you do minister to
love,
That know love's grief by his complexion!

Claudio in *Much Ado About Nothing*,
1.1.312–13

"Grief" = pangs; the lover typically had a pale
appearance ("complexion").

62 All hearts in love use their own
tongues.
Let every eye negotiate for itself,
And trust no agent.

Claudio in *Much Ado About Nothing*,
2.1.177–9

He thinks Don Pedro has wooed Hero for
himself, and not, as he promised, for Claudio.

63 My talk to thee must be how
Benedick
Is sick in love with Beatrice. Of this
matter
Is little Cupid's crafty arrow made,
That only wounds by hearsay.

Hero in *Much Ado About Nothing*,
3.1.20–3

Plotting with Ursula to make Beatrice fall in
love with Benedick.

64 Some Cupid kills with arrows, some
with traps.

Hero in *Much Ado About Nothing*,
3.1.106

Hero's device to make Beatrice admit she
loves Benedick has proved successful.

65 If he be not in love with some
woman, there is no believing old
signs. 'A brushes his hat o'mornings; what should that bode?

Claudio in *Much Ado About Nothing*,
3.2.40–2

On Benedick sprucing himself up.

66 I pray thee now, tell me for which
of my bad parts didst thou first fall
in love with me?

Benedick in *Much Ado About Nothing*,
5.2.59–61

Jokingly to Beatrice.

67 *Beatrice.* But for which of my good
parts did you first suffer love for
me?
Benedick. Suffer love! A good epithet. I do suffer love indeed, for I
love thee against my will.

Much Ado About Nothing, 5.2.64–7

Avoiding sentiment by means of wit.

68 She loved me for the dangers I had
passed,
And I loved her that she did pity
them.

Othello in *Othello*, 1.3.167–8

Speaking about Desdemona.

69   If I be left behind,
A moth of peace, and he go to the
war,

The rites for which I love him are
bereft me,
And I a heavy interim shall support
By his dear absence. Let me go with
him.

Desdemona in *Othello*, 1.3.255–9

Asking the Venetian senate to be allowed to
accompany her husband to Cyprus.

70   The heavens forbid
But that our loves and comforts
should increase
Even as our days do grow!

Desdemona in *Othello*, 2.1.193–5

Greeting Othello on her arrival in Cyprus after
a stormy voyage.

71   Excellent wretch! Perdition catch
my soul
But I do love thee! And when I love
thee not,
Chaos is come again.

Othello in *Othello*, 3.3.90–2

Desdemona has just left the stage; "wretch"
was used as a term of endearment.

72   From forth the fatal loins of these
two foes,
A pair of star-crossed lovers take
their life.

**Chorus in *Romeo and Juliet*, Prologue,
5–6**

The foes are the clans of the Capulets and
Montagues in Verona.

73   Here's much to do with hate, but
more with love.
Why then, O brawling love, O loving hate,

O anything of nothing first create,
O heavy lightness, serious vanity,
Misshapen chaos of well-seeming
forms.

Romeo in *Romeo and Juliet*, 1.1.175–9

On the miseries of unrequited love, hinting
too at the Capulet-Montague quarrel; "create"
= created.

74   Love is a smoke made with the
fume of sighs,
Being purged, a fire sparkling in
lovers' eyes,
Being vexed, a sea nourished with
lovers' tears.

Romeo in *Romeo and Juliet*, 1.1.190–2

A fanciful definition of love: if the "fume" or
smoke of sighs is removed, a lover's eyes
sparkle; if it is stirred up, tears are provoked.

75   Is love a tender thing? It is too
rough,
Too rude, too boisterous, and it
pricks like thorn.

Romeo in *Romeo and Juliet*, 1.4.25–6

He is still infatuated with Rosaline, who will
have nothing to do with him.

76   Did my heart love till now? Forswear it, sight,
For I ne'er saw true beauty till this
night.

Romeo in *Romeo and Juliet*, 1.5.52–3

On seeing Juliet, he dismisses his earlier passion for Rosaline.

77   It is my lady, O, it is my love.
O that she knew she were!

Romeo in *Romeo and Juliet*, 2.2.10–11

Seeing Juliet at her window.

78 With love's light wings did I o'er-
perch these walls,
For stony limits cannot hold love
out,
And what love can do, that dares
love attempt.

Romeo in *Romeo and Juliet*, 2.2.66–8

He has climbed the walls into Capulet's garden in order to watch beneath Juliet's window.

79 This bud of love by summer's
ripening breath
May prove a beauteous flower
when next we meet.

Juliet in *Romeo and Juliet*, 2.2.121–2

Reassuring herself and Romeo that their love
may flourish.

80 My bounty is as boundless as the
sea,
My love as deep. The more I give
to thee
The more I have, for both are infinite.

Juliet in *Romeo and Juliet*, 2.2.133–5

Expressing her devotion to Romeo.

81 Love's heralds should be thoughts,
Which ten times faster glides than
the sun's beams,
Driving back shadows over low'ring
hills.

Juliet in *Romeo and Juliet*, 2.5.4–6

Anxiously expecting her Nurse to return with
news of Romeo.

82 Love moderately: long love doth so.

**Friar Lawrence in *Romeo and Juliet*,
2.6.14**

Giving the hasty Romeo advice.

83 They are but beggars that can count
their worth,
But my true love is grown to such
excess
I cannot sum up sum of half my
wealth.

Juliet in *Romeo and Juliet*, 2.6.32–4

To Romeo as they go off to be married; "sum
up sum" = add up the total.

84   Is it possible
That love should of a sudden take
such hold?

**Tranio in *The Taming of the Shrew*,
1.1.146–7**

His master, Lucentio, has fallen in love at first
sight of Bianca.

85   Of all the men alive
I never yet beheld that special face
Which I could fancy more than any
other.

**Bianca in *The Taming of the Shrew*,
2.1.10–12**

Speaking to her sister Katherine.

86 Kindness in women, not their
beauteous looks,
Shall win my love.

**Hortensio in *The Taming of the
Shrew*, 4.2.41–2**

Deciding he does not want to marry Bianca.

87 Love wrought these miracles.

**Lucentio in *The Taming of the Shrew*,
5.1.124**

Speaking of the devices by which he has
deceived Bianca's father and married her.

88 Let thy song be love. This love will
undo us all.

Helen in *Troilus and Cressida*,
3.1.110–11

Calling on Pandarus to sing; "undo" = ruin.

89 *Helen.* In love, i'faith, to the very tip of the nose.
Paris. He eats nothing but doves, love, and that breeds hot blood, and hot blood begets hot thoughts, and hot thoughts beget hot deeds, and hot deeds is love.

Troilus and Cressida, 3.1.127–30

They are talking about Pandarus; what Paris describes is lechery, not love.

90 This is the monstruosity in love, lady, that the will is infinite and the execution confined; that the desire is boundless, and the act a slave to limit.

Troilus in *Troilus and Cressida*, 3.2.81–3

Speaking to Cressida.

91 They say all lovers swear more performance than they are able, and yet reserve an ability that they never perform; vowing more than the perfection of ten, and discharging less than the tenth part of one.

Cressida in *Troilus and Cressida*, 3.2.84–7

Showing her anxiety about the claims Troilus is making for love.

92 My thoughts were like unbridled children, grown Too headstrong for their mother.

Cressida in *Troilus and Cressida*, 3.2.122–3

Admitting her love for Troilus.

93 Time, force, and death Do to this body what extremes you can, But the strong base and building of my love Is as the very center of the earth, Drawing all things to it.

Cressida in *Troilus and Cressida*, 4.2.101–5

On learning that she must leave Troilus and go to the Greek camp; the center of the earth was thought to act as a powerful magnet.

94 O spirit of love, how quick and fresh art thou.

Orsino in *Twelfth Night*, 1.1.9

"Quick and fresh" = alert and vigorous.

95 O mistress mine, where are you roaming? O stay and hear, your true love's coming, That can sing both high and low. Trip no further, pretty sweeting. Journeys end in lovers meeting, Every wise man's son doth know.

Feste in *Twelfth Night*, 2.3.39–44

His song of love seems to relate to the love-tangles of the play, which do end happily.

96 What is love? 'Tis not hereafter, Present mirth hath present laughter. What's to come is still unsure. In delay there lies no plenty, Then come kiss me, sweet and twenty. Youth's a stuff will not endure.

Feste in *Twelfth Night*, 2.3.47–52

This stanza touches on the brevity of life and traditional "ubi sunt" ("where are they?") theme (as in "where have all the flowers gone?").

97 *Sir Andrew Aguecheek.* Before me,
she's a good wench.
Sir Toby Belch. She's a beagle true
bred, and one that adores me.
What o' that?
Sir Andrew Aguecheek. I was
adored once, too.

Twelfth Night, 2.3.178–81

They speak of Maria; a "beagle" = a small,
intelligent hunting dog; Sir Andrew has his
moment of pathos.

98 There is no woman's sides
Can bide the beating of so strong a
passion
As love doth give my heart; no
woman's heart
So big, to hold so much; they lack
retention.
Alas, their love may be called
appetite.

Orsino in *Twelfth Night,* 2.4.93–7

Speaking to Cesario, really Viola in disguise;
"bide" = endure.

99 Love sought is good, but given
unsought is better.

Olivia in *Twelfth Night,* 3.1.156

100 *Julia.* His little speaking shows his
love but small.
Lucetta. Fire that's closest kept
burns most of all.
Julia. They do not love that do not
show their love.
Lucetta. O, they love least that let
men know their love.

The Two Gentlemen of Verona,
1.2.29–32

101 Sweet love, sweet lines, sweet life!
Here is her hand, the agent of her
heart;
Here is her oath for love, her
honor's pawn.

Proteus in *The Two Gentlemen of
Verona,* 1.3.45–7

He enters reading a love-letter from Julia.

102 O, how this spring of love resem-
bleth
The uncertain glory of an April day,
Which now shows all the beauty of
the sun,
And by and by a cloud takes all
away.

Proteus in *The Two Gentlemen of
Verona,* 1.3.84–7

On being sent away from Verona, and from
his love, Julia.

103 Love is blind.

Speed in *The Two Gentlemen of
Verona,* 2.1.70

Proverbial; Speed, the clown, can see better
than his master Valentine.

104 What, gone without a word?
Ay, so true love should do: it cannot speak,
For truth hath better deeds than
words to grace it.

Proteus in *The Two Gentlemen of
Verona,* 2.2.16–18

Spoken as Julia parts from him.

105 Love is like a child

That longs for everything that he can come by.

Duke in *The Two Gentlemen of Verona*, 3.1.124–5

For as you were when first your eye I eyed,
Such seems your beauty still.

Sonnet 104, 1–3

106 He says he loves my daughter:
I think so too; for never gaz'd the moon
Upon the water as he'll stand and read
As 'twere my daughter's eyes: and, to be plain,
I think there is not half a kiss to choose
Who loves another best.

Shepherd in *The Winter's Tale*, 4.4.171–6

On Perdita and Florizel.

107 But if the while I think on thee, dear friend,
All losses are restored, and sorrows end.

Sonnet 30, 13–14

108 Take all my loves, my love, yea, take them all.
What hast thou then more than thou hadst before?
No love, my love, that thou mayst true love call;
All mine was thine before thou hadst this more.

Sonnet 40, 1–4

Does "all my loves" refer to the speaker's male and female "friends"?

109 To me, fair friend, you never can be old,

110 Let me not to the marriage of true minds
Admit impediments; love is not love
That alters where it alteration finds,
Or bends with the remover to remove.
O no, it is an ever-fixèd mark
That looks on tempests and is never shaken.

Sonnet 116, 1–6

A famous expression of the idea of love: "admit" = concede that there may be; the "alteration" may be in age or other circumstances; "Or bends with the remover to remove" = or changes because of inconstancy in either party. The word "impediment" occurs in the wedding service in the Book of Common Prayer, and the third line sums up the promises made in that ceremony "for better for worse, for richer for poorer, in sickness and in health."

111 Two loves I have of comfort and despair,
Which like two spirits do suggest me still:
The better angel is a man right fair,
The worser spirit a woman colored ill.

Sonnet 144, 1–4

The speaker's mistress, now involved also with his friend, is depicted as a spirit that tempts him (suggests) to evil; other sonnets (130, for instance) describe her having black hair and eyes, or "colored ill" at a time when fair hair, a white skin and grey eyes were prized.

Loyalty

1   He'll go along o'er the wide world
with me.

Celia in *As You Like It*, 1.3.132

Speaking of the clown, Touchstone.

2   I will follow thee
To the last gasp with truth and loyalty.

Adam in *As You Like It*, 2.3.69–70

Spoken by the faithful old servant Adam to
Orlando as they set off for the forest of Arden.

3   A plague upon it when thieves cannot be true one to another!

Falstaff in *Henry IV, Part 1*, 2.2.27–8

His companions have taken his horse, and
Falstaff is too fat to walk far.

4   My heart doth joy that yet in all my
life
I found no man but he was true to
me.

Brutus in *Julius Caesar*, 5.5.34–5

Luck (see also Chance, Fortune)

1   This is the third time; I hope good
luck lies in odd numbers.

**Falstaff in *The Merry Wives of Wind-
sor*, 5.1.2–3**

2   'Tis a lucky day, boy, and we'll do
good deeds on't.

**Shepherd in *The Winter's Tale*,
3.3.138–9**

On finding the gold left with the baby Perdita
by Antigonus.

Lust (see also Desire, Lechery, Luxury, Sex)

1   When you have our roses,
You barely leave our thorns to
prick ourselves,
And mock us with our bareness.

**Diana in *All's Well That Ends Well*,
4.2.18–20**

Resisting Bertram's attempt to seduce her.

2   [Antony] is become the bellows and
the fan
To cool a gipsy's lust.

Philo in *Antony and Cleopatra*, 1.1.9–10

One acerbic view of the love of Antony and
Cleopatra.

3   I was
A morsel for a monarch.

**Cleopatra in *Antony and Cleopatra*,
1.5.30–1**

Recalling her affair with Julius Caesar.

4   What hotter hours,
Unregistered in vulgar fame, you
have
Luxuriously picked out.

**Antony in *Antony and Cleopatra*,
3.13.118–20**

Condemning Cleopatra for her past love
affairs; "luxuriously" relates to lechery.

5   Thou thyself hast been a libertine,
As sensual as the brutish sting itself.

Duke Senior in *As You Like It*, 2.7.65–6

Denying Jaques the moral high ground he has claimed.

6   Rebellious hell,
    If thou canst mutine in a matron's
      bones,
    To flaming youth let virtue be as
      wax
    And melt in her own fire.

Hamlet in *Hamlet*, 3.4.82–5

Reproaching his mother for marrying her late husband's brother, a marriage Hamlet regards as springing from lust.

7   Such is the simplicity of man to
    hearken after the flesh.

Costard in *Love's Labor' Lost*, 1.1.217

Is Costard confusing biblical echoes of such texts as "we all had our conversation in times past in the lusts of the flesh" (Ephesians 2:3)?

8   Lust is but a bloody fire
    Kindled with unchaste desire,
    Fed in heart, whose flames aspire
    As thoughts do blow them, higher
      and higher.

Song by Fairies, *The Merry Wives of Windsor*, 5.5.95–8

9   She knows the heat of a luxurious
      bed.
    Her blush is guiltiness, not mod-
      esty.

Claudio in *Much Ado About Nothing*, 4.1.41–2

Accusing Hero of being unchaste; "luxurious" could mean lecherous.

10   You seem to me as Diana in her
     orb,

As chaste as is the bud ere it be
   blown;
But you are more intemperate in
   your blood
Than Venus, or those pampered
   animals
That rage in savage sensuality.

Claudio in *Much Ado About Nothing*, 4.1.57–61

Rejecting Hero as a bride: Diana, goddess of the moon and of chastity, is contrasted with Venus, goddess of love or sexuality; "blood" = sensual appetite.

11   But we have reason to cool our rag-
    ing motions, our carnal stings, our
    unbitted lusts; whereof I take this
    that you call love to be a sect or
    scion. . . . It is merely a lust of the
    blood and a permission of the will.

Iago in *Othello*, 1.3.329–32, 334–5

Iago cynically reduces all love to lust in speaking to Roderigo.

12   If ever you prove false to one
    another, since I have taken such
    pain to bring you together, let all
    pitiful goers-between be called to
    the world's end after my name; call
    them all Pandars.

Pandarus in *Troilus and Cressida*, 3.2.199–202

On providing Troilus and Cressida with a bedroom in which to make love.

13   This momentary joy breeds months
    of pain,
    This hot desire converts to cold dis-
    dain;
    Pure Chastity is ruffled of her store,
    And Lust, the thief, far poorer than
    before.

***The Rape of Lucrece*, 690–3**

14   Th' expense of spirit in a waste of
shame
Is lust in action, and till action lust
Is perjured, murderous, bloody, full
of blame,
Savage, extreme, rude, cruel, not to
trust,
Enjoyed no sooner but despisèd
straight,
Past reason hunted, and no sooner
had,
Past reason hated as a swallowed
bait
On purpose laid to make the taker
mad;
Mad in pursuit, and in possession
so,
Had, having, and in quest to have
extreme,
A bliss in proof, and proved, a very
woe,
Before a joy proposed, behind a
dream.
All this the world well knows, yet
none knows well
To shun the heaven that leads
men to this hell.

Sonnet 129

The definitive account of the experience of
lust in action; "Th'expense of spirit" = the
pouring out of vital energy, involving the soul
or spirit, not just the body; "not to trust" = not
to be trusted; "in proof, and proved" = during
the experience, and afterwards.

15   Love comforteth like sunshine after
rain,
But lust's effect is tempest after sun;
Love's gentle spring doth always
fresh remain,
Lust's winter comes ere summer
half be done;
Love surfeits not, lust like a glut-
ton dies;
Love is all truth, lust full of forgèd
lies.

Venus and Adonis, 799–804

Adonis tries to repel the lustful advances of
Venus; the contrast between lust and love is a
recurrent topic in Shakespeare's work.

Luxury

1   The beds i'th' East are soft.

Antony in *Antony and Cleopatra*, 2.6.50

Recalling Egyptian luxury in warlike Rome.

2   The devil Luxury, with his fat rump
and potato finger.

**Thersites in *Troilus and Cressida*,
5.2.55–6**

Luxury was not distinguished from lust; pota-
toes, first brought to England in the sixteenth
century, were thought to have aphrodisiac
qualities.

Lying

1   These lies are like their father that
begets them, gross as a mountain,
open, palpable.

**Prince Hal in *Henry IV, Part 1*,
2.4.225–6**

To Falstaff, who has hugely exaggerated his
account of a fight with the disguised Prince
and Poins; "gross" = huge, and hence obvi-
ous.

2   Lord, Lord, how this world is
given to lying!

Falstaff in *Henry IV, Part 1*, 5.4.145–6

No one more than Falstaff himself.

3   For my part, if a lie may do thee
grace,
I'll gild it with the happiest terms I
have.

Prince Hal in *Henry IV, Part 1*,
5.4.157–8

Falstaff claims to have killed Hotspur, and Hal
does not expose the lie; "do thee grace" =
bring you credit.

4 Lord, Lord, how subject we old
men are to this vice of lying!

Falstaff in *Henry IV, Part 2*. 3.2.303–4

Falstaff for once speaks the truth (compare 2
above).

5 If he say so, may his pernicious soul
Rot half a grain a day! He lies to
the heart.

Emilia in *Othello*, 5.2.155–6

She wants Iago to rot slowly; a "grain" is the
smallest measurement of weight.

6 You told a lie, an odious, damnèd
lie;
Upon my soul, a lie, a wicked lie.

Emilia in *Othello*, 5.2.180–1

On learning of Iago's lies about Desdemona.

7 As many lies as will lie in thy paper,
although the sheet were big enough
for the bed of Ware in England.

Sir Toby Belch in *Twelfth Night*,
3.2.46–8

Advising Sir Andrew on writing a challenge;
"the bed of Ware," in Hertfordshire, was
famous, being ten feet square and able to
accommodate twelve people.

Madness

1 Lord Hamlet, with his doublet all
unbraced,
No hat upon his head, his stockings
fouled,
Ungartered, and down-gyvèd to his
ankle,
Pale as his shirt, his knees knocking
each other,
And with a look so piteous in pur-
port
As if he had been loosèd out of hell
To speak of horrors.

Ophelia in *Hamlet*, 2.1.75–81

Describing to Polonius the distraught state of
Hamlet, who appears like a ghost; "down-
gyved" = fallen down like fetters.

2 To define true madness,
What is't but to be nothing else but
mad?

Polonius in *Hamlet*, 2.2.93–4

Explaining Hamlet's madness to Claudius and
Gertrude.

3 He repelled, a short tale to make,
Fell into a sadness, then into a fast,
Thence to a watch, thence into a
weakness,
Thence to a lightness, and by this
declension,
Into the madness wherein now he
raves.

Polonius in *Hamlet*, 2.2.146–50

His idea of the stages of Hamlet's madness;
"watch" = inability to sleep.

4 Though this be madness, yet there
is method in't.

Polonius in *Hamlet*, 2.2.205–6

It dawns on him that Hamlet is not as mad as
he is pretending to be; "method" = logic.

5 I am but mad north-north-west.
When the wind is southerly, I know
a hawk from a handsaw.

Hamlet in *Hamlet*, 2.2.378–9

Quibbling perhaps on "hernshaw" or heron.

6   This is mere madness,
And thus a while the fit will work
    on him.
Anon, as patient as the female dove
When that her golden couplets are
    disclosed,
His silence will sit drooping.

Gertrude in *Hamlet*, 5.1.284–8

On Hamlet's changing moods; "golden couplets" = pair of baby birds with yellow down;
"disclosed" = hatched.

7   My wits begin to turn.

King Lear in *King Lear*, 3.2.67

Realizing he is going mad.

8   O, that way madness lies; let me
    shun that!

King Lear in *King Lear*, 3.4.21

"That way" = thinking about the ingratitude of
his daughters.

9   Why, he was met even now
As mad as the vexed sea, singing
    aloud,
Crowned with rank fumiter and
    furrow-weeds,
With hardocks, hemlock, nettles,
    cuckoo-flowers,
Darnel, and all the idle weeds that
    grow
In our sustaining corn.

Cordelia in *King Lear*, 4.4.1–6

The mad king has crowned himself with useless ("idle") weeds.

10   Why, this is very midsummer madness.

Olivia in *Twelfth Night*, 3.4.56

On Malvolio's strange behavior; the midsummer moon was thought to cause madness (or
"lunacy," from "luna" = moon).

Magic

1   We have the receipt of fern-seed,
we walk invisible.

Gadshill in *Henry IV, Part 1*, 2.1.86–7

"Receipt" = recipe; fern-seed was thought to
make invisible whoever carried it.

2   *Othello.* Make it a darling like your
    precious eye.
To lose't or give't away were such
    perdition
As nothing else could match.
Desdemona. Is't possible?
Othello. There's magic in the web
    of it.

Othello, 3.4.69–73

Their topic is the handkerchief that causes so
much discord between them.

3   If this be magic, let it be an art
Lawful as eating!

Leontes in *The Winter's Tale*, 5.3.110–1

Spoken as what he thinks is a statue of
Hermione comes to life.

Malice (see also Hate)

1   Ill will never said well.

Orleans in *Henry V*, 3.7.113

Proverbial.

2   If I can catch him once upon the
    hip,
I will feed fat the ancient grudge I
    bear him.

**Shylock in *The Merchant of Venice*,
1.3.46–7**

To "have one on the hip," or capable of being
overthrown, is a proverbial phrase, from
wrestling.

Man (see also Men, Men and Women)

1 You might have been enough the
   man you are
   With striving less to be so.

   Volumnia in *Coriolanus*, 3.2.19–20

   Speaking to her warrior son.

2   I'll never
   Be such a gosling to obey instinct,
      but stand
   As if a man were author of himself,
   And knew no other kin.

   Coriolanus in *Coriolanus*, 5.3.34–7

   The gosling, or young goose, was noted for its
   foolishness.

3 I see a man's life is a tedious one.

   Imogen in *Cymbeline*, 3.6.1

   She is tired with traveling on foot disguised as
   a youth.

4 'A was a man, take him for all in
      all;
   I shall not look upon his like again.

   Hamlet in *Hamlet*, 1.2.186–8

   Hamlet sees his father as a real man, a heroic
   figure, in contrast to his uncle Claudius, now
   King of Denmark.

5 What a piece of work is a man!
   How noble in reason, how infinite
   in faculty, in form and moving how
   express and admirable, in action
   how like an angel, in apprehension
   how like a god—the beauty of the
   world, the paragon of animals!

   Hamlet in *Hamlet*, 2.2.303–7

Expressing the confidence of Renaissance
humanism.

6   Thou art e'en as just a man
   As e'er my conversation coped
   withal.

   Hamlet in *Hamlet*, 3.2.54–5

   His friend Horatio is as upright ("just") a man
   as any he has had dealings with ("coped
   withal").

7   What is a man,
   If his chief good and market of his
      time
   Be but to sleep and feed? A beast,
      no more.

   Hamlet in *Hamlet*, 4.4.33–5

   Trying to rouse himself; "market" = profit.

8 There is nothing but roguery to be
   found in villainous man, yet a coward is worse than a cup of sack with
   lime in it.

   Falstaff in *Henry IV, Part 1*, 2.4.124–7

   On being deserted by his friends; lime was
   sometimes added to poor wine to add sparkle;
   "sack" = dry white wine.

9 Is man no more than this? Consider him well. Thou ow'st the
   worm no silk, the beast no hide, the
   sheep no wool, the cat no perfume.
   Here's three on's are sophisticated.
   Thou art the thing itself; unaccommodated man is no more than such
   a poor, bare, forked animal as thou
   art.

   King Lear in *King Lear*, 3.4.102–8

   On meeting Edgar disguised as a mad beggar;
   Lear and his companions are clothed; Poor
   Tom (Edgar) is almost naked ("unaccommo-
   dated").

Manliness

1 I sprang not more in joy at first hearing he was a man-child than now in first seeing he had proved himself a man.

Volumnia in *Coriolanus*, 1.3.15–17

Rejoicing that her son, Caius Martius, is a warrior.

2 I dare do all that may become a man;
Who dares do more is none.

Macbeth in *Macbeth*, 1.7.46–7

Lady Macbeth taunts him with cowardice, but Macbeth replies that there is a limit to what it is fitting for a man to do; he is resisting the idea of murdering Duncan.

3 O that I were a man for his sake, or that I had any friend that would be a man for my sake! But manhood is melted into curtsies, valor into compliment.

Beatrice in *Much Ado About Nothing*, 4.1.317–20

Wishing she could challenge Claudio to a duel.

Manners

1 Thou art too wild, too rude, and bold of voice.

Bassanio in *The Merchant of Venice*, 2.2.181

On the boisterous Gratiano.

Maps

1 A plague upon it!
I have forgot the map.

Hotspur in *Henry IV, Part 1*, 3.1.5–6

The map on which the rebels were to mark out their shares of the kingdom.

2 Give me the map there.

King Lear in *King Lear*, 1.1.37

He intends to mark on it the division of his kingdom into three parts.

Marriage

1 A young man married is a man that's marred.

Parolles in *All's Well That Ends Well*, 2.3.298

Proverbial.

2 Husband, I come!
Now to that name my courage prove my title!

Cleopatra in *Antony and Cleopatra*, 5.2.287–8

Dying, she claims Antony, to whom she was never married, as her husband.

3 As the ox hath his bow, sir, the horse his curb, and the falcon her bells, so man hath his desires; and as pigeons bill, so wedlock would be nibbling.

Touchstone in *As You Like It*, 3.3.79–82

On his desire to marry; "bow" = yoke.

4 This fellow will but join you together as they join wainscot; then one of you will prove a shrunk panel, and like green timber warp, warp.

Jaques in *As You Like It*, 3.3.86–9

To Touchstone, who has invited an illiterate priest to marry him to Audrey.

5   Men are April when they woo,
    December when they wed; maids
    are May when they are maids, but
    the sky changes when they are
    wives.

Rosalind in *As You Like It*, 4.1.147–9

A woman's view of marriage.

6   Tomorrow is the joyful day,
    Audrey, tomorrow will we be
    married.

Touchstone in *As You Like It*, 5.3.1–2

7   Wedding is great Juno's crown,
    O blessed bond of board and bed!
    'Tis Hymen peoples every town,
    High wedlock then be honorèd.
    Honor, high honor, and renown
    To Hymen, god of every town!

Hymen in *As You Like It*, 5.4.141–6

"Hymen" = god of marriage, and "Juno,"
queen of the gods, also protected marriage.

8   Thy loving voyage
    Is but for two months victualled.

Jaques in *As You Like It*, 5.4.191–2

To Touchstone, about to marry Audrey.

9   The beasts, the fishes, and the
        wingèd fowls
    Are their males' subjects and at
        their controls:
    Man, more divine, the master of all
        these,
    Lord of the wide world and wild
        watery seas,
    Indued with intellectual sense and
        souls,
    Or more pre-eminence than fish
        and fowls,
    Are masters to their females, and
        their lords:

Then let your will attend on their
    accords.

**Luciana in *The Comedy of Errors*,
2.1.18–25**

An Elizabethan view of marriage, rejected
with spirit by her sister, Adriana, to whom the
lines are addressed.

10   My decayèd fair
    A sunny look of his would soon
        repair.

**Adriana in *The Comedy of Errors*,
2.1.98–9**

Complaining about her absent husband.

11 The time was once, when thou
        unurged wouldst vow
    That never words were music to
        thine ear,
    That never object pleasing in thine
        eye,
    That never meat sweet-savored in
        thy taste,
    Unless I spake, or looked, or
        touched, or carved to thee.

**Adriana in *The Comedy of Errors*,
2.2.113–18**

She is not, as she supposes, speaking to her
straying husband, but to his twin, Antipholus
of Syracuse.

12   As easy mayst thou fall
    A drop of water in the breaking
        gulf,
    And take unmingled thence that
        drop again,
    Without addition or diminishing,
    As take from me thyself and not me
        too.

**Adriana in *The Comedy of Errors*,
2.2.125–9**

An image of unity in marriage; "fall" = let fall.

13 Thou art an elm, my husband, I a
   vine,
   Whose weakness, married to thy
   stronger state,
   Makes me with thy strength to
   communicate.

Adriana in *The Comedy of Errors*,
2.2.174–6

The image of the vine embracing the elm is
proverbial.

14 And may it be that you have quite
   forgot
   A husband's office? Shall, Antipholus,
   Even in the spring of love, thy love-
   springs rot?

Luciana in *The Comedy of Errors*,
3.2.1–3

Luciana thinks she is talking to her sister's
husband, when it is actually his twin brother.

15   I will remain
   The loyalest husband that did e'er
   plight troth.

Posthumus in *Cymbeline*, 1.1.95–6

To Imogen, his wife, as they are about to be
parted.

16 If thou dost marry, I'll give thee this
   plague for thy dowry: be thou as
   chaste as ice, as pure as snow, thou
   shalt not escape calumny. Get thee
   to a nunnery, farewell! If thou wilt
   needs marry, marry a fool, for wise
   men know what monsters you
   make of them.

Hamlet in *Hamlet*, 3.1.134–9

Caustic advice to Ophelia.

17 Man and wife, being two, are one in
   love.

Queen Isabel in *Henry V*, 5.2.361

18 For what is wedlock forcèd, but a
   hell,
   An age of discord and continual
   strife?
   Whereas the contrary bringeth
   bliss,
   And is a pattern of celestial peace.

Suffolk in *Henry VI, Part 1*, 5.5.62–5

Proposing the king should marry for love.

19 Hasty marriage seldom proveth
   well.

**Richard of Gloucester in *Henry VI,
Part 3*, 4.1.18**

Varying the proverb, "Marry in haste and
repent at leisure."

20   Am I your self
   But as it were in sort or limitation,
   To keep with you at meals, comfort
   your bed,
   And talk to you sometimes?

Portia in *Julius Caesar*, 2.1.282–5

To her husband, Brutus; "in sort" = up to a
point.

21   Dwell I but in the suburbs
   Of your good pleasure? If it be no
   more,
   Portia is Brutus' harlot, not his
   wife.

Portia in *Julius Caesar*, 2.1.285–7

The brothels in Elizabethan London were
located in the suburbs, beyond the jurisdiction
of the city.

22 You are my true and honorable
   wife,
   As dear to me as are the ruddy
   drops
   That visit my sad heart.

Brutus in *Julius Caesar*, 2.1.288–90

To Portia.

23 What's mine is yours, and what is yours is mine.

Duke in *Measure for Measure*, 5.1.537

Offering marriage to Isabella.

24 Your wife would give you little thanks for that
If she were by to hear you make the offer.

Portia in *The Merchant of Venice*, 4.1.288–9

Disguised as a lawyer, she hears Bassanio value Antonio's life above everything, including herself.

25 Let me give light, but let me not be light,
For a light wife doth make a heavy husband.

Portia in *The Merchant of Venice*, 5.1.129–30

Playing on the idea of "light" as wanton or unchaste.

26 If there be no great love in the beginning, yet heaven may decrease it upon better acquaintance, when we are married and have more occasion to know one another.

Slender in *The Merry Wives of Windsor*, 1.1.246–9

Responding to the suggestion that he marry Anne Page.

27 We'll leave a proof, by that which we will do,
Wives may be merry, and yet honest too.

Mistress Page in *The Merry Wives of Windsor*, 4.2.104–5

Plotting to expose Falstaff and remain chaste.

28 But earthlier happy is the rose distilled
Than that which, withering on the virgin thorn,
Grows, lives, and dies in single blessedness.

Theseus in *A Midsummer Night's Dream*, 1.1.76–8

"Rose distilled" means literally distilled to perfume, but figuratively suggests marriage (and happiness on this earth).

29 Lord, I could not endure a husband with a beard on his face! I had rather lie in the woolen.

Beatrice in *Much Ado About Nothing*, 2.1.29–31

"Lie in the woolen" = between rough blankets, without sheets.

30 Wooing, wedding, and repenting, is as a Scotch jig, a measure, and a cinquepace; the first suit is hot and hasty, like a Scotch jig, and full as fantastical; the wedding, mannerly-modest, as a measure, full of state and ancientry; and then comes repentance and, with his bad legs, falls into the cinquepace faster and faster, till he sink into his grave.

Beatrice in *Much Ado About Nothing*, 2.1.73–80

Her cynical view of marriage; "state and ancientry" = stateliness and old-fashioned formality; a "cinquepace" was a lively dance (French "cinq pas" = five paces), with a pun on "sink."

31 *Don Pedro.* Will you have me, lady?
Beatrice. No, my lord, unless I might have another for working-days: your grace is too costly to wear every day.

***Much Ado About Nothing*, 2.1.326–9**

Beatrice neatly turns aside the offer of the Prince of Aragon.

32 When I said I would die a bachelor,
I did not think I should live till I
were married.

Benedick in *Much Ado About Nothing*,
2.3.242–4

Explaining his sudden discovery that he loves
Beatrice.

33 He swore he would never marry,
and yet now, in despite of his heart,
he eats his meat without grudging;
and how you may be converted I
know not, but methinks you look
with your eyes as other women do.

**Margaret in *Much Ado About
Nothing*, 3.4.88–92**

Speaking to Beatrice about Benedick, who
now is content to be a lover ("eats his meat
without grudging").

34 *Don Pedro.* But when shall we set
the savage bull's horns on the sensible Benedick's head?
Claudio. Yes, and text underneath,
"Here dwells Benedick, the married man"?

***Much Ado About Nothing*, 5.1.181–4**

Benedick had boasted earlier that he would
never submit to the yoke of marriage; the
"horns" as usual suggest cuckoldry.

35 Here's our own hands against our
hearts. Come, I will have thee; but,
by this light, I take thee for pity.

Benedick in *Much Ado About Nothing*,
5.4.91–3

To Beatrice; they have both expressed in writing ("hands") the love for each other they
have denied in speech.

36 I would not deny you; but, by this
good day, I yield upon great persuasion; and partly to save your life,
for I was told you were in a consumption.

Beatrice in *Much Ado About Nothing*,
5.4.94–7

Wittily accepting Benedick as a husband on
equal terms.

37 Since I do purpose to marry, I will
think nothing to any purpose that
the world can say against it; and
therefore never flout at me for what
I have said against it; for man is a
giddy thing, and this is my conclusion.

Benedick in *Much Ado About Nothing*,
5.4.105–9

Defending his change from being a confirmed
bachelor.

38 Prince, thou art sad. Get thee a
wife, get thee a wife. There is no
staff more reverend than one tipped
with horn.

Benedick in *Much Ado About Nothing*,
5.4.122–4

Jokingly hinting at the cuckold's horns.

39 A fellow almost damned in a fair
wife.

Iago in *Othello*, 1.1.22

Describing Cassio; we hear no more of this
"wife."

40 But that I love the gentle Desdemona,
I would not my unhousèd free condition
Put into circumscription and confine
For the sea's worth.

Othello in *Othello*, 1.2.25–8

As a soldier Othello has no house or domestic life; "circumscription" = restriction; Othello is fond of such big words, that here make marriage sound a little like imprisonment.

41   O curse of marriage,
That we can call these delicate creatures ours
And not their appetites!
Othello in *Othello*, 3.3.268–70

Thinking of Desdemona.

42 But I do think it is their husbands' faults
If wives do fall.
Emilia in *Othello*, 4.3.86–7

43   Let husbands know
Their wives have sense like them; they see, and smell,
And have their palates both for sweet and sour,
As husbands have. What is it that they do
When they change us for others? Is it sport?
I think it is. And doth affection breed it?
I think it doth. Is't frailty that thus errs?
It is so, too. And have not we affections,
Desires for sport, and frailty, as men have?
Then let them use us well; else let them know,
The ills we do, their ills instruct us so.
Emilia in *Othello*, 4.3.93–103

Emilia's impassioned plea for equal moral standards for men and women.

44 The sweet silent hours of marriage joys.
King Richard in *Richard III*, 4.4.330

Trying to persuade Queen Elizabeth that he is a fit suitor for her daughter's hand.

45 Do thou but close our hands with holy words,
Then love-devouring death do what he dare,
It is enough I may but call her mine.
Romeo in *Romeo and Juliet*, 2.6.6–8

Speaking to Friar Lawrence before his marriage to Juliet, and already foreshadowing the death that will end their love.

46 We will have rings and things, and fine array,
And kiss me, Kate, we will be married o' Sunday.
Petruchio in *The Taming of the Shrew*, 2.1.323–4

"Kiss Me Kate" is the title of a musical based on the play; "we will be married o' Sunday" occurs as a refrain in ballads.

47 *Miranda.* My husband, then?
Ferdinand. Ay, with a heart as willing
As bondage e'er of freedom.
Here's my hand.
Miranda. And mine, with my heart in 't.
The Tempest, 3.1.87–90

The marriage bond for these lovers becomes paradoxically their freedom.

48 Many a good hanging prevents a bad marriage.
Feste in *Twelfth Night*, 1.5.19–20

Probably with a sexual quibble on the idea of being "well hung."

49   Let still the woman take
An elder than herself. So wears she
   to him;
So sways she level in her husband's
   heart.

Orsino in *Twelfth Night*, 2.4.29–31

Giving to his page Cesario (Viola in disguise) advice that is ironically more appropriate to Viola.

Maturity

1   Then the justice,
In fair round belly with good capon
   lined,
With eyes severe and beard of for-
   mal cut,
Full of wise saws and modern
   instances;
And so he plays his part.

Jaques in *As You Like It*, 2.7.153–7

The fifth of the "seven ages" of man, when he is full of wise sayings and trite examples. The capon or fowl suggests he is well fed with meat; or is it possibly a bribe?

2   O, let us have him, for his silver
   hairs
Will purchase us a good opinion,
And buy men's voices to commend
   our deeds.

Metellus in *Julius Caesar*, 2.1.144–6

Recommending that Cicero be invited to join the conspirators against Caesar.

3   It shall be said his judgment ruled
   our hands.
Our youths and wildness shall no
   whit appear,
But all be buried in his gravity.

Metellus in *Julius Caesar*, 2.1.147–9

Arguing for the inclusion of Cicero as one of the conspirators.

4   I speak not like a dotard nor a fool,
As under privilege of age to brag
What I have done being young, or
   what would do
Were I not old.

Leonato in *Much Ado About Nothing*, 5.1.59–62

Old Leonato is about to challenge young Claudio to a duel.

Medicine (see also Sickness)

1   I have seen a medicine
That's able to breathe life into a
   stone.

Lafew in *All's Well That Ends Well*, 2.1.72–3

Referring to the beauty of Helena, as able to cure the sick King of France.

2   I will through and
   through
Cleanse the foul body of the
   infected world
If they will patiently receive my
   medicine.

Jaques in *As You Like It*, 2.7.60–1

Claiming a godlike ability to purge people of their sins.

3   I will not cast away my physic but
on those that are sick.

Rosalind in *As You Like It*, 3.2.358–9

4   I will not let him stir
Till I have used the approvèd
   means I have,
With wholesome syrups, drugs, and
   holy prayers,
To make of him a formal man
   again.

The Abbess in *The Comedy of Errors*, 5.1.102–5

About Antipholus of Ephesus, who is supposedly mad; "formal" = sane.

5   By medicine life may be prolonged, yet death
Will seize the doctor too.

Cymbeline in *Cymbeline*, 5.5.29–30

On hearing that his Queen, who compounded drugs herself, is dead.

6   No medicine in the world can do thee good;
In thee there is not half an hour's life.

Laertes in *Hamlet*, 5.2.314–5

Telling Hamlet he is fatally poisoned.

7   I am bewitched with the rogue's company. If the rascal have not given me medicines to make me love him, I'll be hanged. It could not be else, I have drunk medicines.

Falstaff in *Henry IV, Part 1*, 2.2.17–20

Speaking of Prince Hal or Poins, who has hidden his horse.

8   Kill thy physician, and the fee bestow
Upon the foul disease.

Kent in *King Lear*, 1.1.163–4

Kent himself is the "physician" trying to cure Lear of madness.

9   *Macbeth.* Canst thou not minister to a mind diseased,
Pluck from the memory a rooted sorrow,
Raze out the written troubles of the brain,
And with some sweet oblivious antidote

Cleanse the stuffed bosom of that perilous stuff
Which weighs upon the heart?
Doctor. Therein the patient
Must minister to himself.

Macbeth, 5.3.40–6

"Raze out" = erase; "oblivious" = producing forgetfulness; the "stuff" that weighs on the heart includes guilt for murder.

10   Throw physic to the dogs! I'll none of it.

Macbeth in *Macbeth*, 5.3.47

To the doctor who cannot cure his wife's disease of the mind.

11   What rhubarb, senna, or what purgative drug
Would scour these English hence?

Macbeth in *Macbeth*, 5.3.55–6

Wishing he could get rid of his enemies by purging.

12   Tenderly apply to her
Some remedies for life.

Leontes in *The Winter's Tale*, 3.2.152–3

Anxious as Hermione faints; "for life" = to restore her to life.

Mediocrity

1   *Touchstone.* Art rich?
William. Faith, sir, so-so.
Touchstone. So-so is good, very good, very excellent good. And yet it is not, it is but so-so.

As You Like It, 5.1.25–8

Touchstone is mocking the country bumpkin William, who says he is pretty rich, by changing the meaning of so-so.

Meeting

1 Methinks King Richard and myself
should meet
With no less terror than the elements
Of fire and water, when their thun-
dering shock
At meeting tears the cloudy cheeks
of heaven.

Bolingbroke in *Richard II*, 3.3.54–7

Fire and water were two of the four elements
thought to compose all matter (the others
being earth and air).

Melancholy (see also Moods, Temperament)

1 The melancholy Jaques.

First Lord in *As You Like It*, 2.1.26

The adjective has permanently stuck to the
character.

2 I can suck melancholy out of a
song, as a weasel sucks eggs.

Jaques in *As You Like It*, 2.5.12–13

3 I have neither the scholar's melancholy, which is emulation; nor the
musician's, which is fantastical; nor
the courtier's, which is proud; nor
the soldier's, which is ambitious;
nor the lawyer's, which is politic;
nor the lady's, which is nice; nor
the lover's, which is all these.

Jaques in *As You Like It*, 4.1.10–15

Claiming his brand of melancholy is unique to
himself.

4 It is a melancholy of mine own,
compounded of many simples,
extracted from many objects.

Jaques in *As You Like It*, 4.1.15–17

"Simples" = ingredients.

5 Sweet recreation barred, what doth
ensue
But moody and dull melancholy,
Kinsman to grim and comfortless
despair.

The Abbess in *The Comedy of Errors*, 5.1.78–80

Showing Adriana the state to which she has
supposedly driven her husband.

6 He raised a sigh so piteous and pro-
found
As it did seem to shatter all his bulk
And end his being.

Ophelia in *Hamlet*, 2.1.91–3

Describing Hamlet's behavior to Polonius;
"bulk" = body.

7 *Falstaff.* 'Sblood, I am as melancholy as a gib cat, or a lugged
bear.
Prince Hal. Or an old lion, or a
lover's lute.
Falstaff. Yea, or the drone of a Lin-
colnshire bagpipe.

Henry IV, Part 1, 1.2.73–6

Falstaff swears by Christ's blood; "gib cat" =
tomcat, and a "lugged" bear is one led by a
chain for bear-baiting.

8 The sad companion, dull-eyed
melancholy.

Pericles in *Pericles*, 1.2.2

9   She never told her love,
But let concealment, like a worm i'
 the bud
Feed on her damask cheek. She
 pined in thought,
And with a green and yellow
 melancholy
She sat like patience on a monument,
Smiling at grief. Was not this love
 indeed?

Viola in *Twelfth Night*, 2.4.110–15

Disguised as Cesario, she is forced to conceal
her love for Orsino, to whom she is speaking.

Memory (see also Remembrance)

1 Though yet of Hamlet our dear
  brother's death
 The memory be green.

Claudius in *Hamlet*, 1.2.1–2

"Green" = fresh; he has been dead two
months.

2   Remember thee!
Ay, thou poor ghost, while memory
 holds a seat
In this distracted globe.

Hamlet in *Hamlet*, 1.5.95–7

Hamlet's father's ghost has just left him with
the command, "remember me"; "globe" = his
head (or the Globe Theatre, or the world?).

3 Die two months ago, and not forgotten yet? Then there's hope a
 great man's memory may outlive
 his life half a year.

Hamlet in *Hamlet*, 3.2.130–2

A biting comment in response to Ophelia saying Hamlet's father died "twice two months"
ago.

4 Memory, the warder of the brain.

Lady Macbeth in *Macbeth*, 1.7.65

"Warder" = watchman.

5   I would forget it fain,
But O, it presses to my memory
Like damnèd guilty deeds to sin-
 ners' minds.

Juliet in *Romeo and Juliet*, 3.2.109–11

She would forget that she heard Romeo was
banished; "fain" = gladly.

6   What seest thou else
In the dark backward and abysm of
 time?

Prospero in *The Tempest*, 1.2.49–50

Asking his daughter Miranda what she
remembers of her childhood.

Men (see also Man, Men and Women)

1 In faith, he is a worthy gentleman,
 Exceedingly well read, and profited
 In strange concealments, valiant as
  a lion,
 And wondrous affable, and as
  bountiful
 As mines of India.

Mortimer in *Henry IV, Part 1*, 3.1.163–7

To Hotspur, about Glendower, mocked by
Hotspur; "profited" = proficient; "strange concealments" = occult arts.

2 A fellow of no mark nor livelihood.

King Henry in *Henry IV, Part 1*, 3.2.45

On what he would have been had he behaved
like Prince Hal; "livelihood" = means of
living.

3 Let the end try the man.

Prince Hal in *Henry IV, Part 2,* 2.2.47

"Try" = test, show the true worth of.

4 O miracle of men!

Lady Percy in *Henry IV, Part 2,* 2.3.33

Acclaiming Hotspur as the ideal man.

5 As young as I am, I have observed these three swashers. I am boy to them all three, but all they three, though they would serve me, could not be man to me.

Boy in *Henry V,* 3.2.28–31

Seeing through the swashbuckling Nym, Bardolph and Pistol, who, for all their bravado, are cowards; "boy" = servant.

6 For Nym, he hath heard that men of few words are the best men, and therefore he scorns to say his prayers, lest 'a should be thought a coward.

Boy in *Henry V,* 3.2.36–8

7 You are not wood, you are not stones, but men;
And being men, hearing the will of Caesar,
It will inflame you, it will make you mad.

Mark Antony in *Julius Caesar,* 3.2.142–4

Addressing the people.

8 I dare do all that may become a man;
Who dares do more is none.

Macbeth in *Macbeth,* 1.7.46–7

"Become" = be proper to, or grace, and could be meant in physical or moral terms.

9 When I did first impart my love to you,
I freely told you all the wealth I had
Ran in my veins: I was a gentleman;
And then I told you true.

Bassanio in *The Merchant of Venice,* 3.2.253–6

10 He is the only man of Italy,
Always excepted my dear Claudio.

Hero in *Much Ado About Nothing,* 3.1.92–3

Praising Benedick in the hope of making the listening Beatrice fall in love with him.

11 But men are men; the best sometimes forget.

Iago in *Othello,* 2.3.241

"Men are but men" is proverbial.

12 Nay, we must think men are not gods,
Nor of them look for such observancy
As fits the bridal.

Desdemona in *Othello,* 3.4.148–50

Excusing Othello's anger with her by saying she cannot expect such attentiveness ("observancy") as at her wedding.

Men and Women

1 That man should be at woman's command, and no harm done!

Lavatch in *All's Well That Ends Well,* 1.3.92–3

On being ordered away by the Countess of Rossillion.

2 You are a thousand times a properer man

Than she a woman. 'Tis such fools
as you
That makes the world full of ill-
favored children.

Rosalind in *As You Like It*, 3.5.51–3

Disguised as a man, she advises Silvius, who
loves Phebe, who is in love with Rosalind;
"properer" = more handsome.

3   My way is to conjure you, and I'll
begin with the women. I charge
you, O women, for the love you
bear to men, to like as much of this
play as please you. I charge you, O
men, for the love you bear to
women (as I perceive by your simpering none of you hates them),
that between you and the women,
the play may please.

**Rosalind in *As You Like It*, Epilogue,
11–17**

Appealing to her audience, which included a
lot of women.

4   Rich she shall be, that's certain;
wise, or I'll none; virtuous, or I'll
never cheapen her; fair, or I'll never
look on her; mild, or come not near
me; noble, or not I for an angel; of
good discourse, an excellent musician, and her hair shall be of what
color it please God.

**Benedick in *Much Ado About Nothing*,
2.3.30–5**

Admitting after all that he could care for a
woman—if she has all the graces.

5   They say the lady is fair; 'tis a truth,
I can bear them witness; and virtuous; so, I cannot reprove it; and
wise, but for loving me. By my
troth, it is no addition to her wit,
nor no great argument of her folly,
for I will be horribly in love with
her.

**Benedick in *Much Ado About Nothing*,
2.3.230–5**

On hearing Beatrice loves him, he is prepared
to praise her, and to love her.

6   I cannot be a man with wishing,
therefore I will die a woman with
grieving.

**Beatrice in *Much Ado About Nothing*,
4.1.322–3**

Addressing Benedick, in the hope of persuading him to challenge Claudio.

7   'Tis not a year or two shows us a
man:
They are all but stomachs, and we
all but food;
They eat us hungerly, and when
they are full
They belch us.

Emilia in *Othello*, 3.4.103–6

She may have her husband, Iago, in mind; "all
but" = nothing but; "hungerly" = hungrily.

8   Women may fall when there's no
strength in men.

**Friar Lawrence in *Romeo and Juliet*,
2.3.80**

To Romeo, alluding to St. Paul's conception of
the wife as the "weaker vessel" to be honored
and protected by her husband (I Peter 3:7).

9   Women are angels, wooing;
Things won are done; joy's soul lies
in the doing.
That she beloved knows naught
that knows not this:
Men prize the thing ungained more
than it is.

**Cressida in *Troilus and Cressida*,
1.2.286–9**

She has been holding off against her uncle
Pandarus's attempts to woo her on behalf of
Troilus.

10 Boy, however we do praise ourselves,
   Our fancies are more giddy and
   unfirm,
   More longing, wavering, sooner
   lost and worn,
   Than women's are.

Orsino in *Twelfth Night*, 2.4.32–5

Speaking to Cesario (Viola in disguise) of
men's loves ("fancies") as soon exhausted
("worn").

11 Women will love her, that she is a
   woman
   More worth than any man; men,
   that she is
   The rarest of all women.

Servant in *The Winter's Tale*, 5.1.110–12

On the rare qualities of Perdita.

Mercy (see also Forgiveness)

1 Whereto serves mercy,
  But to confront the visage of
  offense?

Claudius in *Hamlet*, 3.3.46–7

Hoping somehow to be forgiven for murdering old Hamlet.

2 O, let us yet be merciful.

King Henry in *Henry V*, 2.2.47

On pardoning a prisoner against the advice of
others.

3 Use mercy to them all.

King Henry in *Henry V*, 3.3.54

4 Mercy is not itself, that oft looks so;
  Pardon is still the nurse of second
  woe.

Escalus in *Measure for Measure*,
2.1.284–5

Meaning that pardon often leads to more
wrongdoing.

5 Yes, I do think that you might pardon him,
  And neither heaven nor man grieve
  at the mercy.

Isabella in *Measure for Measure*,
2.2.49–50

Pleading for the life of her brother, who is
condemned to death.

6 No ceremony that to great ones
  'longs,
  Not the king's crown, nor the
  deputed sword,
  The marshal's truncheon, nor the
  judge's robe,
  Become them with one half so good
  a grace
  As mercy does.

Isabella in *Measure for Measure*,
2.2.59–63

Arguing for mercy to her condemned brother;
" 'longs" = belongs; "deputed sword" = the
sword of justice entrusted to the ruler or judge
as a mark of office; "truncheon" = baton or
staff.

7 Why, all the souls that were were
  forfeit once,
  And He that might the vantage best
  have took
  Found out the remedy. How would
  you be
  If He which is the top of judgment
  should

But judge you as you are? O, think
   on that,
And mercy then will breathe within
   your lips,
Like man new made.

Isabella in *Measure for Measure,*
2.2.73–9

In pleading for her brother's life, Isabella is
recalling Christ's sermon on the mount,
Matthew 7, beginning "Judge not, that ye be
not judged."

8   Ignominy in ransom and free par-
      don
   Are of two houses; lawful mercy
   Is nothing kin to foul redemption.

Isabella in *Measure for Measure,*
2.4.111–13

Rejecting Angelo's offer of freedom for her
brother at a price (Isabella's chastity).

9   How shalt thou hope for mercy,
    rendering none?

Duke in *The Merchant of Venice,* 4.1.88

To Shylock, who has refused an offer of twice
what he has lent Antonio.

10 The quality of mercy is not
    strained,
   It droppeth as the gentle rain from
    heaven
   Upon the place beneath. It is twice
    blest:
   It blesseth him that gives and him
    that takes.

Portia in *The Merchant of Venice,*
4.1.184–7

Inviting Shylock to be merciful; "strained" =
forced or constrained.

11 Mercy is above this sceptered
    sway,

It is enthronèd in the hearts of
   kings,
It is an attribute to God himself;
And earthly power doth then show
   likest God's
When mercy seasons justice.

Portia in *The Merchant of Venice,*
4.1.193–7

Offering Shylock the chance to show mercy;
"sceptered sway" = earthly rule; "attribute to"
= characteristic of.

12   We do pray for mercy,
   And that same prayer doth teach us
    all to render
   The deeds of mercy.

Portia in *The Merchant of Venice,*
4.1.200–2

Inviting Shylock to be merciful.

13 *Verges.* You have always been
    called a merciful man, partner.
   Dogberry. Truly, I would not hang
    a dog by my will, much more a
    man who hath any honesty in
    him.

Much Ado About Nothing, 3.3.61–4

The two comic constables discuss the law.

14 Mercy but murders, pardoning
    those that kill.

Prince Escalus in *Romeo and Juliet,*
3.1.197

15 Wilt thou draw near the nature of
    the gods?
   Draw near them then in being mer-
    ciful.
   Sweet mercy is nobility's true
    badge.

Tamora in *Titus Andronicus,* 1.1.117–19

Begging Titus for mercy.

Merit (see also Deserving)

1 "Who chooseth me shall get as
   much as he deserves."
   And well said too; for who shall go
   about
   To cozen fortune, and be honorable
   Without the stamp of merit?

   Prince of Aragon in *The Merchant of*
   Venice, 2.9.36–9

   Looking at the silver casket in the hope that he
   will cheat ("cozen") fortune because he has
   the seal of approval ("stamp of merit") in
   being an aristocrat.

2 O that estates, degrees, and offices
   Were not derived corruptly, and
   that clear honor
   Were purchased by the merit of the
   wearer!

   Prince of Aragon in *The Merchant of*
   Venice, 2.9.41–3

   The aristocrat wishes status and rank were
   always the reward of merit, and could not be
   obtained by corrupt means.

Merriment (see also Jokes, Laughter)

1 *Prince Hal.* Shall we be merry?
   Poins. As merry as crickets, my lad.

   Henry IV, Part 1, 2.4.88–9

   Hal and his companions at the tavern in
   Eastcheap.

2 Berowne they call him, but a merrier man,
   Within the limit of becoming
   mirth,
   I never spent an hour's talk withal.

   Rosaline in *Love's Labor's Lost*, 2.1.66–8

   Rosaline's account of meeting with Berowne.

3 Let me play the fool,
   With mirth and laughter let old
   wrinkles come.

   Gratiano in *The Merchant of Venice*,
   1.1.79–80

   Preferring to enjoy life, and rejecting Antonio's melancholy.

4 *Don Pedro.* To be merry best
   becomes you; for, out o'question,
   you were born in a merry hour.
   Beatrice. No, sure, my lord, my
   mother cried; but then there was a
   star danced, and under that was I
   born.

   Much Ado About Nothing, 2.1.331–5

   The stars were thought to influence temperament.

5 From the crown of his head to the
   sole of his foot, he is all mirth.

   Don Pedro in *Much Ado About Noth-*
   ing, 3.2.8–10

   Describing Benedick.

6 Jog on, jog on, the footpath way,
   And merrily hent the stile-a,
   A merry heart goes all the day,
   Your sad tires in a mile-a.

   Autolycus in *The Winter's Tale*,
   4.3.123–6

   Enjoying his success as a trickster; "hent" =
   take hold of.

Middle Age

1   Think on me,
That am with Phoebus' amorous
   pinches black,
And wrinkled deep in time.

Cleopatra in *Antony and Cleopatra*,
1.5.27–8

Acknowledging her age (she was 38) and
experience in love; Phoebus was god of the
sun.

2   What, girl, though grey
Do something mingle with our
   younger brown, yet ha' we
A brain that nourishes our nerves,
   and can
Get goal for goal of youth.

Antony in *Antony and Cleopatra*,
4.8.19–22

To Cleopatra, claiming he can match the
young in fighting.

3   *Lear.* How old art thou?
   Kent. Not so young, sir, to love a
   woman for singing, nor so old to
   dote on her for anything.

King Lear, 1.4.36–8

Kent goes on to say he is 48 years old.

4   I am too old to fawn upon a nurse,
Too far in years to be a pupil now.

Mowbray in *Richard II*, 1.3.170–1

Banished, he feels too old to learn a new language and way of life.

5   He has his health, and ampler
   strength indeed
Than most have of his age.

Florizel in *The Winter's Tale*, 4.4.403–4

Speaking of his father, Polixenes.

Miracles

1   They say miracles are past, and we
have our philosophical persons to
make modern and familiar things
supernatural and causeless. Hence
is it that we make trifles of terrors,
ensconcing ourselves into seeming
knowledge when we should submit
ourselves to an unknown fear.

Lafew in *All's Well That Ends Well*,
2.3.1–6

"Philosophical persons" = scientists who
make what is supernatural and unexplained in
terms of natural causes seem commonplace
("modern and familiar"); "unknown fear" =
awe in the face of what is unknowable.

2   Nothing almost sees miracles
But misery.

Kent in *King Lear*, 2.2.165–6

Those in misery are almost the only people
who see miracles (when anything happens to
bring relief).

3   Ten masts at each make not the
   altitude
Which thou hast perpendicularly
   fell.
Thy life's a miracle.

Edgar in *King Lear*, 4.6.53–5

To his father, who thinks he has jumped off a
cliff.

4   Think that the clearest gods, who
   make them honors
Of men's impossibilities, have preserved thee.

Edgar in *King Lear*, 4.6.73–4

Making his father believe he has fallen off a
cliff and survived.

Misanthropy

1   What should such fellows as I do
crawling between heaven and earth?
We are arrant knaves all, believe
none of us.

Hamlet in *Hamlet*, 3.1.126–8

In Hamlet's anger against Ophelia he
denounces all men, himself included.

2   I have no brother, I am like no
brother;
And this word "love," which greybeards call divine,
Be resident in men like one
another,
And not in me: I am myself alone.

**Richard of Gloucester in *Henry VI,
Part 3*, 5.6.80–3**

3   I had rather hear my dog bark at a
crow than a man swear he loves me.

**Beatrice in *Much Ado About Nothing*,
1.1.131–2**

4   I cannot hide what I am. I must be
sad when I have cause, and smile at
no man's jests.

**Don John in *Much Ado About
Nothing*, 1.3.13–14**

Showing his morose nature.

5   All's obliquy;
There's nothing level in our cursèd
natures
But direct villainy. Therefore be
abhorred
All feasts, societies, and throngs of
men!

Timon in *Timon of Athens*, 4.3.18–21

Timon is expressing his misanthropy;
"obliquy" = obliquity, or deviation from moral
standards.

Misery (see also Affliction, Suffering)

1   When we our betters see bearing
our woes,
We scarcely think our miseries our
foes.
Who alone suffers, suffers most i'
the mind,
Leaving free things and happy
shows behind.
But then the mind much sufferance
doth o'erskip,
When grief hath mates, and bearing
fellowship.

Edgar in *King Lear*, 3.6.102–7

Developing the proverb, "it's good to have
company in misery"; "free" = free from misery; "happy shows" = pleasant sights; "bearing" = endurance.

2   Is wretchedness deprived that benefit
To end itself by death? 'Twas yet
some comfort
When misery could beguile the
tyrant's rage
And frustrate his proud will.

Gloucester in *King Lear*, 4.6.61–4

Stoics like Seneca defended suicide as a way
to cheat ("beguile") the enmity of tyrants like
Nero in ancient Rome.

3   Shall we rest us here,
And by relating tales of others'
griefs,
See if 'twill teach us to forget our
own?

Cleon in *Pericles*, 1.4.1–3

"Griefs" = miseries; Cleon's city is afflicted by
famine.

4 O, the fierce wretchedness that
   glory brings us!
   Who would not wish to be from
   wealth exempt,
   Since riches point to misery and
   contempt?

Flavius in *Timon of Athens*, 4.2.30–2

Commenting on the fall of Timon, abandoned
by his friends.

5 When in disgrace with Fortune and
   men's eyes
   I all alone beweep my outcast
   state,
   And trouble deaf heaven with my
   bootless cries,
   And look upon myself and curse
   my fate,
   Wishing me like to one more rich
   in hope,
   Featured like him, like him with
   friends possessed,
   Desiring this man's art and that
   man's scope,
   With what I most enjoy contented
   least;
   Yet in these thoughts myself almost
   despising,
   Haply I think on thee, and then my
   state
   (Like to the lark at break of day
   arising
   From sullen earth) sings hymns at
   heaven's gate,
   For thy sweet love remembered
   such wealth brings
   That then I scorn to change my
   state with kings.

Sonnet 29

A poignant testimony to the power of his love
for his friend; "in disgrace" = out of favor;
"bootless" = unavailing, useless; "art" = skill
(line 7 is quoted by T.S. Eliot in his poem *Ash
Wednesday*); "haply" = perhaps.

Misogyny

1 Down from the waist they are cen-
   taurs,
   Though women all above;
   But to the girdle do the gods
   inherit,
   Beneath is all the fiends': there's
   hell, there's darkness,
   There is the sulphurous pit, burn-
   ing, scalding,
   Stench, consumption.

King Lear in *King Lear*, 4.6.124–9

The treatment of him by his daughters provokes this outburst of misogyny; centaurs
were legendary creatures, half-human, half-
horse, and notorious for lustfulness.

2 What is he for a fool that betroths
   himself to unquietness?

**Don John in *Much Ado About
Nothing*, 1.3.47–8**

Seeing Claudio as a fool for becoming
engaged to Hero.

3 One woman is fair, yet I am well;
   another is wise, yet I am well;
   another virtuous, yet I am well; but
   till all graces be in one woman, one
   woman shall not come in my grace.

**Benedick in *Much Ado About Nothing*,
2.3.26–30**

Rejecting the idea of loving a woman.

4 There's no true drop of blood in
   him to be truly touched with love;
   if he be sad, he wants money.

**Don Pedro in *Much Ado About Noth-
ing*, 3.2.18–20**

Unable to believe Benedick can fall in love;
"wants" = is in need of, lacks.

Mistakes

1   What error drives our eyes and ears
    amiss?

    Antipholus of Syracuse in *The Comedy of Errors*, 2.2.184

    Amazed to find Adriana, wife of his twin
    Antipholus of Ephesus, treating him as her
    husband.

2   This must be patched
    With cloth of any color.

    Menenius in *Coriolanus*, 3.1.251–2

    Hoping to restore peace after Coriolanus has
    misguidedly angered the people.

3   O hateful Error, Melancholy's
        child,
    Why dost thou show to the apt
        thoughts of men
    The things that are not?

    Messala in *Julius Caesar*, 5.3.67–9

    On the death of Cassius, who mistakenly
    thought the battle lost, and took his own life.

4   You never spoke what did become
        you less
    Than this.

    Camillo in *The Winter's Tale*, 1.2.282–3

    On hearing Leontes accuse his wife of adultery.

Misunderstanding

1   Men may construe things after their
        fashion,
    Clean from the purpose of the
        things themselves.

    Cicero in *Julius Caesar*, 1.3.34–5

    "Construe" = interpret.

2   Your sense pursues not mine.
        Either you are ignorant,
    Or seem so, craftily; and that's not
        good.

    **Angelo in *Measure for Measure*,
    2.4.74–5**

    Isabella does not understand that Angelo
    wants her sexually, and he thinks she is devious, like himself.

Mockery

1   *Amiens.* What's that "ducdame"?
    Jaques. 'Tis a Greek invocation, to
        call fools into a circle.

    ***As You Like It*, 2.5.58–60**

    Jaques is mocking his friends with this meaningless nonsense.

2   The tongues of mocking wenches
        are as keen
    As is the razor's edge invisible.

    Boyet in *Love's Labor's Lost*, 5.2.256–7

    On the court ladies, who have overwhelmed
    the courtiers by mocking them.

3   *Don Pedro.* She cannot endure to
        hear tell of a husband.
    Leonato. O, by no means; she
        mocks all her wooers out of suit.

    ***Much Ado About Nothing*, 2.1.347–50**

    Referring to Beatrice.

Moderation

1   Rather rejoicing to see another
    merry, than merry at anything
    which professed to make him
    rejoice; a gentleman of all temperance.

Escalus in *Measure for Measure,*
3.2.235–7

Describing the Duke's pleasures; 'temperance'
= moderation.

2   They are as sick that surfeit with
too much as they that starve with
nothing. It is no mean happiness
therefore to be seated in the mean.
Nerissa in *The Merchant of Venice,*
1.2.5–8

"In the mean" = between extremes of too
much or too little.

3   Superfluity comes sooner by white
hairs, but competency lives longer.
Nerissa in *The Merchant of Venice,*
1.2.8–9

Over-indulgence or having too much ages
people, while those of moderate means live
longer.

Modesty

1   It is the witness still of excellency
To put a strange face on his own
  perfection.
Don Pedro in *Much Ado About Noth-*
***ing,* 2.3.46–7**

On the singer Balthasar; it is typical of the
truly talented not to seem to be aware of their
own high skill.

2   There's not a note of mine that's
  worth the noting.
Balthasar in *Much Ado About*
***Nothing,* 2.3.55**

Quibbling on "noting" and "nothing," as the
play portrays much ado about noting (observing or listening) and a quarrel that springs
from nothing.

Money (see also Business, Gold, Payment)

1   Poor fellow never joyed since the
price of oats rose, it was the death
of him.
First Carrier in *Henry IV, Part 1,*
2.1.12–13

Remembering Robin, the ostler.

2   A trifle, some eight-penny matter.
Prince Hal in *Henry IV, Part 1,* 3.3.104

The ring Falstaff claims has been stolen from
him.

3   O, I do not like that paying back,
'tis a double labor.
Falstaff in *Henry IV, Part 1,* 3.3.179–80

Prince Hal has returned the money they stole.

4   I can get no remedy against this
consumption of the purse; borrowing only lingers and lingers it out,
but the disease is incurable.
Falstaff in *Henry IV, Part 2,* 1.2.236–8

5   Base is the slave that pays.
Pistol in *Henry V,* 2.1.96

Refusing to pay a gaming debt.

6   For I can raise no money by vile
  means.
Brutus in *Julius Caesar,* 4.3.71

7   *Ford.* If money go before, all ways
  do lie open.
Falstaff. Money is a good soldier,
  sir, and will on.
***The Merry Wives of Windsor,* 2.2.168–70**

Ford, disguised, is exposing Falstaff's corrupt
way of thinking.

8   I hate him for he is a Christian;
But more, for that in low simplicity
He lends out money gratis, and
    brings down
The rate of usance here with us in
    Venice.

Shylock in *The Merchant of Venice*,
1.3.42–5

On Antonio, his rival merchant; "low simplicity" can mean both modest or humble guile-
lessness, or base folly; "usance" = usury.

9   Signior Antonio, many a time and
    oft
In the Rialto you have rated me
About my moneys and my usances.
Still have I borne it with a patient
    shrug
(For sufferance is the badge of all
    our tribe).

Shylock in *The Merchant of Venice*,
1.3.106–10

"Rated" = berated; "usances" = usury.

10   Moneys is your suit.
What should I say to you? Should I
    not say,
"Hath a dog money? Is it possible
A cur can lend three thousand
    ducats?" Or
Shall I bend low and in a bond-
    man's key,
With bated breath and whispering
    humbleness,
Say this:
"Fair sir, you spat on me on
    Wednesday last,
You spurned me such a day,
    another time
You called me dog; and for these
    courtesies
I'll lend you thus much moneys"?

Shylock in *The Merchant of Venice*,
1.3.119–29

Speaking to Antonio, the "merchant" who
needs to borrow from Shylock.

11   Put money in thy purse.

Iago in *Othello*, 1.3.339–40

Proverbial now, implying that anything can be
bought. He is speaking to Roderigo.

12   Why, nothing comes amiss, so
money comes withal.

Grumio in *The Taming of the Shrew*,
1.2.81–2

Arguing that any woman, however old and
ugly, will do for a wife as long as money
comes with her.

13   This is no time to lend money,
especially upon bare friendship
without security.

Lucullus in *Timon of Athens*, 3.1.41–3

Refusing to help Timon.

Monsters

1   Though they are of monstrous
    shape, yet note
Their manners are more gentle,
    kind, than of
Our human generation you shall
    find
Many, nay, almost any.

Gonzalo in *The Tempest*, 3.3.31–4

On the "strange shapes" that offer Alonso and
his courtiers a banquet.

Moods (see also Melancholy, Temperament)

1   Like to the time o'the year between
    the extremes
Of hot and cold, he was nor sad nor
    merry.

Alexas in *Antony and Cleopatra*,
1.5.51–2

Reporting Antony's mood when he sent a message to Cleopatra.

2 I love to cope him in these sullen fits,
For then he's full of matter.
Duke Senior in *As You Like It*,
2.1.67–8

Referring to the melancholy Jaques; "cope" = encounter.

3 *Jaques.* Why, 'tis good to be sad and say nothing.
Rosalind. Why then 'tis good to be a post.
***As You Like It*, 4.1.8–9**

In fact Jaques cannot stop talking.

4 I had rather have a fool to make me merry than experience to make me sad—and to travel for it too!
Rosalind in *As You Like It*, 4.1.27–9

To Jaques, who has been defining his particular melancholy.

5   So to your pleasures,
I am for other than for dancing measures.
Jaques in *As You Like It*, 5.4.92–3

Separating himself from the general happy ending, Jaques returns to the cave in the forest.

6 Why should we in our peevish opposition
Take it to heart?
Claudius in *Hamlet*, 1.2.100–1

Suggesting Hamlet is perverse in continuing to mourn for his father.

7 *Hamlet.* What, looked he frowningly?

Horatio.   A countenance more
In sorrow than in anger.
***Hamlet*, 1.2.231–2**

Describing the expression of the ghost of Hamlet's father.

8 Why hast thou lost the fresh blood in thy cheeks,
And given my treasures and my rights of thee
To thick-eyed musing and cursed melancholy?
Lady Percy in *Henry IV, Part 1*, 2.3.44–6

Her husband, Hotspur, has not told her he is involved in plans for a rebellion against the king.

9 Against ill chances men are ever merry,
But heaviness foreruns the good event.
Archbishop of York in *Henry IV, Part 2*, 4.2.81–2

Anticipating ("against") bad luck men are merry, but sad or heavy before success.

10 In sooth, I know not why I am so sad.
Antonio in *The Merchant of Venice*, 1.1.1

The opening line of this comedy; "sooth" = truth.

11   Let us say you are sad
Because you are not merry; and 'twere as easy
For you to laugh and leap, and say you are merry
Because you are not sad.
Solanio in *The Merchant of Venice*, 1.1.47–50

On Antonio's unexplained melancholy.

12   Why, what's the matter,
That you have such a February face,
So full of frost, of storm and
    cloudiness?

Don Pedro in *Much Ado About Nothing*, 5.4.40–2

He is still angry with his friend Claudio.

13   I am not merry; but I do beguile
The thing I am by seeming other-
    wise.

Desdemona in *Othello*, 2.1.122–3

She is anxiously awaiting the arrival of Othello in Cyprus.

14   I have this while with leaden
    thoughts been pressed.

Cassio in *Othello*, 3.4.177

He is worried about regaining his office as Othello's lieutenant; "pressed" = oppressed.

The Moon

1   How sweet the moonlight sleeps
    upon this bank!
Here will we sit, and let the sounds
    of music
Creep in our ears. Soft stillness and
    the night
Become the touches of sweet har-
    mony.

Lorenzo in *The Merchant of Venice*, 5.1.54–7

To Jessica, while they await the arrival of Portia.

2   The moon, like to a silver bow
New bent in heaven, shall behold
    the night
Of our solemnities.

Hippolyta in *A Midsummer Night's Dream*, 1.1.9–11

To Theseus, whom she is to marry.

3   Tomorrow night, when Phoebe
    doth behold
Her silver visage in the watery glass,
Decking with liquid pearl the
    bladed grass.

Lysander in *A Midsummer Night's Dream*, 1.1.209–11

"Phoebe" is another name for Diana, goddess of the moon and of chastity; "watery glass" = mirror made by water.

4   It is the very error of the moon;
She comes more near the earth than
    she was wont
And makes men mad.

Othello in *Othello*, 5.2.109–11

The term "lunacy" is derived from "luna," Latin for moon, reflecting the popular belief that underlies these lines.

Morning, see Dawn, Sunrise

Mortality (see also Death, Dying)

1   All lovers young, all lovers must
Consign to thee and come to dust.

Guiderius and Arviragus in *Cymbeline*, 4.2.274–5

They address the supposedly dead body of Imogen; "Consign to thee" = share your fate.

2   Where be your gibes now, your
    gambols, your songs, your flashes

of merriment, that were wont to set the table on a roar?

Hamlet in *Hamlet*, 5.1.189–91

Holding the skull of Yorick, the king's jester.

3   *Hamlet.* To what base uses we may return, Horatio! Why may not imagination trace the noble dust of Alexander, till 'a find it stopping a bung-hole?
Horatio. 'Twere to consider too curiously to consider so.

Hamlet, 5.1.202–6

Horatio pinpoints Hamlet's self-indulgence in contemplating death so minutely ("curiously").

4   Imperious Caesar, dead and turned to clay,
Might stop a hole to keep the wind away.
O that that earth which kept the world in awe
Should patch a wall t'expel the winter's flaw!

Hamlet in *Hamlet*, 5.1.213–16

A bleak view of death as mere oblivion, but recalling Genesis 3:19, where man was made of earth by God; "winter's flaw" = gust of cold wind.

5   Do not speak like a death's-head, do not bid me remember mine end.

Falstaff in *Henry IV, Part 2*, 2.4.234–5

"Death's-head" = skull, used as a *memento mori* or reminder that death awaits everyone.

6   Make less thy body hence, and more thy grace.
Leave gormandizing; know the grave doth gape

For thee thrice wider than for other men.

Prince Hal, now King Henry V, in *Henry IV, Part 2*, 5.5.52–4

Advising Falstaff to slim henceforth, abandon gluttony ("gormandizing"), and attend to his soul, to divine influence ("grace").

7   *Gloucester.* O, let me kiss that hand!
Lear. Let me wipe it first, it smells of mortality.
Gloucester. O ruined piece of nature! This great world Shall so wear out to nought.

King Lear, 4.6.132–5

"Piece" = masterpiece, i.e., the old king, now mad and senile.

8   If thou art rich, thou'rt poor,
For like an ass, whose back with ingots bows,
Thou bear'st thy heavy riches but a journey,
And death unloads thee.

Duke in *Measure for Measure*, 3.1.25–8

Preparing Claudio to face death.

9   We are such stuff
As dreams are made on, and our little life
Is rounded with a sleep.

Prospero in *The Tempest*, 4.1.156–8

His famous comment on the insubstantiality and brevity of life; "rounded" may mean rounded off, or possibly crowned.

10   Retire me to my Milan, where Every third thought shall be my grave.

Prospero in *The Tempest*, 5.1.311–12

On returning to resume his role as Duke of Milan, and to contemplate his death.

11 Since brass, nor stone, nor earth,
      nor boundless sea,
    But sad mortality o'ersways their
      power,
    How with this rage shall beauty
      hold a plea,
    Whose action is no stronger than a
      flower?

Sonnet 65, 1–4

A poignant sense of the fragility of mortal beauty: "with this rage" = against this destructive power; "hold a plea" = maintain its cause (as in a legal "action").

Mourning (see also Burials, Epitaphs, Grief, Sorrow)

1 There is nothing left remarkable
   Beneath the visiting moon.

Cleopatra in *Antony and Cleopatra*, 4.15.67–8

Her view of a world without Antony.

2   With fairest flowers
   Whilst summer lasts and I live here,
      Fidele,
   I'll sweeten thy sad grave. Thou
      shalt not lack
   The flower that's like thy face, pale
      primrose, nor
   The azured harebell, like thy veins;
      no, nor
   The leaf of eglantine, whom not to
      slander,
   Outsweetened not thy breath.

Arviragus in *Cymbeline*, 4.2.218–24

Imogen, called Fidele in her disguise as a youth, appears dead.

3 Fear no more the heat o'the sun,
   Nor the furious winter's rages,

Thou thy worldly task hast done,
Home art gone, and ta'en thy
  wages.
Golden lads and girls all must,
As chimney-sweepers, come to
  dust.

Guiderius in *Cymbeline*, 4.2.258–63

First stanza of a song of mourning for Fidele (the disguised Imogen), supposed dead.

4 Fear no more the frown o'the great,
   Thou art past the tyrant's stroke;
   Care no more to clothe and eat,
   To thee the reed is as the oak.
   The scepter, learning, physic, must
   All follow this and come to dust.

Arviragus in *Cymbeline*, 4.2.264–9

Second stanza of a song of mourning for Fidele (Imogen in disguise) supposed dead.

5 No exorciser harm thee.
   Nor no witchcraft charm thee.
   Ghost unlaid forbear thee.
   Nothing ill come near thee.
   Quiet consummation have,
   And renownèd be thy grave.

Guiderius and Arviragus in *Cymbeline*, 4.2.276–81

Last stanza of a song of mourning for Fidele (really Imogen in disguise) supposed dead.

6   With a defeated joy,
   With an auspicious, and a dropping
      eye,
   With mirth in funeral, and with
      dirge in marriage,
   In equal scale weighing delight and
      dole.

Claudius in *Hamlet*, 1.2.10–13

Describing his state of mind in marrying his brother's widow so soon after his brother's death; "dole" = grief.

7 Do not for ever with thy vailèd lids
   Seek for thy noble father in the
     dust.
   Thou know'st 'tis common, all that
     lives must die,
   Passing through nature to eternity.

Gertrude in *Hamlet*, 1.2.70–3

Offering commonplace Christian comfort to
Hamlet, who is in mourning for his father's
death; "vailèd lids" = downcast eyes.

8 'Tis not alone my inky cloak, good
     mother,
   Nor customary suits of solemn
     black,
     . . .
   Together with all forms, moods,
     shapes of grief,
   That can denote me truly.

Hamlet in *Hamlet*, 1.2.77–8, 82–3

Outward shows of mourning do not do justice
to his inward grief for his father's death.

9 They are actions that a man might
     play,
   But I have that within which passes
     show,
   These but the trappings and the
     suits of woe.

Hamlet in *Hamlet*, 1.2.84–6

"Actions" = outward forms of mourning.

10 I cannot choose but weep to think
      they would lay him i'the cold
      ground.

Ophelia in *Hamlet*, 4.5.69–70

Mad and grieving after her father's death.

11 For this I shall have time enough to
      mourn.

Northumberland in *Henry IV, Part 2*,
1.1.136

Bad news prompts him to action, and to put
off mourning.

12   Thy due from me
    Is tears and heavy sorrows of the
      blood,
    Which nature, love, and filial ten-
      derness
    Shall, O dear father, pay thee plen-
      teously.

Prince Hal in *Henry IV, Part 2*,
4.5.37–40

Thinking his father is dead.

13 O world, thou wast the forest to
      this hart,
    And this indeed, O world, the heart
      of thee!
    How like a deer, strucken by many
      princes,
    Dost thou here lie!

Mark Antony in *Julius Caesar*,
3.1.207–10

Mourning over Caesar's dead body.

14 O, pardon me, thou bleeding piece
      of earth,
    That I am meek and gentle with
      these butchers!

Mark Antony in *Julius Caesar*, 3.1.254–5

Looking at the dead body of Caesar, now
earth; compare Genesis 3:19, "dust thou art,
and unto dust shalt thou return."

15   Bear with me;
    My heart is in the coffin there with
      Caesar,
    And I must pause till it come back
      to me.

Mark Antony in *Julius Caesar*, 3.2.105–7

Perhaps shedding, or faking, a tear in his effort
to sway the people.

16　　　　Friends, I owe more tears
To this dead man than you shall see
　　me pay.
I shall find time, Cassius, I shall
　　find time.

Brutus in *Julius Caesar*, 5.3.101–3

17 Howl, howl, howl! O, you are men
　　of stones!
Had I your tongues and eyes, I'd
　　use them so
That heaven's vault should crack.

King Lear in *King Lear*, 5.3.258–60

Carrying on stage the body of his beloved
daughter Cordelia; "men of stones" = statues,
indicating that everyone on stage stands
aghast to see the two of them.

18 Had I but died an hour before this
　　chance,
I had lived a blessèd time; for from
　　this instant
There's nothing serious in mortal-
　　ity.
All is but toys; renown and grace is
　　dead,
The wine of life is drawn, and the
　　mere lees
Is left this vault to brag of.

Macbeth in *Macbeth*, 2.3.91–6

Macbeth mourns in public the man he has just
murdered. "Chance" = mischance, meaning
the death of Duncan; life ("mortality") from
henceforth is trivial ("toys"); the "vault" is the
sky covering the earth.

19 If a man do not erect in this age his
own tomb ere he dies, he shall live
no longer in monument than the
bell rings and the widow weeps.

**Benedick in *Much Ado About Nothing*,
5.2.77–80**

20 No longer mourn for me when I
　　am dead
Than you shall hear the surly sullen
　　bell
Give warning to the world that I am
　　fled
From this vile world with vilest
　　worms to dwell.

***Sonnet* 71, 1–4**

The passing bell was rung once for each year
of the dead person's life.

Murder (see also Assassination)

1 List, list, O list!
If thou didst ever thy dear father
　　love—

　　. . .

Revenge his foul and most unnat-
　　ural murder.

　　. . .

Murder most foul, as in the best it
　　is,
But this most foul, strange, and
　　unnatural.

Ghost in *Hamlet*, 1.5.22–3, 25, 27–8

Calling on Hamlet to revenge (By killing
Claudius? And so committing another "murder most foul"?).

2 For murder, though it have no
　　tongue, will speak
With most miraculous organ.

Hamlet in *Hamlet*, 2.2.593–4

Another way of saying, "Murder will out."

3　　　　So shall you hear
Of carnal, bloody, and unnatural
　　acts,

Of accidental judgments, casual
    slaughters,
Of deaths put on by cunning and
    forced cause,
And in this upshot, purposes mis-
    took
Fallen on th'inventors' heads.

Horatio in _Hamlet_, 5.2.380–5

Summing up his version of the events.

4   There is no sure foundation set on
    blood;
No certain life achieved by others'
    death.

King John in _King John_, 4.2.104–5

On hearing that the nephew he wanted out of
the way is dead.

5   Come, thick night,
And pall thee in the dunnest smoke
    of hell,
That my keen knife see not the
    wound it makes,
Nor heaven peep through the blan-
    ket of the dark
To cry, "Hold, hold!"

Lady Macbeth in _Macbeth_, 1.5.50–4

"Thee" is King Duncan, whom she thinks of
murdering in his bed; hell is proverbially
black or dark; "pall thee" = cover as with a
pall, the cloth spread over a coffin.

6   Withered murder,
Alarumed by his sentinel, the wolf,
Whose howl's his watch, thus with
    his stealthy pace,
With Tarquin's ravishing strides,
    towards his design
Moves like a ghost.

Macbeth in _Macbeth_, 2.1.52–6

The murderer is imagined as roused to action
by the howling of the wolf, and moving like

Tarquin, who raped Lucretia, the wife of Col-
latinus, in ancient Rome.

7   Though in the trade of war I have
    slain men,
Yet do I hold it very stuff o' the
    conscience
To do no contrived murder. I lack
    iniquity
Sometimes to do me service.

Iago in _Othello_, 1.2.1–3

Iago's hypocritical first words to Othello.

8   When I have plucked the
    rose,
I cannot give it vital growth again,
It needs must wither. I'll smell it
    on the tree.

Othello in _Othello_, 5.2.13–15

Desdemona is the rose he is about to pluck, or
kill.

9   Murder's out of tune,
And sweet revenge grows harsh.

Othello in _Othello_, 5.2.115–16

On learning that Iago has failed to kill Cassio.

10   An honorable murderer, if you will,
For naught I did in hate, but all in
    honor.

Othello in _Othello_, 5.2.294–5

After killing Desdemona; "in honor" = from a
sense of integrity, supposing it to be the right
thing to do.

11   The great King of kings
Hath in the table of his law com-
    manded
That thou shalt do no murder.

Clarence in _Richard III_, 1.4.195–7

In the Ten Commandments, Exodus 20:13;
"table" = tablet or list.

12 Murder her brothers and then
    marry her—
Uncertain way of gain, but I am in
So far in blood that sin will pluck
    on sin.

King Richard in *Richard III*, 4.2.62–4

Richard's desperate idea of marrying the
Princess Elizabeth, whose brothers he has had
executed.

13 The tyrannous and bloody deed is
    done,
The most arch deed of piteous mas-
    sacre
That ever yet this land was guilty of.

Tyrell in *Richard III*, 4.3.1–3

Lamenting the murder, ordered by Richard,
of the two young princes in the Tower of
London.

Music

1 Give me some music; music,
    moody food
Of us that trade in love.

Cleopatra in *Antony and Cleopatra*,
2.5.1–2

2 *Jaques.* Have you a song, forester,
    for this purpose?
Second Lord. Yes, sir.
Jaques. Sing it. 'Tis no matter how
    it be in tune, so it make noise
    enough.

As You Like It, 4.2.5–9

The song is to celebrate the killing of a deer.

3 I am advised to give her music o'
    mornings; they say it will penetrate.

Cloten in *Cymbeline*, 2.3.11–12

The buffoon, Cloten, attempts to woo Imogen;
"penetrate" suggests his real desire.

4 It is as easy as lying. Govern these
ventages with your fingers and
thumbs, give it breath with your
mouth, and it will discourse most
eloquent music.

Hamlet in *Hamlet*, 3.2.357–9

To Guildenstern, who cannot play the
recorder; "ventages" are stops on the
instrument.

5 I framed to the harp
Many an English ditty lovely well.

Glendower in *Henry IV, Part 1*,
3.1.121–2

Glendower likes to boast of his accomplish-
ments.

6 Let there be no noise made, my
    gentle friends,
Unless some dull and favorable
    hand
Will whisper music to my weary
    spirit.

King Henry in *Henry IV, Part 2*, 4.5.1–3

The king is sick and close to death; "dull" =
soothing, drowsy.

7 Orpheus with his lute made trees
And the mountain tops that freeze
    Bow themselves when he did sing.
To his music plants and flowers
Ever sprung, as sun and showers
    There had made a lasting spring.

Song in *Henry VIII*, 3.1.3–8

Ancient Greek legend attributed these powers
to Orpheus.

8 In sweet music is such art,
Killing care and grief of heart
Fall asleep, or hearing die.

Song in *Henry VIII*, 3.1.12–14

9 Music oft hath such a
charm

To make bad good, and good provoke to harm.

Duke in *Measure for Measure*, 4.1.15–16

10 Let music sound while he doth
make his choice;
Then if he lose he makes a swan-
like end,
Fading in music.

Portia in *The Merchant of Venice*,
3.2.43–5

The swan was proverbially supposed to sing
before dying.

11 *Jessica.* I am never merry when I
hear sweet music.
Lorenzo. The reason is, your spirits
are attentive.

The Merchant of Venice, 5.1.69–70

"Spirits are attentive" = faculties are engaged.

12 The man that hath no music in
himself,
Nor is not moved with concord of
sweet sounds,
Is fit for treasons, stratagems, and
spoils;
The motions of his spirit are dull as
night,
And his affections dark as Erebus:
Let no such man be trusted.

Lorenzo in *The Merchant of Venice*,
5.1.83–8

"Spoils" = acts of plunder; Erebus was a place
of darkness linked with Hades in classical
mythology.

13 *Titania.* What, wilt thou hear some
music, my sweet love?
Bottom. I have a reasonable good
ear in music. Let's have the tongs
and the bones.

A Midsummer Night's Dream, 4.1.27–9

Bottom's idea of music is to play on metal
tongs and bone clappers.

14 Music, ho, music such as charmeth
sleep!

Titania in *A Midsummer Night's*
Dream, 4.1.83

"Charmeth" = induces like a charm.

15 The general so likes your music,
that he desires you for love's sake to
make no more noise with it.

Clown in *Othello*, 3.1.11–13

Cassio arranged for musicians to play beneath
the window of Othello and Desdemona.

16 An admirable musician! O, she will
sing the savageness out of a bear!

Othello in *Othello*, 4.1.188–9

Praising Desdemona.

17 My mother had a maid called Barbary;
She was in love, and he she loved
proved mad,
And did forsake her. She had a
song of "Willow,"
An old thing 'twas, but it expressed
her fortune,
And she died singing it. That song
tonight
Will not go from my mind.

Desdemona in *Othello*, 4.3.26–31

The willow was the proverbial badge of a forsaken lover.

18   How sour sweet music is
When time is broke, and no pro-
portion kept!
So is it in the music of men's lives.

King Richard in *Richard II*, 5.5.42–4

Reflecting on himself while in prison.

19 How silver-sweet sound lovers'
   tongues by night,
   Like softest music to attending ears!

   Romeo in *Romeo and Juliet*, 2.2.165–6

   Hearing Juliet call to him.

20 *Hortensio.* Madam, my instrument's in tune.
   Bianca. Let's hear. O fie, the treble
   jars.
   Lucentio. Spit in the hole, man, and
   tune again.

   The Taming of the Shrew, 3.1.38–40

   Hortensio's lute was a difficult instrument to
   tune, and Lucentio may be advising him to
   moisten the pegs.

21 Where should this music be? I'
   th'air, or th'earth?
   It sounds no more.

   Ferdinand in *The Tempest*, 1.2.388–9

   On hearing Ariel's spirit-music.

22 This music crept by me upon the
   waters,
   Allaying both their fury and my
   passion
   With its sweet air; thence have I followed it,
   Or it hath drawn me rather.

   Ferdinand in *The Tempest*, 1.2.392–5

   Drawn by Ariel's music; this passage was used
   by T.S. Eliot in *The Waste Land*.

23 Be not afeard; the isle is full of
   noises,
   Sounds and sweet airs, that give
   delight, and hurt not.
   Sometimes a thousand twangling
   instruments
   Will hum about mine ears; and
   sometime voices,

That, if I then had waked after long
   sleep,
   Will make me sleep again.

   Caliban in *The Tempest*, 3.2.135–40

   To Stephano and Trinculo, who are scared by
   Ariel's music.

24 *Alonso.* What harmony is this? My
   good friends, hark!
   Gonzalo. Marvelous sweet music!

   The Tempest, 3.3.18–19

   Hearing "solemn and strange" music, according to the stage direction.

25 If music be the food of love, play
   on,
   Give me excess of it; that surfeiting,
   The appetite may sicken, and so
   die.

   Orsino in *Twelfth Night*, 1.1.1–3

   Hoping to cure his lovesickness.

26 That strain again, it had a dying fall;
   O, it came o'er my ear like the
   sweet sound
   That breathes upon a bank of violets,
   Stealing and giving odor. Enough,
   no more,
   'Tis not so sweet now as it was
   before.

   Orsino in *Twelfth Night*, 1.1.4–8

   Listening to music; "strain" = melody.

27 *Orsino.* How dost thou like this
   tune?
   Viola. It gives a very echo to the
   seat
   Where love is throned.

   Twelfth Night, 2.4.20–2

   Music feeds Orsino's lovesickness.

Mutability (see also Change, Transience, Transformation)

1 This world is not for aye, nor 'tis
not strange
That even our loves should with
our fortunes change.

Player King in *Hamlet*, 3.2.200–1

On the theme of mutability.

2 Sweet love, I see, changing his
property,
Turns to the sourest and most
deadly hate.

Sir Stephen Scroop in *Richard II*,
3.2.135–6

To Richard, who has been cursing his former
favorites; "property" = distinctive nature.

3 When I consider everything that
grows
Holds in perfection but a little
moment;
That this huge stage presenteth
nought but shows
Whereon the stars in secret influence comment. . . .

***Sonnet 15*, 1–2**

On the brevity of life for all things in nature.

4 Ruin hath taught me thus to ruminate,
That Time will come and take my
love away.
This thought is as a death, which
cannot choose
But weep to have that which it
fears to lose.

***Sonnet 64*, 11–14**

The ruins of past ages seem caught up inside
the word "ruminate"; another lament for the
inevitable passage of time.

Myths

1 Now I will believe
That there are unicorns; that in
Arabia
There is one tree, the phoenix'
throne, one phoenix
At this hour reigning there.

Sebastian in *The Tempest*, 3.3.21–4

A strange vision has made him willing to
believe any traveler's tale, of mythical unicorns or the phoenix, said to renew itself peri-
odically from the ashes of its own pyre.

Names

1 *Jaques.* Rosalind is your love's
name?
Orlando. Yes, just.
Jaques. I do not like her name.
Orlando. There was no thought of
pleasing you when she was christened.

***As You Like It*, 3.2.263–7**

2 *Cinna.* I am not Cinna the conspirator.
Fourth Plebeian. It is no matter, his
name's Cinna! Pluck but his
name out of his heart, and turn
him going.

***Julius Caesar*, 3.3.32–4**

Cinna the poet has the misfortune to have the
same name as a conspirator against Caesar.

3 If his name be George I'll call him
Peter,
For new-made honor doth forget
men's names.

**The Bastard Falconbridge in *King
John*, 1.1.186–7**

Falconbridge has just been made a knight.

4   When tongues speak sweetly, then
       they name her name,
    And Rosaline they call her.

Berowne in *Love's Labor's Lost*,
3.1.166–7

Betraying his desire for Rosaline.

5   I cannot tell what the dickens his
    name is.

**Mistress Page in *The Merry Wives of
Windsor*, 3.2.19–20**

"Dickens" is a euphemism for the devil; she
speaks of Robin, Falstaff's page.

6   Peaseblossom, Cobweb, Moth and
    Mustardseed!

**Titania in *A Midsummer Night's
Dream*, 3.1.162**

The names of her fairy attendants; "Moth"
sounded like "mote" or speck.

7   O Romeo, Romeo, wherefore art
       thou Romeo?
    Deny thy father and refuse thy
       name;
    Or, if thou wilt not, be but sworn
       my love,
    And I'll no longer be a Capulet.

Juliet in *Romeo and Juliet*, 2.2.33–6

Realizing that she, a Capulet, has fallen in
love with a Montague, the enemy of her clan.

8   What's in a name? That which we
       call a rose
    By any other name would smell as
       sweet.

Juliet in *Romeo and Juliet*, 2.2.43–4

On loving Romeo, a Montague, and an
enemy.

9   *Ferdinand.* I do beseech you—
       Chiefly that I may set it in my
          prayers—

What is your name?
Miranda. Miranda.—O my father,
I have broke your hest to say so.
Ferdinand. Admired Miranda,
Indeed the top of admiration!
   Worth
What's dearest to the world!

The Tempest, 3.1.34–9

Playing on the meaning of "Miranda," to be
wondered at or admired (from the Latin);
"hest" = command.

Nature

1   How hard it is to hide the sparks of
       nature!

Belarius in *Cymbeline*, 3.3.79

Seeing the innate nobility of the king's sons,
living with him in exile.

2   O thou goddess,
    Thou divine Nature, thou thyself
       thou blazon'st
    In these two princely boys!

Belarius in *Cymbeline*, 4.2.169–71

Speaking of Guiderius and Arviragus, whom
Belarius knows to be the king's sons; to "blazon" is to display, like a coat of arms.

3   Thou, Nature, art my goddess, to
       thy law
    My services are bound.

Edmund in *King Lear*, 1.2.1–2

Rejecting conventional morality in favor of the
law of the jungle, as he is a "natural" child, a
bastard.

4   He loves us not,
    He wants the natural touch. For
       the poor wren,
    The most diminutive of birds, will
       fight,
    Her young ones in the nest, against
       the owl.

Lady Macduff in *Macbeth*, 4.2.8–11

On Macduff, her husband, who has gone to England, and left her and her child unprotected; "wants the natural touch" = lacks natural affection.

5 The earth, that's nature's mother, is her tomb.
What is her burying grave, that is her womb.

Friar Lawrence in *Romeo and Juliet*, 2.3.9–10

"Earth is the mother of us all" was proverbial, but the Friar develops the paradox that everything nature brings to birth also dies.

6 O, mickle is the powerful grace that lies
In plants, herbs, stones, and their true qualities;
For nought so vile that on the earth doth live
But to the earth some special good doth give.

Friar Lawrence in *Romeo and Juliet*, 2.3.15–18

Celebrating the great ("mickle") goodness (as given by divine grace) in natural plants and objects.

7   I have heard it said
There is an art which in their piedness shares
With great creating nature.

Perdita in *The Winter's Tale*, 4.4.86–8

She is thinking of grafting or the cross-breeding that produces parti-colored flowers ("piedness").

8   We marry
A gentler scion to the wildest stock,
And make conceive a bark of baser kind
By bud of nobler race. This is an art

Which does mend nature—change it rather; but
The art itself is nature.

Polixenes in *The Winter's Tale*, 4.4.92–7

Instructing Perdita in the art of grafting, and, paradoxically, arguing that art is nature.

Necessity (see also Fate)

1 Be you not troubled with the time, which drives
O'er your content these strong necessities,
But let determined things to destiny
Hold unbewailed their sway.

Octavius Caesar in *Antony and Cleopatra*, 3.6.82–5

His advice to his sister now that war between him and her husband, Antony, is inevitable.

2 Are these things then necessities?
Then let us meet them like necessities.

King Henry in *Henry IV, Part 2*, 3.1.92–3

Faced with the need to fight a rebel army.

3 The deep of night is crept upon our talk,
And nature must obey necessity.

Brutus in *Julius Caesar*, 4.3.226–7

To Cassius, suggesting they take some sleep.

4 O, reason not the need! our basest beggars
Are in the poorest thing superfluous.
Allow not nature more than nature needs,
Man's life is cheap as beast's.

King Lear in *King Lear*, 2.4.264–7

On being told by Regan that he needs no servants of his own.

5   How dost, my boy? Art cold?
I am cold myself. Where is this
     straw, good fellow?
The art of our necessities is strange
And can make vile things precious.

King Lear in *King Lear*, 3.2.68–71

Out in the storm, he learns there is a hovel
nearby; the "boy" is his Fool.

6   What need the bridge much
      broader than the flood?

Don Pedro in *Much Ado About Nothing*, 1.1.316

Telling Claudio there is no need to do more
than is necessary to achieve his desire; "flood"
= water or river.

7   Teach thy necessity to reason thus:
There is no virtue like necessity.

John of Gaunt in *Richard II*, 1.3.277–8

Trying to comfort his banished son; proverbial
("to make a virtue of necessity").

8   I am sworn brother, sweet,
To grim Necessity, and he and I
Will keep a league till death.

King Richard in *Richard II*, 5.1.20–2

As he is being taken to prison, he meets his
queen.

9   Are you content to be our general,
To make a virtue of necessity
And live as we do in this wilder-
     ness?

**Second Outlaw in *The Two Gentlemen
of Verona*, 4.1.59–61**

Outlaws, having captured Valentine, invite
him to be their leader; it could only happen in
romance. Compare 7 above.

Negotiation

1   In the way of bargain, mark ye me,
I'll cavil on the ninth part of a hair.

Hotspur in *Henry IV, Part 1*, 3.1.137–8

Debating the partition of the country; Hotspur
enjoys the give and take of bargaining.

2   So happy be the issue, brother Eng-
     land,
Of this good day and of this gra-
     cious meeting.

Queen Isabel in *Henry V*, 5.2.12–13

The French Queen hopes for a happy out-
come ("issue") to the negotiations for peace.

3   Haply a woman's voice may do
     some good
When articles too nicely urged be
     stood on.

Queen Isabel in *Henry V*, 5.2.93–4

"Haply" = perhaps; she hopes to mediate if
too much fuss is made about details of an
agreement; "stood on" = insisted on.

News

1   The nature of bad news infects the
     teller.

**Messenger in *Antony and Cleopatra*,
1.2.95**

2   Though it be honest, it is never
     good
To bring bad news.

**Cleopatra in *Antony and Cleopatra*,
2.5.85–6**

3   What's the new news at the new
     court?

Oliver in *As You Like It*, 1.1.96–7

"New court" because Duke Frederick has
banished his brother Duke Senior and usurped
as the new Duke.

4   Thou still hast been the father of
    good news.

Claudius in *Hamlet*, 2.2.42

To Polonius who brings news that peace is
restored between Norway and Denmark;
"still" = always.

5   This advertisement is five days old.

King Henry in *Henry IV, Part 1*, 3.2.172

"Advertisement" = information.

6   *Douglas.* That's the worst tidings
    that I hear of yet.
    Worcester. Ay, by my faith, that
    bears a frosty sound.

***Henry IV, Part 1*, 4.1.127–8**

News that Glendower, one of the leading
rebels, cannot muster his army for fourteen
days.

7   Yea, this man's brow, like to a title-
    leaf,
    Foretells the nature of a tragic vol-
    ume.

**Northumberland in *Henry IV, Part 2*,
1.1.60–1**

The messenger's face, like the title-page of a
book, spells out bad news.

8   Yet the first bringer of unwelcome
    news
    Hath but a losing office, and his
    tongue
    Sounds ever after as a sullen bell,
    Remembered tolling a departing
    friend.

**Northumberland in *Henry IV, Part 2*,
1.1.100–3**

9   Such welcome and unwelcome
    things at once,
    'Tis hard to reconcile.

Macduff in *Macbeth*, 4.3.138–9

Hearing on the one hand that Malcolm is not
fit to rule, and on the other that he is leading
an army against Macbeth.

10 Though news be sad, yet tell them
    merrily;
    If good, thou shamest the music of
    sweet news
    By playing it to me with so sour a
    face.

Juliet in *Romeo and Juliet*, 2.5.22–4

To her Nurse, who is weary rather than sad;
Juliet is anxious for news of Romeo.

Night (see also Darkness)

1   'Tis now the very witching time of
    night,
    When churchyards yawn and hell
    itself breathes out
    Contagion to this world.

Hamlet in *Hamlet*, 3.2.388–90

He is encouraging himself to be stern with his
mother.

2   Let us be Diana's foresters, gentle-
    men of the shade, minions of the
    moon.

Falstaff in *Henry IV, Part 1*, 1.2.25–6

Falstaff prefers stealing by night to working by
day; Diana was goddess of the moon, and
associated with hunting (also, ironically here,
with chastity).

3   Now comes in the sweetest morsel
    of the night, and we must hence
    and leave it unpicked.

Falstaff in *Henry IV, Part 2*, 2.4.367–8

Summoned to the wars, he cannot go to bed
with Doll Tearsheet; "unpicked" = ungath-
ered.

4   And we shall be merry, now comes
     in the sweet o' the night.

Shallow in *Henry IV, Part 2*, 5.3.50–1

As they break out the wine.

5   Now entertain conjecture of a time
     When creeping murmur and the
          poring dark
     Fills the wide vessel of the universe.

Chorus in *Henry V*, 4.Prologue, 1–3

The dark is "poring" because people strain to
see.

6   From camp to camp, through the
          foul womb of night,
     The hum of either army stilly
          sounds.

Chorus in *Henry V*, 4.Prologue, 4–5

"Stilly" = softly; the "foul womb" will give
birth to battle at dawn.

7   The cripple tardy-gaited night,
     Who like a foul and ugly witch doth
          limp
     So tediously away.

Chorus in *Henry V*, 4.Prologue, 20–2

The night seems foul and tedious to the English army knowing they must fight in the
morning.

8   Hung be the heavens with black!
          Yield, day, to night!

Bedford in *Henry VI, Part 1*, 1.1.1

Probably referring to the canopy over the
stage, hung with black drapes for a tragedy.

9   What a fearful night is this!
     There's two or three of us have seen
          strange sights.

Cinna in *Julius Caesar*, 1.3.137–8

On the stormy night before the murder of Caesar.

10   Here's a night pities neither wise
          men nor fools.

Fool in *King Lear*, 3.2.12–13

The stage directions call for "storm and tempest," and the text for thunder and lightning,
wind and rain.

11   Things that love night
     Love not such nights as these.

Kent in *King Lear*, 3.2.42–3

Referring to the wild storm in which Lear
wanders.

12   Now o'er the one half-world
     Nature seems dead, and wicked
          dreams abuse
     The curtained sleep.

Macbeth in *Macbeth*, 2.1.49–51

"Curtained" suggests both bed-curtains, and
the unconsciousness of sleep that shuts off the
control exerted by the conscious mind.

13   Light thickens, and the crow
     Makes wing to the rooky wood.
     Good things of day begin to droop
          and drowse,
     Whiles night's black agents to their
          prey do rouse.

Macbeth in *Macbeth*, 3.2.50–3

Invoking the powers of darkness preparatory
to murdering Banquo.

14   The night is long that never finds
          the day.

Malcolm in *Macbeth*, 4.3.240

For him the "night" is the reign of the tyrant
Macbeth.

15   The moon shines bright. In such a
          night as this,
     When the sweet wind did gently
          kiss the trees,

And they did make no noise, in
    such a night
Troilus methinks mounted the
    Troyan walls,
And sighed his soul toward the
    Grecian tents,
Where Cressida lay that night.

Lorenzo in *The Merchant of Venice*,
5.1.1–6

In Belmont, waiting for the return of Portia,
Lorenzo sets the scene; Cressida turned out to
be faithless to Troilus.

16   Who comes so fast in silence of the
    night?

Lorenzo in *The Merchant of Venice*,
5.1.25

Hearing the sound of a messenger.

17   O weary night, O long and tedious
    night,
Abate thy hours, shine comforts
    from the east.

Helena in *A Midsummer Night's
Dream*, 3.2.431–2

"Abate" = cut short, abridge.

18   O grim-looked night, O night with
    hue so black,
O night which ever art when day is
    not!

Bottom in *A Midsummer Night's
Dream*, 5.1.170–1

As Pyramus, addressing the night.

19   Now the hungry lion roars,
And the wolf behowls the moon,
Whilst the heavy ploughman
    snores,
All with weary task foredone.

Puck in *A Midsummer Night's Dream*,
5.1.371–4

"Foredone" = exhausted.

20   Come, civil night,
Thou sober-suited matron all in
    black.

Juliet in *Romeo and Juliet*, 3.2.10–11

"Civil" = mannerly, observing propriety; Juliet
is now married, and anxiously awaiting nightfall and the coming of Romeo.

21   Come, gentle night, come, loving,
    black-browed night,
Give me my Romeo, and when I
    shall die,
Take him and cut him out in little
    stars
And he will make the face of heaven
    so fine
That all the world will be in love
    with night,
And pay no worship to the garish
    sun.

Juliet in *Romeo and Juliet*, 3.2.20–25

Expressing her adoration of Romeo.

22   The dragon wing of night o'er-
    spreads the earth.

Achilles in *Troilus and Cressida*, 5.8.17

Suggesting doom as well as darkness; he has
just killed Hector.

23   It hath been the longest night
That e'er I watched, and the most
    heaviest.

Julia in *The Two Gentlemen of
Verona*, 4.2.139–40

She has been watching Proteus, who has
sworn his devotion to her, making love to
Sylvia.

24   Sable night, mother of dread and
    fear.

The Rape of Lucrece, 117

Nobility

1   His nature is too noble for the
      world;
    He would not flatter Neptune for
      his trident,
    Or Jove for 's power to thunder.

    Menenius in *Coriolanus*, 3.1.254–6

    Speaking about Coriolanus; "too noble"
    sounds like arrogance.

2   O what a noble mind is here
      o'erthrown!

    Ophelia in *Hamlet*, 3.1.150

    She thinks Hamlet to be mad after his verbal
    attack on her.

3   She's noble born,
    And like her true nobility she has
    Carried herself towards me.

    King Henry in *Henry VIII*, 2.4.142–4

    Praising Katherine, the wife he is about to
    divorce.

4   Well, Brutus, thou art noble, yet I
      see
    Thy honorable mettle may be
      wrought
    From that it is disposed. It is meet
    That noble minds keep ever with
      their likes;
    For who so firm that cannot be
      seduced.

    Cassius in *Julius Caesar*, 1.2.308–12

    Realizing Brutus's spirit ("mettle") may be
    diverted from the course he is disposed to fol-
    low; "meet" = fitting.

5   O, he sits high in all the people's
      hearts;
    And that which would appear
      offense in us

His countenance, like richest
  alchemy,
Will change to virtue and to worthiness.

Casca in *Julius Caesar*, 1.3.157–60

Describing Brutus; "countenance" = appearance, and support; the aim of alchemy was to
transmute base metals into gold.

6   This was the noblest Roman of
      them all.
    All the conspirators save only he
    Did that they did in envy of great
      Caesar.
    He only, in a general honest
      thought
    And common good to all, made
      one of them.

    Mark Antony in *Julius Caesar*, 5.5.68–72

    His eulogy of Brutus.

7   A brother noble,
    Whose nature is so far from doing
      harms
    That he suspects none.

    Edmund in *King Lear*, 1.2.179–81

    On his brother Edgar.

8   I might call him
    A thing divine, for nothing natural
    I ever saw so noble.

    Miranda in *The Tempest*, 1.2.418–20

    Miranda's first sight of a young man, Ferdi-
    nand.

9   This is the prettiest low-born lass
      that ever
    Ran on the green-sward: nothing
      she does or seems
    But smacks of something greater
      than herself,
    Too noble for this place.

Polixenes in *The Winter's Tale*,
4.4.156–9

Speaking of Perdita; he doesn't yet know that she is a princess.

Nonsense

1   This is the silliest stuff that ever I heard.

Hippolyta in *A Midsummer Night's Dream*, 5.1.210

Watching the play of "Pyramus and Thisbe."

Nostalgia

1   If ever you have looked on better days.

Orlando in *As You Like It*, 2.7.113

Asking to be pitied.

2   There lives not three good men unhanged in England, and one of them is fat and grows old.

Falstaff in *Henry IV, Part 1*, 2.4.130–2

The fat one is himself.

3   Jesu, Jesu, the mad days that I have spent! And to see how many of my old acquaintance are dead!

Shallow in *Henry IV, Part 2*, 3.2.33–4

Old justices Shallow and Silence recall their wild youth.

4   We have heard the chimes at midnight, Master Shallow.

Falstaff in *Henry IV, Part 2*, 3.2.214–15

Recalling their youth in London.

5   "Where is the life that late I led?"

Petruchio in *The Taming of the Shrew*, 4.1.140

The newly married Petruchio sings what seems to be the first line of a lost ballad.

Nothing

1   *Kent.* This is nothing, Fool.
    Fool. Then 'tis like the breath of an unfeed lawyer, you gave me nothing for't.

King Lear, 1.4.128–30

Kent is commenting on the Fool's rhymes.

2   Nothing can be made out of nothing.

King Lear in *King Lear*, 1.4.132–3

Proverbial (see also Proverbs)

3   Thou wast a pretty fellow when thou hadst no need to care for her frowning; now thou art an O without a figure. I am better than thou art now; I am a fool, thou art nothing.

Fool in *King Lear*, 1.4.191–4

To King Lear, who has given his lands to his daughters; an "O" is nothing without another figure in front of it.

Oaths (see also Promises, Vows)

1   Swear me, Kate, like a lady as thou art,
    A good mouth-filling oath.

Hotspur in *Henry IV, Part 1*, 3.1.253–4

To his wife, who has sworn she will not sing.

2   I will die a hundred thousand
deaths
Ere break the smallest parcel of this
vow.

Prince Hal in *Henry IV, Part 1,*
3.2.158–9

Vowing his allegiance to his father and determination to overcome their enemy, Hotspur.

3   I have no cunning in protestation—only downright oaths, which
I never use till urged, nor never
break for urging.

King Henry in *Henry V,* 5.2.143–6

Plain speaking in making love to Katherine.

Obscenity

1   If bawdy talk offend you, we'll have
very little of it.

Lucio in *Measure for Measure,* 4.3.178–9

To the Duke, who is trying to get rid of him.

Obstinacy

1   Why should we in our peevish
opposition
Take it to heart

Claudius in *Hamlet,* 1.2.100–1

Suggesting Hamlet is pig-headed in continuing to mourn for his father.

2   A peevish self-willed harlotry,
One that no persuasion can do
good upon.

Glendower in *Henry IV, Part 1,*
3.1.196–7

Speaking playfully of his daughter, who says
she will not be parted from her husband, who
is leaving for the wars; "harlotry" = hussy.

3   'Tis best to give him way, he leads
himself.

Cornwall in *King Lear,* 2.4.298

"Leads himself" = goes where his will leads
him.

4   O sir, to willful men
The injuries that they themselves
   procure
Must be their schoolmasters.

Regan in *King Lear,* 2.4.302–4

Speaking to Gloucester about her father, shut
out in the storm.

The Occult

1   Eye of newt and toe of frog,
Wool of bat and tongue of dog,
Adder's fork and blind-worm's
   sting,
Lizard's leg and owlet's wing,
For a charm of powerful trouble,
Like a hell-broth boil and bubble.

Second Witch in *Macbeth,* 4.1.14–19

The parts of creatures include the forked
tongue of the poisonous adder, and the "sting"
of the blind-worm, a lizard that is in fact
harmless.

2   Double, double, toil and trouble;
Fire burn, and cauldron bubble.

The Witches (Weird Sisters) in *Macbeth,* 4.1.20–1

Casting a spell.

3   *Macbeth.* How now, you secret,
   black, and midnight hags?
What is't you do?
Witches.   A deed without a
name.

Macbeth, 4.1.48–9

Old Age (see also Age)

1   "Let me not live," quoth he
"After my flame lacks oil, to be the
    snuff
Of younger spirits, whose appre-
    hensive senses
All but new things disdain."

**King of France in *All's Well That Ends
Well*, 1.2.58–61**

An old man's wish to die rather than oppress
the young; "snuff" = a burned wick that prevents a candle from flaming brightly.

2   They say an old man is twice a
child.

Rosencrantz in *Hamlet*, 2.2.385

To Hamlet, who has just pointed out Polonius;
proverbial.

3   There lives not three good men
unhanged in England, and one of
them is fat and grows old.

Falstaff in *Henry IV, Part 1*, 2.4.130–2

Referring to himself as "one of them."

4   Your lordship, though not clean
past your youth, have yet some
smack of age in you, some relish of
the saltness of time in you.

Falstaff in *Henry IV, Part 2*, 1.2.96–9

Addressing the Lord Chief Justice.

5   So minutes, hours, days, months,
    and years,
Passed over to the end they were
    created,
Would bring white hairs unto a
    quiet grave.
Ah, what a life were this! How
sweet! How lovely!

**King Henry in *Henry VI, Part 3*,
2.5.38–41**

In a savage civil war the king longs for a quiet
life.

6   An old man, broken with the
    storms of state,
Is come to lay his weary bones
    among ye:
Give him a little earth for charity.

**Griffith, reporting Wolsey's words, in
Henry VIII, 4.2.21–3**

Wolsey's greeting to the Abbot of Leicester.

7   O sir, you are old,
Nature in you stands on the very
    verge
Of her confine.

Regan in *King Lear*, 2.4.146–8

Implying that her father is not competent to
conduct his own affairs.

8   I have lived long enough: my way of
    life
Is fallen into the sere, the yellow
    leaf;
And that which should accompany
    old age,
As honor, love, obedience, troops
    of friends,
I must not look to have.

Macbeth in *Macbeth*, 5.3.22–6

Macbeth's achievement of the throne of Scotland in the end brings him no satisfaction;
"sere" = dry and withered; "as honor" = such
as honor.

9   When thou art old and rich,
Thou hast neither heat, affection,
    limb, nor beauty,
To make thy riches pleasant.

Duke in *Measure for Measure*, 3.1.36–8

Preparing Claudio to face death.

10 A good old man, sir, he will be talking; as they say, "When the age is in, the wit is out."

Dogberry in *Much Ado About Nothing,* 3.5.33–4

On Verges, his assistant; proverbial phrases, though the second alters the proverb, "When the ale (or wine) is in the wit is out."

11 But old folks—many feign as they were dead,
Unwieldy, slow, heavy, and pale as lead.

Juliet in *Romeo and Juliet,* 2.5.16–17

Thinking of her old Nurse; "feign as" = behave as if.

12 Give me a staff of honor for mine age,
But not a scepter to control the world.

Titus in *Titus Andronicus,* 1.1.198–9

Refusing to be made emperor of Rome.

13 Old Nestor—whose wit was mouldy ere your grandsires had nails on their toes.

Thersites in *Troilus and Cressida,* 2.1.104–6

"Wit" = intelligence; Nestor is the oldest of the Greek generals; Thersites is speaking to Achilles and Ajax.

14 Respect and reason wait on wrinkled age.

The Rape of Lucrece, 275

So Tarquin seeks to justify the rape by claiming it is proper for the young to pursue desires.

Omens, see Portents

Opinion

1 Thou art a blessed fellow to think as every man thinks. Never a man's thought in the world keeps the road-way better than thine.

Prince Hal in *Henry IV, Part 2,* 2.2.56–9

Mocking his friend Poins for accepting common opinion as true.

2 Come on my right hand, for this ear is deaf,
And tell me truly what thou think'st of him.

Caesar in *Julius Caesar,* 1.2.213–14

Inviting Antony to say what he thinks of Cassius; the all-powerful ruler has physical weaknesses.

3 Opinion's but a fool that makes us scan
The outward habit for the inward man.

Simonides in *Pericles,* 2.2.56–7

"Outward habit" = external appearance.

Opportunity

1 Who seeks and will not take when once 'tis offered
Shall never find it more.

Menas in *Antony and Cleopatra,* 2.7.83–4

Pompey has just refused his offer to make him emperor by assassinating Antony and Octavius Caesar.

2   There is a tide in the affairs of men
Which, taken at the flood, leads on
    to fortune;
Omitted, all the voyage of their life
Is bound in shallows and in mis-
    eries.
On such a full sea are we now
    afloat,
And we must take the current when
    it serves,
Or lose our ventures.

Brutus in *Julius Caesar*, 4.3.218–24

The idea is that if the moment or opportunity
is neglected ("omitted"), the whole life may be
confined ("bound in") to treading water.

3   Why then, the world's mine oyster,
Which I with sword will open.

**Pistol in *The Merry Wives of Windsor*,
2.2.3–4**

On failing to persuade Falstaff to lend him
money; "the world's my oyster" was proverbial, meaning I'll find wealth somehow.

4   The poor, lame, blind, halt, creep,
    cry out for thee,
But they ne'er meet with opportu-
    nity.

***The Rape of Lucrece*, 902–3**

Lucrece broods on the force of opportunity,
anachronistically referring to the gospels;
compare Luke 14:13, "when thou makest a
feast, call the poor, the maimed, the lame, the
blind."

Order

1   The heavens themselves, the plan-
    ets, and this center
Observe degree, priority, and place.

**Ulysses in *Troilus and Cressida*,
1.3.85–6**

Appealing to a hierarchical concept of the
universe, with the earth at the center, as in the
Ptolemaic concept of astronomy.

2   O, when degree is shaked,
Which is the ladder to all high
    designs,
The enterprise is sick.

**Ulysses in *Troilus and Cressida*,
1.3.101–3**

By "degree" he means hierarchy, the relative
positions of people on a social scale; "enterprise" = social or political project, here the
Trojan war.

3   Take but degree away, untune that
    string,
And hark what discord follows!

**Ulysses in *Troilus and Cressida*,
1.3.109–10**

4   You must confine yourself within
the modest limits of order.

Maria in *Twelfth Night*, 1.3.8–9

Advising Sir Toby Belch not to stay up drinking late at night.

Overconfidence

1   The man that once did sell the
    lion's skin
While the beast lived, was killed
    with hunting him.

King Henry in *Henry V*, 4.3.93–4

Referring to the French, who rashly expect an
easy victory.

Painting

1 Look when a painter would surpass
   the life
   In limning out a well-proportioned
   steed,
   His art with Nature's workmanship
   at strife,
   As if the dead the living should
   exceed,
   So did this horse excel a common
   one,
   In shape, in courage, color, pace
   and bone.

Venus and Adonis, 289–94

"Look" = just as; "limning" = painting.

Paradoxes

1 Fair is foul and foul is fair.

The Witches (Weird Sisters) in *Mac-beth.* 1.1.11

2 Nothing is but what is not.

Macbeth in *Macbeth,* 1.3.141–2

Expressing the confusion in his mind as he
begins to imagine murdering Duncan.

3 And I have found Demetrius, like a
   jewel,
   Mine own, and not mine own.

Helena in *A Midsummer Night's
Dream,* 4.1.191–2

She has "found" him by chance or magic, and
so, like a jewel found by accident, he may be
claimed by someone else.

4 But fare thee well, most foul, most
   fair! Farewell,
   Thou pure impiety and impious
   purity!

Claudio in *Much Ado About Nothing,*
4.1.103–4

Dismissing Hero, whom he was to have married, and believes to have been false to him.

Parents and Children
(see also Boys, Children,
Girls, Youth)

1   Thou hast never in thy life
   Showed thy dear mother any cour-
      tesy,
   When she, poor hen, fond of no
      second brood,
   Has clucked thee to the wars, and
      safely home
   Loaden with honor.

Volumnia in *Coriolanus,* 5.3.160–4

His mother pleads with Coriolanus not to
make war on Rome; a strikingly homely image
for a patrician lady.

2 [*holds her by the hand, silent*] O
   mother, mother!
   What have you done? Behold, the
      heavens do ope,
   The gods look down, and this
      unnatural scene
   They laugh at. O my mother,
      mother! O!
   You have won a happy victory to
      Rome;
   But, for your son, believe it—O,
      believe it—
   Most dangerously you have with
      him prevailed,
   If not most mortal to him.

Coriolanus in *Coriolanus,* 5.3.182–9

The turning-point, when he agrees to spare
Rome, knowing it may lead to his own ruin.

3 That thou art my son I have partly
   thy mother's word, partly my own

opinion, but chiefly a villainous
trick of thine eye and a foolish
hanging of thy nether lip that doth
warrant me.

Falstaff in *Henry IV, Part 1*, 2.4.402–5

Falstaff is play-acting as Prince Hal's father,
and invoking the common idea that one could
never be sure who the father of a child was,
hence the importance of resemblance to
parents.

4   Why, 'tis a happy thing
To be a father unto many sons.

**King Edward in *Henry VI, Part 3*,
3.2.104–5**

He wants to marry Lady Grey, who has sons
by a previous husband.

5   Sir, I love you more than words can
       wield the matter,
Dearer than eyesight, space, and
       liberty,
Beyond what can be valued, rich or
       rare,
No less than life, with grace, health,
       beauty, honor;
As much as child e'er loved, or
       father found,
A love that makes breath poor and
       speech unable.

Goneril in *King Lear*, 1.1.55–60

Overdoing her response to her father's
demand of his daughters, "Which of you shall
we say doth love us most?"

6   Now our joy,
Although our last and least.

King Lear in *King Lear*, 1.1.82–3

Addressing Cordelia, his youngest daughter
(so the Folio text, 1623; the Quarto, 1608, has
"not least").

7   You have begot me, bred me, loved
       me. I
Return those duties back as are
       right fit,

Obey you, love you, and most
    honor you.

Cordelia in *King Lear*, 1.1.96–8

Speaking to her father; the last line curiously
echoes the marriage service.

8   Fathers that wear rags
        Do make their children blind,
     But fathers that bear bags
        Shall see their children kind.

Fool in *King Lear*, 2.4.47–50

"Bear bags" = have wealth.

9   I prithee, daughter, do not make
        me mad.
     I will not trouble thee, my child;
        farewell:
     We'll no more meet, no more see
        one another.
     But yet thou art my flesh, my
        blood, my daughter—
     Or rather a disease that's in my
        flesh,
     Which I must needs call mine.

King Lear in *King Lear*, 2.4.218–23

Speaking to Goneril; he has given his power
to his daughters, and now they use it against
him.

10   I may neither choose who I would,
     nor refuse who I dislike; so is the
     will of a living daughter curbed by
     the will of a dead father.

**Portia in *The Merchant of Venice*,
1.2.23–5**

Playing on "will" as desire and as testament.

11   It is a wise father that knows his
     own child.

**Launcelot Gobbo in *The Merchant of
Venice*, 2.2.76–7**

His blind father fails to recognize him; varying
the proverb, "It is a wise child that knows his
own father."

12 Farewell, and if my fortune be not
      crossed,
    I have a father, you a daughter, lost.

    Jessica in *The Merchant of Venice*,
    2.5.56–7

    Said as her father, Shylock, leaves; she is aim-
    ing to elope with Lorenzo.

13 It is my cousin's duty to make
    curtsy and say, "Father, as it please
    you." But yet for all that, cousin,
    let him be a handsome fellow, or
    else make another curtsy and say,
    "Father, as it please me."

    Beatrice in *Much Ado About Nothing*,
    2.1.52–6

    Speaking of Hero; Beatrice is freer, her father
    being dead.

14 Can no man tell me of my unthrifty
      son?
    'Tis full three months since I did
      see him last.

    King Henry IV in *Richard II*, 5.3.1–2

    Referring to Prince Hal, as he becomes in
    Henry IV; "unthrifty" = spendthrift, prodigal.

15 Earth hath swallowed all my hopes
      but she;
    She is the hopeful lady of my earth.

    Capulet in *Romeo and Juliet*, 1.2.14–15

    On his only daughter, Juliet, the heir to his
    property ("earth").

16   They say we are
    Almost as like as eggs. Women say
      so
    That will say anything.

    Leontes in *The Winter's Tale*, 1.2.129–31

    On the likeness of father and son.

17   Methinks a father
    Is at the nuptial of his son a guest
    That best becomes the table.

    Polixenes in *The Winter's Tale*,
    4.4.394–6

    To Florizel, who has concealed his love for
    Perdita from his father.

18 Thou art thy mother's glass, and
      she in thee
    Calls back the lovely April of her
      prime.

    ***Sonnet* 3, 9–10**

    Addressing his "friend"; "glass" = mirror or
    image.

19 A decrepit father takes delight
    To see his active child do deeds of
      youth.

    ***Sonnet* 37, 1–2**

    Was Shakespeare thinking of himself? His first
    child was born when he was nineteen, in
    1583.

Parting (see also Farewells)

1   Sir, you and I must part, but that's
      not it;
    Sir, you and I have loved, but
      there's not it.

    Cleopatra in *Antony and Cleopatra*,
    1.3.87–8

    Movingly suggesting what cannot be
    expressed.

2   *Jaques.* Let's meet as little as we
      can.
    Orlando. I do desire we may be
      better strangers.

    ***As You Like It*,** 3.2.257–8

3   O the gods!
    When shall we see again?

Imogen in *Cymbeline*, 1.1.123–4

To Posthumus, her husband, as they are about
to be parted; "see" = see one another, meet.

4   There cannot be a pinch in death
    More sharp than this is.

Imogen in *Cymbeline*, 1.1.130–1

On the banishment of her husband,
Posthumus.

5   I would have broke mine eye-
        strings, cracked them, but
    To look upon him, till the diminu-
        tion
    Of space had pointed him sharp as
        my needle;
    Nay, followed him till he had
        melted from
    The smallness of a gnat to air, and
        then
    Have turned mine eye and wept.

Imogen in *Cymbeline*, 1.3.17–22

To Pisanio, who watched her husband,
Posthumus, sail away.

6   *Polonius.* My lord, I will take my
        leave of you.
    Hamlet. You cannot, sir, take from
        me anything that I will not more
        willingly part withal—except my
        life, except my life, except my life.

Hamlet, 2.2.213–16

Hamlet affects madness, but his melancholy
and death-wish are genuine.

7   Come, wilt thou see me ride?
    And when I am a' horseback, I will
        swear
    I love thee infinitely.

Hotspur in *Henry IV, Part 1*, 2.3.100–2

Joking that he will love his wife only when he
leaves her.

8   Art thou gone too? All comfort go
        with thee,
    For none abides with me.

**Duchess of Gloucester in *Henry VI,
Part 2*, 2.4.87–8**

On being forced to part from her husband.

9   For ever and for ever farewell, Cas-
        sius!
    If we do meet again, why, we shall
        smile.
    If not, why then this parting was
        well made.

Brutus in *Julius Caesar*, 5.1.116–18

Before the battle of Philippi; they never do
meet again.

10   Let us not be dainty of leave-taking,
    But shift away.

Malcolm in *Macbeth*, 2.3.144–5

After the murder of their father, Duncan;
"dainty of" = particular about.

11   Stand not upon the order of your
        going,
    But go at once.

Lady Macbeth in *Macbeth*, 3.4.118–19

The nobles at her feast would normally leave
in order of precedence, but Macbeth's wild
behavior on seeing the ghost of Banquo has
made her eager for their departure.

12   Trouble being gone, comfort
    should remain; but when you
    depart from me sorrow abides, and
    happiness takes his leave.

**Leonato in *Much Ado About Nothing*,
1.1.100–2**

An odd way to express pleasure in welcoming
guests.

13 *Queen.* And must we be divided?
    Must we part?
    King Richard. Ay, hand from hand,
    my love, and heart from heart.
    Richard II, 5.1.81–2

    Richard is being sent north to imprisonment.

14 Love goes toward love as school-
    boys from their books,
    But love from love, toward school
    with heavy looks.
    Romeo in *Romeo and Juliet,* 2.2.156–7

    On leaving Juliet.

15 Good night, good night. Parting is
    such sweet sorrow
    That I shall say good night till it be
    morrow.
    Juliet in *Romeo and Juliet,* 2.2.184–5

    Bidding farewell from her window to Romeo
    in the garden below.

16 Wilt thou be gone? It is not yet
    near day.
    It was the nightingale, and not the
    lark,
    That pierced the fearful hollow of
    thine ear;
    Nightly she sings on yond pome-
    granate tree.
    Juliet in *Romeo and Juliet,* 3.5.1–4

    To Romeo, who is anxious to get away at day-
    break; "fearful" = anxious.

Passion

1 What to ourselves in passion we
    propose,
    The passion ending, doth the pur-
    pose lose.
    Player King in *Hamlet,* 3.2.194–5

2   Is this the nature
    Whom passion could not shake?
    Whose solid virtue
    The shot of accident nor dart of
    chance
    Could neither graze nor pierce?
    Lodovico in *Othello,* 4.1.265–8

    Amazed at the angry passion Othello shows.

3   Is your blood
    So madly hot that no discourse of
    reason,
    Nor fear of bad success in a bad
    cause,
    Can qualify the same?
    Hector in *Troilus and Cressida,*
    2.2.115–18

    Questioning the passion his young brother,
    Troilus, has for keeping Helen.

4 An oven that is stopped, or river
    stayed,
    Burneth more hotly, swelleth with
    more rage;
    So of concealèd sorrow may be said
    Free vent of words love's fire doth
    assuage.
    Venus and Adonis, 331–4

    Venus, burning with love for Adonis,
    approaches him.

Patience

1 I laughed him out of patience; and
    that night
    I laughed him into patience.
    Cleopatra in *Antony and Cleopatra,*
    2.5.19–20

    Exemplifying her "infinite variety" (2.2.235).

2 Though patience be a tired mare,
    yet she will plod.
    Nym in *Henry V,* 2.1.23–4

3   With meditating that she must die
     once,
     I have the patience to endure it
     now.

Brutus in *Julius Caesar*, 4.3.191–2

On the death of his wife, Portia.

4   I know not how,
     But I do find it cowardly and vile,
     For fear of what might fall, so to
     prevent
     The time of life—arming myself
     with patience
     To stay the providence of some
     high powers
     That govern us below.

Brutus in *Julius Caesar*, 5.1.102–7

Anticipating the worst, and rejecting for the
moment the idea of suicide; "prevent" =
anticipate.

5   No, I will be the pattern of all
     patience,
     I will say nothing.

King Lear in *King Lear*, 3.2.37–8

Shut out of doors in a violent storm, King Lear
does not remain patient for long.

6   Bear free and patient thoughts.

Edgar in *King Lear*, 4.6.80

Advising his father; "free" = free from guilt or
anxiety.

7   Thou must be patient; we came cry-
     ing hither.
     Thou know'st, the first time that we
     smell the air
     We wawl and cry.

King Lear in *King Lear*, 4.6.178–80

The old king, half-crazed, preaches to the
blind Gloucester.

8   I do oppose
     My patience to his fury, and am
     armed
     To suffer, with a quietness of
     spirit,
     The very tyranny and rage of his.

**Antonio in *The Merchant of Venice*,
4.1.10–13**

Referring to Shylock's cruelty ("tyranny").

9   If then true lovers have been ever
     crossed
     It stands as an edict in destiny.
     Then let us teach our trial
     patience,
     Because it is a customary cross,
     As due to love as thoughts, and
     dreams, and sighs,
     Wishes, and tears—poor fancy's
     followers.

**Hermia in *A Midsummer Night's
Dream*, 1.1.150–5**

Speaking to Lysander; "crossed" = thwarted;
"fancy" suggests both love and the capricious
workings of the imagination.

10   How poor are they that have not
     patience!
     What wound did ever heal but by
     degrees?

Iago in *Othello*, 2.3.370–1

Recommending patience to Roderigo, who
has been beaten by Cassio; "He that has no
patience has nothing" is proverbial.

11   Yet thou dost look
     Like Patience gazing on kings'
     graves, and smiling
     Extremity out of act.

Pericles in *Pericles*, 5.1.137–9

On the sufferings of Marina; "smiling extremity out of act" = making extreme calamities
seem as if they never happened.

12 She sat like Patience on a monument,
 Smiling at grief.

Viola in *Twelfth Night,* 2.4.114–5

She is describing her own concealed love for
Orsino, to whom she is speaking.

Patriotism

1 Who is here so base that would be a
 bondman? If any, speak, for him
 have I offended. Who is here so
 rude that would not be a Roman?
 If any, speak, for him have I
 offended. Who is here so vile that
 will not love his country? If any,
 speak, for him have I offended.

Brutus in *Julius Caesar,* 3.2.29–34

To the people, after the death of Caesar.

2 This England never did, nor never
 shall
 Lie at the proud foot of a conqueror,
 But when it first did help to wound
 itself.
 Now these her princes are come
 home again,
 Come the three corners of the
 world in arms,
 And we shall shock them. Nought
 shall make us rue
 If England to herself do rest but
 true!

The Bastard Falconbridge in *King
John,* 5.7.112–18

A rousing finish to a play much concerned
with civil discords.

Payment (see also Money)

1 Now I will look to his remuneration. Remuneration! O, that's the
 Latin word for three-farthings.

Costard in *Love's Labor's Lost,* 3.1.136–7

Armado's "reward" to him for carrying a letter
to Jaquenetta.

2 He is well paid that is well satisfied.

Portia in *The Merchant of Venice,*
4.1.415

Disguised as Balthasar the lawyer, she refuses
the money offered to her as a fee by her husband Bassanio.

Peace

1 The time of universal peace is near.
 Prove this a prosp'rous day, the
 three-nooked world
 Shall bear the olive freely.

Octavius Caesar in *Antony and
Cleopatra,* 4.6.4–6

Anticipating peace. "Prove this" = If this
prove; "three-nooked" = three-cornered.

2 *Second Servant.* As wars, in some
 sort, may be said to be a ravisher,
 so it cannot be denied but peace is
 a great maker of cuckolds.
 First Servant. Ay, and it makes men
 hate one another.
 Second Servant. Reason: because
 they then less need one another.

Coriolanus, 4.5.227–32

The servants of Aufidius commenting after the
arrival of Coriolanus at his house.

3   Never was a war did cease,
Ere bloody hands were washed,
  with such a peace.

Cymbeline in *Cymbeline*, 5.5.484–5

Having defeated the Romans, Cymbeline agrees to submit to their rule.

4 All you that kiss my Lady Peace at home.

Falstaff in *Henry IV, Part 2*, 1.2.207–8

To the Chief Justice, as Falstaff goes off to fight rebels.

5 The dove and very blessed spirit of peace.

Westmorland in *Henry IV, Part 2*, 4.1.46

On what an archbishop's vestments symbolize.

6 Our peace shall stand as firm as rocky mountains.

Mowbray in *Henry IV, Part 2*, 4.1.186

A rebel hopes to negotiate peace with the king.

7 A peace is of the nature of a conquest,
For then both parties nobly are subdued,
And neither party loser.

Archbishop of York in *Henry IV, Part 2*, 4.2.89–91

He does not know that Prince John is tricking his enemies, and will promptly execute the rebel leaders.

8 Peace puts forth her olive everywhere.

Westmorland in *Henry IV, Part 2*, 4.4.87

The olive branch, a traditional symbol of peace.

9 In peace there's nothing so becomes a man
As modest stillness and humility.

King Henry in *Henry V*, 3.1.3–4

10 Peace to this meeting, wherefore we are met.

King Henry in *Henry V*, 5.2.1

The meeting is to settle peace between England and France.

11   Peace,
Dear nurse of arts, plenties, and joyful births.

Burgundy in *Henry V*, 5.2.34–5

12 For blessèd are the peacemakers on earth.

King Henry in *Henry VI, Part 2*, 2.1.34

13 In her days every man shall eat in safety
Under his own vine what he plants, and sing
The merry songs of peace to all his neighbors.

Archbishop Cranmer in *Henry VIII*, 5.4.33–5

Anticipating the reign of Queen Elizabeth I; the terms recall biblical passages such as Micah 4:3–4.

14   'Tis not hard, I think,
For men so old as we to keep the peace.

Capulet in *Romeo and Juliet*, 1.2.2–3

The prince has bound old Capulet and Montague to keep the peace.

15 I hold the olive in my hand. My
words are as full of peace as matter.

Viola in *Twelfth Night*, 1.5.209–11

Bringing Orsino's message of love to Olivia.

People/Populace

1 Tonight we'll wander through the
streets and note
The qualities of people.

Antony in *Antony and Cleopatra*,
1.1.53–4

An early instance of the popular sport of "peo-
ple-watching."

2   This common body
Like to a vagabond flag upon the
stream,
Goes to and back, lackeying the
various tide
To rot itself with motion.

Octavius Caesar in *Antony and
Cleopatra*, 1.4.44–7

The "vagabond flag" refers to a flag iris drifting; "lackeying" = following, like a lackey or
servant. Octavius shows his contempt for the
people.

3 He's a very dog to the commonalty.

First Citizen in *Coriolanus*, 1.1.28–9

Referring to Caius Martius, later named Coriolanus, one of the patricians against whom
the citizens have begun an uprising; "commonalty" = state or commonwealth.

4 What's the matter, you dissentious
rogues,
That rubbing the poor itch of your
opinion
Make yourselves scabs?

Caius Martius, later Coriolanus, in
Coriolanus, 1.1.164–6

A patrician reveals his contempt for the people and their opinions.

5   He that trusts to you,
Where he should find you lions,
finds you hares;
Where foxes, geese.

Caius Martius, later Coriolanus, in
Coriolanus, 1.1.170–2

A patrician view of the people of Rome, seeing them as cowardly.

6   You are no surer, no,
Than is the coal of fire upon the ice,
Or hailstone in the sun.

Caius Martius, later Coriolanus, in
Coriolanus, 1.1.172–4

A patrician tells the people they cannot be
trusted.

7 With every minute you do change a
mind,
And call him noble that was now
your hate.

Caius Martius, later Coriolanus, in
Coriolanus, 1.1.177–9

A patrician complains that the citizens of
Rome are unstable.

8   He that depends
Upon your favors swims with fins
of lead,
And hews down oaks with rushes.

Caius Martius, later Coriolanus, in
Coriolanus, 1.1.179–81

A patrician view of the people as unreliable.

9 For the mutable, rank-scented
meiny, let them
Regard me as I do not flatter, and
Therein behold themselves.

Coriolanus in *Coriolanus*, 3.1.66

A patrician claims to be telling the truth about
the people, but shows his scorn for them at
the same time; "meiny" = multitude.

10   You speak o'the people
As if you were a god, to punish; not
A man of their infirmity.

Brutus in *Coriolanus*, 3.1.80–2

A tribune of the people sums up the attitude of the patrician Coriolanus.

11   You common cry of curs, whose breath I hate
As reek o'the rotten fens, whose loves I prize
As the dead carcasses of unburied men
That do corrupt my air—I banish you!

Coriolanus in *Coriolanus*, 3.3.120–3

Sicinius, a tribune of the people, has just declared that Coriolanus should be banished.

12   Come, leave your tears. A brief farewell. The beast
With many heads butts me away.

Coriolanus in *Coriolanus*, 4.1.1–2

Coriolanus bids his wife farewell as he goes from Rome, banished by the people (the "beast with many heads").

13   The blunt monster with uncounted heads,
The still-discordant wav'ring multitude.

Rumor in *Henry IV, Part 2*, Induction, 18–19

14   An habitation giddy and unsure
Hath he that buildeth on the vulgar heart.

Archbishop of York in *Henry IV, Part 2*, 1.3.89–90

Complaining that the common people cannot be relied on.

15   See how the giddy multitude do point

And nod their heads and throw their eyes on thee!

Duchess of Gloucester in *Henry VI, Part 2*, 2.4.21–2

To her husband, who stays with her when she is exposed to public shame.

16   Was ever feather so lightly blown to and fro as this multitude?

Jack Cade in *Henry VI, Part 2*, 4.8.55–6

The leader of the mob finds they readily change allegiance.

17   I love the people,
But do not like to stage me to their eyes;
Though it do well, I do not relish well
Their loud applause and aves vehement;
Nor do I think the man of safe discretion
That does affect it.

Duke in *Measure for Measure*, 1.1.67–72

Deputing Angelo to rule Vienna in his place; "aves" = cries of acclaim; "safe" = sound.

18   I will not choose what many men desire,
Because I will not jump with common spirits,
And rank me with the barbarous multitudes.

Prince of Aragon in *The Merchant of Venice*, 2.9.31–3

"Jump" = agree, go along with.

Perception

1   Sits the wind in that corner?

Benedick in *Much Ado About Nothing*, 2.3.98

Is that how things stand?; on overhearing it said that Beatrice loves him.

2   Grief has so wrought on
him,
He takes false shadows for true sub-
stances.

Marcus in *Titus Andronicus*, 3.2.79–80

He thinks Titus is mad to identify a fly with
Aaron the Moor.

3   One face, one voice, one habit, and
two persons,
A natural perspective that is and is
not!

Orsino in *Twelfth Night*, 5.1.216–7

On seeing the twins, Sebastian and Viola
(who is dressed as a man), together for the first
time; "natural perspective" = optical illusion
produced by nature.

Perfection

1   You, O you,
So perfect and so peerless, are cre-
ated
Of every creature's best!

Ferdinand in *The Tempest*, 3.1.46–8

Expressing his love for Miranda.

2   But no perfection is so absolute
That some impurity doth not pol-
lute.

The Rape of Lucrece, 853–4

Lucrece broods on the rape she has suffered.

3   Everything that grows
Holds in perfection but a little
moment.

Sonnet 15, 1–2

Perfume

1   'Tis her breathing that
Perfumes the chamber thus.

Jachimo in *Cymbeline*, 2.2.18–19

Looking at Imogen asleep.

Perplexity

1   My thoughts are whirlèd like a potter's wheel;
I know not where I am , nor what I
do.

Talbot in *Henry VI, Part 1*, 1.5.19–20

He is confused by the unexpected success in
battle of Joan la Pucelle (Joan of Arc).

2   My mind is troubled, like a fountain stirred,
And I myself see not the bottom of
it.

**Achilles in *Troilus and Cressida*,
3.3.308–9**

Perseverance

1   Many strokes, though with a little
axe,
Hews down and fells the hardest-
timbered oak.

Messenger in *Henry VI, Part 3*, 2.1.54–5

Proverbial.

2   I am a kind of burr; I shall stick.

Lucio in *Measure for Measure*, 4.3.179

Determined to stay with the Duke, who wants
to shake him off.

3   Perseverance, dear my
lord,
Keeps honor bright; to have done is
to hang

Quite out of fashion.

Ulysses in *Troilus and Cressida*,
3.3.150–2

He is trying to persuade the great warrior
Achilles to return to the battlefield.

Persuasion

1   But your discretions better can persuade
Than I am able to instruct or teach,
And therefore, as we hither came in
peace,
So let us still continue peace and
love.

King Henry in *Henry VI, Part 1*,
4.1.158–61

Henry is trying to preserve peace among the
quarreling factions in England.

2   What you would work me to, I have
some aim.

Brutus in *Julius Caesar*, 1.2.163

"Aim" = idea.

3   Three parts of him
Is ours already, and the man entire
Upon the next encounter yields
him ours.

Cassius in *Julius Caesar*, 1.3.154–6

Using devious means to win the support of
Brutus.

4   Let me work;
For I can give his humor the true
bent.

Decius in *Julius Caesar*, 2.1.209–10

Claiming he can direct Caesar's inclination
the right way.

5   There is no tongue that moves,
none, none i'the world
So soon as yours, could win me.

Polixenes in *The Winter's Tale*, 1.2.20–1

Leontes is pressing him to continue his visit to
Sicily.

Philosophy

1   They say miracles are past, and we
have our philosophical persons, to
make modern and familiar, things
supernatural and causeless. Hence
is it that we make trifles of terrors,
ensconcing ourselves into seeming
knowledge, when we should submit
ourselves to an unknown fear.

Lafew in *All's Well That Ends Well*,
2.3.1–6

On trusting what is awesome and inexplica-
ble, rather than seeking explanations for
everything; the miracle is Helena's cure of the
king's sickness.

2   This is no flattery: these are coun-
selors
That feelingly persuade me what I
am.

Duke Senior in *As You Like It*, 2.1.10–11

The Duke's philosophy in the face of wind
and cold.

3   A great cause of the night is lack of
the sun.

Corin in *As You Like It*, 3.2.28

The shepherd's homespun philosophy.

4   I earn that I eat, get that I wear, owe
no man hate, envy no man's happiness, glad of other men's good,
content with my harm.

Corin in *As You Like It*, 3.2.73–6

5 *Horatio.* O day and night, but this
is wondrous strange!
Hamlet. And therefore as a
stranger give it welcome.
There are more things in heaven
and earth, Horatio,
Than are dreamt of in your philosophy.

Hamlet in *Hamlet*, 1.5.164–7

After Hamlet's interview with his father's
ghost; Horatio has just returned from Witten-
berg to Denmark, and so is a "stranger."

6 There is nothing either good or
bad, but thinking makes it so.

Hamlet in *Hamlet*, 2.2.249–50

To Rosencrantz and Guildenstern; Hamlet
says Denmark is a prison and they do not
think so.

7 There is something in this more
than natural, if philosophy could
find it out.

Hamlet in *Hamlet*, 2.2.367–8

Commenting on his uncle's popularity as king
with the people who previously decried him.

8 There is some soul of goodness in
things evil,
Would men observingly distill it
out.

King Henry in *Henry V*, 4.1.4–5

"Observingly" = observantly, with watchful
care.

9 Thus may we gather honey from
the weed
And make a moral of the devil himself.

King Henry in *Henry V*, 4.1.11–12

Drawing encouragement from adversity.

10 'Tis good for men to love their present pains
Upon example; so the spirit is
eased.

King Henry in *Henry V*, 4.1.18–19

Soldiers feel better for seeing their betters like
the king enduring their discomforts.

11 There is occasions and causes why
and wherefore in all things.

Fluellen in *Henry V*, 5.1.3–4

The odd grammar hints at Fluellen's Welsh
accent.

12 Of your philosophy you make no
use
If you give place to accidental evils.

Cassius in *Julius Caesar*, 4.3.145–6

To Brutus; "give place to accidental evils" =
are upset by troubles caused by chance.

13 Since the affairs of men rest still
incertain,
Let's reason with the worst that
may befall.

Cassius in *Julius Caesar*, 5.1.95–6

Contemplating battle; "reason" = reckon.

14 'Tis all men's office to speak
patience
To those that wring under the load
of sorrow,
But no man's virtue nor sufficiency
To be so moral when he shall
endure
The like himself.

**Leonato in *Much Ado About Nothing*,
5.1.27–31**

He says everyone has a duty ("office") to
advise patience to those who writhe ("wring")
in suffering, but no one who suffers has the
ability to preach patience to himself.

15   There was never yet philosopher
      That could endure the toothache
      patiently.

Leonato in *Much Ado About Nothing*,
5.1.35–6

Rejecting his brother's attempt to soothe him.

16   To mourn a mischief that is past
      and gone
      Is the next way to draw new mis-
      chief on.

Duke in *Othello*, 1.3.204–5

"Mischief" = misfortune or calamity.

17   The robbed that smiles steals some-
      thing from the thief;
      He robs himself that spends a boot-
      less grief.

Duke in *Othello*, 1.3.208–9

"Spends a bootless grief" = indulges in useless
lamenting.

18   Thoughts tending to content flatter
      themselves
      That they are not the first of for-
      tune's slaves,
      Nor shall not be the last, like silly
      beggars
      Who, sitting in the stocks, refuge
      their shame
      That many have and others must sit
      there,
      And in this thought they find a
      kind of ease.

King Richard in *Richard II*, 5.5.23–8

Meditating in prison; "silly" = simple; "refuge"
= rationalize.

19   What's gone and what's past help
      Should be past grief.

Paulina in *The Winter's Tale*, 3.2.222–3

An elegant variation on the proverb, "never
grieve for that you cannot help."

Pity

1   If ever you have looked on better
     days,
     If ever been where bells have
     knolled to church,
     If ever sat at any good man's feast,
     If ever from your eyelids wiped a
     tear,
     And know what 'tis to pity and be
     pitied,
     Let gentleness my strong enforce-
     ment be.

Orlando in *As You Like It*, 2.7.113–8

Appealing for help for his old servant, Adam.

2   Our hearts you see not; they are
     pitiful;
     And pity to the general wrong of
     Rome—
     As fire drives out fire, so pity pity—
     Hath done this deed on Caesar.

Brutus in *Julius Caesar*, 3.1.169–72

"This deed" = the assassination of Caesar.

3   O, now you weep, and I perceive
     you feel
     The dint of pity.

Mark Antony in *Julius Caesar*,
3.2.193–4

He has succeeded in making the people pity
Caesar.

4   A most poor man, made tame to
     fortune's blows,
     Who by the art of known and feel-
     ing sorrows
     Am pregnant to good pity.

Edgar in *King Lear*, 4.6.221–3

"Pregnant" = prone or predisposed.

5   Pity, like a naked, new-born babe
Striding the blast, or heaven's
cherubins, horsed
Upon the sightless couriers of the
air,
Shall blow the horrid deed in every
eye,
That tears shall drown the wind.

Macbeth in *Macbeth*, 1.7.21–5

The "deed" is the murder of Duncan; in
Psalms 18:10 (Book of Common Prayer), God
"rode upon the cherubins and did fly; he
came flying upon the wings of the wind";
"sightless" = invisible.

6   *Isabella.* Yet show some pity.
Angelo. I show it most of all when I
    show justice;
For then I pity those I do not know,
Which a dismissed offense would
    after gall.

Measure for Measure, 2.2.99–102

Asking mercy for her brother, sentenced to
death; "dismissed offense" = one that goes
unpunished; "after gall" = afterwards injure or
annoy.

7   My story being done,
She gave me for my pains a world
    of sighs;
She swore, in faith 'twas strange,
    'twas passing strange;
'Twas pitiful, 'twas wondrous piti-
ful.

Othello in *Othello*, 1.3.158–61

On his courtship of Desdemona by telling her
the story of his life.

8   But yet the pity of it, Iago! O Iago,
the pity of it, Iago!

Othello in *Othello*, 4.1.195–6

Loving Desdemona even as he plans to murder her.

9   Had not God, for some strong
purpose, steeled

The hearts of men, they must perforce have melted,
And barbarism itself have pitied
him.

York in *Richard II*, 5.2.34–6

Commenting on the harsh treatment of
Richard by the citizens of London.

10   No beast so fierce but knows some
touch of pity.

Lady Anne in *Richard III*, 1.2.71

Plain-Speaking

1   Mark now how a plain tale shall put
you down.

**Prince Hal in *Henry IV, Part 1*,
2.4.254–5**

Telling the true story to expose Falstaff's lies.

2   Out with it boldly; truth loves open
dealing.

Queen Katherine in *Henry VIII*, 3.1.39

She suspects the Cardinals visiting her are not
being open.

3   What a blunt fellow is this grown to
be!
He was quick mettle when he went
to school.

Brutus in *Julius Caesar*, 1.2.295–6

Describing Casca; "quick mettle" = lively in
spirit.

4   This rudeness is a sauce to his good
wit,
Which gives men stomach to digest
his words
With better appetite.

Cassius in *Julius Caesar*, 1.2.300–2

Describing Casca's forthright manner of
speaking.

5   I am no orator, as Brutus is,
    But, as you know me all, a plain
      blunt man
    That love my friend, and that they
      know full well
    That gave me public leave to speak
      of him.

Mark Antony in *Julius Caesar*,
3.2.217–20

Antony is, of course, much the better orator in
speaking of Caesar.

6   Sir, 'tis my occupation to be plain:
    I have seen better faces in my time
    Than stands on any shoulder that I
      see
    Before me at this instant.

Kent in *King Lear*, 2.2.92–5

Addressing his superior, the Duke of Cornwall.

7   He cannot flatter, he,
    An honest mind and plain, he must
      speak truth.
    An they will take it, so; if not, he's
      plain.

Cornwall in *King Lear*, 2.2.98–100

Responding to the disguised Kent's blunt
words; "an they" = if they.

8   Taffeta phrases, silken terms pre-
      cise,
    Three-piled hyperboles, spruce
      affectation,
    Figures pedantical—these summer
      flies
    Have blown me full of maggot
      ostentation.
    I do forswear them, and I here
      protest,
    By this white glove (how white the
      hand, God knows!),

Henceforth my wooing mind shall
  be expressed
In russet yeas and honest kersey
  noes.

Berowne in *Love's Labor's Lost*,
5.2.406–13

"Russet" and "kersey" were plain and rough
kinds of cloth.

9   Honest plain words best pierce the
      ear of grief.

Berowne in *Love's Labor's Lost*, 5.2.753

News of the death of the Princess's father
reduces the courtiers to plain-speaking.

10 Do I entice you? Do I speak you
      fair?
    Or rather do I not in plainest truth
    Tell you I do not nor I cannot love
      you?

**Demetrius in *A Midsummer Night's
Dream*, 2.1.199–201**

Rejecting Helena's love.

11 An honest tale speeds best being
      plainly told.

Queen Elizabeth in *Richard III*, 4.4.358

Proverbial; exposing Richard's hypocrisy.

12 I was not much afeard; for once or
      twice
    I was about to speak, and tell him
      plainly,
    The selfsame sun that shines upon
      his court
    Hides not his visage from our cot-
      tage, but
    Looks on alike.

Perdita in *The Winter's Tale*, 4.4.442–6

As Polixenes separates her from Florizel, his
son and heir to the throne.

Plays (see also Acting, Theater)

He and Prince Hal are interrupted in their improvised play in which each in turn played King Henry and the Prince.

1   If it be true that good wine needs no bush, 'tis true that a good play needs no epilogue.

Rosalind in *As You Like It*, Epilogue, 3–5

It was proverbial that a good wine needed "no bush," or sign hung out to advertise sale of it.

2   My way is to conjure you, and I'll begin with the women. I charge you, O women, for the love you bear to men, to like as much of this play as please you. I charge you, O men, for the love you bear to women (as I perceive by your simpering, none of you hates them), that between you and the women the play may please.

Rosalind in *As You Like It*, Epilogue, 11–17

3   The play, I remember, pleased not the million, 'twas caviare to the general.

Hamlet in *Hamlet*, 2.2.435–7

"Caviare to the general" = too rare a delicacy for the multitude.

4   The play's the thing Wherein I'll catch the conscience of the King.

Hamlet in *Hamlet*, 2.2.604–5

"The play's the thing" is often quoted on its own; for Hamlet it is a means to expose the guilt of Claudius.

5   Play out the play!

Falstaff in *Henry IV, Part 1*, 2.4.484

6   Our wooing doth not end like an old play, Jack hath not Jill.

Berowne in *Love's Labor's Lost*, 5.2.874–5

The courtiers have to practice celibacy for a year before the ladies will have them.

Pleasure

1   There's not a minute of our lives should stretch Without some pleasure now.

Antony in *Antony and Cleopatra*, 1.1.46–7

2   The present pleasure, By revolution lowering, does become The opposite of itself.

Antony in *Antony and Cleopatra*, 1.2.123–5

"By revolution lowering" = losing its appeal as things change; "revolution" suggests the turning of Fortune's wheel.

3   I'th' East my pleasure lies.

Antony in *Antony and Cleopatra*, 2.3.41

Married, and in Rome, Antony yearns for Egypt and Cleopatra.

4   His delights Were dolphin-like, they showed his back above The element they lived in.

Cleopatra in *Antony and Cleopatra*,
5.2.88–90

Her vision of Antony, after his death.

5   Come, madam wife, sit by my
       side
And let the world slip. We shall
   ne'er be younger.

Sly in *The Taming of the Shrew*,
Induction, 2.142–4

Inviting her to forget the world and watch a
play.

6   *Orsino.* There's for thy pains.
    Feste. No pains, sir, I take pleasure
      in singing, sir.
    Orsino. I'll pay thy pleasure then.
    Feste. Truly, sir, and pleasure will
      be paid, one time or another.

Twelfth Night, 2.4.67–71

Feste alludes to the proverbial idea that pleasure must be paid for with pain.

Plots

1   Who cannot be crushed with a
    plot?

Parolles in *All's Well That Ends Well*,
4.3.325

2   O, 'tis most sweet
When in one line two crafts directly
   meet.

Hamlet in *Hamlet*, 3.4.210–1

3   This falls out better than I could
    devise.

Oberon in *A Midsummer Night's
Dream*, 3.2.35

Oberon has succeeded better than he
expected in making Titania fall in love with
an ass.

4   With as little a web as this will I
    ensnare as great a fly as Cassio.

Iago in *Othello*, 2.1.168–9

Iago is observing Cassio's gallant behavior to
Desdemona.

5   *Maria.* Nay, but say true, does it
      work upon him?
    Sir Toby Belch. Like aqua vitae with
      a midwife.

Twelfth Night, 2.5.195–6

"Aqua vitae," the water of life = brandy or
other spirits.

Poetry

1   Hang there, my verse, in witness of
    my love.

Orlando in *As You Like It*, 3.2.1

Hanging poems in praise of Rosalind on the
forest trees.

2   I'll rhyme you so eight years
    together, dinners and suppers and
    sleeping-hours excepted.

Touchstone in *As You Like It*, 3.2.96–7

Mocking Orlando's style of writing love
poetry.

3   If a hart do lack a hind,
    Let him seek out Rosalind.

Touchstone in *As You Like It*, 3.2.101–2

Parodying Orlando's verses to Rosalind.

4   The truest poetry is the most feign-
    ing.

Touchstone in *As You Like It*, 3.3.19–20

Reviving an old argument that poets who
"feign," or make fictions, are liars.

5 *Orlando.* Good day and happiness,
   dear Rosalind!
   Jaques. Nay then, God buy you, an
   you talk in blank verse.

   As You Like It, 4.1.30–2

   "God buy you" spells out "goodbye"; "an" =
   if.

6 I had rather be a kitten and cry
   mew
   Than one of these same meter ballad-mongers.

   Hotspur in Henry IV, Part 1, 3.1.127–8

   Expressing in verse his scorn for it.

7 I had rather hear a brazen canstick
   turned,
   Or a dry wheel grate on the axle-
   tree,
   And that would set my teeth nothing on edge,
   Nothing so much as mincing
   poetry.
   'Tis like the forced gait of a shuffling nag.

   Hotspur in Henry IV, Part 1, 3.1.129–33

   Hotspur, speaking in verse, dismisses poetry
   as affected or effeminate ("mincing"); "canstick" = candlestick; "turned" = on a lathe.

8 O for a Muse of fire, that would
   ascend
   The brightest heaven of invention!
   A kingdom for a stage, princes to
   act,
   And monarchs to behold the
   swelling scene!

   Chorus in Henry V, Prologue, 1–4

   "Invention" = poetic imagination.

9 Never durst poet touch a pen to
   write

Until his ink were tempered with
love's sighs.
O then his lines would ravish savage ears,
And plant in tyrants mild humility.

Berowne in Love's Labor's Lost,
4.3.343–6

Berowne's extravagant idea of the power of
love-poetry.

10 The poet's eye, in a fine frenzy
    rolling,
    Doth glance from heaven to earth,
    from earth to heaven;
    And as imagination bodies forth
    The forms of things unknown, the
    poet's pen
    Turns them to shapes, and gives to
    airy nothing
    A local habitation and a name.

    **Theseus in A Midsummer Night's
    Dream,** 5.1.12–17

    These lines might be Shakespeare's own com-
    ment on creating the fairy world of this play.

11 Marry, I cannot show it in rhyme, I
    have tried; I can find no rhyme to
    "lady" but "baby"—an innocent
    rhyme; for "scorn," "horn"—a hard
    rhyme; for "school," "fool"—a bab-
    bling rhyme; very ominous end-
    ings. No, I was not born under a
    rhyming planet, nor I cannot woo
    in festival terms.

    Benedick in Much Ado About Nothing,
    5.2.36–41

    Trying to express his love for Beatrice.

12 Lascivious meters, to whose venom
    sound
    The open ear of youth doth always
    listen.

York in *Richard II*, 2.1.19–20

Equivalent to the pop songs of modern times?

13   Much is the force of heaven-bred
    poesy.

**Duke in *The Two Gentlemen of
Verona*, 3.2.71**

That is, as an aid in wooing Silvia.

14   I love a ballad in print alife, for
    then we are sure they are true.

Mopsa in *The Winter's Tale*, 4.4.260–1

"Alife" = on my life, dearly; the peasant girl
thinks anything in print must be true.

15   Not marble nor the gilded monu-
    ments
    Of princes shall outlive this power-
    ful rhyme,
    But you shall shine more bright in
    these contents
    Than unswept stone, besmeared
    with sluttish time.

***Sonnet 55*, 1–4**

Shakespeare's confidence that his lines in
praise of his friend would outlast monuments
in stone has been validated by time.

16   Your monument shall be my gentle
    verse,
    Which eyes not yet created shall
    o'er-read,
    And tongues to be your being shall
    rehearse
    When all the breathers of this world
    are dead;
    You still shall live (such virtue
    hath my pen)
    Where breath most breathes, even
    in the mouths of men.

***Sonnet 81*, 9–14**

When those now living ("the breathers of this
world") are dead, the speaker's friend will sur-
vive in remembrance through the power
("virtue") of his poetry.

Poison

1   No medicine in the world can do
    thee good;
    In thee there is not half an hour's
    life.

Laertes in *Hamlet*, 5.2.314–15

He has touched Hamlet with a poisoned
rapier in their fencing match.

2   They love not poison that do poi-
    son need.

King Henry IV in *Richard II*, 5.6.38

Unhappy to learn that Richard II has been
killed at his own suggestion.

3   There is thy gold, worse poison to
    men's souls,
    Doing more murder in this loath-
    some world,
    Than these poor compounds that
    thou mayest not sell.
    I sell thee poison, thou hast sold me
    none.

Romeo in *Romeo and Juliet*, 5.1.80–3

Buying poison from the poor apothecary.

4   I could do this, and that with no
    rash potion,
    But with a lingering dram, that
    should not work
    Maliciously, like poison.

Camillo in *The Winter's Tale*, 1.2.319–21

On first hearing the king, Leontes, urge him to
poison his "enemy," Polixenes.

5   There may be in the cup
A spider steeped, and one may
 drink, depart,
And yet partake no venom, for his
 knowledge
Is not infected; but if one present
Th'abhorred ingredient to his eye,
 make known
How he hath drunk, he cracks his
 gorge, his sides,
With violent hefts. I have drunk,
 and seen the spider.

Leontes in *The Winter's Tale*, 2.1.39–45

Finding the escape of Polixenes to be con-
vincing evidence of his wife's adultery; spiders were thought to be poisonous; "hefts" =
heavings (vomiting out the poison).

Politics (see also Greatness, Power)

1 The time is out of joint—O cursed
 spite,
That ever I was born to set it right!

Hamlet in *Hamlet*, 1.5.188–9

Lamenting not only the disorder of the time,
but his own nativity.

2 The great man down, you mark his
 favorite flies,
The poor advanced makes friends
 of enemies.

Player King in *Hamlet*, 3.2.204–5

"Advanced" = given promotion.

3 I am whipped and scourged with
 rods,
Nettled and stung with pismires,
 when I hear
Of this vile politician Bolingbroke.

Hotspur in *Henry IV, Part 1*, 1.3.239–41

Angry with the king (formerly Henry Bolingbroke), who came to power with the help of
Hotspur's family and now regards them as
rebels; "pismires" = ants; "politician" =
schemer.

4 Be it thy course to busy giddy
 minds
With foreign quarrels, that action,
 hence borne out,
May waste the memory of former
 days.

King Henry in *Henry IV, Part 2*,
4.5.213–5

The king's advice to Prince Hal, that foreign
affairs distract attention from problems at
home, has often been thought sound politics.

5 Hear him debate of commonwealth
 affairs,
You would say it hath been all in all
 his study.

Archbishop of Canterbury in *Henry
V*, 1.1.41–2

Speaking of Prince Hal, now king.

6 Turn him to any cause of policy,
The Gordian knot of it he will
 unloose,
Familiar as his garter.

Archbishop of Canterbury in *Henry
V*, 1.1.45–7

It was said that whoever undid the Gordian
knot would rule Asia, and Alexander the
Great, who cut it with his sword, went on to
great conquests.

7   He was a fool,
For he would needs be virtuous.
 That good fellow,
If I command him, follows my
 appointment.

Cardinal Wolsey in *Henry VIII*,
2.2.131–3

Putting obedience above principle; the "good
fellow" is Gardiner, promoted to be the king's
secretary by Wolsey's scheming.

8   You ever
Have wished the sleeping of this
    business, never desired
It to be stirred, but oft have hin-
    dered, oft
The passages made toward it.

King Henry in *Henry VIII*, 2.4.163–6

Speaking to Wolsey; the "business" is the
divorce proceeding against Katherine of
Aragon.

9   Plague of your policy!

Surrey in *Henry VIII*, 3.2.259

To Wolsey, who contrived to have Surrey sent
off to Ireland; "of" = on.

10   Let me have men about me that are
    fat,
Sleek-headed men, and such as
    sleep a-nights.
Yon Cassius has a lean and hungry
    look;
He thinks too much. Such men are
    dangerous.

Caesar in *Julius Caesar*, 1.2.192–5

Caesar's intuitive feeling about Cassius.

11   Such men as he be never at heart's
    ease
Whiles they behold a greater than
    themselves,
And therefore are they very danger-
    ous.

Caesar in *Julius Caesar*, 1.2.208–10

Referring to Cassius.

12   Let us not break with him,
For he will never follow anything
That other men begin.

Brutus in *Julius Caesar*, 2.1.150–2

Rejecting the idea of asking Cicero to join the
conspiracy against Caesar; "break with" =
confide in.

13   We shall find of him
A shrewd contriver; and, you know,
    his means,
If he improve them, may well
    stretch so far
As to annoy us all.

Cassius in *Julius Caesar*, 2.1.157–60

Arguing for killing Mark Antony as well as
Caesar; "shrewd contriver" = cunning and
dangerous schemer.

14   What compact mean you to have
    with us?
Will you be pricked in number of
    our friends,
Or shall we on, and not depend on
    you?

Cassius in *Julius Caesar*, 3.1.215–7

Speaking to Mark Antony; "compact" = agreement; "pricked" = marked or noted down.

15   Though we lay these honors on
    this man
To ease ourselves of divers slander-
    ous loads,
He shall but bear them as the ass
    bears gold,
To groan and sweat under the busi-
    ness,
Either led or driven as we point the
    way.

Mark Antony in *Julius Caesar*, 4.1.19–23

Speaking of Lepidus; Octavius and Antony
plan to put on him responsibility for what they
may be accused of ("slanderous loads").

16   Get thee glass eyes,
And like a scurvy politician, seem
To see the things thou dost not.

King Lear in *King Lear*, 4.6.170–2

Speaking to the blind Gloucester; "glass eyes"
may mean spectacles.

17   So we'll live,
And pray, and sing, and tell old
 tales, and laugh
At gilded butterflies, and hear poor
 rogues
Talk of court news; and we'll talk
 with them too—
Who loses and who wins; who's in,
 who's out—
And take upon 's the mystery of
 things,
As if we were God's spies.

King Lear in *King Lear*, 5.3.11–17

Imagining being imprisoned with his daughter
Cordelia; "gilded butterflies" probably refers
to extravagantly dressed courtiers.

18 He cannot buckle his distempered
 cause
Within the belt of rule.

Caithness in *Macbeth*, 5.2.15–16

On Macbeth as unable to put his sick or
chaotic ("distempered" may mean both) affairs
in order.

19 If I know how or which way to
 order these affairs
Thus disorderly thrust into my
 hands,
Never believe me.

York in *Richard II*, 2.2.108–11

He has been left to rule England in the
absence of King Richard.

20 The caterpillars of the commonwealth,

Which I have sworn to weed and
 pluck away.

Bolingbroke in *Richard II*, 2.3.166–7

Describing Richard's favorites.

21 Will you enforce me to a world of
 cares?
Call them again, I am not made of
 stones,
But penetrable to your kind
 entreaties,
Albeit against my conscience and
 my soul.

King Richard in *Richard III*, 3.7.223–6

Pretending to be reluctant to accept the
crown.

22 They'll take suggestion as a cat laps
 milk;
They'll tell the clock to any business
 that
We say befits the hour.

Antonio in *The Tempest*, 2.1.288–90

Referring to all the courtiers except Gonzalo.

23 Men must learn now with pity to
 dispense,
For policy sits above conscience.

**First Stranger in *Timon of Athens*,
3.2.86–7**

Commenting on the refusal of Timon's friends
to help him. "Policy" commonly for Shakespeare had a pejorative meaning of expedi-
ency or political cunning.

Popularity

1 And then I stole all courtesy from
 heaven,

And dressed myself in such humility
That I did pluck allegiance from
men's hearts,
Loud shouts and salutations from
their mouths,
Even in the presence of the
crownèd King.

King Henry in *Henry IV, Part 1*,
3.2.50–4

Recalling his popularity before he became
king.

Portents (see also Foreboding)

1   At my nativity
The front of heaven was full of fiery
shapes
Of burning cressets, and at my
birth
The frame and huge foundation of
the earth
Shaked like a coward.

Glendower in *Henry IV, Part 1*,
3.1.13–17

Events which he says foretold that he would
be remarkable; "front" = forehead; "cressets"
= fires in metal baskets on poles.

2   The heavens were all on fire, the
earth did tremble.

Glendower in *Henry IV, Part 1*, 3.1.23

Portents, he claims, at his birth.

3   Comets, importing change of times
and states,
Brandish your crystal tresses in the
sky.

Bedford in *Henry VI, Part 1*, 1.1.2–3

Comets were thought to foretell disasters to
come.

4   It is the part of men to fear and
tremble
When the most mighty gods by
tokens send
Such dreadful heralds to astonish
us.

Casca in *Julius Caesar*, 1.3.54–6

On the ominous storms the night before Caesar is assassinated.

5   The noise of battle hurtled in the
air,
Horses did neigh, and dying men
did groan,
And ghosts did shriek and squeal
about the streets.

Calpurnia in *Julius Caesar*, 2.2.22–4

Hoping, by reporting these strange happen-
ings, to persuade her husband, Caesar, not to
go to the Capitol.

6   When beggars die there are no
comets seen;
The heavens themselves blaze forth
the death of princes.

Calpurnia in *Julius Caesar*, 2.2.30–1

7   These late eclipses in the sun and
moon portend no good to us.

Gloucester in *King Lear*, 1.2.103–4

"Late" = recent.

8   The screech-owl, screeching loud,
Puts the wretch that lies in woe
In remembrance of a shroud.

Puck in *A Midsummer Night's Dream*,
5.1.376–8

The owl was regarded as a bird of ill-omen,
often foreboding death.

9   The bay-trees in our country are all
withered,
And meteors fright the fixèd stars
of heaven.
The pale-faced moon looks bloody
on the earth,
And lean-looked prophets whisper
fearful change.
Rich men look sad, and ruffians
dance and leap;
The one in fear to lose what they
enjoy,
The other to enjoy by rage and war.
These signs forerun the death or fall
of kings.

Welsh Captain in *Richard II*, 2.4.8–15

Possession

1   A poor virgin, sir, an ill-favored
thing, sir, but mine own.

Touchstone in *As You Like It*, 5.4.57–8

Introducing the sluttish Audrey to Jaques.

2   O, these naughty times
Puts bars between the owners and
their rights!

**Portia in *The Merchant of Venice*,
3.2.18–19**

"Naughty" = wicked; "bars" = barriers; she is
regretting that she cannot choose a husband
for herself.

3   Myself, and what is mine, to you
and yours
Is now converted.

**Portia in *The Merchant of Venice*,
3.2.166–7**

Giving herself to Bassanio in love.

Poverty

1   Famine is in thy cheeks,
Need and oppression starveth in
thy eyes,
Contempt and beggary hangs upon
thy back;
The world is not thy friend, nor the
world's law.

Romeo in *Romeo and Juliet*, 5.1.69–72

Speaking to the poor apothecary whose poison he is seeking to buy; "starveth" = are
shown by your look of starvation.

2   *Apothecary.* My poverty, but not
my will, consents.
Romeo. I pay thy poverty, and not
thy will.

Romeo and Juliet, 5.1.75–6

Romeo persuades the apothecary to sell him
poison.

3   His poor self,
A dedicated beggar to the air,
With his disease of all-shunned
poverty,
Walks, like contempt, alone.

**Varro's Second Servant in *Timon of
Athens*, 4.2.12–15**

On the state of the once-rich Timon.

4   *Autolycus.* I am a poor fellow, sir.
Camillo. Why, be so still; here's
nobody will steal that from thee.

The Winter's Tale, 4.4.630–2

Power (see also Greatness, Politics, Tyranny)

1   Realms and islands were
As plates dropped from his pocket.

Cleopatra in *Antony and Cleopatra*,
5.2.91–2

Cleopatra's dream of Antony; "plates" means
coins, of silver or gold.

2   These growing feathers plucked
    from Caesar's wing
    Will make him fly an ordinary
    pitch,
    Who else would soar above the
    view of men,
    And keep us all in servile fearful-
    ness.

Flavius in *Julius Caesar*, 1.1.72–5

Caesar is imaged as a hawk that could be pre-
vented from flying high if its feathers were
plucked.

3   When Caesar says, "Do this," it is
    performed.

Mark Antony in *Julius Caesar*, 1.2.10

Responding to an order given by Caesar.

4   It doth amaze me
    A man of such a feeble temper
    should
    So get the start of the majestic
    world
    And bear the palm alone.

Cassius in *Julius Caesar*, 1.2.128–31

Referring to Caesar, who in spite of physical
ailments outstrips ("get the start of") all other
rulers to bear the palm of victory alone.

5   Why, man, he doth bestride the
    narrow world
    Like a colossus, and we petty men
    Walk under his huge legs and peep
    about
    To find ourselves dishonorable
    graves.

Cassius in *Julius Caesar*, 1.2.135–8

Referring to Caesar; the colossus was a gigan-
tic figure of the sun-god Apollo that stood
astride the entrance to the harbor at Rhodes.

6   Now could I, Casca, name to thee a
    man
    Most like this dreadful night,
    That thunders, lightens, opens
    graves, and roars
    As doth the lion in the Capitol—
    A man no mightier than thyself or
    me
    In personal action, yet prodigious
    grown
    And fearful, as these strange erup-
    tions are.

Cassius in *Julius Caesar*, 1.3.72–8

Referring to Julius Caesar; the audience may
have thought of the lions kept in the Tower of
London.

7   Have I in conquest stretched mine
    arm so far
    To be afeared to tell greybeards the
    truth?

Caesar in *Julius Caesar*, 2.2.66–7

The "greybeards" are the senators of Rome.

8   A power I have, but of what
    strength and nature
    I am not yet instructed.

Escalus in *Measure for Measure*,
1.1.79–80

To Angelo, with whom he is to share the rule
of Vienna.

9   Lord Angelo is precise,
    Stands at a guard with envy, scarce
    confesses
    That his blood flows, or that his
    appetite
    Is more to bread than stone. Hence
    shall we see
    If power change purpose, what our
    seemers be.

Duke in *Measure for Measure*, 1.3.50–4

He knows Angelo as puritanical ("precise"),
and anxious about his reputation ("at a guard
with envy").

10   O, it is excellent
To have a giant's strength; but it is
    tyrannous
To use it like a giant.

Isabella in *Measure for Measure*,
2.2.107–9

Pleading with Angelo for her brother's life.

11 What you will have, I'll give, and
    willing too,
For do we must what force will
    have us do.

King Richard in *Richard II*, 3.3.206–7

What Bolingbroke, later Henry IV, wants is
the kingdom.

12 The eagle suffers little birds to sing,
And is not careful what they mean
    thereby,
Knowing that with the shadow of
    his wings
He can at pleasure stint their
    melody.

Tamora in *Titus Andronicus*, 4.4.83–6

The eagle symbolizes royalty or power.

13 They that have power to hurt, and
    will do none,
That do not do the thing they most
    do show,
Who, moving others, are them-
    selves as stone,
Unmovèd, cold, and to temptation
    slow,
They rightly do inherit heaven's
    graces,
And husband nature's riches from
    expense;
They are the lords and owners of
    their faces,

Others but stewards of their excel-
    lence.

Sonnet 94, 1–8

These great lines link virtue and beauty in suggesting the idea of people who in their bearing show the power they have, but possess the
mastery over themselves to exercise restraint
and preserve the gifts nature has given them
("husband nature's riches").

Praise

1   Other women cloy
The appetites they feed, but she
    makes hungry
Where most she satisfies.

Enobarbus in *Antony and Cleopatra*,
2.2.235–7

Praising Cleopatra.

2 I will praise any man that will
praise me.

Enobarbus in *Antony and Cleopatra*,
2.6.88

3 His face was as the heavens, and
    therein stuck
A sun and moon, which kept their
    course and lighted
The little O, the earth.

Cleopatra in *Antony and Cleopatra*,
5.2.79–81

Cleopatra's image of Antony.

4 His legs bestrid the ocean, his
    reared arm
Crested the world.

Cleopatra in *Antony and Cleopatra*,
5.2.82–3

Cleopatra recalls Antony as if he were a colossal figure overawing the world; Cassius uses a similar image to describe Caesar in *Julius Caesar*; see Power 5.

5   Your praise is come too swiftly home before you.

Adam in *As You Like It*, 2.2.9

Orlando's good reputation has made his brother hate him.

6   I did not think thee lord of such a spirit.
Before, I loved thee as a brother, John,
But now I do respect thee as my soul.

Prince Hal in *Henry IV, Part 1*, 5.4.18–20

Praising his brother's courage.

7   I hear as good exclamation on your worship as of any man in the city.

Dogberry in *Much Ado About Nothing*, 3.5.25–6

Mistaking the word, as usual: "exclamation" = outcry against; he perhaps means "acclamation" in speaking to Leonato, governor of Messina.

8   O slanderous world! Kate like the hazel twig
Is straight and slender, and as brown in hue
As hazelnuts, and sweeter than the kernels.

Petruchio in *The Taming of the Shrew*, 2.1.253–5

Sweet-talking Katherine, who has been abusing him.

9   Thou shalt find she will outstrip all praise

And make it halt behind her.

Prospero in *The Tempest*, 4.1.10–11

Praising his daughter Miranda.

10   The worthiness of praise distains his worth
If that the praised himself bring the praise forth.

Aeneas in *Troilus and Cressida*, 1.3.241–2

"Distains his worth" = taints or loses its value.

11   You are as strong, as valiant, as wise, no less noble, much more gentle, and altogether more tractable.

Agamemnon in *Troilus and Cressida*, 2.3.148–50

Comparing Ajax to Achilles.

12   Praise us as we are tasted, allow us as we prove.

Troilus in *Troilus and Cressida*, 3.2.90–1

"Allow" = commend; he is asking Cressida to let experience show how faithful he will be.

13   One good deed dying tongueless
Slaughters a thousand waiting upon that;
Our praises are our wages.

Hermione in *The Winter's Tale*, 1.2.92–4

On praise as the reward of doing good.

14   Each your doing,
So singular in each particular,
Crowns what you are doing in the present deeds,
That all your acts are queens.

Florizel in *The Winter's Tale*, 4.4.143–6

Praising Perdita; everything she does seems unique ("singular"), and superb; he doesn't yet know that she is in fact royal and a princess.

Prayer

1   We, ignorant of ourselves,
Beg often our own harms, which
the wise powers
Deny us for our good; so find we
profit
By losing of our prayers.

Menecrates in *Antony and Cleopatra*,
2.1.5–8

2   To your protection I commend me,
gods;
From fairies and the tempters of the
night,
Guard me, I beseech ye.

Imogen in *Cymbeline*, 2.2.8–10

As she prepares to sleep; she does not know
that Jachimo is hidden in her bedchamber.

3   Angels and ministers of grace
defend us!

Hamlet in *Hamlet*, 1.4.39

Exclamation on first seeing his father's ghost.

4   Bow, stubborn knees, and heart,
with strings of steel,
Be soft as sinews of the new-born
babe!

Claudius in *Hamlet*, 3.3.70–1

Trying to pray for forgiveness for his murder of
his brother.

5   My words fly up, my thoughts
remain below:
Words without thoughts never to
heaven go.

Claudius in *Hamlet*, 3.3.97–8

6   O God of battles, steel my soldiers'
hearts.

Possess them not with fear. Take
from them now
The sense of reckoning, ere th'
opposèd numbers
Pluck their hearts from them. Not
today, O Lord,
O not today, think not upon the
fault
My father made in compassing the
crown.

King Henry in *Henry V*, 4.1.289–4

Henry IV gained ("compassed") the crown by
devious means; "sense of reckoning" = the
ability to gauge the odds against winning; the
French army is much stronger.

7   God, the best maker of all marriages,
Combine your hearts in one.

Queen Isabel in *Henry V*, 5.2.359–60

On the betrothal of Henry of England and
Katherine of France.

8   O Lord that lends me life,
Lend me a heart replete with thank-
fulness!

King Henry in *Henry VI, Part 2*,
1.1.19–20

9   Now God be praised, that to believing souls
Gives light in darkness, comfort in
despair.

King Henry in *Henry VI, Part 2*,
2.1.64–5

Hearing of a miracle, that a blind man has
regained his sight.

10 O pity, God, this miserable age!

Father in *Henry VI, Part 3*, 2.5.88

On the miseries of civil war; he discovers he
has killed his own son in battle.

11 O, let me not be mad, not mad,
       sweet heaven!
    Keep me in temper, I would not be
       mad!

King Lear in *King Lear*, 1.5.46–7

Lear's first intimation that the ingratitude of his
daughters will drive him into madness.

12   O heavens!
    If you do love old men, if your
       sweet sway
    Allow obedience, if you yourselves
       are old,
    Make it your cause; send down, and
       take my part.

King Lear in *King Lear*, 2.4.189–92

"Allow" = approve; Lear is thinking of the dis-
obedience and ingratitude of his daughters.

13 You ever gentle gods, take my
       breath from me;
    Let not my worser spirit tempt me
       again
    To die before you please!

Gloucester in *King Lear*, 4.6.217–9

Encountering the mad king in worse condition
than himself makes him abandon thoughts of
suicide.

14 *Hermia.* Good night, sweet friend;
       Thy love ne'er alter till thy sweet
       life end!
    Lysander. Amen, amen, to that fair
       prayer say I,
    And then end life when I end loy-
       alty!

***A Midsummer Night's Dream*, 2.2.60–3**

15 When holy and devout religious
       men
    Are at their beads, 'tis much to
       draw them thence,

So sweet is zealous contemplation.

Buckingham in *Richard III*, 3.7.92–4

Richard is staging an appearance between two
bishops, in order to persuade the citizens of
London that he is fit to be king.

16   Now I want
    Spirits to enforce, art to enchant,
    And my ending is despair,
    Unless I be relieved by prayer,
    Which pierces so that it assaults
    Mercy itself, and frees all faults.

**Prospero in *The Tempest*, Epilogue,
13–18**

Addressing the audience, having abandoned
his role as magician.

17 Immortal gods, I crave no pelf;
    I pray for no man but myself.
    Grant I may never prove so fond
    To trust man on his oath or bond.

**Apemantus in *Timon of Athens*,
1.2.62–5**

A cynic's prayer; "pelf" = wealth; "fond" =
foolish.

18 Lend to each man enough, that one
    need not lend to another; for were
    your godheads to borrow of men,
    men would forsake the gods.

Timon in *Timon of Athens*, 3.6.73–5

Timon has been forsaken by his friends now
that he is poor.

19 Upon some book I love I'll pray for
       thee.

**Proteus in *The Two Gentlemen of
Verona*, 1.1.20**

To his friend Valentine, who is off to see the
world; he does not say what book he has in
mind.

Pregnancy

1   Your brother and his lover have
     embraced.
     As those that feed grow full, as blos-
     soming time
     That from the seedness the bare fal-
     low brings
     To teeming foison, even so her
     plenteous womb
     Expresseth his full tilth and hus-
     bandry.

Lucio in *Measure for Measure*, 1.4.40–4

Telling Isabella that Juliet is heavily pregnant
by her brother; the images of plowing, sowing
seeds, and coming to abundance ("foison")
reflect Lucio's coarseness.

2   We have laughed to see the sails
     conceive
     And grow big-bellied with the wan-
     ton wind;
     Which she, with pretty and with
     swimming gait,
     Following (her womb then rich
     with my young squire)
     Would imitate, and sail upon the
     land.

**Titania in *A Midsummer Night's
Dream*, 1.2.128–32**

On the mother of her "changeling boy."

Pride

1   Small things make base men proud.

Suffolk in *Henry VI, Part 2*, 4.1.106

He is angry at being taken prisoner by an
"obscure and lousy swain."

2   Pride must have a fall.

King Richard in *Richard II*, 5.5.88

Proverbial.

3   The elephant hath joints, but none
     for courtesy; his legs are legs for
     necessity, not for flexure.

**Ulysses in *Troilus and Cressida*,
2.3.105–6**

"Flexure" = bending; elephants were thought
to have no joints in their knees. Ulysses refers
to Achilles, who will not bend or show courtesy to the other Greek leaders.

4   He that is proud eats up himself.
     Pride is his own glass, his own
     trumpet, his own chronicle; and
     whatever praises itself but in the
     deed, devours the deed in the
     praise.

**Agamemnon in *Troilus and Cressida*,
2.3.154–7**

Speaking to Ajax, who is as proud as any of
the Greeks.

5   I do hate a proud man as I hate the
     engendering of toads.

Ajax in *Troilus and Cressida*, 2.3.158–9

Nestor wisely comments, "And yet he loves
himself."

6   I see you what you are, you are too
     proud;
     But if you were the devil, you are
     fair.

Viola in *Twelfth Night*, 1.5.250–1

On Olivia; "if" = even if.

Promises (see also Oaths, Vows)

1   The oath of a lover is no stronger
     than the word of a tapster; they are
     both the confirmer of false reckon-
     ings.

Celia in *As You Like It*, 3.4.30–2

A lover's promises are no more to be trusted than an innkeeper's reckonings; on Orlando, who has failed to keep his appointment with Rosalind.

2 O, that's a brave man! He writes
brave verses, speaks brave words,
swears brave oaths, and breaks
them bravely.

Celia in *As You Like It*, 3.4.40–2

Mocking Orlando; "brave" = fine, used ironically.

3 Breaking his oath and resolution
like
A twist of rotten silk.

Aufidius in *Coriolanus*, 5.6.94–5

Accusing Coriolanus of disloyalty to the Volscians.

4 Every drop of blood
That every Roman bears, and nobly
bears,
Is guilty of a several bastardy
If he do break the smallest particle
Of any promise that hath passed
from him.

Brutus in *Julius Caesar*, 2.1.136–40

Expressing his confidence in the idea of being a Roman.

5 I will not hold thee long. If I do
live,
I will be good to thee.

Brutus in *Julius Caesar*, 4.3.265–6

Asking his servant Lucius to play music.

6 He promised to meet me two hours
since, and he was ever precise in
promise-keeping.

Lucio in *Measure for Measure*, 1.2.74–6

To a gentleman, remarking on Claudio's failure to keep an appointment.

7 I'll take thy word for faith, not ask
thine oath;
Who shuns not to break one will
crack them both.

Pericles in *Pericles*, 1.2.120–2

8 Promising is the very air o'the time;
It opens the eyes of expectation.
Performance is ever the duller for
his act.

Painter in *Timon of Athens*, 5.1.22–4

"For his act" = when the performance is carried out.

Promptness

1 You come most carefully upon
your hour.

Francisco in *Hamlet*, 1.1.6

Greeting Barnardo, succeeding him as a guard on the king's castle in Elsinore.

Proof

1 Be sure of it. Give me the ocular
proof.

Othello in *Othello*, 3.3.360

To Iago, demanding to see Desdemona and Cassio making love.

2 Make me to see't, or at the least so
prove it
That the probation bear no hinge
nor loop
To hang a doubt on.

Othello in *Othello*, 3.3.364–6

He seeks proof that Desdemona has committed adultery; "probation" = proof.

Prophecy

1 In nature's infinite book of secrecy
A little I can read.

Soothsayer in *Antony and Cleopatra*,
1.2.10–11

His prophecies turn out to be accurate.

2 *Ghost.* The serpent that did sting
thy father's life
Now wears his crown.
Hamlet.   O my prophetic
soul!
My uncle?
Ghost. Ay, that incestuous, that
adulterate beast.

Hamlet, 1.5.39–42

Hamlet has half-guessed what the ghost
reveals, that old Hamlet was murdered by his
brother, who then married his widow, a marriage regarded as incestuous in Shakespeare's
time.

3 The hope and expectation of thy
time
Is ruined, and the soul of every man
Prophetically do forethink thy fall.

King Henry in *Henry IV, Part 1*,
3.2.36–8

To Prince Hal, heir to the crown, who finds
Falstaff and tavern life more interesting than
the court.

4 The blood weeps from my heart
when I do shape,
In forms imaginary, th' unguided
days
And rotten times that you shall
look upon
When I am sleeping with my ances-
tors.

King Henry in *Henry IV, Part 2*,
4.4.58–61

Anticipating disorder after his death.

5 Over thy wounds now do I proph-
esy
. . .
A curse shall light upon the limbs
of men,
Domestic fury and fierce civil strife
Shall cumber all the parts of Italy.

Mark Antony in *Julius Caesar*, 3.1.259,
262–4

The wounds are those of the assassinated
Julius Caesar.

6 If you can look into the seeds of
time,
And say which grain will grow and
which will not,
Speak then to me.

Banquo in *Macbeth*, 1.3.58–60

Speaking to the three witches.

7 The night has been unruly. Where
we lay,
Our chimneys were blown down,
and, as they say,
Lamentings heard i' th' air, strange
screams of death,
And prophesying with accents terrible
Of dire combustion and confused
events,
New-hatched to the woeful time.

Lennox in *Macbeth*, 2.3.54–9

Describing the night of Duncan's murder;
"combustion" = tumult.

8 Be bloody, bold, and resolute; laugh
to scorn
The power of man; for none of
woman born
Shall harm Macbeth.

Second Apparition in *Macbeth*,
4.1.79–81

A prophecy that makes Macbeth overconfi-
dent.

9 Macbeth shall never vanquished be
    until
    Great Birnam Wood to high Dunsi-
    nane Hill
    Shall come against him.

Third Apparition in *Macbeth*, 4.1.92–4

The "wood" does move, in the form of soldiers carrying a screen of branches.

Prostitution

1 *Escalus.* What do you think of the
    trade, Pompey? Is it a lawful
    trade?
    Pompey. If the law would allow it,
    sir.
    Escalus. But the law will not allow
    it, Pompey; nor it shall not be
    allowed in Vienna.
    Pompey. Does your worship mean
    to geld and spay all the youth of
    the city?
    Escalus. No, Pompey.
    Pompey. Truly, sir, in my poor
    opinion they will to't then.

***Measure for Measure*,** 2.1.225–35

Pompey is defending his trade as a bawd.

Proverbs

1 Neither rhyme nor reason can
    express how much.

Orlando in *As You Like It*, 3.2.398–9

Proverbial; he has been trying to express in
rhymes how much he is in love.

2 He will give the devil his due.

Prince Hal in *Henry IV, Part 1*, 1.2.119

Proverbial; the phrase occurs too in *Henry V*;
see The Devil 4.

3 But since all is well, keep it so, wake
    not a sleeping wolf.

Chief Justice in *Henry IV, Part 2*,
1.2.153–4

Advising Falstaff not to get into trouble with
the law.

4 One for superfluity, and another
    for use.

Prince Hal in *Henry IV, Part 2*,
2.2.17–18

Mockingly suggesting a spare clean shirt is
superfluous, more than his friend Poins needs.

5 *Falstaff.* What wind blew you
    hither, Pistol?
    Pistol. Not the ill wind which blows
    no man to good.

***Henry IV, Part 2*,** 5.3.85–6

Pistol brings news that Hal is now king, bending the proverb, "it's an ill wind that blows no
man good."

6 I did never know so full a voice
    issue from so empty a heart. But
    the saying is true: "The empty ves-
    sel makes the greatest sound."

Boy in *Henry V*, 4.4.67–9

Proverbial; referring to the empty boasting of
Pistol.

7 I shall not want false witness to
    condemn me,
    Nor store of treasons to augment
    my guilt.
    The ancient proverb will be well
    effected:
    "A staff is quickly found to beat a
    dog."

Gloucester in *Henry VI, Part 2*,
3.1.168–71

On being accused of treason.

8 As dead as a doornail.

Jack Cade in *Henry VI, Part 2*, 4.10.40–1

Shakespeare may have established this phrase
as proverbial.

9 Ill blows the wind that profits
nobody.

Soldier in *Henry VI, Part 3*, 2.5.55

10 Courage mounteth with occasion.

Duke of Austria in *King John*, 2.1.82

"Occasion" = emergency, or occasion calling
for action; from a proverb.

11 The better act of purposes mistook
Is to mistake again; though indirect,
Yet indirection thereby grows
direct,
And falsehood falsehood cures, as
fire cools fire
Within the scorchèd veins of one
who burns.

**Cardinal Pandulph in *King John*,
3.1.274–8**

The crafty Cardinal casuistically uses
proverbs, that one deceit ("indirection") drives
out another, just as one fire drives out another
(it was thought burns could be cured by
warmth), to excuse wrongdoing.

12 Nothing will come of nothing.

King Lear in *King Lear*, 1.1.90

13 Striving to better, oft we mar what's
well.

Albany in *King Lear*, 1.4.346

Varying the proverb, "let well alone."

14 We'll set thee to school to an ant, to
teach thee there's no laboring i' the
winter.

Fool in *King Lear*, 2.4.67–8

Proverbs 6:6; Proverbs 30:25.

15 The younger rises when the old
doth fall.

Edmund in *King Lear*, 3.3.25

Varying the proverb, "the rising of one man is
the falling of another."

16 Jesters do oft prove prophets.

Regan in *King Lear*, 5.3.71

Varying the proverb, "there's many a true
word spoken in jest."

17 It will have blood, they say; blood
will have blood.

Macbeth in *Macbeth*, 3.4.121

Proverbial, and echoing Genesis 9:6, "Whoso
sheddeth man's blood, by man shall his blood
be shed."

18 Give me your blessing; truth will
come to light; murder cannot be
hid long; a man's son may, but in
the end truth will out.

**Launcelot Gobbo in *The Merchant of
Venice*, 2.2.78–80**

Comically acknowledging that he is old
Gobbo's son.

19 The old proverb is very well parted
between my master Shylock and
you, sir: you have the grace of God,
sir, and he hath enough.

**Launcelot Gobbo in *The Merchant of
Venice*, 2.2.149–51**

The proverb is "the grace of God is great
enough"; Launcelot means that his father has
grace, and Shylock enough in the sense of
wealth.

First Senator in *Timon of Athens*,
3.5.86–7

The context suggests that Shakespeare did not approve of this strict devotion to capital punishment.

Purgatory

1   *Ghost.*   My hour is almost come
When I to sulph'rous and torment-
   ing flames
Must render up myself.
Hamlet.   Alas, poor ghost!

Hamlet, 1.5.2–4

"Sulph'rous and tormenting flames" = purgatorial fire.

2   But that I am forbid
To tell the secrets of my prison-
   house,
I could a tale unfold whose lightest
   word
Would harrow up thy soul, freeze
   thy young blood.

Ghost in *Hamlet*, 1.5.13–16

Effectively suggesting the horrors of purgatory to Hamlet; "harrow up" = lacerate.

Quarrels

1   I know when seven justices could
not take up a quarrel, but when the
parties met themselves, one of them
thought but of an If, as, "If you said
so, then I said so"; and they shook
hands and swore brothers. Your If
is your only peacemaker; much
virtue in If.

Touchstone in *As You Like It*, 5.4.98–103

"Take up" = settle

2   'Tis dangerous when the baser
   nature comes
Between the pass and fell incensèd
   points
Of mighty opposites.

Hamlet in *Hamlet*, 5.2.60

Hamlet is thinking of himself as opposed to Claudius; "pass" = thrust, as with a sword (hence "points"); "fell" = fierce. The "baser nature" refers to Rosencrantz and Guildenstern, whom he has sent to their deaths.

3   By my troth, this is the old fashion.
You two never meet but you fall to
some discord.

Hostess in *Henry IV, Part 2*, 2.4.55–6

On Falstaff and Doll Tearsheet.

4   How irksome is this music to my
   heart!
When such strings jar, what hope of
   harmony?

King Henry in *Henry VI, Part 2*,
2.1.54–5

Referring to his lords who quarrel at court.

5   Thrice is he armed that hath his
   quarrel just,
And he but naked, though locked
   up in steel,
Whose conscience with injustice is
   corrupted.

King Henry in *Henry VI, Part 2*,
3.2.233–5

Henry's wishful thinking has little effect on his contentious nobles and citizens.

6   Urge me no more, I shall forget
   myself.

Cassius in *Julius Caesar*, 4.3.35

To Brutus; "urge" = provoke.

7   *Cassius.* Must I endure all this?
    Brutus. All this? Ay, more! Fret till
    your proud heart break.

Julius Caesar, 4.3.41–2

Brutus has accused Cassius of being corrupt.

8   Do not presume too much upon
    my love,
    I may do that I shall be sorry for.

Cassius in *Julius Caesar*, 4.3.63–4

Quarreling with Brutus.

9   I am the unhappy subject of these
    quarrels.

**Antonio in *The Merchant of Venice*,
5.1.238**

Fearing he has provoked discord in Belmont.

10 Never since the middle summer's
    spring
    Met we on hill, in dale, forest, or
    mead,
    By pavèd fountain or by rushy
    brook,
    Or in the beachèd margent of the
    sea
    To dance our ringlets to the
    whistling wind,
    But with thy brawls thou hast dis-
    turbed our sport.

**Titania in *A Midsummer Night's
Dream*, 2.1.82–7**

The quarrel between Oberon and Titania has
gone on since the beginning of summer; a
"paved" fountain flows over stones; "margent"
= margin, and "ringlets" are circular dances
that mark the grass with fairy rings.

11 This same progeny of evils comes
    From our debate, from our dissen-
    sion.

**Titania in *A Midsummer Night's
Dream*, 2.1.115–16**

On the disorder resulting from her quarrel
("debate") with Oberon.

12 Who set this ancient quarrel new
    abroach?

Montague in *Romeo and Juliet*, 1.1.104

The quarrel between the clans of the Montagues and Capulets; "abroach" = flowing, as
in opening or broaching a cask.

13 Thou wilt quarrel with a man for
    cracking nuts, having no other rea-
    son but because thou hast hazel
    eyes.

Mercutio in *Romeo and Juliet*, 3.1.18–20

Mocking his friend Benvolio.

14 Thy head is as full of quarrels as an
    egg is full of meat.

Mercutio in *Romeo and Juliet*, 3.1.22–3

The "meat" of the egg is what can be eaten.

15 Be thou armed for some unhappy
    words.

**Baptista in *The Taming of the Shrew*,
2.1.139**

Advising Petruchio what to expect from
Katherine.

16 *Katherine.* Asses are made to bear,
    and so are you.
    Petruchio. Women are made to
    bear, and so are you.
    Katherine. No such jade as you, if
    me you mean.

The Taming of the Shrew, 2.1.199–201

Playing on various senses of "bear," including
bearing children; a "jade" is a worn-out horse,
a hack.

17 No man hath any quarrel to me.
My remembrance is very free and
clear from any image of offense
done to any man.

Viola in *Twelfth Night*, 3.4.226–8

Responding to Sir Toby's demand that she
meet the challenge of Sir Andrew Aguecheek.

Queens, see Royalty

Readiness

1 All things are ready if our minds be
so.

King Henry in *Henry V*, 4.3.71

On being prepared to fight the French.

2 Let's lack no discipline, make no
delay:
For, lords, tomorrow is a busy day.

King Richard in *Richard III*, 5.3.17–18

Preparing to fight the forces of Richmond.

3 I would have been much more a
fresher man
Had I expected thee.

Hector in *Troilus and Cressida*, 5.6.20–1

Hector did not anticipate fighting with
Achilles, who had been sulking in his tent.

Reading (see also Books, Study)

1 *Polonius.* What do you read, my
lord?
Hamlet. Words, words, words.

Hamlet, 2.2.191–2

Hamlet affecting madness answers Polonius's
question literally.

2 He reads much,
He is a great observer, and he looks
Quite through the deeds of men.

Caesar in *Julius Caesar*, 1.2.201–3

Describing Cassius.

3 How well he's read, to reason
against reading!

**King of Navarre in *Love's Labor's Lost*,
1.1.94**

Responding to Berowne's arguments against
poring over a book.

Reason/Reasons (see also Argument)

1 They say every why hath a wherefore.

**Dromio of Syracuse in *The Comedy of
Errors*, 2.2.43**

Meaning another reason can always be found
to support a case.

2 Sure He that made us with such
large discourse,
Looking before and after, gave us
not
That capability and godlike reason
To fust in us unused.

Hamlet in *Hamlet*, 4.4.36–9

Reason is "godlike" as shared with the creator,
and marking the difference between human
beings and beasts.

3 Give you a reason on compulsion?
If reasons were as plentiful as black-
berries, I would give no man a reason upon compulsion, I.

Falstaff in *Henry IV, Part 1*, 2.4.238–40

Evading a direct answer to Poins and Hal;
"reasons" would have sounded like "raisins."

4   O judgment, thou art fled to
        brutish beasts,
     And men have lost their reason!

Mark Antony in *Julius Caesar*, 3.2.104–5

Otherwise, he implies, they would all mourn
for Caesar.

5   Gratiano speaks an infinite deal of
     nothing, more than any man in all
     Venice. His reasons are as two
     grains of wheat hid in two bushels
     of chaff; you shall seek all day ere
     you find them, and when you have
     them, they are not worth the
     search.

**Bassanio in *The Merchant of Venice*,
1.1.114–18**

6   To say the truth, reason and love
     keep little company together nowa-
     days.

**Bottom in *A Midsummer Night's
Dream*, 3.1.143–4**

Amazed that Titania makes love to him.

7   Reason and respect
     Make livers pale, and lustihood
        deject.

**Troilus in *Troilus and Cressida*,
2.2.49–50**

Reason here is matched with "respect" or caution as breeding cowardice (pale livers) and
inertia; Troilus is eager to fight to keep Helen
in Troy.

Rebellion

1   Rebellion lay in his way, and he
     found it.

Falstaff in *Henry IV, Part 1*, 5.1.28

On the Earl of Worcester, who says he did not
seek rebellion.

2   To face the garment of rebellion
     With some fine color that may
        please the eye
     Of fickle changelings and poor dis-
        contents,
     Which gape and rub the elbow at
        the news
     Of hurly-burly innovation.

**King Henry in *Henry IV, Part 1*,
5.1.74–8**

Rebels can always attract support; "face" =
trim; "changelings" are turncoats who greet
with pleasure ("rub the elbow") news of
revolution.

Recklessness

1   If I be foiled, there is but one
     shamed that was never gracious; if
     killed, but one dead that is willing
     to be so.

Orlando in *As You Like It*, 1.2.187–9

Not caring whether he is overthrown
("foiled"), as he volunteers to wrestle with a
deadly professional.

2   I do not set my life at a pin's fee,
     And for my soul, what can it do to
        that,
     Being a thing immortal as itself?

Hamlet in *Hamlet*, 1.4.65–7

He is determined to follow the ghost, not
knowing whether it is a good or evil spirit;
"fee" = worth.

3   I am one, my liege,
     Whom the vile blows and buffets of
        the world
     Hath so incensed that I am reckless
        what
     I do to spite the world.

**Second Murderer in *Macbeth*,
3.1.107–10**

So he is ready to murder Banquo.

Reconciliation

1 Love and be friends, as two such
men should be.

Poet in *Julius Caesar*, 4.3.131

To the quarreling Brutus and Cassius.

2 This was an ill beginning of the
night.
Never come such division 'tween
our souls!

Cassius in *Julius Caesar*, 4.3.234–5

To Brutus, after their quarrel.

3 You must bear with me.
Pray you now, forget and forgive; I
am old and foolish.

King Lear in *King Lear*, 4.7.82–3

Asking forgiveness of his daughter, Cordelia.

4 Come, let's away to prison:
We two alone will sit like birds i'
the cage;
When thou dost ask me blessing,
I'll kneel down
And ask of thee forgiveness.

King Lear in *King Lear*, 5.3.8–11

To his daughter Cordelia when they are taken
prisoner.

5 Now thou and I are new in amity.

**Oberon in *A Midsummer Night's
Dream*, 4.1.87**

Reconciled to his Queen, Titania.

Reformation

1 Like bright metal on a sullen
ground,
My reformation, glitt'ring o'er my
fault,

Shall show more goodly and attract
more eyes
Than that which hath no foil to set
it off.

**Prince Hal in *Henry IV, Part 1*,
1.2.212–15**

Hal plans to humor his companions for a
while, joining in their dissolute life, in order to
cast them off later; "sullen ground" = dark
background.

2 If I do grow great, I'll grow less, for
I'll purge and leave sack, and live
cleanly as a nobleman should do.

Falstaff in *Henry IV, Part 1*, 5.4.163–5

Imagining he may be rewarded for his claim
to have killed Hotspur, he thinks of slimming
and giving up drinking ("sack" = sherry).

3 When wilt thou leave fighting o'
days and foining o' nights, and
begin to patch up thine old body
for heaven?

**Doll Tearsheet in *Henry IV, Part 2*,
2.4.231–3**

To Falstaff, who has just driven ancient Pistol
out of doors; "foining" = fornicating.

4 Presume not that I am the thing I
was.

**Prince Hal, now King Henry V, in
Henry IV, Part 2, 5.5.56**

Marking the change in him now that he is
king.

5 Consideration like an angel came
And whipped th' offending Adam
out of him.

**Archbishop of Canterbury in *Henry
V*, 1.1.28–9**

On Prince Hal's reformation now that he is
king; Adam was guilty of the first, original sin
in disobeying God (see Romans 5:12–14).

Regret

1 What our contempts doth often
   hurl from us,
   We wish it ours again.
   Antony in *Antony and Cleopatra*,
   1.2.123–4

   Regret for what is scorned and thrown away.

2   Things without all remedy
   Should be without regard. What's
   done is done.
   Lady Macbeth in *Macbeth*, 3.2.11–12

   "Be without regard" = not brooded on.

Rejection

1 O that a lady, of one man refused,
   Should of another therefore be
   abused!
   **Helena in *A Midsummer Night's
   Dream*, 2.2.133–4**

   Helena finds herself scorned by both Lysander
   and Demetrius.

2 I have told you enough of this. For
   my part I'll not meddle nor make
   no farther.
   Pandarus in *Troilus and Cressida*,
   1.1.13–14

   "Meddle nor make" was a proverbial phrase,
   "make" meaning "have anything to do with
   it"; he is refusing to help Troilus.

3 I will acquaintance strangle, and
   look strange.
   ***Sonnet 89*, 8**

   Rejecting his friend; "acquaintance strangle" =
   cease to be familiar.

Religion

1 The gross band of the unfaithful.
   Rosalind in *As You Like It*, 4.1.194–5

   To Orlando, merging love and religion.

2 It is religion that doth make vows
   kept.
   Cardinal Pandulph in *King John*,
   1.1.172

3 Hath not a Jew eyes? Hath not a
   Jew hands, organs, dimensions,
   senses, affections, passions; fed with
   the same food, hurt with the same
   weapons, subject to the same diseases, healed by the same means,
   warmed and cooled by the same
   winter and summer, as a Christian
   is?
   Shylock in *The Merchant of Venice*,
   3.1.59–64

   His famous defense of the shared humanity of
   Jews.

4   In religion,
   What damnèd error but some sober
   brow
   Will bless it, and approve it with a
   text,
   Hiding the grossness with fair ornament?
   Bassanio in *The Merchant of Venice*,
   3.2.77–80

   "Approve" = confirm.

5 Whether, if you yield not to your
   father's choice,
   You can endure the livery of a nun,
   For aye to be in shady cloister
   mewed,

To live a barren sister all your life,
Chanting faint hymns to the cold
  fruitless moon.
Thrice blessèd they that master so
  their blood
To undergo such maiden pilgrimage.

**Theseus in *A Midsummer Night's
Dream*, 1.1.69–75**

To Hermia, who has refused to marry
Demetrius, the suitor favored by her father.

6   God save the foundation!

**Dogberry in *Much Ado About
Nothing*, 5.1.318**

On being given money by Leonato, Dogberry
responds as if he had been given alms at some
religious house or foundation.

Remembrance (see also Memory)

1   Praising what is lost
  Makes the remembrance dear.

**King of France in *All's Well That Ends
Well*, 5.3.19–20**

2   *Hamlet.* Methinks I see my father.
  Horatio. Where, my lord?
  Hamlet. In my mind's eye, Hora-
    tio.

***Hamlet*, 1.2.184–5**

Recalling the appearance of the ghost of old
Hamlet in the previous scene.

3   Old men forget; yet all shall be for-
    got,
  But he'll remember, with advan-
    tages,

What feats he did that day.

King Henry in *Henry V*, 4.3.49–51

4   Men's evil manners live in brass,
    their virtues
  We write in water.

Griffith in *Henry VIII*, 4.2.45–6

Speaking of the dead Cardinal Wolsey; "live
in brass" = are long remembered; the idea
was proverbial.

5   After my death I wish no other her-
    ald,
  No other speaker of my living
    actions
  To keep mine honor from corrup-
    tion,
  But such an honest chronicler as
    Griffith.

**Queen Katherine in *Henry VIII*,
4.2.69–72**

Griffith has just spoken of the good qualities
of Wolsey.

6   Remember that you call on me
    today.
  Be near me, that I may remember
    you.

Caesar in *Julius Caesar*, 2.2.122–3

To Trebonius, who is one of the conspirators
plotting to murder Caesar.

7   My love to Hermia,
  Melted as the snow, seems to me
    now
  As the remembrance of an idle
    gaud
  Which in my childhood I did dote
    upon.

**Demetrius in *A Midsummer Night's
Dream*, 4.1.165–8**

"Idle gaud" = worthless plaything.

8 Let us not burden our remembrances
With a heaviness that's gone.

Prospero in *The Tempest*, 5.1.198–9

"Heaviness" = grief.

9 When to the sessions of sweet silent
thought
I summon up remembrance of
things past,
I sigh the lack of many a thing I
sought,
And with old woes new wail my
dear time's waste.

Sonnet 30, 1–4

These famous lines seem to be recalled in the
general title of Marcel Proust's sequence of
novels, *A la recherche du temps perdu*; "dear"
= precious.

Renunciation

1 What must the King do now? Must
he submit?
The King shall do it. Must he be
deposed?
The King shall be contented. Must
he lose
The name of King? A' God's name
let it go.

King Richard in *Richard II*, 3.3.143–6

Anticipating the loss of his throne.

2 I'll give my jewels for a set of beads,
My gorgeous palace for a hermitage,
. . .
And my large kingdom for a little
grave,
A little, little grave, an obscure
grave.

King Richard in *Richard II*, 3.3.147–8,
153–4

Already yielding in mind to his inevitable
deposition from the throne.

3 Now mark me how I will undo
myself.
I give this heavy weight from off my
head,
And this unwieldy scepter from my
hand,
The pride of kingly sway from out
my heart.
With mine own tears I wash away
my balm,
With mine own hands I give away
my crown.

King Richard in *Richard II*, 4.1.203–8

Deposing himself.

4 Graves at my command
Have waked their sleepers, oped,
and let 'em forth
By my so potent art. But this rough
magic
I here abjure.

Prospero in *The Tempest*, 5.1.48–51

Renouncing his magical powers; "oped" =
opened.

5 I'll break my staff,
Bury it certain fathoms in the earth,
And deeper than did ever plummet
sound
I'll drown my book.

Prospero in *The Tempest*, 5.1.54–7

Abandoning his magic powers by discarding
his staff and book; "plummet" = plumb-line, a
line weighted with lead to measure depth.

Repentance

1 Try what repentance can. What
can it not?
Yet what can it, when one cannot
repent?

Claudius in *Hamlet*, 3.3.65–6

Wishing he could find forgiveness for the murder of old Hamlet.

2 Well, I'll repent, and that suddenly,
while I am in some liking. I shall be
out of heart shortly, and then I shall
have no strength to repent.

Falstaff in *Henry IV, Part 1*, 3.3.4–7

"Suddenly" = at once; "in some liking" =
inclined to do it.

3   More will I do,
Though all that I can do is nothing
worth,
Since that my penitence comes after
all,
Imploring pardon.

King Henry in *Henry V*, 4.1.302–5

Nothing he can do in penitence for his past
sins is any use, because ("since that") he still
has to seek pardon.

4 Woe, that too late repents!

King Lear in *King Lear*, 1.4.257

"Woe" = woe to the person; Lear finds
Goneril ungrateful and regrets giving her half
his kingdom.

5 Well, if my wind were but long
enough to say my prayers, I would
repent.

Falstaff in *The Merry Wives of Windsor*, 4.5.102–3

On being cheated and beaten; "wind" =
breath.

Repetition

1 *Richard.* Harp not on that string,
madam, that is past.
Queen Elizabeth. Harp on it still
shall I till heart-strings break.

Richard III, 4.4.364–5

He wants to talk of marriage, but she reminds
him of the murders he has perpetrated.

Reputation (see also Fame, Slander)

1   I have offended reputation,
A most unnoble swerving.

**Antony in *Antony and Cleopatra*,
3.11.49–50**

After turning tail at the battle of Actium.

2 I would to God thou and I knew
where a commodity of good names
were to be bought.

Falstaff in *Henry IV, Part 1*, 1.2.82–3

To Prince Hal, implying they both have a bad
reputation; "commodity" = goods for sale,
supply.

3 My credit now stands on such slip-
pery ground
That one of two bad ways you must
conceit me,
Either a coward or a flatterer.

Mark Antony in *Julius Caesar*, 3.1.191–3

Speaking to the conspirators who have killed
Caesar; "conceit" = think of.

4 He hath honored me of late, and I
have bought
Golden opinions from all sorts of
people,
Which would be worn now in their
newest gloss,
Not cast aside so soon.

Macbeth in *Macbeth*, 1.7.32–5

Resisting the idea of murdering King Duncan
to get the throne.

5   I do know of these
     That therefore only are reputed
        wise
     For saying nothing; when I am very
        sure
     If they should speak, would almost
        damn those ears
     Which hearing them would call
        their brothers fools.

Gratiano in *The Merchant of Venice*,
1.1.95–9

Alluding to Matthew 5:22, "And whosoever
saith unto his brother . . . Fool, shall be worthy to be punished with hell fire." (Geneva
version.)

6   Reputation, reputation, reputation!
     O, I have lost my reputation! I
     have lost the immortal part of
     myself, and what remains is bestial.

Cassio in *Othello*, 2.3.262–4

On being cashiered for drinking and
quarreling.

7   Reputation is an idle and most false
     imposition; oft got without merit,
     and lost without deserving.

Iago in *Othello*, 2.3.268–70

"Imposition" = what is attributed to someone
by other people; this is said for the benefit of
Cassio; see next entries.

8   Good name in man and woman,
        dear my lord,
     Is the immediate jewel of their
        souls.

Iago in *Othello*, 3.3.155–6

Iago praises reputation to Othello, having earlier made little of it to Cassio at 2.3.268–70.

9   He that filches from me my good
        name
     Robs me of that which not enriches
        him,

And makes me poor indeed.

Iago in *Othello*, 3.3.159–61

Provoking Othello to be suspicious of Desdemona.

10   But, alas, to make me
      A fixèd figure for the time of scorn
      To point his slow unmoving finger
         at!

Othello in *Othello*, 4.2.53–5

Imagining everyone will always point him out
as a cuckold.

11   The purest treasure mortal times
         afford
      Is spotless reputation.

Mowbray in *Richard II*, 1.1.177–8

On being accused of treason.

12   The King's name is a tower of
         strength.

King Richard in *Richard III*, 5.3.12

Relying on his reputation in fighting against
Richmond.

13   Perseverance, dear my lord,
      Keeps honor bright; to have done is
         to hang
      Quite out of fashion, like a rusty
         mail,
      In monumental mockery.

Ulysses in *Troilus and Cressida*,
3.3.150–3

"Rusty mail" = rusty suit of armor; addressing
Achilles, who has refused to fight for the
Greeks.

14   Take the instant way,
      For honor travels in a strait so nar-
         row,

Where one but goes abreast. Keep then the path,
For emulation hath a thousand sons
That one by one pursue. If you give way,
Or hedge aside from the direct forthright,
Like to an entered tide, they all rush by
And leave you hindmost.

Ulysses in *Troilus and Cressida*,
3.3.153–60

Depicting life as a rat-race to Achilles in an effort to get him to fight again.

15   I see my reputation is at stake,
My fame is shrewdly gored.

Achilles in *Troilus and Cressida*,
3.3.227–8

"Shrewdly gored" = badly wounded; responding to Ulysses.

16   Thence comes it that my name receives a brand,
And almost thence my nature is subdued
To what it works in, like the dyer's hand.

Sonnet 111, 5–7

As the dyer's hand is stained by his work, so the speaker (Shakespeare himself presumably) is tainted (as with a brand) and conditioned by his work as an actor and writer for the stage.

17   'Tis better to be vile than vile esteemed,
When not to be receives reproach of being.

Sonnet 121, 1–2

It is better to be vile when, not being vicious, one is thought to be so, and reproached for it.

Resignation

1   All strange and terrible events are welcome,
But comforts we despise.

Cleopatra in *Antony and Cleopatra*,
4.15.3–4

Preparing for the worst.

2   Night hangs upon mine eyes; my bones would rest,
That have but labored to attain this hour.

Brutus in *Julius Caesar*, 5.5.41–2

Anticipating his death.

3   Cold indeed, and labor lost:
Then farewell heat, and welcome frost!

Prince of Morocco in *The Merchant of Venice*, 2.7.74–5

Before choosing the wrong casket, he had sworn never to marry.

4   I am a tainted wether of the flock,
Meetest for death; the weakest kind of fruit
Drops earliest to the ground, and so let me.

Antonio in *The Merchant of Venice*,
4.1.114–16

"Tainted wether" literally = sickly castrated ram; Antonio offers himself, as it were, for sacrifice.

5   But why should honor outlive honesty?
Let it go all.

Othello in *Othello*, 5.2.245–6

Having lost his integrity ("honesty") he no longer sees a need to maintain his reputation as a warrior.

6   Here is my journey's end, here is
my butt
And very sea-mark of my utmost
sail.

Othello in *Othello*, 5.2.267–8

Meaning the journey of life; "butt" = goal; a
sea-mark was a beacon or landmark to guide
ships to harbor.

Resistance

1   Fight to the last gasp; I'll be your
guard.

Joan la Pucelle in *Henry VI, Part 1*,
1.2.127

Urging the French to resist the attack by the
English on Orleans.

2   What fates impose, that men must
needs abide;
It boots not to resist both wind and
tide.

King Edward in *Henry VI, Part 3*,
4.4.58–9

He has been taken prisoner; "It boots not" = it
is pointless.

3   I'll not budge an inch.

Sly in *The Taming of the Shrew*,
Induction, I.14

Threatened with the Constable, he refuses to
leave the inn where he has broken some
glasses.

Resolution (see also Determination)

1   I have nothing
Of woman in me; now from head
to foot

I am marble-constant.

Cleopatra in *Antony and Cleopatra*,
5.2.237–40

Cleopatra prepares for death.

2   Thy commandment all alone shall
live
Within the book and volume of my
brain
Unmixed with baser matter.

Hamlet in *Hamlet*, 1.5.102–4

Taking the Ghost's demand for revenge as a
military order (command), and a biblical
injunction (commandment).

3   I am fresh of spirit and resolved
To meet all perils very constantly.

Cassius in *Julius Caesar*, 5.1.90–1

Rejecting the bad omens seen before the battle of Philippi.

4   Put on
The dauntless spirit of resolution.

**The Bastard Falconbridge in *King
John*, 5.1.52–3**

Urging King John to stand firm.

5   I am settled, and bend up
Each corporal agent to this terrible
feat.

Macbeth in *Macbeth*, 1.7.79–80

"Bend up" = brace every nerve in my body
(from bringing a bow into tension); he is ready
to murder Duncan (the "terrible feat").

6   It makes us, or it mars us, think on
that,
And fix most firm thy resolution.

Iago in *Othello*, 5.1.4–5

"Makes or mars" was proverbial = succeed or
be destroyed; to Roderigo, as they ambush
Cassio.

Respect

1   That title of respect
Which the proud soul ne'er pays
  but to the proud.

King Henry in *Henry IV, Part 1*, 1.3.8–9

He thinks he can only earn respect by being tough.

Retirement

1   I could be well content
To entertain the lag end of my life
With quiet hours.

Worcester in *Henry IV, Part 1*, 5.1.23–5

2   'Tis our fast intent
To shake all cares and business
  from our age,
Conferring them on younger
  strengths, while we
Unburdened crawl toward death.

King Lear in *King Lear*, 1.1.38–41

Kings are not expected to retire, and Lear brings disaster when he gives his power to his daughters.

Revels

1   See, Antony, that revels long a-
  nights,
Is notwithstanding up.

Caesar in *Julius Caesar*, 2.2.116–17

Greeting Antony.

2   Revels, dances, masques, and
  merry hours
Forerun fair love, strewing her way
  with flowers.

Berowne in *Love's Labor's Lost*,
4.3.376–7

Berowne's plan to win over the ladies of the court.

3   Come now, what masques, what
  dances shall we have
To wear away this long age of three
  hours
Between our after-supper and bed-
  time?

**Theseus in *A Midsummer Night's
Dream*, 5.1.32–4**

"Masques" were courtly entertainments based on the idea of masked dancers.

4   Say, what abridgement have you for
  this evening?
What masque, what music? How
  shall we beguile
The lazy time if not with some
  delight?

**Theseus in *A Midsummer Night's
Dream*, 5.1.39–41**

"Abridgement" = amusement to make the time pass quickly.

5   I am a fellow o'the strangest mind
i'the world; I delight in masques
and revels sometimes altogether.

**Sir Andrew Aguecheek in *Twelfth
Night*, 1.3.112–14**

He has just changed his mind about staying in Illyria.

Revenge

1   Haste me to know it, that I with
  wings as swift
As meditation, or the thoughts of
  love,
May sweep to my revenge.

Hamlet in *Hamlet*, 1.5.29–31

Impulsively eager to rush to the revenge his father's ghost has demanded; "swift as thought" is proverbial.

2   How all occasions do inform
        against me,
    And spur my dull revenge!

    Hamlet in *Hamlet*, 4.4.32–3

    "Inform against me" = accuse me of inaction.

3   *Salerio.* Why, I am sure if he forfeit
        thou wilt not take his flesh.
        What's that good for?
    Shylock. To bait fish withal—if it
        will feed nothing else, it will feed
        my revenge.

    ***The Merchant of Venice*, 3.1.51–4**

    On the news that ships bearing Antonio's
    goods have been lost.

4   If you prick us, do we not bleed? If
    you tickle us, do we not laugh? If
    you poison us, do we not die? And
    if you wrong us, shall we not
    revenge? If we are like you in the
    rest, we will resemble you in that.
    If a Jew wrong a Christian, what is
    his humility? Revenge. If a Christ-
    ian wrong a Jew, what should his
    sufferance be by Christian example?
    Why, revenge. The villainy you
    teach me, I will execute, and it
    shall go hard but I will better the
    instruction.

    Shylock in *The Merchant of Venice*,
    3.1.64–73

    Intending to demand his pound of flesh from
    Antonio.

5   Nothing can or shall content
        my soul
    Till I am evened with him, wife for
        wife,
    Or failing so, yet that I put the
        Moor
    At least into a jealousy so strong
    That judgment cannot cure.

    Iago in *Othello*, 2.1.298–302

    Imagining Othello has slept with his wife,
    Emilia.

6   All my fond love thus do I blow to
        heaven.
    'Tis gone.
    Arise, black vengeance, from the
        hollow hell!

    Othello in *Othello*, 3.3.445–7

    The turning point, as his love for Desdemona
    turns to hate.

7   Like to the Pontic Sea,
    Whose icy current and compulsive
        course
    Ne'er knows retiring ebb, but keeps
        due on
    To the Propontic and the Helle-
        spont,
    Even so my bloody thoughts with
        violent pace
    Shall ne'er look back, ne'er ebb to
        humble love,
    Till that a capable and wide revenge
    Swallow them up.

    Othello in *Othello*, 3.3.453–60

    The "Pontic Sea" is the Black Sea; the "Pro-
    pontic" or Sea of Marmora, and the "Helle-
    spont," the straits of the Dardanelles, both
    connect the Black Sea with the Aegean Sea in
    the Mediterranean.

8   To revenge is no valor, but to bear.

    First Senator in *Timon of Athens*, 3.5.39

    Claiming that true valor lies in being able to
    endure rather than seek revenge.

9   I'll be revenged on the whole pack
    of you.

    Malvolio in *Twelfth Night*, 5.1.378

    His famous exit-line, after being duped and
    treated as mad.

Revolution

1   Pluck down my officers, break my
    decrees,
    For now a time is come to mock at
    form.

    King Henry in *Henry IV, Part 2*,
    4.5.117–8

    Imagining what will happen when Prince
    Hal becomes king; "form" = ceremony or
    tradition.

Risk

1   Were it good
    To set the exact wealth of all our
    states
    All at one cast? To set so rich a
    main
    On the nice hazard of one doubtful
    hour?
    It were not good, for therein should
    we read
    The very bottom and the soul of
    hope,
    The very list, the very utmost
    bound
    Of all our fortunes.

    Hotspur in *Henry IV, Part 1*, 4.1.45–52

    Convincing himself it is as well to keep the
    forces of his father, who pleads sickness, in
    reserve; "exact wealth of all our states" =
    whole of our resources; "main" = stake; "nice
    hazard" = tricky gamble; "list" = boundary.

2   "Who chooseth me must give and
    hazard all he hath."
    Must give—for what? For lead,
    hazard for lead?
    This casket threatens. Men that
    hazard all
    Do it in hope of fair advantages;

A golden mind stoops not to shows
of dross.

Prince of Morocco in *The Merchant of
Venice*, 2.7.16–20

Reading the message he finds on the leaden
casket.

Rivalry

1   Think not, Percy,
    To share with me in glory any
    more.
    Two stars keep not their motion in
    one sphere.

    Prince Hal in *Henry IV, Part 1*, 5.4.63–5

    To Hotspur; the last line means two stars can-
    not share the same orbit.

Rivers

1   There is a river in Macedon, and
    there is moreover a river in Mon-
    mouth. It is called Wye at Mon-
    mouth, but it is out of my prains
    what is the name of the other river;
    but 'tis all one, 'tis alike as my fin-
    gers is to my fingers, and there is
    salmons in both.

    Fluellen in *Henry V*, 4.7.26–31

    Fluellen's logic is as quaint as his language as
    he "proves" that Henry V is as great a soldier
    as Alexander the Great.

2   Smooth runs the water where the
    brook is deep.

    Suffolk in *Henry VI, Part 2*, 3.1.53

    Accusing Humphrey, Duke of Gloucester, of
    hypocrisy; proverbial.

3 The current that with gentle mur-
   mur glides,
   Thou know'st, being stopped,
   impatiently doth rage;
   But when his fair course is not hin-
   derèd,
   He makes sweet music with th'
   enameled stones,
   Giving a gentle kiss to every sedge
   He overtaketh in his pilgrimage.

   Julia in *The Two Gentlemen of*
   Verona, 2.7.25–30

   She is really thinking of the course of her love
   for Valentine.

Royalty

1   There is gold, and here
   My bluest veins to kiss—a hand
   that kings
   Have lipped, and trembled kissing.

   Cleopatra in *Antony and Cleopatra,*
   2.5.28–30

   Allowing a messenger to kiss the royal hand.

2 Show me, my women, like a queen;
   go fetch
   My best attires. I am again for Cydnus
   To meet Mark Antony.

   Cleopatra in *Antony and Cleopatra,*
   5.2.227–9

   Dressing up to recapture her first glamorous
   meeting with Antony.

3 Give me my robe, put on my
   crown, I have
   Immortal longings in me.

   Cleopatra in *Antony and Cleopatra,*
   5.2.280–1

   Preparing for death as a queen.

4 *First Guard.* Is this well done?
   Charmian. It is well done, and fit-
   ting for a princess
   Descended of so many royal kings.

   Antony and Cleopatra, 5.2.325–7

   Caesar's guards find Cleopatra dead.

5   Never alone
   Did the King sigh, but with a general groan.

   Rosencrantz in *Hamlet,* 3.3.22–3

   The obsequious courtier speaking to Claudius.

6 There's such divinity doth hedge a
   king
   That treason can but peep to what
   it would,
   Acts little of his will.

   Claudius in *Hamlet,* 4.5.124–6

   James I liked to claim that kings were gods on
   earth. It is ironic that Claudius, who murdered King Hamlet, should claim divine protection; "his" = its.

7   Let four captains
   Bear Hamlet like a soldier to the
   stage,
   For he was likely, had he been put
   on,
   To have proved most royally.

   Fortinbras in *Hamlet,* 5.2.395–8

   Hamlet receives a soldier's funeral.

8 The skipping King, he ambled up
   and down,
   With shallow jesters and rash bavin
   wits,
   Soon kindled and soon burnt,
   carded his state,
   Mingled his royalty with cap'ring
   fools.

King Henry in *Henry IV, Part 1*,
3.2.60–3

Speaking to his son of Richard II; "bavin" = brushwood; "carded his state" = weakened his power.

9   No extraordinary gaze,
Such as is bent on sunlike majesty
When it shines seldom in admiring eyes.
King Henry in *Henry IV, Part 1*,
3.2.78–80

Advising Prince Hal that kings should rarely display themselves.

10 The King himself is to be feared as the lion.
Falstaff in *Henry IV, Part 1*, 3.3.149

As the lion is king of the beasts.

11 Uneasy lies the head that wears a crown.
King Henry in *Henry IV, Part 2*, 3.1.31

The king's best-known line.

12 O polished perturbation! Golden care!
That keep'st the ports of slumber open wide
To many a watchful night.
Prince Hal in *Henry IV, Part 2*,
4.5.23–5

Commenting on the crown that lies on his sick father's pillow; "ports" = gates.

13 This new and gorgeous garment, majesty,
Sits not so easy on me as you think.
Prince Hal in *Henry IV, Part 2*, 5.2.44–5

On taking the throne as Henry V.

14 The mirror of all Christian kings.
Chorus in *Henry V*, 2.Prologue, 6

Praising Henry V as the model for all kings.

15 Never was monarch better feared and loved
Than is your Majesty.
Cambridge in *Henry V*, 2.2.25–6

He is about to be exposed as a traitor.

16   Mean and gentle all
Behold, as may unworthiness define,
A little touch of Harry in the night.
Chorus in *Henry V*, 4.Prologue, 45–7

High and low ("mean and gentle") alike are influenced by the king's personality (the familiar "Harry," not Henry); the Chorus apologizes for his "unworthiness" in attempting to describe it.

17 I think the King is but a man, as I am. The violet smells to him as it doth to me.
King Henry in *Henry V*, 4.1.101–2

Henry is in disguise, speaking with common soldiers.

18 Upon the King! Let us our lives, our souls,
Our debts, our careful wives,
Our children, and our sins lay on the King!
We must bear all. O hard condition,
Twin-born with greatness, subject to the breath
Of every fool.
King Henry in *Henry V*, 4.1.230–5

Lamenting the hardship of bearing responsibility.

19 'Tis not the balm, the scepter, and
    the ball,
    The sword, the mace, the crown
    imperial,
    The intertissued robe of gold and
    pearl,
    . . .
    Not all these, laid in bed majestical,
    Can sleep so soundly as the
    wretched slave
    Who with a body filled and vacant
    mind
    Gets him to rest, crammed with
    distressful bread.

    King Henry in *Henry V*, 4.1.260–2,
    267–70

    The poor laborer whose food is earned by
    hard toil (hence "distressful") sleeps easier
    than a king, for all his luxury.

20 I am glad thou canst speak no bet-
    ter English, for if thou couldst, thou
    wouldst find me such a plain king
    that thou wouldst think I had sold
    my farm to buy my crown.

    King Henry in *Henry V*, 5.2.123–6

    Apologizing to Katherine for his roughness.

21 How sweet a thing it is to wear a
    crown,
    Within whose circuit is Elysium
    And all that poets feign of bliss and
    joy.

    Richard of Gloucester in *Henry VI,
    Part 3*, 1.2.29–31

    Elysium was the heaven of Greek mythology,
    where the spirits of the blessed dwelled.

22 *Second Keeper.* But if thou be a
    king, where is thy crown?
    King Henry. My crown is in my
    heart, not on my head;
    Not decked with diamonds and
    Indian stones,

    Nor to be seen: my crown is called
    content;
    A crown it is that seldom kings
    enjoy.

    Henry VI, Part 3, 3.1.61–5

    The king, in disguise, encounters two game-
    keepers; "Indian stones" = precious gems from
    India.

23 I swear again, I would not be a
    queen
    For all the world.

    Anne Boleyn in *Henry VIII*, 2.3.45–6

    Ironic both in relation to the quibble on
    "quean" or whore, and in view of what hap-
    pened to her; she became queen, and was
    later beheaded.

24   Thou art alone
    (If thy rare qualities, sweet gentle-
    ness,
    Thy meekness saintlike, wife-like
    government,
    Obeying in commanding, and thy
    parts
    Sovereign and pious else, could
    speak thee out)
    The queen of earthly queens.

    King Henry in *Henry VIII*, 2.4.137–42

    Praising Katherine, the wife he is divorcing;
    "government" = conduct; her "sovereign
    parts" are her excellent qualities.

25 *Gloucester.* Is't not the King?
    Lear. Ay, every inch a king!
    When I do stare, see how the sub-
    ject quakes!

    King Lear, 4.6.107–8

26 We were not born to sue, but to
    command.

    King Richard in *Richard II*, 1.1.196

27 Four lagging winters and four wanton springs
End in a word: such is the breath of kings.

Bolingbroke in *Richard II*, 1.3.214–5

King Richard has reduced his term of banishment by four years.

28 Not all the water in the rough rude sea
Can wash the balm off from an anointed king;
The breath of worldly men cannot depose
The deputy elected by the Lord.

King Richard in *Richard II*, 3.2.54–7

Alluding to the "divine right" of a king, consecrated with holy oil ("balm"), and God's deputy on earth.

29 Is not the king's name twenty thousand names?
Arm, arm, my name! A puny subject strikes
At thy great glory.

King Richard in *Richard II*, 3.2.85–7

Having no soldiers, he tries to cheer himself up.

30 See, see, King Richard doth himself appear,
As doth the blushing discontented sun
From out the fiery portal of the east.

Bolingbroke in *Richard II*, 3.3.62–4

Richard appears on the battlements of a castle (or balcony on the stage).

31 Yet looks he like a king. Behold, his eye,

As bright as is the eagle's, lightens forth
Controlling majesty.

York in *Richard II*, 3.3.68–70

In defeat Richard still has a good appearance; "lightens forth" = flashes like lightning.

32 She is
The queen of curds and cream.

Camillo in *The Winter's Tale*, 4.4.160–1

Seeing Perdita, really a princess, among the country shepherds and shepherdesses.

33 For princes are the glass, the school, the book
Where subjects' eyes do learn, do read, do look.

***The Rape of Lucrece*, 615–6**

Ruin

1 Leave not the mansion so long tenantless
Lest, growing ruinous, the building fall
And leave no memory of what it was.

Valentine in *The Two Gentlemen of Verona*, 5.4.7–10

Appealing to Sylvia; the "mansion" is his heart.

Rumor

1 Let every feeble rumor shake your hearts.

Coriolanus in *Coriolanus*, 3.3.125

To the people as he goes into exile.

2   *Enter Rumor, painted full of tongues.*
Open your ears; for which of you
will stop
The vent of hearing when loud
Rumor speaks?

Rumor in *Henry IV, Part 2*, Induction, 1–2, and stage direction

The Chorus to the play.

3   Rumor is a pipe
Blown by surmises, jealousies, con-
jectures.

Rumor in *Henry IV, Part 2*, Induction, 15–16

How rumor spreads, like music.

4   From Rumor's tongues
They bring smooth comforts false,
worse than true wrongs.

Rumor in *Henry IV, Part 2*, Induction, 39–40

"They" are people spreading reports.

5   Rumor doth double, like the voice
and echo,
The numbers of the feared.

Warwick in *Henry IV, Part 2*, 3.1.97–8

Referring to the size of a rebel army.

6   I heard a bustling rumor like a fray,
And the wind blows it from the
Capitol.

Portia in *Julius Caesar*, 2.4.18–19

"Bustling rumor like a fray" = confused noise
like a brawl.

Ruthlessness (see also Cruelty)

1   There is no more mercy in him
than there is milk in a male tiger.

Menenius in *Coriolanus*, 5.4.27–8

Referring to Coriolanus, who is threatening to
conquer Rome.

2   Down, down to hell, and say I sent
thee thither—
I that have neither pity, love, nor
fear.

Richard of Gloucester in *Henry VI, Part 3*, 5.6.67–8

Stabbing the already dead King Henry VI.

3   Make thick my blood,
Stop up th' access and passage to
remorse,
That no compunctious visitings of
nature
Shake my fell purpose.

Lady Macbeth in *Macbeth*, 1.5.43–6

If the blood is "thick" no pity or remorse
("compunctious visitings") can flow from the
heart; the "purpose" is murder.

4   I have given suck, and know
How tender 'tis to love the babe
that milks me;
I would, while it was smiling in my
face,
Have plucked my nipple from his
boneless gums
And dashed the brains out, had I so
sworn
As you have done to this.

Lady Macbeth in *Macbeth*, 1.7.54–9

To Macbeth, who is hesitating about murdering Duncan.

5   Tear-falling pity dwells not in this
eye.

King Richard in *Richard III*, 4.2.65

Sacrifice

1   Let us be sacrificers, but not butchers, Caius.

Brutus in *Julius Caesar*, 2.1.166

On the idea of killing Caesar.

2   Upon such sacrifices, my Cordelia, The gods themselves throw incense.

King Lear in *King Lear*, 5.3.20–1

Lear here seems to anticipate the death of Cordelia, who is soon to be hanged in prison.

Safety

1   Would I were in an alehouse in London. I would give all my fame for a pot of ale, and safety.

Boy in *Henry V*, 3.2.12–13

He is with the English forces attacking Harfleur in France; a wry comment on the militarism of Henry V.

2   I am sure 'tis safer to Avoid what's grown than question how 'tis born.

Camillo in *The Winter's Tale*, 1.2.432–3

To Polixenes, who cannot conceive how his old friend, Leontes, should wish to murder him.

Sanity

1   My pulse as yours doth temperately keep time, And makes as healthful music. It is not madness That I have uttered.

Hamlet in *Hamlet*, 3.4.140–2

To Gertrude, who thinks Hamlet is mad.

Scorn (see also Contempt)

1   Disdain and scorn ride sparkling in her eyes, Misprising what they look on, and her wit Values itself so highly that to her All matter else seems weak.

Hero in *Much Ado About Nothing*, 3.1.51–4

Characterizing Beatrice as self-centered in her cleverness ("wit") and despising ("misprising") what anyone else says as trivial.

2   Teach not thy lip such scorn, for it was made For kissing, lady, not for such contempt.

King Richard in *Richard III*, 1.2.171–2

Wooing the Lady Anne, whose father-in-law he killed.

Sea

1   The wild and wasteful ocean.

King Henry in *Henry V*, 3.1.14

2   The murmuring surge, That on th' unnumbered idle pebble chafes, Cannot be heard so high.

Edgar in *King Lear*, 4.6.20–2

Imagining being on the cliffs at Dover.

3   I never did like molestation view On the enchafèd flood.

Second Gentleman in *Othello*, 2.1.16–17

"Like molestation" = disturbance like this; he is looking out to sea ("flood") for the ship bringing Othello.

4   *Gonzalo.* Nay, good, be patient.
     Boatswain. When the sea is.
        Hence! What cares these roarers
        for the name of king?

     The Tempest, 1.1.15–17

     The storm has no respect for social rank.

5   Now would I give a thousand fur-
     longs of sea for an acre of barren
     ground, long heath, brown furze,
     anything.

     Gonzalo in *The Tempest,* 1.1.65–7

     Facing shipwreck.

6   Come unto these yellow sands,
     And then take hands.
     Curtsied when you have and kissed
     The wild waves whist,
     Foot it featly here and there;
     And, sweet sprites, the burden bear.

     Ariel in *The Tempest,* 1.2.375–80

     Summoning spirits to calm the waves into
     silence ("kissed/The wild waves whist"),
     dance, and sing the refrain ("the burden
     bear").

Seasons

1   Here feel we not the penalty of
     Adam,
     The seasons' difference.

     Duke Senior in *As You Like It,* 2.1.6

     There were no seasons until Adam was
     expelled from the Garden of Eden.

2   Freeze, freeze, thou bitter sky,
     That dost not bite so nigh
     As benefits forgot.

     Amiens in *As You Like It,* 2.7.184–6

     Establishing the idea of winter in the forest of
     Arden.

3   It was a lover and his lass,
     With a hey, and a ho, and a hey
        nonino,
     That o'er the green corn-field did
        pass,
     In spring time, the only pretty ring
        time,
     When birds do sing, hey ding a
        ding, ding,
     Sweet lovers love the spring.
     Between the acres of the rye,
     With a hey, and a ho, and a hey
        nonino,
     These pretty country folks would
        lie,
     In spring time.

     Song in *As You Like It,* 5.3.16–25

     One of Shakespeare's best known lyrics.

4   As full of spirit as the month of
        May,
     And gorgeous as the sun at mid-
        summer.

     Vernon in *Henry IV, Part 1,* 4.1.101–2

     Describing Prince Hal and his comrades, in
     armor to fight against the rebel noblemen.

5   In an early spring
     We see th'appearing buds, which to
        prove fruit
     Hope gives not so much warrant, as
        despair
     That frosts will bite them.

     Lord Bardolph in *Henry IV, Part 2,*
     1.3.38–41

     Fear of a killing frost tends to outweigh hope
     for a plentiful crop.

6   The seasons change their manners,
        as the year
     Had found some months asleep
        and leapt them over.

     Gloucester in *Henry IV, Part 2,* 4.4.123–4

     "As" = as if; on unseasonable and strange
     weather.

7 As clear as is the summer's sun.

Archbishop of Canterbury in *Henry V*, 1.2.86

He is "proving" Henry's claim to rule France.

8 Thus sometimes hath the brightest
  day a cloud,
And after summer evermore succeeds
Barren winter, with his wrathful
  nipping cold;
So cares and joys abound, as seasons fleet.

Gloucester in *Henry VI, Part 2,*
2.4.1–4

He has lost his office of Protector of the King,
and his wife has been banished.

9 At Christmas I no more desire a
  rose
Than wish a snow in May's new-
  fangled shows,
But like of each thing that in season
  grows.

Berowne in *Love's Labor's Lost,*
1.1.105–7

Berowne rejects the idea of mature men
devoting themselves to study.

10 When daisies pied and violets blue,
And lady-smocks, all silver-white,
And cuckoo-buds of yellow hue
Do paint the meadows with delight,
The cuckoo then on every tree
Mocks married men, for thus sings
  he:
  Cuckoo!
Cuckoo, cuckoo—O word of fear,
Unpleasing to a married ear.

Spring in *Love's Labor's Lost,*
5.2.894–902

The first stanza of the song of Spring at the
end of the play; the cuckoo's habit of using

the nests of other birds suggests cuckoldry,
and the refrain conflicts with the delights of
spring.

11 When icicles hang by the wall,
And Dick the shepherd blows his
  nail,
And Tom bears logs into the hall,
And milk comes frozen home in
  pail;
When blood is nipped, and ways be
  foul,
Then nightly sings the staring owl:
Tu-whit, tu-whoo!—
A merry note,
While greasy Joan doth keel the
  pot.

Winter in *Love's Labor's Lost,* 5.2.912–20

The first stanza of the song of Winter at the
end of the play; the refrain ends in merriment
in spite of winter.

12 How many things by season seasoned are
To their right praise and true perfection!

Portia in *The Merchant of Venice,*
5.1.107–8

"By season" = by fit occasion, playing on the
notion of seasoning.

13 The seasons alter; hoary-headed
  frosts
Fall in the fresh lap of the crimson
  rose,
And on old Hiems' thin and icy
  crown
An odorous chaplet of sweet summer buds
Is, as in mockery, set.

Titania in *A Midsummer Night's
Dream,* 2.1.107–11

"Hiems" is the personification of winter, hoary
and old.

14   The spring, the summer,
The childing autumn, angry winter
 change
Their wonted liveries, and the
 mazèd world
By their increase now knows not
 which is which.

Titania in *A Midsummer Night's
Dream,* 2.1.111–14

On the confusion brought about by her quarrel with Oberon; "childing" = fruitful; "mazed" = bewildered.

15 Such comfort as do lusty young
 men feel
When well-appareled April on the
 heel
Of limping winter treads.

Capulet in *Romeo and Juliet,* 1.2.26–8

Referring to the feast and dance Capulet is planning.

16 Winter tames man, woman, and
 beast.

Grumio in *The Taming of the Shrew,*
4.1.23–4

17 When daffodils begin to peer,
With heigh, the doxy over the dale,
Why then comes in the sweet o'the
 year,
For the red blood reigns in the winter's pale.

Autolycus in *The Winter's Tale,* 4.3.1–4

The rogue Autolycus bursts in to change the mood from winter to spring, singing of renewed vitality ("red blood") doing away with the paleness of winter; a "doxy" is slang for a wench or, in modern slang, a floozy.

18 That time of year thou may'st in me
 behold
When yellow leaves, or none, or
 few, do hang

Upon those boughs which shake
 against the cold,
Bare ruined choirs where late the
 sweet birds sang.

Sonnet 73, 1–4

The speaker represents himself to his younger lover as aged and close to death (Shakespeare was 45 when the Sonnets were first published in 1609, and they are thought to have been written much earlier).

19 The teeming autumn, big with rich
 increase.

Sonnet 97, 6

Secrets

1 Two may keep counsel when the
 third's away.

Aaron in *Titus Andronicus,* 4.2.144

He kills the nurse he is speaking to so that she cannot betray him; she is the "third" who knows about the birth of his son; proverbial.

2   I have unclasped
To thee the book even of my secret
 soul.

Orsino in *Twelfth Night,* 1.4.13–14

To Cesario (Viola in disguise), whom he is sending to Olivia as his go-between.

Security

1 And you all know security
Is mortals' chiefest enemy.

Hecate in *Macbeth,* 3.5.32–3

Hecate, the goddess of witchcraft, speaks to the Witches.

2   The wound of peace is
 surety,

Surety secure, but modest doubt is
called
The beacon of the wise.

Hector in *Troilus and Cressida*,
2.2.15–16

Arguing that a sense of safety endangers
peace, and that it is best to maintain a moderate degree of wariness ("modest doubt").

Self-Harm

1   Those wounds heal ill that men do
give themselves.

Patroclus in *Troilus and Cressida*,
3.3.229

Referring to Achilles, whose reputation has
been damaged by his idleness.

Self-Importance

1   There are a sort of men whose visages
Do cream and mantle like a standing pond,
And do a willful stillness entertain,
With purpose to be dressed in an
opinion
Of wisdom, gravity, profound conceit,
As who should say, "I am Sir Oracle,
And when I ope my lips let no dog
bark!"

Gratiano in *The Merchant of Venice*,
1.1.88–94

The idea is that their faces take on a set
expression, like the puckered or wrinkled
scum on a stagnant pond; "opinion" = reputation; "conceit" = imagination.

2   Masters, do not forget to specify,
when time and place shall serve,
that I am an ass.

**Dogberry in *Much Ado About
Nothing*,** 5.1.255–6

Dogberry exposes the comic aspects of self-
importance.

3   The best persuaded of himself, so
crammed, as he thinks, with excel-
lencies, that it is his grounds of
faith that all that look on him love
him.

Maria in *Twelfth Night*, 2.3.150–2

On Malvolio; "The best persuaded of himself"
= having the best opinion of himself.

Self-Interest

1   That same purpose-changer, that
sly devil,
That broker that still breaks the
pate of faith,
That daily break-vow, he that wins
of all,
Of kings, of beggars, old men,
young men, maids . . .
That smooth-faced gentleman, tick-
ling commodity,
Commodity, the bias of the world.

**The Bastard Falconbridge in *King
John*,** 2.1.567–9, 573–4

"Commodity" = selfish interest, or concern
with profit; it is imaged as a middleman or
bawd ("broker"), a plausible rogue ("smooth-
faced gentleman"), and as the weight (from
the game of bowls) that influences dealings in
the world.

2   Let me, if not by birth, have lands
by wit;
All with me's meet that I can fashion fit.

Edmund in *King Lear*, 1.2.183–4

Everything that serves his purpose ("can fashion fit") is permissible or justifiable ("meet").

3   That sir which serves and seeks for
     gain,
     And follows but for form,
     Will pack when it begins to rain,
     And leave thee in the storm.

Fool in *King Lear*, 2.4.78–81

"Sir" = man; "pack" = pack up and go.

4   In following him, I follow but
     myself.

Iago in *Othello*, 1.1.58

Referring to Othello.

Self-Knowledge (see also Identity)

1   I will chide no breather in the
     world but myself, against whom I
     know most faults.

Orlando in *As You Like It*, 3.2.280–1

Refusing to join Jaques in abusing the world.

2   Mistress, know yourself, down on
     your knees,
     And thank heaven, fasting, for a
     good man's love.

Rosalind in *As You Like It*, 3.5.57–8

To Phebe, who rejects Silvius's love.

3   Lord, we know what we are, but
     know not what we may be.

Ophelia in *Hamlet*, 4.5.43–4

Wise in her madness.

4   I know myself now, and I feel
     within me
     A peace above all earthly dignities,
     A still and quiet conscience.

**Cardinal Wolsey in *Henry VIII*,
3.2.378–80**

In his downfall he finds peace, and knows his
faults and limitations.

5   Since you know you cannot see
     yourself
     So well as by reflection, I, your
     glass,
     Will modestly discover to yourself
     That of yourself which yet you
     know not of.

Cassius in *Julius Caesar*, 1.2.67–70

Telling Brutus he can, like a mirror ("glass")
reveal discreetly ("modestly discover") what
Brutus fails to understand about himself.

6   'Tis the infirmity of his age, yet he
     hath ever but slenderly known him-
     self.

Regan in *King Lear*, 1.1.293–4

On Lear casting off his daughter Cordelia.

7   To know my deed, 'twere best not
     know myself.

Macbeth in *Macbeth*, 2.2.70

The "deed" is the murder of Duncan.

8   *Duke (in disguise)*. I pray you, sir, of
     what disposition was the Duke?
     Escalus. One that, above all other
     strifes, contended especially to
     know himself.

Measure for Measure, 3.2.230–3

To know oneself was to know how to balance
understanding against the will and the senses;
"strifes" = efforts, endeavors.

9   I have much ado to know myself.

**Antonio in *The Merchant of Venice*,
1.1.7**

He cannot understand why he is melancholy.

10 I do begin to perceive that I am
    made an ass.
    **Falstaff in *The Merry Wives of Wind-
    sor*, 5.5.119**

    Realizing how much he has been fooled.

11   I'll read enough
    When I do see the very book indeed
    Where all my sins are writ, and
        that's myself.
    King Richard in *Richard II*, 4.1.273–5

    On being pressed to read a list of his crimes.

12 *Feste.* The better for my foes and
        the worse for my friends.
    Orsino. Just the contrary: the better
        for thy friends.
    Feste. No, sir, the worse.
    Orsino. How can that be?
    Feste. ... They praise me, and
        make an ass of me. Now my foes
        tell me plainly I am an ass; so that
        by my foes, sir, I profit in the
        knowledge of myself, and by my
        friends I am abused.
    ***Twelfth Night*, 5.1.12–20**

    Feste's friends flatter him, so that he is
    deceived and badly treated ("abused").

Self-Love

1   Self-love, my liege, is not so vile a
        sin
    As self-neglecting.
    Dauphin in *Henry V*, 2.4.74–5

    Advising his father, the King of France, to con-
    front the English invaders.

2   She cannot love,
    Nor take no shape nor project of
        affection,
    She is so self-endeared.
    **Hero in *Much Ado About Nothing*,
    3.1.54–6**

    Commenting on Beatrice in the knowledge
    that she is listening.

3   O, you are sick of self-love, Malvo-
    lio, and taste with a distempered
    appetite.
    Olivia in *Twelfth Night*, 1.5.90–1

    Malvolio has been criticizing Feste; "distem-
    pered" = diseased.

4   Sin of self-love possesseth all mine
        eye,
    And all my soul, and all my every
        part;
    And for this sin there is no remedy,
    It is so grounded inward in my
        heart.
    ***Sonnet* 62, 1–4**

    The aging poet, "chopped with tanned antiq-
    uity," paradoxically sees himself reflected in
    the beauty of his lover, even as he acknowl-
    edges the "sin" of indulging that love.

Self-Pity

1   Here I stand your slave,
    A poor, infirm, weak, and despised
        old man.
    King Lear in *King Lear*, 3.2.19–20

    He is at the mercy of the elements, cast out in
    a storm.

2   I am a man
    More sinned against than sinning.
    King Lear in *King Lear*, 3.2.59–60

    The cry of someone who is as yet unwilling
    fully to acknowledge his own faults?

3   Give me that glass, and therein will
     I read.
     No deeper wrinkles yet? Hath sor-
     row struck
     So many blows upon this face of
     mine
     And made no deeper wounds?
     King Richard in *Richard II*, 4.1.276–9

     Looking at himself in a mirror.

Self-Reliance

1   Our remedies oft in ourselves do lie
     Which we ascribe to heaven.
     Helena in *All's Well That Ends Well*,
     1.1.216–7

2   Simply the thing I am
     Shall make me live.
     Parolles in *All's Well That Ends Well*,
     4.3.333–4

     Bouncing back from humiliation.

Senses

1   Dark night, that from the eye his
          function takes,
     The ear more quick of apprehen-
     sion makes;
     Wherein it doth impair the seeing
     sense
     It pays the hearing double recom-
     pense.
     Hermia in *A Midsummer Night's*
     ***Dream*, 3.2.177–80**

2   The eye of man hath not heard, the
     ear of man hath not seen, man's
     hand is not able to taste, his tongue

to conceive, nor his heart to report
what my dream was!
Bottom in *A Midsummer Night's*
***Dream*, 4.1.211–4**

Bottom mixes up senses in misquoting a passage from I Corinthians 2:9–10, but perhaps
his dream was one of the "things which God
hath prepared for them that love him."

Service

1   I have lost my teeth in your service.
     Adam in *As You Like It*, 1.1.82–3

     The faithful old servant is cast out.

2   O good old man, how well in thee
          appears
     The constant service of the antique
          world,
     When service sweat for duty, not
          for meed!
     Orlando in *As You Like It*, 2.3.56–8

     Imagining a golden age when doing the job
     was its own reward.

3   I had rather be their servant in my
          way
     Than sway with them in theirs.
     Coriolanus in *Coriolanus*, 2.1.203–4

     Responding to his mother's wish that he
     accept the public office of Consul in Rome.

4   My endeavors
     Have ever come too short of my
          desires,
     Yet filed with my abilities.
     Cardinal Wolsey in *Henry VIII*,
     3.2.169–71

     "Filed" = kept pace with; he claims he has
     done the best he could.

5   Had I but served my God with half
      the zeal
      I served my king, he would not in
      mine age
      Have left me naked to mine ene-
      mies.
      Cardinal Wolsey in *Henry VIII*,
      3.2.455–7

6   Remember I have done thee worthy
      service,
      Told thee no lies, made no mistak-
      ings, served
      Without or grudge or grumblings.
      Ariel in *The Tempest*, 1.2.247–9

      Prospero's "airy spirit" reminds Prospero of
      the service he has given.

7   Hear my soul speak:
      The very instant that I saw you, did
      My heart fly to your service, there
      resides
      To make me slave to it.
      Ferdinand in *The Tempest*, 3.1.63–6

      His love makes him a willing "servant" to
      Miranda.

Servitude

1   Our fathers' minds are dead,
      And we are governed with our
      mothers' spirits.
      Our yoke and sufferance show us
      womanish.
      Cassius in *Julius Caesar*, 1.3.82–4

      "Yoke and sufferance" = servitude and patient
      submission to it.

2   Every bondman in his own hand
      bears

The power to cancel his captivity.
Casca in *Julius Caesar*, 1.3.101–2

The ultimate way out of slavery, by suicide.

3   I am all the subjects that you have,
      Which first was mine own king.
      Caliban in *The Tempest*, 1.2.341–2

      To Prospero, who has made him a slave.

Sex (see also Lechery, Lust)

1   *Gertrude.* Come hither, my dear
          Hamlet, sit by me.
      Hamlet. No, good mother, here's
          metal more attractive.
      Hamlet, 3.2.108–9

      Hamlet implies he is drawn like a magnet to
      Ophelia; he wants to be where he can watch
      Claudius at the play, but it is as if he cannot
      leave Ophelia alone. Does he touch or
      embrace her here? Whatever, the phrase
      "here's metal more attractive" has passed into
      common use to indicate any kind of prefer-
      ence. See next entry.

2   *Hamlet.* Lady, shall I lie in your
          lap?
      Ophelia. No, my lord.
      Hamlet. I mean, my head upon
          your lap?
      Ophelia. Ay, my lord.
      Hamlet. Do you think I meant
          country matters?
      Ophelia. I think nothing, my lord.
      Hamlet. That's a fair thought to lie
          between maids' legs.
      Hamlet, 3.2.112–8

      This is Hamlet at his least attractive, vexing
      Ophelia with the obscene pun in "country"
      and sexual innuendo in "fair thought."

3 Come, Kate, thou art perfect in
lying down.
Come, quick, quick, that I may lay
my head in thy lap.

Hotspur in *Henry IV, Part 1*, 3.1.226–7

Teasing his wife, as Mortimer's wife prepares
to sing.

4 Well, while I live I'll fear no other
thing
So sore, as keeping safe Nerissa's
ring.

Gratiano in *The Merchant of Venice*,
5.1.306–7

Pleased to find Nerissa has the ring he thought
he had given away, Gratiano exploits a sexual
play on the word.

5 *Don Pedro.* You have put him
down, lady, you have put him
down.
Beatrice. So I would not he should
do me, my lord, lest I should
prove the mother of fools.

Much Ado About Nothing, 2.1.283–6

Beatrice has outsmarted Benedick, but she
jokingly takes "put him down" literally.

6 *Beatrice.* I am stuffed, cousin, I
cannot smell.
Margaret. A maid, and stuffed!
There's goodly catching of cold.

Much Ado About Nothing, 3.4.64–6

Beatrice is "stuffed" with a cold in the head,
but Margaret takes the word in a bawdy sense.

7 *Beatrice.* Will you go hear this
news, signor?
Benedick. I will live in thy heart, die
in thy lap and be buried in thy
eyes; and moreover, I will go with
thee to thy uncle's.

Much Ado About Nothing, 5.2.101–4

Benedick's witty response to her question
plays on "die" as referring to sexual orgasm, a
common image in poetry of Shakespeare's age.

8 Do not give dal-
liance
Too much the rein. The strongest
oaths are straw
To the fire in the blood.

Prospero in *The Tempest*, 4.1.51–3

Cautioning Ferdinand and Miranda in their
lovemaking.

9 These lovers cry, O ho they die!
Yet that which seems the wound to
kill
Doth turn O ho! to ha, ha, he!
So dying love lives still.

Pandarus in *Troilus and Cressida*,
3.1.121–4

Pandarus's song about sexual consummation.

Shame

1 Alack, when once our grace we
have forgot,
Nothing goes right; we would, and
we would not.

Angelo in *Measure for Measure*,
4.4.33–4

Ashamed, he thinks he has forced Isabella to
have sex with him, and executed her brother
Claudio; "grace" = sense of right, and the
divine grace given to man.

Shiftiness

1 You have been a boggler ever.

Antony in *Antony and Cleopatra*,
3.13.110

Accusing Cleopatra of having been always
shifty and unreliable.

Ships

1 The barge she sat in, like a burnished throne,
Burnt on the water. The poop was
beaten gold;
Purple the sails, and so perfumèd
that
The winds were love-sick with
them.

Enobarbus in *Antony and Cleopatra*,
2.2.191–4

Describing Cleopatra as she first appeared to
Antony, on the River Cydnus; quoted by T.S.
Eliot in *The Waste Land*.

2 Play with your fancies: and in them
behold
Upon the hempen tackle ship-boys
climbing;
Hear the shrill whistle which doth
order give
To sound confused; behold the
threaden sails
Borne with th' invisible and creeping wind.

Chorus in *Henry V*, 3.Prologue, 7–11

Urging the audience to imagine ships sailing
to France; "threaden" = woven with thread.

3 A city on th' inconstant billows
dancing;
For so appears this fleet majestical.

Chorus in *Henry V*, 3.Prologue, 15–16

Imagining the English fleet sailing to France.

4 Ships are but boards, sailors but
men; there be land-rats and water-
rats, water-thieves and land-
thieves, I mean pirates, and then
there is the peril of waters, winds,
and rocks.

Shylock in *The Merchant of Venice*,
1.3.22–5

On Antonio's business ventures, his goods
sent off on various ships; the heavy-handed
joke on "pi-rats" marks Shylock's odd sense of
humor.

5 A rotten carcass of a butt, not
rigged,
Nor tackle, sail, nor mast—the very
rats
Instinctively have quit it.

Prospero in *The Tempest*, 1.2.146–8

Describing to Miranda the miserable boat
("butt" = cask) in which they were exiled from
his dukedom.

6 Light boats sail swift, though
greater hulks draw deep.

Agamemnon in *Troilus and Cressida*,
2.3.266

"Hulks" = larger and clumsier vessels, like
Ajax and Achilles, the great but not very
bright warriors of the Greeks.

Shopping

1 Haply your eye shall light upon
some toy
You have desire to purchase.

Antonio in *Twelfth Night*, 3.3.44–5

Giving his friend Sebastian his purse; "Haply"
= perhaps; "toy" = trifle.

Sickness (see also Medicine)

1 I know the more one sickens the
worse at ease he is.

Corin in *As You Like It*, 3.2.23–4

On the basic facts of life.

2 I am ill, but your being by me
Cannot amend me; society is no
comfort
To one not sociable. I am not very
sick,
Since I can reason of it.

Imogen in *Cymbeline*, 4.2.11–14

She is begging to be left alone.

3 Lay not that flattering unction to
your soul,
That not your trespass but my
madness speaks;
It will but skin and film the ulcerous place,
Whilst rank corruption, mining all
within,
Infects unseen.

Hamlet in *Hamlet*, 3.4.145–9

To Gertrude, who thinks he is mad; "flattering
unction" = soothing ointment of flattery.

4   Diseases desperate grown
By desperate appliance are relieved,
Or not at all.

Claudius in *Hamlet*, 4.3.9–11

Proverbial.

5   How has he the leisure to be
sick
In such a jostling time?

Hotspur in *Henry IV, Part 1*, 4.1.17–18

Referring to his father, who was to have
brought an army to support Hotspur's rebellion
against the king; "jostling time" = time of strife.

6   This sickness doth infect
The very life-blood of our enterprise.

Hotspur in *Henry IV, Part 1*, 4.1.28–9

The enterprise is the rebellion against King
Henry; the sickness of Northumberland prevents him from taking part.

7   Worse than the sun in March,
This praise doth nourish agues.

Hotspur in *Henry IV, Part 1*, 4.1.111–12

On hearing praise of Prince Hal; "agues" =
fevers, thought to come from mists raised by
the sun.

8 It is the disease of not listening, the
malady of not marking, that I am
troubled withal.

Falstaff in *Henry IV, Part 2*, 1.2.121–2

Refusing to heed the advice of the Chief Justice.

9 In poison there is physic, and these
news,
Having been well, that would have
made me sick,
Being sick, have in some measure
made me well.

Northumberland in *Henry IV, Part 2*,
1.1.137–9

Bad news stimulates him to act.

10 A pox of this gout! Or a gout of
this pox! For the one or the other
plays the rogue with my great toe.

Falstaff in *Henry IV, Part 2*, 1.2.243–5

Diseases brought on by lechery ("pox" =
syphilis) and drinking.

11 Before the curing of a strong disease,
Even in the instant of repair and
health,
The fit is strongest.

Lewis the Dauphin in *King John*,
3.4.112–14

"Repair" = restoration, cure.

12 This fever that hath troubled me so
long

Lies heavy on me. O, my heart is sick!

King John in *King John*, 5.3.3–4

Spoken shortly before his death.

13 Infirmity doth still neglect all office
Whereto our health is bound; we are not ourselves
When nature, being oppressed, commands the mind
To suffer with the body.

King Lear in *King Lear*, 2.4.106–9

Ill health makes us neglect the duties ("all office") we are obliged to do when well.

14   Where the greater malady is fixed,
The lesser is scarce felt.

King Lear in *King Lear*, 3.4.8–9

His inner torment prevents Lear from being troubled by the storm raging around him.

15 How now, which of your hips has the most profound sciatica?

First Gentleman in *Measure for Measure*, 1.2.58–9

Greeting the bawd, Mistress Overdone.

16 For let our finger ache, and it endues
Our other healthful members even to a sense
Of pain.

Desdemona in *Othello*, 3.4.146–8

"Endues" = brings.

17   Be cured
Of this diseased opinion, and betimes,
For 'tis most dangerous.

Camillo in *The Winter's Tale*, 1.2.296–8

Realizing Leontes is mentally unbalanced.

Silence

1 Thou art a soldier only, speak no more.

Antony in *Antony and Cleopatra*, 2.2.107

Rebuking his lieutenant Enobarbus.

2 My gracious silence, hail!

Coriolanus in *Coriolanus*, 2.1.175

Returning victorious from battle, he at last notices his wife, Virgilia.

3 Holds her by the hand, silent.

Stage Direction, *Coriolanus*, 5.3.182

This striking gesture to his mother marks the yielding by Coriolanus to her plea that he spare Rome, and leads to his death at the hands of Aufidius.

4 The rest is silence.

Hamlet in *Hamlet*, 5.2.358

Hamlet's last words.

5 Madam, you have bereft me of all words.

Bassanio in *The Merchant of Venice*, 3.2.175

6 Demand me nothing; what you know, you know.
From this time forth I never will speak word.

Iago in *Othello*, 5.2.303–4

7 *Troilus.* You have bereft me of all words, lady.
Pandarus. Words pay no debts, give her deeds.

Troilus and Cressida, 3.2.54–5

Echoing Bassanio, Troilus is overwhelmed by his first encounter with Cressida; see 5 above.

8 I like your silence, it the more
   shows off
   Your wonder.

Paulina in *The Winter's Tale,* 5.3.21–2

Leontes is struck dumb on seeing, as he
thinks, so lifelike a statue of Hermione.

Simplicity

1 How green you are, and fresh in
   this old world!

Cardinal Pandulph in *King John,*
3.4.145

The Cardinal finds the young Dauphin of
France to be politically naive.

2 Never anything can be amiss
   When simpleness and duty tender
   it.

Theseus in *A Midsummer Night's
Dream,* 5.1.82–3

3 Home-keeping youth have ever
   homely wits.

Valentine in *The Two Gentlemen of
Verona,* 1.1.2

Sin

1   I will weep for thee,
   For this revolt of thine methinks is
   like
   Another fall of man.

King Henry in *Henry V,* 2.2.140–2

Speaking to the traitor, Lord Scroop, and referring to Adam's original transgression (Genesis
3).

2 Forbear to judge, for we are sinners
   all.

King Henry in *Henry VI, Part 2,* 3.3.31

On the tormented dying of Cardinal Beaufort.

3 Some sins do bear their privilege on
   earth,
   And so doth yours; your fault was
   not your folly.

The Bastard Falconbridge in *King
John,* 1.1.261–2

The Bastard Falconbridge tells his mother she
is not to blame for her adultery; "do bear their
privilege" = may be excused.

4   I am a man
   More sinned against than sinning.

King Lear in *King Lear,* 3.2.59–60

A dubious claim, as he has not yet come to
terms with his own tyrannical behavior in
casting out his daughter Cordelia.

5 Impose me to what penance your
   invention
   Can lay upon my sin; yet sinned I
   not
   But in mistaking.

Claudio in *Much Ado About Nothing,*
5.1.273–5

Contrite after his public denunciation of Hero,
he invites Leonato to subject him to any
penance.

6 Few love to hear the sins they love
   to act.

Pericles in *Pericles,* 1.1.92

On discovering the incestuous relationship
between King Antiochus and his daughter;
"hear" = hear described.

7 One sin, I know, another doth provoke.

Murder's as near to lust as flame to
smoke.

Pericles in *Pericles*, 1.1.137–8

Fearing for his life now he has revealed the
incest of the King and his daughter.

8   Anything that's mended is but
patched; virtue that transgresses is
but patched with sin, and sin that
amends is patched with virtue.

Feste in *Twelfth Night*, 1.5.47–9

The fool's understanding of human nature as
imperfect.

Sincerity

1   I hold you as a thing enskied, and
sainted,
By your renouncement an immor-
tal spirit,
And to be talked with in sincerity,
As with a saint.

Lucio in *Measure for Measure*, 1.4.34–7

Addressing the novice Isabella at the gate of
the nunnery; "enskied" = in heaven.

2   Pleads he in earnest? Look upon
his face.
His eyes do drop no tears, his
prayers are in jest.
His words come from his mouth;
ours from our breast.
He prays but faintly, and would be
denied;
We pray with heart and soul, and
all beside.

Duchess of York in *Richard II*, 5.3.100–4

Pleading against her husband with Henry IV
to save her traitorous son, Aumerle.

3   His words are bonds, his oaths are
oracles,
His love sincere, his thoughts
immaculate,
His tears pure messengers sent
from his heart,
His heart as far from fraud as
heaven from earth.

**Julia in *The Two Gentlemen of
Verona*, 2.7.75–8**

Mistakenly trusting the unfaithful Proteus.

Singing

1   *Amiens.* My voice is ragged, I know
I cannot please you.
Jaques. I do not desire you to
please me, I do desire you to sing.

***As You Like It*, 2.5.15–18**

2   Warble, child, make passionate my
sense of hearing.

Armado in *Love's Labor's Lost*, 3.1.1–2

Armado's absurd way of asking his page,
Moth, to sing.

3   I love a ballad but even too well, if
it be doleful matter merrily set
down, or a very pleasant thing
indeed, and sung lamentably.

Clown in *The Winter's Tale*, 4.4.188–90

He likes a mixture of emotions in his ballads;
"pleasant" = merry.

4   He has the prettiest love-songs for
maids, so without bawdry, which is
strange.

Servant in *The Winter's Tale*, 4.4.193–4

On Autolycus, who is peddling ballads.

Slander (see also Reputation)

1   For slander lives upon succession,
For ever housèd where it gets possession.

Balthazar in *The Comedy of Errors*, 3.1.105–6

"Lives upon succession" = is handed down from one generation to the next.

2   'Tis slander,
Whose edge is sharper than the sword, whose tongue
Outvenoms all the worms of Nile, whose breath
Rides on the posting winds, and doth belie
All corners of the world.

Pisanio in *Cymbeline*, 3.4.33–7

In early maps the winds were often shown as faces puffing from the four corners; "worms" = snakes, like the asp with which Cleopatra kills herself.

3   Be thou as chaste as ice, as pure as snow, thou shalt not escape calumny.

Hamlet in *Hamlet*, 3.1.135–6

Addressing Ophelia.

4   Upon my tongues continual slanders ride,
The which in every language I pronounce,
Stuffing the ears of men with false reports.

Rumor in *Henry IV, Part 2*, Induction, 6–8

5   No might nor greatness in mortality

Can censure scape; back-wounding calumny
The whitest virtue strikes. What king so strong
Can tie the gall up in the slanderous tongue?

Duke in *Measure for Measure*, 3.2.185–8

Not even the most virtuous can escape ("scape") slander; the Duke, in disguise, has listened to Lucio slandering him.

6   If thou dost slander her and torture me,
Never pray more; abandon all remorse;
On horror's head horrors accumulate;
Do deeds to make heaven weep, all earth amazed;
For nothing canst thou to damnation add
Greater than that.

Othello in *Othello*, 3.3.368–73

An ironic threat against Iago, since he does indeed slander Desdemona.

7   I am disgraced, impeached, and baffled here,
Pierced to the soul with slander's venomed spear.

Mowbray in *Richard II*, 1.1.170–1

He has been accused of being a traitor; "baffled" = publicly denounced.

8   Calumny will sear
Virtue itself.

Leontes in *The Winter's Tale*, 2.1.73–4

Varying the proverb, "envy shoots at the fairest mark."

9   Slander,
Whose sting is sharper than the sword's.

Paulina in *The Winter's Tale*, 2.3.86–7

Convinced that Hermione is wrongly accused
and slandered.

Sleep (see also Dreams)

1   Weariness
       Can snore upon the flint, when
         resty sloth
       Finds the down pillow hard.
       Belarius in *Cymbeline*, 3.6.33–5

"Resty" = lazy, indolent.

2   Thy spirit within thee hath been so
         at war,
       And thus hath so bestirred thee in
         thy sleep,
       That beads of sweat have stood
         upon thy brow,
       Like bubbles in a late-disturbèd
         stream.
       Lady Percy in *Henry IV, Part 1*, 2.3.56–9

Describing Hotspur's troubled state of mind as
he plots a rebellion against the king.

3   She will sing the song that pleaseth
         you,
       And on your eyelids crown the god
         of sleep,
       Charming your blood with pleasing
         heaviness.
       **Glendower in *Henry IV, Part 1*,
       3.1.213–15**

Translating his daughter's words to her husband, Mortimer.

4   Making such difference 'twixt wake
         and sleep
       As is the difference betwixt day and
         night

The hour before the heavenly-har-
  nessed team
Begins his golden progress in the
  east.

**Glendower in *Henry IV, Part 1*,
3.1.216–19**

Describing the effect his daughter's singing
will have on her sleepy husband.

5   Why rather, sleep, liest thou in
         smoky cribs
       . . .
       Than in the perfumed chambers of
         the great,
       Under the canopies of costly state,
       And lulled with sound of sweetest
         melody?
       **King Henry in *Henry IV, Part 2*, 3.1.9,
       12–14**

Sleep comes easier in a smoky hovel ("crib")
than in a palace.

6   Enjoy the honey-heavy dew of
         slumber.
       Thou hast no figures, nor no fan-
         tasies,
       Which busy care draws in the
         brains of men;
       Therefore thou sleep'st so sound.
       Brutus in *Julius Caesar*, 2.1.230–3

To his boy, Lucius, who has no anxieties.

7   I will not do thee so much wrong to
         wake thee.
       Brutus in *Julius Caesar*, 4.3.270

His servant, Lucius, has fallen asleep.

8   Our foster-nurse of nature is
         repose.
       Doctor in *King Lear*, 4.4.12

"Foster-nurse" = what naturally restores us.

9   A heavy summons lies like lead
    upon me,
    And yet I would not sleep.

Banquo in *Macbeth*, 2.1.6–7

Weariness summons him to sleep, but he is
troubled in mind.

10 Methought I heard a voice cry
    "Sleep no more!
    Macbeth does murder sleep," the
    innocent sleep,
    Sleep that knits up the ravelled
    sleave of care,
    The death of each day's life, sore
    labor's bath,
    Balm of hurt minds, great nature's
    second course,
    Chief nourisher in life's feast.

Macbeth in *Macbeth*, 2.2.32–7

"Ravelled sleave" = tangled thread; "second
course" = main and most nourishing course
(feasts had two courses as a rule).

11 You lack the season of all natures,
    sleep.

Lady Macbeth in *Macbeth*, 3.4.140

"Season" may mean necessary period of rest,
or the seasoning that preserves.

12   Thy best of rest is sleep,
    And that thou oft provok'st, yet
    grossly fear'st
    Thy death, which is no more.

Duke in *Measure for Measure*, 3.1.17–19

Disguised as a Friar, he is preparing Claudio
to face death.

13   Sleep, that sometimes shuts up
    sorrow's eye,
    Steal me awhile from mine own
    company.

**Helena in *A Midsummer Night's
Dream*, 3.2.435–6**

Thinking she is abandoned in the woods by
night.

14   Not poppy, nor mandragora,
    Nor all the drowsy syrups of the
    world
    Shall ever medicine thee to that
    sweet sleep
    Which thou owed'st yesterday.

Iago in *Othello*, 3.3.330–3

Opiates were derived from poppy (opium) and
mandragora (mandrake, of the deadly night-
shade family).

15 *Emilia.* How do you, madam? How
    do you, good lady?
    Desdemona. Faith, half asleep.

***Othello*, 4.2.96–7**

Desdemona's reaction to being treated by
Othello as a whore seems wonderfully apt.

16 Thou art inclined to sleep; 'tis a
    good dullness,
    And give it way.

Prospero in *The Tempest*, 1.2.185–6

Putting Miranda to sleep by his magic; "dull-
ness" = drowsiness.

17 *Alonso.* What, all so soon asleep! I
    wish mine eyes
    Would, with themselves, shut up
    my thoughts. I find
    They are inclined to do so.
    Sebastian.   Please you, sir,
    Do not omit the heavy offer of it.
    It seldom visits sorrow; when it
    doth,
    It is a comforter.

***The Tempest*, 2.1.191–6**

Ariel's music has made them drowsy.

18 When will this fearful slumber have
an end?

Titus in *Titus Andronicus*, 3.1.252

Thinking all the horrors that have happened
may be a dream.

19 Weary with toil, I haste me to my
bed,
The dear repose for limbs with
travel tired,
But then begins a journey in my
head
To work my mind when body's
work's expired.

Sonnet 27, 1–4

"Travel" was not distinguished from "travail"
or labor, the spelling in the first edition of
1609.

Sleeplessness

1   O sleep! O gentle sleep!
Nature's soft nurse, how have I
frighted thee,
That thou no more wilt weigh my
eyelids down,
And steep my senses in forgetfulness?

King Henry in *Henry IV, Part 2*, 3.1.5–8

The king, burdened with cares, cannot sleep.

2 I have been up this hour, awake all
night.

Brutus in *Julius Caesar*, 2.1.88

Greeting Cassius and the conspirators against
Caesar.

3 What watchful cares do interpose
themselves
Betwixt your eyes and night?

Brutus in *Julius Caesar*, 2.1.98–9

"Watchful cares" = anxieties preventing sleep.

4 Sleep shall neither night nor day
Hang upon his penthouse lid;
He shall live a man forbid;
Weary sev'n-nights, nine times
nine,
Shall he dwindle, peak and pine;
Though his bark cannot be lost,
Yet it shall be tempest-tossed.

First Witch in *Macbeth*, 1.3.19–25

Putting a curse on a ship's captain; "penthouse lid" = eyelid, that slopes like a penthouse roof; "forbid" = accursed; "peak and
pine" = waste away.

5 Still it cried, "Sleep no more!" to all
the house:
"Glamis hath murdered sleep, and
therefore Cawdor
Shall sleep no more, Macbeth shall
sleep no more!"

Macbeth in *Macbeth*, 2.2.38–40

Imagining he hears a voice; Macbeth by now
is Thane (Lord) of Glamis and Cawdor.

6 For never yet one hour in his bed
Did I enjoy the golden dew of sleep,
But with his timorous dreams was
still awaked.

Lady Anne in *Richard III*, 4.1.82–4

On the misery of being married to Richard III.

7 Care keeps his watch in every old
man's eye,
And where care lodges, sleep will
never lie;
But where unbruisèd youth with
unstuffed brain
Doth couch his limbs, there golden
sleep doth reign.

Friar Lawrence in *Romeo and Juliet*,
2.3.35–8

The old friar is interrupted early in the morning by Romeo.

8   Nor night, nor day, no rest.

Leontes in *The Winter's Tale*, 2.3.1

Obsessed with the idea of his wife's adultery.

Snakes

1   He's speaking now,
Or murmuring, "Where's my ser-
pent of old Nile?"
(For so he calls me).

Cleopatra in *Antony and Cleopatra*,
1.5.24–6

Antony's affectionate phrase also suggests evil
(Satan as serpent), and the "worm" that gives
Cleopatra her death-wound.

2   *Cleopatra.* Hast thou the pretty
worm of Nilus there,
That kills and pains not?
Clown. Truly, I have him; but I
would not be the party that
should desire you to touch him,
for his biting is immortal; those
that do die of it do seldom or
never recover.

Antony and Cleopatra, 5.2.243–8

The Clown is delivering the asps with which
Cleopatra kills herself.

3   Wouldst thou have a serpent sting
thee twice?

Shylock in *The Merchant of Venice*,
4.1.69

The "serpent" is Antonio, whose death he
seeks.

Sobriety

1   This same young sober-blooded
boy doth not love me, nor a man

cannot make him laugh, but that's
no marvel, he drinks no wine.

Falstaff in *Henry IV, Part 2*, 4.3.87–9

Referring to Prince John.

2   Let not the sound of shallow fop-
pery enter
My sober house.

Shylock in *The Merchant of Venice*,
2.5.35–6

Telling his daughter Jessica to close up his
house while he is away, and not listen to the
Christians reveling outside.

Society (see also Fellowship, Hospitality)

1   Company, villainous company,
hath been the spoil of me.

Falstaff in *Henry IV, Part 1*, 3.3.9–10

As usual putting the blame on others; "spoil"
= ruin.

2   It is certain that either wise bearing
or ignorant carriage is caught, as
men take diseases, one of another;
therefore let men take heed of their
company.

Falstaff in *Henry IV, Part 2*, 5.1.75–7

"Carriage" = behavior.

3   He is given
To sports, to wildness, and much
company.

Brutus in *Julius Caesar*, 2.1.188–9

Describing Mark Antony.

4   Society, saith the text, is the happiness of life.

Nathaniel in *Love's Labor's Lost*, 4.2.161

The "text" should be biblical, and possibly the reference is to Ecclesiastes 4:8–12, "Two are better than one," etc.

5   To make society
The sweeter welcome, we will keep
    ourself
Till supper-time alone.

Macbeth in _Macbeth_, 3.1.41–3

6   Nay, I'll go with thee, cheek by
jowl.

Demetrius in _A Midsummer Night's Dream_, 3.2.338

Going off to fight with Lysander.

7   I promise you, but for your company,
I would have been a-bed an hour
ago.

Capulet in _Romeo and Juliet_, 3.4.6–7

To Paris, who has been hoping to see Juliet.

8   I would not wish
Any companion in the world but
    you.

Miranda in _The Tempest_, 3.1.54–5

Admitting her love for Ferdinand.

Soldiers (see also Fighting, War)

1   Then a soldier,
Full of strange oaths, and bearded
    like the pard,
Jealous in honor, sudden, and
    quick in quarrel,
Seeking the bubble reputation
Even in the cannon's mouth.

Jaques in _As You Like It_, 2.7.149–53

The fourth of the "seven ages" of man; he has moustaches (any facial hair was a beard) like a leopard.

2   If you have writ your annals true,
    'tis there
That, like an eagle in a dove-cote, I
Fluttered your Volscians in Cori-
    oles.
Alone I did it.

Coriolanus in _Coriolanus_, 5.3.113–16

Boasting of his achievements in battle.

3   Sharked up a list of lawless res-
    olutes.
For food and diet to some enter-
    prise
That hath a stomach in't.

Horatio in _Hamlet_, 1.1.98–100

Speaking of young Fortinbras of Norway and his way of getting an army together; "sharked up" = collected up indiscriminately.

4   Let four captains
Bear Hamlet like a soldier to the
    stage,
For he was likely, had he been put
    on,
To have proved most royal.

Fortinbras in _Hamlet_, 5.2.395–8

Hamlet's body is treated with respect; "stage" = platform (it is not clear how this was staged); "put on" = tested by becoming king.

5   I will redeem all this on Percy's
    head,
And in the closing of some glorious
    day,
Be bold to tell you that I am your
    son.

Prince Hal in _Henry IV, Part 1_, 3.2.132–4

To his father, boasting that he will defeat the renowned Hotspur.

6   I saw young Harry with his beaver
    on,
    His cuishes on his thighs, gallantly
    armed,
    Rise from the ground like feathered
    Mercury,
    And vaulted with such ease into his
    seat
    As if an angel dropped down from
    the clouds
    To turn and wind a fiery Pegasus,
    And witch the world with noble
    horsemanship.

Vernon in *Henry IV, Part 1*, 4.1.104–10

Prince Hal, ready to fight against the rebels;
"beaver" = helmet; "cuishes" = cuisses, thigh
armor; "Mercury" was the messenger of the
gods, who had winged heels; "wind" = wheel
round; "Pegasus" = mythical flying horse.

7   Tut, tut, good enough to toss, food
    for powder, food for powder; they'll
    fill a pit as well as better. Tush,
    man, mortal men, mortal men.

Falstaff in *Henry IV, Part 1*, 4.2.65–7

Describing his conscripts; "powder" = gun-
powder (compare the modern "cannon fod-
der").

8   I do not think a braver gentleman,
    More active-valiant or more
    valiant-young,
    More daring, or more bold, is now
    alive
    To grace this latter age with noble
    deeds.

Prince Hal in *Henry IV, Part 1*,
5.1.89–92

Praising Hotspur.

9   Be he as he will, yet once ere night
    I will embrace him with a soldier's
    arm
    That he shall shrink under my
    courtesy.

Hotspur in *Henry IV, Part 1*, 5.2.72–4

Promising to fight with Prince Hal.

10 A soldier is better accommodated
    than with a wife.

Bardolph in *Henry IV, Part 2*, 3.2.66–7

Referring to Falstaff who is provided ("accommodated") with Doll Tearsheet as a companion.

11 He hath a killing tongue and a quiet
    sword.

Boy in *Henry V*, 3.2.34

On ancient Pistol.

12   As I am a soldier,
    A name that in my thoughts
    becomes me best.

King Henry in *Henry V*, 3.3.5–6

13 A soldier firm and sound of heart.

Pistol in *Henry V*, 3.6.25

Praising Bardolph, who is to be hanged for
stealing from a church.

14   Art thou officer,
    Or art thou base, common, and
    popular?

Pistol in *Henry V*, 4.1.37–8

Addressing the king, who is disguised.

15 A good old commander and a most
    kind gentleman.

Williams in *Henry V*, 4.1.95–6

On Sir Thomas Erpingham.

16 We are but warriors for the work-
    ing day.
    Our gayness and our gilt are all
    besmirched

With rainy marching in the painful field.

King Henry in *Henry V*, 4.3.109–11

On the bedraggled English army.

17 I speak to thee plain soldier. If thou canst love me for this, take me.

King Henry in *Henry V*, 5.2.149–50

His method of making love to the French Princess Katherine.

18 Your son, my lord, has paid a soldier's debt.

Ross in *Macbeth*, 5.9.5

On young Siward, killed in battle.

19   Mere prattle without practice
Is all his soldiership.

Iago in *Othello*, 1.1.26–7

Abusing Cassio to Roderigo.

20 I have served him, and the man commands
Like a full soldier.

Montano in *Othello*, 2.1.35–6

Referring to Othello.

21 You may relish him more in the soldier than in the scholar.

Cassio in *Othello*, 2.1.165–6

Cassio's account of Iago.

22   A soldier's a man,
O, man's life's but a span,
Why then, let a soldier drink.

Iago in *Othello*, 2.3.71–3

A "span" is literally a hand's breadth from thumb to little finger; here a short time, as in Psalms 38:5 (Book of Common Prayer); the phrase "life's but a span" became proverbial.

23 He's a soldier fit to stand by Caesar
And give direction.

Iago in *Othello*, 2.3.122–3

Praising Cassio to Montano (but see 19 above).

24   'Tis the soldier's life
To have their balmy slumbers waked with strife.

Othello in *Othello*, 2.3.257–8

25   But we are soldiers,
And may that soldier a mere recreant prove,
That means not, hath not, or is not in love.

Agamemnon in *Troilus and Cressida*, 1.3.286–8

Responding to Hector's challenge; "recreant" = traitor.

Solecisms

1 Dost thou infamonize me among potentates?

Armado in *Love's Labor's Lost*, 5.2.678

Getting wrong "infamonize" = defame, and overdoing it with "potentates" in reference to the company with him.

2 I pray, let none of your people stir me; I have an exposition of sleep come upon me.

Bottom in *A Midsummer Night's Dream*, 4.1.38–9

Presumably meaning "a disposition to."

3 *Quince.* He is a very paramour for a sweet voice.

Flute. You must say "paragon." A paramour is, God bless us, a thing of naught.

A Midsummer Night's Dream, 4.2.11–14

Comically alluding to Bottom, who has been temporarily Titania's paramour.

4 *Dogberry.* Are you good men and true?

Verges. Yea, or else it were pity but they should suffer salvation, body and soul.

Much Ado About Nothing, 3.3.1–3

Possibly the earliest comic policemen addressing the watchmen; Verges means to say "damnation."

5 Comparisons are odorous.

Dogberry in *Much Ado About Nothing,* 3.5.16

Meaning "odious," and getting the proverb amusingly wrong.

6 O villain! Thou wilt be condemned into everlasting redemption for this.

Dogberry in *Much Ado About Nothing,* 4.2.56–7

Interrogating his prisoner, Borachio; he means to say "damnation," not "redemption."

Solitude (see also Isolation)

1 I had as lief have been myself alone.

Jaques in *As You Like It,* 3.2.254

Preferring to be left alone.

2 I and my bosom must debate awhile,
And then I would no other company.

King Henry in *Henry V,* 4.1.31–2

Preparing himself for battle.

3 Then how can it be said I am alone
When all the world is here to look on me?

Helena in *A Midsummer Night's Dream,* 2.11

Her world is Demetrius, with whom she is alone.

4 I myself am best
When least in company.

Orsino in *Twelfth Night,* 1.4.37–8

The lovesick Orsino prefers to be alone.

5 Here can I sit alone, unseen of any,
And to the nightingale's complaining notes
Tune my distresses and record my woes.

Valentine in *The Two Gentlemen of Verona,* 5.4.4–6

Sorrow (see also Affliction, Grief, Mourning)

1 When sorrows come, they come not single spies,
But in battalions.

Claudius in *Hamlet,* 4.5.78–9

Proverbial; "spies" = soldiers sent ahead to reconnoiter.

2 One woe doth tread upon another's heel,

So fast they follow.

Gertrude in *Hamlet*, 4.7.163–4

Ophelia's death by drowning follows on the killing of Polonius.

3   Down, thou climbing sorrow,
Thy element's below.

King Lear in *King Lear*, 2.4.57–8

Afraid his heart will burst; "element" = proper place.

4   Let us seek out some desolate shade, and there
Weep our sad bosoms empty.

Malcolm in *Macbeth*, 4.3.1–2

5   Each new morn
New widows howl, new orphans cry, new sorrows
Strike heaven on the face.

Macduff in *Macbeth*, 4.3.4–6

On the affliction Macbeth has brought to Scotland.

6   My particular grief
Is of so flood-gate and o'erbearing nature
That it engluts and swallows other sorrows,
And it is still itself.

Brabantio in *Othello*, 1.3.55–8

Overwhelmed (as if a "flood-gate" were open) by the loss of his daughter, his grief engulfs ("engluts") other feelings.

7   One sorrow never comes but brings an heir
That may succeed as his inheritor.

Cleon in *Pericles*, 1.4.63–4

Proverbial.

8   Sorrow ends not when it seemeth done.

Duchess of Gloucester in *Richard II*,
1.2.61

Lamenting her murdered husband.

9   For gnarling sorrow hath less power to bite
The man that mocks at it and sets it light.

John of Gaunt in *Richard II*, 1.3.292–3

"Gnarling" = biting or snarling; "sets it light" = makes light of it.

10   Sorrow and grief of heart
Makes him speak fondly like a frantic man.

Northumberland in *Richard II*,
3.3.184–5

Reporting the behavior of Richard to Henry Bolingbroke; "fondly" = foolishly.

11 Sorrow breaks seasons and reposing hours,
Makes the night morning and the noontide night.

Brakenbury in *Richard III*, 1.4.76–7

Commenting on Clarence, whose terrible dream kept him awake all night.

12 Griefs of mine own lie heavy in my breast.

Romeo in *Romeo and Juliet*, 1.1.186

Meaning his unrequited love for Rosaline.

13   All these woes shall serve
For sweet discourses in our times to come.

Romeo in *Romeo and Juliet*, 3.5.52–3

Leaving Juliet and Verona as a banished man.

14 Is there no pity sitting in the clouds,
That sees into the bottom of my
grief?

Juliet in *Romeo and Juliet*, 3.5.196–7

To her mother, making grief for her cousin
Tybalt's death a reason for delaying the proposed marriage with Paris.

15 For never was a story of more woe
Than this of Juliet and her Romeo.

**Prince of Escalus in *Romeo and Juliet*,
5.3.309–10**

The Prince of Verona pronouncing an epitaph
on the dead lovers.

16 I have, as when the sun doth light a
storm,
Buried this sigh in wrinkle of a
smile;
But sorrow that is couched in seeming gladness
Is like that mirth fate turns to sudden sadness.

**Troilus in *Troilus and Cressida*,
1.1.37–40**

He has been pretending to be happy in order
to conceal his lovesickness from his brother
and father.

17 If all the world could have seen 't,
the woe had been universal.

**Third Gentleman in *The Winter's
Tale*, 5.2.91–2**

On the reporting of the (supposed) death of
Hermione.

18 Though woe be heavy, yet it seldom
sleeps,
And they that watch see time how
slow it creeps.

***The Rape of Lucrece*, 1574–5**

The Soul

1 I do not set my life at a pin's fee,
And for my soul, what can it do to
that,
Being a thing immortal as itself?

Hamlet in *Hamlet*, 1.4.65–7

Determined to follow the ghost, not knowing
whether it is a good or evil spirit; "fee" =
worth.

2 Well, God's above all; and there be
souls must be saved, and there be
souls must not be saved.

Cassio in *Othello*, 2.3.102–4

Cassio, tipsy, may be recalling such biblical
phrases as "whosoever shall call on the name
of the Lord shall be saved" (Acts 2:21).

3 I think nobly of the soul.

Malvolio in *Twelfth Night*, 4.2.55

Protesting his sanity.

4 Poor soul, the center of my sinful
earth.

***Sonnet* 146, 1**

"Earth" is both the speaker's body ("The first
man is of the earth, earthy," I Corinthians
15:47), and his world.

Speculation

1 In my school-days, when I had lost
one shaft,
I shot his fellow of the self-same
flight
The self-same way with more
advisèd watch
To find the other forth, and by
adventuring both
I oft found both.

Bassanio in *The Merchant of Venice*,
1.1.140–4

The image is from archery; "advised watch" =
careful estimation; "forth" = out.

Speech (see also Eloquence, Talking, Words)

1 What I think I utter, and spend my
malice in my breath.

Menenius in *Coriolanus*, 2.1.53–4

2   His heart's his mouth;
What his breast forges, that his
tongue must vent.

Volumnia in *Coriolanus*, 3.1.256–7

3 Speaking thick, which nature made
his blemish,
Became the accents of the valiant;
For those that could speak low and
tardily
Would turn their own perfection to
abuse
To seem like him.

Lady Percy in *Henry IV, Part 2*, 2.3.24–8

Everyone tried to adopt Hotspur's impetuous
("thick") way of speaking.

4 Good phrases are surely, and ever
were, very commendable.

Shallow in *Henry IV, Part 2*, 3.2.70–1

He is impressed by Bardolph's rather absurd
use of the word "accommodated" in relation
to Falstaff and Doll Tearsheet.

5 Wherefore do you so ill translate
yourself
Out of the speech of peace that
bears such grace,

Into the harsh and boisterous
tongue of war?

**Westmorland in *Henry IV, Part 2*,
4.1.47–9**

On an archbishop transforming (translating)
himself into a soldier, and changing his
speech.

6 Speak on, but be not over-tedious.

Burgundy in *Henry VI, Part 1*, 3.3.43

Allowing Joan la Pucelle (Joan of Arc) to have
her say.

7 For things are often spoke and seldom meant.

Suffolk in *Henry VI, Part 2*, 3.1.268

Claiming that he always means what he says.

8 I have neither wit, nor words, nor
worth,
Action, nor utterance, nor the
power of speech
To stir men's blood; I only speak
right on.

Mark Antony in *Julius Caesar*, 3.2.221–3

He has already stirred the people in speaking
about the killing of Caesar.

9   I cannot heave
My heart into my mouth. I love
your Majesty
According to my bond, no more
nor less.

Cordelia in *King Lear*, 1.1.91–3

"Bond" disturbingly suggests the natural tie
between father and child, but also a formal
agreement or limitation, and a fetter.

10   Mend your speech a little,
Lest you may mar your fortunes.

King Lear in *King Lear*, 1.1.94–5

On Cordelia refusing to say she loves him.

11 Thy youngest daughter does not
love thee least,
Nor are those empty-hearted whose
low sounds
Reverb no hollowness.

Kent in *King Lear*, 1.1.152–4

Proverbial ("the emptiest vessel makes the
greatest sound").

12   Her voice was ever soft,
Gentle, and low, an excellent thing
in woman.

King Lear in *King Lear*, 5.3.273–4

Referring to his daughter Cordelia.

13 It is not enough to speak, but to
speak true.

**Lysander in *A Midsummer Night's
Dream*, 5.1.120**

Quince's misreading of the prologue to "Pyramus and Thisbe" prompts Lysander to think of
this "good moral."

14 She speaks poniards, and every
word stabs.

**Benedick in *Much Ado About Nothing*,
2.1.247–8**

On Beatrice's sharp tongue.

15 If her breath were as terrible as her
terminations, there were no living
near her; she would infect to the
north star.

**Benedick in *Much Ado About Nothing*,
2.1.248–50**

On Beatrice's sharp tongue; "terminations" =
the barbed endings of her sentences.

16 He was wont to speak plain and to
the purpose, like an honest man

and a soldier, and now is he turned
orthography; his words are a very
fantastical banquet, just so many
strange dishes.

**Benedick in *Much Ado About Nothing*,
2.3.18–21**

On Claudio's rhetorical flourishes now he has
become a lover; "turned orthography" =
become pedantic.

17 He hath a heart as sound as a bell
and his tongue is the clapper, for
what his heart thinks, his tongue
speaks.

Don Pedro in *Much Ado About Nothing*, 3.2.12–14

Praising Benedick.

18   Rude am I in my speech,
And little blessed with the soft
phrase of peace.

Othello in *Othello*, 1.3.81–2

Eloquently addressing the Venetian senate.

19   Little of this great world can I
speak
More than pertains to feats of broils
and battle,
And therefore little shall I grace my
cause
In speaking for myself.

Othello in *Othello*, 1.3.86–9

Othello in fact speaks magnificently; "broils"
= quarrels or fights.

20 Soft you, a word or two before you
go.

Othello in *Othello*, 5.2.338

Prefacing his final speech; "soft you" = hold
on, wait a moment.

21 Speak of me as I am; nothing extenuate,
Nor set down aught in malice.

Othello in *Othello*, 5.2.342–3

22 Your fair discourse hath been as
sugar,
Making the hard way sweet and
delectable.

Northumberland in *Richard II*, 2.3.6–7

Flattering Henry Bolingbroke.

23 You never spoke what did become
you less
Than this.

Camillo in *The Winter's Tale*, 1.2.282–3

On hearing Leontes accuse his wife of adultery.

Speechmaking (see also Eloquence)

1 I'll mountebank their
loves,
Cog their hearts from them, and
come home beloved
Of all the trades in Rome.

Coriolanus in *Coriolanus*, 3.2.132–4

Promising his mother he will dissemble like a
quack medicine-man ("mountebank"), and
beguile ("Cog") the citizens into voting for
him.

2 Hear me for my cause, and be
silent, that you may hear.

Brutus in *Julius Caesar*, 3.2.13–14

Opening his speech to the people after the
death of Caesar.

3 In the modesty of fearful duty
I read as much as from the rattling
tongue
Of saucy and audacious eloquence.
Love, therefore, and tongue-tied
simplicity
In least speak most, to my capacity.

**Theseus in *A Midsummer Night's
Dream*, 5.1.101–5**

"To my capacity" = in my judgment.

4 Runs not this speech like iron
through your blood?

**Don Pedro in *Much Ado About Noth-
ing*, 5.1.245**

To Claudio, on learning they were misled into
thinking Hero false.

5 *Katherine.* Where did you study all
this goodly speech?
Petruchio. It is extempore, from my
mother-wit.

The *Taming of the Shrew*, 2.1.262–3

Petruchio has been praising Katherine for
sweetness of temper.

6 I would be loath to cast away my
speech, for besides that it is excellently well penned, I have taken
great pains to con it.

Viola in *Twelfth Night*, 1.5.172–4

Addressing Olivia with a speech on behalf of
Orsino; "con" = learn by heart.

Speed

1 Celerity is never more admired
Than by the negligent.

**Cleopatra in *Antony and Cleopatra*,
3.7.24–5**

"A good rebuke," as Antony remarks.

2 I have speeded hither with the very
   extremest inch of possibility.

Falstaff in *Henry IV, Part 2*, 4.3.34–5

Excusing himself for being late.

3   We may outrun
   By violent swiftness that which we
      run at,
   And lose by over-running.

Norfolk in *Henry VIII*, 1.1.141–3

Varying the proverb, "make haste slowly"
(Latin "festina lente").

4 I will be here again, even with a
      thought.

Titinius in *Julius Caesar*, 5.3.19

Reporting to Cassius on the state of the battle
of Philippi.

5 I drink the air before me, and
      return
   Or ere your pulse twice beat.

Ariel in *The Tempest*, 5.1.102–3

To Prospero, as he is sent off to fetch the captain and boatswain of Alonso's ship.

Sport

1 What sport shall we devise here in
      this garden
   To drive away the heavy thought of
      care?

Queen in *Richard II*, 3.4.1–2

Speaking to the women who attend on her.

2 There be some sports are painful,
      and their labor
   Delight in them sets off.

Ferdinand in *The Tempest*, 3.1.1–2

Forced by Prospero to heave logs, Ferdinand
finds consolation in his love for Miranda.

3 Hark what good sport is out of
      town today.

Aeneas in *Troilus and Cressida*, 1.1.113

By "sport" he means fighting with the Greeks.

Spring, see Seasons

Stoicism

1 A man that Fortune's buffets and
      rewards
   Hath ta'en with equal thanks.

Hamlet in *Hamlet*, 3.2.67–8

Describing his friend Horatio.

2 *Brutus.* Now, as you are a Roman,
      tell me true.
   Messala. Then like a Roman bear
      the truth I tell,
   For certain she is dead, and by
      strange manner.
   Brutus. Why, farewell, Portia. We
      must die, Messala.

***Julius Caesar*, 4.3.187–90**

Brutus's stoic response to the news of the
death of his wife.

Stories

1 If thou didst ever hold me in thy
      heart,
   Absent thee from felicity awhile,
   And in this harsh world draw thy
      breath in pain
   To tell my story.

Hamlet in *Hamlet*, 5.2.346–9

As he lies dying, he prevents Horatio from
committing suicide; Hamlet pleads with him
to live on to tell the world the truth.

2   So shall you hear
Of carnal, bloody, and unnatural
 acts,
Of accidental judgments, casual
 slaughters,
Of deaths put on by cunning and
 forced cause,
And in this upshot, purposes mis-
 took,
Fallen on the inventors' heads.

Horatio in *Hamlet*, 5.2.380–5

Horatio's version of events makes *Hamlet*
sound like a detective fiction.

3   Yet by your gracious
 patience
I will a round unvarnished tale
 deliver
Of my whole course of love.

Othello in *Othello*, 1.3.89–91

Explaining to the Venetian senate his
courtship of Desdemona.

4 If I should tell my history, 'twould
 seem
Like lies, disdained in the reporting.

Marina in *Pericles*, 5.1.118–19

In response to Pericles's questions about her;
"in the reporting" = in the act of telling.

5 For God's sake let us sit upon the
 ground
And tell sad stories of the death of
 kings.

King Richard in *Richard II*, 3.2.155–6

Yielding to despair, and foreshadowing his
own death.

6 *First Lady.* Madam, we'll tell tales.
 Queen. Of sorrow or of joy?
 First Lady. Of either, madam.
 Queen. Of neither, girl.
 For if of joy, being altogether want-
  ing,

It doth remember me the more of
 sorrow.
Or if of grief, being altogether had,
It adds more sorrow to my want of
 joy.

Richard II, 3.4.10–16

"Remember" = remind.

7 In winter's tedious nights, sit by the
 fire
With good old folks, and let them
 tell thee tales
Of woeful ages long ago betid.

King Richard in *Richard II*, 5.1.40–2

Speaking to his queen as if he were a character in an old tale.

8 An honest tale speeds best being
 plainly told.

**Queen Elizabeth in *Richard III*,
4.4.357–8**

Responding to Richard's flattery; "speeds" =
succeeds.

9 I'll to thy closet and go read with
 thee
Sad stories chancèd in the times of
 old.

Titus in *Titus Andronicus*, 3.2.82–3

To his mutilated daughter, Lavinia; "closet" =
private room.

10 *Hermione.* Pray you sit by us,
 And tell's a tale.
 Mamillius. Merry or sad shall't be?
 Hermione. As merry as you will.
 Mamillius. A sad tale's best for
  winter. I have one
 Of sprites and goblins.

The Winter's Tale, 2.1.22–6

Mother and child are talking; a "winter's tale"
was the sort of fable or old wives' tale that
would pass the time on a dark winter evening.

Storms

1
        The southern wind
Doth play the trumpet to his purposes,
And by his hollow whistling in the
   leaves,
Foretells a tempest and a blustering
   day.

Prince Hal in *Henry IV, Part 1,* 5.1.3–6

The day he fights the rebels at the battle of
Shrewsbury.

2
When from thy shore the tempest
   beat us back,
I stood upon the hatches in the
   storm.

Queen Margaret in *Henry VI, Part 2,*
3.2.102–3

Her account of sailing to England.

3
Who ever knew the heavens menace so?

Casca in *Julius Caesar,* 1.3.44

On the night before the assassination of Caesar.

4
Why now, blow wind, swell billow,
   and swim bark!
The storm is up, and all is on the
   hazard.

Cassius in *Julius Caesar,* 5.1.67–8

Anticipating the battle to come.

5
So foul a sky clears not without a
   storm.

King John in *King John,* 4.2.108

He refers to the consequences of the death of
his nephew, young Arthur.

6
Alack, the night comes on, and the
   bleak winds

Do sorely ruffle; for many miles
   about
There's scarce a bush.

Gloucester in *King Lear,* 2.4.300–2

As Lear rushes off into the storm; "ruffle" =
rage.

7
Blow, winds, and crack your
   cheeks! Rage, blow!
You cataracts and hurricanoes,
   spout
Till you have drenched our steeples,
   drowned the cocks!

King Lear in *King Lear,* 3.2.1–3

Cast out in the storm, he welcomes it with a
storm of words; "cocks" = weathercocks.

8
       And thou, all-shaking thun-
   der,
Strike flat the thick rotundity o' the
   world!
Crack nature's molds, all germens
   spill at once
That makes ingrateful man!

King Lear in *King Lear,* 3.2.6–9

Jupiter spoke in thunder, which is the voice of
God in the book of Job too; "molds" are the
forms with which nature creates living beings;
"germens" = seeds.

9
Rumble thy bellyful! Spit, fire!
   Spout, rain!
Nor rain, wind, thunder, fire are
   my daughters.
I tax you not, you elements, with
   unkindness;
I never gave you kingdom, called
   you children.

King Lear in *King Lear,* 3.2.14–17

Welcoming thunder, lightning and rain in his
anger.

10
       Since I was man,
Such sheets of fire, such bursts of
   horrid thunder,

Such groans of roaring wind and
  rain, I never
Remember to have heard. Man's
  nature cannot carry
Th'affliction nor the fear.

Kent in *King Lear*, 3.2.45–9

Describing the storm as more than human
nature can bear ("carry").

11   O my soul's joy,
If after every tempest come such
  calms,
May the winds blow till they have
  wakened death!
And let the laboring bark climb
  hills of seas
Olympus-high, and duck again as
  low
As hell's from heaven!

Othello in *Othello*, 2.1.184–9

On finding Desdemona safe in Cyprus; Mount
Olympus was the seat of the ancient Greek
gods.

12 Yet cease your ire, you angry stars
  of heaven!
Wind, rain, and thunder, remember earthly man
Is but a substance that must yield to
  you.

Pericles in *Pericles*, 2.1.1–3

Seeing the storm that has shipwrecked him as
marking the anger of the heavens.

13 The god of this great vast, rebuke
  these surges,
Which wash both heaven and hell;
  and thou that hast
Upon the winds command, bind
  them in brass,
Having called them from the deep!
  O, still
Thy deaf'ning dreadful thunders,
  gently quench

Thy nimble sulphurous flashes!

Pericles in *Pericles*, 3.1.1–6

Pericles is imagined as on shipboard in a
storm; "vast" = huge desolate sea (suggesting
also "waste").

14 The sky it seems would pour down
  stinking pitch,
But that the sea, mounting to the
  welkin's cheek,
Dashes the fire out.

Miranda in *The Tempest*, 1.2.3–5

Describing the storm she has seen; "welkin's
cheek" = the clouds in the sky.

15 Here's neither bush nor shrub to
  bear off any weather at all. And
  another storm brewing, I hear it
  sing i' the wind. Yond same black
  cloud, yond huge one, looks like a
  foul bombard that would shed his
  liquor. If it should thunder as it did
  before, I know not where to hide
  my head. Yond same cloud cannot
  choose but fall by pailfuls.

Trinculo in *The Tempest*, 2.2.18–24

A "bombard" was a large leather container for
liquor.

16 I will here shroud till the dregs of
  the storm be past.

Trinculo in *The Tempest*, 2.2.40–1

Taking cover under Caliban's cloak.

17 When heaven doth weep, doth not
  the earth o'erflow?
If the winds rage, doth not the sea
  wax mad,
Threatening the welkin with his
  big-swollen face?

Titus in *Titus Andronicus*, 3.1.221–3

Titus is raging at the barbarous mutilation of
his daughter.

18   I never saw
The heavens so dim by day. A savage clamor!

Antigonus in *The Winter's Tale*,
3.3.55–6

The ominous storm bodes the death of
Antigonus.

Strength

1   Then join you with them like a rib
of steel,
To make strength stronger.

Lady Percy in *Henry IV, Part 2*, 2.3.54–5

Advising Northumberland not to join rebels in
fighting the king until he is sure of their
power.

2   O, it is excellent
To have a giant's strength, but it is
tyrannous
To use it like a giant.

Isabella in *Measure for Measure*,
2.2.107–9

3   Love give me strength, and strength
shall help afford!

Juliet in *Romeo and Juliet*, 4.1.125

She needs strength to take the drug Friar
Lawrence has given her.

Study (see also Books, Education, Learning)

1   *Berowne.* What is the end of study,
let me know?
King of Navarre. Why, that to
know which else we should not
know.

Love's Labor's Lost, 1.1.55–6

Speaking of the little academy they propose to
set up.

2   Study is like the heaven's glorious
sun,
That will not be deep searched with
saucy looks;
Small have continual plodders ever
won,
Save base authority from others'
books.

Berowne in *Love's Labor's Lost*, 1.1.84–7

"Small" = little; "base" = second-hand, hack-
neyed.

3   So study evermore is overshot;
While it doth study to have what it
would.
It doth forget to do the thing it
should.

Berowne in *Love's Labor's Lost*,
1.1.142–4

Proposing to keep away from women, his
companions have forgotten a planned visit by
the Princess of France; "is overshot" = misses
the target.

4   No profit grows where is no pleasure ta'en.
In brief, sir, study what you most
affect.

Tranio in *The Taming of the Shrew*,
1.1.39–40

Advising his master Lucentio; "affect" = find
pleasing.

5   My books and instruments shall be
my company,
On them to look and practice by
myself.

Bianca in *The Taming of the Shrew*,
1.1.82–3

To her father Baptista, submitting (for the
moment) to his wishes.

Stupidity

1   O that he were here to write me
    down an ass! But, masters, remem-
    ber that I am an ass; though it be
    not written down, yet forget not
    that I am an ass.

    **Dogberry in *Much Ado About
    Nothing*, 4.2.75–8**

    Keen to have his own stupidity recorded for
    posterity.

2   The plague of Greece upon thee,
    thou mongrel beef-witted lord!

    **Thersites in *Troilus and Cressida*,
    2.1.12–13**

    Bandying insults with Ajax; a diet of beef was
    thought to make people stupid.

3   Thou hast no more brain than I
    have in mine elbows.

    **Thersites in *Troilus and Cressida*,
    2.1.43–4**

    Insulting the slow-witted Ajax.

4   An honest fellow enough, and one
    that loves quails, but he has not so
    much brain as ear-wax.

    **Thersites in *Troilus and Cressida*,
    5.1.51–3**

    His description of Agamemnon, the leader of
    the Greeks.

Suffering (see also Affliction, Grief)

1   You do me wrong to take me out o'
    the grave:
    Thou art a soul in bliss, but I am
    bound
    Upon a wheel of fire, that mine
    own tears

Do scald like molten lead.

King Lear in *King Lear*, 4.7.44–7

Lear thinks he is in hell; in classical and Christian mythology a wheel of fire was a traditional form of torture for the damned.

2   Vex not his ghost. O, let him pass;
    he hates him
    That would upon the rack of this
    tough world
    Stretch him out longer.

    Kent in *King Lear*, 5.3.314–6

    On the dying King Lear; "ghost" = departing
    spirit.

3   He jests at scars that never felt a
    wound.

    Romeo in *Romeo and Juliet*, 2.2.1

    The lover responds to the mockery of Mercu-
    tio and Benvolio.

4   O, I have suffered
    With those that I saw suffer!

    Miranda in *The Tempest*, 1.2.5–6

    She thinks she has seen a ship wrecked, and
    all the crew drowned.

Suicide (see also Death-Wish)

1   There is left us
    Ourselves to end ourselves.

    **Antony in *Antony and Cleopatra*,
    4.14.21–2**

    His despairing last resort.

2   The long day's task is done,
    And we must sleep.

    **Antony in *Antony and Cleopatra*,
    4.14.35–6**

    Deciding to die, on hearing of Cleopatra's
    supposed death.

3
　　　Since the torch is out,
Lie down and stray no further.

Antony in *Antony and Cleopatra*,
4.14.46–7

The "torch" is the light of his life, Cleopatra.

4
　　　I will be
A bridegroom in my death, and run
　　into't
As to a lover's bed.

Antony in *Antony and Cleopatra*,
4.14.99–101

Turning suicide into a fantasy of marriage.

5
　　　None but Antony
Should conquer Antony.

Cleopatra in *Antony and Cleopatra*,
4.15.16–17

For her suicide shows the courage to remain
in control of oneself.

6
　　　Is it sin
To rush into the secret house of
　　death
Ere death dare come to us?

Cleopatra in *Antony and Cleopatra*,
4.15.80–2

Contemplating suicide, and perhaps recalling
oddly the biblical injunction against killing, as
at Matthew 5:21.

7
　　　What's brave, what's noble,
Let's do't after the high Roman
　　fashion,
And make death proud to take us.

Cleopatra in *Antony and Cleopatra*,
4.15.86–8

Determined to control her destiny.

8
　　　It is great
To do that thing that ends all other
　　deeds,

Which shackles accidents and bolts
　　up change.

Cleopatra in *Antony and Cleopatra*,
5.2.4–6

Contemplating suicide after Antony's death, in
the Stoic fashion defended by Seneca as a
positive act.

9
　　　Bravest at the last,
She leveled at our purposes, and
　　being royal
Took her own way.

**Octavius Caesar in *Antony and
Cleopatra*, 5.2.335–7**

Finding Cleopatra dead by her own hand.

10
　　　Against self-slaughter
There is a prohibition so divine
That cravens my weak hand.

Imogen in *Cymbeline*, 3.4.76–8

Alluding to the Christian injunction against
suicide.

11
O that this too too solid flesh would
　　melt,
Thaw, and resolve itself into a dew!
Or that the Everlasting had not
　　fixed
His canon 'gainst self-slaughter!

Hamlet in *Hamlet*, 1.2.129–32

"Canon" = the Sixth Commandment, "Thou
shalt not kill"; "solid" puns on "sullied," cont-
aminated.

12
To be or not to be, that is the ques-
　　tion.

Hamlet in *Hamlet*, 3.1.55

Taken by itself, this most famous of Hamlet's
lines suggests a death-wish, though he goes
on to define the "question" as a choice
between endurance and action (see also
Choice 1).

13
For who would bear the whips and
　　scorns of time,

Th'oppressor's wrong, the proud
   man's contumely,
The pangs of despised love, the
   law's delay,
The insolence of office, and the
   spurns
That patient merit of the unworthy
   takes,
When he himself might his quietus
   make
With a bare bodkin.

Hamlet in Hamlet, 3.1.69–75

A bodkin could mean a dagger, or even a pin for the hair; "contumely" = contemptuous abuse.

14   I am more an antique Roman than
     a Dane.

Horatio in Hamlet, 5.2.341

Meaning he chooses the Stoic path of suicide, recommended by Seneca, rather than the modern Christian one of survival.

15   Life, being weary of these worldly
     bars,
     Never lacks power to dismiss itself.

Cassius in Julius Caesar, 1.3.96–7

A Stoic attitude that sees suicide positively as having power over oneself.

16   Why should I play the Roman fool
     and die
     On my own sword?

Macbeth in Macbeth, 5.8.1–2

Suicide was advocated by the Roman Stoics, notably Seneca.

Summer, see Seasons

Sunrise (see also Dawn)

1   Hark, hark, the lark at heaven's gate
     sings,

And Phoebus 'gins arise,
His steeds to water at those springs
On chaliced flowers that lies;
And winking Mary-buds begin to
   ope their golden eyes;
With everything that pretty is, my
   lady sweet, arise;
Arise, arise!

Song in Cymbeline, 2.3.20–26

Sung to wake Imogen.

2   But we are spirits of another sort.
     I with the morning's love have oft
      made sport,
     And like a forester the groves may
      tread
     Even till the eastern gate, all fiery-
      red,
     Opening on Neptune with fair
      blessèd beams,
     Turns into yellow gold his salt
      green streams.

Oberon in A Midsummer Night's Dream, 3.2.388–93

The fairies, being benign spirits, do not have to disappear with the dawn, but can greet the rising sun that changes the color of the sea (Neptune).

3   All the world is cheered by the
     sun.

King Richard in Richard III, 1.2.129

So, he claims, he is cheered by the beauty of Anne.

4   All so soon as the all-cheering sun
     Should in the farthest east begin to
      draw
     The shady curtains from Aurora's
      bed.

Montague in Romeo and Juliet, 1.1.134–6

5   But soft, what light through yonder
window breaks?
It is the east, and Juliet is the sun.

Romeo in *Romeo and Juliet*, 2.2.2–3

Looking up as a light appears in Juliet's
window.

6   Full many a glorious morning have
I seen
Flatter the mountain tops with sov-
ereign eye.

***Sonnet 33*, 1–2**

The "sovereign eye" is the sun, soon to be
covered by clouds.

7   Lo here the gentle lark, weary of
rest,
From his moist cabinet mounts up
on high,
And wakes the morning, from
whose silver breast
The sun ariseth in his majesty,
Who doth the world so gloriously
behold
That cedar tops and hills seem
burnished gold.

***Venus and Adonis*, 853–8**

In these beautiful lines, the lark is imaged as
soaring from its damp or dewy nest ("moist
cabinet") as the sun (Apollo) rises from the
breast of his lover, the dawn (Aurora).

Sunset

1   The west yet glimmers with some
streaks of day.
Now spurs the lated traveler apace
To gain the timely inn.

First Murderer in *Macbeth*, 3.3.5–7

2   The weary sun hath made a golden
set,
And by the bright track of his fiery
car

Gives token of a goodly day tomorrow.

Richmond in *Richard III*, 5.3.19–21

Cheerfully anticipating victory in the battle
with Richard the next morning.

3   The sun begins to gild the western
sky.

**Eglamour in *The Two Gentlemen of
Verona*, 5.1.1**

The Supernatural

1   *Glendower.* I can call spirits from
the vasty deep.
Hotspur. Why, so can I, or so can
any man.
But will they come when you do
call for them?

***Henry IV, Part 1*, 3.1.52–4**

Glendower's claims undermined; "vasty
deep" = great abyss, the underworld.

2   *First Witch.* When shall we three
meet again?
In thunder, lightning, or in rain?
Second Witch. When the hurly-
burly's done,
When the battle's lost and won.
Third Witch. That will be ere set of
sun.
First Witch. Where the place?
Second Witch.   Upon the
heath.
Third Witch. There to meet with
Macbeth.

***Macbeth*, 1.1.1–7**

"Hurly-burly" = tumult of war.

3   What are these
So withered and so wild in their
attire,
That look not like th' inhabitants o'
th' earth,

And yet are on't?

Banquo in *Macbeth*, 1.3.39–42

On first seeing the three Witches.

4 This supernatural soliciting
Cannot be ill; cannot be good.

Macbeth in *Macbeth*, 1.3.130–1

Reflecting on what the Weird Sisters have told him.

Superstition

1 He is superstitious grown of late,
Quite from the main opinion he
held once
Of fantasy, of dreams, and cere-
monies.

Cassius in *Julius Caesar*, 2.1.195–7

Claiming that Caesar has changed his basic opinion about things imagined ("fantasy"), dreams, and divination based on ceremonial rites.

Suspicion

1 The bird that hath been limèd in a
bush
With trembling wings misdoubteth
every bush.

**King Henry in *Henry VI, Part 3*,
5.6.13–14**

"Limèd" = caught with birdlime; "misdoubteth" = suspects; the idea is proverbial.

2 Is whispering nothing?
Is leaning cheek to cheek? Is meeting noses?
Kissing with inside lip? Stopping
the career
Of laughter with a sigh?—A note
infallible

Of breaking honesty.

Leontes in *The Winter's Tale*, 1.2.284–8

Evidence to him that his wife's chastity ("honesty") is suspect; "career" = full gallop.

Swimming

1 I saw him beat the surges under
him,
And ride upon their backs. He trod
the water,
Whose enmity he flung aside, and
breasted
The surge most swoll'n that met
him.

Francisco in *The Tempest*, 2.1.115–18

Telling Alonso that his son may be safe.

2 His bold head
'Bove the contentious waves he
kept, and oared
Himself with his good arms in lusty
stroke
To the shore.

Francisco in *The Tempest*, 2.1.118–21

Describing Ferdinand swimming from the
shipwreck.

Sympathy

1 Hast thou, which art but air, a
touch, a feeling
Of their afflictions, and shall not
myself,
One of their kind, that relish all as
sharply
Passion as they, be kindlier moved
than thou art?

Prospero in *The Tempest*, 5.1.21–4

To Ariel, who has encouraged Prospero to
have pity on his enemies.

Talking (see also Speech, Words)

1 I love not many words.

Parolles in *All's Well That Ends Well*, 3.6.84

The braggart whose very name means "words" protests that he is not a talker.

2 He talks well—
But what care I for words?

Phebe in *As You Like It*, 3.5.110–1

She is attracted to Rosalind, disguised as a man.

3 These are but wild and whirling words, my lord.

Horatio in *Hamlet*, 1.5.133

Commenting on Hamlet's overexcited response to seeing the ghost of his father.

4 If I chance to talk a little wild, forgive me;
I had it from my father.

Lord Sands in *Henry VIII*, 1.4.26–7

He is being bold with the court ladies.

5 Agèd ears play truant at his tales,
And younger hearings are quite ravishèd,
So sweet and voluble is his discourse.

Rosaline in *Love's Labor's Lost*, 2.1.74–6

Praising Berowne; "play truant" = cease to attend to serious business; "voluble" = lively, quick.

6 A gentleman, Nurse, that loves to hear himself talk, and will speak more in a minute than he will stand to in a month.

Romeo in *Romeo and Juliet*, 2.4.147–9

Describing his friend Mercutio to the Nurse; "stand to" = defend.

7 What, this gentleman will out-talk us all.

Gremio in *The Taming of the Shrew*, 1.2.246

On hearing Tranio, disguised as Lucentio, offering to woo Bianca.

Tears

1 The April's in her eyes, it is love's spring,
And these the showers to bring it on.

Antony in *Antony and Cleopatra*, 3.2.43–4

On Octavia weeping as she parts from her brother, Octavius Caesar.

2 Fall not a tear, I say, one of them rates
All that is won and lost.

Antony in *Antony and Cleopatra*, 3.11.69–70

Spoken to the penitent Cleopatra after the Battle of Actium; "Fall" = let fall.

3 The big round tears
Coursed one another down his innocent nose
In piteous chase.

First Lord in *As You Like It*, 2.1.38–40

Describing the weeping of a wounded stag.

4 At a few drops of women's rheum, which are
As cheap as lies, he sold the blood and labor
Of our great action.

Aufidius in *Coriolanus*, 5.6.45–7

Speaking of Coriolanus, who yielded to the entreaties of his wife and mother to spare Rome; "rheum" = tears.

5   There will be a world of water shed
    Upon the parting of your wives and
      you.

Glendower in *Henry IV, Part 1*, 3.1.93–4

He is to bring the rebels' wives to take leave
before the wars.

6   All my mother came into mine eyes
    And gave me up to tears.

Exeter in *Henry V*, 4.6.31–2

On the death in battle of Suffolk and York.

7   I did not think to shed a tear
    In all my miseries; but thou hast
      forced me,
    Out of thy honest truth, to play the
      woman.

**Cardinal Wolsey in *Henry VIII*,
3.2.428–30**

To his devoted supporter Cromwell.

8   If you have tears, prepare to shed
      them now.

Mark Antony in *Julius Caesar*, 3.2.169

Displaying the body of Caesar to the people.

9   I am ashamed
    That thou hast power to shake my
      manhood thus,
    That these hot tears, which break
      from me perforce,
    Should make thee worth them.

King Lear in *King Lear*, 1.4.296–9

In distress at the way his daughter Goneril has
been treating him.

10   Touch me with noble anger,
    And let not women's weapons,
      water-drops,
    Stain my man's cheeks!

King Lear in *King Lear*, 2.4.276–8

Reacting to the rejection of him by his daughters, Goneril and Regan.

11   You think I'll weep:
    No, I'll not weep.
    I have full cause of weeping, but
      this heart
    Shall break into a hundred thou-
      sand flaws
    Or ere I'll weep.

King Lear in *King Lear*, 2.4.282–6

The old king in fact is impotent to do more
than weep and curse; "flaws" = fragments; "or
ere" = before.

12   You have seen
    Sunshine and rain at once; her
      smiles and tears
    Were like a better way: those happy
      smilets
    That played on her ripe lip seemed
      not to know
    What guests were in her eyes, which
      parted thence
    As pearls from diamonds dropped.

Gentleman in *King Lear*, 4.3.17–22

Cordelia here becomes an emblem of pity;
"like" = alike.

13   How much better is it to weep at
    joy than to joy at weeping!

**Leonato in *Much Ado About Nothing*,
1.1.27–9**

On Claudio's uncle, who weeps for joy that
his nephew is safe.

14   If that the earth could teem with
      woman's tears,
    Each drop she falls would prove a
      crocodile.

Othello in *Othello*, 4.1.245–6

Accusing Desdemona of deception; crocodiles proverbially shed hypocritical tears over
their victims.

15 His tears runs down his beard like
winter's drops
From eaves of reeds.

Ariel in *The Tempest*, 5.1.16–17

Referring to old Gonzalo, whose tears show
his pity for the madness afflicting Alonso.

16 Tears harden lust, though marble
wear with raining.

***The Rape of Lucrece*, 560**

The effect on Tarquin of Lucrece's tears.

Tediousness

1   O, he is as tedious
As a tired horse, a railing wife,
Worse than a smoky house.

Hotspur in *Henry IV, Part 1*, 3.1.157–9

Meaning Glendower.

2 Life is as tedious as a twice-told tale,
Vexing the dull ear of a drowsy
man.

Lewis the Dauphin in *King John*,
3.4.108–9

3 This will last out a night in Russia
When nights are longest there.

Angelo in *Measure for Measure*,
2.1.134–5

Bored with the interrogation of the bawd,
Pompey.

4 *Dogberry.* If I were as tedious as a
king, I could find in my heart to
bestow it all on your worship.
Leonato. All thy tediousness on me,
ha?

***Much Ado About Nothing*, 3.5.21–3**

Dogberry seems to think "tedious" means
"wealthy"; Leonato is indeed finding him very
tedious.

Temperament (see also Melancholy, Moods)

1 My master is of churlish disposition,
And little recks to find the way to
heaven
By doing deeds of hospitality.

Corin in *As You Like It*, 2.4.80–82

"Recks" means cares.

2   Blest are those
Whose blood and judgment are so
well commingled
That they are not a pipe for For-
tune's finger
To sound what stop she please.

Hamlet in *Hamlet*, 3.2.68–71

Referring to Horatio; "blood" = passions;
"commingled" = mixed.

3   Give me that man
That is not passion's slave, and I
will wear him
In my heart's core, ay, in my heart
of heart,
As I do thee.

Hamlet in *Hamlet*, 3.2.71–4

Praising Horatio.

4 I am now of all humors that have
showed themselves humors since
the old days of goodman Adam to
the pupil age of this present twelve
o'clock at midnight.

Prince Hal in *Henry IV, Part 1*,
2.4.92–5

Feeling ready for anything; "goodman" =
farmer or gardener.

Temperance

1   I am sure,
Though you can guess what tem-
     perance should be,
You know not what it is.

Antony in *Antony and Cleopatra*,
3.13.120–2

Criticizing Cleopatra.

Temptation

1   Why do I yield to that suggestion
Whose horrid image doth unfix my
     hair
And make my seated heart knock at
     my ribs
Against the use of nature?

Macbeth in *Macbeth*, 1.3.134–7

The "horrid image" is the idea of murdering
King Duncan.

2   'Tis one thing to be tempted,
     Escalus,
Another thing to fall.

Angelo in *Measure for Measure*,
2.1.17–18

To Escalus, who has been pleading for Claudio, sentenced to death by Angelo for getting
Juliet with child.

3   What's this, what's this? Is it her
     fault or mine?
The tempter, or the tempted, who
     sins most, ha?

Angelo in *Measure for Measure*,
2.2.162–3

Finding he is sexually attracted by the novice,
Isabella.

4   O cunning enemy, that to catch a
     saint,
With saints doth bait thy hook!
     Most dangerous
Is that temptation that doth goad
     us on
To sin in loving virtue.

Angelo in *Measure for Measure*,
2.2.179–82

Angelo imagines Satan (the "enemy") as causing him to be attracted sexually by Isabella.

5   But something may be done that we
     will not,
And sometimes we are devils to
     ourselves,
When we will tempt the frailty of
     our powers,
Presuming on their changeful
     potency.

Troilus in *Troilus and Cressida*, 4.4.94–7

Anxious about Cressida's promise to be faithful to him; "changeful potency" = unstable
strength.

Thanks

1   I thank you. I am not of many
     words, but I thank you.

**Don John in *Much Ado About
Nothing*, 1.1.157–8**

On being welcomed by Leonato, Don John
establishes his taciturn nature.

2   I greet thy love,
Not with vain thanks, but with
     acceptance bounteous.

Othello in *Othello*, 3.3.469–70

Accepting Iago's offer to do anything, even
murder, for him.

3   My recompense is thanks, that's all,
    Yet my good will is great, though
        the gift small.

Thaisa in *Pericles*, 3.4.17–18

To Cerimon, who has brought her back to life.

4   Evermore thanks, the exchequer of
        the poor.

Bolingbroke in *Richard II*, 2.3.65

Having no other reward to give; "exchequer"
= treasury, purse.

5   The poorest service is repaid with
        thanks.

**Petruchio in *The Taming of the Shrew*,
4.3.45**

Demanding that Katherine thank him before
she gets anything to eat.

6   I can no other answer make but
        thanks,
    And thanks.

Sebastian in *Twelfth Night*, 3.3.14–15

Thanking his friend Antonio.

Theater (see also Acting, Plays)

1   The quick comedians
    Extemporally will stage us, and pre-
        sent
    Our Alexandrian revels: Antony
    Shall be brought drunken forth,
        and I shall see
    Some squeaking Cleopatra boy my
        greatness
    I' the posture of a whore.

**Cleopatra in *Antony and Cleopatra*,
5.2.216–21**

A direct allusion to Shakespeare's own theater, in which female characters were played
by boy actors.

2   This wide and universal theatre
    Presents more woeful pageants than
        the scene
    Wherein we play in.

Duke Senior in *As You Like It*, 2.7.136–9

He has just heard from Orlando of Adam's
sufferings from age and hunger; Shakespeare
exploits the traditional idea of the world as a
theater.

3   All the world's a stage,
    And all the men and women merely
        players;
    They have their exits and their
        entrances,
    And one man in his time plays
        many parts,
    His acts being seven ages.

Jaques in *As You Like It*, 2.7.139–43

A most brilliant formulation of a proverbial
idea.

4   I have heard
    That guilty creatures sitting at a
        play
    Have by the very cunning of the
        scene
    Been struck so to the soul, that
        presently
    They have proclaimed their male-
        factions.

Hamlet in *Hamlet*, 2.2.588–92

Thinking of ways to expose Claudius's guilt;
"malefactions" = crimes, evil-doing.

5   O for a Muse of fire, that would
        ascend
    The brightest heaven of invention!

A kingdom for a stage, princes to
act,
And monarchs to behold the
swelling scene!

Chorus in *Henry V*, 1.1–4

"Invention" = poetic imagination.

6   Can this cockpit hold
The vasty fields of France? Or may
we cram
Within this wooden O the very
casques
That did affright the air at Agincourt?

Chorus in *Henry V*, 1.11–14

The "wooden O" refers to multi-sided theaters
like the Globe, where Shakespeare's plays
were staged; "casques" = helmets.

7   Thus with imagined wing our swift
scene flies
In motion of no less celerity
Than that of thought.

Chorus in *Henry V*, 3.1–3

"As swift as thought" was proverbial.

8   Sit and see,
Minding true things by what their
mockeries be.

Chorus in *Henry V*, 4.52–3

Asking the audience to imagine the battle of
Agincourt as it really happened.

9   Thus far with rough and all-unable
pen
Our bending author hath pursued
the story,
In little room confining mighty
men.

Chorus in *Henry V*, 5.Epilogue, 1–3

The "little room" refers to the theater.

10   *Brutus.* How many times shall Caesar bleed in sport,
That now on Pompey's basis lies
along,
No worthier than the dust!
Cassius.   So oft as that shall
be,
So often shall the knot of us be
called
The men that gave their country
liberty.

Julius Caesar, 3.1.114–18

Caesar's body is supposed to have fallen at the
base of the statue of his old enemy, Pompey.

11   *Quince.* Marry, our play is "The
most lamentable comedy and
most cruel death of Pyramus and
Thisbe."
Bottom. A very good piece of work,
I assure you, and a merry.

A Midsummer Night's Dream, 1.2.11–14

Shakespeare was mocking a fashion for elaborate titles that confounded genres, such as the
"Tragical Comedy of Apius and Virginia"
(1575).

12   Here's a marvelous convenient
place for our rehearsal.

Quince in *A Midsummer Night's
Dream*, 3.1.2–3

13   "A tedious brief scene of young
Pyramus
And his love Thisbe, very tragical
mirth"—
Merry and tragical? Tedious and
brief?
That is hot ice and wondrous
strange snow!

Theseus in *A Midsummer Night's
Dream*, 5.1.56–9

The absurd title of the play put on by Bottom,
Quince and their crew parodies the titles of
some earlier Elizabethan plays.

14 A play there is, my lord, some ten
   words long,
   Which is as brief as I have known a
      play,
   But by ten words, my lord, it is too
      long,
   Which makes it tedious.

Philostrate in *A Midsummer Night's*
Dream, 5.1.61–4

Advising Theseus not to watch "Pyramus and
Thisbe."

15 No epilogue, I pray you; for your
   play needs no excuse. Never excuse;
   for when the players are all dead,
   there need none to be blamed.

Theseus in *A Midsummer Night's*
Dream, 5.1.355–7

Speaking to the players after watching "Pyramus and Thisbe"; the players are "dead" at the
end of the tragedy.

16 If we shadows have offended,
   Think but this, and all is mended,
   That you have but slumbered here
   While these visions did appear.

Puck in *A Midsummer Night's Dream*,
5.1.423–6

The word shadow was often opposed to substance; so spirits were shadows, and so were
actors playing roles; the word also suggests
the illusions of the theater.

17 As in a theater the eyes of men,
   After a well-graced actor leaves the
      stage,
   Are idly bent on him that enters
      next,
   Thinking his prattle to be tedious,
   Even so, or with much more con-
      tempt, men's eyes
   Did scowl on gentle Richard.

York in *Richard II*, 5.2.23–8

Commenting on the disrespect shown to
Richard by the people of London.

18 The two hours' traffic of our stage.

Chorus in *Romeo and Juliet*, **Prologue,**
12

Suggesting how swift the action of a play was
on Shakespeare's stage.

19 If this were played upon a stage
   now, I could condemn it as an
   improbable fiction.

Fabian in *Twelfth Night*, 3.4.127–8

Referring to Malvolio's absurd confidence that
Olivia is in love with him.

20 A great while ago the world begun,
   With hey, ho, the wind and the
      rain,
   But that's all one, our play is done,
   And we'll strive to please you every
      day.

Feste in *Twelfth Night*, 5.1.405–8

Bringing the play to an end on a slight note of
melancholy.

Theft

1 *Prince Hal.* I see a good amendment of life in thee, from praying
   to purse-taking.
   Falstaff. Why, Hal, 'tis my vocation, Hal; 'tis no sin for a man to
   labor in his vocation.

Henry IV, Part 1, 1.2.102–5

Falstaff wittily invokes a biblical echo of Ephesians 4:1, "beseech you that ye walk worthy
of the vocation wherewith ye are called."

2 Rob me the exchequer the first
   thing thou dost, and do it with
   unwashed hands too.

Falstaff in *Henry IV, Part 1*, 3.3.183–4

To Prince Hal now that he is reconciled with
the king.

3   They will steal anything, and call it
    purchase.

Boy in *Henry V*, 3.2.41–2

Referring to Nym, Bardolph and Pistol; "purchase" = plunder.

4   They would have me as familiar
    with men's pockets as their gloves
    or their handkerchiefs; which
    makes much against my manhood,
    if I should take from another's
    pocket to put into mine; for it is
    plain pocketing up of wrongs.

Boy in *Henry V*, 3.2.47–51

His employers, Nym, Bardolph and Pistol,
would turn the boy into a pickpocket.

5   To England will I steal, and there
    I'll steal.

Pistol in *Henry V*, 5.1.87

Humiliated in France, he plans to steal off to
England.

6   Thieves for their robbery have
    authority
    When judges steal themselves.

**Angelo in *Measure for Measure*,
2.2.175–6**

The hitherto upright judge finds he cannot
control his lust for Isabella.

7   If you meet a thief, you may suspect
    him, by virtue of your office, to be
    no true man.

**Dogberry in *Much Ado About
Nothing*, 3.3.50–1**

Comically laying down the law.

8   The most peaceable way for you, if
    you do take a thief, is to let him

show himself what he is and steal
out of your company.

**Dogberry in *Much Ado About
Nothing*, 3.3.57–60**

The incompetent constable instructs the
watchmen who patrol the town at night.

9   The robbed that smiles steals some-
    thing from the thief.

Duke in *Othello*, 1.3.208

Advising Brabantio to accept the loss of his
daughter, Desdemona.

10 He that is robbed, not wanting
    what is stolen,
    Let him not know't, and he's not
    robbed at all.

Othello in *Othello*, 3.3.342–3

"Wanting" = missing; the idea became
proverbial.

11   I'll example you with
        thievery:
    The sun's a thief, and with his great
        attraction
    Robs the vast sea; the moon's an
        arrant thief,
    And her pale fire she snatches from
        the sun.

Timon in *Timon of Athens*, 4.3.435–8

Timon seeks to prove everything in nature is a
thief. Nabokov used the phrase "pale fire" as
the title of a novel.

12 My father named me Autolycus,
    who being, as I am, littered under
    Mercury, was likewise a snapper-up
    of unconsidered trifles.

**Autolycus in *The Winter's Tale*,
4.3.24–6**

Mercury was the god of thieves; in the
Odyssey, Autolycus, the grandfather of
Ulysses, was supposed to be a son of Mer-
cury.

Thinness

1 When I was about thy years, Hal, I was not an eagle's talon in the waist, I could have crept into any alderman's thumb-ring. A plague of sighing and grief, it blows a man up like a bladder.

Falstaff in *Henry IV, Part 1*, 2.4.329–33

2 Do I not bate? Do I not dwindle? Why, my skin hangs about me like an old lady's loose gown; I am withered like an old apple-john.

Falstaff in *Henry IV, Part 1*, 3.3.2–4

"Bate" = abate, grow thin; "apple-john" = kind of apple which was kept until the skin shriveled.

3 I am famished in his service; you may tell every finger I have with my ribs.

Launcelot Gobbo in *The Merchant of Venice*, 2.2.106–7

Launcelot is servant to Shylock; "tell" = count.

4 I am not tall enough to become the function well, nor lean enough to be thought a good student.

Feste in *Twelfth Night*, 4.2.6–8

About to put on a gown and pretend to be the curate, Sir Topas; the typical student was assumed to be poor and thin.

5 You'd be so lean that blasts of January
Would blow you through and through.

Perdita in *The Winter's Tale*, 4.4.111–12

To Camillo, who is so taken by her beauty that he says he could feed by staring at her.

Thought

1 *Rosalind.* There's a girl goes before the priest, and certainly a woman's thought runs before her actions.
Orlando. So do all thoughts, they are winged.

As You Like It, 4.1.139–42

Disguised as a man, Rosalind gets Celia to "marry" her to Orlando; does he penetrate her disguise?

2   Pacing through the forest,
Chewing the food of sweet and bitter fancy.

Oliver in *As You Like It*, 4.3.100–1

On Orlando mulling over his thoughts of love ("fancy").

3 Our thoughts are ours, their ends none of our own.

Player King in *Hamlet*, 3.2.213

On the gap between thoughts and deeds.

4 *Prince Hal.* I never thought to hear you speak again.
King Henry. Thy wish was father, Harry, to that thought.

Henry IV, Part 2, 4.5.91–2

The king thinks his son wished him dead.

5 Thus with imagined wing our swift scene flies
In motion of no less celerity
Than that of thought.

Chorus in *Henry V*, 3.Prologue, 1–3

"As swift as thought" was proverbial.

6 In the quick forge and working-house of thought.

Chorus in *Henry V*, 5.Prologue, 23

A fine image of the working of the imagination.

7 My thoughts are whirlèd like a potter's wheel,
I know not where I am, nor what I do.

Talbot in *Henry VI, Part 1*, 1.5.19–20

He is amazed at the power shown by Joan la Pucelle (Joan of Arc) in fighting him.

8 Faster than springtime showers comes thought on thought.

York in *Henry VI, Part 2*, 3.1.337

Brooding on his ambition for the throne.

9 I hear, yet say not much, but think the more.

Richard of Gloucester in *Henry VI, Part 3*, 4.1.83

Richard stirs up quarrels at court while watching for his chance to seize power.

10 My noble friend, chew upon this.

Brutus in *Julius Caesar*, 1.2.171

To Cassius; "chew" = ruminate, reflect.

11 　　　Merciful powers,
Restrain in me the cursèd thoughts that nature
Gives way to in repose!

Banquo in *Macbeth*, 2.1.7–9

"Powers" may refer to the order of angels deputed to resist demons; the orders are listed in John Milton's *Paradise Lost*, V.601, as "Thrones, Dominations, Princedoms, Virtues, Powers."

12 　　　By heaven, he echoes me,
As if there were some monster in his thought

Too hideous to be shown.

Othello in *Othello*, 3.3.106–8

Iago echoes the suspicion already forming in Othello's thought.

13 Thought is free.

Maria in *Twelfth Night*, 1.3.69

To Sir Andrew Aguecheek, meaning "you may think what you like"; proverbial.

14 Thoughts are but dreams till their effects be tried.

***The Rape of Lucrece*, 353**

Thrift

1 Thrift, thrift, Horatio; the funeral baked meats
Did coldly furnish forth the marriage tables.

Hamlet in *Hamlet*, 1.2.180–1

Horatio has remarked that Hamlet's mother married again soon after her first husband's death; "coldly" = when cold.

2 This was a way to thrive, and he was blest;
And thrift is blessing, if men steal it not.

Shylock in *The Merchant of Venice*, 1.3.89–90

Defending usury by reference to Jacob's skill in increasing his flocks of sheep and goats (Genesis 30:32–43).

3 　　　Fast bind, fast find,
A proverb never stale in thrifty mind.

Shylock in *The Merchant of Venice*, 2.5.54–5

Meaning keep things secure and they are readily found.

Time

1   Let's take the instant by the forward
   top;
   For we are old, and on our quick'st
   decrees
   Th'inaudible and noiseless foot of
   time
   Steals ere we can effect them.

**King of France in *All's Well That Ends
Well*, 5.3.40–2**

Being old, he must move quickly if he is to
see the results of his actions; compare the
proverb, "seize Occasion by the forelock, for
she is bald behind."

2   'Tis but an hour ago since it was
   nine,
   And after one hour more 'twill be
   eleven,
   And so from hour to hour, we ripe
   and ripe,
   And then from hour to hour, we
   rot and rot;
   And thereby hangs a tale.

Jaques in *As You Like It*, 2.7.24–8

Quoting Touchstone's basic view of life.

3   Whate'er you are
   That in this desert inaccessible,
   Under the shade of melancholy
   boughs,
   Lose and neglect the creeping hours
   of time.

Orlando in *As You Like It*, 2.7.109–12

Meeting Duke Senior's company in the forest
of Arden, he sees them as wasting time.

4   *Rosalind.* I pray you, what is't
   o'clock?
   Orlando. You should ask me what
   time o' day; there's no clock in the
   forest.

As You Like It, 3.2.299–305

Time is measured by clocks in the world of
business and the court, not in the forest of
Arden.

5   Time travels in divers paces with
   divers persons.

Rosalind in *As You Like It*, 3.2.308–9

Time passes at different speeds according to
the person.

6   *Orlando.* Who stays it still withal?
   Rosalind. With lawyers in the vacation; for they sleep between term
   and term, and then they perceive
   not how Time moves.

As You Like It, 3.2.330–3

On the perception of time, mocking lawyers.

7   There's a time for all things.

**Antipholus of Syracuse in *The Com-
edy of Errors*, 2.2.65**

Proverbial; from Ecclesiastes 3:1, "To every
thing there is a season."

8   Time is a very bankrupt and owes
   more than he's worth to season.
   Nay, he's a thief too: have you not
   heard men say,
   That Time comes stealing on by
   night and day?

**Dromio of Syracuse in *The Comedy of
Errors*, 4.2.58–60**

Time proverbially steals away; "season" =
opportunity, with a quibble on "seizing," link-
ing with "thief."

9   But thoughts, the slaves of life, and
   life, time's fool,
   And time, that takes survey of all
   the world,
   Must have a stop.

Hotspur in *Henry IV, Part 1*, 5.4.80–3

He is dying as he speaks these words.

10 Past and to come seems best; things present, worst.

Archbishop of York in *Henry IV, Part 2*, 1.3.108

Everything seems to be at its worst for the rebels.

11 We are time's subjects, and time bids be gone.

Hastings in *Henry IV, Part 2*, 1.3.110

Time calls on the rebels to act, not to go on talking.

12 Well, thus we play the fools with the time, and the spirits of the wise sit in the clouds and mock us.

Prince Hal in *Henry IV, Part 2*, 2.2.142–3

Recognizing that in fooling with his tavern companions he is wasting time.

13   I feel me much to blame
So idly to profane the precious time.

Prince Hal in *Henry IV, Part 2*, 2.4.361–2

News of war makes Hal realize he is wasting time; "profane" = violate, treat with contempt.

14 We see which way the stream of time doth run.

Archbishop of York in *Henry IV, Part 2*, 4.2.70

Accepting what is inevitable.

15   Now he weighs time
Even to the utmost grain.

Exeter in *Henry V*, 2.4.137–8

Recalling how as Prince Hal, Henry wasted time; a grain is the smallest unit of weight.

16 Old Time the clock-setter, that bald sexton Time!

The Bastard Falconbridge in *King John*, 3.1.324

Referring both to the proverb, "Take occasion/time by the forelock for she/he is bald behind," and also to time as bringing death, since the sexton often doubled as grave-digger.

17 Time shall unfold what plighted cunning hides,
Who covert faults at last with shame derides.

Cordelia in *King Lear*, 1.1.280–1

Compare the proverb, "Time brings truth to light"; "plighted" = pleated.

18   Come what come may,
Time and the hour runs through the roughest day.

Macbeth in *Macbeth*, 1.3.146–7

Recalling the proverb, "time and tide stay for no man."

19 *Seyton.* The Queen, my lord, is dead.
Macbeth. She should have died hereafter;
There would have been a time for such a word.—
Tomorrow, and tomorrow, and tomorrow,
Creeps in this petty pace from day to day,
To the last syllable of recorded time;
And all our yesterdays have lighted fools
The way to dusty death.

Macbeth, 5.5.16–23

Macbeth has lost the ability to feel grief, or any emotion. The lines gain power from the common biblical associations of light with life, and of the body with dust; see, for example, Ecclesiastes 3:20, "All go unto one place; all are of the dust, and all turn to dust again."

20 There are many events in the womb of time which will be delivered.

Iago in *Othello*, 1.3.369–70

21 What, keep a week away? Seven days and nights,
Eightscore-eight hours, and lovers' absent hours
More tedious than the dial eightscore times!
A weary reckoning!

Bianca in *Othello*, 3.4.173–6

On Cassio's neglect of her.

22 I see that Time's the king of men;
He's both their parent, and he is their grave,
And gives them what he will, not what they crave.

Pericles in *Pericles*, 2.3.45–7

After suffering misfortunes, Pericles, against expectations, wins a tournament and a bride.

23 O call back yesterday, bid time return!

Salisbury in *Richard II*, 3.2.69

Reporting that the Welsh have deserted Richard.

24 I wasted time, and now doth time waste me.

King Richard in *Richard II*, 5.5.49

Playing on "waste" as meaning 1. squander; 2. wear away and destroy.

25 Sad hours seem long.

Romeo in *Romeo and Juliet*, 1.1.161

The lovelorn Romeo finds time hangs on his hands.

26 The bawdy hand of the dial is now upon the prick of noon.

Mercutio in *Romeo and Juliet*, 2.4.112–13

Teasing Juliet's nurse, who is something of a bawd.

27 Now is the sun upon the highmost hill
Of this day's journey.

Juliet in *Romeo and Juliet*, 2.5.9–10

It is noon, and she has been waiting three hours for her nurse to return.

28 Time hath, my lord, a wallet at his back,
Wherein he puts alms for oblivion,
A great-sized monster of ingratitudes:
Those scraps are good deeds past, which are devoured
As fast as they are made, forgot as soon
As done.

Ulysses in *Troilus and Cressida*, 3.3.145–50

Trying to persuade the idle Achilles to fight again for the Greeks; Time was often personified as an old man.

29 Time is like a fashionable host,
That slightly shakes his parting guest by the hand,
And with his arms outstretched, as he would fly,
Grasps in the comer: the welcome ever smiles,
And farewell goes out sighing.

Ulysses in *Troilus and Cressida*, 3.3.165–9

Telling Achilles that his past achievements are soon forgotten.

30 For beauty, wit,
High birth, vigor of bone, desert in service,

Love, friendship, charity, are subjects all
To envious and calumniating time.

Ulysses in *Troilus and Cressida*,
3.3.171–4

Inviting Achilles to contemplate the brevity of
life and all human attributes in an effort to get
him to fight.

31 Injurious Time now, with a rob-
ber's haste,
Crams his rich thievery up, he
knows not how;
As many farewells as be stars in
heaven,
With distinct breath and consigned
kisses to them,
He fumbles up into a loose adieu,
And scants us with a single famished kiss,
Distasted with the salt of broken
tears.

Troilus in *Troilus and Cressida*, 4.4.42–8

On parting from Cressida; "he knows not
how" = indiscriminately; numberless
farewells, each with its kisses, are crammed
into a casual ("loose") parting.

32 *Aeneas.* 'Tis the old Nestor.
Hector. Let me embrace thee, good
old chronicle,
That hast so long walked hand in
hand with time.

***Troilus and Cressida*,** 4.5.201–3

Aeneas is introducing Hector to the Greek
warriors during a truce.

33 The end crowns all;
And that old common arbitrator,
Time,
Will one day end it.

Hector in *Troilus and Cressida*,
4.5.224–6

Refusing to accept Ulysses's prophecy that
Troy will fall.

34 What else may hap, to time I will
commit.

Viola in *Twelfth Night*, 1.2.60

"Hap" = chance to happen.

35 O time, thou must untangle this,
not I.
It is too hard a knot for me t'untie.

Viola in *Twelfth Night*, 2.2.40–1

On realizing that Olivia has fallen in love with
her, supposing her to be a man (Cesario).

36 The clock upbraids me with a waste
of time.

Olivia in *Twelfth Night*, 3.1.130

Conscious of spending too much time with
Cesario (the disguised Viola).

37 Thus the whirligig of time brings in
his revenges.

Feste in *Twelfth Night*, 5.1.376–7

Marking the comeuppance afflicted on Malvolio; a "whirligig" is a spinning top.

38 Time is the nurse and breeder of all
good.

**Proteus in *The Two Gentlemen of
Verona*, 3.1.245**

A truism perhaps, but he is in the act of
deceiving his friend Valentine.

39 I that please some, try all, both joy
and terror
Of good and bad, that makes and
unfolds error.

Time in *The Winter's Tale*, 4.1.1–2

Time, the Chorus, proclaims his proverbial
impartiality or indifference in relation to
humanity ("time tries all things").

40 Time's glory is to calm contending kings,
To unmask falsehood and bring truth to light,
To stamp the seal of time in agèd things,
To wake the morn and sentinel the night.

The Rape of Lucrece, 939–42

"Sentinel" = keep guard during.

41 Nothing 'gainst Time's scythe can make defense.

Sonnet 12, 13

A traditional image of time as a reaper.

42 Devouring Time, blunt thou the lion's paws,
And make the earth devour her own sweet brood.

Sonnet 19, 1–2

On Time personified as destructive (Latin "edax rerum," or consuming all things).

43 Like as the waves make towards the pebbled shore,
So do our minutes hasten to their end;
Each changing place with that which goes before,
In sequent toil all forwards do contend.

Sonnet 60, 1–4

The inexorable passage of time is a recurrent theme of Shakespeare's sonnets; here it is as if each minute struggles onward painfully ("in sequent toil").

44 No, Time, thou shalt not boast that I do change;

Thy pyramids built up with newer might
To me are nothing novel, nothing strange;
They are but dressings of a former sight.
Our dates are brief, and therefore we admire
What thou dost foist upon us that is old,
And rather make them born to our desire
Than think that we before have heard them told.

Sonnet 123, 1–8

The pyramids recall ancient Egypt, and may refer also to obelisks or other buildings set up in London; new constructions seem recreations ("dressings") of old ones, and we admire old forms by reinventing them to our taste rather than remembering how we have heard them described ("told").

45 Make use of time, let not advantage slip;
Beauty within itself should not be wasted.
Fair flowers that are gathered in their prime
Rot and consume themselves in little time.

Venus and Adonis, 129–32

Venus is seeking to seduce Adonis by a common plea of lovers; "advantage" = opportunity.

Time of Day

1 In the dead waste and middle of the night.

Horatio in *Hamlet*, 1.2.198

He describes the time when he saw the ghost of Hamlet's father; "waste" suggests barrenness, and could be heard also as "waist" or middle. The earliest text has "vast."

2   But soft, methinks I scent the
morning air,
Brief let me be.

Ghost in *Hamlet*, 1.5.58–9

The ghost has to return to his "prison-house"
by day.

3   The glow-worm shows the matin to
be near,
And 'gins to pale his uneffectual
fire.

Ghost in *Hamlet*, 1.5.89–90

Signaling the end of the interview between
Hamlet and the ghost of his father as day
approaches.

4   What time of day is it, lad?

Falstaff in *Henry IV, Part 1*, 1.2.1

Addressing Prince Hal as "lad" shows the
close relationship between them.

5   What a devil hast thou to do with
the time of the day? Unless hours
were cups of sack, and minutes
capons, and clocks the tongues of
bawds, and dials the signs of leaping-houses, and the blessed sun
himself a fair hot wench in flame-
colored taffeta, I see no reason why
thou shouldst be so superfluous to
demand the time of the day.

Prince Hal in *Henry IV, Part 1*, 1.2.6–12

On Falstaff's feckless way of life, consisting of
drinking ("sack"), eating ("capons" or fowl)
and lechery; "leaping-houses" = brothels.

6   From the rising of the lark to the
lodging of the lamb.

Dauphin in *Henry V*, 3.7.31–2

That is, from dawn to dusk, when the lamb
lies down to sleep.

7   *Macbeth.* What is the night?
Lady Macbeth. Almost at odds with
morning, which is which.

***Macbeth*, 3.4.125–6**

8   The iron tongue of midnight hath
told twelve.
Lovers, to bed; 'tis almost fairy
time.

**Theseus in *A Midsummer Night's
Dream*, 5.1.363–4**

"Iron tongue" = clapper of a bell.

9   'Tis fresh morning with me
When you are by at night.

Ferdinand in *The Tempest*, 3.1.33–4

To Miranda, whom he loves; "by" = nearby.

Timeserving

1   A hovering temporizer,
that
Canst with thine eyes at once see
good and evil,
Inclining to them both.

Leontes in *The Winter's Tale*, 1.2.302–4

His misguided perception of his good coun-
selor, Camillo.

Torture

1   I fear you speak upon the rack,
Where men enforcèd do speak anything.

**Portia in *The Merchant of Venice*,
3.2.32–3**

She fears Bassanio may not be honest in his
protestations of love.

2 What studied torments, tyrant, hast
  for me?
  What wheels, racks, fires? What
   flaying, boiling
  In leads or oils? What old or newer
   torture
  Must I receive, whose every word
   deserves
  To taste of thy most worst?

Paulina in *The Winter's Tale*, 3.2.175–9

Emphasizing what a tyrant Leontes has been, but knowing that he is not really going to punish her now he has come to his senses.

Transformation (see also Change, Mutability)

1   I do not shame
  To tell you what I was, since my
   conversion
  So sweetly tastes, being the thing I
  am.

Oliver in *As You Like It*, 4.3.135–7

Saved from death by his brother, Orlando, the malicious Oliver suddenly becomes gentle and loving.

2   Something have you heard
  Of Hamlet's transformation; so I
   call it,
  Since not th' exterior nor the
   inward man
  Resembles that it was.

Claudius in *Hamlet*, 2.2.4–7

To Rosencrantz and Guildenstern, summoned to try to find out what is troubling Hamlet.

3 Full fathom five thy father lies,
  Of his bones are coral made;
  Those are pearls that were his eyes;
  Nothing of him that doth fade,
  But doth suffer a sea-change

Into something rich and strange.
Sea-nymphs hourly ring his knell:
 Ding-dong.
Hark! Now I hear them—ding-
 dong bell.

Ariel in *The Tempest*, 1.2.397–405

Ariel's best-known song, for Ferdinand's benefit, misleading him about his father, who is not dead; the idea of change or transformation is important in the play.

Transience (see also Change, Mutability)

1 The sun of Rome is set. Our day is
  gone;
  Clouds, dews, and dangers come;
   our deeds are done.

Titinius in *Julius Caesar*, 5.3.63–4

On finding Cassius dead at the battle of Philippi.

2 Swift as a shadow, short as any
  dream,
  Brief as the lightning in the collied
   night,
  That in a spleen unfolds both
   heaven and earth,
  And, ere a man hath power to say
   "Behold!,"
  The jaws of darkness do devour it
   up.
  So quick bright things come to con-
   fusion.

Lysander in *A Midsummer Night's Dream*, 1.1.144–9

On the nature of human love, and life; "collied" = blackened (as with coal dust); "in a spleen" = fit of temper.

3 His rash fierce blaze of riot cannot
  last,
  For violent fires soon burn out
   themselves;

Small showers last long, but sudden
   storms are short.

John of Gaunt in *Richard II*, 2.1.33–5

Referring to Richard.

4 O momentary grace of mortal men,
   Which we more hunt for than the
      grace of God!

Hastings in *Richard III*, 3.4.96–7

Playing on the meanings of "grace" = 1. the
condition of being in favor; 2. divine grace.
Hastings has just been sentenced to death.

5 These violent delights have violent
      ends,
   And in their triumph die, like fire
      and powder,
   Which as they kiss consume.

**Friar Lawrence in *Romeo and Juliet*,
2.6.9–11**

On Romeo and Juliet as they rush into marriage; the Friar's words seem to anticipate
their death.

6 The cloud-capped towers, the gor-
      geous palaces,
   The solemn temples, the great globe
      itself,
   Yea, all which it inherit, shall dis-
      solve,
   And, like this insubstantial pageant
      faded,
   Leave not a rack behind.

Prospero in *The Tempest*, 4.1.152–6

The "globe" may have made Shakespeare's
audience think of the Globe Theatre as well as
the world.

7 When forty winters shall besiege
      thy brow
   And dig deep trenches in thy
      beauty's field,
   Thy youth's proud livery, so gazed
      on now,

Will be a tattered weed of small
   worth held.

***Sonnet* 2, 1–4**

On the speed with which the good looks of
his friend will fade.

Travel

1 *Rosalind.* Well, this is the forest of
      Arden.
   Touchstone. Ay, now am I in
      Arden, the more fool I. When I
      was at home, I was in a better
      place, but travelers must be con-
      tent.

***As You Like It*, 2.4.15–18**

2 I fear you have sold your own lands
   to see other men's; then to have
   seen much, and to have nothing, is
   to have rich eyes and poor hands.

Rosalind in *As You Like It*, 4.1.22–5

To Jaques, defining the true traveler.

3 I'll view the manners of the town,
   Peruse the traders, gaze upon the
      buildings,
   And then return and sleep within
      mine inn,
   For with long travel I am stiff and
      weary.

**Antipholus of Syracuse in *The Com-
edy of Errors*, 1.2.12–15**

On arriving in Ephesus.

4   I will go lose myself,
   And wander up and down to view
      the city.

**Antipholus of Syracuse in *The Com-
edy of Errors*, 1.2.30–1**

The city is Ephesus.

5 They say this town is full of cozenage:
As nimble jugglers that deceive the
eye,
Dark-working sorcerers that change
the mind,
Soul-killing witches that deform the
body,
Disguisèd cheaters, prating mountebanks,
And many such-like liberties of sin.

**Antipholus of Syracuse in *The Com-
edy of Errors*, 1.2.97–102**

The reputation of Ephesus, where Antipholus
has just arrived; "mountebanks" were quack
doctors or charlatans.

6 O for a horse with wings!

Imogen in *Cymbeline*, 3.2.48

Imogen learns that her husband, Posthumus, is
at Milford-Haven.

7 Whither I go, thither shall you go
too;
Today will I set forth, tomorrow
you.

Hotspur in *Henry IV, Part 1*, 2.3.115–16

Leaving his wife, without telling her that he is
going to lead a rebellion against the king.

8 Thou and I
Have thirty miles to ride yet ere
dinner-time.

**Prince Hal in *Henry IV, Part 1*,
3.3.197–8**

To Peto, on their way to fight with rebels.

9 I hope to see London once ere I die.

Davy in *Henry IV, Part 2*, 5.3.60

Davy, a servant, has lived all his life in the
country.

10 'Tis ever common
That men are merriest when they
are from home.

King Henry in *Henry V*, 1.2.271–2

11 Now sits the wind fair, and we will
aboard.

King Henry in *Henry V*, 2.2.12

Preparing to sail for France.

12 A man of travel, that hath seen the
world.

Armado in *Love's Labor's Lost*, 5.1.107–8

Making the claim for himself.

13 Come away!
For you shall hence upon your
wedding day.

**Portia in *The Merchant of Venice*,
3.2.310–11**

Sending Bassanio off with money to pay his
friend Antonio's debts.

14 I'll put a girdle round about the
earth
In forty minutes!

**Puck in *A Midsummer Night's Dream*,
2.1.175–6**

Puck travels at fairy speed to serve Oberon.

15 We the globe can compass soon,
Swifter than the wandering moon.

**Puck and Oberon in *A Midsummer
Night's Dream*, 4.1.97–8**

On the power of fairies to circle the earth in
no time.

16 My travel's history,
Wherein of antres vast and deserts
idle,

Rough quarries, rocks, and hills
whose heads touch heaven,
It was my hint to speak—such was
my process—
And of the cannibals that each
other eat,
The anthropophagi, and men
whose heads
Do grow beneath their shoulders.

Othello in *Othello*, 1.3.139–45

On his exotic past; "antres" = caves; "rough
quarries" = rugged precipices; "anthropophagi," or cannibals, and headless men
were reported by Pliny, and figured in travel-
books still in the 16th century.

17 All places that the eye of heaven visits
Are to a wise man ports and happy
havens.

John of Gaunt in *Richard II*, 1.3.275–6

Advising his banished son, Bolingbroke.

18 These high wild hills and rough
uneven ways
Draws out our miles and makes
them wearisome.

Northumberland in *Richard II*, 2.3.4–5

He is a stranger in Gloucestershire.

19 *Hortensio.* What happy gale
Blows you to Padua here from old
Verona?
Petruchio. Such wind as scatters
young men through the world
To seek their fortunes farther than
at home,
Where small experience grows.

The Taming of the Shrew, 1.2.48–52

20 Crowns in my purse I have, and
goods at home,
And so am come abroad to see the
world.

Petruchio in *The Taming of the Shrew*,
1.2.57–8

He has just arrived in Padua from Verona.

21 All torment, trouble, wonder, and
amazement
Inhabits here. Some heavenly
power guide us
Out of this fearful country!

Gonzalo in *The Tempest*, 5.1.104–6

Concerned at the distraction suffered by
Alonso; the "country" is Prospero's island.

22 *Olivia.* There lies your way, due
west.
Viola. Then westward ho!

***Twelfth Night*, 3.1.134**

Viola picks up on the cry of watermen who
ferried people across the Thames to Westminster.

23   What's to do?
Shall we go see the relics of this
town?

Sebastian in *Twelfth Night*, 3.3.18–19

To Antonio, on arriving in Illyria; "relics" =
antiquities.

24 I pray you let us satisfy our eyes
With the memorials and the things
of fame
That do renown this city.

Sebastian in *Twelfth Night*, 3.3.22–4

Anxious to see the sights of Illyria.

25 Beguile the time, and feed your
knowledge
With viewing of the town.

Antonio in *Twelfth Night*, 3.3.41–2

Urging Sebastian to look around Illyria.

26 Alas, the way is wearisome and
    long.

**Lucetta in *The Two Gentlemen of
Verona*, 2.7.8**

Trying to persuade Julia not to follow her "loving Proteus" from Verona to Milan.

27 The climate's delicate, the air most
    sweet,
    Fertile the isle, the temple much
    surpassing
    The common praise it bears.

**Cleomenes in *The Winter's Tale*,
3.1.1–3**

Describing their visit to the oracle at Delphos.

Treachery

1 I fear me you but warm the starvèd
   snake,
   Who, cherished in your breasts, will
   sting your hearts.

York in *Henry VI, Part 2*, 3.1.343–4

Plotting rebellion.

Treason

1 Treason is not inherited, my lord.

Rosalind in *As You Like It*, 1.3.61

Protesting her innocence after her father has
been banished.

2 Suspicion all our lives shall be stuck
   full of eyes;
   For treason is but trusted like the
   fox,
   Who never so tame, so cherished
   and locked up,
   Will have a wild trick of his ances-
   tors.

Worcester in *Henry IV, Part 1*, 5.2.8–11

The rebels should not make terms with the
king since they will always be watched and
never trusted.

3 Treason and murder ever kept
   together,
   As two yoke-devils sworn to either's
   purpose.

King Henry in *Henry V*, 2.2.105–6

"Yoke-devils" = devils in partnership, yoked
together.

4 O, what a fall was there, my countrymen!
   Then I, and you, and all of us fell
   down,
   Whilst bloody treason flourished
   over us.

Mark Antony in *Julius Caesar*, 3.2.190–2

On the death of Caesar.

Trees

1 Under an oak, whose antique root
   peeps out
   Upon the brook that brawls along
   this wood.

First Lord in *As You Like It*, 2.1.31–2

2 Under an old oak, whose boughs
   were mossed with age
   And high top bald with dry antiquity.

Oliver in *As You Like It*, 4.3.104–5

3 There is a willow grows aslant a
   brook
   That shows his hoar leaves in the
   glassy stream.

Gertrude in *Hamlet*, 4.7.166–7

"His" = its; "hoar" = frost; the undersides of willow leaves are greyish white, like frost.

Trials

1   Let your fair eyes and gentle wishes go with me to my trial.
    Orlando in *As You Like It*, 1.2.185–7

Addressing Rosalind and Celia before he wrestles with Charles.

Truisms

1   The property of rain is to wet and fire to burn.
    Corin in *As You Like It*, 3.2.26–7

The shepherd's common sense.

2   *Hamlet.* There's never a villain dwelling in all Denmark
    But he's an arrant knave.
    Horatio. There needs no ghost, my lord, come from the grave
    To tell us this.
    ***Hamlet*, 1.5.123–6**

Hamlet fends off questions about his interview with his father's ghost.

3   Every cloud engenders not a storm.
    Clarence in *Henry VI, Part 3*, 5.3.13

Trust

1   Constant you are,
    But yet a woman, and for secrecy
    No lady closer, for I well believe
    Thou wilt not utter what thou dost
    not know,

And so far will I trust thee, gentle Kate.
Hotspur in *Henry IV, Part 1*, 2.3 108–12

Refusing to tell his wife about his involvement in rebellion against the king.

2   There's no more faith in thee than in a stewed prune.
    Falstaff in *Henry IV, Part 1*, 3.3.112–13

Insulting the Hostess, who denies he has been robbed in her tavern; stewed prunes were associated with brothels, where regular food could not be served.

3   I took him for the plainest harmless creature
    That breathed upon the earth a Christian;
    Made him my book, wherein my soul recorded
    The history of all her secret thoughts.
    King Richard in *Richard III*, 3.5.25–8

Protesting his love for Hastings, whose execution he has just plotted.

4   My trust,
    Like a good parent, did beget of him
    A falsehood in its contrary, as great
    As my trust was; which had indeed no limit,
    A confidence sans bound.
    Prospero in *The Tempest*, 1.2.93–7

On being betrayed by his brother Antonio; recalling the proverb, "trust is the mother of deceit."

5   I wonder men dare trust themselves with men.
    Apemantus in *Timon of Athens*, 1.2.43

Seeing that Timon's guests are destroying him.

Truth (see also Honesty, Integrity)

1 If circumstances lead me, I will find
Where truth is hid, though it were
hid indeed
Within the center.

Polonius in *Hamlet*, 2.2.157–9

Boasting of his political skills.

2 I can teach thee, coz, to shame the
devil
By telling truth: tell truth and
shame the devil.

Hotspur in *Henry IV, Part 1*, 3.1.57–8

To Glendower ("coz" = cousin), who has
been claiming supernatural powers; "tell truth
and shame the devil" was proverbial (as the
devil was the father of lies).

3 Whom I most hated living, thou
hast made me
With thy religious truth and modesty,
Now in his ashes honor.

Queen Katherine in *Henry VIII*, 4.2.73–5

Changing her opinion of Cardinal Wolsey;
"modesty" = moderation.

4 What in the world should make me
now deceive,
Since I must lose the use of all
deceit?
Why should I then be false, since it
is true
That I must die here and live hence
by truth?

Melune in *King John*, 5.3.26–9

Melune, wounded and at the point of death,
develops the proverb "Dying men speak true"
to include the idea of an afterlife in which he
will have to "live . . . by truth."

5 Truth is truth
To the very end of reckoning.

Isabella in *Measure for Measure*, 5.1.45–6

6 Promise me life, and I'll confess the
truth.

Bassanio in *The Merchant of Venice*, 3.2.34

To Portia, who is anxious to be assured of his
love.

7 Methinks the truth should live
from age to age,
As 'twere retailed to all posterity,
Even to the general all-ending day.

Prince Edward in *Richard III*, 3.1.76–8

"Retailed" = handed down; by the "all-ending
day" he means doomsday.

Twins

1 Methinks you are my glass, and not
my brother:
I see by you I am a sweet-faced
youth.

Dromio of Ephesus in *The Comedy of Errors*, 5.1.418–19

The twins meet at last.

2 We came into the world like
brother and brother;
And now let's go hand in hand, not
one before another.

Dromio of Ephesus in *The Comedy of Errors*, 5.1.425–6

To his twin, Dromio of Syracuse, at the end of
the play.

3 So we grew together
Like to a double cherry, seeming
parted,

But yet an union in partition,
Two lovely berries molded on one
    stem.

**Helena in *A Midsummer Night's
Dream*, 3.2.208–11**

4   An apple cleft in two is not more
    twin
Than these two creatures.

Antonio in *Twelfth Night*, 5.1.223–4

The twins, Viola and Sebastian, are at last
revealed, and meet one another.

Tyranny (see also Power)

1   For how can tyrants safely govern
    home,
Unless abroad they purchase great
    alliance?

**Queen Margaret in *Henry VI, Part 3*,
3.3.69–70**

2   Brutus had rather be a villager
Than to repute himself a son of
    Rome
Under these hard conditions as this
    time
Is like to lay upon us.

Brutus in *Julius Caesar*, 1.2.172–5

Expecting that Caesar may turn out to be a
tyrant; "is like" = may well.

3   That part of tyranny that I do bear
I can shake off at pleasure.

Cassius in *Julius Caesar*, 1.3.99–100

He means by taking his own life.

4   Thy brother by decree is banishèd.
If thou dost bend, and pray, and
    fawn for him,
I spurn thee like a cur out of my
    way.

Caesar in *Julius Caesar*, 3.1.44–6

To Metellus, who pleads for his exiled
brother; "spurn" = kick.

5   I begin to find an idle and fond
bondage in the oppression of aged
tyranny, who sways, not as it hath
power, but as it is suffered.

Gloucester in *King Lear*, 1.2.49–51

"Suffered" = allowed, by the young who
could seize power.

6   'Tis time to fear when tyrants seem
    to kiss.

Pericles in *Pericles*, 1.2.79

After discovering the guilty secret of Antiochus's incest with his own daughter, Pericles
distrusts the tyrant's honeyed words.

7   The orphan pines while the oppres-
    sor sleeps.

***The Rape of Lucrece*, 905**

After being raped, Lucrece thinks of the injustice in the world.

Unkindness

1   Hath homely age th' alluring beauty
    took
From my poor cheek? Then he
    hath wasted it.
Are my discourses dull? Barren my
    wit?
If voluble and sharp discourse be
    marred,
Unkindness blunts it more than
    marble hard.

**Adriana in *The Comedy of Errors*,
2.1.89–93**

On her absent husband; "wasted" = squan-
dered and laid waste to.

2   My decayèd fair
A sunny look of his would soon
   repair.

Adriana in *The Comedy of Errors*,
2.1.98–9

Complaining about her absent husband.

3   Unkindness may do much,
And his unkindness may defeat my
   life,
But never taint my love.

Desdemona in *Othello*, 4.2.159–61

On Othello's harsh treatment of her; "defeat"
= destroy.

4   In nature there's no blemish but the
      mind;
None can be called deformed but
   the unkind.

Antonio in *Twelfth Night*, 3.4.367–8

Mistaking Cesario (the disguised Viola) for
Sebastian, he accuses him/her of being unnatural and ungrateful ("unkind").

Utopias

1   I'the commonwealth I would by
      contraries
Execute all things; for no kind of
   traffic
Would I admit; no name of magis-
   trate;
Letters should not be known;
   riches, poverty,
And use of service, none; contract,
   succession,
Bourn, bound of land, tilth, vine-
   yard, none;
No use of metal, corn, or wine, or
   oil;

No occupation; all men idle, all,
And women too, but innocent and
   pure.

Gonzalo in *The Tempest*, 2.1.148–56

His utopian vision of himself as king in a
golden age with no rules or private property
("Bourn, bound of land"); "traffic" = trade;
"use of service" = employment of servants.

Valor (see also Courage)

1   I will reward thee
Once for thy sprightly comfort, and
   tenfold
For thy good valor.

Antony in *Antony and Cleopatra*,
4.7.14–16

The "comfort" is news of victory.

2   O infinite virtue, com'st thou smil-
      ing from
The world's great snare uncaught?

Cleopatra in *Antony and Cleopatra*,
4.8.17–18

On Antony returning from his one defeat of
Octavius's army; "virtue" here = valor.

3   He is a lion
That I am proud to hunt.

**Caius Martius, later Coriolanus, in
Coriolanus, 1.1.235–6**

A warrior's admiration for his rival, Tullus
Aufidius, leader of the Volsces.

4   He is himself alone,
To answer all the city.

First Soldier in *Coriolanus*, 1.4.51–2

On Caius Martius, who has fought his way
alone into the city of Corioli.

5   It is held
That valor is the chiefest virtue, and
Most dignifies the haver.

Cominius in *Coriolanus*, 2.2.83–5

Praising Coriolanus for his courage in battle
("haver" = possessor).

6   O, the blood more stirs
To rouse a lion than to start a hare!

Hotspur in *Henry IV, Part 1*, 1.3.197–8

Imagining himself as the lion; the hare was
proverbially fearful.

7 There's no more valor in that Poins
than in a wild duck.

Falstaff in *Henry IV, Part 1*, 2.2.101

After a robbery, from which Poins was absent
by design.

8 The better part of valor is discretion, in the which better part I have
saved my life.

Falstaff in *Henry IV, Part 1*, 5.4.119–20

Falstaff's "discretion" means avoiding danger
on the battlefield by pretending to be dead.

9 His valors shown upon our crests
  today
Have taught us how to cherish such
  high deeds
Even in the bosom of our adversaries.

**Prince Hal in *Henry IV, Part 1*,
5.5.29–31**

Freeing the prisoner, Douglas, who has fought
heroically.

10 Thou wilt be as valiant as the
wrathful dove or most magnanimous mouse.

Falstaff in *Henry IV, Part 2*, 3.2.159–60

On recruiting little Feeble, a tailor, as a
soldier.

11 That's a valiant flea that dare eat his
breakfast on the lip of a lion.

Orleans in *Henry V*, 3.7.145–6

Seeing the English as foolish to engage the
French army.

12 'Tis much he dares,
And to that dauntless temper of his
  mind,
He hath a wisdom that doth guide
  his valor
To act in safety.

Macbeth in *Macbeth*, 3.1.50–3

Describing Banquo.

13 In a false quarrel there is no true
valor.

**Benedick in *Much Ado About Nothing*,
5.1.120**

To Don Pedro and Claudio, and their mockery
of old Leonato's quarrel with them.

14 He is as valiant as the lion, churlish
as the bear, slow as the elephant.

**Alexander in *Troilus and Cressida*,
1.2.20–1**

Describing the huge but dim-witted Ajax.

15 To awake your dormouse valor, to
put fire in your heart, and brimstone in your liver.

Fabian in *Twelfth Night*, 3.2.19–21

Trying to provoke Sir Andrew to challenge
Cesario (Viola); "brimstone" = sulphur.

Value

1   The jewel that we find, we stoop
    and take it
    Because we see it; but what we do
    not see
    We tread upon and never think of
    it.

Angelo in *Measure for Measure*, 2.1.24–6

2   What we have we prize not to the
    worth
    Whiles we enjoy it, but being lacked
    and lost,
    Why, then we rack the value, then
    we find
    The virtue that possession would
    not show us
    Whiles it was ours.

**Friar Francis in *Much Ado About
Nothing*, 4.1.218–22**

He says we do not value at its true worth what
we possess, but when we lose a possession,
we exaggerate ("rack") its value; he is thinking
of Claudio's harsh treatment of Hero.

3   What, is the jay more precious than
    the lark
    Because his feathers are more beau-
    tiful?
    Or is the adder better than the eel
    Because his painted skin contents
    the eye?

**Petruchio in *The Taming of the Shrew*,
4.3.175–8**

"Painted" = brightly colored.

4   What's aught but as 'tis valued?

Troilus in *Troilus and Cressida*, 2.2.52

The Trojans are debating whether to keep
Helen or return her to the Greeks.

5   Value dwells not in particular
    will;

It holds his estimate and dignity
As well wherein 'tis precious of
    itself
As in the prizer.

Hector in *Troilus and Cressida*, 2.2.53–6

Arguing that value depends on intrinsic worth,
not on the particular preference of any individual; the debate is about keeping Helen or
returning her to the Greeks.

6   Is she worth keeping? Why, she is a
    pearl
    Whose price hath launched above a
    thousand ships.

Troilus in *Troilus and Cressida*, 2.2.81–2

Referring to Helen, whose rape by Paris
caused the Trojan war, and echoing a famous
passage in Christopher Marlowe's play, *Doctor Faustus*.

7   Nature, what things
    there are
    Most abject in regard, and dear in
    use!
    What things again most dear in the
    esteem
    And poor in worth!

**Ulysses in *Troilus and Cressida*,
3.3.127–30**

Pointing out that things of low esteem may
have great practical value, while what is
highly esteemed may be of little use.

Vanity

1   There was never yet fair woman but
    she made mouths in a glass.

Fool in *King Lear*, 3.2.35–6

2   Light vanity, insatiate cormorant,
    Consuming means, soon preys on
    itself.

John of Gaunt in *Richard II*, 2.1.38–9

Prophesying that the extravagance of King Richard, by devouring the means of sustaining life, will lead to disaster; the cormorant is noted for its gluttony.

3   A lover may bestride the gossamers
    That idles in the wanton summer
      air,
    And yet not fall; so light is vanity.

Friar Lawrence in *Romeo and Juliet*,
2.6.18–20

On Juliet's arrival, "light of foot"; "wanton" = playful.

4   What a sweep of vanity comes this
      way!

Apemantus in *Timon of Athens*, 1.2.132

A cynic's comment on the arrival at Timon's feast of a group of dancers dressed as Amazons.

Vegetables

1   I am qualmish at the smell of leek.

Pistol in *Henry V*, 5.1.21

He is insulting Fluellen, who wears a leek to identify himself as Welsh (usually worn on St. David's Day, the patron saint of Wales).

2   Midnight mushrooms.

Prospero in *The Tempest*, 5.1.39

"Mushrumps" in the original text, imagined as brought into being by Prospero's spirits.

Vertigo

1   How fearful
    And dizzy 'tis, to cast one's eyes so
      low!

The crows and choughs that wing
    the midway air
Show scarce so gross as beetles.
    Half way down
Hangs one that gathers samphire,
    dreadful trade!

Edgar in *King Lear*, 4.6.11–15

Imagining the prospect from the cliffs at Dover; "choughs" = crows or jackdaws; "gross" = large; "samphire" is an herb used in pickling.

Vice

1   When we in our viciousness grow
      hard
    (O, misery on't!), the wise gods seel
      our eyes,
    In our own filth drop our clear
      judgments, make us
    Adore our errors, laugh at us while
      we strut
    To our confusion.

Antony in *Antony and Cleopatra*,
3.13.111–5

"Seel" = blind (a term from hawking; the eyes of the hawk are covered in order to train it).

2   That reverend Vice, that grey Iniq-
    uity, that father Ruffian, that Van-
    ity in years.

Prince Hal in *Henry IV*, Part 1,
2.4.453–4

Meaning Falstaff; "Vice," "Iniquity," "Ruffian," and "Vanity" are type names suggesting a morality play.

3   Virtue itself turns vice, being mis-
    applied,
    And vice sometime by action digni-
    fied.

Friar Lawrence in *Romeo and Juliet*,
2.3.21–2

4 There is no man hath a virtue that he hath not a glimpse of, nor any man an attaint but he carries some stain of it.

Alexander in *Troilus and Cressida*, 1.2.24–6

Referring to Ajax; "attaint" = vice.

5 O what a mansion have those vices got
Which for their habitation chose out thee,
Where beauty's veil doth cover every blot,
And all things turns to fair that eyes can see!

***Sonnet 95*, 9–12**

"All things turns to fair" = makes all appear beautiful.

Victory

1 The harder matched, the greater victory.

King Edward in *Henry VI, Part 3*, 5.1.70

The king is about to engage in battle; the idea is based on the proverb, "The more danger the more honor."

2 A victory is twice itself when the achiever brings home full numbers.

Leonato in *Much Ado About Nothing*, 1.1.8–9

On a battle won with almost no loss of life.

3 Now are our brows bound with victorious wreaths.

King Richard in *Richard III*, 1.1.5

At the end of the civil wars that plagued the reign of Henry VI.

Vigilance

1 I am as vigilant as a cat to steal cream.

Falstaff in *Henry IV, Part 1*, 4.2.58–9

Villainy

1 O villain, villain, smiling, damned villain!
My tables—meet it is I set it down
That one may smile, and smile, and be a villain!

Hamlet in *Hamlet*, 1.5.106–8

Brooding on his uncle Claudius, the "villain" who murdered his father; "tables" = writing tables.

2 I like not fair terms and a villain's mind.

Bassanio in *The Merchant of Venice*, 1.3.179

On Shylock's offer to lend Antonio 3,000 ducats.

3 Though I cannot be said to be a flattering honest man, it must not be denied but I am a plain-dealing villain.

Don John in *Much Ado About Nothing*, 1.3.30–2

Showing his true nature to his companion, Conrade.

4 If I had my mouth, I would bite; if I had my liberty, I would do my liking. In the meantime, let me be that I am, and seek not to alter me.

Don John in *Much Ado About Nothing*, 1.3.34–7

If he cannot do any harm, he can be morose and surly.

5   We have here recovered the most dangerous piece of lechery that ever was known in the commonwealth.

Second Watchman in *Much Ado About Nothing*, 3.3.167–8

The comic watchman means to say "discovered" and "treachery."

6   He is composed and framed of treachery,
And fled he is upon this villainy.

Don Pedro in *Much Ado About Nothing*, 5.1.249–50

On Don John, who set up the plot to ruin the marriage of Claudio and Hero.

7   Since I cannot prove a
      lover
To entertain these fair well-spoken days,
I am determinèd to prove a villain
And hate the idle pleasures of these days.

King Richard in *Richard III*, 1.1.28–31

Announcing his intentions in his opening soliloquy.

Virginity (see also Chastity)

1   Man is an enemy to virginity. How may we barricado it against him?

Helena in *All's Well That Ends Well*, 1.1.112–3

She is somewhat oddly seeking advice of the corrupt Parolles.

2   It is not politic in the commonwealth of nature to preserve virginity. Loss of virginity is rational increase, and there was never virgin got till virginity was first lost.

Parolles in *All's Well That Ends Well*, 1.1.126–8

The sardonic response of Parolles to Helena.

3   The imperial votaress passed on,
In maiden meditation, fancy-free.

Oberon in *A Midsummer Night's Dream*, 2.1.163–4

On Cupid's arrow missing the vestal virgin or "imperial votaress," perhaps Queen Elizabeth.

Virtue (see also Goodness)

1   Where an unclean mind carries virtuous qualities, there commendations go with pity; they are virtues and traitors too.

Countess of Rossillion, *All's Well That Ends Well*, 1.1.41–3

Virtuous qualities become "traitors" if they are used for wicked purposes.

2   Honesty coupled to beauty is to have honey a sauce to sugar.

Touchstone in *As You Like It*, 3.3.30–1

Trying to persuade her not to be virtuous ("honest").

3   Our virtues
Lie in the interpretation of the time.

Aufidius in *Coriolanus*, 4.7.49–50

The leader of the Volscians finds his abilities no longer appreciated now that he shares authority with Coriolanus.

4 Thou wrong'st a gentleman, who is as far
From thy report as thou from honor, and
Solicits here a lady that disdains
Thee and the devil alike.

Imogen in *Cymbeline*, 1.6.145–8

Rejecting Jachimo's account of Posthumus's unfaithfulness.

5 Virtue itself scapes not calumnious strokes.

Laertes in *Hamlet*, 1.3.39–40

Warning Ophelia against Hamlet.

6 But virtue, as it never will be moved,
Though lewdness court it in a shape of heaven,
So lust, though to a radiant angel linked,
Will sate itself in a celestial bed
And prey on garbage.

Ghost in *Hamlet*, 1.5.53–7

Accusing his widow Gertrude of lust in marrying a brother he despises, a marriage he regards as incestuous; "shape of heaven" = angelic form; "sate itself" = gratify its appetite to the point of disgust.

7 *Polonius.* What do you think of me?
Claudius. As of a man faithful and honorable.

Hamlet, 2.2.129–30

Appealing to Claudius for confirmation of his integrity.

8 My heart laments that virtue cannot live
Out of the teeth of emulation.

Artemidorus in *Julius Caesar*, 2.3.13–14

Thinking of Caesar; "Out of the teeth of emulation" = beyond the bite of envious rivalry.

9 Fairest Cordelia, that art most rich being poor,
Most choice forsaken, and most loved despised,
Thee and thy virtues here I seize upon.

King of France in *King Lear*, 1.1.250–2

Taking her in marriage with no dowry and hated by her father.

10 This Duncan
Hath borne his faculties so meek, hath been
So clear in his great office, that his virtues
Will plead like angels, trumpet-tongued, against
The deep damnation of his taking-off.

Macbeth in *Macbeth*, 1.7.16–20

Duncan has wielded power so mildly ("meek"), and been blameless ("clear") as king, hence the "deep damnation" of killing him.

11 The king-becoming graces,
As justice, verity, temperance, stableness,
Bounty, perseverance, mercy, lowliness,
Devotion, patience, courage, fortitude,
I have no relish of them.

Malcolm in *Macbeth*, 4.3.91–5

Malcolm denigrates himself, afraid that Macduff may be a spy.

12 Heaven doth with us as we with
   torches do,
Not light them for themselves; for if
   our virtues
Did not go forth of us, 'twere all
   alike
As if we had them not.

Duke in *Measure for Measure*, 1.1.32–5

Echoing various injunctions of Jesus in the
gospels, as at Matthew 5:14–16 and Luke
8:16, e.g., "Let your light so shine before men,
that they may see your good works"; "all
alike" = just the same.

13 The hand that hath made you fair
hath made you good.

Duke in *Measure for Measure*, 3.1.180–1

Greeting the novice Isabella; the hand is
God's.

14 Virtue is bold, and goodness never
fearful.

Duke in *Measure for Measure*, 3.1.208

Varying the proverb, "innocence is bold."

15 He who the sword of heaven will
   bear
Must be as holy as severe;
Pattern in himself to know,
Grace to stand, and virtue go.

Duke in *Measure for Measure*, 3.2.261–4

The last two lines may be understood as
meaning he must know himself as a model for
judging others, stand firm with grace, and act
with virtue.

16 Your father was ever virtuous, and
holy men at their death have good
inspirations.

Nerissa in *The Merchant of Venice*,
1.2.27–8

Defending the will made by Portia's father
that restricts her choice in marriage.

17 Virtue? A fig! 'Tis in ourselves that
we are thus or thus. Our bodies are
our gardens, to the which our wills
are gardeners.

Iago in *Othello*, 1.3.319–21

"A fig!" implies the scornful gesture of thrust-
ing the thumb between the first and second
fingers.

18 She is of so free, so kind, so apt, so
blessed a disposition, she holds it a
vice in her goodness not to do more
than she is requested.

Iago in *Othello*, 2.3.319–22

A perceptive description of Desdemona.

19   If Cassio do remain,
He hath a daily beauty in his life
That makes me ugly.

Iago in *Othello*, 5.1.18–20

Meaning "if Cassio remains alive."

20 Virtue itself turns vice, being mis-
   applied,
And vice sometime's by action dig-
   nified.

Friar Lawrence in *Romeo and Juliet*,
2.3.21–2

21 Is it a world to hide virtues in?

Sir Toby Belch in *Twelfth Night*,
1.3.131–2

Encouraging the foolish Sir Andrew to show
how well he can dance.

22 Anything that's mended is but
patched; virtue that transgresses is
but patched with sin, and sin that
amends is patched with virtue.

Feste in *Twelfth Night*, 1.5.47–9

23 *Sir Toby Belch.* Dost thou think
   because thou art virtuous there
   shall be no more cakes and ale?
   Feste. Yes, by Saint Anne, and ginger shall be hot i'the mouth, too.
   Twelfth Night, 2.3.114–18

   Referring to Malvolio's puritanical streak;
   "cakes and ale" were associated with church
   feasts, the ale often spiced with ginger.

24 Virtue is beauty, but the beauteous
   evil
   Are empty trunks o'erflourished by
   the devil.
   Antonio in *Twelfth Night*, 3.4.369–70

   That is, those who are beautiful on the outside
   but evil within are like vacant bodies or chests
   covered over with ornament.

Vows (see also Oaths, Promises)

1 'Tis not the many oaths that makes
   the truth,
   But the plain single vow that is
   vowed true.
   What is not holy, that we swear not
   by,
   But take the Highest to witness.
   Diana in *All's Well That Ends Well*,
   4.2.21–2

   Rejecting Bertram's protestations of love as
   unholy.

2 I swear to thee by Cupid's strongest
   bow,
   By his best arrow with the golden
   head,
   By the simplicity of Venus' doves,
   By that which knitteth souls and
   prospers loves,
   . . .

By all the vows that ever men have
broke
(In number more than ever women
spoke).
**Hermia in *A Midsummer Night's
Dream*,** 1.1.169–72, 175–6

Cupid used arrows of gold to cause love, and
lead to repel it; doves were sacred to Venus,
as symbolizing fidelity and freedom from
deceit ("simplicity").

3 For, ere Demetrius looked on Her-
   mia's eyne,
   He hailed down oaths that he was
   only mine,
   And when this hail some heat from
   Hermia felt,
   So he dissolved, and showers of
   oaths did melt.
   **Helena in *A Midsummer Night's
   Dream*,** 1.1.242–5

   "Eyne" = eyes.

4 *Romeo.* Lady, by yonder blessèd
   moon I vow,
   That tips with silver all these fruit
   tree tops—
   Juliet. O, swear not by the moon,
   th' inconstant moon,
   That monthly changes in her cir-
   cled orb,
   Lest that thy love prove likewise
   variable.
   Romeo and Juliet, 2.2.107–11

5 It is the purpose that makes strong
   the vow,
   But vows to every purpose must
   not hold.
   Cassandra in *Troilus and Cressida*,
   5.3.23–4

   She is trying to persuade Hector to break for
   one day an engagement he has made to fight
   the Greeks.

War (see also Fighting, Soldiers)

1   Wars is no strife
     To the dark house and the detested
     wife.

Bertram in *All's Well That Ends Well*, 2.3.291–2

Preferring the risks of war to being at home.

2   They come like sacrifices in their
     trim,
     And to the fire-eyed maid of smoky
     war
     All hot and bleeding will we offer
     them.

Hotspur in *Henry IV, Part 1*, 4.1.113–15

Expecting to defeat Prince Hal and his army; "fire-eyed maid" = Bellona, goddess of war.

3   I would 'twere bed-time, Hal, and
     all well.

Falstaff in *Henry IV, Part 1*, 5.1.125

Showing his fear of dying in battle.

4   Sound all the lofty instruments of
     war,
     And by that music let us all
     embrace,
     For, heaven to earth, some of us
     never shall
     A second time do such a courtesy.

Hotspur in *Henry IV, Part 1*, 5.2.97–100

5   God keep lead out of me!

Falstaff in *Henry IV, Part 1*, 5.3.34

Referring to bullets.

6   O yet for God's sake, go not to
     these wars!

Lady Percy in *Henry IV, Part 2*, 2.3.9

Hotspur's widow begs her father-in-law not to fight.

7   The hideous god of war.

Lady Percy in *Henry IV, Part 2*, 2.3.35

Mars seems hideous to her now that her husband has been killed in battle.

8   In cases of defense 'tis best to weigh
     The enemy more mighty than he
     seems.

Dauphin in *Henry V*, 2.4.43–4

Advising the King of France not to underestimate the strength of English forces.

9   He bids you . . . to take mercy
     On the poor souls for whom this
     hungry war
     Opens his vasty jaws.

Exeter in *Henry V*, 2.4.93, 103–5

Henry's message to the King of France.

10   Once more unto the breach, dear
     friends, once more.

King Henry in *Henry V*, 3.1.1

Henry's famous battle-cry at the gap or breach in the walls of Harfleur.

11   When the blast of war blows in our
     ears,
     Then imitate the action of the
     tiger;
     Stiffen the sinews, conjure up the
     blood,
     Disguise fair nature with hard-
     favored rage;
     Then lend the eye a terrible aspect.

King Henry in *Henry V*, 3.1.5–9

Encouraging his soldiers to fight.

12 I see you stand like greyhounds in
   the slips,
   Straining upon the start. The
   game's afoot!
   Follow your spirit, and upon this
   charge
   Cry, "God for Harry, England and
   Saint George!"

King Henry in *Henry V*, 3.1.31–4

Seeing his troops as like greyhounds leashed
("in the slips") and waiting to be loosed to
hunt game. St. George is the patron saint of
England.

13 What is it then to me, if impious
   War,
   Arrayed in flames like to the prince
   of fiends,
   Do with his smirched complexion
   all fell feats
   Enlinked to waste and desolation?

King Henry in *Henry V*, 3.3.15–18

Blaming war rather than individuals for the
cruelty ("fell feats") and devastation it brings.

14 Advantage is a better soldier than
   rashness.

Montjoy in *Henry V*, 3.6.120

Better to wait for a favorable opportunity than
act rashly in war; so the French King makes
the best of losing Harfleur to the English.

15 Gentlemen in England now abed
   Shall think themselves accursed
     they were not here,
   And hold their manhoods cheap
     whiles any speaks
   That fought with us upon Saint
   Crispin's Day.

King Henry in *Henry V*, 4.3.64–7

Encouraging his army to fight the French;
Saint Crispin was martyred on 25th October,
the date of the Battle of Agincourt.

16 Caesar's spirit, ranging for
     revenge,
   With Ate by his side, come hot
     from hell,
   Shall in these confines, with a
     monarch's voice,
   Cry "Havoc!" and let slip the dogs
     of war.

Mark Antony in *Julius Caesar*, 3.1.270–3

Ate was the Greek goddess of discord and
destruction; the cry "Havoc!" was the signal
to kill and pillage without mercy.

17 I pray you, how many hath he
   killed and eaten in these wars? But
   how many hath he killed? For
   indeed, I promised to eat all of his
   killing.

**Beatrice in *Much Ado About Nothing*,
1.1.42–5**

Mocking Benedick's achievement as a soldier.

18 The tyrant custom, most grave sen-
     ators,
   Hath made the flinty and steel
     couch of war
   My thrice-driven bed of down.

Othello in *Othello*, 1.3.229–31

As a soldier, he is used to living rough.

19 Farewell the neighing steed and the
     shrill trump,
   The spirit-stirring drum, th' ear-
     piercing fife,
   The royal banner and all quality,
   Pride, pomp, and circumstance of
     glorious war!

Othello in *Othello*, 3.3.351–4

Bidding farewell to the glamour and ceremony ("circumstance") of his profession as a
general; "trump" = trumpet. Edward Elgar
chose to name his famous marches with the
phrase "pomp and circumstance."

20   He is come to open
The purple testament of bleeding
war.

King Richard in *Richard II*, 3.3.93–4

On Henry Bolingbroke; blood was often
described as purple.

21 Contumelious, beastly, mad-
brained, war.

Timon in *Timon of Athens*, 5.1.174

His response to the senators of Athens when
they want him to defend them against Alcibiades; "contumelious" = insolent.

22 She is a theme of honor and
renown,
A spur to valiant and magnanimous
deeds,
Whose present courage may beat
down our foes,
And fame in time to come canonize
us.

**Hector in *Troilus and Cressida*,
2.2.199–202**

Hector's reasons for keeping Helen in Troy.

23 All the argument is a whore and a
cuckold, a good quarrel to draw
emulous factions and bleed to
death upon!

**Thersites in *Troilus and Cressida*,
2.3.72–4**

A cynic's view of the Trojan war; Helen is the
"whore," and Menelaus the "cuckold";
"draw" = attract.

Weakness

1   Frailty, thy name is woman!
Hamlet in *Hamlet*, 1.2.146

Generalizing from Gertrude, his mother, and
her hasty marriage to her dead husband's
brother.

2   We are all men,
In our own natures frail and capa-
ble
Of our flesh.

**Lord Chamberlain in *Henry VIII*,
5.2.45–7**

"Capable" = susceptible to temptation. Compare Matthew 26:41, "the spirit indeed is willing, but the flesh is weak."

3   We are all frail.
Angelo in *Measure for Measure*, 2.4.121

Proverbial, from the apocryphal Ecclesiasticus
8:5; frail means liable to sin, rather than phys-
ically weak. See also Psalms 39:4.

4   Bear with my weakness. My old
brain is troubled.
Be not disturbed with my infirmity.

Prospero in *The Tempest*, 4.1.159–60

5   Now my charms are all o'erthrown,
And what strength I have's mine
own,
Which is most faint.

**Prospero in *The Tempest*, Epilogue,
1–3**

Appealing to the audience in his epilogue.

6   I am weaker than a woman's tear,
Tamer than sleep, fonder than
ignorance,
Less valiant than the virgin in the
night,
And skilless as unpracticed infancy.

Troilus in *Troilus and Cressida*, 1.1.9–12

"Fonder" = more foolish; his love for Cressida
prevents him from fighting against the Greeks.

Weariness

1   Weariness
Can snore upon the flint, when
   resty sloth
Finds the down pillow hard.
Belarius in *Cymbeline*, 3.6.33–5

"Resty" = sluggish.

2   By my troth, Nerissa, my little body
is aweary of this great world.
**Portia in *The Merchant of Venice*,
1.2.1–2**

Portia's first words in the play.

3   I can go no further, sir.
My old bones aches.
Gonzalo in *The Tempest*, 3.3.1–2

The third person plural ending in "s," as in
"aches," was very common in Shakespeare's
day. Gonzalo has been helping to search the
island for Ferdinand.

Weather

1   *Hamlet.* The air bites shrewdly, it is
   very cold.
Horatio. It is a nipping and an
   eager air.
Hamlet, 1.4.1–2

On the battlements of the castle, waiting for
the ghost to appear; "shrewdly" = keenly;
"eager" = sharp, bitter.

2   Is not their climate foggy, raw and
   dull,
On whom, as in despite, the sun
   looks pale,
Killing their fruit with frowns?
Constable in *Henry V*, 3.5.16–18

On the English climate.

3   Many can brook the weather that
love not the wind.
Nathaniel in *Love's Labor's Lost*, 4.2.33

Proverbial, meaning we must endure
("brook") much we may not like.

4   So foul and fair a day I have not
   seen.
Macbeth in *Macbeth*, 1.3.38

5   Men judge by the complexion of
   the sky
The state and inclination of the day.
**Sir Stephen Scroop in *Richard II*,
3.2.194–5**

His gloomy looks match the bad news he
brings.

6   The skies look grimly
And threaten present blusters.
Mariner in *The Winter's Tale*, 3.3.3–4

7   The day frowns more and more.
Antigonus in *The Winter's Tale*, 3.3.54

8   Like a red morn that ever yet beto-
   kened
Wrack to the seaman, tempest to
   the field,
   Sorrow to shepherds, woe unto
      the birds,
   Gusts and foul flaws to herdsmen
      and to herds.
Venus and Adonis, 453–6

It was proverbial that a red sky in the morning
heralded bad weather; "wrack" = shipwreck;
"flaws" = blasts of wind.

Weeping, see Tears

Welcome (see also Greetings)

1   At first
And last, the hearty welcome.
Macbeth in *Macbeth*, 3.4.1–2

"At first/And last" = once and for all.

2   What's past and what's to come is
    strewed with husks
And formless ruin of oblivion;
But in this extant moment, faith
    and truth,
Strained purely from all hollow
    bias-drawing,
Bids thee, with most divine
    integrity,
From heart of very heart, great
    Hector, welcome!
Agamemnon in *Troilus and Cressida*, 4.5.166–71

Greeting Hector with pleasure in a moment of truce, free from all insincerity or deviation from truth ("hollow bias-drawing").

3   Pray you bid
These unknown friends to 's wel-
    come, for it is
A way to make us better friends,
    more known.
Shepherd in *The Winter's Tale*, 4.4.64–6

On the arrival of the disguised Polixenes and Camillo; "to's" = each to his.

4   Welcome hither,
As is the spring to th' earth.
Leontes in *The Winter's Tale*, 5.1.151–2

Welcoming Florizel at his court.

Wilderness

1   Thou wilt be a wilderness again,
Peopled with wolves, thy old inhab-
    itants!
King Henry in *Henry IV, Part 2*, 4.5.136–7

Referring to his kingdom.

2   The commonwealth of Athens is
become a forest of beasts.
Apemantus in *Timon of Athens*, 4.3.347–8

His cynical view of the state of Athens.

3   Dost thou not perceive
That Rome is but a wilderness of
    tigers?
Titus in *Titus Andronicus*, 3.1.53–4

Speaking to his son, Lucius, who has just been banished from Rome.

Winter, see Seasons

Wisdom

1   Thus men may grow wiser every
day.
Touchstone in *As You Like It*, 1.2.137

On hearing the destruction of three young men by a wrestler described as sport for ladies; Touchstone is being ironic.

2   The fool doth think he is wise, but
the wise man knows himself to be a
fool.
Touchstone in *As You Like It*, 5.1.30–2

3   Wisdom cries out in the streets, and
     no man regards it.

     Prince Hal in *Henry IV, Part 1*, 1.2.88–9

     Echoing the Bible, Proverbs 1:23–4.

4   I never knew so young a body with
     so old a head.

     **Duke in *The Merchant of Venice*,
     4.1.163–4**

     Citing the letter commending the legal ability
     of the disguised Portia.

5   There's not one wise man among
     twenty that will praise himself.

     **Beatrice in *Much Ado About Nothing*,
     5.2.73–5**

     To Benedick, varying the proverb, "he must
     praise himself since no-one else will."

6   You are wise,
     Or else you love not, for to be wise
        and love
     Exceeds man's might.

     **Cressida in *Troilus and Cressida*,
     3.2.155–7**

     Speaking to Troilus.

Wit

1   Make the door upon a woman's
     wit, and it will out at the casement;
     shut that, and 'twill out at the key-
     hole; stop that, 'twill fly with the
     smoke out at the chimney.

     Rosalind in *As You Like It*, 4.1.161–4

2   Brevity is the soul of wit.

     Polonius in *Hamlet*, 2.2.90

     Ironically, he is tediously long-winded him-
     self; "wit" could mean wisdom, but shades
     into its modern meaning.

3   I am not only witty in myself, but
     the cause that wit is in other men.

     Falstaff in *Henry IV, Part 2*, 1.2.9–10

     In this play Falstaff becomes the butt of other
     men's wit.

4   Thy wit is as quick as the grey-
     hound's mouth; it catches.

     **Benedick in *Much Ado About Nothing*,
     5.2.11–12**

     To Margaret, who seizes on unintended mean-
     ings as quick as a hound catches its prey.

5   A college of wit-crackers cannot
     flout me out of my humor. Dost
     thou think I care for a satire or an
     epigram?

     **Benedick in *Much Ado About Nothing*,
     5.4.100–2**

     Having sworn he would never marry, he is
     teased by Don Pedro for agreeing to marry
     Beatrice; "college" = assembly.

6   Look, he's winding up the watch of
     his wit; by and by it will strike.

     Sebastian in *The Tempest*, 2.1.12–13

     Scornfully referring to Gonzalo, who is trying
     to comfort Alonso; "wit" = intelligence or
     thought.

7   A sentence is but a cheveril glove to
     a good wit. How quickly the wrong
     side may be turned outward!

     Feste in *Twelfth Night*, 3.1.11–13

     A "sentence" could be any utterance or opin-
     ion; "cheveril" = kidskin, noted for being pli-
     able.

Women (see also Men and Women)

1   No more but e'en a woman, and
     commanded

By such poor passion as the maid
  that milks
And does the meanest chares.

Cleopatra in *Antony and Cleopatra*,
4.15.73–5

In grief the queen discovers her common
humanity.

2 Those that she makes fair she scarce
makes honest, and those that she
makes honest she makes very ill-
favoredly.

Celia in *As You Like It*, 1.2.37–9

Discussing with Rosalind Fortune's contrary
gifts to women.

3 Alas, what danger will it be to us,
Maids as we are, to travel forth so
  far!
Beauty provoketh thieves sooner
  than gold.

Rosalind in *As You Like It*, 1.3.108–10

Celia has suggested that they go to the forest
of Arden.

4 I must comfort the weaker vessel, as
doublet and hose ought to show
itself courageous to petticoat.

Rosalind in *As You Like It*, 2.4.5–7

Rosalind is dressed as a man, and refers to
Celia in the biblical phrase as a woman or
"weaker vessel" (Paul's first epistle to Peter
3:7).

5 Dost thou think, though I am
caparisoned like a man, I have a
doublet and hose in my disposition?

Rosalind in *As You Like It*, 3.2.194–7

Dressed as a man, but with a woman's heart,
she is eager for Celia to tell her who has been
posting verses about her.

6 Do you not know I am a woman?
When I think, I must speak.

Rosalind in *As You Like It*, 3.2.249–50

7 I thank God I am not a woman, to
be touched with so many giddy
offenses as he hath generally taxed
their whole sex withal.

Rosalind in *As You Like It*, 3.2.347–50

She is disguised as a boy, and mocks her own
sex in speaking to Orlando.

8 I know a wench of excellent discourse,
Pretty and witty; wild, and yet, too,
  gentle.

**Antipholus of Ephesus in *The Comedy
of Errors*,** 3.1.109–10

9 Alas, poor women, make us but
  believe
(Being compact of credit) that you
  love us;
Though others have the arm, show
  us the sleeve;
We in your motion turn, and you
  may move us.

Luciana in *The Comedy of Errors*,
3.2.21–4

Speaking to Antipholus of Syracuse; "compact
of credit" = quick to believe; "motion" refers
to the orbit of a heavenly sphere.

10 My gracious silence, hail!
Wouldst thou have laughed had I
  come coffined home,
That weep'st to see me triumph?

Coriolanus in *Coriolanus*, 2.1.175

To his wife, Virgilia, who weeps with relief
that he has returned alive from battle.

11 Is there no way for men to be, but
    women
  Must be half-workers?

Posthumus in *Cymbeline*, 2.5.1–2

Beginning Posthumus's outburst of misogyny
when he falsely believes Imogen to be
unfaithful; "half-workers" = accessories, part
responsible.

12   There's no motion
  That tends to vice in man, but I
    affirm
  It is the woman's part.

Posthumus in *Cymbeline*, 2.5.20–22

Posthumus turns against all women, falsely
believing Imogen to be unfaithful; "motion" =
impulse.

13 I have heard of your paintings, too,
  well enough. God hath given you
  one face, and you make yourselves
  another.

Hamlet in *Hamlet*, 3.1.142–4

To Ophelia, in his misogyny denouncing her
and women in general.

14 Now get you to my lady's chamber,
  and tell her, let her paint an inch
  thick, to this favor she must come;
  make her laugh at that.

Hamlet in *Hamlet*, 5.1.192–5

Addressing the skull of Yorick, the king's
jester.

15   Constant you are,
  But yet a woman, and for secrecy,
  No lady closer, for I well believe
  Thou wilt not utter what thou dost
    not know,
  And so far will I trust thee, gentle
    Kate.

Hotspur in *Henry IV, Part 1*, 2.3.108–12

Refusing to tell her his purpose of armed
rebellion against the king.

16 She's beautiful, and therefore to be
    wooed;
  She is a woman, therefore to be
    won.

Suffolk in *Henry VI, Part 1*, 5.3.78–9

Seeing Margaret of France as a match for King
Henry.

17 You, that have so fair parts of
    woman on you,
  Have too a woman's heart, which
    ever yet
  Affected eminence, wealth, sover-
    eignty;
  Which, to say sooth, are blessings.

Old Lady in *Henry VIII*, 2.3.27–30

To Anne Boleyn, who has said she does not
want to be queen; "affected" = desired.

18 Alas, I am a woman friendless,
    hopeless!

Queen Katherine in *Henry VIII*, 3.1.80

Divorced by Henry and bullied by Cardinal
Wolsey.

19 I grant I am a woman; but withal
  A woman that Lord Brutus took to
    wife.
  I grant I am a woman; but withal
  A woman well-reputed, Cato's
    daughter.
  Think you I am no stronger than
    my sex,
  Being so fathered and so hus-
    banded?

Portia in *Julius Caesar*, 2.1.292–7

Cato was noted for his integrity; he supported
Pompey against Caesar, and committed suicide rather than submit to Caesar.

20 How hard it is for women to keep
    counsel.

Portia in *Julius Caesar*, 2.4.9

21   Ay me, how weak a thing
    The heart of woman is!

Portia in *Julius Caesar*, 2.4.39–40

22 *Cassio.* The divine Desdemona.
    Montano.   What is
      she?
    Cassio. She that I spake of, our
      great captain's captain.

Othello, 2.1.73–4

Implying that Desdemona now commands
Othello.

23 She that was ever fair, and never
      proud,
    Had tongue at will, and yet was
      never loud,
    . . .
    She that could think, and ne'er dis-
      close her mind,
    See suitors following, and not look
      behind.
    She was a wight, if ever such wight
      were—
    . . .
    To suckle fools and chronicle small
      beer.

Iago in *Othello*, 2.1.148–9, 156–8, 160

Any woman ("wight") so perfect would be fit
only to have fools for children and be concerned with trivialities ("small beer"); Iago's
litany ends characteristically in contempt.

24 O, the world hath not a sweeter
    creature! She might lie by an
    emperor's side and command him
    tasks.

Othello in *Othello*, 4.1.183–5

Praising Desdemona.

25 A woman moved is like a fountain
      troubled,
    Muddy, ill-seeming, thick, bereft of
      beauty,
    And while it is so, none so dry or
      thirsty
    Will deign to sip or touch one drop
      of it.

Katherine in *The Taming of the Shrew*,
5.2.142–5

Katherine lectures the angry ("moved")
Widow; "ill-seeming" = ugly.

26   Now I see our lances are but
      straws,
    Our strength as weak, our weakness
      past compare,
    That seeming to be most which we
      indeed least are.

Katherine in *The Taming of the Shrew*,
5.2.173–5

Saying, for the benefit of the headstrong
Widow and Bianca, that women's weapons
(words, temper, anger) are weak, offering a
mere appearance of strength.

27 *Orsino.* For women are as roses,
      whose fair flower
    Being once displayed, doth fall that
      very hour.
    Viola. And so they are. Alas, that
      they are so:
    To die even when they to perfection
      grow.

Twelfth Night, 2.4.38–41

Transience, the swift passage of life, is a recurrent topic in the play; the image of a woman
as a rose, fading as soon as it is full-blown
("displayed") is common.

28 *Lucetta.* Of many good, I think
    him best.
    Julia. Your reason?
    Lucetta. I have no other but a
    woman's reason:
    I think him so because I think him
    so.
    The Two Gentlemen of Verona, 1.2.21–4

Wonder

1 I was seven of the nine days out of
   the wonder before you came.
   Rosalind in As You Like It, 3.2.174–5

   The wonder was caused by Rosalind finding
   the love-rhymes Orlando hung on trees in the
   forest of Arden; alluding to the proverb "a
   wonder lasts but nine days."

2   You are made
   Rather to wonder at the things you
      hear
   Than to work any.
   Posthumus in Cymbeline, 5.3.53–5

   To a British Lord, astonished that two boys
   and an old man could win a battle against the
   Romans.

3 That would be ten days' wonder at
   the least.
   **Richard of Gloucester in Henry VI,
   Part 3,** 3.2.113

   On King Edward IV's idea of marrying Lady
   Grey; a ten days' wonder would be one more
   than the proverbial nine.

4   Be collected.
   No more amazement. Tell your
      piteous heart
   There's no harm done.
   Prospero in The Tempest, 1.2.13–15

   The storm his daughter Miranda witnessed
   was created by his magic.

Words (see also Speech, Talking, Words and Deeds)

1   Oft
   When blows have made me stay, I
   fled from words.
   Coriolanus in Coriolanus, 2.2.71–2

   The warrior would rather fight than deal in
   words.

2 That ever this fellow should have
   fewer words than a parrot, and yet
   the son of a woman!
   Prince Hal in Henry IV, Part 1,
   2.4.98–9

   Meaning Francis, the apprentice tapster;
   Prince Hal has given him little chance to talk.

3 Zounds, I was never so bethumped
      with words
   Since I first called my brother's
      father 'dad'!
   **The Bastard Falconbridge in King
   John,** 2.1.466–7

   On hearing the long speech of Hubert in an
   effort to make peace between France and England; he prefers war.

4 I marvel thy master hath not eaten
   thee for a word, for thou art not so
   long by the head as honorificabilitudinitatibus.
   Costard in Love's Labor's Lost,
   5.1.39–41

   The last word is said to be the longest known;
   the dative plural of a medieval term meaning
   the condition of being loaded with honors.

5 *Holofernes.* Goodman Dull, thou
      hast spoken no word all this
      while.

Dull. Nor understood none, neither.

Love's Labor's Lost, 5.1.149–51

An apt response to the absurdly learned dialogue of Holofernes, Nathaniel and Armado.

6 How every fool can play upon the word!

Lorenzo in *The Merchant of Venice*, 3.5.43

On Launcelot Gobbo.

7 Thou wilt be like a lover presently
And tire the hearer with a book of words.

Don Pedro in *Much Ado About Nothing*, 1.1.306–7

To Claudio, who waxes lyrical in praise of Hero, the woman he wants to marry.

8 Thou hast frighted the word out of his right sense, so forcible is thy wit.

Benedick in *Much Ado About Nothing*, 5.2.55–6

To Beatrice, who has deliberately twisted Benedick's attempt to persuade her to accept a kiss.

9 You cram these words into mine ears against
The stomach of my sense.

Alonso in *The Tempest*, 2.1.107–8

To Gonzalo, who has been trying to comfort him; he fears his son is drowned.

10 Words, words, mere words, no matter from the heart.

Troilus in *Troilus and Cressida*, 5.3.108

On receiving a letter from Cressida, whose love for Diomedes he has witnessed.

Words and Deeds

1 'Tis a kind of good deed to say well,
And yet words are no deeds.

King Henry in *Henry VIII*, 3.2.153–4

2 Your words and performances are no kin together.

Roderigo in *Othello*, 4.2.182–3

On the gap between what Iago promises and what he does.

3 Talkers are no good doers. Be assured,
We go to use our hands and not our tongues.

First Murderer in *Richard III*, 1.3.350–1

Assuring Richard they will not listen to Clarence before murdering him.

4   A true knight,
Not yet mature, yet matchless, firm of word,
Speaking in deeds, and deedless in his tongue.

Ulysses in *Troilus and Cressida*, 4.5.96–8

Describing Troilus as one who keeps his promises ("firm of word"), and who lets his actions speak for themselves.

5 His insolence draws folly from my lips,
But I'll endeavor deeds to match these words.

Hector in *Troilus and Cressida*, 4.5.258–9

Realizing it is stupid to boast as Achilles has done about what he will do in battle.

Work

1 I am indeed, sir, a surgeon to old shoes; when they are in great danger I recover them.

Cobbler in *Julius Caesar*, 1.1.23–4

Playing on "recover" as cure and resole.

2 When workmen strive to do better than well,
They do confound their skill in covetousness,
And oftentimes excusing of a fault,
Doth make the fault worse by the excuse.

Pembroke in *King John*, 4.2.28–31

"Confound their skill in covetousness" = spoil what they are skilled at by emulation, or trying to be too clever.

3 I cannot draw a cart, nor eat dried oats;
If it be man's work, I'll do't.

Captain in *King Lear*, 5.3.38–9

Accepting a commission to kill Lear and Cordelia.

4 The labor we delight in physics pain.

Macbeth in *Macbeth*, 2.3.50

"Physics pain" = relieves pain, or the trouble we have taken.

5 Now have I done a good day's work.

King Edward in *Richard III*, 2.1.1

Thinking he has reconciled his quarreling nobles.

6 These sweet thoughts do even refresh my labors.

Ferdinand in *The Tempest*, 3.1.14

Thoughts, i.e., of Miranda, with whom he is in love.

The World

1 His face was as the heav'ns, and therein stuck
A sun and moon, which kept their course, and lighted
The little O, th' earth.

Cleopatra in *Antony and Cleopatra*, 5.2.79–81

The dead Antony becomes godlike in her imaginative recall.

2 His legs bestrid the ocean, his reared arm
Crested the world.

Cleopatra in *Antony and Cleopatra*, 5.2.82–3

Her magnificent, inflated vision of the dead Antony as superman, a colossus.

3 This goodly frame, the earth, seems to me a sterile promontory.

Hamlet in *Hamlet*, 2.2.298–9

4 This most excellent canopy, the air, look you, this brave o'erhanging firmament, this majestical roof fretted with golden fire, why, it appeareth nothing to me but a foul and pestilent congregation of vapors.

Hamlet in *Hamlet*, 2.2.299–303

Hamlet may be telling his old school fellows, whom he now knows were sent for to spy on him, what he wants them to think.

5   World, world, O world!
But that thy strange mutations make us hate thee,
Life would not yield to age.

Edgar in *King Lear*, 4.1.9–11

"Life would not yield to age" = we would not be reconciled to growing old.

6   This world's a city full of straying
      streets,
    And death the market-place where
      each one meets.

Third Queen in *The Two Noble Kinsmen*, 1.5.15–16

Writing

1   Devise, wit; write, pen; for I am for
    whole volumes in folio.

Armado in *Love's Labor's Lost*, 1.2.184–5

To express his love for the country wench, Jaquenetta.

Wrongdoing (see also Crime, Evil)

1   I'll so offend to make offense a skill,
    Redeeming time when men least
      think I will.

Prince Hal in *Henry IV, Part 1*, 1.2.216–17

Planning to make up for wasted time.

2   Didst thou never hear
    That things ill got had ever bad success?

King Henry in *Henry VI, Part 3*, 2.2.45–6

Varying the proverb, "evil-gotten goods never prove well."

3   How oft the sight of means to do ill
      deeds

Make ill deeds done!

King John in *King John*, 4.2.219

Claiming that it was seeing Hubert as his agent that made him think of killing his nephew, Arthur.

4   I cannot wish the fault undone, the
    issue of it being so proper.

Kent in *King Lear*, 1.1.17–18

On learning that the handsome ("proper") Edmund is the "issue" of Gloucester's adultery.

5   *Don Pedro.* Officers, what offense
      have these men done?
    Dogberry. Marry, sir, they have
      committed false report; moreover
      they have spoken untruths; secon-
      darily, they are slanders; sixth and
      lastly, they have belied a lady;
      thirdly, they have verified unjust
      things; and, to conclude, they are
      lying knaves.

Much Ado About Nothing, 5.1.213–19

Dogberry's list is wonderfully muddled; by "slanders" he means slanderers.

6   Thus to persist
    In doing wrong extenuates not
      wrong,
    But makes it much more heavy.

Hector in *Troilus and Cressida*, 2.2.186–8

Seeing that the Trojans are wrong to want to keep Helen.

7   I see this is the time that the unjust
    man doth thrive.

Autolycus in *The Winter's Tale*, 4.4.673–4

He has benefited by an exchange of clothes with Prince Florizel.

8 Think but how vile a spectacle it
   were
   To view thy present trespass in
   another,
   Men's faults do seldom to themselves appear;
   Their own transgressions partially
   they smother.

The Rape of Lucrece, 631–4

Lucrece pleads with Tarquin, who intends to
rape her.

9 No more be grieved at that which
   thou hast done:
   Roses have thorns, and silver foun-
   tains mud;
   Clouds and eclipses stain both sun
   and moon,
   And loathsome canker lives in
   sweetest bud.

Sonnet 35, 1–4

On some wrong the loved friend has done
him; the "canker" is a worm that blights the
rose, symbol of beauty.

Youth (see also Boys, Girls, Parents and Children)

1 This thorn
   Doth to our rose of youth rightly
   belong.

**Countess of Rossillion in *All's Well
That Ends Well***, 1.3.129–30

The "thorn" is Helena's unrequited love.

2 If the quick fire of youth light not
   your mind,
   You are no maiden, but a monument.

When you are dead, you should be
such a one
As you are now; for you are cold
and stern.

Bertram in *All's Well That Ends Well*,
4.2.5–9

Bertram, married to Helena, attempts to
seduce the chaste Diana.

3 My salad days,
   When I was green in judgment,
   cold in blood,
   To say as I said then!

Cleopatra in *Antony and Cleopatra*,
1.5.73–5

Dismissing her earlier love for Julius Caesar.

4 He wears the rose
   Of youth upon him.

Antony in *Antony and Cleopatra*,
3.13.20–1

Referring to the young Octavius.

5 Briefly die their joys
   That place them on the truth of
   girls and boys.

Lucius in *Cymbeline*, 5.5.106

Imogen, disguised as his page, abandons him
for the man she loves, Posthumus.

6 In the morn and liquid dew of
   youth
   Contagious blastments are most
   imminent.
   Be wary then; best safety lies in fear.
   Youth to itself rebels, though none
   else near.

Laertes in *Hamlet*, 1.3.41–4

Warning his sister Ophelia against Hamlet's
advances; "contagious blastments" = disease-
bringing blights.

7   In the very May-morn of his youth,
     Ripe for exploits and mighty enter-
        prises.
     Bishop of Ely in _Henry V_, 1.2.120–1

     On the newly-crowned Henry V.

8   Now all the youth of England are
        on fire,
     And silken dalliance in the
        wardrobe lies.
     Chorus in _Henry V_, 2.Prologue, 1–2

9   For who is he, whose chin is but
        enriched
     With one appearing hair, that will
        not follow
     These culled and choice-drawn cav-
        aliers to France?
     Chorus in _Henry V_, 3.Prologue, 22–4

     On the English army sailing to France;
     "choice-drawn" = carefully chosen.

10   So wise so young, they say, do never
        live long.
     King Richard in _Richard III_, 3.1.79

     Commenting on the clever talk of the young
     Prince Edward; reformulating a proverb, "too
     soon wise to live long."

11   Not yet old enough for a man, nor
     young enough for a boy; as a
     squash is before 'tis a peascod, or a
     codling when 'tis almost an apple.
     'Tis with him in standing water
     between boy and man.
     Malvolio in _Twelfth Night_, 1.5.156–9

     Describing Cesario, Orsino's page (the dis-
     guised Viola); a "squash" was an unripe pea-
     pod; and a "codling" an unripe apple.

12   I would there were no age between
     ten and three-and-twenty, or that
     youth would sleep out the rest; for
     there is nothing in the between but
     getting wenches with child, wrong-
     ing the ancientry, stealing, fighting.
     Shepherd in _The Winter's Tale_,
     3.3.59–63

     "Ancientry" = old people.

13   Would any but these boiled-brains
     of nineteen and two-and-twenty
     hunt this weather?
     Shepherd in _The Winter's Tale_,
     3.3.63–5

     That is, in the gloom of a great storm.

Character Index

Duke (Measure for Measure):
Death 26; Freedom 6; Greatness 8; Happiness 5; Hypocrisy 9; Justice 10, 13, 14; Love 45; Marriage 23; Mortality 8; Music 9; Old Age 9; People 17; Power 9; Self-Knowledge 8; Slander 5; Sleep 12; Virtue 12, 13, 14, 15

Duke (The Merchant of Venice):
Cruelty 5; Mercy 9; Wisdom 4

Duke (Othello):
Philosophy 17; Theft 9

Duke (The Two Gentlemen of Verona):
Love 105; Poetry 13

Duke of Austria (King John):
Proverbs 10

Duke Senior (As You Like It):
Adversity 2; Country Life 2; Exile 1; Lust 5; Moods 2; Philosophy 2; Punishment 1; Seasons 1; Theater 2

Dull (Love's Labor's Lost):
Words 5

Dumaine (Love's Labor's Lost):
Love 41

Duncan (Macbeth):
Appearance 2; Castles 1

Edgar (King Lear):
Affliction 5; Demons 1; Devil 5; Doomsday 2; Dying 12; Endurance 3; Experience 1; Hope 2; Justice 8; Laughter 2; Miracles 3, 4; Misery 1; Patience 6; Pity 4; Sea 2; Vertigo 1; World 5

Edmund (King Lear):
Astrology 1, 2; Bastardy 1; Fortune 16; Nature 3; Nobility 7; Proverbs 15; Self-Interest 2

Egeon (The Comedy of Errors):
Grief 2, 3

Eglamour (The Two Gentlemen of Verona):
Sunset 3

Emilia (Othello):
Desire 14; Dying 14; Jealousy 11; Lying 5, 6; Marriage 42, 43; Men and Women 7; Sleep 15

Enobarbus (Antony and Cleopatra):
Argument 1; Beauty 1; Charm 1, 2; Desire 2; Folly 2; Praise 1, 2; Ships 1

Escalus (Measure for Measure):
Injustice 1; Mercy 4; Moderation 1; Power 8; Prostitution 1; Self-Knowledge 8

Evans (The Merry Wives of Windsor):
Food 9

Exeter (Henry V):
Government 2; History 1; Time 15; Tears 6; War 9

Exeter (Henry VI, Part 1):
Civil War 2; Curses 1

Fabian (Twelfth Night):
Challenges 2; Cowardice 7; Foolery 4; Theater 19; Valor 15

Fairies (The Merry Wives of Windsor):
Lust 8

Fairy (A Midsummer Night's Dream):
Fairies 1, 2, 3, 4

Falstaff (Henry IV, Part 1):
Age 7, 8, 9; Character 3; Clothing 5; Courage 2; Cowardice 3; Death 12; Excuses 2, 3; Faces 3, 4; Fatness 3; Fellowship 1; Fighting 1; Government 1; Honor 5, 6; Improvement 1; Instinct 1; Insults 3, 6, 7; Law 2; Leisure 2; Loyalty 3; Lying 2; Man 8; Medicine 7; Melancholy 7; Money 3; Night 2; Nostalgia 2; Old Age 3; Parents and Children 3; Plays 5; Reason 3; Rebellion 1; Reformation 2; Repentance 2; Reputation 2; Royalty 10; Society 1; Soldiers 7; Theft 1, 2; Thinness 1, 2; Time of Day 4; Trust 2; Valor 7, 8; Vigilance 1; War 3, 5

Falstaff (Henry IV, Part 2):
Action 5; Age 10, 11, 13, 14, 15; Body 3; Business 4; Conquest 2; Countries 4; Drinking 9, 10, 11, 12; Extravagance 1; Impatience 2; Insults 9; Laughter 1; Love 36; Lying 4; Money 4; Mortality 5; Night 3; Nostalgia 4; Old Age 4; Peace 4; Proverbs 5; Sickness 8, 10; Sobriety 1; Society 2; Speed 2; Valor 10; Wit 3

Falstaff (The Merry Wives of Windsor):
Clothing 8; Curses 6; Drinking 19; Luck 1; Money 7; Repentance 5; Self-Knowledge 10

Father (Henry VI, Part 3):
Prayer 10

Feeble (Henry IV, Part 2):
Death 14

Ferdinand (The Tempest):
Marriage 47; Music 21, 22; Names 9; Perfection 1; Service 7; Sport 2; Time of Day 9; Work 6

Feste (Twelfth Night):
Boys 4; Death 40; Drinking 28; Foolery 3; Fools 11, 12, 13, 14; Graves 2; Ignorance 2; Love 95, 96; Marriage 48; Pleasure 6; Proverbs 30; Self-Knowledge 12; Sin 8; Theater 20; Thinness 4; Time 37; Virtue 22, 23; Wit 7

First Carrier (Henry IV, Part 1):
Cleverness 1; Money 1

First Citizen (Coriolanus):
People 3

First Fairy (A Midsummer Night's Dream):
Creatures 3, 4

First Fisherman (Pericles):
Begging 2; Fish 1; Food 13

First Gentleman (Measure for Measure):
Sickness 15

First Guard (Antony and Cleopatra):
Royalty 4

First Lady (Richard II):
Stories 7

First Lady (The Winter's Tale):
Appearances 13

First Lord (All's Well That Ends Well):
Comfort 1; Life 1

First Lord (As You Like It):
Cities 1; Melancholy 1; Tears 3; Trees 1

First Murderer (Macbeth):
Sunset 1

First Murderer (Richard III):
Conscience 5; Words and Deeds 3

First Plebeian (Julius Caesar):
Civil War 3

Play Index

Time 15; Time of Day 6; Travel 10, 11; Treason 3; Valor 11; Vegetables 1; War 8, 9, 10, 11, 12, 13, 14, 15; Weather 2; Youth 7, 8, 9

Henry VI, Part 1
Anxiety 3; Birds 4, 5; Chastity 7; Chivalry 1; Civil War 1, 2; Curses 1; Delay 3; Duty 3; Fear 4; Flowers 4; Glory 1; God 4; Hospitality 1; Law 3, 4; Marriage 18; Night 8; Perplexity 1; Persuasion 1; Portents 3; Pride 1; Resistance 1; Speech 6; Thought 7; Women 16

Henry VI, Part 2
Ambition 3; Animals 5; Books 1; Education 1, 2; Farewells 9; Fear 5; Gardens 3, 4; God 5, 6, 7; Grief 7; Heaven 2; Honor 11; Innocence 3; Kissing 7; Language 4; Lawyers 1; Loss 2; Parting 8; Peace 12; People 15, 16; Prayer 8, 9; Proverbs 7, 8; Quarrels 4, 5; Rivers 2; Seasons 8; Sin 2; Speech 7; Storms 2; Thought 8; Treachery 1

Henry VI, Part 3
Action 7, 8; Afterlife 5; Animals 6, 7; Aspiration 1; Beauty 8; Body 4; Courage 3, 4; Courtship 12; Cruelty 1; Duplicity 1, 2, 3; Dying 8, 9; Encouragement 1; Fate 4; Fear 6; Fire 1; Happiness 3; Hypocrisy 3; Identity 6; Law 5; Misanthropy 2; Old Age 5; Parents and Children 4; Perseverance 1; Prayer 10; Proverbs 9; Resistance 2; Royalty 21, 22; Ruthlessness 2; Suspicion 1; Thought 9; Truisms 3; Tyranny 1; Victory 1; Wonder 3; Wrongdoing 2

Henry VIII
Action 9, 10, 11; Advice 9; Ambition 4, 5, 6; Beauty 9, 10, 11; Betrayal 1; Conscience 3; Contempt 1; Corruption 4; Devotion 1; Downfall 1, 2, 3; Dying 10; Eating 6; Eloquence 5; Enemies 3; Envy 1; Farewells 10; Fashion 5; Forgiveness 4; God 8; Goodness 1; Happiness 4; Haste 1; Hypocrisy 4; Innocence 4; Innovation 1; Integrity 1; Justice 3; Law 6; Learning 1; Music 7, 8; Nobility 3; Old Age 6; Peace 13; Plain-Speaking 2; Politics 7, 8, 9; Remembrance 4, 5; Royalty 23, 24; Self-Knowledge 4; Service 4, 5; Speed 3; Talking 4; Tears 7; Truth 3; Weakness 2; Women 17, 18; Words and Deeds 1

Julius Caesar
Acting 15, 16; Affliction 2; Ambition 7, 8, 9, 10; Anger 2; Anxiety 4, 5; Apologies 2; Apparitions 4, 5; Assassination 1, 2; Burial 4; Caesar 1, 2, 3, 4, 5; Cause 1, 2, 3; Chaos 1; Civil War 3; Conspiracy 2, 3, 4, 5, 6; Constancy 1, 2; Constraint 1; Contempt 2, 3; Corruption 5, 6; Councils 1, 2, 3; Courage 5; Criticism 1, 2; Cruelty 2; Danger 5, 6, 7, 8, 9; Death 17, 18, 19; Death-Wish 6; Defeat 1; Dismissal 1; Education 3; Enemies 4; Epitaphs 8, 9, 10, 11, 12; Evil 3; Eyes 7; Farewells 11; Fate 5, 6; Faults 6, 7; Fear 7, 8; Fire 2; Fitness 1; Flattery 4; Foolery 2; Forbearance 1, 2, 3; Foreboding 8; Fortune 11; Freedom 3, 4, 5; Friendship 12, 13, 14, 15, 16 17; Greatness 6, 7; Greetings 2, 3, 4; Health 1; History 2; Honor 12, 13, 14, 15, 16, 17; Hypocrisy 5; Idleness 1; Ingratitude 3, 4; Insults 10; Integrity 2; Invitations 1; Judgment 1; Justice 4; Language 5; Last Words 2; Life 6; Loss 3; Love 37; Loyalty

4; Marriage 20, 21, 22; Maturity 2, 3; Men 7; Mistakes 3; Misunderstanding 1; Money 6; Mourning 13, 14, 15, 16; Names 2; Necessity 3; Night 9; Nobility 4, 5, 6; Opinion 2; Opportunity 2; Parting 9; Patience 3, 4; Patriotism 1; Persuasion 2, 3, 4; Philosophy 12, 13; Pity 2, 3; Plain-Speaking 3, 4, 5; Politics 10, 11, 12, 13, 14, 15; Portents 4, 5, 6; Power 2, 3, 4, 5, 6, 7; Promises 4, 5; Prophecy 5; Quarrels 6, 7, 8; Reading 2; Reason 4; Reconciliation 1, 2; Remembrance 6; Reputation 3; Resignation 2; Resolution 3; Revels 1; Rumor 6; Sacrifice 1; Self-Knowledge 5; Servitude 1, 2; Sleep 6, 7; Sleeplessness 2, 3; Society 3; Speech 8; Speechmaking 2; Speed 4; Stoicism 2; Storms 3, 4; Suicide 15; Superstition 1; Tears 8; Theater 10; Thought 10; Transience 1; Treason 4; Tyranny 2, 3, 4; Virtue 8; War 16; Women 19, 20, 21; Work 1

King John
Anger 3; Comfort 4; Danger 10; Death-Wish 7; Dying 11; Encouragement 2; Extravagance 4; Fear 9, 10; Fortune 12; Grief 8, 9; Hypocrisy 6; Murder 4; Names 3; Patriotism 2; Proverbs 10, 11; Religion 2; Resolution 4; Self-Interest 1; Sickness 11, 12; Simplicity 1; Sin 3; Storms 5; Tediousness 2; Time 16; Truth 4; Words 3; Work 2; Wrongdoing 3

King Lear
Adultery 1; Advice 10; Affliction 3, 4, 5, 6; Age 20, 21, 22, 23, 24, 25, 26, 27; Anarchy 1; Anger 4; Aphorisms 2, 3; Astrology 1, 2, 3; Authority 6, 7; Bastardy 1; Capriciousness 2; Cause 4; Ceremony 3; Country Life 11; Danger 11; Death 20, 21; Demons 1; Desire 8; Devil 5; Disorder 1, 2; Dogs 3; Doomsday 2; Duty 4; Dying 12; Endurance 3; Evil 4; Experience 1; Eyes 8; Farewells 12; Fashion 6; Fear 11; Flattery 5; Fools 8; Forgetfulness 3; Fortune 13, 14, 15, 16; Gods and Goddesses 1; Gold 4; Homelessness 1, 2; Honesty 3; Hope 2; Humanity 3; Hypocrisy 7; Identity 3, 4; Improvement 2; Ingratitude 5, 6, 7, 8; Insults 11; Justice 5, 6, 7, 8; Laughter 2; Lawyers 2; Love 38, 39, 40; Madness 7, 8, 9; Man 9; Maps 2; Medicine 8; Middle Age 3; Miracles 2, 3, 4; Misery 1, 2; Misogyny 1; Mortality 7; Mourning 17; Nature 3; Necessity 4, 5; Night 10, 11; Nobility 7; Nothing 1, 2, 3; Obstinacy 3, 4; Old Age 7; Parents and Children 5, 6, 7, 8, 9; Patience 5, 6, 7; Pity 4; Plain-Speaking 6, 7; Politics 16, 17; Portents 7; Prayer 11, 12, 13; Proverbs 12, 13, 14, 15, 16; Reconciliation 3, 4; Repentance 4; Retirement 2; Royalty 25; Sacrifice 2; Sea 2; Self-Interest 2, 3; Self-Knowledge 6; Self-Pity 1, 2; Sickness 13, 14; Sin 4; Sleep 8; Sorrow 3; Speech 9, 10, 11, 12; Storms 6, 7, 8, 9, 10; Suffering 1, 2; Tears 9, 10, 11, 12; Time 17; Tyranny 5; Vanity 1; Vertigo 1; Virtue 9; Work 3; World 5; Wrongdoing 4

Love's Labor's Lost
Affectation 1; Argument 3, 4; Arithmetic 1; Beauty 12, 13; Books 2; Charity 2; Cheerfulness 1; Clothing 6; Devil 6; Endings 2; Fame 2; Fashion 7; Ignorance 1; Jokes 1, 2, 3; Language 6; Light 1; Love 41, 42, 43, 44; Lust 7; Merriment 2; Mockery 2; Names 4; Payment 1; Plain-Speaking 8, 9; Plays 6; Poetry 9; Reading 3;

Theft 7, 8; Valor 13; Value 2; Victory 2; Villainy 3, 4, 5, 6; Wisdom 5; Wit 4, 5; Words 7, 8; Wrongdoing 5

Othello

Action 14; Advice 14; Affliction 8, 9, 10; Aphorisms 10, 11; Appearance 8; Beauty 16, 17, 18; Cause 5; Chance 1; Character 4; Constancy 5; Courtship 16; Criticism 4; Deceit 11, 12, 13, 14; Desire 14; Devil 9; Devotion 5; Drinking 20, 21, 22, 23; Duty 5; Dying 14; Education 4; Endings 3; Evil 10; Farewells 14; Fate 7; Fighting 4, 5; Foreboding 11; Friendship 24; Greatness 9; Greetings 9, 10; Grief 12; Happiness 6; Hell 5, 6; Honesty 5, 6, 7; Hypocrisy 11, 12; Inconstancy 5; Infidelity 1; Jealousy 5, 6, 7, 8, 9, 10, 11, 12; Joy 4; Lament 1; Lechery 3; Light 2; Loss 6, 7; Love 68, 69, 70, 71; Lust 11; Lying 5, 6; Magic 2; Marriage 39, 40, 41, 42, 43; Men 11, 12; Men and Women 7; Money 11; Moods 13, 14; Moon 4; Murder 7, 8, 9, 10; Music 15, 16, 17; Passion 2; Patience 10; Philosophy 17; Pity 7, 8; Plots 4; Proof 1, 2; Proverbs 23; Reputation 6, 7, 8, 9, 10; Resignation 5, 6; Resolution 6; Revenge 5, 6, 7; Sea 3; Self-Interest 4; Sickness 16; Silence 6; Slander 6; Sleep 14, 15; Soldiers 19, 20, 21, 22, 23, 24; Sorrow 6; Soul 2; Speech 18, 19, 20, 21; Stories 3; Storms 11; Tears 14; Thanks 2; Theft 9, 10; Thought 12; Time 20, 21; Travel 16; Unkindness 3; Virtue 17, 18, 19; War 18, 19; Women 22, 23, 24; Words and Deeds 2

Pericles

Appearance 9; Beauty 19, 20; Begging 2; Birth and Death 1; Cities 2; Death 32; Deceit 15; Fish 1; Fishing 3; Food 13; Gifts 2, 3; Honor 18; Life 9; Melancholy 8; Misery 3; Opinion 3; Patience 11; Promises 7; Sin 6, 7; Sorrow 7; Stories 4; Storms 12, 13; Thanks 3; Time 22; Tyranny 6

Richard II

Advice 15; Affliction 11; Angels 2; Anger 8; Animals 9, 10; Betrayal 2; Castles 2; Civil War 4; Confusion 7; Conspiracy 7, 8; Countries 5, 6, 7; Cowardice 5; Death 33, 34, 35; Death-Wish 9; Deserving 3; Despair 4, 5, 6; Devil 10; Discontent; Disorder 3; Eating 11; Eloquence 6; Endings 4; Epitaphs 13, 14; Exile 3, 4, 5, 6, 7; Farewells 15; Fashion 9; Flattery 6; Flowers 7; Foreboding 12; Friendship 25; Futility 1; Gardens 5, 6, 7, 8, 9; Grace 1; Greetings 11; Grief 13, 14; Holidays 2; Honor 19, 20; Humanity 6; Hypocrisy 13; Identity 5; Imagination 6; Innovation 2; Integrity 3; Language 7; Last Words 3, 4; Lateness 3; Letters 3; Life 10; Loss 8; Meeting 1; Middle Age 4; Music 18; Mutability 2; Necessity 7, 8; Parents and Children 14; Parting 13; Philosophy 18; Pity 9; Poetry 12; Poison 2; Politics 19, 20; Portents 9; Power 11; Pride 2; Proverbs 24; Renunciation 1, 2, 3; Reputation 11; Royalty 26, 27, 28, 29, 30, 31; Self-Knowledge 11; Self-Pity 3; Sincerity 2; Slander 7; Sorrow 8, 9, 10; Speech 22; Sport 1; Stories 5, 6, 7; Thanks 4; Theater 17; Time 23, 24; Transience 3; Travel 17, 18; Vanity 2; War 20; Weather 5

Richard III

Acting 26; Animals 11; Apologies 4; Appearances 10; Boys 3; Brevity 2; Change 1; Conscience 4, 5, 6, 7, 8; Courtship 17, 18; Cowardice 6; Curses 7; Dancing 2;

Danger 14; Death 36; Deceit 16, 17, 18, 19, 20; Decline 2; Dejection 4; Deserving 4; Despair 7; Desperation 1; Dreams 8, 9, 10, 11; Duplicity 6, 7; Eloquence 7; Excuses 4; Execution 1; Fame 4; Foreboding 13; Gifts 4; Government 4; Grace 2; Greatness 10; Hope 4; Hypocrisy 14, 15, 16; Improvement 3; Insults 18; Judgment 6; Last Words 5; Marriage 44; Murder 11, 12, 13; Pity 10; Plain-Speaking 11; Politics 21; Prayer 15; Proverbs 25, 26; Punishment 3; Readiness 2; Repetition 1; Reputation 12; Ruthlessness 5; Scorn 2; Sleeplessness 6; Sorrow 11; Stories 8; Sunrise 3; Sunset 2; Transience 4; Trust 3; Truth 7; Victory 3; Villainy 7; Words and Deeds 3; Work 5; Youth 10

Romeo and Juliet

Adoration 1; Adversity 4, 5; Advice 16; Affliction 12; Anticipation 3; Anxiety 9; Apologies 5; Appetite 1; Beauty 21, 22; Cooking 2; Courtesy 2; Courtship 19; Curses 8; Dancing 3; Dawn 5,6, 7; Death 37, 38; Death-Wish 10; Deceit 21, 22, 23; Despair 8; Devotion 6; Dreams 12, 13, 14; Dying 15; Evil 11; Exile 8, 9; Eyes 13; Farewells 16, 17, 18, 19; Fear 15; Fire 3; Futility 2; Haste 2; Impatience 3; Inevitability 2; Infatuation 9; Jokes 4; Last Words 6; Love 72, 73, 74, 75, 76, 77, 78, 79, 80, 81, 82, 83; Marriage 45; Memory 5; Men and Women 8; Mercy 14; Music 19; Names 7, 8; Nature 5, 6; News 10; Night 20, 21; Old Age 11; Parents and Children 15; Parting 14, 15, 16; Peace 14; Poison 3; Poverty 1, 2; Quarrels 12, 13, 14; Seasons 15; Sleeplessness 7; Society 7; Sorrow 12, 13, 14, 15; Strength 2; Suffering 3; Sunrise 4, 5; Talking 6; Theater 18; Time 25, 26, 27; Transience 5; Vanity 3; Vice 3; Virtue 20; Vows 4

The Taming of the Shrew

Acting 27; Choice 8; Clothing 9, 10; Courtship 20; Death 39; Eating 12; Education 5; Falconry 1; Fashion 10; Fire 4; Food 14; Friendship 26, 27; Giddiness 1; Insults 19; Kissing 9; Lateness 4; Learning 4; Love 84, 85, 86, 87; Marriage 46; Money 12; Music 20; Nostalgia 5; Pleasure 5; Praise 8; Quarrels 15, 16; Resistance 3; Speechmaking 5; Study 4, 5; Talking 7; Thanks 5; Travel 19; Value 3; Women 25

The Tempest

Acting 28; Air 2; Astrology 4; Beauty 23; Blessings 5, 6; Books 3, 4; Clothing 11; Comfort 6; Darkness 3; Dreams 15; Drinking 24, 25, 25; Education 6, 7; Exercise 1; Eyes 14, 15; Fairies 8, 9; Fellowship 3; Fish 2; Forgiveness 5; Freedom 7, 8, 9; Gardens 10; Goodness 4; Government 5; Humanity 7; Joy 5; Language 8; Life 11; Marriage 47; Memory 6; Monsters 1; Mortality 9, 10; Music 21, 22, 23, 24; Myths 1; Names 9; Nobility 8; Perfection 1; Politics 22; Praise 9; Prayer 16; Proverbs 27; Remembrance 8; Renunciation 4, 5; Sea 4, 5, 6; Service 6, 7; Servitude 3; Sex 8; Ships 5; Sleep 16, 17; Society 8; Speed 5; Sport 2; Storms 14, 15, 16; Suffering 4; Swimming 1, 2; Sympathy 1; Tears 15; Time of Day 9; Transformation 3; Transience 6; Travel 21; Trust 4; Utopias 1; Vegetables 2; Weakness 4, 5; Weariness 3; Wit 6; Wonder 4; Words 9; Work 6

Poem Index

Keyword Index

advantage (cont'd.)
  let not a. slip (Proverbs 33)
adversaries:
  do as a. do in law (Friendship 27)
adversary:
  answer a stony a. (Cruelty 5)
adversity:
  a.'s sweet milk, philosophy (Adversity 4)
  sweet are the uses of a. (Adversity 2)
  wretched soul, bruised with a. (Adversity 3)
advertisement:
  this a. is five days old (News 5)
advice:
  this a. is free I give (Advice 14)
advise:
  thou dost a. me (Advice 17)
afeared:
  be not a. (Music 23)
  I was not much a. (Plain-Speaking 12)
affairs:
  a tide in the a. of men (Opportunity 2)
  hear him debate of commonwealth a. (Politics 5)
  since the a. of men (Philosophy 13)
  which way to order these a. (Politics 19)
affection:
  I weigh my friend's a. (Friendship 30)
  that ceremonious a. (Ceremony 3)
affections:
  have not we a.? (Marriage 43)
  yet have I fierce a. (Desire 1)
affliction:
  a. is enamored of thy parts (Affliction 12)
  a. may subdue the cheek (Affliction 13)
  henceforth I'll bear a. (Affliction 6)
  pleased heaven to try me with a. (Affliction 9)
afflictions:
  hast thou ... a feeling of their a.? (Sympathy 1)
agate:
  in shape no bigger than an a. stone (Dreams 12)
age:
  a. cannot wither her (Charm 3)
  a. is unnecessary (Age 26)
  a staff of honor for mine a. (Old Age 12)
  beauty doth varnish a. (Beauty 13)
  be comfort to my a. (Age 2)
  beyond the promise of his a. (Courage 5)
  ease in waning a. (Ambition 14)
  hath homely a. th'alluring beauty took (Unkindness 1)
  have some smack of a. in you (Old Age 4)
  help time to furrow me with a. (Grief 13)
  how full of changes his a. is (Age 20)
  I would there were no a. (Youth 12)
  meat ... he cannot endure in his age (Experience 22)
  my a. is as a lusty winter (Age 3)
  old a., that ill layer-up of beauty (Age 19)
  pity, God, this miserable a. (Prayer 10)
  respect and reason wait on wrinkled a. (Old Age 14)
  separate a. and covetousness (Age 13)
  settled a. his sables (Clothing 4)

the sixth a. shifts (Age 4)
unregarded a. (Age 1)
weariest ... life that a. ... can lay (Death 30)
when went there by an a. (History 2)
your lordship ... have yet some smack of a. (Age 10)
agent:
  bend up each corporal a. (Resolution 5)
agents:
  night's black a. (Night 13)
ague-proof:
  I am not a. (Flattery 5)
agues:
  this praise doth nourish a. (Sickness 7)
aim:
  the a. of all is but to nurse the life (Ambition 14)
air:
  a. is delicate (Birds 7)
  a. sweetly recommends itself (Castles 1)
  fog and filthy a. (Air 1, Confusion 2)
  I am fire and a. (Dying 2)
  I drink the a. before me (Speed 5)
  infected be the a. whereon they ride (Curses 3)
  I scent the morning a. (Dawn 2, Time of Day 2)
  it is as the a., invulnerable (Ghosts 4)
  melted into a.(Acting 26)
  the a., a chartered libertine, is still (Eloquence 3)
  the a. bites shrewdly (Weather 1)
  the a. breathes upon us (Air 2)
  this most excellent canopy, the a. (World 4)
alabaster:
  smooth as monumental a. (Beauty 16)
alack:
  a., the night comes on (Storms 4)
  a., when once our grace (Shame 10)
alacrity:
  I have not that a. of spirit (Dejection 4)
Alas:
  a., poor Yorick (Epitaphs 4)
  a., 'tis true, I have gone here and there (Folly 5)
  a., why ... you heap this care on me? (Hypocrisy 16)
alderman:
  agate stone on the forefinger of an a. (Dreams 12)
alehouse:
  would I were in an a. in London (Safety 1)
Alexandrian:
  this is not yet an A. feast (Feasts 1)
all:
  a. is uneven (Confusion 7)
  a. shall be well (Proverbs 21)
  a. so soon as the all-cheering sun (Sunrise 4)
  a. strange and terrible events (Resignation 1)
  a.'s well (Achievement 1)
  a.'s well that ends well (Endings 1)
  a. that glisters is not gold (Gold 5)
  a. the faith, the virtue of my heart (Devotion 2)
  a. the world is cheered by the sun (Sunrise 3)
  a. you that kiss my lady peace (Peace 4)
  did you say a.? O hell-kite! All? (Cruelty 4)
allegiance:
  pluck a. from men's hearts (Humility 3)

alliance:

Good lord, for a. (Celibacy 3)

all-seer:

that high a. which I dallied with (Punishment 3)

alone:

here can I sit a. (Solitude 5)

how can it be said I am a. (Solitude 3)

Alps:

on the A. ... thou didst eat strange flesh (Eating 1)

altitude:

the a. which thou hast ... fell (Miracles 3)

amaze:

it doth a. me that such a man (Power 4)

amazed:

I am a. ... and lose my way (Danger 10)

amazement:

be collected. No more a. (Wonder 4)

ambition:

a.'s debt is paid (Ambition 8)

a., the soldier's virtue (Ambition 1)

art not without a. (Ambition 11)

become a churchman better than a. (Ambition 6)

death for his a.(Caesar 3)

fling away a. (Ambition 5)

ill-weaved a. (Ambition 2)

lowliness is young a.'s ladder (Ambition 7)

the big wars that makes a. virtue (Farewells 14)

thriftless a. (Ambition 13)

vaulting a. (Ambition 12)

virtue is choked with foul a. (Ambition 3)

ambitious:

the very substance of the a. (Dreams 4)

Amen:

a., a. to that fair prayer (Prayer 14)

amend:

do thou a. thy face, and I'll a. my life (Faces 3)

amendment:

I see a good a. of life (Theft 1)

amiable:

O a., lovely Death! (Death-Wish 5)

amity:

now thou and I are new in a. (Reconciliation 4)

the a. that wisdom knits not (Friendship 31)

anatomy:

a mere a. (Character 1)

angel:

art thou... some angel (Apparitions 5)

a. is like you, Kate (Courtship 8)

better a. is a man (Love 111)

how like an a. (Man 5)

she is an a. (Beauty 11)

speak again, bright a. (Adoration 1)

though a. on the outward side (Hypocrisy 9)

angels:

a. and ministers of grace (Prayer 3)

a. are bright still (Angels 1)

flights of a. sing thee to thy rest (Epitaphs 5)

if a. fight weak men must fall (Angels 2)

anger:

a.'s my meat (Anger 1)

contempt and a. of his lip (Contempt 4)

more in sorrow than in a. (Moods 7)

to be in a. is impiety (Anger 9)

touch me with noble a. (Tears 10)

angle:

give me mine a. (Fishing 1)

angling:

pleasant'st a. is to see the fish (Fishing 2)

angry:

be a. when you will (Forbearance 1)

when she is a. she is keen (Anger 5)

animal:

a poor., bare, forked a. (Man 9)

animals:

the paragon of a. (Man 5)

annals:

if you have writ your a. true (Soldiers 2)

answer:

still a. nay and take it (Deceit 19)

your a., sir, is enigmatical (Answers 1)

ant:

set thee to school to an a. (Proverbs 14)

anthropophagi:

the a., and men whose heads (Travel 16)

antic:

there the a. sits (Death 35)

antiquity:

every part ... blasted with a. (Age 12)

Antony:

A. that revels long a-nights (Revels 1)

as she would catch another A. (Death 6)

bear the weight of A. (Horses 1)

none but A. should conquer A. (Suicide 5)

to imagine an A. (Imagination 1)

when I forget to send to A. (Letters 1)

anything:

a. that's mended is but patched (Virtue 22, Sin 8)

ape:

like an angry a. (Authority 9)

Apollo:

A. a poor humble swain (Gods 5)

apothecary:

O true a. (Last Words 6)

apparel:

a. oft proclaims the man (Clothing 3)

a. vice like virtue's harbinger (Deceit 1)

fashion wears out more a. (Fashion 8)

appetite:

a. an universal wolf (Anarchy 1)

cloy the hungry edge of a. (Imagination 6)

good digestion wait on a. (Eating 7)

sharpen with cloyless sauce his a. (Food 2)

taste with a distempered a. (Self-Love 3)

their l. may be called a. (Love 98)

who riseth from a feast with that keen a. (Eating 8)

appetites:

curb those a. (Law 11)

other women cloy the a. (Praise 1)

applause:

their loud a. and aves vehement (People 17)

apple:
a goodly a. rotten at the heart (Duplicity 4)
an a. cleft in twain (Twins 4)
apple-john:
I am withered like an old a. (Thinness 2)
apples:
small choice in rotten a. (Choice 8)
apricots:
feed him with apricots (Food 11)
go bind ... yon dangling a. (Gardens 5)
April:
a day in A. never came so sweet (Anticipation 2)
he smells A. and May (Courtship 13)
men are A. when they woo (Marriage 5)
the A.'s in her eyes (Tears 1)
uncertain glory of an A. day (Love 102)
aqua-vitae:
like a. with a midwife (Plots 5)
arch:
the wide a. of the ranged empire fall (Empire 1)
Arden:
in the forest of A. (Country Life 1)
now I am in A., the more fool I (Travel 1)
argument:
all the a. is a whore (War 23)
finer than the staple of his a. (Argument 4)
are:
a. you good men and true? (Solecisms 4)
Aristotle:
A. thought unfit to hear ... philosophy (Argument 3)
armed:
be thou a. for some unhappy words (Quarrels 15)
armor:
the very a. he had on (Ghosts 1)
arms:
a., take your last embrace (Farewells 19)
my father's spirit in a.! (Foreboding 5)
take a. against a sea of troubles (Choice 1)
arrest:
Death is strict in his a. (Death 9)
art:
a. made tongue-tied (Censorship 1)
a. of our necessities (Necessity 5)
a. which does change nature (Nature 8)
a. which in their piedness shares (Nature 7)
a. with nature's workmanship at strife (Painting 1)
desiring this man's a. (Misery 5)
in sweet music is such a. (Music 8)
I want that glib and oily a. (Hypocrisy 7)
let it be an a. lawful as eating (Magic 3)
more matter with less a. (Eloquence 2)
no a. to find the mind's construction (Appearance 2)
artery:
makes each petty a. in this body (Fate 1)
Arthur's bosom:
(Afterlife 4)
arts:
had I but followed the a. (Language 9)
peace, dear nurse of a. (Peace 11)

asleep:
faith, half a. (Sleep 15)
what, all so soon a. (Sleep 17)
ass:
forget not that I am an a. (Stupidity 1)
I ... perceive that I am made an a. (Self-Knowledge 10)
my foes tell me plainly I am an a. (Self-Knowledge 12)
specify ... that I am an a. (Self-Importance 2)
that any man turn a. (Country Life 5)
you are an a. (Insults 17)
assays:
with a. of bias (Deviousness 1)
assassination:
if th' a. could trammel up (Action 12)
asses:
a. are made to bear (Quarrels 16)
tenderly led by the nose as a. are (Deceit 12)
Athens:
seemed A. as a paradise (Love 53)
atomies:
eyes ... shut their coward gates on a. (Eyes 1)
attention:
tongues of dying men enforce a. (Last Words 3)
attribute:
much a. he hath (Fame 5)
aught:
what's a. but as 'tis valued? (Value 4)
augmentation:
new map with the a. of the Indies (Faces 6)
Aurora:
yonder shines A's harbinger (Dawn 4)
authorities:
manage those a. (Age 21)
when two a. are up (Confusion 1)
authority:
art made tongue-tied by a. (Censorship 1)
a., though it err like others (Authority 10)
man ... dressed in a little brief a. (Authority 9)
the demigod, a. (Authority 8)
the great image of a. (Authority 5)
there is no fettering of a. (Authority 1)
though a. be a stubborn bear (Authority 11)
what a. and show of truth (Deceit 9)
wrest once the law to your a. (Law 7)
you have that in your countenance ... a. (Authority 6)
autumn:
the childing a. (Seasons 14)
the teeming a. (Seasons 19)
an a. ... that grew the more by reaping (Generosity 1)
avoided:
what can be a., whose end is purposed? (Fate 4)
away:
a. and mock the time (Deceit 5)
awe:
live to be in a. of such a thing (Freedom 2)
aweary:
Cassius is a. of the world (Criticism 2)

axe:
let the great a. fall (Punishment 2)
babbled:
'a b. of green fields (Dying 6)
babe:
how tender 'tis to love the b. (Infancy 1, Ruthlessness 4)
pity like a naked new-born b. (Pity 5)
babes:
old fools are b. again (Age 25)
baby:
dost thou not see my b.? (Infancy 1)
bachelor:
b. of threescore (Celibacy 1)
when I said I would die a b. (Marriage 32)
backward:
dark b. and abysm of time (Memory 6)
bait:
your b. of falsehood takes this carp (Deviousness 1)
ballad:
I love a b. in print (Poetry 14, Singing 3)
ballad-mongers:
these same meter b. (Poetry 6)
balm:
I wash away my b. (Renunciation 3)
'tis not the b., the scepter and the ball (Royalty 19)
band:
the gross b. of the unfaithful (Religion 1)
banishment:
Ha, b.? Be merciful, say death (Exile 8)
bankrupt:
time is a very b. (Time 8)
Banquo:
B, thy soul's flight (Death 24)
bar:
any b., any cross (Hindrance 1)
barbarism:
b. itself have pitied him (Pity 9)
Barbary:
a maid called B. (Music 16)
barber's:
I must to the b. (Hair 3)
barefoot:
walked b. to Palestine (Desire 14)
bargain:
in the way of b. (Business 2, Negotiation 1)
barge:
the b. she sat in (Ships 1)
barnes:
b. are blessings (Children 1)
bars:
life being weary of these worldly b. (Suicide 15)
base:
art thou b., common, and popular? (Soldiers 14)
b. is the slave that pays (Money 5)
who is here so b.? (Patriotism 1)
bastard:
that same wicked b. of Venus (Love 23)
I am a bastard too (Bastardy 2)

bastardizing:
star...twinkled on my b. (Astrology 2)
bastards:
gods, stand up for b. (Bastardy 1)
bat:
ere the b. hath flown (Evil 7)
bate:
do I not b.? (Thinness 2)
battle:
the noise of b. hurtled (Portents 5)
when the b.'s lost and won (Supernatural 2)
battlements:
entrance of Duncan under my b. (Foreboding 9)
bawdy:
if b. talk offend you (Obscenity 1)
bay-trees:
the b. ... are all withered (Portents 9)
be:
be it thy course to busy giddy minds (Politics 4)
be not afeared (Music 22)
be not easily won (Deceit 19)
be you not troubled with the time (Necessity 1)
to be or not to be (Choice 1, Suicide 12)
beacon:
modest doubt ... the b. of the wise (Security 2)
beagle:
a b., true-bred (Love 97)
bear:
exit pursued by a b. (Animals 12)
b. free and patient thoughts (Patience 6)
b. with me good boy (Forbearance 3)
b. with my weakness (Weakness 4)
sing the savageness out of a b. (Music 15)
though authority be a stubborn b. (Authority 11)
beard:
a husband with a b. on his face (Marriage 29)
black b. will turn white (Courtship 11)
he that hath a b. (Celibacy 2)
what a b. hast thou got (Appearance 4)
younger ... by the loss of a b. (Appearance 6)
bearing:
either wise b. or ignorant carriage (Society 2)
bears:
wolves and b. (Creatures 5)
beast:
a b., no more (Man 7)
Caesar should be a b. without a heart (Fear 8)
he is little better than a b. (Drinking 15)
no b. so fierce (Animals 11, Pity 10)
the b. with many heads (People 12)
unkindest b. more kinder than mankind (Kindness 4)
beasts:
gods ... have taken the shapes of b. (Gods 5)
here comes a pair of very strange b. (Fools 6)
the b., the fishes and the wingèd fowls (Marriage 9)
beating:
b. and hanging are terrors to me (Afterlife 6)
beautiful:
she's b., and therefore to be wooed (Women 16)

beauty:
 b. and honor in her (Beauty 10)
 b. doth varnish age (Beauty 13)
 b. itself doth of itself persuade (Beauty 29)
 b. my prize (Desire 19)
 b. provoketh thieves (Women 3)
 b.'s ensign yet is crimson (Death 38)
 b.'s rose might never die (Beauty 30)
 b. too rich for use (Beauty 22)
 b. within itself should not be wasted (Time 45)
 for b. lives with kindness (Beauty 27)
 for b., wit, high birth (Time 30)
 grief, that's b.'s canker (Beauty 23)
 he hath a daily b. in his life (Virtue 19)
 how much more doth b. beauteous seem (Beauty 32)
 I ne'er saw true b. (Love 70)
 look on b., and you shall see (Beauty 14)
 most radiant, exquisite ... b. (Beauty 24)
 my b., though but mean (Beauty 12)
 O b., till now I never knew thee (Beauty 9)
 orators are dumb when b. pleadeth (Eloquence 8)
 'tis b. that doth oft make women proud (Beauty 8)
 unmask her b. to the moon (Chastity 5)
 virtue is b. (Virtue 24)
 were b. under twenty locks (Proverbs 32)
bed:
 heat of a luxurious b. (Lust 9)
 how bravely thou becom'st thy b. (Beauty 5)
 I haste me to my b. (Sleep 19)
 made his pendant b.(Birds 7)
 never yet one hour in his b. (Sleeplessness 6)
 run into't as to a lover's b. (Death 1)
bedfellows:
 misery acquaints a man with strange b. (Fellowship 3)
beds:
 the b. i'th' east are soft (Luxury 1)
bed-time:
 I would 'twere b.-time (War 3)
bee:
 where the b. sucks there suck I (Fairies 9)
beef:
 I am a great eater of b. (Eating 13)
 what say you to a piece of b.? (Food 14)
beer:
 show vilely in me to desire small b. (Drinking 8)
beetle:
 poor b. that we tread upon (Death 27)
 shard-borne b. with his drowsy hums (Evil 7)
beetles:
 b. black approach not near (Creatures 4)
beggar:
 a dedicated b. to the air (Poverty 3)
 farmer's dog bark at a b. (Authority 7)
 whiles I am a b. I will rail (Hypocrisy 6)
beggars:
 our basest b. (Necessity 4)
 they are but b. (Love 83)
 when b. die there are no comets (Portents 6)

beggary:
 there's b. in the love (Love 5)
begging:
 here's them ... gets more with b. (Begging 2)
begot:
 you have b. me (Parents and Children 7)
beguile:
 to b. the time (Deceit 4)
believe:
 b. me for mine honor (Honor 14)
 b. not that the ... dart of love (Love 45)
 I might not this b. (Belief 1)
 make thee b. I love (Courtship 1)
bell:
 she strike upon the b. (Bells 1)
 the b. invites me (Bells 2)
 the sullen, surly b. (Mourning 20)
bellman:
 the fatal b. (Birds 8)
bellows:
 the b. and the fan (Lust 2)
bells:
 like sweet b. jangled (Dejection 4)
bellyful:
 rumble thy b. (Storms 9)
benefits:
 we are born to do b. (Friendship 29)
benison:
 God's b. go with you (Blessings 1)
beseech:
 b. you sir, be merry (Joy 5)
best:
 the b. persuaded of himself (Self-Importance 3)
 the b. in this kind (Acting 25)
 'tis b. to give him way (Obstinacy 3)
 when he is b. (Drinking 15)
betray :
 to b. us in deepest consequence (Evil 5)
betrothed:
 to her ... was I b. (Devotion 3)
better:
 b. a little chiding (Chiding 1)
 b. a witty fool than a foolish wit (Fools 11)
 b. once than never (Lateness 4)
 b. three hours too soon (Lateness 2)
 I could have b. spared a b. man (Farewells 7)
betters:
 when we see our b. (Misery 1)
bid:
 b. that welcome which comes to punish (Endurance 2)
big:
 looked b. and spit at him (Cowardice 8)
big-bellied:
 see the sails conceive and grow b. (Pregnancy 2)
bird:
 b. of dawning singeth (Festivals 1)
 sweet b.'s throat (Country Life 3)
 the b. that hath been limèd (Suspicion 1)

this b. hath made his procreant bed (Birds 7)

thou art a summer b. (Birds 3)

birds:

the eagle suffers little b. to sing (Birds 14, Power 12)

birth:

bring this monstrous b. to the world's light (Evil 10)

birthday:

it is my b. (Birthdays 1)

biting:

his b. is immortal (Death 4, Snakes 1)

blanket:

heaven peep through the b. (Murder 5)

blastments:

contagious b. are most imminent (Chastity 6)

blasts:

b. of January would blow you (Thinness 5)

many b. to shake them (Greatness 10)

blaze:

rash fierce b. of riot (Transience 3)

blazon:

eternal b. must not be (Afterlife 1, Eternity 2)

blessedness:

lives and dies in single b. (Marriage 28)

blessings:

barnes are b. (Children 1)

blest:

b. are those whose blood (Temperament 2)

blind:

b. fear that seeing reason leads (Fear 16)

he that is strucken b. (Eyes 13)

now you strike like the b. man (Anger 6)

blindworms:

newts and b. do no wrong (Creatures 4)

blocks:

you b., you stones (Insults 10)

blood:

every drop of blood (Promises 4)

here's the smell of the b. still (Guilt 8)

his b. is very snow-broth (Asceticism 1)

I am in b. stepped in so far (Crime 2)

I am in so far in b. (Murder 12)

I'll not shed her b. (Beauty 18)

is your b. so madly hot (Passion 3)

it will have b. ... b. will have b. (Proverbs 17)

lost the fresh b. in thy cheeks (Moods 8)

make thick my b. (Ruthlessness 3)

Neptune's ocean wash this b. (Guilt 5)

no sure foundation set on b. (Murder 4)

no true drop of b. in him (Misogyny 4)

the b. more stirs to rouse a lion (Valor 6)

the b. weeps from my heart (Prophecy 4)

the warming of the b. (Drinking 10)

those whose b. and judgment (Temperament 2)

bloody:

be b. , bold and resolute (Prophecy 8)

blossom:

I pluck this pale and maiden b. here (Flowers 4)

O that this b. could be kept from cankers (Flowers 3)

blow:

that but this b. might be the be-all (Action 12)

blows:

oft when b. have made me stay (Words 1)

words before b. (Councils 3)

boast:

now b. thee, death (Death 5)

boats:

fortune brings in some b. (Fortune 6)

light b. sail swift (Ships 6)

bodies:

our b. are our gardens (Virtue 17)

bodkin:

his quietus make with a bare b. (Suicide 13)

body:

bear your b. more seeming (Body 2)

done with the dead b. (Burial 1)

make less thy b. hence (Mortality 6)

my little b. is aweary (Weariness 2)

so young a b. with so old a head (Wisdom 4)

the foul b. of the infected world (Body 1)

this common b. (People 2)

what is the b.? (Body 4)

boggler:

you have been a b. ever (Shiftiness 1)

boiled-brains:

would any but these b. (Youth 13)

bold:

that which hath made them drunk hath made me b. (Drinking 13)

bolt:

a fool's b. is soon shot (Fools 7)

marked I where the b. of Cupid fell (Flowers 5)

bolting-hutch:

that b. of beastliness (Fatness 4)

bombard:

that huge b. of sack (Fatness 4)

bombast:

my sweet creature of b. (Fatness 2)

bond:

b. cracked 'twixt son and father (Disorder 1)

I'll have my b. (Determination 2)

natural b. of sisters (Love 7)

tear to pieces that great b. (Evil 8)

bondage:

as b. e'er of freedom (Marriage 47)

I begin to find an idle ... b. (Tyranny 5)

bondman:

checked like a b. (Criticism 2)

every b. in his own hand bears (Servitude 2)

who ... would be a b.? (Patriotism 1)

bonds:

my b. in thee are all determinate (Farewells 21)

bones:

my old b. aches (Weariness 3)

book:

painfully to pore upon a b. (Books 2)

shut the b. and sit him down and die (Despair 2)

book (cont'd.)
that one might read the b. of fate (Fate 3)
upon some b. I love (Prayer 19)
was ever b. containing such vile matter (Deceit 23)
when I do see the very b. (Self-Knowledge 11)
your face, my thane, is as a b. (Faces 6)

books:
finds b. in the running brooks (Country Life 2)
forefathers had no other b. (Books 1)
knowing I loved my b. (Books 4)
my b. and instruments (Study 5)

booties:
fortune ... drops b. in my mouth (Fortune 24)

boots:
so be these b. too (Clothing 12)

born:
who's b. that day (Letters 1)

borrower:
neither a ... nor a b. be (Advice 6)

bosom:
cleanse the stuffed b. (Medicine 9)

bosoms:
two b. and a single troth (Love 58)

bounds:
of all these b. ... we make thee lady (Country Life 11)

bounty:
for his b., there was no winter in't (Generosity 1)
my b. is as boundless (Love 80)
no villainous b. yet hath passed my heart (Generosity 5)
the more merit is in your b. (Generosity 2)

bow:
b. is bent and drawn (Danger 11)
b., stubborn knees (Prayer 4)
moon, like to a silver b. (Moon 2)

boy:
b., however we do praise ourselves (Men and Women 10)
nor young enough for a b. (Youth 11)
the b. disdains me (Boys 2)
this same young sober-blooded b. (Sobriety 1)
'tis a parlous b. (Boys 3)
trusts in ... a b.'s love (Aphorisms 2)
when that I was and a little tiny b. (Boys 4)

boys:
as flies to wanton b. (Gods 1)
the truth of girls and b. (Girls 2)

brain:
ascends me into the b. (Drinking 9)
b. him with his lady's fan (Cowardice 2)
not so much b. as ear-wax (Stupidity 4)
the children of an idle b. (Dreams 13)
thou hast no more brain (Stupidity 3)

brains:
poor and unhappy b. for drinking (Drinking 20)
to steal away their b. (Drinking 22)

branches:
superfluous b. we lop away (Gardens 7)

brass:
since b., nor stone (Mortality 11)

brave:
what's b., what's noble (Suicide 7)

bravest:
b. at the last (Suicide 9)

brawls:
with thy b. thou hast disturbed (Quarrels 10)

breach:
more honored in the b. (Custom 2)
once more unto the b. (War 10)

bread:
eating the bitter b. of banishment (Exile 7)
I live with b. like you (Humanity 6)
one half-penny-worth of b. (Drinking 7)

break:
b. my heart (Grief 6)
let us not b. with him (Politics 12)

breakfast:
then to b. with what appetite (Eating 6)

breast:
on her left b. a mole (Beauty 6)

breasts:
come to my woman's b. (Evil 4)

breath:
an after-dinner's b. (Exercise 2)
foul wind is but foul b. (Kissing 7)
if her b. were as terrible (Speech 15)
O for b. to utter (Insults 7)

breathing:
'tis her b. that perfumes the chamber (Perfume 1)

breed:
this happy b. of men (Countries 6)

brevity:
b. is the soul of wit (Brevity 1, Wit 2)

bribes:
contaminate ... with base b. (Corruption 6)

bridegroom:
I will be a b. in my death (Death 2, Suicide 4)

bridge:
what need the b. much broader (Necessity 6)

brief:
what, so b.? (Brevity 2)

briefly:
b. die their joys (Girls 2, Youth 4)

briers:
full of b. (Adversity 1)

bringer:
the first b. of unwelcome news (News 8)

Britain:
hath B. all the sun? (Countries 1)
i'the world's volume our B. seems (Countries 2)

brothel-house:
hang me up at the door of a b. (Love 60)

brother:
a b. noble (Nobility 7)
friend or b., he forfeits (Punishment 4)
I have no b. (Misanthropy 2)
like a b. toiled in my affairs (Friendship 9)

we came into the world like b. and b. (Twins 2)

thy b. by decree is banishèd (Tyranny 4)

your b. and his lover have embraced (Pregnancy 1)

your b. and my sister no sooner met (Love 26)

brothers:

we happy few, we band of b. (Fellowship 2)

brow:

grace was seated on this b. (Beauty 7)

show thy dangerous b. by night (Conspiracy 5)

this man's b. ... foretells (News 7)

brows:

black b. ... become some women (Beauty 28)

b. full of discontent (Conspiracy 7)

our b. bound with victorious wreaths (Victory 3)

your inky b. (Beauty 3)

Brute:

et tu, B. (Last Words 1)

Brutus:

B. had rather be a villager (Tyranny 2)

B. says he was ambitious (Ambition 9)

found like B., like himself (Integrity 2)

bubukles:

his face is all b. and whelks (Faces 5)

buckle:

he cannot b. his distempered cause (Politics 18)

bud:

as chaste as is the b. (Lust 10)

buds:

shakes all our b. from growing (Kissing 4)

bug:

the b. that you would fright me with (Death-Wish 11)

build:

when we mean to b. (Building 1)

bulls:

wild as young b. (Animals 4)

burial:

with all respect and rites of b. (Burial 3)

buried:

she shall be b. by her Antony (Epitaphs 3)

burr:

I am a kind of b., I shall stick (Perseverance 2)

burrs:

they are b. ... they'll stick (Constancy 6)

bush:

here's neither b. nor shrub (Storms 15)

how easy is a b. supposed a bear (Imagination 5)

business

a man to double b. bound (Indecision 2)

know the end of this day's b. (Foreboding 8)

my b. was great (Apologies 5)

our hands are full of b. (Business 3)

to b. that we love (Business 1)

wished the sleeping of this b. (Politics 8)

but:

b. yet madam - I do not like "b. yet" (Foreboding 1)

butchers:

let us be sacrificers but not b. (Sacrifice 1)

butt:

a rotten carcass of a b. (Ships 5)

here is my b. and very sea-mark (Resignation 6)

buttock:

converses ... with the b. of the night (Drinking 4)

buy:

b. with you, sell with you (Business 7)

by-paths:

by what b. and indirect crooked ways (Deviousness 3)

cabin:

make me a willow c. at your gate (Courtship 23)

cabined:

now I am c., cribbed, confined (Anxiety 7)

Caesar:

always I am C. (Caesar 1)

as C. loved me (Caesar 3)

C. doth not wrong (Caesar 2)

C. is more dangerous than he (Danger 8)

C. should be a beast without a heart (Fear 8)

C.'s spirit, ranging for revenge (War 16)

had you rather C. were living? (Freedom 5)

here was a C. (Caesar 4)

I come to bury C. (Epitaphs 10)

Imperious C. (Mortality 4)

O Julius C., thou art mighty (Caesar 5)

O mighty C.! Dost thou lie so low (Epitaphs 8)

when C. says, "do this" (Power 3)

cage:

not to sing in my c. (Constraint 2)

cakes:

no more c. and ale (Virtue 23)

calamity:

thou art wedded to c. (Affliction 12)

calendar:

give me a c. (Foreboding 13)

stand aye accursèd in the c. (Curses 2)

calumny:

back-wounding c. (Slander 5)

c. will sear virtue itself (Slander 8)

thou shalt not escape c. (Slander 1)

came:

c. saw, and overcame (Conquest 2)

camp:

from c. to c. (Night 6)

can:

an unfilled c. (Lateness 5)

candle:

c. singed the moth (Disappointment 2)

how far that little c. throws his beams (Goodness 3)

out, out, brief c. (Life 7)

candles:

night's c. are burnt out (Dawn 7)

their c. are all out (Darkness 2)

candy:

what a c. deal of courtesy (Flattery 1)

canker:

grief, that's beauty's c. (Beauty 23)

cankers:

that this blossom could be kept from c. (Flowers 3)

cannibals:

the c. that each other eat (Travel 16)

canopy:

this most excellent c. (World 4)

cantle:

the greater c. of the world is lost (Empire 2)

cantons:

loyal c. of contemnèd love (Courtship 23)

capability:

that c. and godlike reason (Reason 1)

capers:

he c., he dances (Courtship 13)

he c. nimbly in a lady's chamber (Dancing 2)

true lovers run into strange c. (Love 12)

captain:

our great c.'s c. (Women 22)

captains:

let four c. bear Hamlet (Royalty 7, Soldiers 4)

caraways:

we will eat ... a dish of c. (Eating 5)

carcass:

a rotten c. of a butt (Ships 5)

care:

buy it with much c. (Anxiety 8)

c. is no cure (Anxiety 3)

c. keeps his watch (Sleeplessness 7)

c.'s an enemy to life (Hedonism 1)

no c., no stop; so senseless of expense (Extravagance 3)

wan with c. (Anxiety 2)

what though c. killed a cat (Encouragement 3)

why would you heap this c. on me (Hypocrisy 16)

career:

down the hill he holds his fierce c. (Evil 2)

cares:

be not with mortal c. oppressed (Providence 1)

enforce me to a world of c. (Politics 21)

forfeited to c. for ever (Anxiety 1)

intent to shake all c. ... from our age (Retirement 2)

what watchful c. do interpose (Sleeplessness 3)

carnations:

the fairest flowers ... are our c. (Flowers 10)

carp:

bait of falsehood takes this c. of truth (Deviousness 1)

cart:

I cannot draw a c. (Work 3)

Cassius:

C. is aweary of the world (Criticism 2)

cast:

set the exact wealth ... all at one c. (Risk 1)

castle:

this c. hath a pleasant seat (Castles 1)

there stands the c. (Castles 2)

castles:

though c. topple (Chaos 2)

cat:

harmless necessary c. (Animals 8)

I am as melancholy as a gib c. (Melancholy 7)

poor c. i' th' adage (Cowardice 4)

the c. will mew (Animals 3)

vigilant as a c. (Vigilance 1)

what though care killed a c. (Encouragement 3)

catalogue:

in the c. ye go for men (Dogs 4)

cataracts:

you c. and hurricanoes, spout (Storms 7)

caterpillars:

the c. of the commonwealth (Politics 20)

cattle:

get your living by the copulation of c. (Country Life 6)

Caucasus:

thinking on the frosty C. (Imagination 6)

cause:

a great c. of the night (Philosophy 1)

hear me for my c. (Speechmaking 2)

he cannot buckle his distempered c. (Politics 18)

I know no personal c. (Cause 1)

is there any c. in nature? (Cause 4)

it is the c. (Cause 5)

love him, not without c. (Cause 3)

on the cause ... have glozed (Argument 5)

the c. is in my will (Cause 2)

wrenching the true c. the false way (Deviousness 2)

caviare:

'twas c. to the general (Plays 3)

cavil:

c. on the ninth part of a hair (Business 2)

celerity:

c. is never more admired (Speed 1)

cell:

death ... thine eternal cell (Death 10)

cellarage:

you hear this fellow in the c. (Ghosts 10)

censure:

c. me in your wisdom (Judgment 1)

no might nor greatness ... can c. scape (Slander 5)

censurers:

to cope malicious c. (Action 9)

ceremony:

c. was but devised at first (Ceremony 5)

love...useth an enforcèd c. (Hypocrisy 5, Love 37)

no c. that to great ones 'longs (Mercy 6)

the sauce to meat is c. (Ceremony 4)

thou idol, c. (Ceremony 2)

what have kings ... save c. (Ceremony 1)

Cesario:

C., by the roses of the spring (Infatuation 10)

chalice:

th'ingredients of our poisoned c. (Justice 9)

challenge:

here's the c. (Challenges 2)

chamber:

get you to my lady's c. (Women 14)

chameleon:

add colors to the c. (Duplicity 2)

the c. love can feed on the air (Food 15)

chance:

c. as fair (Choice 7)

in the reproof of c. (Chance 2)

the slaves of c. (Chance 3)

chances:
against ill c. (Moods 9)

change:
the lamentable c. is from the best (Hope 2, Laughter 2)

changes:
full of c. (Age 20)

chaos:
misshapen c. (Love 73)
c. is come again (Love 71)

chapmen:
you do as c. do (Business 10)

character:
thy fair and outward c. (Appearance 11)

charity:
am so near the lack of c. (Hate 1)
bound in c. against it (Contempt 1)
c. itself fulfills the law (Charity 2)
melting c. (Charity 1)
'twere good you do so much for c. (Charity 3)

charm:
for a c. of powerful trouble (Occult 1)
music oft hath such a c. (Music 9)

charmers:
O you heavenly c. (Gods and Goddesses 4)

charms:
now my c. are all o'erthrown (Weakness 5)

charter:
I must have ... as large a c. (Freedom 1)
the c. of thy worth gives thee releasing (Farewells 21)

chase:
this is the c. (Last Words 7)

chaste:
be thou as c. as ice (Slander 1)
c. and immaculate (Chastity 7)
c. as the icicle (Chastity 1)

chastity:
cold, my girl, even like thy c. (Affliction 10)
pure c. is ruffled (Lust 13)

cheer:
receive what c. you may (Aphorisms 6)
small c. and great welcome (Feasts 3)

cheese:
my c., my digestion, (Fools 10)

cherry:
we grew together, like to a double c. (Twins 3)

cherubins:
still quiring to the young-eyed c. (Heaven 3)

chestnut:
c. the only color (Hair 1)

chew:
my noble friend, c. upon this (Thought 10)

chickens:
all my pretty c. (Cruelty 4)

chiding:
better a little c. than ... heartbreak (Chiding 1)

child:
an impatient c. (Impatience 3)

as much as c. e'er loved (Parents and Children 5)
grief fills the room up of my absent c. (Grief 9)
love is like a c. (Love 105)
old man is twice a c. (Old Age 2)
to have a thankless c. (Ingratitude 7)
to see his active c. do deeds (Parents and Children 19)
wise father that knows his own c. (Parents and Children 11)
woe to that land that's governed by a c. (Government 4)

childbed:
a terrible c. (Birth and Death 1)

childhood:
eye of c. fears a painted devil (Death 22)

childishness:
second c. and mere oblivion (Age 5)

childness:
his varying c. (Children 2)

children:
fathers ... make their c. blind (Parents and Children 7)
thoughts like unbridled c. (Love 92)
when scepters are in c's hands (Cities 2)

chimes:
we have heard the c. at midnight (Nostalgia 4)

chin:
who is he whose c. (Youth 9)

choice:
there's small c. in rotten apples (Choice 8)

choirs:
bare ruined c. where late (Seasons 18)

choler:
your rash c. (Anger 2)

choose:
fools, when they do c. (Choice 4)
here c. I (Choice 6)
here do I c. (Choice 3)
I may neither c. who I would (Parents and Children 7)
let me c. (Choice 5)
you that c. not by the view (Choice 7)

choughs:
russet-pated c. (Hunting 2)

Christ:
so Judas did to C. (Betrayal 2)

Christian:
as I am a C. faithful man (Dreams 8)
I hate him for he is a C. (Money 8)

Christians:
making of C. will raise the price of hogs (Food 8)

chronicle:
let me embrace thee, good old c. (Time 32)

chronicles:
abstracts and brief c. (Acting 5)
time's doting c. (Age 16)

chrysolite:
world of one entire and perfect c. (Constancy 5)

church:
I can see a c. by daylight (Eyes 12)

when beggars die there are no c. (Portents 6)

comfort:

all c. go with thee (Parting 8)

be c. to my age (Age 2)

c. should remain (Parting 12)

c.'s in heaven (Affliction 11)

he receives c. like cold porridge (Comfort 6)

I beg cold c. (Comfort 4)

I must c. the weaker vessel (Comfort 3)

my c. is that old age ... no more spoil (Age 19)

of c. no man speak (Despair 5)

reward thee ... for thy sprightly c. (Comfort 1, Valor 1)

society is no c. (Sickness 2)

such c. as do lusty young men feel (Seasons 15)

that spring whence c. seemed to come (Confusion 3)

this must my c. be (Exile 3)

two loves I have of c. and despair (Love 111)

what c. have we now? (Despair 6)

comforts:

we make us c. of our losses (Comfort 2)

command:

achievement is c. (Desire 15)

exactly do at all points my c. (Freedom 5)

commander:

a good old c. (Soldiers 15)

commandment:

thy c. all alone shall live (Resolution 2)

commodity:

c. the bias of the world (Self-Interest 1)

turn diseases to c. (Business 4)

common:

thou know'st 'tis c. (Mourning 7)

commonwealth:

caterpillars of the c. (Politics 20)

i'the c. I would by contraries (Utopias 1)

the c. of Athens is become a forest (Wilderness 2)

worm that gnaws the bowels of the c. (Civil War 1)

compact:

what c. mean you to have with us? (Friendship 14)

companion:

I scorn you, scurvy c. (Insults 8)

I would not wish any c. (Society 8)

sad c., dull-eyed melancholy (Melancholy 8)

companions:

in c. that do converse (Friendship 19)

the prince but studies his c. (Language 2)

company:

best when least in c. (Solitude 4)

but for your c. I would have been in bed (Society 7)

c., villainous c. hath been the spoil (Society 1)

he is given to sports ... and much c. (Society 3)

he is too disputable for my c. (Argument 2)

I cannot live out of her c. (Friendship 1)

I would no other c. (Solitude 2)

let men take heed of their c. (Society 2)

my books and instruments shall be my c. (Study 5)

comparisons:

c. are odorous (Solecisms 5)

compass:

my life is run his c. (Life 5)

competency:

c. lives longer (Moderation 3)

complexion:

c. of the element (Conspiracy 3)

mislike me not for my c. (Appearance 3)

the best thing about him is his c. (Faces 1)

compliment:

demonstrate ... my heart in c. externe (Deceit 10)

comrade:

to be a c. with the wolf (Homelessness 1)

concealment:

let c. like a worm i'the bud (Melancholy 9)

conceits:

dangerous c. are ... poisons (Jealousy 10)

conclusion:

lame and impotent c.! (Endings 3)

concord:

sweet milk of c.(Chaos 3)

condition:

unhousèd, free c. (Marriage 40)

confine:

spirit hies to his c. (Ghosts 6)

confusion:

c. now hath made his masterpiece (Confusion 5)

how soon c. may enter (Confusion 1)

conquest:

a peace is of the nature of a c. (Peace 7)

death makes no c. of this conqueror (Fame 4)

have I in c. stretched mine arm? (Power 7)

made a shameful c. of itself (Countries 7)

conquests:

are all thy c. ... shrunk (Epitaphs 8)

conscience:

c. is born of love (Conscience 10)

c. is but a word (Conscience 8)

for policy sits above c. (Politics 23)

haunt thee like a wicked c. (Conscience 9)

hulling in the wild sea of my c. (Conscience 3)

my c. hath a thousand several tongues (Conscience 7)

O coward c. (Conscience 6)

their best c. is not to leave't undone (Deceit 14)

the worm of c. (Conscience 4)

thus c. does make cowards (Conscience 2)

where's thy c. now? (Conscience 5)

consecrate:

did I my soul and fortunes c. (Devotion 4)

consent:

government ... doth keep in one c. (Government 2)

consider:

'twere to c. too curiously (Mortality 3)

consideration:

c. like an angel came (Reformation 5)

conspiracy:

for c., I know not how it tastes (Conspiracy 9)

heinous, strong and bold c. (Conspiracy 8)

security gives way to c. (Conspiracy 6)

cowardice:

    patience is pale cold c. (Cowardice 5)

cowards:

    a plague of all c. (Cowardice 3)

    as many other mannish c. do (Cowardice 1)

    conscience doth make c. (Conscience 2)

    c. die many times before their deaths (Death 17)

    word that c. use (Conscience 8)

cowslip:

    crimson drops i'the bottom of a c. (Beauty 6)

    hang a pearl in every c.'s ear (Fairies 2)

    in a c.'s bell I lie (Fairies 9)

    the freckled c., burnet and green clover (Farming 2)

cozenage:

    this town is full of c. (Corruption 1)

Crab:

    I think C., my dog, be the sourest-natured (Dogs 7)

crabs:

    bring thee where c. grow (Education 6)

cracks:

    now c. a noble heart (Epitaphs 5)

cradle:

    procreant c. (Birds 7)

crafts:

    in one line two c. directly meet (Plots 2)

crannies:

    creep in c. (Insects 1)

creature:

    I took him for the plainest ... c. (Trust 3)

    there is no c. loves me (Despair 7)

    the world hath not a sweeter c. (Women 24)

    wine is a good familiar creature (Drinking 23)

creatures:

    call these delicate c. ours (Marriage 41)

    from fairest c. we desire increase (Beauty 30)

    guilty c. sitting at a play (Theater 4)

    home, you idle c. (Idleness 1)

    how many goodly c. are there here (Humanity 7)

    those wicked c. yet do look (Evil 4)

credit:

    my c. now stands (Reputation 3)

crickets:

    as merry as c. (Merriment 1)

crimes:

    the foul c. done in my days of nature (Ghosts 9)

cripple:

    c. tardy-gaited night (Night 7)

Crispian:

    this day is called the feast of C. (Festivals 3)

    tomorrow is Saint C. (Festivals 4)

critical:

    I am nothing if not c. (Criticism 4)

crocodile:

    what manner o'thing is your c.? (Creatures 1)

cross:

    delivered me to my sour c. (Hypocrisy 13)

crow:

    c. doth sing as sweetly as the lark (Birds 10)

    c. makes wing to the rooky wood (Night 13)

    waked the ribald c. (Dawn 8)

crown:

    by what ... crooked ways I met this c. (Deviousness 3)

    from the c. of his head (Merriment 5)

    how sweet ... it is to wear a c. (Royalty 21)

    my c. is in my heart (Royalty 22)

    put on my c. (Death-Wish 3, Royalty 3)

    the sword, the mace, the c. imperial (Royalty 19)

    uneasy lies the head that wears a c. (Royalty 11)

    within the hollow c. (Death 35)

    with mine own hands I give away my c. (Renunciation 3)

crowns:

    c. in my purse I have (Travel 20)

cruel:

    c. are the times (Confusion 6)

cruelty:

    fill me ... top-full of direst c. (Cruelty 3)

    'tis a c. to load a falling man (Downfall 3)

cry:

    c. woe, destruction, ruin (Death 33)

    you common c. of curs (People 11)

crying:

    we came c. hither (Patience 7)

cuckolds:

    have been c. ... ere now (Adultery 2)

cuckoo:

    as the c. is in June (Birds 1)

    c., c. - O word of fear (Seasons 10)

    hedge-sparrow fed the c. (Ingratitude 5)

    plainsong c. grey (Birds 13)

    the c.'s bird useth the sparrow (Birds 2)

cue:

    were it my c. to fight (Fighting 4)

cup:

    there may be in the c. a spider (Poison 5)

Cupid:

    C. himself would blush (Love 46)

    C. is a knavish lad (Gods 3)

    I saw ... C. all armed (Gods 2)

    little C.'s crafty arrow (Love 63)

    marked I where the bolt of C. fell (Flowers 5)

    sign of blind C. (Love 60)

    some C. kills with arrows (Love 64)

    winged C. painted blind (Love 54)

cur:

    this cruel-hearted c. (Dogs 7)

cure:

    care is no c. (Anxiety 3)

current:

    the c. that with gentle murmur (Rivers 3)

curs:

    like to village c., bark (Enemies 3)

    you common cry of c. (People 11)

curse:

    a c. shall light upon the limbs (Prophecy 5)

    I know how to c. (Language 8)

    shall we c. the planets (Curses 1)

d., d.! O amiable, lovely d.! (Death-Wish 7)
d. is a fearful thing (Death 29)
d. lies on her like an untimely frost (Death 37)
d. makes no conquest of this conqueror (Fame 4)
d. may usurp on nature (Death 32)
d. once dead there's no more dying then (Eternity 4)
d., that hath sucked the honey (Death 38)
d. the market-place (World 6)
downy sleep. d.'s counterfeit (Death 23)
drop into the rotten mouth of d. (Decline 2)
for restful d. I cry (Death-Wish 12)
grim d., how foul (Death 39)
I will be a bridegroom in my d. (Death 2)
keeps d. his court (Death 35)
love-devouring d. (Marriage 45)
nothing we can call our own but d. (Death 34)
now boast thee, d. (Death 5, Epitaphs 2)
O proud d., what feast is toward (Death 10)
set honor in one eye and d. i'th' other (Honor 12)
the sense of d. (Death 27)
the stroke of d. is as a lover's pinch (Dying 3)
the worst is d. (Death 33)
this fell sergeant, d. (Death 9)
thou owest God a d. (Death 12)
through the hollow eyes of d. (Life 10)
we owe God a d. (Death 14)
what sights of ugly d. within mine eyes (Dreams 9)
where art thou, d.? (Death 3)

death's head:
do not speak like a d. (Mortality 5)

deaths:
d. put on by cunning (Murder 3)

debt:
ambition's d. is paid (Ambition 8)

debts:
he that dies pays all d. (Proverbs 27)

decay:
this muddy vesture of d. (Heaven 3)

deceit:
that d. should steal such gentle shape (Deceit 16)
the fairest show means most d. (Deceit 15)

deceits:
the tongues of men are full of d. (Deceit 3)

deceived:
she has d. her father (Deceit 11)

December:
D.'s bareness (Absence 3)
D. when they are wed (Marriage 5)
makes a July's day short as D. (Children 2)
rain and wind beat dark D. (Country Life 10)

decrees:
break my d. (Revolution 1)

deed:
a little water clears us of this d. (Guilt 6)
one good d. dying (Praise 13)
so shines a good d. (Goodness 3)
this d. is chronicled in hell (Devil 10)
'tis a kind of good d. to say well (Action 11)
to know my d. (Self-Knowledge 7)
tyrannous and bloody d. (Murder 13)

deeds:
a spur to valiant ... d. (War 22)
foul d. will rise (Foreboding 5)
give her d. (Silence 7)
hot d. is love (Love 89)
I'll endeavor d. (Words and Deeds 5)
pity choked with custom of fell d. (Cruelty 2)
speaking in deeds (Words and Deeds 4)
the sight of means to do ill d. (Wrongdoing 3)
unnatural d. (Guilt 9)
words are no d. (Action 11, Words and Deeds 1)

deer:
what shall he have that killed the d. (Hunting 1)

defeatures:
written strange d. on my face (Grief 3)

defect:
make d. perfection (Charm 2)

defense:
in cases of d. 'tis best to weigh (War 8)

deformed:
he is d., crooked (Insults 2)

defy:
what man, d. the devil (Devil 11)

degree:
take but d. away (Order 3)
the heavens ... observe d. (Order 1)
when d. is shaked (Order 2)

degrees:
d. were not derived corruptly (Merit 2)

deject:
I of ladies most d. (Dejection 3)

delays:
d. have dangerous ends (Delay 3)

delight:
all for your d. (Acting 24)

delights:
all d. are vain (Books 2)
his d. were dolphin-like (Pleasure 4)
these violent d. have violent ends (Transience 5)

demand:
d. me nothing (Silence 6)

demigod:
d. authority (Authority 8)

denial:
he's fortified against any d. (Determination 4)

deny:
I would not d. you (Marriage 36)

Denmark:
rotten in the state of D. (Corruption 2)

depraved:
who lives that's not d. ? (Corruption 6, Humanity 8)

Desdemona:
the divine D. (Women 22)

desert:
in this d. inaccessible (Time 3)
use every man after your own d. (Deserving 2, Generosity 2)

deserts:
not my d., but what I will deserve (Deserving 4)

deserve:
  well you d. (Deserving 3)
deserves:
  get as much as he d. (Choice 2)
deservings:
  make foul the clearness of our d. (Deserving 1)
desire:
  a great d. for a bottle of hay (Eating 9)
  can one d. to much of a good thing (Desire 5)
  d. is boundless (Love 90)
  d. my pilot is (Desire 19)
  d. should ... outlive performance (Desire 7)
  gain what many men d. (Desire 12, 13)
  how far I am from the d. of this (Deceit 20)
  I hope it is no dishonest d. (Desire 6)
  in night ... d. sees best of all (Desire 21)
  provokes the d. (Drinking 14)
  so sweet as when d. did sue (Desire 15)
  tend upon the ... times of your d. (Devotion 7)
  the trustless wings of false d. (Desire 17)
desires:
  my black and deep d. (Desire 9)
  my d., like fell and cruel hounds (Desire 16)
  thy d. are wolvish (Cruelty 7)
  your heart's d. be with you (Desire 3)
desolation:
  a careless d. (Love 15)
despair:
  grim and comfortless d. (Melancholy 5)
  I shall d. (Despair 7)
  I will d. and be at enmity (Despair 4)
  two loves ... of comfort and d. (Love 111)
despise:
  how much I could d. this man (Contempt 1)
despising:
  d. for you the city (Exile 2)
destruction:
  cry woe, d., ruin (Death 33)
device:
  who ... cannot see this palpable d. (Deceit 18)
devil:
  a d., a born d. (Education 7)
  a d. more damned to top Macbeth (Hell 3)
  art thou ... some d. (Apparitions 5)
  d., he's an enemy to mankind (Devil 11)
  eye of childhood fears a painted d. (Death 22)
  give the d. his due (Devil 4, Proverbs 2)
  he must needs go that the d. drives (Devil 1)
  hypocrisy against the d. (Devil 9)
  I perceive the d. understands Welsh (Devil 3)
  sugar o'er the d. himself (Hypocrisy 1)
  the d. can cite scripture (Devil 8)
  the d. damn thee black (Curses 4)
  the d. take one party (Curses 6)
  the d. that told me I did well (Devil 10)
  the spirit ... may be the d. (Devil 2)
  what a d. hast thou to do (Time of Day 5)
  what, can the d. speak true (Devil 7)

what man, defy the d. (Devil 11)
devil-porter:
  I'll d. it no further (Hell 2)
devils:
  d. soonest tempt (Devil 6)
  when d. ... the blackest sins put on (Hypocrisy 12)
  whip me, ye d. (Hell 6)
devouring:
  d. time, blunt thou the lion's paws (Time 42)
devout:
  a most d. coward (Cowardice 7)
dewdrops:
  I must go seek some d. (Fairies 2)
devices:
  our d. all are overthrown (Fate 1)
devil:
  seem a saint when most I play the d. (Hypocrisy 14)
devotion:
  with d.'s visage (Hypocrisy 1)
dial:
  the bawdy hand of the d. (Time 26)
Dian:
  as D. in her orb (Lust 10)
  icicle ... hangs on D.'s temple (Chastity 1)
Diana:
  D's lip is not more rubious (Androgyny 1)
  let us be D.'s foresters (Night 2)
die:
  all shall d. (Death 13)
  a man can d. but once (Death 14)
  d. all, d. merrily (Death 11, Doomsday 1)
  d. two months ago (Memory 3)
  find myself so apt to d. (Death-Wish 6)
  if it were now to die (Happiness 6)
  lovers cry, O ho they d. (Sex 9)
  that we shall d. we know (Death 19)
  'tis a vile thing to d. (Death 36)
  to d. and go we know not where (Graves 1)
  to d., to sleep, perchance to dream (Death 7)
died:
  he d. as one ... studied in his death (Dying 13)
dies:
  he that d. pays all debts (Proverbs 27)
difference:
  O the d. of man and man! (Desire 8)
digestion:
  good d. wait on appetite (Eating 7)
  things sweet to taste prove in d. sour (Eating 11)
digestions:
  unquiet meals make ill d. (Eating 2)
diminution:
  a d. in our captain's brain (Folly 2)
dine:
  will you d. with me? (Invitations 1)
dinner:
  I will make an end of my d. (Food 9)
disasters:
  make guilty of our d. the sun (Astrology 1)

discipline:
 let's lack no d. (Readiness 2)
discontent:
 brows full of d. (Conspiracy 7)
 now is the winter of our d. (Improvement 3)
discord:
 fall to some d. (Quarrels 3)
 hark what d. follows (Order 3)
 so musical a d. (Hunting 3)
discourse:
 so sweet and voluble is his d. (Talking 3)
 your fair d. hath been as sugar (Speech 22)
discretion:
 the better part of valor is d. (Valor 8)
discretions:
 your d. better can persuade (Persuasion 1)
disdain:
 d. and scorn ride sparkling (Scorn 1)
 my dear lady d. (Greetings 8)
disease:
 before the curing of a strong d. (Sickness 11)
 the d. of not listening (Sickness 8)
diseases:
 d. desperate grown (Sickness 4)
 turn d. to commodity (Business 4)
disgrace:
 when in d. with fortune (Misery 5)
disposition:
 a more coming on d. (Courtship 3)
 antic d. (Acting 4)
 I know our country d. well (Deceit 14)
 of what d. was the duke? (Self-Knowledge 8)
 so blessed a d. (Virtue 18)
 the bitter d. of the time (Inevitability 3)
 this robe ... does change my d. (Clothing 13)
dispraise:
 d. the thing that they desire to buy (Business 10)
disputable:
 he is too d. for my company (Argument 1)
dissembling:
 d. courtesy (Deceit 2)
ditties:
 sweet as d. highly penned (Language 1)
divided:
 must we be d.? (Parting 13)
divine:
 a good d. (Advice 11)
 more needs she the d. (Guilt 9)
divinity:
 d. of hell (Hypocrisy 12)
 such d. doth hedge a king (Royalty 6)
 there's a d. that shapes our ends (Providence 2)
division:
 envy breeds unkind d. (Civil War 2)
 never come such d. (Reconciliation 2)
 the woefullest d. (Civil War 4)
do:
 do not for ever with thy vailèd lids (Mourning 7)

do not give dalliance too much the rein (Sex 6)
 that we would do we should do (Delay 2)
docks:
 nothing teems but hateful d. (Farming 2)
doers:
 talkers are no good doers (Words and Deeds 3)
dog:
 a d.'s obeyed in office (Authority 7)
 a d. will have his day (Animals 3)
 as familiar with me as my d. (Dogs 1)
 be a d. and bay the moon (Corruption 6)
 hath a d. money? (Money 10)
 hear my d. bark at a crow (Misanthropy 3)
 he's a very d. to the commonalty (People 3)
 I think Crab, my d. (Dogs 7)
 I would not hang a d. (Mercy 13)
 thou call'st me d. (Insults 13)
 why should a d. ... have life? (Death 21)
dogs:
 d. must eat (Hunger 1)
 the little d. and all (Dogs 3)
 throw physic to the d. (Medicine 10)
doing:
 each your d., so singular (Praise 14)
dolor:
 think their d. others have endured (Affliction 14)
dolphin-like:
 his delights were d. (Pleasure 4)
done:
 what is d. cannot now be amended (Excuses 4)
 what's d. cannot be undone (Aphorisms 7)
 what's d. is d. (Aphorisms 4)
doom:
 bears it out even to the edge of d. (Constancy 12)
 line stretch out to the crack of d. (Doom 3)
doomsday:
 d. is near, die all (Death 11, Doomsday 1)
 stare as it were d. (Chaos 1)
door:
 make the d. upon a woman's wit (Wit 1)
dormouse:
 to awake your d. valor (Valor 15)
dotage:
 lose myself in d. (Infatuation 3)
dotard:
 I speak not like a d. (Maturity 4)
double:
 d., d. toil and trouble (Occult 2)
doublet:
 d. and hose (Comfort 3)
 dost thou think ... I have a d. and hose (Women 5)
 with his d. all unbraced (Madness 1)
doubt:
 d. not, my lord, I'll play the orator (Eloquence 7)
 d. thou the stars are fire (Love 30)
 modest d. ... the beacon of the wise (Security 2)
doubting:
 d. things go ill often hurts more (Doubts 1)

doubts:

bound in to saucy doubts (Anxiety 7)

our d. are traitors (Doubts 2)

dove:

change a raven for a d. (Inconstancy 2)

dove (cont'd.)

d. and very blessèd spirit (Peace 5)

harmless d. (Innocence 3)

patient as the female d. (Madness 6)

doves:

d. will peck in safeguard (Courage 3)

he eats nothing but d. (Love 89)

down:

d., d. to hell (Ruthlessness 2)

d., thou climbing sorrow (Sorrow 3)

you have put him d. (Sex 5)

downy:

d. windows close (Death 5)

dowry:

give thee this plague for thy d. (Marriage 16)

dragon:

come not between the d. (Anger 4)

compounded...under the dragon's tail (Astrology 2)

d. wing of night (Night 22)

dread:

sable night, mother of d. (Night 24)

dream:

a d. itself is but a shadow (Dreams 4)

fierce vexation of a d. (Dreams 5)

had thee as a d. doth flatter (Dreams 17)

I dreamt a d. tonight (Dreams 12)

I have had a d. (Dreams 6)

I have bad d. (Dreams 3)

phantasma or hideous d. (Anxiety 4)

to sleep, perchance to d. (Death 7)

dreamer:

he is a dreamer (Danger 5)

dreaming:

in d. the clouds methought would open (Dreams 15)

dreams:

d. are toys (Dreams 16)

I talk of d. (Dreams 13)

my d. presage some joyful news (Dreams 14)

night so full of fearful d. (Dreams 8)

one that d. on sovereignty (Aspiration 1)

thoughts are but d. (Thought 14)

dreamt:

I d. there was an emperor (Dreams 1)

drink:

I d. the air before me (Speed 5)

we'll teach you to d. deep (Drinking 5)

we shall d. down all unkindness (Drinking 17)

what three things does d. ... provoke? (Drinking 14)

when my d. is ready (Bells 1)

drinking:

unhappy brains for d. (Drinking 20)

droop:

wherefore do you d.? (Encouragement 2)

drops:

at a few d. of women's rheum (Tears 4)

dropsies:

that parcel of d. (Fatness 4)

drown:

methought what pain it was to d. (Dreams 9)

drug:

what purgative d. (Medicine 11)

drugs:

thy d. are quick (Last Words 6)

drunk:

he is d. now (Drinking 25)

he's d. nightly in your company (Drinking 27)

he's d., Sir Toby, an hour agone (Drinking 28)

I'll ne'er be d. (Drinking 16)

that which hath made them d. (Drinking 13)

ducats:

O my d. (Loss 4)

ducdame:

what's that d. (Mockery 1)

due:

give the Devil his d. (Devil 4)

dumb show:

who can converse with a d.? (Conversation 2)

Duncan:

D. is in his grave (Death 25)

this D. hath borne (Virtue 10)

dungeon:

Nor airless d. ... can be retentive (Constraint 1)

dust:

compounded it with d. (Burial 1)

d. on antique time would lie unswept (Custom 1)

give to d. that is a little gilt (Fashion 11)

this quintessence of d. (Humanity 1)

trace the noble d. of Alexander (Mortality 3)

duty:

ceremonious d. (Humanity 6)

d. never yet did want his meed (Duty 6)

every subject's d. is the king's (Duty 2)

I do perceive here a divided d. (Duty 5)

in the modesty of fearful d. (Speechmaking 3)

I owe him little d. (Duty 3)

think'st thou that d. shall have dread? (Duty 4)

urge thy d. (Apologies 2)

dwarf:

stirring d. (Action 15)

dwell:

d. I but in the suburbs (Marriage 21)

dye:

that dye is on me (Innocence 4)

dyer:

like the d.'s hand (Reputation 16)

dying:

I am d., Egypt, d. (Dying 1)

each:

e. new morn new widows howl (Sorrow 5)

e. one ... answer to his part (Acting 31)

eagle:

gaze an e. blind (Love 42)

like an e. in a dovecote (Soldiers 2)

the e. suffers little birds to sing (Birds 14, Power 12)

ear:

a jest's prosperity lies in the e. (Jokes 3)

give every man thy e. (Advice 5)

this e. is deaf (Opinion 2)

early:

the reason I was up so e. (Lateness 1)

earn:

I e. that I eat (Contentment 1)

earnest:

I love no man in good e. (Love 8)

pleads he in e.? (Sincerity 2)

ears:

aged e. play truant at his tales (Talking 5)

lend me your e. (Epitaphs 10)

O that men's e. should be to counsel deaf (Flattery 8)

shake your Rome about your e. (Authority 3)

to e. of flesh and blood (Afterlife 1)

earth:

beauty for ... e. too dear (Beauty 22)

canst work i'th' e. so fast? (Ghosts 11)

e. hath swallowed all my hopes (Parents and Children 15)

e.'s increase, foison plenty (Blessings 6)

from the four corners of the e. (Fame 3)

greet I thee, my e. (Greetings 11)

lards the lean e. as he walks along (Fatness 1)

lay her i'th'e. (Burial 3)

teeming e. is with a kind of colic pinched (Earth-quakes 1)

the e. that's nature's mother (Nature 5)

this goodly frame, the e. (World 3)

thou bleeding piece of e. (Mourning 14)

earthlier:

e. happy is the rose distilled (Marriage 28)

ease:

take mine e. in mine inn (Leisure 2)

east:

e., west, north, south (Home 1)

from the e. to western Inde (Love 14)

i'th' e. my pleasure lies (Pleasure 3)

easy:

as e. mayst thou fall (Marriage 12)

eat:

e. no onions nor garlic (Eating 10)

nothing but sit and sit, and e. and e. (Eating 12)

we will e. a last year's pippin (Eating 5)

eaten:

he hath e. me out of house and home (Eating 4)

eater:

I am a great e. of beef (Eating 13)

eating:

e. the bitter bread of banishment (Exile 7)

eclipse:

should be now a huge e. (Loss 7)

eclipses:

these late e. in the sun (Portents 7)

ecstasy:

allay thy e. (Love 51)

restless e. (Anxiety 6)

the very e. of love (Love 29)

Eden:

this other E., demi-paradise (Countries 5)

edict:

it stands as an e. in destiny (Patience 9)

egg:

full of quarrels as an e. is full of meat (Quarrels 14)

thou art damned, like an ill-roasted e. (Food 4)

eglantine:

with sweet musk-roses and with e. (Flowers 6)

Egypt:

I am dying, E., dying (Dying 1)

Egyptian:

he will to his E. dish again (Desire 2)

eight:

eyes were set at e. i' the morning (Drinking 28)

elbow:

my e. itched (Insults 16)

elements:

I tax you not, you e. (Storms 9)

life consist of the four e. (Hedonism 2)

the e. so mixed in him (Epitaphs 12)

to the e. be free (Freedom 9)

unfriendly e. forgot thee (Birth and Death 1)

with no less terror than the e. (Meeting 1)

elephant:

the e. hath joints (Pride 3)

elm:

thou art an e., my husband (Marriage 13)

eloquence:

action is e. (Action 1)

more e. in a sugar touch (Eloquence 4)

saucy and audacious e. (Speechmaking 3)

she uttereth piercing e. (Courtship 20)

Elsinore:

what make you at E.? (Friendship 4)

elves:

ye e. of hills, brooks, standing lakes (Fairies 8)

Elysium:

my brother he is in E. (Countries 8)

emulation:

e. hath a thousand sons (Reputation 14)

encounterers:

these e., so glib of tongue (Lechery 5)

end:

bid me remember mine e. (Mortality 5)

here is my journey's e. (Resignation 6)

is this the promised e.? (Doomsday 2)

let the e. try the man (Men 3)

the e. crowns all (Time 33)

whose e. is purposed by the mighty gods (Fate 6)

endeavors:

my e. have ever come too short (Service 4)

ends:

delays have dangerous e. (Delay 3)

more are men's e. marked (Endings 3)

endure:

men must e. their going hence (Endurance 2)

must I e. all this? (Quarrels 7)

enemies:
bayed about with many e. (Danger 9)
our e. have beat us to the pit (Defeat 1)
such men my friends than e. (Enemies 4)
you have many e. (Enemies 3)

enemy:
common e. of man (Damnation 1)
easier ... than fight with mine e. (Fighting 3)
if the e. is an ass and a fool (Enemies 2)
my nearest and dearest e. (Enemies 1)
O cunning e. (Temptation 4)
put an e. into their mouths (Drinking 22)
security is mortals' chiefest e. (Security 2)
though mine e. (Honor 20)

engendered:
I have 't. It is e. (Evil 10)

enginer:
have the e. hoist with his own petard (Justice 1)

England:
E. breeds very valiant creatures (Dogs 2)
if E. to herself do rest but true (Patriotism 2)
old Robin Hood of E. (Country Life 1)
save back to E. all the world's my way (Exile 5)
that E. that was wont to conquer (Countries 7)
then E.'s ground farewell (Exile 6)
this blessed plot, this E. (Countries 6)
this E. never did (Patriotism 2)
to E. will I steal (Theft 5)
why was he sent into E.? (Countries 3)

English:
my native E. I must now forgo (Language 7)
trick of our E. nation (Countries 4)

Englishman:
though banished, yet a true-born E. (Exile 6)

enigmatical:
your answer, sir, is e. (Meaning 1, Answers 1)

enjoy:
e. the honey-heavy dew of slumber (Sleep 6)

enmity:
be at e. with any cozening hope (Despair 4)

enough:
lend to each man enough (Prayer 18)

entice:
do I e. you? (Plain-Speaking 10)

entrails:
of intolerable e. (Insults 14)
turns our swords in our own proper e. (Caesar 5)

entrance:
the fatal e. of Duncan (Foreboding 9)

envy:
e. breeds unkind division (Civil War 2)
men that make e. ... nourishment (Envy 1)

Epicurean:
E. cooks sharpen ... his appetite (Food 2)

epilogue:
no e., I pray you (Theater 15)

epithet:
singular and choice e. (Affectation 1)
suffer love! a good e. (Love 67)

Eros:
unarm E. (Death-Wish 1)

error:
e. of our eye (Inconstancy 6)
mountainous e. be ... heaped (Custom 1)
O hateful e. (Mistakes 3)
the very e. of the moon (Moon 4)
what e. drives our eyes and ears amiss? (Mistakes 1)

eruption:
this bodes some strange e. (Foreboding 3)

eruptions:
earth breaks out in strange e. (Earthquakes 1)

eschewed:
what cannot be e. (Inevitability 1)

esperance:
stands still in e. (Hope 2)

essence:
his glassy e. (Authority 9)

estate:
what thinks he of our e.? (Danger 4)
wish th'e. o'the world were now undone (Despair 3)

estates:
O that e. ... were not derived corruptly (Merit 2)

et:
et tu Brute (Last Words 2)

eternal:
this e. blazon must not be (Afterlife 1, Eternity 2)
thy e. summer shall; not fade (Eternity 3)

eternity:
e. was in our lips and eyes (Eternity 1)
make us heirs of all e. (Fame 2)
who ... sells e. to gain a toy? (Desire 18)

evening:
how still the e. is (Evening 1)

events:
many e. in the womb of time (Time 20)

ever:
e. till now when men were fond (Infatuation 7)
for e. and for e. farewell (Parting 9)

everyone:
e. can master a grief (Aphorisms 9)

everything:
e. that grows holds in perfection (Perfection 3)

evil:
e. soul producing holy witness (Duplicity 1)
obscures the show of e. (Hypocrisy 10)
the beauteous e. (Virtue 24)
the e. that men do (Epitaphs 10)

evils:
pitch our e. there (Building 3)
this same progeny of e. (Quarrels 11)

example:
things done without e. (Innovation 1)

excellent:
e. wretch! (Love 71)
so e. a king (Excellence 1)

excess:
is wasteful and ridiculous e. (Extravagance 2)

face (cont'd.):
    when I do see your f. (Love 56)
    your f., my thane, is as a book (Faces 6)
faces:
    we know each other's f. (Deceit 17)
    ye have angels' f. (Hypocrisy 4)
faction:
    leave the f. of fools (Folly 4)
factious:
    be f. for redress of ... griefs (Conspiracy 2)
fail:
    if we should f. (Courage 6)
fair:
    as a f. day in summer (Beauty 20)
    f. is foul (Confusion 2, Paradoxes 1)
    most foul, most f. (Paradoxes 2)
    my decayèd f. (Unkindness 2, Marriage 10)
    those that she makes f. (Women 2)
fairies:
    we f. that do run (Fairies 6)
fairy:
    hand in hand with f. grace (Fairies 7)
    no f. takes, nor witch hath power (Festivals 1)
faith:
    no tricks in plain and simple f. (Hypocrisy 5)
    there's no more f. in thee (Trust 2)
    there's no room for f., truth, nor honesty (Fatness 5)
    wears his f. but as the fashion (Inconstancy 3)
falcon:
    f. towering in her pride (Birds 9)
    my f. now is sharp (Falconry 1)
fall:
    f. not a tear (Tears 2)
    what a f. was there (Treason 4)
falling-off:
    what a f. was there! (Decline 1)
falls:
    this f. out better (Plots 1)
false:
    if I be f. (Constancy 8)
    if she be f. (Inconstancy 5)
falsehood:
    f. f. cures, as fire cools fire (Proverbs 11)
    what a goodly outside f. hath (Duplicity 5)
Falstaff:
    F. sweats to death (Fatness 1)
fame:
    let f. that all hunt after (Fame 2)
    my f. is shrewdly gored (Reputation 15)
    now he lives in f. (Fame 4)
    paragons description and wild f.(Beauty 16)
    unregistered in vulgar f. (Lust 4)
familiar:
    as f. with me as my dog (Dogs 1)
famine:
    f. is in thy cheeks (Poverty 1)
famished:
    I am f. in his service (Thinness 3)
fan:
    brain him with his lady's f. (Cowardice 2)

fancies:
    our f. are more giddy (Men and Women 10)
    play with your f. (Ships 2)
fancy:
    all impediments in f.'s course (Love 4)
    my idolatrous f. (Infatuation 2)
    tell me where is f. bred (Love 50)
    the f. outwork nature (Beauty 1)
    the food of sweet and bitter f. (Love 25)
    the power of f. (Love 19)
fangs:
    beware my f. (Insults 13)
fantasied:
    I find the people strangely f. (Fear 10)
fantasy:
    dreams ... begot of nothing but vain f. (Dreams 13)
    is not this something more than f.? (Fear 1)
fardels:
    who would f. bear (Afterlife 2)
fare:
    f. thee well, dame (Farewells 1)
    f. thee well, great heart (Farewells 6)
    well, f. thee well (Farewells 8)
farewell:
    f., a long f. (Farewells 10)
    f. thee well, most foul (Paradoxes 4)
    f. the neighing steed (War 19)
    f. the tranquil mind (Farewells 14)
    f., thou art too dear (Farewells 21)
    our everlasting f. take (Farewells 11)
    poor Jack, f. (Farewells 7)
    sweets to the sweet, f. (Farewells 5)
    yet now f., and f. life (Farewells 9)
farewells:
    as many f. as be stars in heaven (Time 31)
fashion:
    a man in all the world's new f. (Fashion 7)
    f. it thus (Conspiracy 4)
    I see that the f. wears out (Fashion 8)
    the f. of the world is to avoid cost (Generosity 4)
    the glass of f. (Fashion 2)
    thou art not for the f. of these times (Fashion 1)
    'tis just the f. (Cities 1)
fashions:
    old f. please me best (Fashion 10)
    report of f. in proud Italy (Fashion 9)
fast:
    f. bind, f. find (Thrift 3)
faster:
    f. than springtime showers (Thought 8)
fat:
    men about me that are f. (Politics 10)
fate:
    comfort ... succeeds in unknown f. (Happiness 5)
    my f. cries out (Fate 1)
    that one might read the book of f. (Fate 3)
    who can control his f.? (Fate 7)
fates:
    men ... are masters of their f. (Fate 5)
    our wills and f. (Fate 1)

what f. impose (Fate 4, Resistance 2)

father:

a decrepit f. takes delight (Parents and Children 19)

a f.'s at the nuptial of his son (Parents and Children 17)

as a f. to my youth (Advice 8)

I am glad thy f.'s dead (Grief 12)

I am thy f.'s spirit (Ghosts 9)

I have a f., you a daughter lost (Parents and Children 12)

my f. did something smack (Lechery 2)

my f. named me Autolycus (Theft 12)

my f. will grant precious things (Generosity 7)

she has deceived her f. (Deceit 11)

to be a f. unto many sons (Parents and Children 4)

wise f. that knows his own child (Parents and Children 11)

your f. was ever virtuous (Virtue 16)

fathers:

f. that wear rags (Parents and Children 7)

fathom:

full f. five thy father lies (Transformation 3)

how many f. deep I am in love (Love 22)

fatter:

would he were f. (Fear 7)

fault:

Fie, 'tis a f. to heaven (Faults 5)

I cannot wish the f. undone (Wrongdoing 4)

if sack and sugar be a f. (Age 9)

is it her f. or mine? (Temptation 3)

pardon this f. (Apologies 3)

the f., dear Brutus, is not in our stars (Faults 6)

the worst f. you have (Faults 4)

think not upon the f. (Prayer 6)

this f. I find (Inconstancy 6)

faults:

all his f. observed (Criticism 2)

a man who is the abstract of all f. (Faults 1)

best men are molded out of f. (Faults 8)

f. that are rich are fair (Generosity 5)

I do not like your f. (Faults 7)

if little f. ... shall not be winked at (Crime 1)

myself, against whom I know most f. (Self-Knowledge 1)

one error fills him with f. (Inconstancy 7)

who covert f. ... with shame derides (Time 17)

you gods will give us some f. (Faults 3)

favors:

he that depends upon your f. (People 8)

remember the f. of these men (Betrayal 2)

fear:

blind f. that seeing reason (Fear 16)

f. is most accursed (Fear 4)

f. no more the frown (Mourning 4)

f. no more the heat (Mourning 3)

I f. him not (Fear 7)

if he should stay at home ... for f. (Fear 8)

I have a faint cold f. (Fear 15)

know not what we f. (Confusion 5)

'tis time to fear (Tyranny 6)

to be feared than what I f. (Caesar 1)

true nobility is exempt from f. (Fear 5)

you may f. too far (Fear 11)

fearful:

how f. and dizzy 'tis (Vertigo 1)

fears:

he that but f. the thing (Fear 3)

I have almost forgot the taste of f. (Fear 14)

not mine own f. (Anxiety 11)

our f. do make us traitors (Fear 13)

present f. are less (Fear 12)

feast:

buy for our sheep-shearing f. (Feasts 4)

not yet an Alexandrian f. (Feasts 1)

one f., one house (Happiness 7)

proud death, what f. is toward (Death 10)

small cheer ... makes a merry f. (Feasts 3)

the beginning of a f. (Fighting 1)

the f. of Crispian (Festivals 2)

who riseth from a f. with that keen appetite (Eating 8)

feasts:

be abhorred all f. (Misanthropy 5)

feather:

I am a f. for each wind (Indecision 4)

the swan's down f. (Indecision 1)

was ever f. so lightly blown (People 16)

feathers:

these growing f. plucked (Power 2)

February:

such a F. face (Moods 12)

fee:

the golden f. for which I plead (Eloquence 7)

feeble:

not enough to help the f. up (Helping 2)

feed:

f. him with apricots and dewberries (Food 11)

felicity:

absent thee from f. (Stories 1)

fellow:

a barren-spirited f. (Contempt 3)

a f. almost damned (Marriage 39)

a f. of a good respect (Honor 17)

a f. of infinite jest (Epitaphs 3)

a f. of no mark (Men 2)

an honest f. enough (Stupidity 4)

a very tainted fellow (Evil 1)

ignorant, unweighing f. (Insults 12)

love a f. of this temper (Courtship 10)

poor f. never joyed (Money 1)

that ever this f. should have fewer words (Words 2)

this f. is wise enough to play the fool (Fools 15)

this f.'s of exceeding honesty (Honesty 6)

this f. will but join you (Marriage 4)

thou art a blessed f. (Opinion 1)

thou art a f. of a good respect (Honor 17)

what a blunt f. is this grown (Plain-Speaking 3)

fellows:

nature hath framed strange f. (Humanity 4)

what should such f. as I do? (Humanity 2, Misanthropy 1)

fortune (cont'd.)

f. is painted blind (Fortune 9)

f. knows we scorn her most (Fortune 2)

f. now to my heart's hope (Fortune 20)

f. reigns in the gifts of the world (Fortune 4)

f.'s bastard be unfathered (Constancy 13)

f.'s buffets and rewards (Fortune 7, Stoicism 1)

good f. then (Fortune 18)

greatness once fallen out with f. (Decline 3)

herein f. shows herself more kind (Fortune 21)

if f. be a woman (Fortune 19)

if my f. be not crossed (Parents and Children 12)

I see f. would not suffer me (Fortune 24)

I thank my f. for it (Business 6)

joy for his f. (Caesar 3)

mock the good huswife f. (Fortune 3)

most dejected thing of f. (Hope 2)

O lady f., stand you (Fortune 23)

one out of suits with f. (Fortune 5)

poor man made tame to f.'s blows (Pity 4)

since this f. falls to you (Choice 7)

slings and arrows of outrageous f. (Choice 1)

some unborn sorrow ripe in f.'s womb (Foreboding 12)

tide leads on to f. (Opportunity 2)

to cozen f. (Merit 1)

when f. means to men most good (Fortune 12)

when in disgrace with f. (Misery 5)

will f. never come (Fortune 8)

fortunes:

all my f. at thy foot I'll lay (Devotion 6)

f. will ever after droop (Astrology 4)

least rub in your f. (Betrayal 1)

loves should with our f. change (Mutability 1)

make content with his f. fit (Fortune 15)

fortune-teller:

one Pinch ... a f. (Character 1)

foster-nurse:

our f. of nature is repose (Sleep 8)

foul:

f. is fair (Confusion 2)

most f., most fair (Paradoxes 2)

so f. and fair a day I have not seen (Weather 4)

foundation:

God save the f.! (Religion 6)

no sure f. set on blood (Murder 4)

fountain:

f. from the which my current runs (Loss 6)

troubled like a f. stirred (Perplexity 2)

four:

f. lagging winters (Royalty 27)

fowler:

geese that the creeping f. eye (Hunting 2)

fox:

the f. barks not when he would steal (Animals 5)

when the f. hath once got in his nose (Animals 6)

frail:

we are all f. (Weakness 3)

frailty:

f., thy name is woman (Weakness 1)

I have more flesh ... and therefore more f. (Excuses 3)

frame:

this goodly f., the earth (World 3)

France:

churlish turf of F. (Age 18)

fray:

latter end of a f. (Fighting 1)

free:

be as f. as mountain winds (Freedom 7)

to the elements be f. (Freedom 9)

freedom:

f., high-day! high-day f.! (Freedom 8)

liberty! f.! (Freedom 4)

freeze:

f., f. thou bitter sky (Seasons 2)

French:

I will tell thee in F. (Language 3)

fret:

f. till your proud heart break (Quarrels 4)

friend:

a f. i'the court (Friendship 11)

a f. should bear his f.'s infirmities (Friendship 17)

f. or brother, he forfeits (Punishment 4)

he was my f., faithful and just to me (Friendship 16)

if I had a f. that loved her (Courtship 16)

I weigh my f.'s affection (Friendship 30)

my noble f., chew upon this (Thought 10)

think on thee, dear f. (Love 107)

to me, fair f., you never can be old (Love 109)

friends:

come, I'll be f. with thee (Friendship 8)

eat and drink as f. (Friendship 27)

f. am I with you all, and love you all (Friendship 15)

f., I owe more tears (Mourning 16)

f., Romans, countrymen (Epitaphs 10)

good f., go in (Friendship 13)

good morrow, f. (Greetings 6)

happy ... in remembering my good f. (Friendship 25)

I had rather have such men my f. than enemies (Enemies 4)

joy, gentle f. (Greetings 7)

love and be f. (Reconciliation 1)

make f. and give your heart to (Betrayal 1)

make f. of foes (Blessings 1)

make f. with speed (Diplomacy 1, Letters 2)

my f. were poor, but honest (Love 2)

pity two such f. should be long foes (Friendship 32)

pricked in number of our f. (Friendship 14)

those f. thou hast (Friendship 3)

'twixt such f. as we few words suffice (Friendship 26)

what need we have any f.? (Friendship 28)

you dare easier be f. with me (Fighting 3)

friendship:

f. is constant in all other things (Friendship 23)

if I do vow a f. (Friendship 24)

in the beaten way of f. (Friendship 4)

love cools, f. falls off (Disorder 1)

most f. is feigning (Disillusion 1)

there is flattery in f. (Flattery 3)

where there is true f. (Ceremony 5)

frost:
>   death lies on her like an untimely f. (Death 37)
>   the third day comes a f., a killing f. (Farewells 10)

frown:
>   fear no more the f. (Mourning 4)

frowningly:
>   what, looked he f.? (Faces 2)

fruit:
>   the ripest f. first falls (Epitaphs 13)

full:
>   f. fathom five (Transformation 2)
>   f. many a glorious morning (Sunrise 6)

full-gorged:
>   my falcon ... must not be f. (Falconry 1)

function:
>   f. is smothered in surmise (Confusion 4)

funeral:
>   come I to speak in Caesar's f. (Honor 15)
>   with mirth in f. (Mourning 6)

furnace:
>   heat not a f. for your foe (Advice 9)

fury:
>   fires ... consume the thing that feeds their f. (Fire 4)

gaberdine:
>   my Jewish g. (Anti-Semitism 1)

gain:
>   sir which serves and seeks for g. (Self-Interest 3)

gale:
>   what happy g. blows you to Padua? (Travel 19)

gallop:
>   g. apace, you fiery-footed steeds (Anticipation 3)

gap:
>   sleep out this great g. of time (Forgetfulness 2)

garden:
>   old Adam's likeness, set to dress this g. (Gardens 8)
>   our sea-walled g. the whole land (Disorder 3)
>   this world ... 'tis an unweeded g. (Dejection 1)

gardener:
>   Adam was a g. (Gardens 4)

garland:
>   withered is the g. of the war (Epitaphs 1)

garlic:
>   eat no onions nor g. (Eating 10)

garment:
>   this new and gorgeous g. (Royalty 13)

garments:
>   our g. poor (Clothing 10)

garter:
>   knights of the g. (Chivalry 1)

garters:
>   hang thyself in thine own ... g. (Insults 3)

gasp:
>   fight to the last g. (Resistance 1)

gauds:
>   all, with one consent, praise new-born g. (Fashion 11)

gaudy:
>   let's have one other g. night (Feasts 2)

gaze:
>   no extraordinary g. (Royalty 9)

geese:
>   wild g. that the creeping fowler eye (Hunting 2)

geld:
>   g. and spay all the youth (Prostitution 1)

gem:
>   never so rich a g. (Jewels 2)

general:
>   are you content to be our g.? (Necessity 9)
>   the g. so likes your music (Music 15)

gentleman:
>   a g. ... that loves to hear himself talk (Talking 6)
>   a most kind g. (Soldiers 15)
>   he is a worthy g. (Men 1)
>   I do not think a braver g. (Soldiers 8)
>   I was a g. (Men 9)
>   prince of darkness is a g. (Devil 5)
>   smooth-faced g., tickling commodity (Self-Interest 1)
>   the g. is learned (Eloquence 5)
>   this g. will out-talk us all (Talking 7)
>   thou wrong'st a g. (Virtue 4)

gentlemen:
>   g. in England now abed (War 15)

gentleness:
>   I have not from your eyes that g. (Friendship 12)
>   the g. of all the gods go with thee (Farewells 20)

germens:
>   all g. spill at once (Storms 6)

get:
>   g. you hence, sirrah! (Dismissal 1)

ghost:
>   I'll make a g. of him that lets me (Determination 1)
>   there needs no g., my lord (Truisms 2)

giant:
>   excellent to have a g.'s strength (Strength 2)
>   pang as great as when a g. dies (Death 27)
>   sleeping g. (Action 15)

gibes:
>   where be your g. now? (Mortality 2)

giddy:
>   he that is g. (Giddiness 1)

gift:
>   action did outsell her g. (Action 2)
>   make my g. the more delayed (Providence 1)
>   this rich and precious g. (Gifts 1)
>   though the g. small (Gifts 3)

gifts:
>   the g. she looks from me (Gifts 6)
>   why do you make us love your goodly g.? (Gifts 2)
>   win her with g. (Gifts 5)

gild:
>   to g. refinèd gold (Extravagance 2)

gillyvors:
>   our carnations and streaked g. (Flowers 10)

ginger:
>   and g. shall be hot (Virtue 23)

girdle:
>   but to the g. do the gods inherit (Misogyny 1)
>   I'll put a g. round about the earth (Travel 14)

girl:
>   an unlessoned g., unschooled (Girls 3)

girl (cont'd.)
  there's a g. goes before the priest (Thought 1)
girls:
  the truth of g.'s and boys (Girls 2)
  those g. of Italy (Girls 1)
give:
  g. me my robe (Death-Wish 3)
  g. me that glass (Self-Pity 3)
  g. me that man that is not passion's slave (Freedom 5)
  g. me the map there (Maps 2)
  g. the Devil his due (Devil 4)
glass:
  fair woman but she made mouths in a g. (Vanity 1)
  give me that g. (Self-Pity 3)
  he was the mark and g., copy and book (Fashion 4)
  methinks you are my g. (Twins 1)
  the g. of fashion and the mold of form (Fashion 2)
  the g. wherein the noble youth (Fashion 3)
globe:
  th'affrighted g. (Loss 7)
  this distracted g. (Memory 2)
  we the g. can compass soon (Travel 15)
glory:
  fierce wretchedness that g. brings (Misery 4)
  g. is like a circle in the water (Glory 1)
  greater g. dim the less (Comparisons 2)
  think not ... to share with me in g. (Rivalry 1)
  times's g. is to calm (Time 40)
  uncertain g. of an April day (Love 102)
glove:
  a cheveril g. to a good wit (Wit 7)
gloves:
  g. as sweet as damask roses (Clothing 15)
glow-worm:
  g. shows the matin to be near (Dawn 3, Time of Day 3)
gnats:
  let foolish g. make sport (Insects 1)
go:
  he must needs go that the devil drives (Devil 1)
goats:
  as prime as g. (Lechery 3)
  wanton as youthful g. (Animals 4)
goblin:
  be thou ... a g. damned (Ghosts 7)
God:
  an attribute to G. himself (Mercy 9)
  art thou some g. (Apparitions 5)
  for G.'s sake go not to these wars (War 6)
  for G.'s sake let us sit (Stories 5)
  G. doth know and you may partly see (Deceit 20)
  G. is our fortress (God 4)
  G. keep lead out of me (War 5)
  G. keep your worship (Blessings 4)
  G.'s above all (Soul 2)
  G. save the foundation! (Religion 6)
  G.'s benison go with you (Blessings 1)
  G. shall be my hope (God 7)

G. the best maker of all marriages (Prayer 7)
  had I but served my G. (Service 4)
  had not G. for some strong purpose (Pity 9)
  in apprehension how like a g. (Man 5)
  I thank G. I am not a woman (Women 7)
  make the service greater than the g. (Idolatry 1)
  now G. be praised (God 5, Prayer 9)
  O G. of battles (Prayer 6)
  O G., that men should put an enemy (Drinking 22)
  O G., that one might read the book of fate (Fate 3)
  O G., thy arm was here (God 3)
  O pity, G., this miserable age! (Prayer 10)
  the g. of this great vast (Storms 13)
  the hideous g. of w. (War 7)
  thou owest G. a death (Death 12)
  we are in G.'s hands (God 2)
  we owe G. a death (Death 14)
  what kind of g. art thou (Ceremony 2)
godheads:
  were your g. to borrow of men (Prayer 18)
gods:
  as flies ... are we to the g. (Gods 1)
  draw near the nature of the g. (Mercy 15)
  g. are just (Justice 8)
  g. stand up for bastards (Bastardy 1)
  g. themselves humbling their deities (Gods 5)
  g., why do you make us love your ... gifts (Gifts 2)
  immortal g., I crave no pelf (Prayer 17)
  nature of the g. (Mercy 5)
  the clearest g. ... have preserved thee (Miracles 4)
  the voice of all the g. (Love 44)
  to your protection I commend me, g. (Prayer 2)
  you ever gentle g. (Prayer 13)
goers-between:
  let all pitiful g. (Lust 12)
gold:
  all that glisters is not g. (Gold 5)
  g., worse poison to men's souls (Poison 3)
  g., yellow, glistering, precious g. (Gold 6)
  I am not covetous for g. (Honor 9)
  plate sin with g. (Gold 4)
  poop was beaten g. (Ships 2)
  saint-seducing g. (Courtship 19)
  the g. bides still (Gold 1)
  there is g. (Royalty 1)
  'tis g. which makes the true man killed (Gold 2)
  when g. becomes her object (Avarice 1, Gold 3)
golden age:
  t'excel the g. (Government 5)
golden world:
  carelessly as they did in the g. (Golden Age 1)
gone:
  art thou g. too ? (Parting 8)
  wilt thou be g.? (Parting 16)
good:
  g. fortune then! To make me blest (Fortune 18)
  g. friends, go in and taste some wine (Friendship 13)
  g. Hamlet, cast thy nighted color (Clothing 2)
  I never did repent for doing g. (Goodness 2)

it is not, nor it cannot come to g. (Grief 6)

make g. of bad (Blessings 1)

so shines a g. deed (Goodness 3)

the g. is oft interrèd with their bones (Epitaphs 10)

the g. I stand on (Integrity 1)

they should be g. men (Goodness 1)

'tis g. for men to love their ... pains (Philosophy 10)

to do g. accounted dangerous folly (Innocence 4)

goodly:

a g. portly man, i'faith (Fatness 3)

good will:

my g. w. is great (Gifts 3)

when g. w. is showed (Acting 1)

goodness:

g. to the vile seem vile (Aphorisms 3)

some soul of g. in things evil (Philosophy 8)

goose:

when every g. is cackling (Birds 11)

gorgeous:

nature needs not what thou g. wear'st (Fashion 5)

gosling:

I'll never be such a g. (Man 2)

gossamers:

lover may bestride the g. (Vanity 3)

gout:

a pox of this g. (Sickness 10)

govern:

I would with such perfection g. (Government 5)

government:

g., though high and low (Government 2)

we be men of good g. (Government 1)

gowns:

one that hath two g. (Dignity 1)

grace:

g. and remembrance be to you (Flowers 9)

g. me no g. (Grace 1)

g. of heaven ... enwheel thee round (Greetings 10)

heaven such g. did lend her (Beauty 26)

he does it with a better g. (Fools 12)

her strong toil of g. (Death 6)

if a lie may do thee g. (Lying 3)

in all external g. (Constancy 11)

mickle is the powerful g. (Nature 6)

O momentary g. of mortal men (Grace 2, Transience 4)

things foul would wear the brows of g. (Angels 1)

this action ... is for my better g. (Action 16)

what a g. was seated on this brow (Beauty 7)

when once our g. we have forgot (Shame 1)

you have the g. of God (Proverbs 19)

graces:

g. her subjects (Beauty 19)

the king-becoming g. (Virtue 11)

grain:

'tis in g. ... 'twill endure wind (Beauty 25)

grass:

how lush and lusty the g. looks (Gardens 10)

grave:

a little g., an obscure g. (Renunciation 2)

do me wrong to take me out o' the g. (Suffering 1)

Duncan is in his g. (Death 25)

every third thought shall be my g. (Mortality 10)

no g. upon the earth shall clip (Epitaphs 3)

renownèd be thy g. (Mourning 5)

still as the g. (Proverbs 23)

sweeten thy sad g. (Mourning 2)

the g. doth gape for thee (Mortality 6)

thy ignominy sleep with thee in the g. (Epitaphs 7)

tomorrow you shall find me a g. man (Dying 15)

true lover never find my g. (Graces 2)

graves:

bears not one spurn to their g. (Corruption 7)

g. at my command (Renunciation 4)

g. stood tenantless (Apparitions 3)

let's talk of g. (Despair 5)

the g. all gaping wide (Ghosts 14)

grave-stone:

let my g-stone be your oracle (Epitaphs 15)

gravity:

g. out of his bed at midnight (Age 7)

great:

g. thing of us forgot! (Forgetfulness 3)

he was g. of heart (Greatness 9)

if I do grow g., I'll grow less (Reformation 2)

it is g. to do that thing (Suicide 8)

rightly to be g. (Greatness 2)

some are born g. (Greatness 11)

thou wouldst be g. (Ambition 11)

what g. ones do the less will prattle of (Gossip 1)

greatest:

g. scandal waits on g. state (Greatness 12)

greatness:

a long farewell to all my g. (Farewells 10)

g. going off (Greatness 1)

g. knows itself (Greatness 5)

g. once fallen out with fortune (Decline 3)

possessed he is with g. (Arrogance 2)

some achieve g. (Greatness 11)

th'abuse of g. (Greatness 6)

touched the highest point of all my g. (Downfall 1)

Greece:

in our country of G. (Begging 2)

Greek:

it was G. to me (Language 5)

green:

how g. you are, and fresh (Simplicity 1)

greenwood:

under the g. tree (Country Life 3)

greeting:

bear my g. to the senators (Greetings 3)

grey:

though g. do something mingle (Middle Age 2)

greyhound:

fawning g. then did proffer (Flattery 1)

greyhounds:

I see you stand like g. (War 12)

grief:

crosses, cares and g. (Affliction 11)

grief (cont'd.)
  everyone can master a g. (Aphorisms 9)
  full of g. as age (Affliction 4)
  g. fills the room up (Grief 9)
  g. has so wrought on him (Perception 2)
  g. hath changed me (Grief 3)
  he robs himself that spends a bootless g. (Philosophy 17, Theft 9)
  I have that honorable g. (Grief 15)
  it were a g. ... to part with thee (Farewells 17)
  my g. lies all within (Grief 14)
  my g.'s so great (Grief 8)
  my heart of g. (Grief 7)
  my particular g. (Sorrow 6)
  pure g. shore his old thread (Grief 12)
  something stained with g. (Beauty 23)
  speak comfort to that g. (Experience 3)
  the g. that does not speak (Grief 10)
griefs:
  factious for redress of all these g. (Conspiracy 2)
  g. of mine own lie heavy (Sorrow 12)
  great g., I see, medicine the less (Grief 4)
  relating tales of others' g. (Misery 3)
  sick of many g. (Affliction 2)
  suffer'st ... mortal g. (Ceremony 2)
  to speak my g. unspeakable (Grief 2)
grieved:
  no more be g. (Wrongdoing 8)
grim:
  g. death, how foul (Death 39)
gross:
  in the g. and scope of mine opinion (Foreboding 3)
ground:
  having waste g. enough (Building 3)
  the hopes we have in him touch g. (Disappointment 1)
  lay him in the cold g. (Burial 2)
grudge:
  the ancient g. I bear him (Malevolence 2)
guest:
  beginning of a feast ... fits ... a keen g. (Fighting 1)
guests:
  unbidden g. (Hospitality 1)
guilt:
  they whose g. within their bosoms lie (Guilt 11)
  full of artless jealousy is g. (Guilt 4)
gulfs:
  wash me in steep-down g. (Hell 6)
gull:
  that ungentle g. (Birds 2)
guts:
  thou clay-brained g. (Insults 4)
habit:
  costly thy h. as thy purse can buy (Clothing 3)
  honor peereth in the meanest h. (Clothing 10)
  how use doth breed a h. (Custom 5)
habitation:
  an h. giddy and unsure (People 14)

hags:
  secret, black and midnight h. (Occult 3)
hail:
  h. to thee, lady (Greetings 10)
hair:
  h. shall be of what color it please God (Men and Women 4)
  his very h. is of the dissembling color (Hair 1)
  many a man has more h. than wit (Hair 2)
hairs:
  his silver h. (Maturity 2)
  if h. be wires (Beauty 33)
  spread ... thy golden h. (Courtship 4)
  white h. (Age 8, 17)
half:
  one h. of me is yours (Love 48)
half-world:
  now o'er the one h. (Night 12)
hand:
  each man render me his bloody h. (Greetings 4)
  h. in h. with fairy grace (Fairies 7)
  I saw her h. ... a leathern h. (Insults 1)
  let me kiss that h. (Mortality 7)
  the bawdy h. of the dial (Time 26)
  the eye wink at the h. (Desire 9)
  the fairest h. I ... touched (Beauty 9)
  the h. that hath made you fair (Virtue 13)
  what if this cursèd h. were thicker (Forgiveness 3)
hands:
  close our h. with holy words (Marriage 45)
  give me your h. all over (Greetings 2)
  our own h. against our hearts (Marriage 35)
  these h. do lack nobility (Assault 1)
handy-dandy:
  h., which is the justice (Justice 6)
hang:
  h. me up at the door of a brothel-house (Love 60)
  h. there like fruit (Love 28)
  h. there, my verse (Poetry 1)
  h. thyself (Insults 3)
hanging:
  beating and h. are terrors to me (Afterlife 6)
  h. and wiving goes by destiny (Proverbs 20)
  many a good h. prevents a bad marriage (Marriage 48)
happiness:
  envy no man's h. (Contentment 1)
  look into h. through another man's eyes (Happiness 1)
  one mutual h. (Happiness 7)
  society ... is the h. of life (Society 4)
happy:
  h. thou art not (Happiness 5)
  methinks it were a h. life (Happiness 3)
  so h. be the issue (Negotiation 2)
  'twere now to be most h. (Happiness 6)
harbinger:
  apparel vice like virtue's h. (Deceit 1)

shines Aurora's h. (Dawn 4)

harder:
the h. matched, the greater victory (Victory 1)

hark:
h., h., the lark at heaven's gate (Sunrise 1)
h. what good sport is out of town (Sport 3)

harlot:
Portia is Brutus's h. (Marriage 21)

harlotry:
peevish, self-willed h. (Obstinacy 2)

harm:
I have done no h. (Innocence 5)
know'st thou any h.'s intended (Foreboding 7)

harmony:
hushed on purpose to grace h. (Evening 1)
make heaven drowsy with the h. (Love 44)
such h. is in immortal souls (Heaven 3)
what h. is this? (Music 24)

harp:
h. not on that string (Repetition 1)
I framed to the h. (Music 5)

hart:
if a h. do lack a hind (Poetry 3)
that instant was I turned into a h. (Desire 16)

hast:
h. thou, which art but air (Sympathy 1)

haste:
h. still pays h. (Justice 14)
pray God we may make h. (Lateness 3)

hat:
'a brushes his h. o'mornings (Love 65)
as the fashion of his h. (Inconstancy 3)

hate:
lesser hide his love or h. (Appearance 10)
much to do with h. (Love 73)
naught I did in h. (Murder 10)

haunt:
h. thee like a wicked conscience (Conscience 9)

have:
they well deserve to h. (Deserving 2)
to h. what we would h. (Desire 11)

hawk:
I soar, I am a h. (Horses 2)

hay:
a bottle of h. Good h., sweet h. (Eating 9)

hazard:
give and h. all he hath (Risk 2)
the nice h. of one doubtful hour (Risk 1)

he:
he bids you ... to take mercy (War 9)
he does me double wrong (Flattery 6)
he does smile his face (Faces 7)
he hath a heart as sound as a bell (Speech 17)
he hath borne himself (Courage 7)
he hath disgraced me (Anti-Semitism 2)
he hath honored me (Reputation 4)
he hath ribbons of all the colors (Clothing 14)
he is as valiant as the lion (Valor 14)

he is come to open the purple testament (War 20)
he is composed and framed of treachery (Villainy 6)
he is himself alone (Valor 4)
he is too disputable (Argument 2)
he repelled ... fell into a sadness (Madness 3)
he's as tall a man (Appearance 12)
he seemed to find his way without his eyes (Eyes 6)
he's truly valiant (Endurance 4)
he talks well (Talking 2)
he that but fears the thing (Fear 3)
he that depends upon your favors (People 8)
he that filches from me (Reputation 9)
he that is strucken blind (Eyes 13)
he that loves to be flattered (Flattery 7)
he that of greatest works is finisher (God 1)
he that plays the king (Acting 5)
he that shall see this day (Festivals 4)
he that trusts to you (the People 5)
he was wont to speak plain (Speech 16)
he who the sword of heaven will bear (Justice 13,
Virtue 15)
he will to his Egyptian dish (Desire 2)

head:
his bold h. 'bove the ... waves (Swimming 2)
no house to put his h. in (Homelessness 3)
off with his h. (Execution 1)
thy h. is as full of quarrels (Quarrels 14)
uneasy lies the h. (Royalty 11)
what is the body when the h. is off? (Body 4)

health:
as in h. come to my natural taste (Devotion 3)
h. and fair time of day (Greetings 1)
he has his h. (Middle Age)

healths:
with drinking h. to my niece (Drinking 27)

hear:
h. him debate of commonwealth affairs (Politics 5)
h. me for my cause (Speechmaking 2)

heart:
a good h. is the sun and the moon (Courtship 11)
a kind h. he hath (Kindness 3)
a light h. lives long (Cheerfulness 1)
a merry h. goes all the way (Endurance 5)
break, my h. (Grief 6)
did my h. love till now? (Love 76)
fare thee well, great h.! (Farewells 6)
he has my h. yet (Devotion 1)
he hath a h. as sound as a bell (Speech 17)
he was great of h. (Greatness 9)
his flawed h., alack too weak (Dying 12)
his h.'s his mouth (Speech 2)
how ill all's here about my h. (Foreboding 6)
how weak a thing the h. of woman is (Women 20)
I cannot heave my h. (Speech 9)
infinite h.'s ease (Ceremony 1)
I saw his h. in his face (Faces 8)
I will live in thy h. (Sex 7)
I would eat his h. (Anger 7)

heart (cont'd.)

just as high as my h. (Height 1)

like none for constant h. (Constancy 11)

my h. doth joy (Loyalty 4)

my h. hath one poor string (Dying 11)

my h. is in the coffin (Mourning 15)

my h. is turned to stone (Affliction 8)

my h. laments that virtue (Virtue 8)

my h. prays for him (Forgiveness 1)

my h.'s subdued (Devotion 4)

my h. unto yours is knit (Love 58)

my old h. is cracked (Affliction 3)

no matter from the h. (Words 10)

now cracks a noble h. (Epitaphs 5)

one h., one bed (Love 57)

O serpent h. (Deceit 22)

show his eyes and grieve his h. (Eyes 10)

the poor h. would fain deny (Curses 5)

thy breast encloseth my poor h. (Courtship 17)

wear him in my h.'s core, ay, in my h. of h. (Friend-ship 5)

wear my h. upon my sleeve (Deceit 10)

what the false h. doth know (Deceit 5)

where I have garnered up my h. (Loss 6)

whispers the o'er-fraught h. (Grief 10)

with a h. as willing (Marriage 47)

your h's desires be with you (Desire 3)

heart-break:

better a little chiding than ... h. (Chiding 1)

hearts:

all h. in love (Love 62)

for our h., he knows no more of mine (Deceit 17)

he sits high in all the people's h. (Nobility 5)

let our h. stir up their servants (Assassination 2)

makes these hard h. (Cause 4)

our h. you see not (Pity 2)

our own hands against our h. (Marriage 35)

heat:

the h. of a luxurious bed (Lust 9)

heaven:

comfort's in h. (Affliction 11)

either in h. or hell (Afterlife 3)

h. doth with us as we with torches (Virtue 12)

h. give thee joy (Blessings 2)

h. give you ... merry days (Blessings 3)

he hath turned a h. unto a hell (Love 53)

he who the sword of h. will bear (Justice 13)

h. is above all yet (God 8)

h. mocks itself (Inconstancy 5)

h. still guards the right (Angels 2)

hurl my soul from h. (Affliction 10)

leave her to h. (Conscience 1)

lightning seemed to open the breast of h. (Courage 5)

make h. drowsy (Love 44)

make my h. in a lady's lap (Courtship 12)

my sole earth's h. (Courtship 5)

plays tricks before high h. (Authority 9)

steep and thorny way to h. (Advice 4)

summons thee to h. (Bells 2)

that kiss which is my h. to have (Kissing 2)

the front of h. was full of fiery shapes (Portents 1)

the help of h. we count the act of men (Arrogance 1)

there's husbandry in h. (Darkness 2)

thy soul's flight, if it find h. (Death 24)

when h. doth weep (Storms 17)

heavens:

do as the h. have done (Forgiveness 6)

his face was as the h. (Praise 3)

hung be the h. with black (Night 8)

if that the h. do not their visible spirits (Anarchy 1)

I never saw the h. so dim (Storms 18)

the h. forbid but that our loves (Love 70)

the h. hold firm the walls (Chastity 2, Wishes 2)

the h. themselves blaze forth (Portents 6)

the h. themselves ... observe degree (Order 1)

the h. were all on fire (Portents 2)

who ever knew the h. menace so? (Storms 3)

Hecate:

the triple H.'s team (Fairies 6)

Hecuba:

What's H. to him, or he to H.? (Acting 8)

hedgehogs:

thorny h. (Creatures 3)

hedge-sparrow:

the h. fed the cuckoo so long (Ingratitude 5)

heigh-ho:

sing h. unto the green holly (Disillusion 1)

height:

with her h. ... she hath prevailed (Comparisons 1)

heir:

folly helped her to an h. (Aphorisms 10)

hell:

all h. shall stir for this (Hell 1)

could not believe but that I was in h. (Dreams 11)

down, down to h. (Ruthlessness 2)

either in heaven or h. (Afterlife 3)

h. is murky (Hell 4)

he's not in h. (Afterlife 4)

keeps the gate of h. (Hell 5)

loosèd out of h. (Madness 1)

not in the legions of horrid h. (Hell 3)

rebellious h. (Lust 6)

summons thee to ... h. (Bells 2)

there's h., there's darkness (Misogyny 1)

this place is too cold for h. (Hell 2)

wedlock forcèd but a h. (Marriage 18)

hell-fire:

I never see thy face but I think upon h. (Faces 4)

help:

it appears you need my h. (Help 1)

there is no h. (Inevitability 3)

'tis not enough to h. the feeble (Help 2)

hen:

she, poor h., has clucked thee (Parents and Children 1)

herald:

I wish no other h. (Remembrance 5)

the lark, the h. of the morn (Dawn 6)

heralds:

love's h. should be thoughts (Love 81)

herbs:
> choke the h. for want of husbandry (Gardens 3)
> small h. have grace (Proverbs 25)

Hercules:
> I was with H. and Cadmus once (Hunting 3)

here:
> h. can I sit alone (Solitude 5)
> h. is everything (Life 11)
> h. is my journey's end (Resignation 6)
> h. will I set up my everlasting rest (Death-Wish 10)

hereafter:
> h. in a better world than this (Farewells 2)

herein:
> h. fortune shows herself more kind (Fortune 21)

herring:
> a plague on these pickle h. (Eating 14)

hill:
> over h., over dale (Fairies 1)

hills:
> these high wild h. (Travel 18)
> to climb steep h. (Haste 2)

hind:
> h. that would be mated by the lion (Love 1)

hip:
> catch him once upon the h. (Malevolence 2)

hips:
> which of your h. has ... sciatica (Sickness 15)

history:
> if I should tell my h. (Stories 4)
> there is a h. in all men's lives (Life 5)

hobgoblin:
> those that h. call you and sweet Puck (Fairies 4)

hogs:
> raise the price of h. (Food 8)

holiday:
> a while to work, and after, h. (Holidays 2)
> is this a h.? (Idleness 1)
> he speaks h. (Courtship 13)

holidays:
> if all the year were playing h. (Holidays 1)

hollow:
> within the h. crown (Death 35)

home:
> a h. to fly unto (Investment 1)
> each hurries toward his h. (Home 1)
> h. you idle creatures (Idleness 1)
> to feed were best at h. (Ceremony 4)
> your praise is come too swiftly h. (Praise 5)

honest:
> an h. tale speeds best (Plain-Speaking 11, Stories 8)
> h. as the skin between his brows (Honesty 4)
> h. plain words best pierce (Plain-Speaking 9)
> if I had a mind to be h. (Fortune 24)
> though I am not naturally h. (Honesty 9)
> to be h., as this world goes (Honesty 2)
> where I could not be h. (Honesty 3)

honesty:
> h. coupled to beauty (Virtue 2)
> lov'st to make thine h. a vice (Honesty 7)

> my truth and h. (Integrity 1)
> neither h., manhood, nor ... fellowship (Courage 2)
> rich h. dwells like a miser (Honesty 1)
> this fellow's of exceeding h. (Honesty 6)
> thou art full of love and h. (Honesty 5)
> what a fool h. is (Honesty 8)
> why should honor outlive h.? (Resignation 5)

honey:
> Death ... hath sucked the h. (Death 38)
> sweetest h. ... is loathsome (Appetite 1)
> they surfeited with h. (Eating 3)
> thus may we gather h. (Philosophy 9)

honey-bees:
> so work the h. (Government 3)

honor:
> as far from thy report as thou from h. (Virtue 4)
> beauty and h. ... mingled (Beauty 10)
> believe me for mine h. (Honor 14)
> from the book of h. rasèd quite (Honor 23)
> high sparks of h. (Honor 20)
> hold firm the walls of thy dear h. (Chastity 2)
> h. for his valor (Caesar 3)
> h. is the subject of my story (Honor 13)
> h. peereth in the meanest (Clothing 10)
> h. pricks me on (Honor 5)
> h. riches, marriage-blessing (Blessings 5)
> h.'s thought reigns solely (Honor 7)
> h. travels in a strait so narrow (Reputation 14)
> if it be a sin to covet h. (Honor 9)
> if you were born to h. (Honor 18)
> in thy face I see the map of h. (Honor 11)
> I would not lose so great an h. (Honor 10)
> mine h. is my life (Honor 19)
> not a man ... hath any h. (Honor 21)
> perseverance ... keeps h. bright (Reputation 13)
> set h. in one eye (Honor 12)
> she is a theme of h. (War 22)
> sign and semblance of her h. (Appearance 7)
> the dear man holds h. far more precious-dear (Honor 22)
> the fewer men, the greater share of h. (Honor 8)
> the h. of a maid is her name (Honor 2)
> thou art the king of h. (Honor 4)
> thy life hath had some smatch of h. (Honor 17)
> to pluck bright h. from the pale-faced moon (Honor 3)
> what is h.? A word (Honor 6)
> what loss your h. may sustain (Chastity 4)
> when h.'s at the stake (Greatness 2)
> why should h. outlive honesty? (Resignation 5)

honorable:
> thou couldst not die more h. (Honor 16)
> Brutus is an h. man (Honor 15)

honorificabilitudinitatibus:
> (Words 4)

honors:
> he gave his h. to the world again (Dying 10)
> his taints and h. waged equal (Faults 2)
> h. thrive (Honor 1)
> though we lay these h. on this man (Politics 15)

hoods:
all h. make not monks (Goodness 1)
hop:
I saw her ... h. forty paces (Charm 2)
hope:
be at enmity with any cozening h. (Despair 4)
fortune now, to my heart's h. (Fortune 20)
God shall be my h. (God 7)
likelihoods and forms of h. (Hope 1)
no other medicine but only h. (Hope 3)
past h., past help, past cure (Despair 8)
the h. and expectation (Prophecy 3)
true h. is swift (Hope 4)
hopes:
earth hath swallowed all my h. (Parents and Children 15)
the full prospect of my h. (Confidence 2)
the h. we have in him touch ground (Disappointment 1)
horn:
the h., the h., the lusty h. (Hunting 1)
horns:
set the savage bull's h. (Marriage 34)
horrors:
I have supped full with h. (Fear 14)
on h.'s head h. accumulate (Slander 6)
horse:
an two men ride of a h. (Proverbs 22)
my kingdom for a h. (Desperation 1, Last Words 5)
I will not change my h. (Horses 2)
O for a h. with wings (Travel 6)
O happy h. (Horses 1)
trusts ... a h.'s health (Aphorisms 2)
horses:
when we talk of h. (Imagination 3)
hose:
your h. should be ungartered (Love 15)
host:
play the humble h. (Hospitality 2)
time is like a fashionable h. (Time 29)
hostess:
the h. of the meeting (Hospitality 4)
Hotspur:
H. of the north (Action 4)
hounds:
desires like fell and cruel h. (Desire 16)
my h. are bred out of the Spartan kind (Dogs 6)
the music of my h. (Dogs 5)
hour:
from h. to h, we ripe and ripe (Time 2)
jump at this dead h. (Ghosts 2)
my h. is almost come (Purgatory 1)
this pernicious h. (Curses 2)
'tis but an h. ago (Time 2)
hours:
better three h. too soon (Lateness 2)
h. seem short (Action 14)
sad h. seem long (Time 25)
what hotter h. (Lust 4)

house:
he hath eaten me out of h. and home (Eating 4)
no h. to put his head in (Homelessness 3)
raise this h. against this h. (Civil War 4)
you take my h. (Life 8)
houses:
a plague on both your h. (Curses 8)
how:
h. do you, madam? (Sleep 15)
h. is it that the clouds still hang (Grief 5)
h. like a fawning publican (Humility 4)
h. low am I? (Insults 15)
h. many times shall Caesar bleed (Theater 10)
h. mightily sometimes we make comforts (Comfort 1)
h. much better it is to weep (Tears 13)
h. now, Horatio? You tremble (Fear 1)
h. now, my sweet creature of bombast? (Fatness 2)
h. should I your true love know (Love 32)
h. strange or odd (Acting 4)
h. sweet a thing it is (Royalty 21)
h. weary, stale, flat and unprofitable (Dejection 1)
howl:
h., h., h. (Mourning 17)
hulks:
greater h. draw deep (Ships 6)
humanity:
a rarer spirit never did steer h. (Faults 3)
h. must perforce prey on itself (Anarchy 1)
the middle of h. thou never knewest (Humanity 9)
humble:
h. as the ripest mulberry (Humility 1)
humility:
dressed myself in such h. (Humility 3)
I thank my God for my h. (Hypocrisy 15)
the very base string of h. (Humility 2)
humor:
I am in a holiday h. (Courtship 2)
I can give his h. the true bent (Persuasion 4)
my chief humor is for a tyrant (Acting 19)
the career of his h. (Aphorisms 8)
was ever woman in this h. wooed? (Courtship 18)
when that rash h. that my mother gave me (Forbearance 2)
humors:
I am now of all h. (Temperament 4)
hums:
the shard-borne beetle with his drowsy h. (Evil 7)
hunger:
h. broke stone walls (Hunger 1)
hunt:
the h. is up (Hunting 4)
husband:
cry heigh-ho for a h. (Celibacy 3)
endure a h. with a beard (Marriage 29)
forgot a h.'s office (Marriage 14)
h. I come! (Courage 1, Marriage 2)
light wife doth make a heavy h. (Marriage 25)
loyall'st h. (Marriage 15)
my h. then? (Marriage 47)

prove to Desdemona a most dear h.(Character 4)
shall I live ... like a deceivèd h. (Deceit 24)
she cannot endure to hear of a h. (Mockery 3)
sways she ... in her h.'s heart (Marriage 49)
thou art an elm, my h. (Marriage 13)
while I play the good h. at home (Education 5)

husbandry:
all her h. doth lie on heaps (Farming 1)
both healthful and good h. (Business 5)
choke the herbs for want of h. (Gardens 3)
dulls the edge of h.(Advice 6)
there's h. in heaven (Darkness 2)

husbands:
fools are like h. (Fools 13)
it is their h.'s' faults (Marriage 42)
let h. know (Marriage 43)

huswife:
doth fortune play the h. with me now? (Fortune 10)
mock the good h. Fortune (Fortune 3)

Hymen:
'tis H. peoples every town (Marriage 7)

hymns:
chanting faint h. (Religion 5)

hyperboles:
three-piled h. (Plain-Speaking 8)

Hyperion:
H.'s curls (Beauty 7)
was to this H. to a satyr (Excellence 1)

hypocrisy:
it is h. against the devil (Devil 9)

I:
am I your self (Marriage 20)
had I but died (Mourning 18)
had I but served my God (Service 5)
I am a bastard too (Bastardy 2)
I am a kind of burr (Perseverance 2)
I am all the subjects that you have (Servitude 3)
I am a man more sinned against (Self-Pity 2, Sin 4)
I am ambitious for a motley coat (Fools 3)
I am ashamed that thou hast power (Tears 9)
I am as poor as Job (Impatience 2)
I am a tainted wether (Resignation 4)
I am a wise fellow (Dignity 1)
I am bewitched (Medicine 7)
I am but mad north-north-west (Madness 5)
I am determinèd to prove a villain (Villainy 7)
I am disgraced, impeached (Slander 7)
I am dying, Egypt, dying (Dying 1)
I am fire and air (Dying 2)
I am fresh of spirit (Resolution 3)
I am giddy; expectation whirls (Anticipation 4)
I am glad I was up so late (Lateness 1)
I am glad thou canst speak (Royalty 20)
I am gone for ever (Last Words 7)
I am indeed not her fool (Fools 14)
I am more an antique Roman (Suicide 14)
I am myself alone (Identity 6, Misanthropy 2)
I am not ague-proof (Flattery 5)
I am not bid for love (Invitations 2)
I am not Cinna (Names 2)

I am not in the giving vein (Gifts 4)
I am not only witty in myself (Wit 3)
I am nothing if not critical (Criticism 4)
I am now of all humors (Temperament 4)
I am not tall enough (Thinness 4)
I am old, I am old (Love 36)
I am one ... whom the vile blows (Recklessness 3)
I am qualmish at the smell of leek (Vegetables 1)
I am settled, and bend up (Resolution 5)
I am so lated in the world (Despair 1)
I am stuffed, cousin (Sex 6)
I am sure 'tis safer (Safety 2)
I am the unhappy subject (Quarrels 9)
I am well acquainted with your manner (Deviousness 2)
I am whipped and scourged with rods (Politics 3)
I and my bosom must debate (Solitude 2)
I as free forgive you (Forgiveness 3)
I beg cold comfort (Comfort 4)
I can add colors to the chameleon (Duplicity 2)
I can counterfeit (Acting 26)
I can express no kinder sign (Kissing 7)
I can go no further (Weariness 3)
I cannot choose but weep (Burial 2, Mourning 10)
I cannot flatter (Friendship 6)
I cannot heave my heart (Speech 9)
I cannot hide what I am (Misanthropy 4)
I cannot live out of her company (Friendship 1)
I cannot show it in rhyme (Poetry 11)
I cannot tell what the dickens (Names 5)
I cannot wish the fault undone (Wrongdoing 4)
I can see yet without spectacles (Eyes 11)
I can suck melancholy (Melancholy 2)
I can teach thee, coz (Truth 2)
I care not for you (Hate 1)
I could be bounded in a nutshell (Dreams 3)
I could be well content (Retirement 1)
I could do this (Poison 4)
I count myself in nothing else so happy (Friendship 25)
I dare do all (Manliness 2, Men 8)
I did not think thee lord (Praise 6)
I did not think to shed a tear (Tears 7)
I do begin to perceive (Self-Knowledge 10)
I do hate a proud man (Pride 5)
I do know of these ... reputed wise (Reputation 5)
I do not know why yet I live (Delay 1)
I do not like that paying back (Money 3)
I do not like your faults (Faults 7)
I do not relish well their loud applause (People 17)
I do not set my life at a pin's fee (Recklessness 2, Soul 1)
I do not shame to tell you (Transformation 1)
I do not think a braver gentleman (Soldiers 8)
I do perceive here a divided duty (Duty 5)
I do suspect the lusty Moor (Jealousy 5)
I do the wrong (Duplicity 7)
I do wander everywhere (Fairies 1)
I draw the sword myself (Death-Wish 2)
I dreamt there was an emperor (Dreams 1)

I (cont'd.)

I earn that I eat (Philosophy 4)
I fear me you but warm the starvèd snake (Treachery 1)
I fear you have sold your own lands (Travel 2)
I fear you speak upon the rack (Torture 1)
I feel me much to blame (Time 13)
if I can cross him any way (Hate 2)
I found you as a morsel (Food 3)
I 'gin to be aweary of the sun (Despair 3)
I had as lief have been myself alone (Solitude 1)
I had as lief not be (Freedom 3)
I had rather be a kitten (Poetry 6)
I had rather be their servant (Service 3)
I had rather hear my dog (Misanthropy 3)
I hate ingratitude (Ingratitude 10)
I have a faint cold fear (Fear 15)
I have a good eye (Eyes 12)
I have almost forgot the taste of fears (Fear 14)
I have been up this hour (Sleeplessness 2)
I have ... buried this sigh (Sorrow 16)
I have done no harm (Innocence 5)
I have drunk and seen the spider (Poison 5)
I have given suck (Ruthlessness 4, Infancy 3)
I have heard that guilty creatures (Theater 4)
I have lived long enough (Old Age 8)
I have lost my teeth in your service (Service 1)
I have lost my way for ever (Despair 1)
I have much ado to know myself (Self-Knowledge 9)
I have neither the scholar's (Melancholy 3)
I have neither wit, nor words (Speech 8)
I have not ... that gentleness (Friendship 12)
I have nothing of woman in me (Resolution 1)
I have no spur (Ambition 12)
I have not that alacrity of spirit (Dejection 4)
I have no way (Eyes 8)
I have offended reputation (Reputation 1)
I have of late ... lost all my mirth (Dejection 2)
I have passed a miserable night (Dreams 8)
I have served him (Soldiers 20)
I have sounded the very base string (Humility 2)
I have speeded hither (Speed 2)
I have suffered (Suffering 4)
I have supped full with horrors (Fear 14)
I have't. It is engendered (Evil 10)
I have unclasped to thee (Secrets 2)
I have very poor and unhappy brains (Drinking 20)
I hear as good exclamation (Praise 7)
I heard a bustling rumor (Rumor 6)
I hold the olive in my hand (Peace 15)
I hold you as a thing (Sincerity 1)
I hope it is no dishonest desire (Desire 6)
I hope to see London (Travel 9)
I know a bank where the wild thyme blows (Flowers 6)
I know a lady in Venice (Desire 14)
I know myself now (Self-Knowledge 4)
I know not where I am (Perplexity 1)
I know our country disposition (Deceit 14)
I know thee not, old man (Age 17)

I know the more one sickens (Sickness 1)
I know thou'rt full of love (Honesty 5)
I know when seven justices (Quarrels 1)
I laughed him out of patience (Patience 1)
I like not fair terms (Villainy 2)
I like your silence (Silence 8)
I'll be revenged on the whole pack (Revenge 9)
I'll cross it though it blast me (Ghosts 3)
I'll go with thee (Society 6)
I'll ne'er be drunk (Drinking 16)
I'll never be such a gosling (Man 2)
I'll not budge an inch (Resistance 3)
I'll read enough (Self-Knowledge 11)
I'll so offend (Wrongdoing 1)
I'll take your word for faith (Promises 7)
I love not many words (Talking 1)
I love thee so (Infatuation 10)
I marvel thy master hath not eaten thee (Words 4)
I may neither choose (Parents and Children 10)
I must be patient (Authority 1)
I must comfort the weaker vessel (Women 4)
I must from this enchanting queen (Infatuation 4)
I must have liberty (Freedom 2)
I must to the barber's (Hair 3)
I myself am best (Solitude 4)
I never did repent for doing good (Goodness 2)
I never knew so young a body (Wisdom 4)
I never thought to hear you speak (Thought 4)
I of ladies most deject and wretched (Dejection 3)
I owe him a little duty (Duty 3)
I pluck this pale and maiden blossom (Flowers 4)
I pray for no man but myself (Prayer 17)
I pray, let none of your people (Solecisms 2)
I pray you, how many hath he killed (War 17)
I pray you, let us satisfy our eyes (Travel 24)
I prithee let me bring thee (Education 6)
I promise you, but for your company (Society 7)
I saw him beat the surges (Swimming 1)
I saw young Harry with his beaver on (Soldiers 6)
I scorn you, scurvy companion (Insults 8)
I see before me, man (Eyes 4)
I see still a diminution (Folly 2)
I see that time's the king (Time 22)
I see the jewel best enameled (Gold 1)
I see this is the time (Wrongdoing 7)
I see you what you are (Pride 6)
I shall be loved (Absence 2)
I speak not like a dotard (Maturity 4)
I speak to thee plain soldier (Soldiers 17)
I sprang not more in joy (Manliness 1)
I stole all courtesy (Humility 1)
I swear to thee (Vows 2)
I thank my God for my humility (Hypocrisy 15)
I that please some, try all (Time 39)
I think he only loves the world for me (Friendship 18)
I think nobly of the soul (Soul 2)
I think she means to tangle my eyes (Eyes 2)
I think there's never a man (Appearance 10)
I took him for the plainest ... creature (Trust 3)

I understand thy kisses (Kissing 5)
I was not much afeared (Plain-Speaking 12)
I was seeking for a fool when I found you (Fools 4)
I wasted time (Time 24)
I weigh my friend's affection (Friendship 30)
I will acquaintance strangle (Rejection 3)
I will aggravate my voice (Acting 21)
I will a round unvarnished tale (Stories 3)
I will be here again (Speed 4)
I will believe thou hast a mind (Appearance 11)
I will be the pattern (Patience 5)
I will chide no breather (Self-Knowledge 1)
I will despair (Despair 4)
I will embrace him with a soldier's arm (Soldiers 9)
I will follow thee (Loyalty 2)
I will go lose myself (Travel 4)
I will here shroud (Storms 16)
I will keep where there is wit stirring (Folly 4)
I will live in thy heart (Sex 7)
I will make an end of my dinner (Food 9)
I will not choose (People 18)
I will not do thee so much wrong (Sleep 7)
I will not hold thee long (Promises 5)
I will not let him stir (Medicine 4)
I will praise any man (Praise 2)
I will redeem all this (Soldiers 5)
I will reward thee (Comfort 2)
I will through and through (Medicine 2)
I wonder men dare trust themselves (Trust 5)
I would be loath to cast away (Speechmaking 6)
I would have been ... a fresher man (Readiness 3)
I would have broke mine eye-strings (Parting 5)
I would not be a queen (Royalty 23)
I would not deny you (Marriage 36)
I would not hang a dog (Mercy 11)
I would not lose so great an honor (Honor 10)
I would not wish any companion (Society 8)
I would there were no age (Youth 12)
I would to God thou and I (Reputation 2)
though I cannot be said to be ... honest (Villainy 3)

icicle:
    chaste as the i. (Chastity 1)
icicles:
    when i. hang by the wall (Seasons 11)
Ides:
    beware the I. of March (Danger 5)
idol:
    thou i. ceremony (Ceremony 2)
idolatry:
    'tis mad i. (Idolatry 1)
if:
    if all the world could have seen't (Sorrow 17)
    if Cassio do remain (Virtue 19)
    if ever you have looked (Nostalgia 1, Pity 1)
    if ever you prove false (Lust 12)
    if I be foiled (Recklessness 1)
    if I be left behind (Love 69)
    if I can catch him (Malevolence 2)
    if I chance to talk a little wild (Talking 4)

if I had a mind to be honest (Fortune 24)
    if I know how or which way (Politics 19)
    if I must die (Death 28)
    if I should tell my history (Stories 4)
    if it be my luck (Fortune 22)
    if ... I think on thee, dear friend (Love 107)
    if it were done when 'tis done (Action 12)
    if I were as tedious as a king (Tediousness 4)
    if she first meet the curlèd Antony (Kissing 2)
    if that the earth could teem (Tears 14)
    if there be no great love (Marriage 26)
    if this be magic (Magic 3)
    if this were played upon a stage (Theater 19)
    if thou didst ever hold me (Stories 1)
    if thou dost slander her (Slander 6)
    if we shall stand still (Action 10)
    if we should fail (Courage 6)
    if ye should lead her in a fool's paradise (Deceit 21)
    if you can look into the seeds of time (Prophecy 6)
    if you had but looked big (Cowardice 8)
    if you have tears (Tears 8)
    if you were born to honor (Honor 18)
    your if is your only peacemaker (Quarrels 1)
ignominy:
    i. in ransom and free pardon (Mercy 8)
    thy i. sleep with thee in the grave (Epitaphs 7)
ignorance:
    i. the common curse of mankind (Curses 9)
    i. is the curse of God (Education 2)
    O thou monster i. (Ignorance 1)
    there is no darkness but i. (Ignorance 2)
ill:
    I am i., but your being by me (Sickness 2)
    i. blows the wind (Proverbs 9)
    how i. all's here about my heart (Foreboding 6)
    there is some i. a-brewing (Foreboding 10)
ill-doing:
    knew not the doctrine of i. (Innocence 6)
ills:
    the i. we do, their i. instruct us to (Marriage 43)
illumineth:
    it i. the face (Drinking 11)
illusion:
    stay, i.! (Ghosts 3)
Illyria:
    This is I., lady (Countries 8)
image:
    Death, how foul ... is thine i. (Death 39)
imagine:
    to i. an Antony (Imagination 1)
imagination:
    are of i. all compact (Imagination 4)
    as i. bodies forth (Poetry 10)
    bare i. of a feast (Imagination 6)
    if i. amend them (Acting 25)
    such tricks hath strong i. (Imagination 5)
imaginings:
    present fears are less than horrible i. (Fear 12)

Italy:
  fashions in proud I. (Fashion 9)
  those girls of I. (Girls 1)
itching:
  condemned to have an i. palm (Corruption 5)
Jack:
  J. hath not Jill (Endings 1)
  J. shall have Jill (Proverbs 21)
Jacks:
  abused with silken, sly, insinuating J. (Duplicity 6)
jay:
  is the j. more precious than the lark? (Value 3)
jealous:
  are to the j. confirmation strong (Jealousy 9)
  clamors of a j. woman (Jealousy 2)
  j. complexion (Jealousy 4)
  j. souls will not be answered (Jealousy 11)
  one not easily j. (Jealousy 12)
  thy j. fits (Jealousy 3)
jealousy:
  beware, my lord, of j. (Jealousy 6)
  how many fond fools serve mad j. (Jealousy 1)
  my tribe defend from j. (Jealousy 8)
  put the Moor ... into a j. (Revenge 5)
Jerusalem:
  meet ... in sweet J. (Afterlife 5)
jest:
  a j.'s prosperity lies in the ear (Jokes 3)
  a mirth-moving j. (Jokes 1)
  not a word with him but a j. (Jokes 2)
jester:
  how ill white hairs become a ... j. (Age 17)
jesters:
  ambled up and down with shallow j. (Royalty 8)
  j. do oft prove prophets (Proverbs 16)
jests:
  he j. at scars (Jokes 4)
Jesu:
  J., J., the mad days (Nostalgia 3)
Jew:
  hath not a J. eyes? (Religion 3)
  his reason? I am a J. (Anti-Semitism 2)
  if a J. wrong a Christian (Revenge 4)
jewel:
  he hath got the j. that I loved (Liberality 1)
  I see the j. best enameled (Gold 1)
  mine eternal j. (Damnation 1)
  no j. is like Rosalind (Love 14)
  precious j. (Adversity 2)
  the j. that we find (Jewels 1, Value 1)
jewels:
  dumb j. ... move a woman's mind (Gifts 5)
  give my j. for a set of beads (Renunciation 2)
jig:
  Scotch j. (Marriage 30)
Job:
  as poor as J. (Impatience 2)
jocund:
  j. day stands tiptoe (Dawn 7)

jog:
  j. on, j. on, the footpath way (Endurance 5, Merriment 6)
join:
  then j. you with them (Strength 1)
journeys:
  j. end in lovers' meeting (Love 95)
Jove:
  the front of J. (Beauty 7)
joy:
  a froth of fleeting j. (Desire 18)
  but that a j. past j. calls out to me (Farewells 17)
  heaven give thee j. (Blessings 2)
  how much better it is to weep at j. (Tears 13)
  if he be sick with j. (Joy 2)
  I have no j. of this contract (Anxiety 9)
  I sprang not more in j. (Manliness 1)
  I wish you all j. of the worm (Joy 1)
  j. be the consequence (Choice 6)
  j. for his fortune (Caesar 3)
  j. gentle friends, j. and fresh days of love (Greetings 7)
  j.'s soul lies in the doing (Men and Women 9)
  night will hide our j. no longer (Dawn 8)
  now, our j., although our last (Parents and Children 6)
  O my soul's j. (Storms 9)
  one j. crown another (Joy 6)
  their j. waded in tears (Joy 6)
  the perfectest herald of j. (Joy 3)
  this momentary j. (Lust 13)
  treasury of everlasting j. (Heaven 2)
  with a defeated j. (Mourning 6)
  you have cause ... of j. (Joy 5)
joys:
  briefly die their j. (Girls 2, Youth 5)
  hours of marriage j. (Marriage 44)
Judas:
  so J. did to Christ (Betrayal 2)
  so J. kissed his master (Duplicity 3)
Judean:
  like the base J. (Jealousy 12)
judge:
  a j. that no king can corrupt (God 8)
  to offend and j. are distinct offices (Judgment 2)
  wise and upright j. (Appearance 5)
judgment:
  a Daniel come to j. (Judgment 5)
  head unmellowed, but his j. is ripe (Experience 5)
  he which is the top of j. (Mercy 7)
  his j. ruled our hands (Maturity 3)
  j. hath repented o'er his doom (Justice 12)
  O j., thou art fled to brutish beasts (Reason 4)
  reserve thy j. (Advice 5)
  seven times tried that j. is (Judgment 3)
  some shallow spirit of j. (Law 4)
  the urging of that word j. (Judgment 6)
  what j. shall I dread? (Judgment 4)
judgments:
  accidental j. (Murder 3)
  eyes are sometimes, like our j., blind (Eyes 5)

juggler:
a threadbare j. (Character 1)

jugglers:
nimble j. that deceive the eye (Corruption 1)

July:
makes a J.'s day short (Children 2)

June:
as the cuckoo is in J. (Birds 1)

Juno:
wedding is great J.'s crown (Marriage 7)

Juno (cont'd.)
sauced our broths as J. had been sick (Cooking 1)

Jupiter:
J. became a bull (Gods 5)

jury:
the j. passing on the prisoner's life (Justice 11)

just:
the gods are j. (Justice 8)

justice:
desire you do me right and j. (Justice 3)
great Julius bleed for j. sake (Justice 4)
j. is feasting while the widow weeps (Justice 16)
liberty plucks j. by the nose (Freedom 6, Justice 10)
may shove by j. (Law 1)
see how yon j. rails (Justice 6)
then the j. (Maturity 1)
the strong lance of j. (Justice 7)
this even-handed j. (Justice 9)
thou shalt have j. (Justice 15)
what's open made to j. (Justice 11)
when mercy seasons j. (Mercy 11)

jutty:
no j., frieze, buttress (Birds 7)

keep:
k. up your bright swords (Fighting 4)

kernel:
there can be no k. in this light nut (Clothing 1)

kill:
k. thy physician (Medicine 8)
let's k. him boldly (Assassination 1)

kin:
more than k., and less than kind (Kinship 1)

kind:
a k. heart he hath (Kindness 3)

kindness:
beauty lives with k. (Beauty 27)
k. in women (Love 86)
k. nobler ever than revenge (Kindness 1)
the milk of human k. (Kindness 2)

kindred:
our k. ... are constant being won (Constancy 6)

king:
crown that rounds the mortal temples of a k. (Death 35)
every inch a k. (Royalty 25)
he that plays the k. (Acting 5)
if thou be a k., where is thy crown (Royalty 22)
in sleep a k., but waking no such matter (Dreams 17)
is not the k.'s name? (Royalty 29)
judge that no k. can corrupt (God 7)

k. of courtesy (Courtesy 1)
K. Richard doth himself appear (Royalty 30)
never alone did the k. sigh (Royalty 5)
O that I were a mockery k. (Death-Wish 9)
our sins lay on the k. (Royalty 18)
substitute shines brightly as a k. (Comparisons 2)
such divinity doth hedge a k. (Royalty 6)
the great K. of k. (Murder 11)
the k. himself is to be feared (Royalty 10)
the k. is but a man, as I am (Royalty 17)
the k.'s name is a tower of strength (Reputation 12)
the skipping k., he ambled (Royalty 8)
thou art the k. of honor (Honor 4)
thou wouldst find me such a plain k. (Royalty 20)
wash the balm off from an anointed k. (Royalty 28)
what must the k. do now? (Renunciation 1)
yet looks he like a k. (Royalty 31)

kingdom:
a k. ... was too small a bound (Ambition 2)
my k. for a horse (Desperation 1)
say, is my k. lost? (Loss 8)
state of man like to a little k. (Anxiety 4)
teach the act of order to a peopled k. (Government 3)

kingdoms:
k. are clay (Kissing 1)
we have kissed away k. and provinces (Empire 2)

kings:
a princess descended of ... k. (Royalty 4)
heart's ease must k. neglect (Ceremony 1)
k. it makes gods (Hope 3)
nice customs curtsy to great k. (Custom 4)
such is the breath of k. (Royalty 27)
the mirror of all Christian k. (Royalty 14)

kiss:
give him that parting k. (Kissing 3)
I k. thee with a most constant heart (Kissing 6)
k. me, Kate (Marriage 46)
O, a k., long as my exile (Kissing 3)
spend that k. (Kissing 2)
there is not half a k. to choose (Love 106)
thereupon I will k. thee (Kissing 8)
this is a soldier's k. (Farewells 1)
this kind k. (Kissing 7)
witness the loving kiss I give (Duplicity 3)

kisses:
I understand thy k. (Kissing 5)
my k. bring again (Inconstancy 1)

kites:
instruct the k. and ravens (Creatures 5)

knavery:
k's plain face is never seen (Deceit 13)

knaves:
we are arrant k. all (Misanthropy 1)

knife:
that my keen k. see not (Murder 5)

knell:
k. that summons thee to heaven (Bells 2)

knight:
a true k. (Words and Deeds 4)
the k.'s in admirable fooling (Fools 12)

law (cont'd.)
  like a poor man's right in the l. (Fishing 3)
  make a scarecrow of the l. (Law 7)
  old father antic the l. (Law 2)
  pity is the virtue of the l. (Law 10)
  sharp quillets of the l. (Law 4)
  the l. hath not been dead (Law 8)
  the l. I bear no malice (Law 6)
  thou know'st no l. (Animals 11)
  wicked prize ... buys out the l. (Law 1)
  wrest once the l. (Law 9)
lawn:
  l. as white as driven snow (Clothing 15)
lawyer:
  the breath of an unfeed l. (Lawyers 2)
lawyers:
  let's kill all the l. (Lawyers 1)
  with l. in the vacation (Time 6)
lay:
  l. on, Macduff (Fighting 2)
lead:
  God keep l. out of me! (War 5)
lean:
  l. enough to be thought a good student (Thinness 4)
  you'd be so l. (Thinness 5)
leap:
  methinks it were an easy l. (Honor 1)
Lear:
  this is not L. (Identity 3)
learning:
  O this l., what a thing it is! (Learning 4)
leave:
  I will take my l. of you (Parting 6)
  l. not the mansion ... tenantless (Ruin 1)
leave-taking:
  let us not be dainty of l. (Parting 10)
lechery:
  l., l. still wars and l. (Lechery 6)
  l., sir, it provokes and unprovokes (Drinking 14)
  the most dangerous piece of l. (Villainy 5)
leek:
  I am qualmish at the smell of l. (Vegetables 1)
leg:
  a good l. will fall (Courtship 11)
legacy:
  no l. is so rich as honesty (Honor 2)
legion:
  methought a l. of foul fiends (Dreams 11)
legs:
  his l. are l. for courtesy (Pride 3)
  his l. bestrid the ocean (Praise 4, World 2)
leisure:
  how has he the l. to be sick? (Sickness 5)
  when thou hast l. (Leisure 1)
lend:
  l. to each man enough (Prayer 18)
lender:
  neither a borrower nor a l. be (Advice 6)
Lent:
  what's a joint of mutton or two in a whole L. (Food 7)

leopards:
  lions make l. tame (Animals 9)
leprosy:
  make the hoar l. adored (Gold 6)
lesson:
  any hard l. that may do thee good (Friendship 22)
let:
  l. every feeble rumor shake (Rumor 1)
  l. me, if not by birth (Self-Interest 2)
  l. us ... mock the good huswife fortune (Fortune 3)
  l. us not break with him (Politics 12)
  l. us not burden our remembrances (Remembrance 8)
  l. us seek out some desolate shade (Sorrow 4)
Lethe:
  weed that roots itself ... on L. wharf (Action 3)
letter:
  thou unnecessary l. (Insults 11)
letters:
  get posts and l. (Letters 2)
liberal:
  I will become as l. as you (Liberality 1)
  where you are l. of your loves (Betrayal 1)
  you are l. in offers (Begging 1)
libertine:
  reckless l. (Advice 4)
  the air, a chartered l. is still (Eloquence 3)
  thou thyself hast been a l. (Lust 5)
liberty:
  I must have l. (Freedom 2)
  l.! freedom! tyranny is dead (Freedom 4)
  l. plucks justice by the nose (Freedom 6, Justice 10)
library:
  furnished me from mine own l. (Books 4)
  make choice of all my l. (Books 5)
  my l. was dukedom large enough (Books 3)
lids:
  with thy vailèd l. (Mourning 7)
lie:
  if a l. may do thee grace (Lying 3)
  you told a l. ... a wicked l. (Lying 6)
lies:
  as many l. as will lie in thy paper (Lying 7)
  he l. to the heart (Lying 5)
  these l. are like their father (Lying 1)
life:
  after l.'s fitful fever (Death 25)
  aim of all is but to nurse the l. (Ambition 14)
  all the courses of my l. do show (Greatness 3)
  a man's l.'s but a span (Soldiers 22)
  care's an enemy to l. (Hedonism 1)
  entertain the lag-end of my l. (Retirement 1)
  everything advantageous to l. (Life 10)
  farewell l. (Farewells 9)
  fie upon this quiet l. (Action 4)
  for the l. to come (Afterlife 6)
  grunt and sweat under a weary l. (Afterlife 2)
  his l. was gentle (Epitaphs 12)
  I do not set my l. at a pin's fee (Recklessness 2)
  I love long l. (Life 2)

I spy l. peering (Life 10)

l. being weary of these worldly bars (Suicide 15)

l. consists of the four elements (Hedonism 2)

l. every man holds dear (Honor 22)

l. is as tedious (Tediousness 2)

l. itself, my wife and all the world (Friendship 20)

l.'s but a walking shadow (Life 7)

l.'s uncertain voyage (Life 12)

l., time's fool (Time 9)

merriment ... lengthens l. (Acting 27)

methinks it were a happy l. (Happiness 3)

mine honor is my l. (Honor 17)

my l. is run his compass (Life 6)

our little l. (Mortality 9)

promise me l., and I'll confess (Truth 6)

reason thus with l. (Death 25)

sands are numbered that makes up my l. (Dying 8)

the time of l. is short (Life 4)

the web of our l. (Life 1)

this l. is nobler (Country Life 9)

this our l., exempt from public haunt (Country Life 2)

to me can l. be no commodity (Death-Wish 11)

very vile l. (Country Life 7)

weariest ... worldly l. (Death 30)

we'd jump the l. to come (Action 12)

when a painter would surpass the l. (Painting 1)

where is the l. (Nostalgia 5)

you take my l. (Life 8)

light:

God ... give l. in darkness (God 5)

let me give l. (Marriage 25)

let not l. see my black and deep desires (Desire 9)

l., seeking l. (Light 1)

l. thickens, and the crow (Night 13)

put out the l. (Light 2)

what l. through yonder window breaks (Sunrise 5)

lightning:

brief as the l. (Transience 2)

the cross blue l. (Courage 5)

too like the l. (Anxiety 9)

like:

so l. you 'tis the worse (Proverbs 31)

likelihood:

l. and forms of hope (Hope 1)

lilies:

l. that fester smell far worse (Flowers 14)

lily:

fresh l. (Beauty 5)

to paint the l. (Extravagance 2)

limitation:

your self but ... in sort or l. (Marriage 20)

limits:

stony l. cannot hold love out (Love 78)

line:

will the l. stretch out? (Doomsday 3)

lion:

doing ... the feats of a l. (Courage 7)

hardy as the Nemean l.'s nerve (Fate 2)

he is a l. I am proud to hunt (Valor 3)

he is as valiant as the l. (Valor 14)

hind that would be mated by the l. (Love 1)

l. dying ... wounds the earth (Animals 10)

l. will not touch the true prince (Instinct 1)

now the hungry l. roars (Night 19)

the blood more stirs to rouse a l. (Valor 6)

the king ... is to be feared as the l. (Royalty 10)

when the l. fawns upon the lamb (Animals 7)

lioness:

a l. with udders all drawn dry (Animals 1)

lions:

l. make leopards tame (Animals 9)

two l. littered in one day (Danger 8)

lip:

for a touch of his nether l. (Desire 14)

lips:

eternity was in our l. and eyes (Eternity 1)

take those l. away (Inconstancy 1)

liquor:

this grand l. that hath gilded 'em (Drinking 25)

liquors:

I never did apply hot ... l. (Drinking 2)

list:

l., l., O list (Murder 1)

little:

a l. fire is quickly trodden out (Fire 1)

a l. more than a l. is by much too much (Eating 3)

a very l. (Action 6)

l. of this great world can I speak (Speech 19)

live:

let me not l. (Old Age 1)

l., and deal with others better (Forgiveness 2)

l. a thousand years (Death-Wish 6)

l. we how we can, yet die we must (Dying 9)

so we'll l., and pray (Politics 17)

this queen will l. (Life 8)

livery:

light and careless l. (Clothing 4)

lives:

a history in all men's l. (Life 5)

living:

there is no l., none (Infatuation 1)

lo:

lo, here the gentle lark (Sunrise 7)

locks:

never shake thy gory l. at me (Ghosts 13)

loins:

from forth the fatal l. (Love 72)

London:

I hope to see L. (Travel 9)

longings:

I have immortal l. in me (Death-Wish 3)

look:

l., I draw the sword myself (Death-Wish 4)

l. so piteous in purport (Madness 1)

l. to her, Moor (Deceit 11)

l. what a wardrobe here is for thee (Clothing 11)

l. what is done cannot now be amended (Excuses 4)

looks:

elder than thy l. (Appearance 5)

loon:
    thou cream-faced l. (Curses 4)
Lord:
    L. Angelo is precise (Power 9)
    L. Hamlet with his doublet (Madness 1)
    L., L., how this world is given (Lying 2)
    l. of the wide world (Marriage 9)
    L., what fools these mortals be (Fools 9, Humanity 5)
    O L. that lends me life (Prayer 8)
    remember what the L. hath done (God 6)
loser:
    give the l. leave to chide (Loss 2)
loss:
    O insupportable and touching l. (Loss 3)
    what l. is it to be rid of care? (Loss 8)
    wise men ne'er sit and wail their l. (Encouragement 1)
losses:
    all l. are restored (Love 107)
love:
    a braver place in my heart's l. (Friendship 6)
    all hearts in l. (Love 62)
    Benedick is sick in l. (Love 63)
    but that I l. the gentle Desdemona (Marriage 40)
    can lesser hide his l. (Appearance 10)
    canst l. a fellow of this temper (Courtship 10)
    chameleon l. can feed on air (Food 15)
    course of true l. (Love 52)
    did my heart l. till now? (Love 76)
    do not fall in l. with me (Love 20)
    do not presume too much upon my l. (Quarrels 8)
    do you not l. me? (Love 35)
    even in the spring of l. (Marriage 14)
    ever I lose more blood with l. (Love 60)
    first fall in l. (Love 66)
    first suffer l. for me (Love 67)
    for his verity in l. (Love 17)
    have you not l. enough to bear with me? (Forbearance 2)
    hind ... must die for l. (Love 1)
    honest, so's my l. (Love 2)
    how deep I am in l. (Love 23)
    how many fathom deep I am in l. (Love 22)
    how should I your true l. know (Love 32)
    how this spring of l. (Love 102)
    if ever thou shalt l. (Constancy 9)
    if he be not in l. (Love 65)
    if it be l. indeed (Love 5)
    if music be the food of l. (Music 25)
    if my dear l. were but the child of state (Constancy 13)
    if there be no great l. (Marriage 26)
    if you do l. me (Love 49)
    I l. her heartily (Love 47)
    I l. thee better (Love 36)
    I l. you more than words (Parents and Children 5)
    in l., i'faith (Love 89)
    innocent mansion of my l., my heart (Death-Wish 4)
    I owe him a little duty and less l. (Duty 2)
    is l. a tender thing? (Love 75)
    it is my l. (Love 77)

I will be horribly in l. with her (Men and Women 5)
let thy song be l. (Love 88)
l. all (Advice 1)
l. and be friends (Reconciliation 1)
l. and be silent (Love 38)
l. and meekness (Ambition 6)
l. breaks through (Proverbs 32)
l. comforteth like sunshine (Lust 15)
l. cools, friendship falls off (Disorder 1)
l. friendship, charity are subjects all (Time 30)
l. give me strength (Strength 3)
l. goes toward l. as schoolboys (Parting 14)
l. is a smoke (Love 74)
l. is begun by time (Love 33)
l. is blind (Love 46, 103)
l. is holy (Love 3)
l. is like a child (Love 105)
l. is merely a madness (Love 16)
l. is not l. (Love 110)
l. is too young (Conscience 10)
l. looks not with the eyes (Love 54)
l. me ... Fridays and Saturdays and all (Courtship 3)
l. moderately (Love 82)
l. no man in good earnest (Love 8)
l.'s feeling is more soft (Love 43)
l. said to be a child (Love 55)
l.'s heralds should be thoughts (Love 81)
l.'s keen arrows (Love 19)
l.'s not l. when it is mingled (Love 40)
l.'s not Time's fool (Constancy 12)
l. sought is good (Love 99)
l. that comes too late (Loss 1)
l. thyself last (Corruption 4)
l. whose month is ever May (Love 41)
l. wrought these miracles (Love 87)
loyal cantons of contemnèd l. (Courtship 23)
men have died ... but not for l. (Dying 5)
minister to l. (Love 61)
monstruosity in l. (Love 90)
my l. as deep (Love 80)
my l. doth so approve him (Devotion 5)
my l. is thine to teach (Friendship 22)
my l. shall hear the music of my hounds (Dogs 5)
my l.'s more ponderous (Love 39)
my l. to Hermia melted (Remembrance 7)
my true l. is grown (Love 83)
never doubt I l. (Love 30)
no kinder sign of l. (Kissing 7)
O brawling l. (Love 73)
O l., be moderate (Love 51)
O spirit of l. (Love 94)
ostentation of our l. (Love 6)
prosperity the very bond of l. (Affliction 13)
reason and l. keep little company (Reason 6)
rites for which I l. him (Love 69)
seat where l. is throned (Music 27)
she cannot l. (Self-Love 2)
she could not l. me (Love 24)
she never told her l. (Melancholy 7)

show out a flag and sign of l. (Hypocrisy 11)
strong base and building of my l. (Love 93)
sweet l., I see (Mutability 2)
sweet l. sweet lines (Love 101)
tell this youth what 'tis to l. (Love 27)
that l. should ... take such hold (Love 84)
the dribbling dart of l. (Love 45)
their l. may be called appetite (Love 98)
the lease of my true l. control (Anxiety 11)
they l. least (Love 100)
this bud of l. (Love 79)
this l. will undo us all (Love 88)
thou hast my l. (Desire 4)
thy l. ne'er alter (Prayer 14)
thy sweet l. remembered (Misery 5)
'tis brief. ... As woman's l. (Love 31)
l. is too young to know what conscience is (Conscience 10)
to swear I l. thee (Love 59)
true l....cannot speak (Love 104)
very ecstasy of l. (Love 29)
very flame of l. (Love 34)
we cannot fight for l. (Courtship 14)
what graces in my l. do dwell (Love 53)
what is l.? (Love 96)
when I did first impart my l. (Men 9)
when I l. thee not, chaos is come (Love 71)
when l. begins to sicken (Hypocrisy 5, Love 37)
when l. speaks (Love 44)
who can sever l. from charity? (Charity 2)
with l.'s light wings (Love 78)
worst fault you have is to be in l. (Faults 4)
you all did l. him once (Cause 3)
your true l.'s coming (Love 95)
love-cause:
   no man died in a l. (Dying 4)
loved:
   no sooner looked but they l. (Love 26)
   she l. me for the dangers (Love 68)
   whoever l. that l. not at first sight (Love 21)
love-in-idleness:
   maidens call it l. (Flowers 5)
lover:
   a l. may bestride the gossamers (Vanity 3)
   a l.'s eyes will gaze (Love 42)
   as true a l. (Love 10)
   it was a l. and his lass (Seasons 3)
   the l. sighing like a furnace (Love 13)
   the oath of a l. is no stronger (Promises 1)
   thou wilt be like a l. presently (Words 7)
lovers:
   all l. swear more (Love 91)
   all l. young (Mortality 1)
   a pair of star-crossed l. (Love 72)
   if true l. ever have been crossed (Patience 9)
   l. and madmen (Imagination 4)
   these l. cry, O ho they die (Sex 9)
   the sight of l. (Love 18)
   we that are true l. (Love 12)

loves:
   he says he l. my daughter (Love 106)
   l. are dearer (Love 9)
   our l. and comforts (Love 70)
   take all my l. (Love 108)
   two l. I have (Love 111)
love-songs:
   he has the prettiest l. (Singing 4)
love-suit:
   terms such as will ... plead his l. (Courtship 7)
love-thoughts:
   l. lie rich (Flowers 8)
loving:
   most l. mere folly (Disillusion 1)
lowliness:
   l. young ambition's ladder (Ambition 7)
loyalty:
   follow thee ... with truth and l. (Loyalty 2)
   map of honor, truth and l. (Honor 11)
Lucifer:
   when he falls, he falls like L. (Downfall 2)
luck:
   good l. lies in odd numbers (Luck 1)
   if it be my l., so (Fortune 22)
lucky:
   'tis a l. day, boy (Luck 2)
lunatic:
   l., the lover and the poet (Imagination 4)
lure:
   she never looks upon her l. (Falconry 1)
lust:
   cool a gipsy's l. (Lust 2)
   love ... is merely a l. of the blood (Lust 11)
   l. in action (Lust 14)
   l. is but a bloody fire (Lust 8)
   l.'s winter comes (Lust 15)
   l., the thief (Lust 13)
   murder's as near to l. (Sin 7)
   tears harden l. (Tears 16)
lute:
   lascivious pleasing of a l. (Dancing 2)
lying:
   how this world is given to l. (Lying 2)
   it is as easy as l. (Music 4)
   Kate, thou art perfect in l. down (Sex 1)
   let me have no l. (Business 11)
   this vice of l. (Lying 4, Age 15)
Mab:
   I see Queen M. hath been with you (Dreams 12)
Macbeth:
   M. shall never vanquished be (Prophecy 9)
Machiavel:
   set the murderous M. to school (Duplicity 2)
machinations:
   m., hollowness, treachery (Disorder 2)
mad:
   as m. as the vexed sea (Madness 9)
   I am but m. north-north-west (Madness 5)
   O let me not be m. (Prayer 11)

mad (cont'd.):

    sent into England? ... because 'a was mad (Countries 3)

madam:

    m., you have bereft me (Silence 5)

madman:

    frighted when a m. stares (Anger 2)

madness:

    draw you into m. (Ghosts 8)

    it is not m. I have uttered (Sanity 1)

    love is merely a m. (Love 16)

    midsummer m. (Madness 10)

    that way m. lies (Madness 8)

    the m. wherein now he raves (Madness 3)

    this is mere m. (Madness 6)

    though this be m. (Madness 4)

    to define true m. (Madness 2)

magic:

    if this be m., let it be an art (Magic 3)

    there's m. in the web of it (Magic 2)

    this rough m. I here abjure (Renunciation 5)

maid:

    a m., and stuffed (Sex 6)

    chariest m. is prodigal (Chastity 5)

    he hath achieved a m. (Beauty 16)

    m. that paragons description (Beauty 16)

    play the m.'s part (Deceit 19)

maids:

    m. are May when they are m. (Marriage 5)

majesty:

    gaze such as is bent on ... m. (Royalty 9)

    I am unfit for state and m. (Hypocrisy 16)

    m. might never yet endure (Authority 5)

    this new and gorgeous garment, m. (Royalty 13)

make:

    m.'t a darling (Magic 2)

    m. me to see it (Proof 2)

    m. the door upon a woman's wit (Wit 1)

    m. thick my blood (Ruthlessness 3)

    m. use of time (Time 45)

makes:

    it m. us or it mars us (Resolution 6)

malady:

    the m. of not marking (Sickness 8)

    where the greater m. is fixed (Sickness 14)

malice:

    men that make ... m. nourishment (Envy 1)

    spend my m. in my breath (Speech 1)

    the law I bear no m. for my death (Law 6)

maltworms:

    these mad, mustachioed m. (Drinking 6)

man:

    a goodly portly m., i'faith (Fatness 3)

    a good m.'s fortune may grow (Fortune 13)

    all that may become a m. (Men 8)

    a m. faithful and honorable (Virtue 7)

    a m. in all the world's new fashion (Fashion 7)

    a m. loves the meat in his youth (Experience 2)

    a m. may rot even here (Endurance 3)

a m. may see how this world goes (Justice 6)

a m. of such a feeble temper (Power 4)

a m.'s life is a tedious one (Man 3)

a m. that apprehends death (Death 31)

a m. that fortune's buffets and rewards (Fortune 7, Stoicism 1)

a m. who is the abstract of all faults (Faults 1)

a m. whom fortune hath cruelly scratched (Fortune 1)

a merrier m. (Merriment 2)

a most poor m. (Pity 4)

an honester and truer-hearted m. (Farewells 8)

a properer m. than she a woman (Beauty 4)

as tall a m. as any (Appearance 12)

a thousand times a properer m. (Men and Women 2)

'a was a m., take him for all in all (Man 4)

Brutus is an honorable m. (Ambition 9)

can no m. tell me? (Parents and Children 14)

cannot a plain m. live (Duplicity 6)

could I, Casca, name to thee a m. (Power 6)

dispute it like a m. (Grief 11)

every m. shall eat in safety (Peace 12)

give me that m. (Friendship 5, Temperament 3)

hath no beard is less than a m. (Celibacy 2)

he has proved himself a m. (Manliness 1)

he is a little worse than a m. (Drinking 15)

he is the only m. of Italy (Men 10)

he'll make a proper m. (Faces 1)

I am a m. more sinned against (Self-Pity 2, Sin 4)

I cannot be a m. with wishing (Men and Women 6)

I dare do all that may become a m. (Manliness 2)

I found no m. but he was true (Loyalty 4)

I play the m. I am (Identity 2)

I would have been ... a fresher m. (Readiness 3)

is m. no more but this? (Man 9)

laugh to scorn the power of m. (Prophecy 8)

let each m. render me his bloody hand (Greetings 4)

let the end try the m. (Men 3)

make of him a formal m. again (Medicine 4)

m. and wife, being two (Marriage 17)

m. delights not me (Humanity 1)

m. hath his desires (Marriage 3)

m. is a giddy thing (Marriage 37)

m. is an enemy to virginity (Virginity 1)

m. is but an ass (Dreams 6)

m., more divine (Marriage 9)

m., proud man (Authority 7)

m.'s life's but a span (Soldiers 22)

m.'s nature cannot carry th'affliction (Storms 8)

m. that once did sell the lion's skin (Overconfidence 1)

m. the image of his maker (Ambition 5)

mightier m., the mightier is the thing (Greatness 12)

more loathed than an effeminate m. (Effeminacy 3)

my single state of m. (Confusion 4)

Nature might say... "This was a m." (Epitaphs 12)

no m. hath any quarrel to me (Quarrels 17)

not a m. ... hath any honor (Honor 21)

not yet old enough for a m. (Youth 11)

O God, that I were a m. (Anger 7)

O, see the monstrousness of m. (Ingratitude 9)
O that I were a m. (Manliness 3)
O, that's a brave m. (Promises 5)
O, the difference of m. and m. (Desire 8)
ruins of the noblest m. (Epitaphs 9)
slight, unmeritable m. (Contempt 2)
stand as if a m. were author of himself (Man 2)
state of m. like to a little kingdom (Anxiety 4)
suffer the worst that m. can breathe (Endurance 4)
that a m. might know the end (Foreboding 8)
that I might see but such another m. (Dreams 1)
that m. should be at woman's command (Men and Women 1)
that m. that hath a tongue (Courtship 24)
that's a brave m. (Promises 2)
the great m. down (Politics 2)
the m. nearest my soul (Friendship 9)
the m. shall have his mare again (Proverbs 21)
the m. that hath no music (Music 12)
there is no m. hath a virtue (Vice 4)
there's not one wise m. among twenty (Wisdom 5)
there's place and means for every m. (Foolery 1)
the simplicity of m. (Lust 7)
the time that the unjust m. doth thrive (Wrongdoing 7)
think you there ... might be such a m.? (Dreams 2)
this is the state of m. (Farewells 10)
thou art e'en as just a m. (Man 6)
though I am caparisoned like a m. (Women 5)
'tis not a year or two shows us a m. (Men and Women 7)
to be a well-favored m. (Learning 2)
turns she every m. the wrong side out (Criticism 3)
unaccommodated m. (Man 9)
villainous m. (Man 8)
were m. but constant (Inconstancy 7)
what a piece of work is a m. (Man 5)
what is a m. (Man 7)
what m. may within him hide (Hypocrisy 9)
what wouldst thou do, old m.? (Duty 4)
who is m. that is not angry (Anger 9)
winter tames m. (Seasons 16)
you might have been enough the m. (Man 1)
young m. married (Marriage 1)

mandragora:
give me to drink m. (Forgetfulness 2)

manhood:
m. is melted into curtsies (Manliness 3)

mankind:
he's an enemy to m. (Devil 11)
how beauteous m. is! (Humanity 7)
the common curse of m. (Curses 9)

manners:
I'll view the m. of the town (Travel 3)
men's evil m. live in brass (Remembrance 4)
their m. are more gentle (Monsters 1)
we are the makers of m. (Custom 4)

mansion:
innocent m. of my love (Death-Wish 2)

leave not the m. so long tenantless (Ruin 1)
Timon hath made his everlasting m. (Epitaphs 15)
what a m. have those vices got (Vice 5)

mantle:
morn in russet m. clad (Dawn 1)

map:
give me the m. there (Maps 2)
I have forgot the m. (Maps 1)
new m. with the augmentation (Faces 7)

marble:
not m. nor the gilded monuments (Poetry 15)

marigold:
the m. that goes to bed with the sun (Flowers 11)

mark:
a fellow of no m. (Men 2)
he was the m. and glass (Fashion 3)
love ... is an ever-fixèd m. (Love 110)
m. how a plain tale (Plain-Speaking 1)

market-maid:
you are come a m. to Rome (Love 6)

markets:
not for all m. (Advice 3)

marmoset:
snare the nimble m. (Education 6)

marriage:
a good hanging prevents a bad m. (Marriage 48)
hasty m. seldom proveth well (Marriage 19)
let me not to the m. (Love 110)
O curse of m. (Marriage 41)
sweet silent hours of m. joys (Marriage 44)
with dirge in m. (Mourning 6)

marriage-blessing:
honor, riches, m. (Blessings 5)

marriages:
God, the best maker of all (Prayer 7)

married:
a young man m. (Marriage 1)
Benedick, the m. man (Marriage 34)
we will be m. o' Sunday (Marriage 46)

marry:
he swore he would never m. (Marriage 33)
if thou dost m. (Marriage 16)
if thou wilt needs m., m. a fool (Marriage 16)
since I do purpose to m. (Marriage 37)

Mars:
an eye like M. (Beauty 7)
think what Venus did with M. (Desire 1)
this seat of M. (Countries 5)

martlet:
the temple-haunting m. (Birds 6)

masks:
m. for faces (Clothing 15)

masons:
the singing m. (Building 2)

masque:
what m., what music? (Revels 4)

masques:
I delight in m. (Revels 5)
what m., what dances shall we have (Revels 3)

m. are flesh and blood (Constancy 2)
m. are m. (Men 11)
m. are merriest when they are from home (Travel 10)
m. are not gods (Men 12)
m. at some time are masters of their fates (Fate 5)
m. have died from time to time (Dying 5)
m. judge by the complexion of the sky (Weather 5)
m. may construe things (Misunderstanding 1)
m. must endure their going hence (Endurance 3)
m. must learn now with pity to dispense (Politics 23)
m. must needs abide (Fate 4)
m. of few words are the best (Men 6)
m. prize the thing ungained (Men and Women 9)
m.'s evil manners live in brass (Remembrance 3)
m. shall deal unadvisedly sometimes (Excuses 4)
m. should be what they seem (Appearance 8)
m. shut their doors against a setting sun (Downfall 4)
m. that make envy ... nourishment (Envy 1)
m. that she is the rarest (Men and Women 11)
m. that talk of a noun and a verb (Language 4)
m. were deceivers ever (Inconstancy 4)
m., wives, and children stare (Chaos 1)
m. would forsake the gods (Prayer 18)
most strange that m. should fear (Death 18)
of all the m. alive (Love 85)
O miracle of m. (Men 4)
such m. as he be never at heart's ease (Politics 11)
that we women had m.'s privilege (Courtship 22)
there are a sort of m. (Self-Importance 1)
there lives not three good m. unhanged (Nostalgia 2, Old Age 3)
the true proof of m. (Chance 2)
they should be good m. (Goodness 1)
thus m. may grow wiser (Wisdom 1)
tongues of m. are full of deceits (Deceit 3)
to willful m. the injuries (Obstinacy 4)
we are all m. (Weakness 2)
what m. dare do (Action 13)
when holy and devout religious m. (Prayer 15)
when there's no strength in m. (Men and Women 8)
wise m. ne'er sit and wail (Encouragement 1)
you are m. of stones (Mourning 17)
you are not stones, but m. (Men 7)
mend:
m. when thou canst (Improvement 2)
merchants:
like m. show our foulest wares (Business 9)
merciful:
O let us yet be m. (Mercy 2)
Mercury:
rise from the ground like feathered M. (Soldiers 6)
mercy:
half so good a grace as m. (Mercy 6)
how shalt thou hope for m.? (Mercy 9)
lawful m. (Mercy 6)
m. but murders, pardoning (Mercy 14)
m. is above this sceptered sway (Mercy 11)

m. is not itself that oft looks so (Mercy 4)
m. then will breathe (Mercy 7)
nor man grieve at the m. (Mercy 5)
quality of m. (Mercy 10)
sweet m. is nobility's true badge (Mercy 15)
there is no more m. in him (Ruthlessness 1)
use m. to them all (Mercy 3)
we do pray for m. (Mercy 12)
void ... from any dram of m. (Cruelty 5)
whereto serves m.? (Mercy 1)
meridian:
from that full m. of my glory (Downfall 1)
merit:
honorable without the stamp of m. (Merit 1)
purchased by the m. (Merit 2)
merrier:
a m. man (Merriment 2)
merriment:
mirth and m. (Acting 27)
your flashes of m. (Mortality 2)
merry:
a m. heart goes all the day (Merriment 6)
I am never m. when I hear (Music 11)
I am not m. (Moods 13)
men are ever m. (Moods 9)
neither sad nor m. (Moods 1)
rejoicing to see another m. (Moderation 1)
shall we be m.? (Merriment 1)
to be m. best becomes you (Merriment 4)
we shall be m. (Night 4)
you are m. because you are not sad (Moods 11)
message:
horrid m. for a challenge (Challenges 3)
metal:
here's metal more attractive (Sex 1)
meteors:
m. fright the fixèd stars (Portents 9)
meters:
lascivious m. to whose venom sound (Poetry 12)
methinks:
m. I see my father (Remembrance 2)
m. it were an easy leap (Honor 3)
m. King Richard and myself (Meeting 1)
m. the truth should live (Truth 7)
mettle:
thy honorable m. may be wrought (Nobility 4)
method:
there's m. in't (Madness 4)
mickle:
O, m,. is the powerful grace (Nature 6)
middle:
the m. of humanity thou never knewest (Humanity 9)
midnight:
out of his bed at m.(Age 7)
the iron tongue of m. (Time of Day 8)
to be up after m. (Lateness 5)
midsummer:
as gorgeous as the sun at m. (Seasons 4)
this is very m. madness (Madness 10)

murder:

a brother's m. (Guilt 1)

conscience to do no contrived m. (Murder 7)

most sacrilegious m. (Confusion 5)

m. cannot be hid (Proverbs 18)

m. her brothers (Murder 12)

m. most foul (Murder 1)

m.'s as near to lust (Sin 7)

m.'s out of tune (Murder 9)

m., though it have no tongue (Murder 2)

m. yet is but fantastical (Confusion 3)

thou shalt do no m. (Murder 11)

withered m. (Murder 6)

murderer:

an honorable m. (Murder 10)

murderers:

purgers, not m. (Assassination 2)

muse:

O for a m. of fire (Poetry 8, Theater 5)

mushrooms:

midnight m. (Vegetables 2)

music:

discourse most eloquent m. (Music 4)

give me some m. (Music 1)

how irksome is this m. (Quarrels 4)

how sour sweet m. is (Music 18)

I am advised to give her m. (Music 3)

if m. be the food of love (Music 25)

in sweet m. is such art (Music 8)

I will play the swan and die in m. (Dying 14)

let m. sound (Music 10)

let the sounds of m. creep (Moon 1)

like softest m. (Music 19)

marvelous sweet m. (Music 24)

much m. ... in this little organ (Character 2)

m. at the close ... is sweetest last (Endings 3)

m., ho! m. such as charmeth (Music 14)

m. oft hath such a charm (Music 9)

my love shall hear the m. of my hounds (Dogs 5)

never merry when I hear sweet m. (Music 11)

the general so likes your m. (Music 15)

the man that hath no m. (Music 12)

this m. crept by me (Music 22)

to his m. plants and flowers (Music 7)

where should this m. be (Music 21)

whisper m. to my weary spirit (Music 6)

wilt thou hear some m.? (Music 13)

musician:

an admirable m. (Music 16)

musk-roses:

with sweet m. and with eglantine (Flowers 6)

mustachioed:

these mad, m. maltworms (Drinking 6)

mustard:

his wit's as thick as Tewkesbury m. (Insults 9)

Mustardseed:

Peaseblossom, Cobweb, Moth, and M. (Fairies 6)

mutable:

m. rank-scented meiny (People 9)

mutations:

world! but that thy strange m. (World 5)

mutinies:

in cities m. (Disorder 1)

mutton:

what's a joint of m. or two in a whole Lent (Food 7)

muzzle:

I am trusted with a m. (Constraint 2)

myself:

m. and what is mine (Possession 3)

mystery:

m. in the soul of state (Government 6)

pluck out the heart of my m. (Character 2)

take upon's the m. of things (Politics 17)

naked:

n. in bed, Iago, and not mean harm? (Devil 9)

when he was n. (Body 3)

name:

good n. in man and woman (Reputation 8)

he that filches from my good n. (Reputation 9)

his n.'s Cinna (Names 2)

I do not like her n. (Names 1)

if his n. be George (Names 3)

if my n. were liable to fear (Fear 7)

is not the king's n. (Royalty 29)

my n. receives a brand (Reputation 16)

refuse thy n. (Names 7)

the king's n. is a tower of strength (Reputation 12)

they n. her n. and Rosaline they call her (Names 4)

to that n. my courage prove my title (Courage 1)

what is your n.? (Names 9)

what's in a n.? (Names 8)

what the dickens his n. is (Names 5)

names:

where a commodity of good n. (Reputation 2)

nation:

a law in each well-ordered n. (Law 11)

trick of our English n. (Countries 4)

native:

though I am n. here (Custom 2)

nativity:

at my n. the front of heaven (Portents 1)

n. was under Ursa Major (Astrology 2)

natural:

I do it more n. (Fools 12)

natural:

he wants the n. touch (Nature 4)

something in this more than n. (Philosophy 7)

nature:

allow not n. more (Necessity 4)

all the good gifts of n. (Character 5)

any cause in n. (Cause 4)

crack n.'s molds (Storms 8)

cunning'st pattern of excelling n. (Light 2)

death may usurp on n. (Death 32)

diseasèd n. oft breaks out (Earthquakes 1)

face with n.'s own hand painted (Androgyny 2)

fancy outwork n. (Beauty 1)

great creating n. (Nature 7)

hard to hide the sparks of n. (Nature 1)
his n. is too noble (Nobility 1)
how that might change his n. (Cause 1)
I do fear thy n. (Kindness 2)
in n.'s infinite book of secrecy (Prophecy 1)
is this the n.? (Passion 2)
life that age ... can lay on n. (Death 30)
Moor is of a free and open n. (Deceit 12)
Moor is of a ... noble n. (Character 3)
n. awakes (Life 9)
n. hath framed strange fellows (Humanity 4)
n. in you stands on the very verge (Old Age 7)
n. might stand up and say (Epitaphs 12)
n. must obey necessity (Necessity 2)
n. needs not what thou gorgeous wear'st (Fashion 6)
n. quickly falls into revolt (Avarice 1)
n. seems dead (Night 12)
n.'s germens tumble (Chaos 2)
n.'s own sweet and cunning hand (Beauty 25)
n. stands on the very verge of his confine (Age 25)
n., what things there are (Value 7)
n. whom passion could not shake (Passion 1)
one touch of n. makes the whole world kin (Fashion 11)
O ruined piece of n. (Mortality 7)
the art itself is n. (Nature 8)
the earth, that's n.'s mother (Nature 5)
things rank and gross in n. (Dejection 1)
thou goddess, thou divine n.! (Nature 2)
thou, N. art my goddess (Nature 3)
use amost can change the stamp of n. (Custom 3)
violet in the youth of primy n. (Flowers 1)
when the baser n. comes (Quarrels 2)
would you have me false to my n. (Identity 2)
natures:
men, in our own n. frail (Weakness 2)
necessities:
are these things then n.? (Necessity 2)
art of our n. is strange (Necessity 5)
call in question our n.(Councils 2)
these strong n. (Necessity 1)
necessity:
brother, sweet, to grim n. (Necessity 8)
for n. of present life (Hypocrisy 11)
make a virtue of n. (Necessity 9)
nature must obey n. (Necessity 3)
n.'s sharp pinch (Homelessness 1)
teach thy n. to reason thus (Necessity 7)
need:
reason not the n. (Necessity 4)
never so few and never yet more n. (Diplomacy 1)
neighbor:
our bad n. makes us early stirrers (Business 5)
pond fished by his n. (Adultery 2)
neighborly:
is not that n. (Desire 4)
Nemean:
hardy as the N. lion's nerve (Fate 2)

Neptune:
the green N. a ram (Gods 5)
ye that ... do chase the ebbing N. (Fairies 8)
nettle:
out of this n., danger (Danger 1)
the strawberry grows underneath the n. (Gardens 2)
never:
n. anything can be amiss (Simplicity 2)
n. come such division (Reconciliation 2)
n. durst poet touch a pen (Poetry 9)
n., never, never, never, never (Death 21)
n. since the middle summer's spring (Quarrels 10)
n. so much as in a thought unborn (Innocence 2)
n. was a story of more woe (Sorrow 15)
n. was a war did cease (Peace 3)
new-born:
met'st ... with things n. (Birth and Death 2)
news:
first bringer of unwelcome n. (News 8)
never good to bring bad n. (News 2)
the father of good n. (News 4)
the nature of bad n. (News 1)
though n. be sad (News 10)
what's the new n.? (News 3)
newts:
n. and blindworms (Creatures 4)
night:
come, civil n. (Night 20)
come, gentle n. (Night 21)
come, seeling n. (Evil 6)
comes in the sweet o' the n. (Night 4)
comes so fast in silence of the n. (Night 16)
come, thick n. (Murder 5)
converses with the buttock of the n. (Drinking 4)
cripple tardy-gaited n. (Night 7)
dark n. that from the eye (Senses 1)
dragon wing of n. (Night 22)
foul womb of n. (Night 6)
here's a n. pities neither wise men (Night 10)
in n. ... desire sees best of all (Desire 21)
in such a n. as this (Night 15)
it hath been the longest n. (Night 23)
it is not n. when I do see (Love 56)
let's have one other gaudy n. (Feasts 2)
n. is long that never finds the day (Aphorisms 6, Night 14)
nor n. nor day no rest (Sleeplessness 8)
now it is the time of n. (Ghosts 14)
n.'s black agents to their preys do rouse (Night 13)
n.'s candles are burnt out (Dawn 7)
O grim-looked n. (Night 18)
O weary n. (Night 17)
sable n., mother of dread (Night 24)
smiles on the frowning n. (Dawn 5)
sweetest morsel of the n. (Night 3)
the n. comes on, and the bleak winds (Storms 6)
the n. has been unruly (Prophecy 7)
things that love n. (Night 11)
this is the n. (Chance 1)

night (cont'd.)

this will last out a n. in Russia (Tediousness 3)

to dwell in solemn shades of endless n. (Exile 4)

usurp'st this time of n. (Apparitions 2)

very witching time of n. (Night 1)

what a fearful n. is this! (Night 9)

what is the n.? (Time of Day 7)

yield day to n. (Night 8)

nightingale:

it was the lark ... no n. (Dawn 6)

it was the n. and not the lark (Parting 16)

she sings as sweetly as a n. (Courtship 20)

the n., if she should sing by day (Birds 11)

night-shriek:

senses would have cooled to hear a n. (Fear 14)

nit:

thou flea, thou n. (Insults 19)

nobility:

hands do lack n. (Assault 1)

mercy is n.'s true badge (Mercy 15)

true n. is exempt from fear (Fear 4)

noble:

a brother n. (Nobility 7)

his nature is too n. (Nobility 1)

nothing natural I ever saw so n. (Nobility 8)

she's n. born (Nobility 3)

too n. for this place (Nobility 9)

well, Brutus, thou art n. (Nobility 4)

what a n. mind is here o'erthrown (Nobility 2)

nobleness:

the n. of life is to do thus (Kissing 1)

noblest:

this was the n. Roman (Nobility 6)

noise:

let there be no n. (Music 6)

the n. of b. hurtled in the air (Portents 5)

noises:

the isle is full of n. (Music 23)

none:

n. can truly say he gives (Generosity 5)

north:

tyrannous breathing of the n. (Kissing 4)

Norway:

when he the ambitious N. combated (Ghosts 1)

nose:

his n. was a sharp as a pen (Dying 6)

nose-painting:

drink especially provoke? ... n. (Drinking 14)

note:

not a n. of mine that's worth noting (Modesty 2)

nothing:

before I knew thee, I knew n. (Character 3)

demand me n. (Silence 6)

Gratiano speaks an infinite deal of n. (Reason 5)

I am a fool; thou art n. (Nothing 3)

n. almost sees miracles (Miracles 2)

n. but sit and sit, and eat and eat (Eating 12)

n. brings me all things (Dying 16)

n. can be made out of n. (Nothing 2)

n. can come between me and ... my hopes (Confidence 2)

n. can ... content my soul (Revenge 5)

n. can we call our own but death (Death 34)

n. comes amiss so money comes (Money 12)

n. either good or bad (Philosophy 6)

n. extenuate (Speech 21)

n. 'gainst time's scythe (Time 41)

n. ill can dwell in such a temple (Goodness 4)

n. in his life became him (Dying 13)

n. is but what is not (Confusion 4, Paradoxes 2)

n. left remarkable (Mourning 1)

nor any man ... with n. shall be pleased (Discontent 1)

n. will come of n. (Proverbs 12)

reputed wise for saying n. (Reputation 5)

this is n., Fool (Lawyers 2, Nothing 1)

thou talk'st of n. (Dreams 13)

nought:

n.'s had, all's spent (Desire 10)

n. shall go ill (Proverbs 21)

now:

n. could I, Casca, name to thee (Power 6)

n. he weighs time (Time 15)

n. is the sun upon the highmost hill (Time 27)

n. is the winter of our discontent (Improvement 3)

n. let it work (Evil 3)

n. mark me how I will undo myself (Renunciation 3)

n. the hungry lion roars (Night 19)

n. thou and I are new in amity (Reconciliation 5)

n. would I give a thousand furlongs (Sea 5)

nun:

endure the livery of a n. (Religion 5)

nunnery:

get thee to a n. (Marriage 16)

nurse:

dear n. of arts (Peace 11)

mewling and puking in the n.'s arms (Infancy 2)

time is the n. and breeder of all good (Time 38)

nurture:

on whose nature n. can never stick (Education 7)

nut:

sweetest n. hath sourest rind (Food 5)

nuts:

quarrel with a man for cracking n. (Quarrels 13)

nutshell:

I could be bounded in a n. (Dreams 3)

O:

cram within this wooden O (Theater 6)

O beware, my lord, of jealousy (Jealousy 6)

O God of battles (Prayer 6)

O God, that men should put an enemy (Drinking 22)

O good old man, how well (Service 2)

O heavens! If you do love old men (Prayer 12)

O how I love thee (Infatuation 8)

O how much more doth beauty (Beauty 32)

O lady fortune, stand you auspicious (Fortune 23)

O let me clip ye in arms as sound (Friendship 2)

O let me not be mad (Prayer 11)

O let us have him (Maturity 2)

O let us yet be merciful (Mercy 1)
O Lord, methought what pain it was to drown (Dreams 9)
O Lord that lends me life (Prayer 8)
O mighty Caesar! Dost thou lie so low (Epitaphs 8)
O mischief, thou art swift (Evil 9)
O pity, God (Prayer 10)
O, sir, your presence is too bold (Authority 5)
O that a lady of one man refused (Rejection 1)
O that I were a fool (Fools 3)
O that I were a man (Manliness 3)
O that I were a mockery king (Death-Wish 9)
O that's a brave man (Promises 2)
O that this too too solid flesh (Suicide 11)
O, 'tis most sweet (Plots 2)
O, what a goodly outside (Duplicity 5)
O, what damnèd minutes tells he o'er (Jealousy 7)
O, what men dare do (Action 13)
the little O, the earth (Praise 3)
thou art an O without a figure (Nothing 3)

oak:
  under an o., whose antique root (Trees 1)
  under an old o. (Trees 2)
oars:
  fish cut with her golden o. the silver stream (Fishing 2)
oath:
  breaking his o. and resolution (Promises 3)
  never more break an o. (Apologies 3)
  swear me ... a good mouth-filling o. (Oaths 1)
  the o. of a lover is no stronger (Promises 1)
oaths:
  downright o. (Oaths 3)
  he hailed down o. that he was only mine (Vows 3)
  his o. are oracles (Sincerity 3)
  soldier, full of strange o. (Soldiers 1)
  the strongest o. are straw (Sex 6)
  'tis not the many o. that makes the truth (Vows 1)
oats:
  I could munch your good dry o. (Eating 9)
  since the price of o. rose (Money 1)
object:
  o. and pleasure of mine eye (Devotion 2)
objects:
  one that feeds on o. (Contempt 3)
oblivion:
  blind o. swallowed cities up (Constancy 8)
  formless ruin of o. (Welcome 2)
  my o. is a very Antony (Forgetfulness 1)
  second childishness and mere o. (Age 5)
  the dust of old o. (History 1)
obloquy:
  all's o. (Misanthropy 5)
observer:
  he is a great o. (Reading 2)
observers:
  the observed of all o. (Fashion 2)
obstruction:
  to lie in cold o. (Graves 1)
occasions:

how all o. do inform (Revenge 2)
there is o. and causes (Philosophy 11)
occupation:
  'tis my o. to be plain (Plain-Speaking 6)
ocean:
  his legs bestrid the o. (Praise 4)
  the wild and wasteful o. (Sea 1)
  water that in the o. seeks another drop (Identity 1)
  will all great Neptune's o. wash (Guilt 5)
oceans:
  drinking o. dry (Futility 1)
offend:
  to o. and judge are distinct offices (Judgment 2)
offense:
  confront the visage of o. (Mercy 1)
  every nice o. bear his comment (Criticism 1)
  my o. is rank (Guilt 1)
  o.'s gilded hand (Law 1)
  some sick o. within your mind (Anxiety 5)
  so offend to make o. a skill (Wrongdoing 1)
  what o. have these men done (Wrongdoing 5)
  where the o. is (Punishment 2)
offenses:
  I would I could quit all o. (Excuses 1)
  made old o. of affections new (Folly 5)
  make us pay down for our o. (Authority 6)
office:
  infirmity doth still neglect all o. (Sickness 13)
  save in the o. and affairs of love (Friendship 23)
  the o. opposite Saint Peter (Hell 5)
  'tis all men's o. to speak patience (Philosophy 14)
officer:
  art thou o.? (Soldiers 14)
offices:
  o. were not derived corruptly (Merit 2)
  sell and mart your o. for gold (Corruption 5)
oftentimes:
  o. to win us to our harm (Evil 5)
old:
  a good o. man, sir (Old Age 10)
  an o. man broken (Old Age 6)
  an o. man, sir, and his wits are not so blunt (Honesty 4)
  foolish fond o. man (Age 27)
  how o. art thou? (Middle Age 3)
  I am o., I am o. (Love 36)
  I am too o. to fawn (Middle Age 4)
  I confess that I am o. (Age 26)
  o. and reverend (Age 23)
  o., cold, withered (Insults 14)
  o. fashions please me best (Fashion 9)
  o. folks ... unwieldy, slow (Old Age 11)
  o. man is twice a child (Old Age 2)
  o. men forget (Remembrance 3)
  o. Nestor (Old Age 13)
  o. till thou hadst been wise (Age 24)
  one of them is fat and grows o. (Old Age 3)
  she cannot choose but be o. (Age 14)
  sir, you are old (Age 25, Old Age 7)

palm:
    bear the p. alone (Power 4)
palpable:
    who cannot see this p. device? (Deceit 18)
Pandars:
    call them all p. (Lust 12)
pansies:
    there is p., that's for thoughts (Flowers 2)
pantaloon:
    lean and slippered p. (Age 4)
pantler:
    she was both p., butler, cook (Hospitality 3)
pants:
    ride on the p. triumphing (Love 7)
paper:
    as many lies as will lie in thy p. (Lying 7)
    let p. show (Letters 3)
paradise:
    lead her in a fool's p. (Deceit 21)
paramour:
    he's a very p. for a sweet voice (Solecisms 3)
parasites:
    most smiling, smooth, detested p. (Flattery 9)
pardon:
    free p. (Mercy 8)
    p. is still the nurse (Mercy 4)
    p. me, thou bleeding piece of earth (Mourning 14)
    you might p. him (Mercy 5)
part:
    answer to his p. (Acting 31)
    his p. is played (Epitaphs 17)
    I have forgot my p. (Acting 3)
    I must bear a p. (Acting 30)
    it is the p. of men to fear (Portents 4)
    lion's p. (Acting 20)
    more willingly p. withal (Parting 6)
    must we p.? (Parting 13)
    p. to tear a cat in (Acting 19)
    question's out of my p. (Acting 29)
    sir, you and I must p. (Parting 1)
    speak all your p. at once (Acting 23)
    stage where every man must play a p. (Acting 17)
    you have put me to such a p. (Acting 2)
parted:
    'A p. even just between twelve and one (Dying 6)
particular:
    why seems it so p. (Appearance 1)
parting:
    p. is such sweet sorrow (Parting 15)
    this p. was well made (Parting 9)
parts:
    for which of my bad p. (Love 66)
    for which of my good p. (Love 67)
    three p. of him is ours (Persuasion 3)
passages:
    in p. of proof (Love 33)
passion:
    hot p. of distempered blood (Argument 6)
    man that is not p.'s slave (Friendship 5)
    nature whom p. could not shake (Passion 2)

nor wit nor reason can my p. hide (Infatuation 10)
    the beating of so strong a p. (Love 98)
    'twixt two extremes of p., joy and grief (Dying 12)
    what to ourselves in p. we propose (Passion 1)
passions:
    of all base p., fear (Fear 4)
past:
    p. and to come seems best (Time 10)
    what's p. and what's to come (Welcome 2)
patched:
    p. with cloth of any color (Mistakes 2)
patience:
    all men's office to speak p. (Philosophy 14)
    arming myself with p. (Patience 4)
    found ... a drop of p. (Affliction 9)
    how poor are they that have not p. (Patience 10)
    I have the p. to endure it (Patience 3)
    I laughed him out of p. (Patience 1)
    I will be the pattern of all p. (Patience 5)
    I will with p. hear (Consideration 1)
    let us teach our trial p. (Patience 9)
    like p. gazing on kings' graves (Patience 11)
    oppose my p. to his fury (Patience 8)
    p. is pale cold cowardice (Cowardice 5)
    sat like p. on a monument (Melancholy 9, Patience
      12)
    though p. be a tired mare (Patience 2)
patient:
    bear free and p. thoughts (Patience 6)
    p. must minister to himself (Medicine 9)
    thou must be p. (Patience 7)
patiently:
    if you will p. dance in our round (Dancing 1)
pattern:
    I will be the p. of all patience (Patience 5)
pause:
    stand in p. where I shall first begin (Indecision 2)
peace:
    a moth of p. (Love 69)
    a p. is of the nature of a conquest (Peace 7)
    blessed spirit of p. (Peace 5)
    for men as old as we to keep the p. (Peace 14)
    frighted p. to pant (Anxiety 1)
    I feel within me a p. (Self-Knowledge 4)
    in p. there's nothing (Peace 9)
    kiss my lady p. at home (Peace 4)
    my words are as full of p. (Peace 15)
    our p. shall stand as firm (Peace 6)
    p., dear nurse of arts (Peace 11)
    p. is a great maker of cuckolds (Peace 2)
    p., p! dost thou not see? (Infancy 1)
    p. puts forth her olive (Peace 8)
    p. to this meeting (Peace 10)
    the merry songs of p. (Peace 13)
    the wound of p. is surety (Security 2)
    time of universal p. (Peace 2)
    uproar the universal p. (Chaos 3)
    we, to gain our p., have sent to p. (Anxiety 6)
peacemakers:
    blessèd are the p. on earth (Peace 12)

pearl:
    she is a p. whose price (Value 6)
    threw a p. away (Jealousy 12)
pearls:
    those are p. (Transformation 3)
peascod-time:
    these twenty-nine years, come p. (Farewells 8)
Peaseblossom:
    P., Cobweb, Moth, and Mustardseed (Fairies 5,
    Names 6)
pelf:
    I crave no p. (Prayer 17)
pen:
    with rough and all-unable p. (Theater 9)
    write, p. (Writing 1)
penalty:
    here feel we not the p. of Adam (Punishment 1)
penance:
    I go woolward for p. (Clothing 6)
    impose me to what p. (Sin 5)
penitence:
    my p. comes after all (Repentance 3)
penny:
    friend i'the court is better than a p. in purse (Friend-
    ship 11)
pens:
    quirks of blazoning p. (Beauty 16)
people:
    I find the p. strangely fantasied (Fear 10)
    I love the p. (People 17)
    note the qualities of p. (People 1)
    thus play I ... many people (Identity 5)
    you speak o' the p. (People 10)
pepper:
    vinegar and p. in't (Challenges 2)
perdition:
    p. catch my soul (Love 71)
perfect:
    thou art p. in lying down (Sex 3)
    you so p. (Perfection 1)
perfection:
    holds in p. but a little moment (Perfection 3)
    I would with such p. govern (Government 5)
    no p. is so absolute (Perfection 2)
    put a strange face on his own p. (Modesty 1)
performance:
    eke out our p. (Acting 14)
    p. is ever the duller for his act (Promises 8)
    swear more p. than they are able (Love 91)
    that desire should outlive p. (Desire 7)
performances:
    words and p. are no kin (Words and Deeds 2)
perfumèd:
    he was p. like a milliner (Effeminacy 1)
perfumes:
    all the p. of Arabia (Guilt 8)
    her breathing that p. the chamber (Perfume 1)
perils:
    open p. surest answered (Councils 1)
    what p. past, what crosses to ensue (Despair 2)

perseverance:
    p. keeps honor bright (Reputation 13)
person:
    did I keep my p. fresh and new (Greatness 4)
perspective:
    a natural p. (Perception 3)
persuade:
    your discretions better can p. (Persuasion 1)
persuasion:
    with what p. did he tempt thy love? (Courtship 6)
person:
    p. beggared all description (Beauty 1)
personage:
    her tall p. (Comparisons 1)
perturbation:
    O polished p.! (Royalty 12)
pestilence:
    she purged the air of p. (Desire 16)
petard:
    hoist with his own p. (Justice 1)
philosopher:
    never yet p. that could endure (Philosophy 15)
philosophical:
    we have our p. persons (Philosophy 1)
philosophy:
    adversity's sweet milk, p. (Adversity 4)
    if p. could find it out (Philosophy 7)
    more things than are dreamt of in your p. (Philoso-
    phy 5)
    of your p. you make no use (Philosophy 12)
    unfit to hear moral p. (Argument 5)
Phoebe:
    when P. doth behold (Moon 3)
Phoebus:
    ere they can behold bright P. (Flowers 13)
    golden P. never be beheld (Death 5)
    with P.'s amorous pinches black (Middle Age 1)
phoenix:
    in Arabia ... one p. (Myths 1)
    were man as rare as p. (Love 24)
phrases:
    good p. are surely ... commendable (Speech 4)
    hath a mint of p. in his brain (Fashion 7)
physic:
    in poison there is p. (Sickness 9)
    I will not cast away my p. (Medicine 3)
    take p. pomp (Justice 5)
    throw p. to the dogs (Medicine 10)
physician:
    kill thy p. (Medicine 8)
    more needs she the divine than the p. (Guilt 9)
pick-purse:
    I think he is not a p. (Love 17)
pie:
    no man's p. is freed (Ambition 4)
piece:
    nature's p. 'gainst fancy (Imagination 1)
    thou bleeding p. of earth (Mourning 14)
piece out:
    p. our imperfections (Imagination 2)

Pilate:
some of you, with P. wash (Hypocrisy 13)
pilchards:
fools are like husbands as p. are to herrings (Fools 12)
pilgrimage:
his time is spent; our p. must be (Epitaphs 13)
pillar:
the triple p. of the world transformed (Folly 1)
pillow:
sighed upon a midnight p. (Love 8)
pilot:
desire my p. is (Desire 19)
pinch:
as a lover's p., which hurts and is desired (Dying 3)
there cannot be a p. in death (Parting 4)
they brought one P. (Character 1)
pinches:
Phoebus' amorous p. (Middle Age 1)
pink:
I am the very p. of courtesy (Courtesy 2)
pipe:
rumor is a p. blown by surmises (Rumor 3)
pippin:
a last year's p. of my own grafting (Eating 5)
pippins:
there's p. and cheese to come (Food 9)
pirates:
water-thieves ... I mean p. (Ships 4)
pit:
enemies have beat us to the p. (Defeat 1)
she is fallen into a p. of ink (Guilt 10)
pitchers:
p. have ears (Proverbs 26)
pitiful:
'twas p., 'twas wondrous p. (Pity 7)
pity:
am pregnant to good p. (Pity 4)
a tear for p. (Charity 1)
but yet the p. of it, Iago! (Pity 8)
I perceive you feel the dint of p. (Pity 3)
is there no p. sitting in the clouds (Sorrow 14)
know what 'tis to p. and be pitied (Pity 1)
men must learn now with p. to dispense (Politics 23)
p. choked with custom of fell deeds (Cruelty 2)
p. is the virtue of the law (Law 10)
p. like a naked new-born babe (Pity 5)
p. to the general wrong of Rome (Pity 2)
p. two such friends ... be long foes (Friendship 32)
showing an outward p. (Hypocrisy 13)
tear-falling p. dwells not (Ruthlessness 5)
wretch uncapable of p. (Cruelty 5)
yet show some p. (Pity 6)
place:
dost thou not suspect my p. (Insults 17)
here's a marvelous convenient p. (Theater 12)
this p. is too cold for hell (Hell 2)
places:
all p. that the eye of heaven visits (Travel 17)
plague:
a p. on these pickle herring (Eating 14)

a p. of sighing and grief (Thinness 1)
a p. upon it! (Maps 1)
a p. upon it when thieves (Loyalty 3)
p. of all cowards (Cowardice 3)
p. of your policy (Politics 9)
p. on both your houses (Curses 8)
the p. of Greece upon thee (Stupidity 2)
the p. that needs must (Ingratitude 3)
plain:
an honest mind and p. (Plain-Speaking 7)
a p. tale shall put you down (Plain-Speaking 1)
honest p. words best pierce (Plain-Speaking 9)
'tis my occupation to be p. (Plain-Speaking 6)
planets:
curse the p. of mishap (Curses 1)
play:
a good p. needs no epilogue (Plays 1)
a p. there is ... some ten words long (Theater 14)
guilty creatures sitting at a p. (Theater 4)
I see the p. so lies (Acting 30)
like as much of this p. as please you (Men and
Women 3, Plays 2)
our p. is done (Theater 20)
our wooing doth not end like an old p. (Plays 6, Endings 6)
p. out the p. (Plays 5)
p. with your fancies (Ships 2)
the p. ... pleased not the million (Plays 3)
the p.'s the thing (Plays 4)
thought it good you hear a p. (Acting 27)
thus play I in one person (Identity 5)
your p. needs no excuse (Theater 15)
you would p. upon me (Character 2)
player:
a poor p. that struts (Life 7)
players:
harlotry p. (Acting 12)
p. well bestowed (Acting 7)
playing:
the purpose of p. (Acting 11)
plead:
p. what I will be (Deserving 4)
pleads:
p. he in earnest? (Sincerity 2)
pleasure:
I take p. in singing (Pleasure 6)
i' th'east my p. lies (Pleasure 3)
lives should stretch without some p. (Pleasure 1)
my lawful p. she restrained (Chastity 3)
p. and action (Action 14)
p. and revenge have ears (Argument 6)
the present p. by revolution lowering (Pleasure 2)
what other p. can the world afford? (Courtship 12)
pleasures:
so to your p. (Moods 5)
plodders:
small have continual p. ever won (Study 2)
plot:
first survey the p. (Building 1)
who cannot be crushed with a p. (Plots 1)

pluck:
  p. down my officers (Revolution 1)
  p. out the heart of my mystery (Character 1)
plummet:
  deeper than did ever p. sound (Renunciation 5)
pockets:
  familiar with men's p. (Theft 4)
poesy:
  the force of heaven-bred p. (Poetry 13)
poet:
  never durst p. touch a pen (Poetry 9)
  the lunatic, the lover and the p. (Imagination 5)
  the p.'s eye, in a fine frenzy (Poetry 10)
poetry:
  mincing p. (Poetry 7)
  the truest p. (Poetry 4)
poison:
  gold, worse p. to men's souls (Poison 3)
  I feed myself with most delicious p. (Food 1)
  in p. there is physic (Sickness 9)
  they love not p. who do p. need (Poison 2)
pole:
  the soldier's p. is fallen (Epitaphs 1)
policy:
  fears not p. that heretic (Constancy 13)
  for p. sits above conscience (Politics 23)
  plague of your p. (Politics 9)
  turn him to any cause of p. (Politics 6)
politic:
  not p. ... to preserve virginity (Virginity 2)
politician:
  like a scurvy p. (Politics 16)
pomp:
  p. and circumstance (War 19)
  why what is p., rule, reign? (Dying 9)
pond:
  mantle like a standing p. (Self-Importance 1)
poniards:
  she speaks p. (Speech 14)
Pontic:
  like to the P. sea (Revenge 7)
poop:
  p. was beaten gold (Ships 2)
poor:
  I am a p. fellow (Poverty 4)
  if thou art rich thou art p. (Mortality 8)
  p. and content is rich (Aphorisms 11)
  p. soul, the center of my sinful earth (Eternity 3)
  thanks, the exchequer of the p. (Thanks 4)
  the p. ... cry out for thee (Opportunity 4)
  when that the p. have cried (Ambition 10)
  why should the p. be flattered (Flattery 1)
poppy:
  not p. nor mandragora (Sleep 14)
pork-eaters:
  if we all grow to be p. (Food 8)
porpentine:
  like quills upon the fretful p. (Horror 1)
porridge:
  receives comfort like cold p. (Comfort 6)

possessing:
  Farewell, thou art too dear for my p. (Farewells 21)
possible:
  is it p. that love (Love 84)
posts:
  get p. and letters (Diplomacy 1, Letters 2)
posy:
  p. of a ring (Love 31)
potations:
  to forswear thin p. (Drinking 12)
potent:
  most p. grave and reverend signiors (Greetings 9)
potion:
  with no rash p. (Poison 4)
pound:
  p. of flesh (Cruelty 6)
pourquoi:
  what is p.? Do or not do? (Language 9)
poverty:
  disease of all-shunned p. (Poverty 3)
  my p., but not my will, consents (Poverty 2)
power:
  a p. I have, but of what strength (Power 8)
  disjoins remorse from p. (Greatness 4)
  had I p. (Chaos 3)
  p. into will, will into appetite (Anarchy 2)
  p. that I have on you is to spare you (Forgiveness 2)
  see if p. change purpose (Power 9)
  some heavenly p. guide us (Travel 21)
  there is no p. in ... man to alter me (Determination 3)
  they that have p. to hurt (Power 13)
  when p. to flattery bows (Duty 4)
powers:
  if powers divine behold (Innocence 8)
  merciful p. restrain in me (Thought 11)
pox:
  a p. of this gout (Sickness 10)
practice:
  a p. as full of labor (Fools 15)
praise:
  I will p. any man (Praise 2)
  painted flourish of your p. (Beauty 12)
  p. us as we are tasted (Praise 12)
  she will outstrip all p. (Praise 9)
  take thy p. with thee to heaven (Epitaphs 6)
  the worthiness of p. (Praise 10)
  your p. is come too swiftly (Praise 5)
praises:
  our p. are our wages (Praise 13)
prattle:
  mere p. without practice (Soldiers 19)
pray:
  I'll p. for thee (Prayer 19)
  p. you bid these unknown friends w. (Welcome 3)
  p. you now, forget and forgive (Reconciliation 3)
  watch tonight, p. tomorrow (Fellowship 1)
  we do p. for mercy (Mercy 12)
prayer:
  amen to that fair p. say I (Prayer 14)
  turned my feignèd p. on my head (Punishment 3)

unless I be relieved by p. (Prayer 16)

prayers:

fall to thy p. (Age 17)

find we profit by losing of our p. (Prayer 1)

he has my heart yet and shall have my p. (Devotion 1)

my wind were but long enough to say my p. (Repentance 6)

when thou hast leisure, say thy p. (Leisure 1)

presence:

what p. must not know (Letters 3)

your p. is too bold (Authority 5)

presume:

do not p. too much (Quarrels 8)

p. not that I am the thing I was (Reformation 4)

presumption:

most it is p. in us (Arrogance 1)

prick:

if you p. us (Revenge 4)

pricked:

will you be p. in number? (Friendship 14)

pricking:

by the p. of my thumbs (Evil 9)

price:

make what p. they will (Business 8)

pride:

p. is his own glass (Pride 4)

p. must have a fall (Pride 2)

p. that quarrels at self-breath (Arrogance 2)

primrose:

p. path of dalliance (Advice 4)

p. way to the everlasting bonfire (Hell 2)

primroses:

pale p., that die unmarried (Flowers 13)

prince:

p., thou art sad (Marriage 38)

the p. of darkness (Devil 5)

princes:

for p. are the glass, the school (Royalty 33)

princess:

p. descended from ... royal kings (Royalty 4)

principle:

the first humane p. I should teach (Drinking 12)

printing:

caused p. to be used (Books 1)

prison:

come, let's away to p. (Reconciliation 4)

prison-house:

tell the secrets of my p. (Horror 1, Purgatory 1)

privilege:

impatience hath his p. (Anger 3)

profit:

find we p. by losing of our prayers (Prayer 1)

no p. grows where is no pleasure (Study 4)

progeny:

this same p. of evils (Quarrels 11)

prologue:

is this a p. (Love 31)

promise:

p. me life and I'll confess (Truth 6)

smallest particle of any p. (Promises 4)

promised:

he p. to meet me (Promises 6)

promising:

p. is the very air o'the time (Promises 8)

promontory:

like one that stands upon a p. (Aspiration)

promotion:

none will sweat but for p. (Fashion 1)

prompter:

I should have known it without a p. (Fighting 4)

proof:

give me the ocular p. (Proof 1)

the true p. of men (Chance 2)

we'll leave a p. (Marriage 27)

property:

sweet love, changing his p. (Mutability 2)

prophesy:

over thy wounds now do I p. (Prophecy 5)

prophesying:

p. with accents terrible (Prophecy 7)

prophetic:

O my p. soul! (Prophecy 2)

proportion:

a like p. of lineaments (Friendship 19)

prosperity:

Death ... thou hate and terror to p. (Death-Wish 5)

p. begins to mellow (Decline 2)

p.'s the very bond of love (Affliction 13)

protestation:

I have no cunning in p. (Oaths 3)

proud:

he that is p. eats up himself (Pride 4)

I do hate a p. man (Pride 5)

small things make base men p. (Pride 1)

you are too p. (Pride 6)

prove:

p. that ever I lose more blood (Love 60)

so p. it that the probation bear (Proof 2)

provender:

a peck of p. (Eating 9)

proverb:

fast find, fast bind, a p. never stale (Thrift 3)

lay the old p. to your charge (Proverbs 31)

the country p. known (Proverbs 21)

the old p. ... you have the grace (Proverbs 19)

proverbs:

they ... sighed forth p. (Hunger 1)

providence:

special p. in the fall (Providence 3)

prune:

no more faith in thee than in a stewed p. (Trust 2)

psalmist:

death, as the p. saith (Death 13)

publican:

how like a fawning p. he looks (Humility 4)

Puck:

those that hobgoblin call you and sweet P. (Fairies 4)

pudding:

ox with the p. in his belly (Fatness 4)

r. and love keep little company (Reason 6)
r. and respect make livers pale (Reason 7)
r. not the need (Necessity 4)
respect and r. wait on wrinkled age (Old Age 14)
r. ... whose common theme is death (Faults 5)
that noble and most sovereign r. (Dejection 4)
we have r. to cool our raging motions (Lust 11)
with my nobler r. 'gainst my fury (Forgiveness 5)
your r.? I have no other but a woman's r. (Women 28)

reasons:
his r. are as two grains of wheat (Reason 5)
r. you allege (Argument 6)
your r. at dinner (Argument 3)

rebellion:
r. lay in his way (Rebellion 1)
to face the garment of r. (Rebellion 2)

receipt:
we have the r. of fern-seed (Magic 1)

reckoning:
a trim r. (Honor 4)
I am ill at r. (Arithmetic 1)

recompense:
my r. is thanks (Thanks 3)

recreation:
sweet r. barred (Melancholy 5)

redemption:
condemned into everlasting r. (Solecisms 6)
nothing kin to foul r. (Mercy 6)

reeling:
Trinculo is r. ripe (Drinking 25)

reflection:
the eye sees not itself but by r. (Eyes 7)
you cannot see yourself but by r. (Self-Knowledge 5)

reformation:
my r. glittering o'er my fault (Reformation 1)

rehearsal:
convenient place for our r. (Theater 12)

rehearse:
r. most obscenely (Acting 22)

rein:
what r. can hold licentious wickedness? (Evil 2)

relics:
sanctify his r. (Infatuation 2)
shall we go see the r. of this town ? (Travel 23)

relief:
for this r., much thanks (Foreboding 2)

religion:
in r. what damnèd error (Religion 4)
it is r. that doth make vows kept (Religion 2)

religions:
knit and break r. (Gold 6)

relish:
imaginary r. is so sweet (Anticipation 4)

remedies:
apply to her some r. (Medicine 12)
our r. oft in ourselves do lie (Self-Reliance 1)

remedy:
no r. against this consumption (Money 4)
things without all r. (Aphorisms 4, Regret 2)

remember:
I well r. the favors (Betrayal 2)
r. I have done thee worthy service (Service 6)
r. March, the Ides of March r. (Justice 4)
r. that you call on me today (Remembrance 6)
r. thee! Ay, thou poor ghost (Memory 2)

remembrance:
as the r. of an idle gaud (Remembrance 7)
I summon up r. of things past (Remembrance 9)
praising makes the r. dear (Remembrance 1)
rosemary, that's for r. (Flowers 2)
rue ... in the r. of a weeping queen (Gardens 9)
writ in r. more than things long past (Endings 4)

remembrances:
let us nor burden our r. (Remembrance 8)

remorse:
greatness ... disjoins r. from power (Greatness 4)
stop up th' access ... to r. (Ruthlessness 3)

remuneration:
now I will look to his r. (Payment 1)

rendezvous:
a r., a home to fly unto (Investment 1)

renown:
r. and grace is dead (Mourning 18)

rents:
what are thy r.? (Ceremony 2)

repent:
I'll r., and that suddenly (Repentance 2)

repentance:
try what r. can (Repentance 1)

repents:
woe, that too late r. (Repentance 4)

report:
r. of fashions in proud Italy (Fashion 9)

repose:
our foster-nurse of nature is r. (Sleep 8)
r. you here in rest (Epitaphs 16)

reproof:
in the r. of chance (Chance 2)

reputation:
I have offended r. (Reputation 1)
I see my r. is at stake (Reputation 15)
r., r., r.! O I have lost my r. (Reputation 6)
r. is an idle ... imposition (Reputation 7)
seeking the bubble r. (Soldiers 1)
spotless r. (Reputation 11)

resist:
it boots not to r. both wind and tide (Resistance 2)

resolutes:
a list of lawless r. (Soldiers 3)

resolution:
breaking his oath and r. (Promises 3)
fix most firm thy r. (Resolution 6)
native hue of r. (Conscience 2)
r. thus fubbed with ... the law (Law 2)
the dauntless spirit of r. (Resolution 4)

respect:
is there no r. of place ... in you ? (Disorder 5)
men so noble ... should find r. (Downfall 3)

respect (cont'd.)

reason and r. make livers pale (Reason 7)

r. and reason wait on wrinkled age (Old Age 14)

that title of r. (Respect 1)

throw away r. (Humanity 6)

too much r. upon the world (Anxiety 7)

use him with all r. (Burial 4)

rest:

the r. is silence (Last Words 1)

nor night, nor day, no r. (Sleeplessness 8)

set up my everlasting r. (Death-Wish 10)

thy best of r. is sleep (Sleep 12)

retire:

r. me to my Milan (Mortality 10)

retirement:

a comfort of r. (Investment 1)

return:

at your r. visit our house (Friendship 10)

r. to her? (Homelessness 1)

returning:

r. were as tedious as go o'er (Crime 2)

revels:

Antony that r. long a-nights (Revels 1)

I delight in masques and r. (Revels 5)

our r. now are ended (Acting 28)

r., dances, masques (Revels 2)

see our moonlight r. (Dancing 1)

revenge:

a capable and wide r. (Revenge 7)

Caesar's spirit, ranging for r. (War 16)

I ... may sweep to my r. (Revenge 1)

it will feed my r. (Revenge 3)

kindness, nobler than r. (Kindness 1)

pleasure and r. (Argument 6)

r. his foul and most unnatural murder (Murder 1)

spur my dull r. (Revenge 2)

sweet as my r. (Kissing 3)

sweet r. grows harsh (Murder 9)

to r. is no valor (Revenge 8)

what should his sufferance be? ... Why, r. (Revenge 4)

revenged:

I'll be r. on the whole pack (Revenge 9)

reverend:

as you are old and r. (Age 23)

reversion:

remains a sweet r. (Investment 1)

revolution:

pleasure by r. lowering (Pleasure 2)

see the r. of the times (Fate 3)

rhubarb:

what r., senna (Medicine 11)

rhyme:

I cannot show it in r. (Poetry 11)

I'll r. you so eight years (Poetry 2)

neither r. nor reason (Proverbs 1)

outlive this powerful r. (Poetry 15)

Rialto:

in the R. you have rated me (Money 9)

ribbons:

r. of all the colors (Clothing 14)

rich:

art r.? (Mediocrity 1)

if thou art r. thou art poor (Mortality 8)

poorly rich ... pineth still for more (Avarice 2)

r. she shall be (Men and Women 4)

riches:

honor, r., marriage-blessing (Blessings 5)

show r. ready to drop upon me (Dreams 15)

since r. point to misery (Misery 4)

r. strewed herself in the streets (Cities 2)

ride:

come, wilt thou see me r.? (Parting 7)

rigol:

from this golden r. hath divorced (Death 15)

ring:

keeping safe Nerissa's r. (Sex 4)

look how my r. encompasseth thy finger (Courtship 17)

r. parts from this finger (Constancy 3)

rings:

we will have r. and things (Marriage 46)

riot:

his rash fierce blaze of r. (Transience 3)

ripeness:

r. is all (Endurance 3)

rising:

from the r. of the lark (Time of Day 6)

rite:

observe the r. of May (Festivals 5)

river:

there is a r. in Macedon (Rivers 1)

roarers:

what cares these r. for the name (Sea 4)

rob:

r. me the exchequer (Theft 2)

robbed:

he that is r. (Theft 10)

the r. that smiles (Philosophy 17, Theft 9)

robbers:

what makes r. bold? (Law 5)

robbery:

thieves for their r. have authority (Theft 6)

robe:

giant's r. upon a ... thief (Clothing 7)

give me my r. (Death-Wish 3, Royalty 3)

like a r. pontifical (Greatness 4)

this r. of mine does change my disposition (Clothing 13)

robes:

r. and furred gowns hide all (Justice 7)

Robin:

sprite called R. Goodfellow (Fairies 3)

Robin Hood:

old R.H. of England (Country Life 1)

rock:

I stand as one upon a r. (Isolation 1)

rods:
   whipped and scourged with r. (Politics 3)
rogue:
   satirical r. (Age 6)
roguery:
   nothing but r. (Man 8)
rogues:
   you dissentious r. (People 4)
Roman:
   a R. thought hath struck him (Duty 1)
   like a R. bear the truth (Stoicism 2)
   more an antique R. than a Dane (Suicide 14)
   R. actors (Acting 15)
   the noblest R. of them all (Nobility 6)
Romans:
   the last of all the R., fare thee well (Epitaphs 11)
Rome:
   be to R. as is the osprey to the fish (Authority 4)
   high and palmy state of R. (Apparitions 3)
   let R. in Tiber melt (Empire 1)
   shake your R. about your ears (Authority 2)
   that ever Brutus will go bound to R. (Greatness 7)
Romeo:
   wherefore art thou R.? (Names 7)
roofs:
   singing masons building r. of gold (Building 2)
Rosalind:
   R. is your love's name (Names 1)
rose:
   a r. by any other name (Names 8)
   beauty's r. might never die (Beauty 30)
   earthlier happy is the r. distilled (Marriage 28)
   he wears the r. of youth (Youth 4)
   this thorn doth to our r. of youth (Youth 1)
   when I have plucked the r. (Murder 8)
   when you have our r. (Lust 1)
rosemary:
   there's r. and rue (Flowers 9)
   there's r., that's for remembrance (Flowers 2)
roses:
   as clear as morning r. (Courtship 20)
   r. have thorns (Wrongdoing 8)
   women are as r. (Women 27)
rot:
   a man may r. even here (Endurance 3)
rotten:
   something is r. in the state of Denmark (Corruption 2)
round:
   dance in our r. (Dancing 1)
royal:
   this r. throne of kings (Countries 5)
royally:
   likely ... to have proved most r. (Royalty 7)
royalty:
   mingled his r. with cap'ring fools (Royalty 8)
rub:
   there's the r. (Death 7)

rude:
   r. am I in my speech (Speech 18)
rudeness:
   this r. is a sauce (Plain-Speaking 4)
rue:
   I'll set a bank of r. (Gardens 9)
   there's rosemary and r. (Flowers 9)
ruin:
   r. hath taught me (Mutability 4)
ruins:
   thou art the r. of the noblest man (Epitaphs 9)
rumble:
   r. thy bellyful (Storms 9)
rumor:
   Enter R., painted full of tongues (Rumor 2)
   from r's tongues they bring (Rumor 4)
   hold r. from what we fear (Confusion 6)
   I heard a bustling r. (Rumor 6)
   let every feeble r. shake (Rumor 1)
   r. doth double, like the voice (Rumor 5)
   r. is a pipe, blown by surmises (Rumor 3)
run:
   now bid me r. (Fitness 1)
   r., r., Orlando (Infatuation 5)
   r. to your houses (Ingratitude 3)
runs:
   r. not this speech like iron (Speechmaking 4)
russet:
   morn in r. mantle clad (Dawn 1)
   r. yeas and honest kersey nos (Plain-Speaking 8)
Russia:
   last out a night in R. (Tediousness 3)
sack:
   addict themselves to s. (Drinking 12)
   brew me a pottle of s. (Drinking 19)
   this intolerable deal of s. (Drinking 7)
   you love s. and so do I (Drinking 18)
sacrificers:
   let us be s., but not butchers (Sacrifice 1)
sacrifices:
   they come like s. (War 2)
   upon such s., my Cordelia (Sacrifice 2)
sad:
   experience to make me s. (Moods 4)
   he was nor s. nor merry (Moods 1)
   if you find him s. (Capriciousness 1)
   I know not why I am so s. (Moods 10)
   I must be s. when I have cause (Misanthropy 4)
   let us say you are s. (Moods 11)
   'tis good to be s. (Moods 3)
safer:
   'tis s. to avoid what's grown (Safety 2)
safety:
   give all ... for a pot of ale and s. (Safety 1)
   we pluck this flower, s. (Danger 1)
sails:
   behold the threaden s. (Ships 2)
   laughed to see the s. conceive (Pregnancy 2)

saint:

  seem a s. when ... I play the devil (Hypocrisy 14)

  this mortal-breathing s. (Fame 3)

  to catch a s. with saints doth bait (Temptation 4)

  tomorrow is S. Valentine's day (Festivals 2)

salad:

  my s. days, when I was green (Youth 3)

salvation:

  pity but they should suffer s. (Solecisms 4)

samphire:

  hangs one that gathers s. (Vertigo 1)

sanctuary:

  shall we desire to raze the s.? (Building 3)

sand:

  as men wrecked upon a s. (Danger 4)

sands:

  numbering s. and drinking oceans (Futility 1)

  the s. are numbered (Dying 8)

Satan:

  I charge thee, S. (Exorcism 1)

Saturn:

  warmed old S. (Chastity 3)

satyr:

  Hyperion to a s. (Excellence 1)

saucy:

  s. fellow, hence! (Dismissal 1)

savior:

  our s.'s birth is celebrated (Festivals 1)

saws:

  full of wise s. (Maturity 1)

say:

  s., is my kingdom lost? (Loss 8)

saying:

  the ancient s. is no heresy (Proverbs 20)

  the old s. is "the third pays for all" (Proverbs 30)

scab:

  I thought there would a s. follow (Insults 16)

scaffold:

  this unworthy s. (Acting 13)

scandal:

  greatest s. waits on greatest state (Greatness 12)

scarecrow:

  make a s. of the law (Law 7)

scarf:

  beauteous s. veiling an Indian beauty (Deceit 8)

  s. up the tender eye of pitiful day (Evil 8)

scars:

  he jests at s. that never felt a wound (Jokes 4)

scene:

  allowing him ... a little s. (Death 35)

  a tedious brief s. (Theater 13)

  last s. of all (Age 5)

  our swift s. flies (Thought 5, Theater 7)

  this our lofty s. (Acting 16)

scepters:

  when s. are in children's hands (Civil War 2)

scholar:

  he was a s. (Learning 1)

  I have neither the s.'s melancholy (Melancholy 3)

more in the soldier than in the s. (Soldiers 21)

thou'rt a s. (Hedonism 2)

school:

  in erecting a grammar s. (Education 1)

  like a s. broke up (Home 1)

schoolboy:

  the whining s. (Boys 1)

school-days:

  in my s. when I had lost a shaft (Speculation 1)

sciatica:

  has the most profound s. (Sickness 15)

scion:

  we marry a gentler s. (Nature 8)

scope:

  the fated sky gives us free s. (Freedom 1)

scorched:

  we have s. the snake (Danger 13)

score:

  no other books but the s. (Books 1)

scorn:

  disdain and s. ride sparkling (Scorn 1)

  teach not thy lip such s. (Scorn 2)

  what a deal of s. looks beautiful (Contempt 4)

scorpions:

  full of s. ... is my mind (Affliction 7)

screech-owl:

  the s., screeching loud (Portents 8)

scripture:

  the devil can cite s. (Devil 8)

sea:

  all scattered in the bottom of the s. (Dreams 10)

  a wilderness of s. (Isolation 1)

  be patient. When the s. is (Sea 4)

  boundless as the s. (Love 80)

  drenched me in the s. (Danger 15)

  float upon a wild and violent s. (Confusion 6)

  give a thousand furlongs of s. (Sea 5)

  horns whelked ... like the enridgèd s. (Demons 1)

  wild s. of my conscience (Conscience 3)

  wish you a wave o' the s. (Dancing 4)

sea-change:

  suffer a s. (Transformation 3)

sea-monster:

  more hideous ... than the s. (Ingratitude 6)

seas:

  the multitudinous s. incarnadine (Guilt 5)

season:

  ever 'gainst that s. comes (Festivals 1)

  how many things by s. seasoned are (Seasons 12)

  like of each thing that in s. grows (Seasons 9)

  you lack the s. of all natures (Sleep 11)

seasons:

  feel we not ... the s.'s difference (Seasons 1)

  sorrow breaks s. (Sorrow 11)

  the s. alter (Seasons 13)

  the s. change their manners (Seasons 6)

seat:

  castle hath a pleasant s. (Castles 1)

secrecy:

  nature's infinite book of s. (Prophecy 1)

secrets:
 s. of my prison-house (Horror 1)
secure:
 s. from worldly chances and mishaps (Epitaphs 16)
security:
 s. gives way to conspiracy (Conspiracy 6)
 you all know s. (Security 1)
see:
 s. how the giddy multitude (People 15)
 s. where she comes (Beauty 19)
 when shall we s. again? (Parting 3)
seeks:
 who s. and will not take (Opportunity 1)
seeling:
 come, s. night (Evil 8)
seeming:
 bear your body more s. (Body 2)
 these keep s. and savor (Flowers 9)
seems:
 why s. it so particular? (Appearance 1)
self:
 to thine own s. be true (Advice 7)
self-endeared:
 she is so s. (Self-Love 2)
self-love:
 O, you are sick of s. (Self-Love 3)
 s. ... is not so vile a sin (Self-Love 1)
 she cannot love (Self-love 2)
 sin of s. (Self-love 4)
self-slaughter:
 against s. there is a prohibition (Suicide 10)
sell:
 buy with you, s. with you (Business 7)
 s. when you can (Advice 3)
senators:
 bear my greeting to the s. (Greetings 3)
sense:
 s. of death is most in apprehension (Death 27)
 stings and motions of the s. (Asceticism 1)
 the s. aches at thee (Beauty 17)
 your s. pursues not mine (Misunderstanding 2)
sentence:
 a s. is but a cheveril glove (Wit 7)
sentinel:
 murder, alarumed by his s. (Murder 6)
sergeant:
 this fell s., Death (Death 9)
sermons:
 finds ... s. in stones (Country Life 2)
serpent:
 innocent flower ... be the s. under it (Deceit 4)
 O s. heart (Deceit 22)
 the s. that did sting thy father's life (Prophecy 2)
 think him as a s.'s egg (Danger 7)
 'tis a strange s. (Creatures 2)
 where's my s. of old Nile? (Snakes 1)
 wouldst thou have a s. sting thee? (Snakes 3)
servant:
 I had rather be their s. in my way (Service 3)

served:
 had I but s. my God (Service 5)
service:
 did my heart fly to your s. (Service 7)
 I have done thee worthy s. (Service 6)
 I have lost my teeth in your s. (Service 1)
 the constant s. of the antique world (Service 2)
 the poorest s. is repaid with thanks (Thanks 5)
 to make the s. greater than the god (Idolatry 1)
services:
 to thee a woman's s. are due (Desire 8)
sessions:
 the s. of sweet silent thought (Remembrance 9)
sex:
 ah, poor our s. (Inconstancy 6)
shade:
 seek out some desolate s. (Sorrow 4)
shadow:
 a dream itself is but a s. (Dreams 4)
 Lear's s. (Identity 4)
 swift as a s. (Transience 2)
shadows:
 he takes false s. for true (Perception 2)
 if we s. have offended (Theater 16)
 some there be that s. kiss (Judgment 3)
 the best in this kind are but s. (Acting 25)
shaft:
 make from the s. (Danger 11)
 when I had lost one s. (Speculation 1)
shake:
 s. off this downy sleep (Death 23)
shall:
 his absolute "shall" (Authority 2)
 s. I compare thee (Beauty 31)
shame:
 a waste of s. (Lust 14)
shape:
 deceit should steal such gentle s. (Deceit 16)
 devil hath power t'assume a pleasing s. (Devil 2)
 thou com'st in such a questionable s. (Ghosts 7)
 though they are of monstrous s. (Monsters 1)
sharked:
 s. up a list (Soldiers 3)
she:
 is s. worth keeping? (Value 6)
 s. is a theme of honor (War 22)
 s. is of so free ... a disposition (Virtue 18)
 s. knows the heat (Lust 9)
 s.'s gone for ever (Death 20)
 s. speaks! O, speak again (Adoration 1)
 s. thanked me (Courtship 16)
 s. that was ever fair (Women 23)
 that s. was never yet (Desire 15)
 the chaste, the inexpressive s. (Infatuation 5)
sheep-shearing:
 to buy for our s. feast (Feasts 4)
shepherd:
 alas, poor s., searching of thy wound (Love 11)
 dead s. (Love 21)
 good s., tell this youth (Love 27)

sherris:
second property of your excellent s. (Drinking 10)
this valor comes of s. (Drinking 11)
sherris-sack:
a good s. hath a twofold operation (Drinking 9)
ships:
s. are but boards (Ships 4)
shirt:
I have no s. (Clothing 6)
not a s. ... in all my company (Clothing 5)
shirts:
rammed me in with foul s. (Clothing 8)
shore:
the varying s. o' the world (Darkness 1)
show:
fool multitude that choose by s. (Desire 13)
mock the time with fairest s. (Deceit 5)
s. his eyes and grieve his heart (Eyes 10)
who makes the fairest s. (Deceit 15)
shows:
so may the outward s. be least themselves (Deceit 6)
sick:
has he the leisure to be s.? (Sickness 5)
I am not very s. (Sickness 2)
if he be s. with joy (Joy 2)
O, my heart is s. (Sickness 12)
that would have made me s., being s. (Sickness 9)
they are as s. that surfeit (Moderation 2)
'tis bitter cold and I am s. at heart (Foreboding 2)
sickens:
the more one s. (Sickness 1)
sickness:
my long s. ... now begins to mend (Dying 16)
this s. doth infect (Sickness 6)
siege:
stay the s. of loving terms (Courtship 19)
sigh:
he raised a s. so piteous (Melancholy 6)
s. no more, ladies (Inconstancy 4)
sight:
at the first s. they have changed eyes (Eyes 15)
how oft the s. of means to do ill (Wrongdoing 3)
the s. of lovers (Love 18)
this is a sorry s. (Eyes 9)
signior:
s. Antonio, many a time (Money 9)
signiors:
most potent, grave and reverend s. (Greetings 9)
silence:
be checked for s. (Advice 2)
I like your s. (Silence 8)
my gracious s., hail! (Silence 2, Women 10)
s. is the perfectest herald of joy (Joy 3)
s. often of pure innocence persuades (Innocence 7)
the rest is s. (Silence 4, Last Words 1)
silent:
holds her by the hand, s. (Silence 3)
silk:
like a twist of rotten s. (Promises 6)
rustling in unpaid for s. (Country Life 9)

Silvia:
who is S.? (Beauty 26)
simplicity:
such is the s. of man (Lust 7)
tongue-tied s. (Speechmaking 3)
true as truth's s. (Constancy 7)
simpleness:
when s. and duty tender it (Simplicity 2)
simply:
s. the thing I am (Self-Reliance 2)
sin:
ambition ... by that s. fell the angels (Ambition 5)
as s.'s true nature is (Guilt 4)
if to be old and merry be a s. (Age 9)
is it s. to rush (Suicide 6)
one s. ... another doth provoke (Sin 7)
penance your invention can lay upon my s. (Sin 5)
plate s. with gold (Gold 4, Justice 7)
show of truth can cunning s. cover itself (Deceit 9)
s. that amends (Virtue 22)
s. will pluck on s. (Murder 12)
some rise by s. (Injustice 1)
teach s. the carriage of a holy saint (Deceit 1)
sincerity:
talked with in s. (Sincerity 1)
sinner:
too weak to be a s. (Drinking 26)
sinners:
we are s. all (Sin 2)
sinning:
a man more sinned against than s. (Sin 4)
sins:
few love to hear the s. (Sin 6)
some s. do bear the privilege (Sin 3)
sir:
s., spare your threats (Death-Wish 11)
s., you and I must part (Parting 1)
that s. which serves and seeks for gain (Self-Interest 3)
siren:
sing, s., for thyself (Courtship 4)
sit:
s. and see, minding true things (Theater 8)
s. we close about this taper (Councils 2)
sits:
he s. high in all the people's hearts (Nobility 5)
skies:
the s. look grimly (Weather 6)
skin:
whiter s. than snow (Beauty 18)
sky:
freeze, thou bitter s. (Seasons 2)
men judge by the complexion of the s. (Weather 5)
so foul a s. clears not (Storms 5)
the fated s. gives us free scope (Freedom 1)
the s. ... would pour down stinking pitch (Storms 14)
slain:
I am s. by a fair cruel maid (Death 40)
slander:
if thou dost s. her (Slander 6)

rude am I in my s. (Speech 18)
runs not this s. like iron (Speechmaking 4)
speak the s. (Acting 9)
the power of s. to stir men's blood (Speech 8)
translate yourself out of the s. of peace (Speech 5)
where did you study ... this goodly s.? (Speechmaking 5)

sphere:
O sun, burn the great s. (Darkness 1)

spider:
bottled s. whose deadly web (Danger 14, Insults 18)
I have drunk and seen the s. (Poison 5)
in the cup a s. steeped (Poison 5)

spiders:
weaving s., come not here (Creatures 4)

spirit:
a rarer s. never did steer humanity (Faults 3)
as full of s. as the month of May (Seasons 4)
be thou a s. of health (Ghosts 7)
extravagant and erring s. (Ghosts 6)
I am fresh of s. (Resolution 3)
I am passing light in s. (Happiness 2)
I am thy father's s. (Ghosts 9)
if the ill s. have so fair a house (Goodness 4)
I have not that alacrity of s. (Dejection 4)
let not my worser s. tempt me (Prayer 13)
lord of such a s. (Praise 6)
my father's s. in arms! (Foreboding 5)
no s. dare walk abroad (Festivals 1)
O s. of love (Love 94)
rest, rest, perturbed s. (Ghosts 12)
retentive to the strength of s. (Constraint 1)
there's a great s. gone (Death 1)
the s. that I have seen may be the devil (Devil 2)
the worser s. a woman (Love 111)
th'expense of s. (Lust 14)
thou invisible s. of wine (Drinking 21)
thy s. walks abroad (Caesar 5)
thy s. within thee (Sleep 2)

spirits:
come, you s. (Cruelty 3)
devils ... tempt resembling s. of light (Devil 6)
draw my s. from me (Affliction 1)
entame my s. to your worship (Beauty 4)
I can call s. from the vasty deep (Supernatural 1)
now I want s. to enforce (Prayer 16)
s. are not finely touched (Greatness 8)
the s. o'the dead may walk again (Ghosts 15)
we are s. of another sort (Sunrise 2)

spoils:
sluttish s. of opportunity (Lechery 5)

spoke:
you never s. what did become you (Mistakes 4, Speech 23)

sport:
hark what good s. is out of town (Sport 3)
'tis the s. to have the enginer (Justice 1)
to s. would be as tedious as to work (Holidays 1)
what s. shall we devise (Sport 1)

sporting-place:
each hurries towards his home and s. (Home 1)

sports:
he is given to s. (Society 3)
there be some s. are painful (Sport 2)

spot:
out damned s. (Guilt 7)
black and grainèd s. (Guilt 3)

spring:
from that s. ... discomfort swells (Confusion 3)
in an early s. (Seasons 5)
in s. time, the only pretty ring time (Seasons 3)
now 'tis the s. (Gardens 3)
she comes, apparelled like the s. (Beauty 19)
s. come to you at the farthest (Blessings 6)
the s., the summer, the ... autumn (Seasons 14)

springe:
a woodcock to mine own s. (Justice 2)

sprite:
every one lets forth his s. (Ghosts 14)
you are that shrewd and knavish s. (Fairies 3)

spur:
I have no s. (Ambition 12)

staff:
a s. is quickly found to beat a dog (Proverbs 7)
give me a s. of honor (Old Age 12)
I'll break my s. (Renunciation 5)

stage:
a kingdom for a s. (Theater 5)
all the world's a s. (Theater 3)
a s. where every man (Acting 17)
frets his hour upon the s. (Life 7)
if this were played upon a s. (Theater 19)
this huge s. presenteth (Mutability 3)
two hours' traffic of our s. (Theater 18)

stake:
we are at the s. (Danger 9)

stale:
drink the s. of horses (Endurance 1)

stalk:
with martial s. hath he gone by (Ghosts 2)

stand:
s. not upon the order (Parting 11)

star:
a s. danced (Merriment 4)
constant as the northern s. (Constancy 1)
love a bright particular s. (Infatuation 1)
most auspicious s. (Astrology 4)
she would infect to the north s. (Speech 15)

stars:
cut him out in little s. (Night 21)
s., hide your fires (Desire 9)
the fault, dear Brutus, is not in our s. (Faults 6)
the s., the s. above us (Astrology 3)
two s. keep not their motion (Rivalry 1)
you chaste s. (Cause 5)

starveling:
you s., you eel-skin (Insults 6)

state:
beweep my outcast s. (Misery 5)

state (cont'd.)

    greatest scandal waits on greatest s. (Greatness 12)

    I am unfit for s. (Hypocrisy 16)

    my s. ... showed like a feast (Greatness 4)

    mystery in the soul of s. (Government 6)

state-statues:

    sit s. only (Action 10)

stature:

    what s. is she of? (Height 1)

staying:

    when you sued s. (Eternity 1)

steal:

    they will s. anything (Theft 3)

    to England will I s., and there I'll s. (Theft 5)

steeds:

    you fiery-footed s. (Anticipation 3)

stench:

    death ... thou odoriferous s. (Death-Wish 7)

sticking-place:

    screw your courage to the s. (Courage 6)

still:

    s. as the grave (Proverbs 23)

    s. it cried "sleep no more" (Sleeplessness 5)

sting:

    sensual as the brutish s. (Lust 5)

    slander, whose s. is sharper (Slander 9)

stirrers:

    bad neighbor makes us early s. (Business 5)

stomach:

    my s. is not constant (Drinking 24)

stone:

    heart is turned to s. (Affliction 8)

stones:

    you are men of s. (Mourning 17)

stories:

    sad s. chancèd in the times of old (Stories 9)

    tell sad s. of the death of kings (Stories 5)

storm:

    another s. brewing (Storms 15)

    every cloud engenders not a s. (Truisms 3)

    shroud till the dregs of the s. be past (Storms 16)

    so foul a sky clears not without a s. (Storms 5)

    the pelting of this pitiless s. (Homelessness 2)

    the s. is up, and all is on the hazard (Storms 4)

story:

    draw thy breath in pain to tell my s. (Stories 1)

    my s. being done (Pity 7)

    never was a s. of more woe (Sorrow 15)

    our bending author hath pursued the s. (Theater 9)

    tell my s. and that would woo her (Courtship 16)

    the subject of my s. (Honor 13)

strain:

    that s. again (Music 26)

strange:

    this is wondrous s. (Philosophy 5)

strangers:

    desire we may be better s. (Parting 2)

straw:

    to find quarrel in a s. (Greatness 1)

strawberry:

    the s. grows underneath the nettle (Gardens 2)

straws:

    a mighty fire begin it with weak s. (Fire 2)

stray:

    now no way can I s. (Exile 5)

stream:

    which way the s. of time doth run (Time 14)

strength:

    excellent to have a giant's s. (Strength 2)

    love give me s. (Strength 3)

    rib of steel to make s. stronger (Strength 1)

strike:

    s. a meaner than myself (Assault 1)

    s. now (Action 7)

string:

    harp not on that s. (Repetition 1)

striving:

    s. to better oft we mar (Proverbs 13)

stroke:

    the s. of death is as a lover's pinch (Dying 3)

strokes:

    many s. ... fells the...oak (Perseverance 1)

strong:

    you are as s. (Praise 11)

stubbornness:

    his s., his checks, ... have grace (Devotion 5)

student:

    lean enough to be thought a good s. (Thinness 4)

studied:

    one that had been s. in his death (Dying 13)

study:

    s. evermore is overshot (Study 3)

    s. is like the heaven's glorious sun (Study 2)

    s. what you most affect (Study 4)

    what is the end of s.? (Study 1)

stuff:

    this is the silliest s. (Nonsense 1)

    we are such s. as dreams are made on (Mortality 9)

stuffed:

    I am s., cousin (Sex 6)

stumble:

    they s. that run fast (Haste 2)

subjects:

    I am all the s. that you have (Servitude 3)

substance:

    the very s. of the ambitious (Dreams 4)

substitute:

    s. shines brightly as a king (Comparisons 2)

suburbs:

    dwell I but in the s. (Marriage 21)

succession:

    slander lives upon s. (Slander 1)

sudden:

    he's s. (Action 8)

sufferance:

    in corporal s. finds a pang (Death 27)

    s. is the badge of all our tribe (Money 9)

suffered:

    I have s. with those that I saw s. (Suffering 4)

suffers:
who alone s. (Misery 1)
sugar:
why strew'st thou s. on that...spider (Danger 14)
suggestion:
they'll take s. as a cat laps milk (Politics 22)
why do I yield to that s. (Temptation 1)
suitor:
I am a humble s. (Law 10)
suits:
customary s. of solemn black (Mourning 8)
sulphur:
burn like the mines of s. (Jealousy 10)
roast me in s. (Hell 6)
summer:
after s. evermore succeeds (Seasons 8)
as a fair day in s. (Beauty 20)
as clear as is the s.'s sun (Seasons 7)
a s. bird (Birds 3)
costly s. (Anticipation 2)
fantastic s.'s heat (Imagination 6)
shall I compare thee to a s.'s day? (Beauty 31)
s.'s lease hath too short a date (Beauty 31)
s.'s ripening breath (Love 79)
the spring, the s., the childing autumn (Seasons 14)
this guest of s. (Birds 6)
thy eternal s. shall not fade (Eternity 3)
summons:
a guilty thing upon a fearful s. (Ghosts 5)
a heavy s. lies like lead (Sleep 9)
ere to black Hecate's s. (Evil 7)
sun:
all so soon as the all-cheering s. (Sunrise 4)
all the world is cheered by the s. (Sunrise 3)
hath Britain all the s.? (Countries 1)
I am too much i'the s. (Grief 5)
I 'gin to be aweary of the s. (Despair 3)
Juliet is the s. (Sunrise 5)
men shut their doors against a setting s. (Downfall 4)
now is the s. upon the highmost hill (Time 27)
O s., burn the great sphere (Darkness 1)
O, 'tis the s. that maketh all things shine (Beauty 13)
the all-seeing s. (Infatuation 9)
the blushing, discontented s. (Royalty 30)
the setting s. and music at the close (Endings 4)
the s. ariseth in his majesty (Sunrise 7)
the s. begins to gild the western sky (Sunset 3)
the s. of Rome is set (Transience 1)
the s. that warms you here (Exile 3)
the s. was not more true (Constancy 4)
the weary s. hath made a golden set (Sunset 2)
when the s. shines (Insects 1)
who ... loves to live i' the s. (Country Life 4)
who saw the s. today? (Foreboding 13)
sunburning:
face is not worth s. (Courtship 10)
sunburnt:
I am s. (Celibacy 3)
sunshine:
you have seen s. and rain (Tears 12)

superfluity:
one for s. and another for use (Proverbs 4)
s. comes sooner by white hairs (Moderation 3)
superflux:
shake the s. to them, (Justice 5)
superstitious:
he is s. grown of late (Superstition 1)
superstitiously:
s. I will be squared by this (Dreams 16)
sure:
s. He that made us (Reason 2)
surer:
you are no s. (People 6)
surety:
the wound of peace is s. (Security 2)
surfeit:
a s. of the sweetest things (Food 10)
surge:
the murmuring s. (Sea 2)
surgeon:
I am ... a s. to old shoes (Work 1)
surges:
I saw him beat the s. (Swimming 1)
suspicion:
s. all our lives shall be (Treason 2)
s. always haunts the guilty mind (Fear 6)
swain:
happy life to be ... a homely s. (Happiness 3)
swallow:
daffodils that come before the s. dares (Flowers 12)
hope ... flies with s.'s wings (Hope 4)
swan:
in a great pool a s.'s nest (Countries 2)
play the s. and die in music (Dying 14)
the s. her downy cygnets save (Birds 5)
swashers:
I have observed these three s. (Men 5)
swashing:
a s. and a martial outside (Cowardice 1)
swear:
s. me, Kate, like a lady (Oaths 1)
sweep:
what a s. of vanity comes this way (Vanity 4)
sweet:
how s. the moonlight sleeps (Moon 1)
s. peace conduct his soul (Epitaphs 14)
sweetest:
s. nut hath sourest rind (Food 5)
sweetness:
began to loathe the taste of s. (Eating 3)
sweets:
s. to the sweet, farewell (Farewells 5)
the s. we wish for (Desire 20)
swift:
s. as a shadow (Transience 2)
swoop:
at one fell s. (Cruelty 4)
sword:
a killing tongue and quiet s. (Soldiers 11)
he who the s. of heaven (Justice 13, Virtue 15)

sword (cont'd.)

I draw the s. myself (Death-Wish 4)

slander, whose edge is sharper than the s. (Slander 2)

swords:

keep up your bright s. (Fighting 4)

sympathy:

would you desire better s.? (Drinking 18)

taffeta:

t. phrases, silken terms (Plain-Speaking 8)

taint:

t. not thy mind (Conscience 1)

taints:

his t. and honors waged equal (Faults 2)

take:

t., o, t. those lips away (Inconstancy 1)

t. the instant way (Reputation 14)

tale:

an honest t. speeds best (Plain-Speaking 11, Stories 8)

a plain t. shall put you down (Plain-Speaking 1)

a round unvarnished t. (Stories 3)

a sad t.'s best for winter (Stories 10)

a t. told by an idiot (Life 7)

I could a t. unfold (Purgatory 2)

tales:

aged ears play truant at his t. (Talking 5)

Madam, we'll tell t. (Stories 7)

relating t. of others' griefs (Misery 3)

tell thee t. of woeful ages (Stories 6)

talk:

if I chance to t. a little wild (Talking 4)

loves to hear himself t. (Talking 6)

my t. to thee must be (Love 63)

talkers:

t. are no good doers (Words and Deeds 3)

talks:

he t. well (Talking 2)

tall:

he is not very t. (Height 2)

tallow-catch:

obscene, greasy t. (Insults 4)

talon:

not an eagle's t. in the waist (Thinness 1)

tame:

be not too t. neither (Acting 8)

tangle:

she means to t. my eyes (Eyes 2)

taper:

how ill this t. burns (Apparitions 4)

sit we close about this t. (Councils 2)

the flame o'the t. bows toward her (Eyes 3)

tapster:

the spirit of a t. (Arithmetic 1)

task:

a heavier t. could not have been imposed (Grief 2)

the long day's t. is done (Death-Wish 1, Suicide 2)

the t. he undertakes is numbering sands (Futility 1)

taste:

things sweet to t. prove in digestion sour (Eating 11)

taught:

he must be t. and trained (Contempt 3, Education 3)

teach:

t. not thy lip such scorn (Scorn 2)

those that do t. young babes (Education 4)

we'll t. you to drink deep (Drinking 5)

teaching:

follow mine own t. (Advice 11)

tear:

a t. for pity (Charity 1)

fall not a t. (Tears 2)

here did she fall a t. (Gardens 9)

I did not think to shed a t. (Tears 7)

tears:

ask some t. (Acting 18)

come, leave your t. (People 12)

earth could teem with women's t. (Tears 14)

gave me up to t. (Tears 6)

her smiles and t. were like (Tears 12)

his t. run down his beard (Tears 15)

if you have t. (Tears 8)

t. harden lust (Tears 16)

the big round t. (Tears 3)

there is t. for his love (Caesar 3)

these hot t. that break from me (Tears 9)

thy due from me is t. (Mourning 12)

tedious:

he is as t. as a tired horse (Tediousness 1)

if I were as t. as a king (Tediousness 4)

life is as t. (Tediousness 2)

so t. is this day (Impatience 3)

'tis better, sir, than to be t. (Brevity 2)

tell:

t. me where is fancy bred (Love 50)

temper:

that dauntless t. of his mind (Valor 12)

temperance:

a gentleman of all t. (Moderation 1)

you cannot guess what t. should be (Temperance 1)

tempest:

if after every t. come such calms (Storms 11)

the southern wind ... foretells a t. (Storms 1)

this t. in my mind (Ingratitude 8)

when from thy shore the t. beat us (Storms 2)

temple:

nothing ill can dwell in such a t. (Goodness 4)

temporizer:

a hovering t. (Timeserving 1)

tempt:

devils soonest t. (Devil 6)

t. the frailty of our powers (Temptation 5)

temptation:

is that t. that doth goad us on? (Temptation 4)

tempted:

'tis one thing to be t. (Temptation 2)

tempter:

the t. or the tempted, who sins most (Temptation 3)

tenderly:

t. apply some remedies (Medicine 12)

terms:

buy t. divine (Eternity 4)

thanks:

evermore t., the exchequer of the poor (Thanks 4)
I greet thy love not with vain t. (Thanks 2)
my recompense is t. (Thanks 3)
no other answer make but t., and t. (Thanks 6)
the poorest service is repaid with t. (Thanks 5)

that:

t. thou art my son (Parents and Children 3)
t. we would do we should do (Delay 2)

theater:

as in a t. the eyes of men (Theater 17)
this wide and universal t. (Theater 2)

theme:

she is a t. of honor and renown (War 22)

there:

t. be some sports are painful (Sport 2)
t. is left us ourselves (Suicide 1)
t. is no creature loves me (Despair 7)
t. is nothing but roguery (Man 5)
t. is nothing either good or bad (Philosophy 6)
t. is not one among them (Absence 3)
t. is some soul of goodness (Philosophy 8)
t. is something in this (Philosophy 7)
t. is thy gold (Poison 3)
t. may be in the cup a spider (Poison 5)
t.'s neither honesty, manhood ... in thee (Courage 2)
t.'s no room for faith, truth, nor honesty (Fatness 5)
t.'s not a minute of our lives (Pleasure 1)
t. will be a world of water shed (Tears 5)

therefore:

t. is love said to be a child (Love 55)

they:

t. have seemed to be together (Friendship 33)
t. say best men are molded (Faults 8)
t. say we are ... as like as eggs (Parents and Children 16)
t. stumble that run fast (Haste 2)
t. that have power to hurt (Power 13)
t. that stand high have many blasts (Greatness 10)
t. told me I was everything (Flattery 5)
t. will steal anything (Theft 3)
t. would have me as familiar (Theft 4)

thief:

giant's robe upon a dwarfish t. (Clothing 7)
if you do take a t. (Theft 8)
if you meet a t. (Theft 7)
steals something from the t. (Philosophy 17, Theft 9)
the sun's a t. (Theft 11)
the t. doth fear each bush an officer (Fear 6)

thievery:

I'll example you with t. (Theft 11)

thieves:

beauty provoketh t. (Beauty 2)
t. for their robbery have authority (Theft 6)
when t. cannot be true (Loyalty 3)

thing:

can one desire too much of a good t.? (Desire 5)
death is a fearful t. (Death 29)
great t. of us forgot! (Forgetfulness 3)
has this t. appeared (Apparitions 1)

it started like a guilty t. (Ghosts 5)
simply the t. I am (Self-Reliance 2)
this t. of darkness (Darkness 3)
'tis a vile t. to die (Death 36)
why yet I live to say "This t.'s to do" (Delay 1)

things:

all t. are ready (Readiness 1)
all t. that are (Anticipation 1)
a surfeit of the sweetest t. (Food 10)
can such t. be? (Apparitions 8)
construe t. after their fashion (Misunderstanding 1)
grant precious t. as trifles (Generosity 7)
I will strive with t. impossible (Fitness 1)
more t. in heaven and earth (Philosophy 5)
remember such t. were (Grief 11)
small t. make base men proud (Pride 1)
so quick bright t. come to confusion (Transience 2)
such welcome and unwelcome t. (News 9)
sweetest t. turn sourest (Flowers 14)
t. are often spoke and seldom meant (Speech 8)
t. at the worst will cease (Comfort 5)
t. bad begun (Aphorisms 5)
t. base and vile (Love 54)
t. done without example (Innovation 1)
t. ill got had ever bad success (Wrongdoing 2)
t. past redress (Proverbs 24)
t. rank and gross in nature (Dejection)
t. sweet to taste (Eating 11)
t. that love night (Night 11)
t. without all remedy (Aphorisms 4, Regret 2)
t. won are done (Men and Women 9)
thou met'st with t. dying (Birth and Death 2)
what t. there are most abject (Value 7)

think:

t. as every man thinks (Opinion 1)
t. but how vile a spectacle it were (Wrongdoing 9)
t. not, thou noble Roman (Greatness 7)
t. on me (Middle Age 1)

third:

the t. pays for all (Proverbs 30)

this:

t. did I fear (Greatness 9)
t. falls out better (Plots 3)
t. is mere madness (Madness 6)
t. is the chase (Last Words 7)

thorn:

this t. doth to our rose of youth (Youth 1)

thorns:

leave our t. to prick ourselves (Lust 1)
t. and dangers of this world (Danger 10)
t. that in her bosom lodge (Conscience 1)
t. we stand upon (Anxiety 10)

those:

t. that do teach young babes (Education 4)
t. that with haste will make a mighty fire (Fire 2)

thou:

t. art e'en as just a man (Man 6)
t. art inclined to sleep (Sleep 16)
t. art not for the fashion (Fashion 1)
t. art too wild (Manners 1)

thou (cont'd.)
t. canst not say I did it (Ghosts 13)
t. hast my love (Desire 4)
t.'lt come no more (Death 21)
t. shalt be as free (Freedom 7)
t. shalt find she will outstrip (Praise 9)
t. still hast been the father (News 4)
t. wilt be like a lover (Words 7)
t. wouldst be great (Ambition 11)

though:
t. some of you, with Pilate (Hypocrisy 13)

thought:
a Roman t. hath struck him (Duty 1)
as if there were some monster in his t. (Thought 12)
a woman's t. runs before her actions (Thought 1)
comes t. on t. (Thought 8)
every third t. shall be my grave (Mortality 10)
honor's t. reigns solely (Honor 7)
in a t. unborn (Innocence 2)
of no less celerity than that of t. (Thought 5)
pale cast of t. (Conscience 2)
quick forge and working-house of t. (Thought 6)
t. is free (Thought 13)
t. whose murder yet is but fantastical (Confusion 4)
thy wish was father ... to that t. (Thought 4)

thoughts:
fair t. and happy hours (Farewells 13)
hot blood begets hot t. (Love 89)
I have ... with leaden t. been pressed (Moods 13)
my bloody t. with violent pace (Revenge 7)
my t. are whirled (Perplexity 1, Thought 7)
my t. remain below (Prayer 5)
my t. were like unbridled children (Love 92)
our t. are ours, their ends (Thought 3)
pansies, that's for t. (Flowers 2)
swift to enter in the t. of men (Evil 9)
the cursèd t. that nature gives way to (Thought 11)
these sweet t. do even refresh my labors (Work 6)
t. are but dreams (Thought 14)
t. tending to content (Philosophy 18)
t. that would thick my blood (Children 2)
t. the slaves of life (Time 9)
what, in ill t. again? (Endurance 3)
words without t. never to heaven go (Prayer 5)
your t. must deck our kings (Imagination 3)

thread:
he draweth out the t. (Argument 4)

threats:
sir, spare your t. (Death-Wish 11)

three:
t. parts of him is ours (Persuasion 3)

thrice:
t. is he armed (Quarrels 5)

thrift:
t. is blessing (Thrift 2)
t., t., Horatio (Food 6, Thrift 1)

thrive:
t. I as I may (Choice 3)

throne:
like a burnished t. (Ships 1)

throstle:
t. with his note so true (Birds 12)

thunder:
such bursts of horrid t. (Storms 10)
thou all-shaking t. (Storms 8)

thunderbolt:
some innocents scape not the t. (Innocence 1)

thus:
t. play I in one person (Identity 5)

thyme:
a bank whereon the wild t. grows (Flowers 6)

thyself:
t. mine own self's better part (Courtship 5)

Tiber:
wine with not a drop of allaying T. (Drinking 3)

tide:
a t. in the affairs of men (Opportunity 2)
on the swell at full of t. (Indecision 1)
'tis with my mind as with the t. (Indecision 3)
washed off at the next t. (Danger 4)

tidings:
the worst t. that I hear of (News 6)

tiger:
milk in a male t. (Ruthlessness 1)
t.'s heart wrapped in a woman's hide (Cruelty 1)

time:
bank and shoal of t. (Action 11)
beguile the t. (Travel 25)
be you not troubled with the t. (Necessity 1)
bid t. return (Time 23)
bitter disposition of the t. (Inevitability 3)
clock upbraids me with a waste of t. (Time 36)
companions that ... waste the t. (Friendship 19)
creeping hours of t. (Time 3)
dark backward and abysm of t. (Memory 6)
devouring t., blunt thou (Time 42)
envious and calumniating t. (Time 30)
fleet the t. carelessly (Golden Age 1)
had I but t. (Death 9)
help t. to furrow me with age (Grief 13)
his t. is spent (Epitaphs 13)
I have no precious t. to spend (Devotion 7)
inaudible and noiseless foot of t. (Time 1)
injurious t. (Time 31)
in such a t. as this (Criticism 1)
I shall find t., Cassius (Mourning 16)
I shall have t. enough (Mourning 11)
I wasted t. (Time 24)
look into the seeds of t. (Prophecy 6)
love's not T.'s fool (Constancy 12)
make use of t. (Proverbs 33, Time 45)
many events in the womb of t. (Time 20)
mock the t. with fairest show (Deceit 5)
nothing 'gainst t.'s scythe can make defense (Time 41)
no, t., thou shalt not boast (Time 44)
now he weighs t. (Time 15)
old folk, t.'s doting chronicles (Age 16)
old t. the clock-setter (Time 16)
O t., thou must untangle this (Time 35)

perceive not how t. moves (Time 6)
relish of the saltness of t. (Age 10)
so idly to profane the precious t. (Time 13)
so long walked hand in hand with t. (Time 32)
spite of cormorant devouring t. (Fame 2)
subject to t.'s love (Constancy 13)
that old common arbitrator, t. (Time 33)
that t. of year thou may'st in me behold (Seasons 18)
there's a t. for all things (Time 7)
there would have been a t. (Time 19)
the t. is out of joint (Politics 1)
the t. of life is short (Life 3)
the t. was once (Marriage 11)
the whirligig of t. (Time 37)
this great gap of time (Forgetfulness 3)
this is no t. to lend money (Money 13)
though t. seem so adverse (Endings 1)
t. and the hour runs through (Time 18)
t. comes stealing on (Time 8)
t., force and death (Love 93)
t. hath, my lord, a wallet (Time 28)
t. is a very bankrupt (Time 8)
t. is like a fashionable host (Time 29)
t. is the nurse and breeder (Time 38)
t. ... must have a stop (Time 9)
t. of universal peace (Peace 2)
t. qualifies the spark (Love 33)
t.'s deformèd hand (Grief 3)
t.'s glory is to calm (Time 40)
t. shall unfold (Time 17)
t.'s the king of men (Time 22)
t. travels in divers paces (Time 5)
t. will come and take my love (Mutability 4)
'tis but the t. ... that men stand upon (Death 19)
to beguile the t., look like the t. (Deceit 4)
trencher-friends, t.'s flies (Flattery 7)
we are t.'s subjects (Time 11)
we have seen the best of our t. (Disorder 2)
we play the fools with the t. (Time 12)
what else may hap, to t. I will commit (Time 34)
what hast thou to do with the t. (Time of Day 5)
what t. of day is it, lad? (Time of Day 4)
when t. is old (Constancy 8)
which way the stream of t. doth run (Time 14)
who would bear the whips and scorns of t. (Suicide 13)
wide gap of t. (Acting 31)
witching t. of night (Night 1)
you shall have t. to wrangle in (Argument 1)
times:
but cruel are the t. (Confusion 6)
how many t. shall Caesar (Theater 10)
O these naughty t. (Possession 2)
Timon:
T. hath made his everlasting mansion (Epitaphs 15)
T. will to the woods (Kindness 4)
tinkers:
to gabble like t. (Disorder 4)
tiptoe:
jocund day stand t. (Dawn 7)

tired:
t. with all these (Death-Wish 12)
Titania:
proud T. (Greetings 5)
title:
his t. hang loose about him (Clothing 7)
that t. of respect (Respect 1)
titles:
all thy other t. thou hast given away (Fools 8)
toad:
foul bunch-backed t. (Insults 18)
like the t., ugly and venomous (Adversity 2)
poisonous bunch-backed t. (Curses 7)
toads:
foul t. to knot and gender in (Loss 6)
I hate the engendering of t. (Pride 5)
together:
they have seemed to be t. (Friendship 33)
toil:
in her strong t. of grace (Death 6)
tombs:
gilded t. do worms infold (Gold 5)
tomorrow:
such a day t. as is today (Boys 5)
t., and t., and t. (Time 19)
t. is Saint Valentine's day (Festivals 2)
t. is the joyful day (Marriage 6)
t. night, when Phoebe (Moon 3)
tongs:
the t. and the bones (Music 13)
tongue:
deedless in his t. (Words and Deeds 3)
he hath a killing t. (Soldiers 11)
I must hold my t. (Grief 6)
like a strange t. (Language 2)
love's more ponderous than my t. (Love 39)
murder, though it have no t. (Murder 2)
no power in the t. of man to alter me (Determination 3)
that man that hath a t. (Courtship 24)
the iron t. of midnight (Time of Day 8)
there is no t. that moves (Persuasion 5)
t.'s sweet air (Beauty 15)
trippingly on the t. (Acting 7)
thy t. makes Welsh as sweet (Language 1)
wounds me with the flatteries of his t. (Flattery 4)
tongues:
bestowed that time in the t. (Language 9)
conscience hath a thousand t. (Conscience 7)
finds t. in trees (Country Life 2)
how silver-sweet sound lovers' t. (Music 19)
t. of dying men (Last Words 3)
t. of men are full of deceits (Deceit 3)
t. of mocking wenches (Mockery 2)
upon my t. continual slanders ride (Slander 4)
tonight:
t. we'll wander through the streets (People 1)
tooth:
a mad dog's t. (Jealousy 2)
sharper than a serpent's t. (Ingratitude 7)

torch:
 since the t. is out (Suicide 3)
torches:
 she doth teach the t. (Beauty 21)
torments:
 what studied t., tyrant (Torture 2)
touch:
 a little t. of Harry in the night (Royalty 16)
 one t. of nature (Fashion 11)
 t. me with noble anger (Tears 10)
tower:
 nor stony t., nor walls (Constraint 1)
towers:
 the cloud-capped t. (Transience 6)
town:
 this t. is full of cozenage (Travel 5)
toy:
 your eye shall light upon some t. (Shopping 1)
toys:
 all is but t. (Mourning 18)
 dreams are t. (Dreams 16)
trade:
 what think you of the t.? (Prostitution 1)
tradesmen:
 lying ... becomes none but t. (Business 11)
traffic:
 the two hours t. of our stage (Theater 18)
tragedian:
 counterfeit the deep t.(Acting 26)
traitor:
 thou art a t. Off with his head (Execution 1)
traitors:
 our doubts are t. (Doubts 2)
 our fears do make us t. (Fear 9)
tranquil:
 farewell the t. mind (Farewells 14)
 times when we are t. (Confusion 6)
transformation:
 Hamlet's t. (Transformation 2)
trappings:
 these but the t. (Mourning 9)
travel:
 a man of t. (Travel 12)
 my t.'s history, wherein of antres vast (Travel 16)
 with long t. I am stiff (Travel 3)
travelers:
 t. must be content (Travel 1)
treachery:
 he is composed ... of t. (Villainy 6)
 justly killed with mine own t. (Justice 1)
treason:
 innocent from meaning t. (Innocence 3)
 t. and murder ever kept together (Treason 3)
 t. can but peep to what it would (Royalty 6)
 t. is but trusted like the fox (Treason 2)
 t. is not inherited (Treason 1)
 whilst bloody t. flourished (Treason 4)
treasure:
 the purest t. mortal times afford (Reputation 11)

 who fears sinking where such t. lies? (Desire 19)
treasury:
 the t. of everlasting joy (Heaven 2)
tree:
 I love the t. from whence (Duplicity 3)
 sighing by a sycamore t. (Lament 1)
trees:
 by yon tuft of trees (Castles 2)
tremble:
 you t. and look pale (Fear 1)
trencher:
 a morsel, cold upon dead Caesar's t. (Food 3)
trencher-friends:
 fools of fortune, t. (Flattery 7)
trial:
 go with me to my t. (Trials 1)
trick:
 I know a t. (Cleverness 1)
 t. of our English nation (Countries 4)
tricks:
 such t. hath strong imagination (Imagination 5)
trifle:
 a t., some eight-penny matter (Money 2)
 the dearest thing ... as 'twere a careless t. (Dying 13)
trifles:
 she prizes not such t. (Gifts 6)
 snapper-up of unconsidered t. (Theft 12)
 t. light as air (Jealousy 9)
 win us with honest t. (Evil 5)
Triton:
 this T. of the minnows (Authority 2)
troops:
 farewell the plumèd t. (Farewells 14)
trouble:
 t. being gone comfort should remain (Parting 12)
trowel:
 that was laid on with a t. (Exaggeration 1)
true:
 can the devil speak t.? (Devil 7)
 had she been t. (Constancy 5)
 supposing thou art t. (Deceit 24)
 t. as truth's simplicity (Constancy 7)
 wrenching the t. cause (Deviousness 2)
truepenny:
 art thou there, t.? (Ghosts 10)
truly:
 t., I would not hang a dog (Mercy 13)
 t., thou art damned (Food 4)
trumpet:
 the southern wind doth play the t. (Storms 1)
trunk:
 that t. of humors (Fatness 4)
trust:
 fear too far. Safer than t. too far (Fear 11)
 I wonder men dare t. themselves (Trust 5)
 my t., like a good parent (Trust 4)
 t. a few (Advice 1)
 what a fool honesty is, and t. (Honesty 8)

trusts:

he that t. to you (People 5)

truth:

bear the t. I tell (Stoicism 2)

good I stand on is my t. (Integrity 1)

he found t. in one (Betrayal 2)

his simple t. must be abused (Duplicity 3)

I'll confess the t. (Truth 6)

I must ... live hence by t. (Truth 4)

I will find where t. is hid (Truth 1)

methinks the t. should live (Truth 7)

seeming t. that cunning times put on (Deceit 8)

show of t. can cunning sin cover itself (Deceit 9)

swerve a hair from t. (Constancy 8)

tell t. and shame the devil (Truth 2)

that sweet ornament which t. (Beauty 32)

the map of honor, t. and loyalty (Honor 11)

the naked t. of it is (Clothing 6)

they breathe t. that breathe ... in pain (Last Words 3)

to seek the light of t. (Books 2)

trust the flattering t. of sleep (Dreams 14)

t. hath a quiet breast (Integrity 3)

t. hath better deeds (Love 104)

t. is truth (Truth 5)

t. loves open dealing (Plain-Speaking 2)

t. will come to light (Proverbs 18)

with thy religious t. (Truth 3)

tuck:

vile standing t. (Insults 7)

tune:

how dost thou like this t.? (Music 27)

turf:

at his head a grass-green t. (Death 8)

one t. shall serve as pillow (Love 57)

turn:

a t. or two I'll walk (Exercise 1)

do not t. me about (Drinking 24)

t. him to any cause (Politics 4)

turquoise:

it was my t. (Loss 5)

turtle-doves:

a pair of loving t. (Birds 4)

tut:

t. man, one fire burns out another's (Fire 3)

t., t., good enough to toss (Soldiers 7)

twig:

Kate, like the hazel t., is straight (Praise 8)

two:

an t. men ride of a horse (Proverbs 22)

t. may keep counsel (Secrets 1)

tyrannous:

the t. and bloody deed (Murder 13)

tyranny:

liberty! freedom! t. is dead (Freedom 3)

that part of t. that I do bear (Tyranny 3)

the oppression of aged t. (Tyranny 5)

tyrant:

how fine this t. can tickle (Deceit 2)

tyrants:

fear when t. seem to kiss (Tyranny 6)

how can t. safely govern home (Tyranny 1)

ulcerous:

skin and film the u. place (Sickness 2)

unarm:

u. Eros, the long day's task is done (Dying 1)

unction:

lay not that flattering u. (Corruption 3, Sickness 2)

underlings:

the fault ... that we are u. (Faults 6)

undeserver:

u. may sleep (Action 5)

undeservers:

sell ... offices for gold to u. (Corruption 5)

undone:

u. and forfeited to cares (Anxiety 1)

uneasy:

u. lies the head (Royalty 11)

uneven:

all is uneven (Confusion 7)

unfaithful:

the gross band of the u. (Religion 1)

unhand:

u. me gentlemen (Determination 1)

unicorns:

I will believe that there are u. (Myths 1)

university:

spend all at the u. (Education 5)

unkindness:

drink down all u. (Drinking 17)

u. blunts it (Unkindness 1)

u. may do much (Unkindness 3)

unnecessary:

age is u. (Age 26)

unpin:

prithee u. me (Devotion 5)

unquietness:

betroths himself to u. (Misogyny 2)

unsex:

u. me here (Cruelty 3)

unstaid:

u. and skittish in all motions else (Constancy 9)

urge:

u. me no more (Quarrels 6)

Ursa Major:

nativity was under U. (Astrology 2)

use:

abject in regard and dear in u. (Value 7)

how u. doth breed a habit (Custom 5)

make u. of time (Proverbs 33)

u. almost can change (Custom 3)

uses:

to what base u. (Mortality 3)

utterance:

with all the gracious u. thou hast (Eloquence 6)

Valentine:

Saint V. is past (Greetings 6)

to be your V. (Festivals 2)

valiant:

he is as v. as the lion (Valor 14)

he's truly v. (Endurance 4)

valiant (cont'd.)

  I never yet was v. (Honesty 3)

  that's a v. flea (Valor 11)

  the v. never taste of death (Death 17)

valor:

  awake your dormouse v. (Valor 15)

  honor for his v. (Caesar 3)

  in a false quarrel there is no true v. (Valor 13)

  reward thee ... for thy v. (Comfort 2, Valor 1)

  the better part of v. is discretion (Valor 8)

  there's no more v. in that Poins (Valor 7)

  this v. comes of sherris (Drinking 11)

  to revenge is no v. (Revenge 8)

  v. is the chiefest virtue (Valor 5)

  wisdom that doth guide his v. (Valor 12)

valors:

  his v. shown upon our crests (Valor 9)

value:

  then we rack the v. (Value 1)

  v. dwells not in particular will (Value 5)

valued:

  what's aught but as 'tis v. (Value 4)

vanity:

  light v., insatiable cormorant (Vanity 2)

  so light is v. (Vanity 3)

  that v. in years (Vice 2)

  what a sweep of v. comes this way (Vanity 4)

  when there is no need of such v. (Learning 3)

variety:

  custom stale her infinite v. (Charm 3)

vast:

  shook hands as over a v. (Friendship 33)

  the god of this great v. (Storms 13)

vein:

  I am not in the giving v. (Gifts 4)

veins:

  fear thrills though my v. (Fear 11)

  my bluest v. to kiss (Royalty 1)

vengeance:

  arise, black v. (Revenge 6)

  rarer action is in virtue than in v. (Forgiveness 5)

Venice:

  in V. they let God see the pranks (Deceit 14)

vent:

  free v. of words (Passion 4)

ventures:

  my v. are not in one bottom (Business 6)

Venus:

  more intemperate ... than V. (Lust 10)

  o'erpicturing that V. (Beauty 1)

  think what V. did with Mars (Desire 1)

  wicked bastard of V. (Love 23)

verbosity:

  draweth out the thread of his v. (Argument 4)

Verona:

  there is no world without V. walls (Exile 9)

verse:

  an you talk in blank v. (Poetry 5)

  hang there, my v. (Poetry 1)

  your monument shall be my gentle v. (Poetry 16)

verses:

  tear him for his bad v. (Civil War 3)

vessel:

  comfort the weaker v. (Comfort 3, Women 4)

  empty v. makes the greatest sound (Proverbs 6)

vesture:

  this muddy v. of decay (Heaven 3)

vexation:

  the fierce v. of a dream (Dreams 5)

vice:

  any taint of v. (Ingratitude 10)

  apparel v. like virtue's harbinger (Deceit 1)

  make thine honesty a v. (Honesty 7)

  medicine that skins the v. (Authority 10)

  no v. so simple (Deceit 7)

  that reverend v. (Vice 2)

  v. of lying (Age 15, Lying 4)

  virtue itself turns v. (Vice 3, Virtue 20)

  with a virtuous visor hide deep v. (Deceit 16)

vices:

  great v. do appear (Justice 7)

  of our pleasant v. (Justice 8)

  what a mansion have those v. got (Vice 5)

viciousness:

  when we in our v. grow hard (Vice 1)

victory:

  a v. is twice itself (Victory 2)

  the harder matched, the greater v. (Victory 1)

victuals:

  I am ... nourished by my v. (Food 15)

vigilant:

  I am a v. as a cat to steal cream (Vigilance 1)

vile:

  'tis a v. thing to die (Death 36)

  'tis better to be v. than v. esteemed (Reputation 17)

villager:

  Brutus had rather be a v. (Tyranny 2)

villain:

  every tale condemns me for a v. (Conscience 7)

  fair terms and a v.'s mind (Villainy 2)

  hungry lean-faced v. (Character 1)

  I am a plain-dealing v. (Villainy 3)

  I am determinèd to prove a v. (Villainy 7)

  I play the v. (Advice 14)

  O v.! thou wilt be condemned (Solecisms 6)

  O v., v. smiling, damnèd v. (Villainy 1)

  there's never a v. living (Truisms 2)

  you are a v. (Challenges 1)

  v. with a smiling cheek (Duplicity 3)

villains:

  v. on necessity (Astrology 1)

  when rich v. have need of poor ones (Business 8)

villainy:

  Falstaff do in the days of v. (Excuses 2)

  in our cursed natures but direct v. (Misanthropy 5)

  thus I clothe my naked v. (Hypocrisy 14)

vine:

  thou art an elm ... I a v. (Marriage 13)

vinegar:

  v. and pepper in't (Challenges 2)

viol:

    he plays o' the v.-de-gamboys (Character 5)

violet:

    a v. in the youth of primy nature (Flowers 1)

    to throw a perfume on the v. (Extravagance 2)

    where oxlips and the nodding v. grows (Flowers 6)

violets:

    breathes upon a bank of v. (Music 26)

    may v. spring (Burial 3)

    who are the v. now (Flowers 7, Innovation 2)

virgin:

    a poor v., sir ... but mine own (Possession 1)

    a v. from her very infancy (Chastity 7)

virginity:

    loss of v. is rational increase (Virginity 2)

    man is an enemy to v. (Virginity 1)

virtue:

    according to his v. (Burial 4)

    but v., as it never will be moved (Virtue 6)

    calumny will sear v. itself (Slander 8)

    grace to stand and v. go (Virtue 15)

    I will not change for your best v. (Faults 4)

    king of every v. (Beauty 19)

    let v. be as wax (Lust 6)

    my heart laments that v. cannot live (Virtue 8)

    no v. like necessity (Necessity 6)

    O infinite v. (Valor 2)

    some by v. fall (Injustice 1)

    the devil their v. tempts (Devil 9)

    the rarer action is in v. than in vengeance (Forgiveness 5)

    there is no man hath a v. (Vice 3)

    thy fair v.'s force (Love 59)

    valor is the chiefest v. (Valor 5)

    vice ... assumes some mark of v. (Deceit 7)

    v.? a fig! 'tis in ourselves (Virtue 17)

    v. cannot live out of the teeth (Virtue 8)

    v. is beauty (Virtue 24)

    v. is bold (Virtue 14)

    v. itself scapes not calumnious strokes (Virtue 5)

    v. itself turns vice (Virtue 20)

    v. that transgresses (Virtue 22)

virtues:

    his v. will plead like angels (Virtue 10)

    if our v. did not go forth of us (Virtue 12)

    is it a world to hide v. in? (Virtue 21)

    our v. lie in the interpretation (Virtue 3)

    thee and thy v. here I seize upon (Virtue 9)

    they are v. and traitors (Virtue 1)

virtuous:

    a fool for he would needs be v. (Politics 7)

    dost think, because thou art v. (Virtue 23)

    your father was ever v. (Virtue 16)

visage:

    I saw Othello's v. in his mind (Devotion 4)

    mask thy monstrous v. (Conspiracy 5)

visages:

    men whose v. do cream (Self-Importance 1)

vision:

    fatal v. (Apparitions 7)

I have had a most rare v. (Dreams 6)

visor:

    with a virtuous v. hide deep vice (Deceit 16)

vixen:

    she was a v. (Anger 5)

vocation:

    why, Hal, 'tis my v. (Theft 1)

voice:

    a woman's v. may do some good (Negotiation 3)

    give ... few thy v. (Advice 5)

    her v. was ever soft (Speech 12)

    I will aggravate my v. (Acting 21)

    my v. is ragged (Singing 1)

    so full a v. from so empty a heart (Proverbs 6)

volubility:

    I'll commend her v. (Courtship 20)

votaress:

    the imperial v. passed on (Virginity 3)

vouchsafe:

    v. to teach a soldier terms (Courtship 7)

vow:

    break the smallest parcel of this v. (Oaths 2)

    by yonder blessèd moon I vow (Vows 4)

    the purpose that makes strong the vow (Vows 5)

    the plain single v. (Vows 1)

vows:

    by all the v. that ever men have broke (Vows 2)

    sucked the honey of his music v. (Dejection 3)

voyage:

    thy loving v. (Marriage 8)

    life's uncertain v. (Life 12)

wages:

    our praises are our wages (Praise 13)

wainscot:

    join you as they join w. (Marriage 4)

waist:

    from the w. they are centaurs (Misogyny 1)

wake:

    do thee so much wrong to w. thee (Sleep 7)

wallet:

    time hath ... a w. at his back (Time 28)

wanderer:

    I am that merry w. of the night (Fairies 4)

war:

    impious w. (War 13)

    in the trade of w. I have slain men (Murder 7)

    let slip the dogs of w. (War 16)

    never was a w. did cease (Peace 3)

    pomp, and circumstance of glorious w. (War 19)

    the fire-eyed maid of smoky w. (War 2)

    the flinty and steel couch of w. (War 18)

    the hideous god of w. (War 7)

    the lofty instruments of w. (War 4)

    the purple testament of bleeding w. (War 20)

    this hungry w. opens his vasty jaws (War 9)

    when the blast of w. blows (War 11)

warble:

    w. , child, make passionate (Singing 2)

warder:

    memory, the w. of the brain (Memory 4)

wardrobe:

look what a w. here is for thee (Clothing 11)

wares:

show our foulest w. (Business 9)

warrior:

the painful w. famousèd for fight (Honor 23)

warriors:

we are but w. for the working day (Soldiers 16)

wars:

as w. ... may be said to be a ravisher (Peace 2)

go not to these w. (Wars 6)

how many hath he killed ... in these w.? (War 17)

still w. and lechery (Lechery 6)

the big w. that makes ambition virtue (Farewells 14)

thou art going to the wars (Friendship 8)

w. is no strife to the dark house (War 1)

waste:

in the dead w. (Time of Day 1)

your w. is great (Extravagance 1)

watch:

he's winding up the w. of his wit (Wit 6)

some must w. while some must sleep (Life 3)

w. tonight, pray tomorrow (Fellowship 1)

water:

a little w. clears us of this deed (Guilt 6)

as false as w. (Infidelity 1)

a world of w. shed (Tears 5)

fall a drop of w. in the breaking gulf (Marriage 12)

honest w. (Drinking 26)

I to the world am like a drop of w. (Identity 1)

like a circle in the w. (Glory 1)

not all the w. in the rough rude sea (Royalty 28)

smooth runs the w. (Rivers 2)

w. in a sieve (Advice 13)

w. that ne'er left man i' the mire (Drinking 26)

what dreadful noise of w. in my ears (Dreams 9)

wave:

I wish you a w. o'the sea (Dancing 4)

waves:

as the w. make towards the pebbled shore (Time 43)

head 'bove the contentious w. (Swimming 2)

way:

in the beaten w. of friendship (Friendship 4)

my w. is to conjure you (Men and Women 3, Plays 2)

my w. of life is fallen into the sere (Old Age 8)

take the instant w. (Reputation 14)

there lies your w. (Travel 22)

the w. is wearisome (Travel 26)

this w. a w. to thrive (Thrift 2)

ways:

by what ... crooked w. (Deviousness 3)

waywardness:

unruly w. (Capriciousness 2)

we:

so we grew together (Twins 3)

we are all frail (Weakness 3)

we are all men (Weakness 2)

we are oft to blame in this (Hypocrisy 1)

we do not come (Acting 24)

we few, we happy few (Fellowship 2)

we have here recovered (Villainy 5)

we have laughed to see the sails (Pregnancy 2)

we have seen the best of our time (Disorder 2)

we, ignorant of ourselves (Prayer 1)

we know each other's faces (Deceit 17)

we know what we are (Self-Knowledge 3)

we'll set thee to school to an ant (Proverbs 14)

we two alone will sing (Reconciliation 4)

we were not born to sue (Royalty 26)

we were the first ... of your friends (Friendship 7)

we wound our modesty (Deserving 1)

weak:

how w. a thing the heart of woman is (Women 21)

weaker:

I am w. than a woman's tear (Weakness 6)

weakness:

bear with my w. (Weakness 4)

our w. past compare (Women 26)

'twere childish w. to lament (Courage 4)

wealth:

all the w. I had (Men 9)

sum up sum of half my w. (Love 83)

weapon:

thought he had no w. (Greatness 9)

weariness:

w. can snore upon the flint (Sleep 1)

weary:

how w., flat, stale and unprofitable (Dejection 1)

weapons:

women's w., water-drops (Tears 9)

wear:

w. this for me (Fortune 5)

weariness:

w. can snore upon the flint (Weariness 1)

weary:

w. with toil, I hast me (Sleep 19)

weather:

many can brook the w. (Weather 3)

web:

with as little a w. as this (Plots 4)

wedding:

the w. mannerly-modest (Marriage 30)

w. is great Juno's crown (Marriage 7)

wedges:

blunt w. rive hard knots (Proverbs 28)

w. of gold, great anchors (Dreams 10)

wedlock:

high w. then be honorèd (Marriage 7)

w. would be nibbling (Marriage 3)

what is w. forcèd (Marriage 18)

weed:

fat w. that roots itself (Action 3)

thou w. who art so lovely fair (Beauty 17)

weeds:

all the idle w. that grow (Madness 9)

great w. do grow apace (Proverbs 25)

I will go root away the noisome w. (Gardens 6)

lilies that fester smell far worse than w. (Flowers 14)

most subject is the fattest soil to w. (Gardens 1)

w. are shallow-rooted (Gardens 3)

week:

what, keep a w. away (Time 21)

weep:

come w. with me (Despair 8)

how much better is it to w. at joy (Tears 13)

I cannot choose but w. (Mourning 10, Burial 2)

you think I'll w. (Tears 11)

weeping:

I am not prone to w. (Grief 15)

welcome:

at first and last, the hearty w. (Welcome 1)

bid that w. which comes to punish (Endurance 2)

bid these unknown friends to's w. (Welcome 3)

great Hector, w.! (Welcome 2)

great w. makes a merry feast (Feasts 3)

such w. and unwelcome things (News 9)

the w. ever smiles (Time 29)

w. hither as is the spring (Welcome 4)

well:

the hurt ... is not so deep as a w. (Dying 15)

since all is w., keep it so (Proverbs 3)

Welsh:

the devil understands W. (Devil 3)

thy tongue makes W. as sweet (Language 1)

wench:

I know a w. of excellent discourse (Women 8)

ill-starred w. (Affliction 10)

she's a good w. (Love 97)

wenches:

tongues of mocking w. (Mockery 2)

west:

the w. yet glimmers (Sunset 1)

w. of this place (Country Life 8)

westward:

then w. ho! (Travel 22)

wether:

I am a tainted w. of the flock (Resignation 4)

what:

w., all so soon asleep? (Sleep 17)

w. a pair of spectacles (Eyes 16)

w. a piece of work is a man (Man 5)

w. are these, so withered? (Supernatural 3)

w. can be avoided? (Fate 6)

w. cannot be eschewed (Inevitability 1)

w. else may hap (Time 34)

w., frighted with false fire? (Fear 2)

w., girl, though grey (Middle Age 2)

w., gone without a word? (Love 104)

w. is a man (Man 7)

w. is it then to me (War 13)

w. I think I utter (Speech 1)

w., keep a week away? (Time 21)

w. must be shall be (Inevitability 2)

w. says she, fair one? (Deceit 3)

w. say you to a piece of beef (Food 14)

w. seest thou else (Memory 6)

w.'s gone and w.'s past help (Philosophy 19)

w. shall Cordelia speak? (Love 38)

w.'s mine is yours (Marriage 23)

w. to ourselves in passion we propose (Passion 1)

w. we have we prize not (Value 2)

w. win I if I gain the thing I seek? (Desire 17)

w. you will have, I'll give (Power 11)

wheel:

fortune ..., turn thy wheel (Fortune 14)

I am bound upon a w. of fire (Suffering 1)

the w. is come full circle (Fortune 16)

thoughts are whirlèd like a potter's w. (Perplexity 1)

w. runs down a hill (Advice 10)

when:

w. holy and devout religious men (Prayer 15)

w. icicles hang by the wall (Seasons 11)

w. I consider everything (Mutability 3)

w. I have plucked the rose (Murder 8)

w. I tell him he hates flatterers (Flattery 4)

w. shall we three meet again? (Supernatural 12)

w. thou hast leisure (Leisure 1)

w. to the sessions of sweet silent thought (Remembrance 9)

w. we in our viciousness grow hard (Vice 1)

w. will this fearful slumber (Sleep 18)

w. you depart from me (Parting 12)

where:

w. did you study? (Speechmaking 5)

w. should this music be? (Music 21)

while:

w. I live I'll fear (Sex 4)

whipping:

who should 'scape w.? (Generosity 2)

whips:

who would bear the w. and scorns of time (Suicide 13)

whirligig:

the w. of time brings ... revenges (Time 37)

whispering:

is w. nothing? (Suspicion 2)

whisperings:

foul w. are abroad (Guilt 9)

whither:

w. I go, thither shall you (Travel 7)

who:

w. are the violets now? (Innovation 2, Flowers 7)

w. can control his fate? (Fate 7)

w. can converse with a dumb show? (Conversation 2)

w. cannot be crushed? (Plots 1)

w. chooseth me must give (Risk 2)

w. chooseth me shall gain (Desire 12, 13)

w. chooseth me shall get (Merit 1)

w. comes so fast? (Night 16)

w. dares not stir by day (Fear 9)

w. is it that can tell me who I am? (Identity 4)

w. is Silvia? (Beauty 26)

w. lives that's not depravèd (Corruption 7, Humanity 8)

w. makes the fairest show (Deceit 15)

w.'s born that day when I forget (Letters 1)

w. cries out in the streets (Wisdom 3)

wise:

not one w. man among twenty (Wisdom 5)

so w., so young, they say (Youth 10)

the fool doth think he is w. (Fools 5)

the w. man knows himself to be a fool (Wisdom 2)

to be w. and love exceeds man's might (Wisdom 6)

too w. to woo peaceably (Courtship 15)

w. men put on their cloaks (Change 1)

you are w. or else you love not (Wisdom 6)

wisely:

w. and slow (Haste 2)

wiser:

men may grow w. (Wisdom 1)

wishes:

let your fair eyes and gentle w. go (Trials 1)

wit:

a cheveril glove to a good w. (Wit 7)

better a witty fool than a foolish w. (Fools 10)

brevity is the soul of w. (Wit 1)

devise, w. (Writing 1)

good w. ... make use of anything (Business 4)

have you no w., manners, nor modesty (Disorder 4)

he's winding up the watch of his w. (Wit 6)

he that has and a little tiny w. (Fortune 15)

his w.'s as thick as Tewkesbury mustard (Insults 9)

I believe that does harm to my w. (Eating 13)

I have neither w., nor words (Speech 4)

I will keep where there is w. stirring (Folly 4)

make the door upon a woman's w. (Wit 1)

many a man has more hair than w. (Hair 2)

the cause that w. is in other men (Wit 3)

thy w. is as quick as the greyhound's mouth (Wit 4)

when the age is in the w. is out (Old Age 10)

witch:

no w. hath power to charm (Festivals 1)

witchcraft:

you have w. in your lips, Kate (Eloquence 4)

witches:

soul-killing w. that deform (Corruption 1)

witching:

w. time of night (Night 1)

wit-crackers:

a college of w. cannot flout (Wit 5)

withered:

so w. and so wild (Supernatural 3)

w. is the garland of the war (Epitaphs 1)

witness:

I shall not want false w. (Proverbs 7)

the w. still of excellency (Modesty 1)

wits:

if our w. run the wild-goose chase (Futility 2)

my w. begin to turn (Madness 7)

witty:

I am not only w. in myself (Wit 3)

wives:

if w. do fall (Marriage 42)

revolted w. (Adultery 3)

wives and children stare (Chaos 1)

w. may be merry (Marriage 27)

woe:

cry w., destruction, ruin (Death 33)

fellowship in w. doth w. assuage (Fellowship 4)

never was a story of more w. (Sorrow 15)

one w. doth tread upon another's heel (Sorrow 2)

the w. had been universal (Sorrow 17)

though w. be heavy (Sorrow 18)

w., that too late repents (Repentance 4)

woes:

all these w. shall serve (Sorrow 13)

ne'er wail their w. (Advice 15)

wolf:

be a comrade with the w. (Homelessness 1)

the w. behowls the moon (Night 19)

trusts in the tameness of a w. (Aphorisms 2)

wake not a sleeping w. (Proverbs 3)

wolves:

as salt as w. in pride (Lechery 3)

howling of Irish w. (Animals 2)

w. and bears ... done offices of pity (Creatures 5)

woman:

alas, I am a w. friendless (Women 18)

a properer man than she a w. (Beauty 4, Men and Women 2)

a w. and therefore may be wooed (Courtship 21)

a w. impudent and mannish grown (Effeminacy 3)

a w. moved is like a fountain troubled (Women 25)

a w.'s thought runs before her actions (Thought 1)

constant you are, but yet a w. (Women 15)

desire to be a w. of the world (Desire 6)

do you not know I am a w. (Women 6)

fair w. but she made mouths in a glass (Vanity 1)

how weak a thing the heart of w. is (Women 21)

if fortune be a w. (Fortune 19)

I grant I am a w. (Women 19)

I have no other but a w.'s reason (Women 28)

I have nothing of w. in me (Resolution 1)

I thank God I am not a w. (Women 7)

I will die a w. with grieving (Men and Women 6)

jewels ... move a w.'s mind (Gifts 3)

let still the w. take (Marriage 49)

no more but e'en a w. (Women 1)

one w. is fair (Misogyny 3)

semblative a w.'s part (Androgyny 1)

she is a w., therefore may be won (Women 21)

that man should be at w.'s command (Men and Women 1)

there is no w.'s sides (Love 98)

tiger's heart wrapped in a w's hide (Cruelty 1)

venom clamors of a jealous w. (Jealousy 2)

vice ... it is the w.'s part (Women 12)

was ever w. in this humor wooed (Courtship 18)

w.'s face ... gentle heart (Androgyny 2)

w.'s voice may do some good (Negotiation 3)

you that have so fair parts of w. (Women 17)

women:

alas, poor w., make us but believe (Women 9)

yoke:

our y. and sufferance show us womanish (Servitude 1)

shake the y. of inauspicious stars (Death-Wish 9)

Yorick:

alas, poor Y. (Epitaphs 4)

you:

y. are as strong, as valiant (Praise 11)

y. are my true and honorable wife (Marriage 22)

y. are no surer (People 6)

y. are not wood (Men 7)

y. call me misbeliever (Anti-Semitism 1)

y. come most carefully (Promptness 1)

y. common cry of curs (People 11)

y. dare easier be friends with me (Fighting 3)

y.'d be so lean (Thinness 5)

y. ever have wished the sleeping (Politics 5)

y. have bereft me of all words (Silence 7)

y. have both said well (Argument 5)

y. have some sick offense (Anxiety 5)

y. have too much respect (Anxiety 8)

y. have put him down, lady (Sex 5)

y. have put me to such a part (Acting 2)

y. have seen sunshine and rain (Tears 12)

y. may relish him more (Soldiers 21)

y. might have been enough the man (Man 1)

y. must confine yourself (Order 4)

y. never spoke what did become you (Mistakes 4, Speech 23)

y., O y., so perfect (Perfection 1)

y. shall have time to wrangle in (Argument 1)

y. shall hence upon your wedding day (Travel 13)

y. speak o' the people (People 10)

y. take my house (Life 8)

y., that have so fair parts of woman (Women 17)

y. think I'll weep (Tears 11)

y. two never meet (Quarrels 3)

y. yourself are much condemned (Corruption 5)

young:

as y. as I am (Men 5)

a y. man married (Marriage 1)

so wise so y. (Youth 10)

we that are y. shall never see so much (Experience 1)

younger:

the y. rises when the old doth fall (Proverbs 15)

youth:

flaming y. (Lust 6)

he that is more than a y. (Celibacy 2)

he wears the rose of y. (Youth 4)

home-keeping y. have ever homely wits (Simplicity 3)

in my y. I never did apply (Drinking 2)

in the morn and liquid dew of y. (Chastity 6, Youth 6)

in the very may-morn of his y. (Youth 7)

like a thankful and reverend y.(Condescension 2)

now all the y. of England (Youth 8)

the happiest y., viewing his progress (Despair 2)

the quick fire of y. (Youth 2)

this thorn doth to our rose of y. belong (Youth 1)

thou hast ... corrupted the y. of the realm (Education 1)

though not clean past your y. (Old Age 4)

y. no less becomes (Clothing 4)

y.'s a stuff will not endure (Love 96)

y. to itself rebels (Youth 5)

zed:

thou whoreson z. (Insults 11)

zenith:

z. doth depend upon a ... star (Astrology 4)

zounds:

z., I was never so bethumped (Words 3)